The ICJ and the Evolution International Law

In 1949 the International Court of Justice (ICJ) handed down its first judgment in the *Corfu Channel* case. In diffusing an early Cold War dispute, the Court articulated a set of legal principles which continue to shape our appreciation of the international legal order. Many of the issues dealt with by the Court in 1949 remain central questions in international law, including due diligence, forcible intervention and self-help, maritime operations, navigation in international straits and the concept of elementary considerations of humanity. The Court's decision has been cited on numerous occasions in subsequent international litigation. Indeed, the relevance of this judgment goes far beyond the subject matter dealt with by the Court in 1949, extending to pressing problems such as transboundary pollution, terrorism and piracy. In short, it was and remains a thoroughly modern decision – a landmark for international law; and one which today still warrants examination sixty years later.

Taking a critical approach, *The ICJ and the Evolution of International Law* examines the decision's influence on international law generally and on some fields of international law such as the law of the sea and the law of international responsibility specifically. The book collects the commentary of a distinguished set of international law scholars, including four well-known international judges. The contributors consider not only the history of the *Corfu Channel Judgment* and its contribution to the development of international law, but also its resonance in many contemporary issues in the field of international law.

This book will be of particular interest to academics and students of International Law, International Relations and Legal History.

Karine Bannelier is Associate Professor at the Faculty of Law of the University of Grenoble, France and Director of the Master Degree on International Security and Defense Studies.

Theodore Christakis is Professor of International Law and Director of the Centre for International Security and European Studies of the University of Grenoble, France.

Sarah Heathcote is Senior Lecturer at the Australian National University College of Law, Canberra, Australia.

Routledge Research in International Law

Available:

International Law and the Third World
Reshaping justice
Richard Falk, Balakrishnan Rajagopal and Jacqueline Stevens (eds.)

International Legal Theory
Essays and engagements, 1966–2006
Nicholas Onuf

The Problem of Enforcement in International Law
Countermeasures, the non-injured state and the idea of international community
Elena Katselli Proukaki

International Economic Actors and Human Rights
Adam McBeth

The Law of Consular Access
A documentary guide
John Quigley, William J. Aceves and Adele Shank

State Accountability under International Law
Holding states accountable for a breach of *jus cogens* norms
Lisa Yarwood

International Organisations and the Idea of Autonomy
Institutional independence in the international legal order
Richard Collins and Nigel D. White (eds)

Self-Determination in the Post-9/11 Era
Elizabeth Chadwick

Participants in the International Legal System
Multiple perspectives on non-state actors in international law
Jean d'Aspremont

Sovereignty and Jurisdiction in the Airspace and Outer Space
Legal criteria for spatial delimitation
Gbenga Oduntan

International Law in a Multipolar World
Matthew Happold (ed.)

The Law on the Use of Force
A feminist analysis
Gina Heathcote

The ICJ and the Evolution of International Law
The enduring impact of the *Corfu Channel* case
Karine Bannelier, Theodore Christakis and Sarah Heathcote (eds)

Forthcoming titles in this series include:

International Law, Regulation and Resistance
Critical spaces
Zoe Pearson

The Right to Self-determination under International Law
"Selfistans," secession, and the Great Powers' rule
Milena Sterio

The Cuban Embargo under International Law
El bloqueo
Nigel D. White

Threats of Force
International law and strategy
Francis Grimal

Asian Approaches to International Law and the Legacy of Colonialism and Imperialism
The law of the sea, territorial disputes and international dispute settlement
Jin-Hyun Paik, Seok-Woo Lee and Kevin Y. L. Tan (eds)

The ICJ and the Evolution of International Law

The enduring impact of the *Corfu Channel* case

Edited by Karine Bannelier,
Theodore Christakis and Sarah Heathcote

LONDON AND NEW YORK

First published 2012
by Routledge
2 Park Square, Milton Park, Abingdon, Oxon OX14 4RN

Simultaneously published in the USA and Canada
by Routledge
711 Third Avenue, New York, NY 10017

Routledge is an imprint of the Taylor & Francis Group, an informa business

First issued in paperback 2013

© 2012 Karine Bannelier, Theodore Christakis and Sarah Heathcote selection and editorial material; individual chapters, the contributors

The right of Karine Bannelier, Theodore Christakis and Sarah Heathcote to be identified as editors of this work has been asserted by them in accordance with sections 77 and 78 of the Copyright, Designs and Patents Act 1988.

All rights reserved. No part of this book may be reprinted or reproduced or utilised in any form or by any electronic, mechanical, or other means, now known or hereafter invented, including photocopying and recording, or in any information storage or retrieval system, without permission in writing from the publishers.

Trademark notice: Product or corporate names may be trademarks or registered trademarks, and are used only for identification and explanation without intent to infringe.

British Library Cataloguing in Publication Data
A catalogue record for this book is available from the British Library

Library of Congress Cataloging in Publication Data
  The ICJ and the development of international law : the lasting impact of the *Corfu Channel* case / [edited by] Karine Bannelier, Théodore Christakis, Sarah Heathcote.
    p. cm. — (Routledge research in international law)
  Includes bibliographical references and index.
  ISBN 978-0-415-60597-7 (hardback) — ISBN 978-0-203-61068-8 (e-book)   1. International Court of Justice.   2. International law. 3. Corfu Channel case.   4. Law of the sea.   5. Government liability (International law)   I. Bannelier, Karine.   II. Christakis, Théodore. III. Heathcote, Sarah.
  KZ6275.I25 2011
  341—dc22
                                                                                            2011016348
ISBN: 978-0-415-87019-1 (pbk)
ISBN: 978–0–415–60597–7 (hbk)
ISBN: 978–0–203–61068–8 (ebk)

Typeset in Garamond
by RefineCatch Limited, Bungay, Suffolk

Contents

List of contributors xi
Preface xv

PART I
Views from the Bench: the legacy of the *Corfu Channel* case 1

1 An international contentious case on the threshold of the Cold War 3
  MOHAMMED BEDJAOUI

2 The *Corfu Channel* case and the concept of sovereignty 16
  MOHAMED BENNOUNA

3 The bar 21
  JEAN-PIERRE COT

PART II
The historical and institutional framework 39

4 The *Corfu Channel* case in perspective: the factual and political background 41
  ARISTOTELES CONSTANTINIDES

5 The International Court of Justice and the Security Council: disentangling Themis from Ares 60
  GIOVANNI DISTEFANO AND ETIENNE HENRY

PART III
Procedural and evidential issues before the World Court 85

6 The basis of the Court's jurisdiction and the scope and usefulness of *forum prorogatum* 87
  HENRY BURMESTER

7   The International Court of Justice and standards of proof   98
    KATHERINE DEL MAR

8   'Naval secrets', public interest immunity and open justice   124
    KENNETH J. KEITH

PART IV
Law of the Sea   147

9   International straits: still a matter of contention?   149
    STUART KAYE

10 Dangerous waters and international law: the *Corfu Channel* case, warships, and sovereignty irritants   164
    ROB MCLAUGHLIN

11 Peacetime maritime operations   181
    DONALD R. ROTHWELL

PART V
Fundamental rules of international law   199

12 The Court's decision *in silentium* on the sources of international law: its enduring significance   201
    AKIHO SHIBATA

13 Intervention and self-help   211
    THEODORE CHRISTAKIS

14 A policy of force   226
    CHRISTINE GRAY

15 Foundational judgment or constructive myth? The Court's decision as a precursor to international environmental law   242
    KARINE BANNELIER

16 The interaction between international humanitarian law and human rights law and the contribution of the ICJ   256
    DJAMCHID MOMTAZ AND AMIN GHANBARI AMIRHANDEH

17 Elementary considerations of humanity   264
    MATTHEW ZAGOR

PART VI
Issues of state responsibility   293

18 State omissions and due diligence: aspects of fault, damage and contribution to injury in the law of state responsibility   295
SARAH HEATHCOTE

19 The limits of complicity as a ground for responsibility: lessons learned from the *Corfu Channel* case   315
OLIVIER CORTEN AND PIERRE KLEIN

20 Reparation and compliance   335
PIERRE D'ARGENT

21 Conclusion   357
HILARY CHARLESWORTH

Index   363

Contributors

Amin Ghanbari Amirhandeh is the recipient of the 2009 SATA prize of the Asian Society of International Law and a research fellow at the Center for International Space Law Studies at the University of Tehran.

Karine Bannelier has a PhD in International Law from the University of Paris-Sorbonne, and is Associate Professor at the Faculty of Law of the University of Grenoble and Director of the Master Degree on *International Security and Defense Studies*. She has published or edited five books and more than 20 articles and book chapters on international law. Her research interests include the Law of Armed Conflict, International Criminal Law and International Environmental Law.

Mohammed Bedjaoui is the former President of the International Court of Justice, Member emeritus of the Institut de Droit International, former Ambassador, former Minister of Foreign Affairs of Algeria, former President of the Algerian Constitutional Council, Member of many Academies and Scholarly Societies, Holder of *Doctorats Honoris Causa* from several universities, and the holder of many national and foreign decorations.

Mohamed Bennouna has been a Judge of the International Court of Justice since 2006 and is a Professor of International Law, Member of the Institute of International Law. He was Ambassador, Permanent Representative of the Kingdom of Morocco to the United Nations (2001–6). He was also a judge of the International Criminal Tribunal for the Former Yugoslavia at The Hague (1998–2001) and a member of the United Nations International Law Commission, Geneva (1986–98). He is the author of numerous books, essays and articles on International Law.

Henry Burmester, QC, is former Chief General Counsel in the Australian Government Solicitor's office, and before that Head of the Office of International Law in the Australian Attorney-General's Department. He has appeared as Counsel for Australia in the International Court. He is a graduate of the Australian National University and the University of Virginia.

Hilary Charlesworth is Professor and Director of the Centre for International Governance and Justice, Regulatory Institutions Network, Australian National University (ANU), and an ARC Laureate Fellow. She is also Professor at the ANU College of Law and has held visiting appointments at US and European universities.

Theodore Christakis is Professor of International Law and Director of the Centre for International Security and European Studies (CESICE: http://cesice. upmf-grenoble.fr) at the University of Grenoble. He has published or edited seven books and more than 35 articles and book chapters on various subjects of international law. His research areas include International and European Human Rights Law, self-determination and minority rights, issues relating to the use of force under international law and the law of international responsibility.

Aristoteles Constantinides, received his PhD in International Law from Aristotle University of Thessaloniki, Greece. He is Assistant Professor in International Law and Human Rights and founding member of the Department of Law of the University of Cyprus, and a member of several academic networks, including the ILA Committee on non-state actors.

Olivier Corten is Professor of International Law at the Centre of International Law at the Université libre de Bruxelles in Belgium. He is the author of numerous books and articles on a broad variety of topics of international law including, recently, *The Law Against War* (Hart, 2010). His research areas include the theory of international law and issues relating to the use of force under international law.

Jean-Pierre Cot is Emeritus Professor of the University of Paris-I Panthéon-Sorbonne. He was advocate and counsel in a number of cases before the International Court of Justice. He is presently a judge at the International Tribunal for the Law of the Sea and *ad hoc* judge in cases before the International Court of Justice. Cot is president of the *Société française pour le droit international*.

Pierre d'Argent is Professor of International Law at the University of Louvain and invited Professor at the University of Leiden. He was First Secretary of the International Court of Justice (2009–11).

Katherine Del Mar is a Teaching and Research Assistant at the Faculty of Law, the University of Geneva, and a PhD candidate in international law at the Graduate Institute of International and Development Studies, Geneva. She has been an Advisor to States in advisory and contentious proceedings before the International Court of Justice.

Giovanni Distefano is Professor at the Law Faculty of the University of Neuchâtel. He also teaches public international law and international law related to the use of force at the Geneva Academy of International Humanitarian Law and Human Rights.

Christine Gray is Professor of International Law at the University of Cambridge. Her main research interests concern, first, international law and the use of force and, second, the role of the International Court of Justice. Her principal publications include *International Law and the Use of Force* (3rd edn, 2008) and *Judicial Remedies in International Law* (1990).

Sarah Heathcote is Senior Lecturer at the Australian National University College of Law. She previously worked for the University of Geneva and Boston University and has published primarily on issues of general international law.

Etienne Henry holds a Master of Law (Neuchâtel) and a Certificate of Advanced Studies in Human Rights (Geneva). He is Teaching and Research Assistant at the University of Neuchâtel and previously worked in the Federal Office of Justice in Berne.

Stuart Kaye is currently Dean and Winthrop Professor of Law at the University of Western Australia. He previously held a Chair in Law at the University of Melbourne (2006–10), and was Dean and Professor of Law at the University of Wollongong (2002–06).

Kenneth J. Keith is judge of the International Court of Justice (2006–), judge of the New Zealand Court of Appeal and Supreme Court (1996–2006), member and President of the New Zealand Law Commission (1986–96), and law faculty member, Victoria University of Wellington (1962–64, 1966–91).

Pierre Klein is Professor of International Law and Director of the Centre of International Law at the Université libre de Bruxelles, Belgium. He has published extensively on various subjects of international law and recently co-edited with Olivier Corten a *Commentary Article by Article of the Vienna Conventions on the Law of Treaties* (Oxford University Press, 2011). His research interests include the law of international organizations and the law of international responsibility.

Rob McLaughlin has a PhD from Cambridge, and is a Captain in the Royal Australian Navy. He is an Associate Professor at the Australian National University College of Law, and has previously served as Director Operations and International Law for the Department of Defence, and Director Naval Legal Service. He has served both at sea and ashore in East Timor, Iraq, and on maritime law enforcement operations.

Djamchid Momtaz is Professor of Public International Law at the University of Tehran, member of the Institut de Droit International, member of the

Curatorium of The Hague Academy of International Law and former Chairman to the International Law Commission. He is a legal advisor to the Iranian Ministry of Foreign Affairs.

Donald R. Rothwell is Professor of International Law at the ANU College of Law, Australian National University. He has written on international security law, the law of the sea, and the law of the polar regions. His most recent book is *The International Law of the Sea* (Hart, 2010).

Akiho Shibata is a Professor of International Law at the Graduate School of International Cooperation Studies, Kobe University, Japan. His main fields of study are international law-making, the Antarctic Treaty System and international environmental law. He served as a legal consultant for Japan's Ministry of Foreign Affairs (2001–10) and was a research fellow at the Australian National University School of Law (2009).

Matthew Zagor is a Senior Lecturer at the ANU College of Law where he teaches refugee law, human rights, environmental and public law. In 2010 he was Deputy Director of the Australian National University's Centre for European Studies. His recent research has focused upon the principle of legality and judicial rhetoric, the rediscovery of constitutional 'faith' in the United Kingdom, the potential role of the European notion of constitutional patriotism in Australian legal thought, the construction of refugee identity through legal narrative, and perspectives of legality in the Occupied Palestinian Territories. He has worked as a community and government lawyer, refugee advocate, and part-time Member of the Migration and Refugee Review Tribunal.

Preface

Just over sixty years ago, in 1949, the International Court of Justice (ICJ) handed down its first judgment in the *Corfu Channel* case. In diffusing an early Cold War dispute, the Court articulated a set of legal principles which, some sixty years later, continue to shape our appreciation of the international legal order.

Many of the issues dealt with by the Court in 1949 remain central questions of international law, including due diligence, forcible intervention and self-help, maritime operations, navigation in international straits and the concept of elementary considerations of humanity. The Court's decision has been cited on numerous occasions both in the literature and in international litigation.[1] In a short essay written in 2002, Malgosia Fitzmaurice described the *Corfu Channel Judgment* as 'one of the finest and one of the most important, if not prophetic, in the history of the World Court'.[2] The word 'prophecy' was also used to describe the *Corfu Channel Judgment* by Judge Simma in the *Oil Platforms* case.[3] Indeed, the relevance of this judgment goes far beyond the subject matter dealt with by the Court in 1949, extending to pressing contemporary problems such as trans-boundary pollution, terrorism or piracy. In short, it was and remains a thoroughly modern decision – a landmark for international law; and one which today warrants reconsideration.

Taking a critical approach, this book examines the decision's influence on international law generally and on some fields of international law in particular, such as the law of the sea or State responsibility. The book collects the commentary of a distinguished set of international law scholars, including several current and former international Judges. The aim is to consider not only the history of the

---

1 As former ICJ President Bedjaoui explains in Chapter 1: 'The solutions developed for the resolution of the *"Corfu Case"* attracted a seal of approval and became the *benchmark for later jurisprudence*. In no less than *18 cases*, did the Court continue to be influenced by the *Corfu Channel case.*'
2 M. Fitzmaurice, 'The *Corfu Channel Case* and the Development of International Law', in N. Ando, E. McWhinney, and R. Wolfrum (eds) *Liber amicorum Judge Shigeru Oda* (The Hague: Kluwer, 2002), Vol. 1, p. 119.
3 *Oil Platforms (Islamic Republic of Iran v. United States of America)*, Judgment of 6 November 2003, *ICJ Reports* 2003, Separate Opinion of Judge Simma, p. 327, para. 5.

Corfu Channel Judgment and its contribution to the development of international law, but also its resonance in many contemporary problems of international law.

The book is divided into six parts. Part I is presented in the form of a 'roundtable': 'Views from the Bench: the legacy of the *Corfu Channel* case'. In this part, a former ICJ President (Mr Mohammed Bedjaoui, Algeria), a current member of the ICJ (Judge Mohamed Bennouna, Morocco), and a current member of the International Tribunal for the Law of the Sea (Judge Jean-Pierre Cot, whose father Pierre Cot was lead Counsel for Albania in this case) address various aspects of the case, providing respectively, an overview of the case's importance for international law in general; its legal relevance to an important specific contemporary topic; and finally, how this case is, from the perspective of the Bar, to be distinguished from the conduct of international litigation today. Together these contributions explain why this Judgment has become one of the most often quoted pieces of international case law.

Part II, 'The historical and institutional framework', presents the history of this case and provides a perspective on the relations and interactions between the ICJ and the United Nations Security Council.

Part III, 'Procedural and evidential issues before the World Court', presents three contributions (including one by Sir Kenneth Keith, Judge at the ICJ and another by M. Henry Burmester, Chief Counsel (retired), Australian Government Solicitor) concerning some important 'Procedural and evidential issues before the World Court', issues that are still of a great interest for international lawyers today.

The last three parts of the book present twelve chapters discussing substantive subject matters and the resonance of the *Corfu Channel Judgment* in some important fields of contemporary international law such as the 'Law of the Sea' (Part IV); some of the 'Fundamental Rules of International Law' (Part V), including those relative to the use of force and recourse to self-help, or those concerning trans-boundary harm or the concept of 'elementary considerations of humanity'. The final part considers 'Issues of state responsibility' raised by the 1949 decision and still highly topical today, such as the limits of complicity as a ground for responsibility, aspects of fault, damage and contribution to injury in the law of State responsibility as well as problems in relation to reparations and compliance with ICJ Judgments.

This book is the result of a collaboration between the ANU College of Law of the Australian National University[4] and the Centre for International Security and European Studies (CESICE) of the Law Faculty, University of Grenoble, France.[5] It brings together many of the papers presented on 29 October 2009 at an international workshop organized and hosted by the ANU College of Law, Australian National University, in collaboration with the Centre for International Security and European Studies (CESICE) of the University of Grenoble and with the support of the French Embassy in Australia.

4 See http://law.anu.edu.au/.
5 See http://cesice.upmf-grenoble.fr.

Part I

Views from the Bench

The legacy of the *Corfu Channel* case

1 An international contentious case on the threshold of the Cold War*

Mohammed Bedjaoui

> I recall, once more, that formula from British Admiralty: 'to learn to behave oneself'. All nations, Mr. President, large and small, strong and weak, must learn to behave themselves. They must learn by looking to the International Court of Justice which, in its wisdom, can teach them how.
> (Concluding words of Pierre Cot in his oral pleadings as Counsel on behalf of Albania, January 22, 1949)[1]

I am very grateful to the editors of this book on the *Corfu Channel* case, whose topicality, some sixty years after the event, remains relevant today. It provides me with an opportunity, which is greatly appreciated, to reread after a long time, the three judgments to which this dispute gave rise and to rediscover with delight, the well-established merits of these historical decisions.

1.1 Tense exchanges in the Security Council

To learn the most from this case, one needs to recall its context: the Cold War was just beginning. At this war's frontline, in the months of February to April 1947, the superpowers were already vigorously flexing their muscles. To my mind, the moment when the *Corfu Channel* dispute first went before the Security Council was integral to the legal history of what was already a set of tense exchanges between the superpowers. The Security Council was in its very first year of existence. This case was the first and last time that this central organ of the United Nations would recommend that two States refer their dispute to the International Court of Justice to resolve their differences. Sir Alexander Cadogan, the Permanent Representative of the United Kingdom to the United

---

* Initial translation from the French by Reia Anquet.
1 A loose translation by L. Gardiner, *The Eagle Spreads His Claws: A History of the Corfu Channel Dispute and of Albania's Relations with the West*, Edinburgh and London: William Blackwood and Sons Ltd, 1966, p. 211. The original French version can be found in *ICJ Pleadings, Oral Arguments, Documents: The Corfu Channel case*. Oral proceedings (first part), Vol. IV, p. 699.

Nations in New York, used modern – and today fashionable – terminology, when he accused Albania, in a failed draft resolution, of having committed a *crime against humanity* by not having told States that a danger existed in navigating the Channel which was awash with naval mines. In these words one can hear the first echoes of present-day international criminal law. But the *Corfu Channel* case would also distinguish itself at this point by being the first time that the veto was used. This highly ranked British diplomat, disappointed to see his proposed resolution crushed by a Soviet veto, rashly remarked that its use was regrettable.[2] This was an unexpected criticism of a use of the right of veto by one of its holders. Andrei Gromyko's was delighted. Savouring the poignancy of the moment, he reminded Cadogan that it was in fact the United States and the United Kingdom that had first suggested that a right of veto be included in the United Nations Charter. It was then the turn of the Colombian Representative to remind the Council that it was due to the *obstinacy* of the superpowers that this mechanism was introduced and locked into the system.[3]

1.2 A perfect trial

But the *Corfu Channel* case also has a number of other distinguishing features. First, it was *the first contentious case to be officially filed with the newly created International Court of Justice*,[4] which was also taking its first steps. It is, above all, a case in which a jurist can find all the different possible facets of a contentious case: a first set of hearings where the Court's *jurisdiction* is questioned, resulting in a first

---

2 *Official Records of the Security Council, Second Year, Hundred and twenty-fifth Meeting*, April 3rd 1947, no. 32, p. 684.
3 On this bitter debate which lasted three months, Leslie Gardiner wrote:

> When the first awkward tussle before the Security Council ended at Lake Success, it might have been thought, by a novice in such affairs, that every aspect of the situation and every shade of opinion had already been weighed and sifted and taken account of; that the decision, to recommend Albania and the United Kingdom to take their quarrel to the International Court, was for a mere formal pronouncement of guilt or innocence, in an atmosphere of judicial calm, undisturbed by political considerations, uncorrupted by nationalistic and ideological threats and sulks. So one might have thought.
>
> (Gardiner, 1966, p. 195)

The author demonstrates his writing skills in 'telling the tale' of the case. One can admire the 'show room' of the Table of Contents: I. Corfu: These yellow sands, II. The Mainland: A hint of woe; III. Recommended routes: Sour-eyed disdain; IV. Cruisers under fire: Too rash a trail; V. Mischief in the Channel: Some tricks of desperation; VI. Home with '*Volage*': Exposed unto the sea; VII. A show of force: Enter mariners; VIII. Veto at Lake Success: A confused noise within; IX. The Yugoslavian's tale: Observation strange; X. Justice at The Hague: All sanctimonious ceremonies; XI. Time to pay: The strongest oaths are straw; XII. After the storm: Calm seas, auspicious gales.
4 This contentious case had been preceded by the request for an advisory opinion on the *Conditions of Admission of a State to Membership in the United Nations (Article 4 of the Charter)*. But the priority was given to the *Corfu Channel case* which was attributed the top position in the Court's General List.

judgment (dated March 25, 1945) rejecting the preliminary objection raised by a contesting party; a second set of hearings in which a *detailed examination* is undertaken and which is concluded by a second judgment (dated April 9, 1949); and finally a third set of hearings focused on the assessment of the amount of compensation for the injury sustained by a party, which resulted in the judgment of 15 December, 1949.[5] The case is in this respect valuable, for it constitutes what can be called a 'comprehensive' or 'complete' case.

The unique nature of the case is not, however, limited to these features. Albania, having contested the International Court's jurisdiction to set the amount of compensation, refused to appear for the third set of hearings. Consequently, the Court applied, and this too would be 'a first', the procedure by default found in Article 53 of the Statute.[6] Perhaps because it was the Court's first case, it felt obliged to handle the case's 'every aspect'.

1.3 A memorable year

The year in which the Court handed down its final judgment in the *Corfu Channel* case distinguishes itself from others. In the Court's history, 'the vintage year of 1949' is to be remembered. Indeed, the Court prospered throughout the course of the whole year. With its General List successfully full, the Court could have been but delighted with promise of productivity, which boded well for the fulfillment of its mission of legal activity of the highest order. The Court was far from envisaging the long, miserable and barren years to come. At this point, it could savour its moment of full and prolific activity, as in that single year of 1949 it was able to hand down no less than 12 judgments![7]

---

5 One could even consider that the *Corfu Channel case* also had a fourth phase, that [....] concerning the *Case of the monetary gold removed from Rome in 1943 (Preliminary Question), Judgment of June 15th, 1954: ICJ Reports 1954*, in which the United Kingdom [....] was awarded this gold as partial compensation owed by Albania under the *Corfu Channel* judgment.

6 The Court had already well defined its role and that of an appearing party (*ICJ Reports 1949*, pp. 237–238, 245, 246, 247, 252 and following pages).

7 *Corfu Channel case, Judgment of April 9th, 1949: ICJ Reports 1949*, p.4; *Corfu Channel case, Order of April 9th, 1949: ICJ Reports 1949*, p. 171 (Assessment of the amount of compensation due from the People's Republic of Albania); *Reparation for injuries suffered in the services of the United Nations, Advisory Opinion: ICJ Reports 1949*, p. 174; *Corfu Channel case, order of June 24th, 1949: ICJ Reports 1949*, p. 222 (Assessment of the amount of compensation due from the People's Republic of Albania); *Colombian-Peruvian Asylum case, Order of October 20th, 1949: ICJ Reports 1949*, p. 225; *Interpretation of Peace Treaties, Order of November 7th, 1949: ICJ Reports 1949*, p. 229; *Anglo-Norwegian fisheries case, Order of November 9th, 1949: ICJ Reports 1949*, p. 233; *Corfu Channel case, Order of November 19th, 1949: ICJ Reports 1949*, p. 237; *Competence General Assembly (admission new Members), Order of December 2nd, 1949: ICJ Reports 1949*, p. 241; *Corfu Channel case, Judgment of December 15th 1949: ICJ Reports 1949*, p. 244 (Assessment of the amount of compensation due from the People's

1.4 In record time

Another feature of the *Corfu Channel* case is that it reflects a perfect example of the meticulous processing of a case by the Court in optimum time. Beginning with a notice of unilateral application by the United Kingdom against Albania on 22 May, 1947, the case finished on 15 December, 1949, thus lasting a mere two and a half years. What is all the more striking concerning this short processing period is that the case produced three judgments: the first relative to jurisdiction, the second on the merits, and the last on compensation. Moreover, the case generated, during the period of written proceedings, an exhaustive exchange of written documents, both parties having submitted Memorials, Counter-Memorials, written Replies and Rejoinders; the amount of documents being the same for the first judgment as for the second. This all-inclusive case additionally required the opinions of witnesses and experts, and even the participation of a third State in proceedings, participating as a kind of *amicus curiae*.

1.5 A bounty of solutions

Richly endowed in all the above features as well as in many others, the *Corfu Channel* case, on which the International Court of Justice cut its teeth, would provide this court of law with an opportunity to issue solutions, which would subsequently prosper, both in respect of procedure and indeed in terms of substantive law. Built as it was, the case would challenge the judges' acumen on a number of significant problems. Armed only with the jurisprudence of its predecessor, this new International Court would successfully establish for the future a whole range of procedural rules, as well as a foundation in a great number of areas, while fortuitously strengthening some legal principles for the good of a world that was about to find itself in a period of strong ideological rivalry. It would even boldly develop international law, notably within the area of environmental protection.

1.6 A benchmark for jurisprudence

The new Court, placed by benevolent Providence on such a perfect launching pad, could not wish for better tools with which to begin in style a very promising career. The solutions it developed for the resolution of the '*Corfu Case*' gained the seal of approval and became the benchmark for later jurisprudence.

Republic of Albania); *Colombian-Peruvian Asylum* case, *Order of December 17th, 1949: ICJ Reports 1949*, p. 267; *International Status of South-West Africa, Order of December 30th, 1949: ICJ Reports 1949*, p. 270. The Court worked right up until the last day of the year!

In no less than 18 cases, did the Court continue to be influenced by the *Corfu Channel* case.[8] The solutions provided in this case particularly influenced the Court's decisions in the case concerning *Military and Paramilitary Activities (Nicaragua v. USA)*, twice for the Jurisdiction and Admissibility phase of the case and at least six times for the Merits phase. In the *Genocide case (Bosnia and Herzegovina v. Serbia and Montenegro)*, the jurisprudence of the *Corfu Channel* case was followed at least four times.[9]

1.7 Instituting proceedings on several levels

The distinctive features of the *Corfu Channel* case can also be found in the area of the institution of proceedings at the International Court of Justice. The case was introduced to the Court using different means, as if in this first case, the World Court was trying to test all the possible grounds for jurisdiction foreseen by its Statute. In this way the *Corfu Channel* case offered a preview of all the different problems concerning the Court's jurisdiction.

---

8 The jurisprudence of the *Corfu Channel case* was used in: the *Nottebohm case (Preliminary Objection). Judgments of November 18th 1953: ICJ Reports 1953*, p. 119; *Judgments of the Administrative Tribunal of the ILO upon complaints made against the UNESCO, Advisory Opinion of October 23rd, 1956: ICJ Reports 1956*, p. 100; in the *Case concerning Right of Passage over Indian Territory (Merits), Judgment of 12 April 1960: ICJ Reports 1960* p. 13; in *North Sea Continental Shelf, Judgment, ICJ Reports 1969*, p. 49; in *United States Diplomatic and Consular Staff in Tehran, Judgment ICJ Reports 1980*, p. 9; in the *Military and Paramilitary Activities in and against Nicaragua (Nicaragua v. United States of America), Jurisdiction and Admissibility, Judgment, ICJ Reports 1984*, pp. 435 and 437; in the *Military and Paramilitary Activities in and against Nicaragua (Nicaragua v. United States of America) Merits, Judgment, ICJ Reports 1986*, where the Corfu Channel Judgment is quoted no less than six times on pp. 24–25, 42, 106, 112, and 114!); in the *Arbitral Award of 31 July 1989 Judgment, ICJ Reports 1991*, p. 70; in the judgment in the *Land, Island and Maritime Frontier Dispute (El Salvador/Honduras: Nicaragua Intervening), ICJ Reports 1992*, p. 584; in the advisory opinion on the *Legality of the Threat or Use of Nuclear Weapons, (ICJ Reports 1996*, p. 257; in the *Application of the Convention on the Prevention and Punishment of the Crime of Genocide Preliminary Objections Judgment, ICJ Reports 1996*, p. 621; in the *Kasikili/Sedudu Island (Botswana/Namibia), Judgment, ICJ Reports 1999*, P. 1076; in *Armed Activities on the Territory of the Congo (New Application: 2002) (Democratic Republic of the Congo v. Rwanda), Jurisdiction and Admissibility, Judgment, ICJ Reports 2006*, pp. 18–19); *Armed Activities on the Territory of the Congo (Democratic Republic of the Congo v. Uganda), Judgment, ICJ Reports 2005* p. 262; in the *Application of the Convention on the Prevention and Punishment of the Crime of Genocide (Bosnia and Herzegovina v. Serbia and Montenegro), Judgment, ICJ Reports 2007*, where the *Corfu Channel case* is referred to four times at pp. 91–92, 95–96, 129 and 234; and finally in the *Certain Questions of Mutual Assistance in Criminal Matters (Djibouti v. France), Judgment, ICJ Reports 2008*, where the *Corfu Channel case* is mentioned twice, on pp. 200–201 and 204.

9 As a point of comparison, it should be noted that the vast case concerning *Military and Paramilitary Activities in and against Nicaragua*, with its three decisions (Jurisdiction and Admissibility, Provisional Measures and Merits), has only been used 22 times in the Court's subsequent jurisprudence, which is not many more times than the use made of the *Corfu Channel case* (even if we take into consideration that the *Corfu* case took place some 35 years before the *Nicaragua* case).

The United Kingdom brought the case before the Court by *unilateral application*, thinking that in this way it was complying with the Security Council's recommendation that the two States refer their dispute to the International Court of Justice. What once again singles out the *Corfu Channel* case was that this was the first and last time that the Security Council would decide to use this highly appropriate mechanism to push disputing parties towards the International Court. This strategy of submitting a unilateral application was very much connected to the mechanism of *forum prorogatum*: the United Kingdom expected that normally Albania would be even more willing to consent to the Court's jurisdiction as it was authorised to participate in Security Council debates on this case only on condition that it accept in advance all the obligations incumbent upon a Member State of the United Nations, and notably the obligation to carry out the Security Council's decisions.

Security Council recommendations, unilateral application by the United Kingdom, *forum prorogatum*, the list does not end there. In its letter dated July 2nd, 1947, Albania accused the United Kingdom of having acted unilaterally by filing an application, Albania considering that the case could only be introduced to the Court by way of a *special agreement*. Albania stated that the Security Council had put forward a simple recommendation and certainly not a 'decision' which would have been of a mandatory nature if it had been adopted under Chapter VII of the Charter. For Albania, the invocation of Article 25 of the Charter by the United Kingdom was incorrect in this particular case. The United Kingdom maintained that this case could constitute an example of compulsory jurisdiction.

The Court specified that, be that as it may, Albania had nevertheless not rejected the Security Council's recommendation in its letter dated July 2nd, 1947. Avoiding giving a ruling on the possibility of compulsory jurisdiction being used in this specific case, the Court declared that it had jurisdiction based on this Albanian letter.

At this point in the proceedings, the tone of the case had been set and would not wane. On the very day that the Court handed down its judgment on Albania's preliminary objection (March 25th, 1948) in which the Court stated with all the authority of *res judicata* that it had jurisdiction to hear the case, the two litigating parties, in all haste, filed a special agreement by which both States granted the Court jurisdiction to rule on two specific questions which summed up the issues of the case.

The multiple grounds of jurisdiction put forward in this first 'historic' case revealed how an international legal system based exclusively on 'consent' would always encounter State disagreements as soon as it appeared unlikely that a special agreement would be concluded by the parties. Some of the complexities of this highly sensitive question of jurisdiction, which today is at the centre of international justice, emerged in the *Corfu Channel* case, and sounded a warning of many others that would arise in the future. Did the Security Council's recommendation enable the parties to avoid the provisions of the Court's Statute concerning rules of jurisdiction? While clearly and correctly declaring that the Council resolution could only be implemented in strict compliance with the Statute, the Court put an end to any further debate, ruling that the Albanian letter dated July 2nd, 1947 removed any potential impediments as it contained a clear acceptance of the Court's jurisdiction. It was the unquestionable expression of consent which prevailed. The *Corfu Channel* case would thus immediately provide clear signposts for tracking consensualism.[10]

1.8 Elusive evidence

The question of evidence was very important in this case. Had there been a minefield in Albanian territorial waters, or had there only been a few individual mines, of which two had caused the known damage to the two British navy destroyers (one of them, the *Saumarez*, would sink), killing a number of people, and wounding others? How could it be that between the date of this serious event (October 22nd, 1946) and that of the Channel's demining (November 12th–13th, 1946), numerous ships had sailed in these waters without incident? Had the minefield been laid by Nazi troops during the war or by Albania itself? Was there enough evidence permitting either the United Kingdom or Albania to insinuate that other States had laid the mines (the former considering that the minefield had been positioned by Yugoslavia; and the latter that it was Greece)? The United Kingdom further claimed that the mooring of the mines by Yugoslavia had been carried out either with the support or knowledge of Albania. During the Second World War, the United Kingdom had laid mines in France and Norway without these States being aware of it. Thus, was it possible to lay mines in an area close to Albania's coast without the government knowing what was happening? How could the mines have been moored so close to the Albanian coast without the collusion of Albania, and especially when this nation had shown itself to be highly jealous of its rights when it came to questions of sovereignty over its territorial waters? And all this, after similar and previous incidents had taken place. These are many of the important questions which needed to be answered and would thus determine whether the question of international responsibility would be brought into play.

The *Corfu Channel* case provides a preview of the whole range of rules concerning the regime of evidence in international trials which would be refined in later cases. The distribution of roles between judges and litigating parties at the International Court of Justice took shape as soon as the 'Corfu'

---

10 This case gave the Court the opportunity to clarify with precision the notion of consent which must be 'voluntary and indisputable' *Corfu Channel case, Judgment on Preliminary Objection: ICJ Reports 1948*, p. 27. There is no need for it 'to be expressed in any particular form' (ibid.). Once given, it cannot be withdrawn (ibid., p. 19, 28ss. and 42–44ss.); The Court cannot . . . hold to be irregular a proceeding which is not precluded by any provision in . . . texts (ibid., p. 28); etc.

case began. The judge was responsible for outlining to the litigating parties the rules concerning the submission of evidence and the conditions of its admission, before then proceeding to a fastidious investigation. Confronted with the parties' contentions, the judge needs to be armed with an arsenal of legal rules relative to all issues that might arise in the hearings and then lead the trial by proceeding with a series of investigations to be carried out rigorously and with a critical eye to the evidence. The value to be accorded evidence belongs to his or her discretionary power, while the litigating parties bear the obligation to prove their allegations and collaborate in good faith towards the elucidation of the truth.[11]

The *Corfu Channel* case is so abundant in examples of the regime of evidence that only a few will be mentioned here. Concerning the burden of proof the Court clearly established that the party seeking to establish another State's responsibility must demonstrate:

1 the existence of the international obligation upon which it seeks to rely; and
2 that this obligation has been breached, through an action or omission.

The principle of *actori incumbit probatio* was naturally given pride of place, making Albania the respondent State. This did not change with the conclusion of the special agreement later signed by the two parties. However, although respondent in the case, Albania became the claimant in relation to its allegation that the United Kingdom had violated its territorial sovereignty during *Operation Retail*. Nothing could be more normal.

When it was impossible for the injured State to provide direct proof of the unlawful acts at hand, the Court resorted to concordant inferences of fact and circumstantial evidence, which constituted indirect evidence. Nonetheless, such methods only serve as probative evidence when they are 'based on a series of facts linked together and leading logically to a single conclusion'.[12] The Court needed to establish if the mines were either laid by the Albanian authorities or whether they had been laid in a manner placing blame on Albania. But the international responsibility of a State, which is an extremely serious matter, should never be assumed. Consequently all assumptions in this regard must be meticulously verified. The Court declared that:

> It cannot be concluded from the mere fact of the control exercised by a State over its territory and waters that that State necessarily knew, or ought to have known, of any unlawful act perpetrated therein, nor yet

---

11 Cf. G. Niyungeko, *La preuve devant les juridictions internationales* (Bruxelles: Bruylant, 2005), 480 p., *passim*.
12 *ICJ Reports 1948*, p. 18.

that it necessarily knew, or should have known, the authors. This fact, by itself and apart from other circumstances, neither involves *prima facie* responsibility nor shifts the burden of proof.[13]

The judge must reach a certain level of satisfactory conviction, and this cannot be determined in the abstract. This stems from the principle of the judge's free and sovereign assessment of evidence (or inference from facts).

The obligation of the two parties to cooperate to assist in finding evidence was affirmed in the *Corfu Channel* case decision. The Court had effectively asked British officials to produce specific documents (known as the XCU documents), but the United Kingdom refused to do so, pleading naval secrecy.[14] The Court determined that this refusal needed to be duly justifiable. With such a refusal the Court could have handed down an unfavorable decision in respect of the uncooperative State. But in the *Corfu Channel* case the Court was very careful in this regard.[15]

More generally the *Corfu Channel Judgment* offered a panorama of the regime of evidence. Indeed, the Court was a trailblazer in this field. It did the following:

- applied the doctrine of '*res ipsa loquitur*';[16]
- allowed the use of documentary evidence, conferring upon itself the right to require the production of the original;[17]
- allowed the use of evidence submitted by a witness and organised the hearing of witnesses;[18]
- received expert evidence and distinguished between the status of experts and witnesses;
- examined evidence coming from a third State – Yugoslavia, which had sent its experts to Sibenik to report to the Court;[19]
- admitted a late presentation of documents, which could be received only if they were presented in an 'original and complete' form;[20] and
- prohibited the preferment of illegally acquired evidence. To justify its demining operation in breach of Albanian sovereignty, the United Kingdom claimed that it was acting to secure evidence before Albania could destroy it.

---

13 Ibid.
14 Ibid., p. 32.
15 Ibid., p. 32.
16 Ibid., p. 18.
17 Ibid., p. 8.
18 In this case there are two large volumes (vols III and IV of the written proceedings) concerning the hearing of the witnesses.
19 Ibid., pp. 16–17. The Court found it unnecessary to express an opinion on the probative value of those documents. See also pp. 152 ss.
20 Ibid., p. 8.

In conclusion, the Court conscientiously plowed through the field of evidence from its very first case. The legal sanction attached to the obligation to produce evidence was the immediate rejection of the unproven allegations.[21] This lack of evidence featured as an important element in the Court's decision.

The combined interplay of direct evidence, inferences of fact and circumstantial evidence, as well as the use of other indirect evidence, led the Court to declare that Albania must have at least known of the existence of a minefield in its territorial waters. Having failed to warn States of its existence for the benefit of navigation in general, Albania breached its obligations under international law. Those obligations arose from:

> certain general and well-recognized principles, namely: elementary considerations of humanity, even more exacting in peace than in war; the principle of the freedom of maritime communication; and every State's obligation not to allow knowingly its territory to be used for acts contrary to the rights of other States.[22]

1.9 Armed and ready: an 'innocent' passage

The Albanian Government claimed that it had special rights of sovereignty over its territorial waters, even when these waters were part of an international highway that linked two zones of high seas. It had refused the right of passage through these waters to ships of other States, whether they were merchant or war vessels. It contested the existence of a right of passage by the British warships, even if it was innocent in nature. Albania maintained that in any case the United Kingdom had neither asked for nor obtained authorisation from Albania for the passage.

This case then became the occasion for the Court to remind States of certain general legal principles and of certain customs and to clarify, legally speaking, certain notions such as vessels, channel, innocent passage, international navigation, which would make this case a point of reference for the Geneva Conference that would take place nine years later as well as for the Third Conference on the Law of the Sea. The Court had in particular found that Albania had no basis on which to prohibit the passage of British vessels or to subject them to prior authorisation. A passage can be 'innocent' even if it involves an armed warship and even if it is ready to return fire.[23] Everything depends on the circumstances and the precautionary measures taken by a State to guarantee passage of its vessels and this must be assessed according to what is 'reasonable': a demonstration of force could simply be intended to

---

21 Ibid., pp. 14–15 and 16–17.
22 Ibid., p. 22.
23 Ibid., p. 31.

dissuade a coastal State from hostile acts. This was a broad and highly lenient interpretation of the right to innocent passage, handed down by the Court during the Cold War.

1.10 The hardship of responsibility

Yet it is above all in the field of international responsibility that the Court handed down important findings, some of which constituted innovative and important landmarks. First of all, simple presumptions unsupported by other related inferences of fact were insufficient to establish Albania's responsibility. In international law no *prima facie* responsibility exists; the international responsibility of a State cannot be presumed. Additionally, the State upon whose territory an internationally unlawful act takes place (such as when foreigners suffer damage on a State's territory), cannot simply assert 'that it is ignorant of the circumstances of the act and of its authors'. Up to a certain point the State may be obliged to supply particulars of the use made by it of the means of information and inquiry at its disposal.[24] This obligation to carry out the necessary measures of inquiry and investigation was not in itself new, but its innovative feature can be found in the fact that the Court was much more exacting than previously.

1.11 An obligation to warn others

Albania was bound by an 'obligation to warn others'. According to the Court, Albania should have notified all States that there was a minefield in its waters. What is the legal grounds upon which this decision rests? 'The Hague Convention VIII of 1907,' answered the United Kingdom. The Court responded with a 'No' to this claim, knowing that this legal instrument is applied only in times of war. The Court stated that 'elementary considerations of humanity' is the principle which should first be applied in this case, that it was unsuitable and dangerous during a period of inter-State tensions for this principle to be ignored. The Court then followed up by ruling that: 'the principle of the freedom of maritime navigation and communication' is a necessity for all and, last but not least, that it was high time to accept the principle that a State's territory must not be dangerous for other States! Such a simple and pragmatic view of living in a community, but one that is so profoundly humanist in its expression, would thus allow international law to take on a new dignity. Even if a State does not have a specific and express obligation to act, it cannot escape its responsibilities vis-à-vis the international community from the moment that the required action carries a 'social good' for all. The 'obligation of good neighbourliness' sums up this point and consolidates the full meaning of this important 'social responsibility'.

---

24 Ibid., p. 18.

1.12 Allergic to intervention

By carrying out mine clearing operations on 12–13 November, 1946, against Albania's will, the United Kingdom breached Albanian sovereignty. The jurisprudence of the *Corfu* case forecasts, like a lightning bolt, the jurisprudence of *Military and Paramilitary Activities in and against Nicaragua*. The right of intervention, the Court said in a clear and powerful way, has no place in modern international law, even if it was undertaken in order to secure possession of evidence which is likely to disappear on the territory of another State.

The Court begins this famous passage of its judgment with an ambitious and brave step by stating and recalling the undeniable truth that international society is first and foremost composed of sovereign States that must respect one another: 'Between independent States, respect for territorial sovereignty is an essential foundation of international relations.'[25] This sovereignty includes exclusivity of jurisdiction which means that a State cannot carry out acts of constraint (of which forced mine clearance is one such example) in a foreign territory, even under the pretext of looking for evidence for a possible breach of international law by another State.

Thus, the Court found that the United Kingdom had engaged in a forcible intervention, which had absolutely no justification in international law. The famous '*obiter dictum*' struck like lightning:

> The Court can only regard the alleged right of intervention as the manifestation of a policy of force, such as has, in the past, given rise to most serious abuses and such as cannot, whatever be the present defects in international organization, find a place in international law.[26]

To measure the impact of this dictum, it is necessary to place this particularly strong statement in the context of the times, then threatened by numerous storms: the Cold War was undermining international solidarity. It is against this background that lucid and courageous individuals in The Hague warned nations of the mortal danger of breaching State sovereignty in a divided world. Such was the Court's firm and solemn message.

1.13 Necessary compensation

Its international responsibility having been engaged by virtue of its grave omission of not notifying others of the presence of the minefield, Albania thus had to make reparation for the injury suffered by the United Kingdom.

As Albania did not appear in the final public hearings, the Court applied Article 53 of its Statute which regulates non-appearance.

---

25 Ibid., p. 35.
26 Ibid.

Once more the question of jurisdiction arose. Was it clear that the special agreement between the United Kingdom and Albania on the question of responsibility also conferred on the Court the power to determine the amount of reparations? The Court replied in the affirmative, first of all to enable the special agreement's provisions to produce their 'appropriate effects'; second, to achieve a more balanced appreciation between the two questions in the *compromis*; and finally to demonstrate that neither of the parties had prevented the Court from handing down a judgment on compensation. To sum up, the Court declared, and the previous PCIJ '*Chorzow Factory*' judgment impelled it to do so, that when a special agreement confers on the Court the power to determine whether compensation is due, this also means that the Court has the power to decide upon the amount of compensation. Borrowing from '*Chorzow*', '*Corfu*' would continue to give rise to the jurisprudence of the future.

1.14 A 'prophetic' decision

Some authors consider the *Corfu Channel* case to be 'prophetic' in the Court's history.[27] The judgment of 1949 not only influenced, established and formatted the subsequent jurisprudence of the Court, it also established its role in the development of international law. The modern principle according to which 'no State has the right to use or permit the use of its territory in such a manner as to cause damage to others', upon which the new environmental law bases its principles, had its foundation in the 'fertile' 1949 judgment. When the Court asserted 'every State's obligation not to allow knowingly its territory to be used for acts contrary to the rights of other States', it was affirming that States must be increasingly aware that jurisdiction over their own territory must necessarily be limited by the need to avoid acts harmful to other States or the international community. Environmental law would thus eventually take off from where *Corfu Channel* left off.[28]

Homage must be paid to the memory of the first generation of judges of those post-war years:

> They knew how to serve the law.
> They knew how to serve world peace.
> They were grand.

---

27 P. Birnie and A. Boyle, *International Law and the Environment* (Oxford: Oxford University Press, 1992), p. 89; M. Fitzmaurice, 'The *Corfu Channel case* and the Development of International Law', *Liber Amicorum Judge Shigeru Oda* (The Hague: Kluwer Law International, 2002), p. 119.
28 Cf. *Legality of the Threat or Use of Nuclear Weapons, ICJ Reports 1996*, p. 242: 'The existence of the general obligation of States to ensure that activities within their jurisdiction and control respect the environment of other States or of areas beyond national control is now part of the corpus of international law relating to the environment.' Cf. also *Gabcikovo-Nagymaros Project (Hungary/Slovakia), Judgment, ICJ Reports 1997*, p. 41. para. 53.

2 The *Corfu Channel* case and the concept of sovereignty

Mohamed Bennouna

Among the areas of international law on which the Judgment in the *Corfu Channel* case is said to have had a lasting influence, M. A. Fitzmaurice has included the concept of State sovereignty, without really pursuing this further in her article.[1] I would like to take this opportunity to return to this important aspect of the Judgment, which also proved to be prophetic in relation to the development of the concept of sovereignty in connection with a putative right or duty of humanitarian intervention; and the affirmation of the existence of a 'responsibility to protect'.

Relying on the traditional concept of sovereignty based on a State's effective control over its entire territory, control which, of course, may be more or less stringent depending on the physical and human features of the territory,[2] the Court affirmed in the *Corfu Channel* case that the territorial State is under an 'obligation not to allow knowingly its territory to be used for acts contrary to the rights of other States'.[3] This obligation is neither abstract nor absolute, it is, on the contrary, contingent upon the State's actual or constructive knowledge of events occurring in its territory and liable to violate other States' rights. Knowledge of the risk is therefore the trigger of the due diligence obligation of the territorial State towards the foreign State or nationals thereof who may be affected; in other words, it is by omission that the territorial State's responsibility is engaged.

In his individual opinion appended to the *Corfu Channel Judgment*, Judge Alvarez drew attention to this new approach to sovereignty based on what he referred to as 'social interdependence', having the following characteristics[4]:

---

1 M. A. Fitzmaurice, 'The Corfu Channel and the Development of International Law', in N. Ando *et al.* (eds), *Liber Amicorum, Judge Shigeru Oda*, vol. 1 (The Hague: Kluwer Law International, 2002), p. 119.
2 *Legal Status of Eastern Greenland, Judgment, 1933, PCIJ,* Series A/B, No. 53, p. 46.
3 *Corfu Channel case, Judgment of April 9th, 1949, Merits, ICJ Reports 1949,* p. 22.
4 (*ICJ Reports 1949*, p. 44)

1   Every State is bound to preserve in its territory such order as is indispensable for the accomplishment of its international obligations: for otherwise its responsibility will be involved.
2   Every State is bound to exercise proper vigilance in its territory. This vigilance does not extend to uninhabited areas; and it is not of the same nature in the terrestrial part of the territory as in the maritime, aerial or other parts.

But does an omission to act by the territorial State, in full knowledge of the situation, entitle another State on its own initiative to act in its stead? Such was the case when the Royal Navy decided to carry out minesweeping operations (*Operation Retail*) in the Albanian waters of the Corfu Channel, in reliance on a purported right of the British Government to do so given the urgency, even without the consent of the territorial State. This is what led the Court to state clearly, in a famous *obiter dictum*, its conception of respect for State sovereignty:

> The Court can only regard the alleged right of intervention as the manifestation of a policy of force, such as has, in the past, given rise to most serious abuses and such as cannot, whatever be the present defects in international organization, find a place in international law.[5]

The Court here alludes to all the policies of force which had, in the past, tried to justify armed intervention, particularly in a number of Latin American countries, based on the right to protect nationals of certain Great Powers and their property. But, by framing its statement so generally, the Court goes beyond this and foretells the future development of international law regarding new forms of intervention, i.e. 'humanitarian' intervention. It has indeed been asserted that, when massive human rights violations are being committed within a country, foreign States have a right or even a duty to intervene militarily to restore international legality.

It is in fact accepted that certain human rights violations constitute serious breaches of peremptory norms (*jus cogens*), which are binding upon all States. (This is true, in particular, of crimes against humanity and genocide.) Granted, under the International Law Commission's draft Articles on Responsibility of States for Internationally Wrongful Acts, such a breach by a State entails an obligation for all other States to co-operate to bring the breach to an end; not to recognize as lawful the situation created by the breach; and not to render aid or assistance in maintaining that situation.[6]

---

5 *Corfu Channel case, ICJ Reports 1949*, p. 35.
6 Draft Articles on the Responsibility of States for Internationally Wrongful Acts, International Law Commission, annexed to Resolution 56/83 of the General Assembly of the United Nations, 12 Dec. 2001, A/RES/56/83.

But can such breaches justify military intervention, thereby forming an exception to the general prohibition of the use of force laid down in Article 2, paragraph 4, of the United Nations Charter, except in the case of self-defence?

The doctrine of humanitarian intervention (*ingérence humanitaire*) was first championed by certain non-governmental organizations active in the fields of public health and providing disaster aid and assistance. It aims at justifying intervention, even forcible, that would 'otherwise be wrongful' where 'the lives of the recipients are in imminent danger'.[7]

This might be considered as nothing more than a return to the old doctrine of humanitarian intervention (*intervention d'humanité*), invoked in the nineteenth century to justify all sorts of attempts at domination, whether in a colonial context or otherwise.

Human rights have by now evolved to a point where they can no longer be considered as being part of the exclusive jurisdiction of the State. State sovereignty not only confers prerogatives on the State but also imposes on it responsibilities towards those living in its territory, whether its own nationals or foreigners. Regarding the 'principles and rules concerning the basic rights of the human person', 'all States . . . have a legal interest in their protection', as the International Court of Justice pointed out in the *Barcelona Traction* case.[8]

But to proceed from there to contending that, if the territorial State fails in its mission, any other State can act in its stead, even against its will, is tantamount to saying that such intervention is 'from the nature of things, . . . reserved for the most powerful States',[9] as the Court observed in the *Corfu Channel* case. Obviously, this would be contrary to one of the founding principles of international society today: the sovereign equality of States (Article 2, paragraph 1, of the Charter of the United Nations).

This debate was to give rise to renewed discussion of the concept of sovereignty, with respect not only to the power actually exercised by an authority in a territory within delimited boundaries but also to that authority's responsibility to ensure the 'human security' of the entire population, whether nationals or foreigners, and to safeguard its rights.

This approach has been cited by the International Court of Justice as the basis for diplomatic protection:

> Owing to the substantive development of international law over recent decades in respect of the rights it accords to individuals, the scope *ratione materiae* of diplomatic protection, originally limited to alleged violations

---

7 M. Bettati and B. Kouchner, *Le devoir d'ingérence: Peut-on les laisser mourir?* (Paris: Denoël, 1987); M. Bettati, 'Un droit d'ingérence?', *RGDIP*, 95 (1991): 650.
8 *Barcelona Traction, Light and Power Company, Limited (Belgium v. Spain), Second Phase, Judgment, ICJ Reports 1970*, p. 32, paras 33–34.
9 *Corfu Channel case, ICJ Reports 1949*, p. 35.

of the minimum standard of treatment of aliens, has subsequently widened to include, *inter alia*, internationally guaranteed human rights.[10]

Following NATO's intervention in Kosovo (in March 1999) and the bombing of Belgrade, the Secretary-General of the United Nations drew the General Assembly's attention to the conflicting views within the international community on reconciling the need to prevent massive human rights violations and the constraints on 'humanitarian' intervention in the context of State sovereignty.[11]

Canada then went on to take the initiative, in September 2000, in establishing an International Commission on Intervention and State Sovereignty, which published a report called *The Responsibility to Protect* in December 2001.[12] The report stresses that priority in authorising military intervention should lie with the Security Council, but adds that, if the Council is stymied by the exercise of the veto power, it might fall *in fine* to ad hoc coalitions or to individual States to do so; here, the report is, however, based more on considerations of pragmatism than of legality.

Remaining unresolved, the issue of legality was to come up again, within the context of the United Nations reform process, when the Secretary-General established a High-level Panel on Threats, Challenges and Change in 2003.

In its report of 1 December 2004, entitled *A More Secure World: Our Shared Responsibility*, the Panel re-examined the issue from the perspective of the *Corfu Channel Judgment* and the United Nations Charter. It observed that: 'It cannot be assumed that every State will always be able, or willing, to meet its responsibilities to protect its own people and avoid harming its neighbours.'[13] It deemed that in any case it was for the collective security system of the United Nations to step in, even if this system needed improvement to respond more effectively to the challenges of the contemporary world.

In keeping with the *Corfu Channel Judgment*, the Panel concluded that a State cannot, acting on its own initiative, take another State's place for the purpose of enforcing law and order in the latter's territory.

In the end, this approach to the concept of sovereignty was endorsed under the heading 'Responsibility to protect populations from genocide, war crimes, ethnic cleansing and crimes against humanity' in the 2005 World Summit Outcome adopted by the General Assembly.[14] This document reiterated that

---

10 *Ahmadou Sadio Diallo (Republic of Guinea v. Democratic Republic of the Congo)*, Preliminary Objections, Judgment, *ICJ Reports 2007*, p. 17, para. 39.
11 See, in particular, the Secretary-General's Millennium Report, entitled, 'We the peoples: the role of the United Nations in the twenty-first century', Doc. A/54/2000, 27 Mar. 2000, p. 35, para. 217.
12 Report of the International Commission on Intervention and State Sovereignty, *The Responsibility to Protect* (Ottawa: International Development Research Centre, 2001).
13 General Assembly Doc. A/59/565, 2 Dec. 2004, para. 29.
14 General Assembly Resolution A/RES/60/1, 24 Oct. 2005.

the State bears the primary responsibility to protect its population, through prevention, with assistance, if needed, from the international community. But, if a State does not fulfil this responsibility, it is for the Security Council, and the Security Council alone, to authorize collective action under Chapter VII of the Charter, possibly in conjunction with regional organizations; acting in a manner consistent with the purposes and principles of the United Nations. (Chap. VIII).

Thus, the only exception allowing the use of force, in case of massive human rights violations, is exclusively for the Security Council acting under Chapter VII of the United Nations Charter, such violations having been characterised in Security Council practice as threats to international peace and security. The proposed reforms to the Charter, suspending the five permanent members' veto power in respect of situations involving genocide, crimes against humanity, war crimes or ethnic cleansing, were not adopted. Therein lies one of the weaknesses of the current system of collective security.

Nevertheless, the notion of a responsibility to protect can be considered to be the outcome of the fruitful reflection initiated in the *Corfu Channel Judgment* on the concept of State sovereignty in today's world; a State's obligations *vis-à-vis* its own population have by now been placed, as it were, under international watch.

3 The bar

Jean-Pierre Cot

3.1 Introduction

This contribution assesses the position of the bar in the *Corfu Channel* case some sixty years since the Court at The Hague handed down its decision. This is all the more interesting, given the changes, for better or worse, of the bar's current practice before the Court.[1]

To appreciate the situation, the political context needs to be recalled. The *Corfu Channel* incident was one of the first incidents of the Cold War. The initial problem was triggered by an Albanian battery in the vicinity of Saranda opening fire on 15 May 1946 on the British cruisers *Orion* and *Superb*. The United Kingdom protested, stating that innocent passage through straits is a right recognised by international law. To prove the point, the Admiralty sent the cruisers *Mauritius* and *Leander* and the destroyers *Saumarez* and *Volage* through the North Corfu Strait on 22 October 1946. The *Saumarez* and the *Volage* struck mines and were heavily damaged. Forty-four British officers and men were killed and a further 42 sailors were injured. Three weeks later, on 22 November 1946, the North Corfu Channel was swept by British minesweepers and 22 moored mines were cut (*Operation Retail*). The British government then brought the incident to the attention of the United Nations Security Council. On 9 April 1947, the Security Council recommended that the dispute be submitted to the International Court of Justice. Proceedings were instituted by the United Kingdom on 22 May 1947. The Court delivered its decisions respectively on 25 March 1948 (*Preliminary Objection*), 9 April 1949 (*Merits*) and 5 December 1949 (*Compensation*).

In parallel, the Cold War settled in. Churchill coined the expression in 1946. On 12 March 1947, President Truman announced $400 million of U.S. military assistance to Greece and Turkey (the Truman Doctrine). The Prague

---

[1] This note is limited to an overview of the Parties' strategies and tactics. Issues of substance are only touched on when necessary for the purpose of this overview and are otherwise dealt with in the learned and substantive contributions to this volume. References to the relevant literature will be found in the substantive contributions.

coup and the Berlin Blockade were staged in 1948. The Korean War started in 1950.

More specifically, the Albanian regime was at the forefront of the Cold War. Enver Hodja eliminated all democratic opposition early in 1946. He was a staunch ally of the Soviet Union and of Yugoslavia, of Stalin and of Tito. Albania was in fact considered a Yugoslav protectorate. The Greek civil war was developing, with the Greek Communist Party supported by the Soviet Union, and the Greek government supported by the United Kingdom and the United States. To compound the tension in the area, Greece voiced claims on Northern Epirus.

The rift between Stalin and Tito intervened in 1948, in the midst of the *Corfu Channel* proceedings before the Court. Hodja clearly sided with Stalin. The decision had direct consequences on the judicial proceedings.

The oral pleadings were consequently conducted in this highly antagonistic context. The tension was reflected in the style and content of the pleadings: 'wholly reckless allegations . . . irresponsible abuse . . . [a] clumsy and deliberate piece of forgery'.[2] Nevertheless, counsel maintained a polite and courteous stance as well as a good working relationship on the production of documents and the examination of witnesses. This obviously did not preclude some remarks *in cauda venenum*.[3] The atmosphere was quite different from proceedings in other fora, whether before the Security Council or before domestic courts. Interestingly, one of Albania's counsel, Joë Nordmann, was during the same period counsel for the French Communist Party and principal advocate before the French courts in a highly political case of libel, involving Victor Kravchenko, a Soviet defector who had written a book on the Gulag. The proceedings in Paris were not nearly as polite as those in The Hague.[4]

The technical setting was quite different to current ones before the International Court of Justice. At the time, simultaneous interpretation was unknown in The Hague Court. Interpretation followed statements every few sentences. Proceedings were protracted, with a greater immediate concentration on oratory and, when necessary, there was an immediate correction by the speaker of any errors of interpretation.

The teams were small when compared to present practice. Two or three counsel appeared for each party with a back-up of two or three more, including technical advice.

The lead counsel for both Parties on the Merits had comparable backgrounds. Sir Hartley Shawcross, appearing for the United Kingdom, was the

---

2 H. Shawcross, *Pleadings, Oral Arguments, Documents*, vol. III, CR 49.1, pp. 203–204.
3 'I think no impartial observer would deny that the case for Albania has been well presented by Professor Cot and Mr. Nordmann . . . If such arguments are insufficient to extricate Albania from complicity in the commission of this outrage, then there is nothing more that could possibly be urged on Albania's behalf.' F. Soskice, *Pleadings, Oral Arguments, Documents*, vol. IV, CR 49.2, p. 471.
4 N. Berberova, *L'affaire Kravtchenko*, translated from Russian (Paris: Actes Sud, 1990).

Attorney General. He was a brilliant barrister and had been appointed the youngest KC in British history at the age of 35. He did not have any particular training in international law, but was involved in foreign affairs early on as an MP and as member of the Labour Government from 1945 to 1951. He was the chief prosecutor for Britain at the Nuremberg Trials and his Government's delegate to the Security Council during proceedings relating to the *Corfu Channel* incident. An independent personality, he retired from politics in 1958, was expected to join the Conservative Party and sat as a cross-bencher in the House of Lords.

Appearing for Albania, Pierre Cot had also started his career as a brilliant barrister. At the age of 27, he graduated first in the *Concours d'Agrégation de Droit Public* (professorship), the *Conférence du Stage des Avocats au Barreau de Paris* and the *Conférence des Avocats aux Conseils* (Supreme Courts). He was trained in public law, but did not specialise particularly in international law. After a few years as an academic, he concentrated on the bar and was a close associate of Raymond Poincaré, then President of Council and Minister of Foreign Affairs. Elected as a Radical-Socialist MP, he closely followed foreign affairs in Parliament and was member of French Governments before World War II. As independent-minded as Sir Hartley Shawcross, he quit the Radical-Socialist Party after the War and led a small pro-Communist party in Parliament from 1946 to 1958.

The clash of talent and of personalities enlivened the oral proceedings before the Court. But it was short-lived. Sir Hartley had to leave after the initial statements to attend to his duties in Government. Pierre Cot noted that he had enlightened the Court for but a brief moment, as the meteor that he was.

If the lead counsel had similar backgrounds, the rest of the teams were quite different. After the departure of Shawcross, Sir Frank Soskice, then Solicitor General, took over as lead counsel. He was a domestic barrister with no particular involvement in international law or international affairs. He did have considerable experience at the bar and proved a very able advocate, in particular when examining the witnesses and highlighting the documents produced by the Parties.

The brunt of the legal argumentation fell upon Legal Counsel for the Foreign Office, Sir Eric Beckett. Beckett was a talented barrister, but also an important international lawyer in his own right. He had the benefit of a formidable back-up team, including Hersch Lauterpacht in the Preliminary Exceptions phase; Humphrey Waldock, R. O. Wilberforce, Mervyn Jones and E. Reed in the Merits phase. It was quite an impressive group of international scholars.[5]

---

5 The Australian Minister for External Affairs, H. V. Evatt, offered to join the team. His offer obviously embarrassed the Foreign Office, as he could not have held a position other than as lead counsel. Sir Eric Beckett suggested that he would rather that Evatt represent the

The Albanians were at pains to line up such a team. During the Preliminary Exceptions phase, Albania was represented by Professor Wochac, of the University of Prague and by Professor Lapenna, of the University of Zagreb. As a result of the rift with Yugoslavia in 1948, the Albanian Government changed the team. Pierre Cot was seconded by Joë Nordmann, Marc Jacquier and Paul Villard, respected domestic barristers and members of – or closely associated with – the French Communist Party, but with little experience in international law.[6]

Certain newspapers criticised French lawyers for acting on behalf of Albania and against the United Kingdom, a staunch ally of France. Such an issue would not be raised today. But in the context of the Cold War, Cot found it necessary to state that, when small States were accused by a Great Power before an international court, there would always be a French lawyer ready to act on their behalf.[7]

The balance between the two teams was somewhat unequal. Pierre Cot made the point, stressing the difficulty for small countries with limited means to appear before the Court. He noted that small States did not have the technical back-up of big States, could not retrieve documents, locate witnesses or call upon the advice of experts so easily. He gave the example of the principal expert witness for Albania, Admiral Moullec, who did not have time to examine the issues at length, unlike his British counterparts. More specifically, he noted that the argument developed by Sir Eric Beckett, justifying *Operation Retail* on the United Kingdom's need to gather the evidence before it disappeared, was to the advantage of Great Powers. One could hardly imagine the Albanian navy minesweeping British territorial waters in similar circumstances . . .[8]

The remark was part of an overall strategy, seeking to portray Albania as a small country with little capacity to stand up to the United Kingdom, a major power with an imperial outlook and an impressive naval force. To accuse Albania of aggressive intent in the incident lacked credibility. Cot's point

---

British position in the advisory proceedings on the issue of *Conditions of Admission of a State to Membership in the United Nations (Article 4 of the Charter)*. Evatt did not take up the offer and dropped the idea. Cf. L. W. Maher, 'Herbert Vere Evatt, the Rule of International Law and the *Corfu Channel case*', *Australian Journal of Legal History* (2005), available at: http://www.austlii.edu.au/au/journals/AJLH/2005/3.html (accessed 25 November 2010).

6 Joë Nordmann had joined the French prosecution team at the Nuremberg trial. Aside from this brief venture by Nordmann into the arena of international criminal law, none of the other members of the Albanian delegation had any prior contact with international law. Single-handed, if one may say, Pierre Cot took on the imposing British team, backed by the Foreign Office in London; a situation quite unimaginable today before The Hague Court.

7 CR 49.2, p. 662.

8 CR 49.2, p. 678.

registered with the Court and was to some extent reflected in the Court's decision in its legal characterisation of *Operation Retail*.

This chapter will concentrate on the Merits phase and on the oral proceedings. The Merits phase was the most lengthy and thorough one. It was in that phase that the Parties argued the main questions of international law and the Court's decision on that phase was an important contribution to essential aspects of the law. Moreover, the Albanian team changed between the proceedings on Preliminary Exceptions and the Merits phase, and Albania was not represented in the Compensation phase.

The Special Agreement between the Parties put two questions to the Court: (1) is Albania responsible for under international law for the explosions that occurred on 22 October 1946 and is there a duty to pay compensation?; and (2) has the United Kingdom violated the sovereignty of Albania by reason of the passage of ships of the Royal Navy on 22 October and on 12–13 November (*Operation Retail*) and is there any duty to give satisfaction? Sir Hartley Shawcross and Professor Pierre Cot, as lead counsel, addressed both questions in their oral pleadings. Sir Frank Soskice and Mr Joë Nordmann concentrated on question no. 1, Sir Eric Beckett and Pierre Cot on question no. 2.

The oral pleadings were by far more important than the written pleadings in the case. Written pleadings were very concise by current standards. For the United Kingdom: 2 pages for the Application, 18 pages for the Memorial, 67 pages for the Reply. For Albania, 11 pages for the Counter-Memorial, 63 pages for the Rejoinder. By contrast, the oral pleadings filled two volumes, amounting respectively to 529 pages and 697 pages.[9]

Beyond the statistics, the drama was in the oral proceedings. It was a fine tournament, with the production of documents, the examination of witnesses and exchange of legal arguments. Perhaps more to the point, the oral proceedings were not a mere repetition of the written pleadings. They were an amplification, an exposition of the summary written arguments. They also provided an opportunity to produce new documents and cross-examine witnesses with effective results. There was no impression of *déjà vu*, as is so often the case today.

The oral proceedings were lengthy, yet they were rarely verbose. The exchange of arguments contributed to focusing on the main points of disagreement and dispensing with secondary points. Sir Frank Soskice was very effective in progressively pinning down the issue of connivance as the main ground for Albania's responsibility. Cot was equally effective in addressing the essentials concerning the resort to force in relation to *Operation Retail*. In both examples, secondary issues were brushed aside early in the day in order to concentrate on principal differences.

---

9 The Merits phase lasted from 9 November 1948 to 9 April 1949, with 16 sittings in 1948 and 10 sittings in 1949.

3.2 Issues of evidence

Issues of evidence were paramount in the Parties' pleadings. Facts were essential to prove the main points of the respective arguments. Both Parties started with affirmations or innuendos wide of the mark. The United Kingdom initially accused Albania of laying the minefield, whereas Albania did not have a naval force, much less a capacity to lay mines.[10] Albania aired the possibility that Greece or uncontrolled Greek forces had laid the mines or even that British secret services had done so ...[11] These far-fetched allegations were dropped early on to concentrate on the facts of the case, i.e. connivance in the laying or knowledge by the Albanian Government of the minefield.

Opposition was not really on questions of principle. Albania naturally insisted that the claimant, i.e. the United Kingdom, shoulder the burden of the proof. The United Kingdom did not contest this and accepted that it had to come up with the supporting evidence. Albania insisted on the need for watertight evidence to incriminate a sovereign State. The United Kingdom countered this with the concept of evidence 'beyond reasonable doubt'.[12]

Sir Hartley Shawcross insisted, in his introductory statement, on the difficulty for a claimant to present evidence concealed by a sovereign State:

> A government in a matter of this kind has a very great advantage over an individual. It can use its powers to prevent impartial police investigation within its own territory, as, indeed, Albania did not hesitate to do when there was the question of the minesweeping immediately after the accident. It can cover up and conceal its clandestine activity in a way in which it would be quite impossible for an individual under surveillance of the police in ordinary circumstances to do. Consequently, in a case like this involving disputes of fact between States, evidence must largely be of a circumstantial nature.[13]

But the skirmishes on points of principle did not go much further than that, as Albanian counsel conceded that, in the end, the question was one of 'intimate conviction' for the Court.[14] The real problems arose with the examination of witnesses and experts.

---

10 Declaration of Sir Alexander Cadogan before the Security Council, CR 49.1, p. 306; United Kingdom submission no. 2, *ICJ Reports 1949*, p. 10.
11 J. Nordmann, CR 49.1, pp. 334–335; CR 49.2, p. 612; *ICJ Reports 1949*, p. 17.
12 Shawcross, CR 49.1, p. 259; Soskice, CR 49.2, p. 480.
13 Shawcross, CR 49.1, p. 259
14 According to Shawcross, CR 49.1, pp. 260–261:

> In a case like this, where indeed there is no balance of evidence, but where the evidence is overwhelmingly in favour of the claimants in this matter, the Court will adopt a

Examination of witnesses was a crucial step in the proceedings. The differences between the British and the French, the Anglo-Saxon and the Continental approaches to the subject were striking. The procedure before the Court is strongly tainted by the common law tradition in this matter, even if it is 'liberal', to quote the then acting President.[15] In preliminary phases, the common law allows, indeed instructs, counsel to 'prepare' the witness, to agree on the subject matters to be raised during examination. The Continental tradition strictly prohibits any preliminary contact between witnesses and counsel.

The point was made in relation to the intention, of the Albanian Government, to call the Yugoslav Chargé d'Affaires as a witness.[16] Sir Hartley Shawcross pointed out the difficulty:

> The Albanian Government is going to call the Chargé d'Affaires as a witness. They would not call him as a witness unless they knew what he was going to say, and I want to know what he is going to say, as the Rules of the Court entitle me to know, before I make further comments on the communiqué which has been submitted by the Yugoslav Government ... I don't want him to study what I say and then adapt his evidence accordingly. I want the evidence first.[17]

Pierre Cot answered that he did not know what the Chargé d'Affaires was going to say.[18] He recalled the French tradition and added that the Rules of the Court only called for 'indications in general terms of the point or points to which their evidence will be directed'. He then offered to produce the list of

> standard of proof which seems consistent with doing justice between the two Parties. On the other hand, of course, the Court must not give judgment lightly against a sovereign State in an important matter, and all cases which come before this Court are important.
>
> (CR 49.1, pp. 260–261)

Cot stated:

> Ici encore, sur le principe, pas de difficulté entre nous. Il n'existe pas, en droit, de système de preuves obligatoires analogue à ce que nous appelons, en droit français, le régime des preuves légales. Le seule système applicable et, si vous me permettez de le dire, le seul convenable quand il s'agit d'une aussi haute juridiction que la vôtre, c'est évidemment le système de l'intime conviction du juge, c'est-à-dire en réalité l'acte de confiance que la communauté internationale fait aux juges de la Cour internationale de Justice. L'adoption de cette règle sans réserve, sans limites, est un hommage rendu à la dignité de votre juridiction.
>
> (CR 49.1, 353)

15 CR 49.1, p. 428.
16 CR 49.1, pp. 245–250.
17 Ibid., pp. 245–246.
18 'Conformément à nos habitudes françaises, nous ne voyons pas les témoins avant de les faire entendre, et nous sommes incapables de dire en quel sens ils déposeront' (ibid., p. 246).

questions he intended to put to the witness. *In fine*, Albania decided not to call the Chargé d'Affaires, as the Yugoslav communiqué was accepted as authentic by the opposing party and the Chargé d'Affaires was not a direct witness to the incident itself.

The United Kingdom called six witnesses, all navy officers, three additional witnesses being examined as experts. Albania called three witnesses and two experts. Examination of the witnesses took place from 22 November 1948 to 14 December 1948, in 20 sittings of the Court. The examination and cross-examination proceeded courteously. For example, before proceeding to the cross-examination of Admiral Moullec, an expert called by Albania, Sir Frank Soskice paid tribute, on behalf of the United Kingdom delegation, to the expert's distinguished war service with the Free French Naval Forces and the Royal Navy.[19]

That being said, the examination of witnesses encapsulated all the *dramatis personae* of a domestic criminal trial, with its strategies and uncertainties. It was magnified by the talent of the opposing barristers and complicated by the opposition of two procedural traditions.

Pierre Cot noted, in his final statement, that the examination of the witnesses had taken much of the Court's time. He felt partially responsible for the length of the proceedings, due to his lack of familiarity with the British procedures adopted by the Court. He hinted that, in the future, the Court might reconsider its procedure and follow Continental principles, which were perhaps more adapted to the requirements of international courts.[20]

As to procedural skills, Cot was thrown off balance by the experience of Sir Frank Soskice. During examination and cross-examination, common law rules are far more exacting than Continental ones. Whereas Soskice sailed through his examinations without any objections by the Albanian party, Cot was bogged down by the intricacies of the common law and wryly remarked, at one point, that, had he known better, he would have opposed to the British examination the very objections Soskice repeatedly voiced during the cross-examination of Commander Kovacic.[21]

But Albanian counsel succeeded in casting doubt on the credibility of the witness. He insisted on his belated appearance and even more so that of a last-minute witness, Zizan Pavlov, called to confirm Kovacic's questionable statements. Both witnesses were defectors from the Yugoslav armed forces. Their declarations were contradicted by the official communications of the Yugoslav Government. The Court could not rely on them without questioning the veracity of Yugoslav authorities. Cot put the dilemma before the Court: either you accept the information provided by a sovereign State, Yugoslavia, or you

---

19 CR 49.2, p. 443.
20 CR 49.2, p. 613.
21 CR 49.2, p. 560.

challenge that information on the basis of declarations made by private persons with a political, albeit honourable, bias.

The Court conceded the point to Albania. In its Judgment, it stated:

> Without deciding as to the personal sincerity of the witness Kovacic, or the truth of what he said, the Court finds that the facts stated by the witness from his personal knowledge are not sufficient to prove what the United Kingdom Government considered them to prove.[22]

The Court went on to consider that 'in the light of the information now available, the authors of the minelaying remain unknown.'[23]

The point made by Pierre Cot was part of a broader argument on that point. If Kovacic was correct in asserting that the Yugoslav Navy had laid the minefield, why was it that the United Kingdom had not addressed its claim to Yugoslavia, instead of little Albania, quite incapable of such an operation?

Nevertheless, British counsel was yet to have the last word. Sir Frank Soskice, in his reply, noted that Albania had concentrated its efforts on the Kovacic statement. But that evidence was only supplementary. In Sir Frank's words, '[I]important as this evidence certainly is, it is not essential to our case that it should be accepted.'[24] The Court agreed and went on to declare that 'From all the facts and observations mentioned above, the Court draws the conclusion that the laying of the minefields which caused the explosions on October 22nd, 1946, could not have been accomplished without the knowledge of the Albanian Government.'[25]

3.3 Experts

Experts played an important part in the case. Both Parties called experts as witnesses to the bar. The Acting President pointed out the difference between experts and witnesses. The United Kingdom called naval officers to the stand. Some had been actual witnesses to the incidents, but were also asked questions on the basis of their expertise. Acting President Guerrero asked them to make two separate declarations, one as witness, according to Article 53(1) of the Rules of the Court as then drafted, the other as expert, according to then Article 53(2) of the Rules.

Albania presented a different situation. On one hand, it called Albanian witnesses with no particular qualifications. On the other, it called two naval officers who had not been witness to the events, but did offer comments as experts. Acting President Guerrero noted that the two officers were members of

---

22 *ICJ Reports 1949*, p. 16.
23 *ICJ Reports 1949*, p. 17.
24 CR 49.2, p. 512.
25 *ICJ Reports 1949*, p. 22.

the Albanian delegation. He asked if they expected to participate in the examination of the witnesses called by the United Kingdom. If that were the case, they were not to make the solemn Article 53(2) declaration, but were to be considered as counsel. Joë Nordmann, for Albania, announced that they would not appear as counsel, but as experts. Accordingly, they made an Article 53(2) declaration.

Quite early on, the Court considered appointing its own panel of experts. Before the examination of witnesses and experts, Acting President Guerrero announced that subsequently, the Court might hear other experts designated by itself, but that no final decision had been taken by the Court on that point.[26] After having heard the witnesses and experts called by the Parties, the Court decided, on 17 December 1948, to appoint three experts pursuant to Article 50 of the Statute and Article 57 of the then Rules. The experts filed their report on 8 January 1949. The Parties commented on the report in their Reply and Rejoinder. In particular, Pierre Cot insisted on a certain number of confusions in the report and suggested that the experts confirm, *in situ*, their conclusions.[27] The Court decided on an inspection by the experts in the vicinity of Sibenik and the Bay of Saranda. The second report of the experts was produced on 8 February with supplementary answers on 12 February 1949. It basically confirmed the British position. The minefield could not have been laid without the knowledge of the Albanian authorities.

The expert report put an end to the argument on Question no. 1; namely, the issue of Albanian responsibility. If Albania had knowledge, Albania should have notified the minefield to all concerned and in particular to the British Admiralty in view of the 22 October passage through the North Corfu Channel. Albanian counsel lamely tried to interpret the Hague Convention of 1907 as placing the responsibility of notification solely on the authority that had effectively laid the minefield. United Kingdom counsel opposed this with a more extensive interpretation of the clause. *In fine*, Albanian counsel recognised that, if Albania had been informed of the operation before the incidents and in time to warn the British vessels, her responsibility would be engaged.[28] The Court brushed aside the arguments, noting that the Convention was only applicable in time of war and the obligation to notify was based on certain general and well-recognised principles, namely elementary considerations of humanity, even more exacting in peace than in war, etc.[29]

3.4 Innocent passage

If the first question put to the Court hinged largely on issues of evidence, the second question was more a matter of law. In fact, two separate questions were

---

26 Minutes of the sittings, 20th public sitting, 19 November 1948, CR 49.1, p. 172.
27 CR 49.2, pp. 644–650.
28 Cot, CR 49.2, pp. 635–636; *ICJ Reports 1949*, p. 22.
29 *ICJ Reports 1949*, p. 22.

put to the Court regarding the sovereignty of the Albanian People's Republic. The passage of the Royal Navy on 22 October 1946 involved the legal characterisation of the right of innocent passage through international straits. *Operation Retail* of 12 and 13 November raised the problem of the use of force.

The passage of 22 October 1946 was triggered by the following preceding incident. While passing southward through the North Corfu Channel on 15 May 1945, the British cruisers *Orion* and *Superb* were fired upon by an Albanian battery in the vicinity of Saranda. The ships were not hit and did not return fire. But the British Government protested and diplomatic correspondence ensued. The Albanian Government subjected the passage of warships to previous notification and authorisation. The British Government maintained its view on the right of innocent passage.

The characterisation of the Channel as an international strait was not all that clear at the time. There was no agreed definition of an international strait. Pierre Cot noted that international traffic was very limited in the Northern Channel, as access to the port of Corfu was essentially through the Southern Channel. The Northern Channel could in no way qualify as a major international route. Sir Eric Beckett insisted, on the contrary, on the importance of the Channel. He added that the definition of an international strait was a strictly geographical one. The Court followed Beckett's argument and considered the geographical situation of the Channel, connecting two parts of the high seas, and being used for international navigation, as decisive as to the characterisation.

That was not the end of the matter. Pierre Cot argued that there was no general regime as to passage of warships through international straits. Major straits were subject to international treaties' organisation of the passage through straits. Cot quoted Hyde: 'There are straits and straits.'[30] He considered that passage of warships, in the absence of a treaty, was a question of comity, not of legal obligation. The coastal State had the right to refuse passage or to issue regulations as to the passage of warships. Beckett did not deny the right of the coastal State to issue regulations, but considered that that right stopped short of prohibiting innocent passage.

In the end, the matter boiled down to the definition of innocent passage. For Pierre Cot, any unauthorised passage by a warship could not be considered as an innocent passage. By definition, passage of a warship without authorisation amounted to hostile intent and could not be construed as innocent. He repeatedly referred to the authority of Elihu Root: 'Warships may not pass without consent because they threaten; merchant ships may pass because they do not threaten.'[31] The Court did not accept the Albanian argument and considered that the right of passage for warships through international straits was to be upheld.

30 CR 49.1, p. 382.
31 CR 49.1, p. 377.

The question was then the manner in which the passage was carried out. Albania argued that the ships were sailing in diamond formation of combat, that the positions of the guns were not consistent with innocent passage, that the crew was at action stations. Beckett argued successfully that the ships were not in combat formation, but in line and that the guns were in line with the ships. The crew were at action stations and ready to retaliate in case of Albanian fire, but this measure of precaution was not unreasonable, given the firing from the Albanian battery on May 15.

The decisive question was that of intent. The British Government admitted that the passage of warships through the straits was not only for purposes of navigation, but to test Albania's attitude. Pierre Cot quoted the Admiralty telegram of 21 September specifying that 'His Majesty's Government ... wish to know whether the Albanian Government have learnt to behave themselves' and asked when the Commander-in-Chief, Mediterranean, intended to instruct ships under his command to pass through the North Corfu Strait. Quoting Walter Schücking at the 1930 Hague Codification Conference, Cot noted that such a passage was obviously a demonstration of force and could not, in any way, be characterised as 'innocent'. Sir Eric Beckett agreed that passage, to be innocent, should respect the sovereignty of the coastal State and should not be used to inspect coastal defences for example. He then addressed the issue of intent: 'The first and primary test is an objective one: the question is decided on what was done and not on what might have been done or even intended to be done.'[32]

The Court accepted Sir Eric's argument. It considered that the Government of the United Kingdom was not bound to abstain from exercising its right of passage, which the Albanian Government had illegally denied.[33] It did not characterise the intention but focused on the manner in which the passage was carried out.

An issue of evidence opposed the Parties in relation to the 22 October passage. The British Memorial made reference to the Admiralty instructions contained in a document XCU (standing for 'Exercise Corfu'). The Albanian Party and the Court requested that the British Government produce the document. The United Kingdom refused, pleading naval secrecy. Sir Eric Beckett explained at length that the document did not contain any relevant information for the case. He added: 'We recognize that the Court may take note of our refusal. We recognize too that the Court may – it is not obliged to – draw inferences from our refusal.'[34]

The Court did take note, and did not draw any inferences. Rightly so, as the British archives show today. As Anthony Carty has noted, XCU did envisage certain British reactions should its vessels be fired upon on 22 October, but it

---

32 CR 49.2, p. 564.
33 *ICJ Reports 1949*, p. 30.
34 CR 49.2, p. 564.

did not in any way anticipate the possible existence of a minefield.[35] Indeed, the reactions of the vessels hit by the mines were very moderate. Their action was aimed at limiting the consequences of the disaster and certainly not at any form of retaliation against Albania.

As to the production of the document, it appears there was quite a controversy between Shawcross and Beckett. Shawcross felt the document should have been produced and, had he known of its existence, he would have hesitated to go to the Court. He was overruled by the Prime Minister. In terms of efficiency, Beckett was correct. If XCU had been annexed to the Memorial, it probably would not have been a decisive factor in the Court's determinations. Produced at a later stage, it would have unnecessarily focused the attention of Albanian counsel and of the Court to the detriment of the British case. But the issue did cast a doubt on the reality of the British Navy's intentions and on the Court's readiness to accept the explanations of the United Kingdom counsel without drawing any inferences from the refusal to produce the document.[36]

3.5 *Operation Retail* and the right of intervention

The last issue addressed by the Parties was *Operation Retail*, the minesweeping of the Corfu Channel by the British fleet on 12–13 November 1946. The operation was carried out under the protection of an important covering force composed of an aircraft carrier, cruisers and other war vessels. Throughout the operation the covering force remained at a certain distance to the west of the Channel, except for the frigate *St. Bride's Bay*, which was stationed in the Channel south-east of Cape Kiephali. The sweep began on the morning of 13 November, at about 9 o'clock, and ended in the afternoon near nightfall. The area swept was in Albanian territorial waters, and within the limits of the Channel previously swept.[37]

The Parties' submissions are an interesting indication of the way they respectively intended to address the issue. Albania, claimant on this issue, submitted that:

> (7) The British naval authorities were not entitled to proceed, on November 12 and 13, 1946, to sweep mines in Albanian territorial waters

---

35 A. Carty, 'The *Corfu Channel case* – and the Missing Admiralty Orders', *The Law and Practice of International Courts and Tribunals*, 3 (2004): 1–35.
36 Carty, ibid., p. 29, considers that Sir Eric Beckett, in his last statement, 'misled the Court about the probable contents of the document'. Whether Beckett was correct in arguing for refusal to produce the document is one matter. But, the British Government having decided to refuse production of XCU, Beckett could not be more explicit about its content and I do not see where he misled the Court. If someone is to blame, it is rather the Court, which declined to draw any negative inferences from the refusal to produce the document and stood by its definition of innocent passage as being passage that appears as innocent, the question of intention being set aside.
37 *ICJ Reports 1949*, p. 33.

without the previous consent of the Albanian authorities. (8) That the Court should find that, on both these occasions, the Government of the United Kingdom of Great Britain and Northern Ireland committed a breach of the rules of international law and that the Albanian Government has a right to demand that it should give satisfaction therefor.[38]

The British submission was oral and terse: 'I demand that the Court decide that on neither head of the counterclaim has Albania made out her case, and that there is no ground for the Court to award nominal damages of one farthing or one franc.'[39]

The British defence of the operation was developed in the written Reply.[40] The United Kingdom put forward two arguments. First, the Corfu Channel was located in the sub-area allocated to Greece for minesweeping purposes by the regional mine clearance organisations set up after World War II, in particular the Medzon (Mediterranean Zone) Board. The Greek Government had the authority to sweep the Channel or to authorise the Government of the United Kingdom to do so. The Greek Government consented to the minesweeping. The United Kingdom conceded that Albania was not a party to the minesweeping agreement. But, as the Channel is an international highway subject to the right of innocent passage, neither Greece nor Albania had the right to prevent the passage of traffic or to prevent the clearance of obstructions to this passage. The Court disposed of this first line of defence in a brief paragraph, noting that the allocation of the sector to Greece was merely nominal and that Albania was not consulted at the time despite the fact that the Channel passed through Albanian territorial waters.[41]

The second line of defence was more developed and gave rise to an important debate among the Parties and within the Court. To quote the United Kingdom's Reply:

> (b) as, on 22nd October, His Majesty's ships had been struck by mines in the Channel in circumstances which created justifiable suspicion that these mines had been deliberately placed there, and that His Majesty's ships had been deliberately allowed by the Albanian authorities to run into them, the Government of the United Kingdom was entitled to sweep the Channel, both to remove an immediate source of danger to shipping and to investigate whether there was any foundation for these suspicions, and to do so without delay to prevent the removal of the evidence, if there was any, justifying these suspicions.[42]

---

38 *ICJ Reports 1949*, p. 12.
39 Ibid.
40 *Pleadings, Oral Arguments, Documents*, vol. II, Reply of the United Kingdom, pp. 280 ff.
41 *ICJ Reports 1949*, p. 34.
42 *Pleadings, Oral Arguments, Documents*, vol. II, Reply of the United Kingdom, pp. 280–281.

The British Government noted a threat to the shipping of all nations and a manifest breach of the Hague Convention VIII of 1907. 'Either of these grounds was in itself sufficient to justify intervention by the United Kingdom, the State which had suffered from it.'[43] The reply then developed an unabashed defence of the traditional right of intervention in international law. It referred to Oppenheim, Hall, Fauchille-Bontemps, Blüntschli, as justifying the right of a State to intervene in such a situation. It added an interesting quotation by Moore ('*Principles of American Diplomacy*'), referring to the invasion of Cuba by the United States in 1898:

> The intervention of the United States in Cuba . . . rested upon the ground that there existed in Cuba conditions so injurious to the United States that they could no longer be endured. Its action was analogous to what is known in private law as the abatement of a nuisance. On this ground the intervention was justified by Rivier, one of the eminent publicists in Europe; and on this ground its justification must continue to rest.[44]

In others words, a legal justification consisting of a big stick in the backyard . . . The British Reply concluded on the point that 'the situation . . . thus clearly falls within the class of situation recognized by international law as justifying intervention.' It added that:

> In view of the secrecy with which these mines had been laid in the Channel there was ample reason to suppose that the *corpora delicti* would be removed, if opportunity to do so was given, before the necessary evidence to enable reparation to be obtained, could be recovered. The right of self-help or intervention was thus justified by the immediate necessity to secure the evidence before it was removed.

Finally, as to the manner in which the operation was conducted, the Government of the United Kingdom 'took the utmost precautions to ensure that all aggressive and provocative acts were avoided and that Albanian sovereign rights were not infringed'.[45]

The Albanian Rejoinder noted that the references offered by the British Government were somewhat outdated:

> The right of intervention has been studied by many authors in international law. A closer analysis of these authors leads one to believe that that the said right belongs more to the past than to the present, or

---

43 Ibid., p. 282.
44 Ibid.
45 Ibid., p. 286.

more exactly that the 'individual' right of States has been replaced, in most cases, by the 'collective' right of international organizations . . . It becomes apparent that the issue of intervention has therefore been presented by reference to an international context that today no longer exists.[46]

The Rejoinder added that the right of intervention, as allowed and recognised in the past by customary international law, did not correspond to the then current state of international relations. It was the expression of the primitive right to render justice unto one's self. This primitive law favoured the more powerful.

Returning to the case before the Court, the Rejoinder noted that Albania could herself never have organised a similar operation off the British coast and imposed its will on British authorities within 48 hours under the pretext of seizing relevant evidence. To warrant being characterised as the law, a right must be equal for all parties. In the relations between large and small States, the so-called right of intervention did not deserve to be characterised as law.[47]

In his oral statement, Sir Eric Beckett did not develop on the initial written arguments at length or try to reply to the Albanian Rejoinder. He mainly referred the Court to the United Kingdom's written Reply. He nevertheless put up a spirited defence of a qualified right of intervention to fill in international law's loopholes. He readily admitted that the Charter of the United Nations had changed the context, but insisted on the upholding of a right of intervention or self-help, noting that the Security Council could be rendered powerless by a single vote and that, consequently '[I]t is only natural that the rights of self-defence and of self-help which are recognized in municipal law should have a somewhat greater importance in international law.'[48] As to the argument that States were unequally able to resort to such methods, Beckett noted that, in domestic law, a healthy young man would more readily avail himself of the right of self-defence against a burglar than a weak old lady . . .

Sir Eric went on to describe the right of intervention within the limits of the Charter. He considered that such a right existed only in certain specific circumstances. He argued:

---

46 *Duplique du Gouvernement albanais*, ibid., p. 372:

> Le droit d'intervention a été étudié par de nombreux auteurs de droit international. Une étude attentive de ces auteurs conduit à penser qu'il appartient plus au passé qu'au présent, ou plutôt que le droit 'individuel' des Etats a été peu à peu remplacé, du moins dans la plupart des cas, par le droit 'collectif' des organisations internationales . . . on s'aperçoit que le problème de l'intervention est traité en fonction d'un état de choses international aujourd'hui disparu.
>
> (Translation from French by the author)

47 CR 49.2, p. 373.
48 CR 49.1, p. 296.

I say that when State A has suffered damage and State A has good reason to suspect that State B has committed against it a serious offence – an illegality under international law – and State A wished to bring that offence before the appropriate international organization, if the evidence justifies its suspicions, State A may take action – which in other circumstances would be an infringement of the rights of B – to investigate the cause of the loss and to preserve the evidence if it is found – if State A has good reason to think that, if it does not do this, State B will cause the evidence to disappear, always provided that the action taken is not disproportionate to the suspected offence. It is this contention, and this alone, that we seek to justify.[49]

Sir Eric added that, as far as he knew, this was '*absolutely the first case* where a State has taken action outside its ordinary rights with the motive of obtaining and preserving evidence'.[50]

Sir Eric then considered the manner in which *Operation Retail* had been implemented. He considered the British force as reasonable, given the circumstances. He noted that the British operation did not contravene the stipulations of Article 2, paragraph 4 of the Charter, requiring members of the Organisation 'to refrain in their international relations from the threat, or use, of force against the territorial integrity or the political independence of any State, or in any other manner inconsistent with the purposes of the United Nations'. He stated that Albania had suffered neither territorial loss nor political independence as a result of *Operation Retail*.

In his oral Statement,[51] Pierre Cot noted that the 'famous' *Operation Retail* was presented by the British Government as a sort of judicial operation performed on behalf of the international community. Albania considered it as a resort to force contrary to international law. The violation of Albanian sovereignty was *prima facie* beyond doubt. Britain argued the theory of intervention. Not an easy task, remarked Pierre Cot: intervention is, after all, the rule that 'might is right' ('*la raison du plus fort*') applied to international relations. Sir Eric had tried hard to confer an innocent hue to the theory. He did concede that the traditional theory of intervention was no longer acceptable in international law, but argued that resort to intervention was inevitable if the Security Council was unable to fulfil its responsibilities. Referring to a character in one of Molière's plays, Pierre Cot commented that the British Government thus appeared under two hats: as a party to the litigation and as a sort of police officer arresting the culprit in order to sue him in a private capacity.

---

49 CR 49.2, p. 579.
50 Ibid.
51 CR 49.1, pp. 5 and ff.

Beckett had tried to justify the right of intervention. An impossible task, as intervention was just a hard fact, beyond the realm of law; a task all the more impossible with the Charter of the United Nations as it stood. Cot conceded that that the international organisation was far from perfect. But Sir Eric's remedy was worse still, as it reserved to more powerful States alone, the possibility of correcting the lacunae in international society. Sir Eric tried in vain to convince the Court that his remedy was open to all members of the international community. But could one seriously imagine Albania organising an 'Operation Retail' against the United Kingdom? He insisted: 'Members of the Court, what the British Government is asking of you, is to affirm the right, not for any State, but only for the more powerful, to consider themselves as the rightful executants of international justice.'[52]

He then addressed the plea of mitigation advanced by the British Government. Was the operation 'reasonable'? He noted the size of the British fleet, impressive to say the least: an aircraft carrier, *Ocean*, carrying some 40 planes; 2 cruisers, *Mauritius*, equipped with 12 large guns and lesser ones, *Ajax*, equipped with 8 large guns and lesser ones, 3 destroyers, *Cheviot* (4 large guns), *Childers* (4 large guns), *Raider* (4 large guns); 2 corvettes, *St. Austell Bay* (4 large guns), *St. Bride's Bay* (4 large guns); 2 submarines and a support vessel. The firepower of the fleet overwhelmed the limited Albanian coastal defences. The force was out of proportion with the justification advanced.

The name of the operation, 'Retail', implied the idea of retaliation, especially in Scottish dialect; Cot wondered if the commanding officer of the operation, Admiral Kinahan, was a Scot . . .

Cot wound up his final Reply by recalling the expression used by the British Admiralty in relation to the incident: 'His Majesty's Government wish to know whether the Albanian Government have learnt to behave themselves.' He noted: 'All States, whether small or large, must learn to behave better. But it is up to the International Court, and no one else, to lecture us on this point.'[53]

The Court decided in favour of Great Britain on the issues of compensation for the explosions and for the characterisation of the 22 October passage as innocent; in favour of Albania on *Operation Retail*. Both Parties had deserved to learn a lesson.

But what a fine tournament it was!

---

52 CR 49.1, p. 408: 'Songez-y, Messieurs, ce que le Gouvernement britannique vous demande, c'est de consacrer le droit, non pas pour n'importe quel Etat, mais pour les Etats les plus forts et pour ceux-là seuls, de se considérer comme les gérants d'affaires de la justice internationale.'
53 CR 49.2, p. 699. 'Tous les Etats, grands ou petits, ont besoin d'apprendre à se mieux conduire. Mais c'est la Cour internationale de Justice qui a seule qualité pour nous donner, à nous et à vous, de semblables leçons.'

Part II
The historical and institutional framework

4 The *Corfu Channel* case in perspective
The factual and political background

Aristoteles Constantinides

4.1 Introduction

The facts of the *Corfu Channel* case relate primarily to two incidents involving vessels of the British Royal Navy in the North Corfu Channel in late 1946. The Corfu Channel (or Straits of Corfu) lies between the Greek island of Corfu to the west and the coasts of Greece and Albania to the east. The North Corfu Channel separates Corfu from the southern coastline of Albania; it varies in width from 1 mile at its narrowest, northern, point to about 6 miles at other points, thus lying within the territorial waters of both coastal states, Albania and Greece.

The first incident took place on 22 October 1946 when two British warships struck mines in the North Corfu Channel. This incident gave rise to the first question submitted to the International Court of Justice (ICJ) by the United Kingdom (UK) and Albania in their Special Agreement of 25 March 1948.[1] The second incident occurred on 12 and 13 November 1946 when British mine-sweepers swept a minefield in the same area in Albanian territorial waters. That incident gave rise to the second question in the Special Agreement.[2]

These two incidents were neither undisputed nor isolated.[3] They were connected to other developments and disputed events that occurred in the

---

1 'Is Albania responsible under international law for the explosions which occurred on the 22nd October 1946 in Albanian waters and for the damage and loss of human life which resulted from them and is there any duty to pay compensation?', *Corfu Channel case (United Kingdom v. Albania), Judgment of April 9th 1949, ICJ Reports 1949*, p. 12 (hereinafter *ICJ Judgment*).
2 'Has the United Kingdom under international law violated the sovereignty of the Albanian People's Republic by reason of the acts of the Royal Navy in Albanian waters on the 22nd October and on the 12th and 13th November 1946 and is there any duty to give satisfaction?', ibid., p. 26.
3 The Corfu Channel *incident* is sometimes described as also including an earlier incident that occurred on 15 May 1946, when two Royal Navy ships were fired upon by an Albanian coastal battery while on passage through the Channel. See P. E. Wynn, 'Corfu Channel Incident', in B. A. Cook (ed.), *Europe since 1945: An Encyclopedia*, vol. I (New York: Garland, 2001), p. 224. In describing the facts of the *Corfu Channel case*, however, this chapter will follow the questions of the Special Agreement which relate to the two (subsequent) incidents of October and November 1946.

immediate aftermath of World War II (WWII), and also involved States other than the United Kingdom and Albania. Indeed, one of the biggest challenges the ICJ faced in deciding its first contentious case was to establish the complicated facts which, at the Merits phase, were still in dispute by the parties.[4] The standards it laid down on various aspects of evidence and fact-finding account significantly for the continued relevance of the judgment for contemporary international law,[5] and are extensively discussed in other chapters of this book.

Section 4.2 will briefly present the political context and the main events preceding and surrounding the two incidents as well as the discussions that followed in the United Nations (UN) Security Council. The main factual findings of the ICJ will then be presented. Finally, Section 4.4 will give a brief account of post-judgment developments that eventually led to the settlement of the dispute in the 1990s and will also address questions that still remain unanswered today.

4.2 The facts and the political context of the dispute

4.2.1 *The political background: relations between Albania, Yugoslavia, Greece and the United Kingdom*

Albania proclaimed its independence from the Ottoman Empire on 28 November 1912. The new State was very weak and soon came under the strong influence of Italy. In 1939, Italy invaded and occupied Albania. In November 1944, communist partisans, led by Enver Hoxha, liberated Albania from German troops and assumed control of the country.[6] They carried out a programme of political and social Marxist reorientation and in January 1946 Albania was declared a People's Republic.[7] One main feature of communist Albania was its close association with a larger communist State. From 1944 to 1948, Albania was aligned with (then) Yugoslavia.[8] Yugoslavia wished to isolate Albania from the West so as to strengthen her own influence over its smaller neighbour.[9] The two States signed a Treaty of Friendship and Mutual Assistance on 9 June 1946,[10] followed by an Economic Agreement on

---

4 M. Fitzmaurice, 'The *Corfu Channel case* and the Development of International Law', in N. Ando (ed.), *Liber amicorum Judge Shigeru Oda* (The Hague: Kluwer, 2002), p. 120.
5 See M. Waibel, '*Corfu Channel case*', in R. Wolfrum (ed.), *The Max Planck Encyclopedia of Public International Law*, 2010, paras 25–27, 30. Online edition. Available at: www.mpepil.com (accessed 5 June 2010).
6 E. E. Jacques, *The Albanians: An Ethnic History from Prehistoric Times to the Present* (Jefferson, NC: McFarland, 1995), p. 424.
7 Ibid., p. 429 *et seq*.
8 Albania's close links with Yugoslavia lasted only until the latter's rift with the Soviet Union in 1948. Albania was then aligned with the Soviets until 1961 and with China from 1961 to 1978.
9 Jacques, op. cit., p. 462.
10 *United Nations Treaty Series*, vol. 1, 1946–1947, p. 88.

27 November 1946.[11] The former provided the framework for very close political and military cooperation, while the latter, *inter alia*, established a customs union, causing foreign observers to speculate over a possible Yugoslav-Albanian federation.[12]

On the other hand, relations with Greece, Albania's southern neighbour, were tense from the outset. The main reasons were the fate and treatment of the Greek minority in that part of south Albania which borders the Northern Corfu Channel and which in Greece is called Northern Epirus,[13] and the (unsuccessful) Greek efforts to be awarded that region during the negotiations of the post-World War II peace treaty with Italy.[14] These negotiations took place throughout 1946 and the Greek claims were supported by the United Kingdom. Both Greece and the UK were also opposed to Albania's application for membership of the United Nations.[15] The United Kingdom was backing the right-wing governmental forces in the Greek civil war against the communist forces backed by Yugoslavia, Bulgaria and Albania. Albania and Greece were in a state of war at the time and were frequently accusing each other of cross-border incursions.

The United Kingdom had recognized the new Albanian regime on 10 November 1945. However, relations between the two States soon deteriorated as the Cold War loomed. Any and all official British presence in Albania was withdrawn in April 1946.[16] Nevertheless, negotiations were taking place with the Albanian mission in Belgrade to resume diplomatic relations but were broken off as a result of the Corfu Channel incidents.

4.2.2 *The situation in the North Corfu Channel prior to the mine explosions*

At the end of the WWII hostilities in Europe in May 1945, approximately 20,000 of the hundreds of thousands of mines laid in the Mediterranean and in the waters of north-western Europe had been swept. The task of coordinating the removal of the remaining mines was assigned to the International Central Mine Clearance Board established by an Agreement between the Soviet Union (USSR), the United States of America, the UK and France in November 1945. The Agreement also provided that coordination of mine-sweeping in the

---

11 The Agreement is reproduced in English in *ICJ Pleadings, Corfu Channel case*, vol. V, p. 68.
12 O. Pearson, *Albania as Dictatorship and Democracy: From Isolation to the Kosovo War* (New York: I. B. Tauris, 2006), p. 52.
13 Certain aspects of that treatment had come before the Permanent Court of International Justice: *Minority Schools in Albania, Advisory Opinion No. 26 of 6 April 1935, PCIJ*, Series A/B, No. 64, p. 4.
14 Northern Epirus was initially awarded to Greece at the Paris Peace Conference of 1919 but was eventually ceded to Albania in 1921.
15 For a summary of the Greek and British arguments, see Pearson, op. cit., p. 69.
16 On the history of the British Embassy in Tirana, see http://ukinalbania.fco.gov.uk/en/about-us/our-embassy/embassy-history/full-embassy-history-part-two (accessed 15 June 2010).

Mediterranean would be the task of a Mediterranean Zone Board consisting of representatives of France, Greece, the USSR, the UK, the USA and Yugoslavia. Certain other governments were also invited to send observers, but the four Powers did not invite Albania because she possessed no minesweeping forces.[17]

During the War the Corfu Channel had been extensively mined by the Axis Powers. They had, however, established and maintained a mile-wide swept channel for the purposes of navigation. Further to the west (closer to Corfu), old German minefields still existed but they posed no danger to the swept channel.[18] On the evidence produced, the Court found that the North Corfu Channel was swept by the British Navy in October 1944 and no mines were found. A safe route through the Channel was thus announced in November 1944. In January and February 1945, the Channel was check-swept by the British Navy with negative results.[19] Between October 1945 and October 1946, Mediterranean Route Instructions (MEDRI) Charts and pamphlets showing the safe areas and routes for shipping in the Mediterranean were produced by the competent organisation, the International Routing and Reporting Authority, and were communicated to Albania. Albania was apparently receiving all MEDRI booklets and had raised no objection to the charts which showed the swept North Corfu Channel as a safe area for navigation.[20] Until May 1946, navigation in the Channel was indeed unhindered.

On 15 May 1946, however, two British cruisers, the *Superb* and *Orion*, were fired upon from the Albanian shore while passing through the swept channel from North to South in the vicinity of Saranda.[21] There were no hits and the British vessels did not retaliate; they did, however, record the positions of the batteries which had attacked them. The British government protested immediately to the Albanian government and requested an apology. In the ensuing diplomatic correspondence Albania asserted that foreign warships had no right of passage through her territorial waters without her authorisation,

---

17 L. W. Maher, 'Half Light Between War and Peace: Herbert Vere Evatt, the Rule of International Law, and the *Corfu Channel case*', *Australian Journal of Legal History*, 9 (2005): 48–49.
18 H. Munro, 'The Case of the Corfu Minefield', *Modern Law Review*, 10 (1947): 366.
19 *ICJ Judgment*, op. cit., pp. 13–14.
20 The only exception was a remaining issue in relation to the MEDRI Charts, dated 7 September 1946, which was sent to Albania but was returned with the indication that the office to which it was addressed had closed down. See the reply submitted by the United Kingdom, *ICJ Pleadings, Corfu Channel case*, vol. II, p. 247.
21 While Wynn, op. cit., p. 224, asserts that the *Orion* and *Superb* were 'the *first warships* to pass through the swept Corfu Channel following reopening of the straits' (emphasis added), it was vaguely stated in the UK Memorial that 'until May 1946 *shipping of all kinds* regularly used the Channel without hindrance . . . and without encountering any mines'. *ICJ Pleadings, Corfu Channel case*, vol. I, p. 24 (emphasis added). This point was not taken up by the ICJ, nor was any relevant data provided by UK counsel during the oral pleadings.

whereas the British Government replied that they could not agree to give prior notification of passage through the Channel and warned that 'if Albanian coastal batteries in the future opened fire on any British warship passing through the Corfu Channel, the fire would be returned'.[22]

4.2.3 The core of the dispute: the mine explosions and the mine-sweeping operation

In the early afternoon of 22 October 1946, a squadron of British warships, the cruisers *Mauritius* and *Leander* and the destroyers *Saumarez* and *Volage*, left the port of Corfu and proceeded northward through the swept channel. No mine detection devices were used. The cruiser *Mauritius* was leading, followed by the destroyer *Saumarez*; after a gap of about 2 miles came the cruiser *Leander* followed by the destroyer *Volage*. Contrary to Albania's contentions, the ships were not sailing in combat formation and were not manoeuvring; they carried their usual detachment of marines and their guns were in the normal mode.[23]

While passing through the swept channel, outside the Bay of Saranda, *Saumarez* struck a mine at 14:53 pm and was heavily damaged.[24] One officer and 35 men were killed either by the explosion or trapped in the fire that raged, and many were injured, including the Captain and two officers. *Volage* was ordered to give assistance and to take *Saumarez* in tow. While passing the tow to *Saumarez*, *Volage* was approached by a motor launch flying the Albanian ensign and also a white flag. A man, claiming to be the port officer, made some enquiries but received no reply. He remained in the area for about half an hour and then returned to shore without offering assistance.[25] While towing the damaged ship, *Volage* also struck a mine and was considerably damaged. Seven were killed, including one officer, and three were wounded, one of whom later died. Overall, 44 seamen lost their lives and 42 were injured. Nevertheless, *Volage* succeeded in towing *Saumarez* back to Corfu, arriving at 03:15 am on 23 October.

The ships had been on a well-organised mission, called *Exercise Corfu*, aimed 'to test the Albanian reactions' to the above diplomatic notes.[26] The mission was apparently authorised at the highest level of the British government 'who [wished] to know whether the Albanian Government have learnt to behave

---

22 *ICJ Judgment*, op. cit., p. 27.
23 Ibid., p. 31.
24 For a detailed account of the explosions, the reaction of the crew and the return to Corfu, see H. A. L. H. Wade, 'Two Destroyers', *The RUSI Journal*, 99 (1954): 65–71.
25 Ibid., p. 67.
26 See Memorandum No. 0321/13 of 5 October 1946 on 'The Use of the North Channel, Corfu' (short title XCU), reproduced in A. Carty, 'The *Corfu Channel case* – And the Missing Admiralty Orders', *The Law and Practice of International Courts and Tribunals*, 3 (2004): 30.

themselves.'[27] However, the British took pains to keep their motives behind the 22 October mission secret and declined to produce the relevant Admiralty orders before the ICJ, pleading naval secrecy.[28] This attitude continued throughout the Cold War.[29] When the documents were finally disclosed in the early 2000s, they revealed that the British were eager to conceal their ulterior motives out of fear that the ICJ would consider British passage through the Strait not to be innocent.[30] These fears were, however, proven unjustified since the Court ultimately ruled that the passage would be innocent regardless of whether testing Albania's attitude was one of the purposes of the passage.[31]

Immediately after the explosions, the British informed the Albanian government of their intention to sweep the Corfu Channel soon. Albania protested both to the UK and to the United Nations against the alleged violation of its territorial waters, and replied that they would not consent to the sweeping unless it took place outside Albanian territorial waters. The Albanian position was formulated in consultation with the Yugoslav government.[32] In view of this protest, the British Prime Minister, at a Cabinet meeting of 31 October, was reluctant to authorise the mine-sweeping operation before receiving the views of his Foreign Secretary and information about the USSR's position on the issue at the Mediterranean Zone Board.[33] The Board had recommended a check sweep of the North Corfu Channel on 28 October, but the Central International Mine Clearance Board decided in a resolution of 1 November that a further sweep of the Channel would be subject to Albania's consent.[34] On 10 November, the UK informed Albania that the proposed

---

27 Telegram sent on 21 September 1946 by the British Admiralty to the Commander-in-Chief, Mediterranean, reproduced verbatim in the *ICJ Judgment*, op. cit., p. 28.
28 Carty, op. cit., p. 2. On this point see the contribution by Sir Kenneth Keith in this book (Chapter 8).
29 In a reply to Lord Avebury in the House of Lords on 9 February 1981, the British Foreign Secretary Lord Carrington stated: 'One hundred and one items of Foreign Office records and six of Admiralty records from 1946 to 1950 have been withheld ... Twelve are retained in the Foreign and Commonwealth Office ... for a period yet to be determined. It would not be appropriate to publish a detailed list.' See *House of Lords Debates*, vol. 417, 9 February 1981, cc 124–125.
30 Carty, op. cit., p. 28 notes that the Law Officers, the Foreign Office and the Admiralty were debating for three months whether to produce the top secret XCU document.
31 *ICJ Judgment*, op. cit., p. 30 ('the object of sending the warships through the Strait was not only to carry out a passage for purposes of navigation, but also to test Albania's attitude ... The legality of this measure ... cannot be disputed, provided that it was carried out in a manner consistent with the requirements of international law.') But see the *Dissenting opinion of Judge Krylov, ICJ Reports 1949*, p. 75.
32 P. Kola, *The Search for Greater Albania* (London: Hurst, 2003), p. 74.
33 Document extract from the British National Archives, Catalogue Reference: CAB/128/6, Secret C.M. (46), 93rd Conclusions, Cabinet 93 (46), p. 109.
34 *ICJ Judgment*, op. cit., p. 33. On the controversy over the resolution of the Board, see Munro, op. cit., pp. 373–374.

sweep would take place on 12 November, but the Albanian government replied on the 11th, protesting against this 'unilateral decision'. Albania did not rule out the sweeping of the Channel by the UK, but proposed the establishment of a Mixed Commission by the United Nations for the purpose of determining those parts of the Channel to be swept. It ended by stating that any sweeping undertaken without Albania's consent outside the Channel thus constituted, would be considered a deliberate violation of Albanian territory and sovereignty.[35]

After this exchange of notes, *Operation Retail* took place on 12 and 13 November 1946. On British request, Commander Mestre of the French Navy was present at the sweep as an observer. The operation was carried out under the protection of an important covering force composed of an aircraft carrier, cruisers and other war vessels. This force remained throughout the operation at a certain distance to the west of the Channel. The sweep began in the morning of 13 November, at about 9 am, and ended in late afternoon. The area swept was in Albanian territorial waters. Twenty-two mines were cut. Many of them were sunk by rifle fire, others drifted ashore and two were taken to Malta for expert examination and were later used as exhibits before the Security Council.[36]

The two incidents left a number of questions of fact in dispute: who laid the mines that caused the explosions and when? Did those mines belong to the minefield discovered on 13 November? What type of mines were they? Did the Albanian authorities know of the mines before the explosion?

4.2.4 The Corfu Channel question before the UN Security Council

The UK government addressed a detailed note to the Albanian government dated 9 December 1946, accusing Albania of causing the damage and casualties sustained by the explosions of 22 October and requesting an apology and compensation. The UK government added that if no satisfactory reply was received within 14 days, it would bring the matter before the Security Council.[37] The Albanian response of 21 December expressed regret for the mine explosions but denied responsibility and blamed those who did not want to see friendly relations re-established between the UK and Albania.[38] The British government regarded the reply as unsatisfactory.

By a letter dated 10 January 1947, the UK submitted the 'Corfu Channel question' to the UN Security Council as a dispute under Article 35 of the UN

---

35 Maher, op. cit., p. 52.
36 Munro, op. cit., p. 365.
37 The text of the note was reproduced in a parliamentary debate of 11 December 1946. See *House of Commons Debates*, vol. 431, 11 December 1946, cc 1168–1175.
38 Maher, op. cit., p. 54.

Charter,[39] although in the diplomatic note of 9 December 1946 it had contemplated 'bring[ing] the matter ... as a serious threat to, and a breach of, international peace and security'.[40] The Soviet representative objected to the inclusion of the question on the agenda on the ground that no proper effort had been made by the UK to bring about a settlement of the dispute in accordance with Article 33 of the Charter.[41] The UK representative replied that his government had resorted to a direct diplomatic exchange of views, but that in light of the unsatisfactory result, they had decided to bring the dispute before the Council.[42] The Council ultimately placed the dispute on its agenda by a vote of ten in favour, the USSR abstaining.[43] The Council also decided pursuant to Article 32 of the Charter to invite Albania (who at the time was not a member of the United Nations) to participate in the proceedings relating to the dispute, on condition that Albania accept for the purposes of the dispute, all the obligations incumbent upon a UN Member.[44] Albania accepted the Security Council's decision and the dispute was subsequently considered at ten Council meetings between 20 January and 9 April 1947.[45]

The Security Council heard the arguments of the parties on 18 and 19 February 1947. On 24 February, the Australian representative proposed the appointment of a Sub-Committee to examine the material presented by the parties and to report to the Council on its findings.[46] By Resolution 19 of 27 February 1947, the Council appointed three Security Council members (Australia, Colombia and Poland) to the Sub-Committee to examine all the available evidence and to report to the Council on the facts of the case.[47] Resolution 19 was adopted by eight votes in favour, with three abstentions (Poland, Syria, the USSR).[48]

---

39 UN Doc. S/247, *Official Records of the Security Council*, Second Year, Suppl. No. 3, 107th meeting, p. 36.
40 *House of Commons Debates*, vol. 431, 11 December 1946, c 1175.
41 The Soviet representative pointed to the British rejection of the Albanian proposal of 11 November 1946 for the establishment of a mixed commission. The UK representative replied that the mixed commission had been proposed for the limited purpose of defining the Channel, not for the settlement of the whole dispute. *Repertoire of the Practice of the Security Council 1946–1951* (New York: United Nations, Department of Political and Security Council Affairs, 1954), p. 378 (hereinafter *Repertoire*).
42 Ibid.
43 *Yearbook of the United Nations 1946–47* (New York: United Nations, Department of Public Information, 1947), p. 392.
44 *Repertoire*, op. cit., p. 127.
45 Ibid., p. 313.
46 For a detailed account of Australia's position and the role of Herbert Vere Evatt, the Australian Deputy Prime Minister, Minister for Foreign Affairs and Attorney-General at the time, see Maher, op. cit., pp. 54 *et seq*. See also G. Distefano and E. Henry's contribution to this book (Chapter 5).
47 *Repertoire*, op. cit., p. 313.
48 Ibid., p. 204.

The Sub-Committee held ten meetings and submitted its Report on 15 March 1947. A minority Report by the Polish representative was included as an appendix.[49] The Sub-Committee emphasised that it was neither a commission of investigation nor a fact-finding sub-committee in the strict sense of the word, and that its main duty was to examine the statements and evidence already submitted to the Security Council and to ascertain whether additional evidence existed.[50] The members of the Sub-Committee and of the Council were divided. The Colombian and Australian members of the Sub-Committee, joined by the Belgian, American, French and Chinese representatives at the Council, endorsed the British version of the facts (but not the British contention that the mines were laid by Albania), whereas the Polish member, joined by the Soviet representative at the Council, endorsed the Albanian version, and the Syrian representative argued that the matter needed further study.[51]

A draft Resolution submitted by the UK was defeated on 25 March 1947 by a vote of seven in favour, two against (Poland and the USSR, a permanent member), one abstention (Syria) and one Member (the UK) not participating in the vote. The draft Resolution would have recommended that the United Kingdom and Albania should settle the dispute on the basis of the Council's findings that an un-notified minefield was laid in the Corfu Channel with the knowledge of the Albanian authorities.[52]

On 3 April, the UK submitted a second draft Resolution to recommend that the dispute be referred to the ICJ. The representatives of Brazil and Australia spoke in favour and the Soviet representative spoke against this proposal.[53] Security Council Resolution 22 was finally adopted on 9 April 1947, with eight votes in favour, the USSR and Poland abstaining and the UK, being a party to the dispute, not participating in the vote. The Resolution's only operative paragraph notoriously recommended that 'the United Kingdom and the Albanian Governments should immediately refer the dispute to the International Court of Justice in accordance with the provisions of the Statute of the Court.' The proceedings before the Security Council were thus terminated.

Acting on the Council's recommendation the United Kingdom instituted proceedings before the ICJ on 13 May 1947. In reaching the ICJ, these combined actions of the Security Council and of the United Kingdom were rightly seen as having successfully defused the tension arising out of the original incident.[54]

---

49 *Yearbook of the United Nations 1946–47*, op. cit., p. 393.
50 UN Doc. S/300, *Official Records of the Security Council*, Second Year, 120th meeting, Suppl. No. 10, p. 544.
51 See UN Doc. S/PV/121 of 21 March 1947 and UN Doc. S/PV/122 of 25 March 1947.
52 *Repertoire*, op. cit., p. 413.
53 Ibid., pp. 413–414.
54 S. Rosenne, 'A Role for the International Court of Justice in Crisis Management?', in G. Kreijen (ed.), *State, Sovereignty, and International Governance* (Oxford: Oxford University Press, 2002), p. 210.

4.3 The ICJ's factual findings: questions (un)answered

4.3.1 Questions unanswered: who laid the mines and when?

Such were the main facts and circumstances upon which the Court had to pronounce judgment with a view to answering the two questions posed by the parties. With regard to the first question, the UK submitted that Albania's responsibility for the mine explosions could be established on three possible grounds: if (it was proven that) the mines were laid (1) by Albania or (2) (by Yugoslavia) with the connivance of Albania or (3) with the knowledge of Albania. The Court dealt with each ground in turn. Thus, in deciding on Albania's responsibility, the Court did not need to give a definite answer to the questions of who laid the mines and (exactly) when. It could still hold Albania responsible if it was established that the Albanian government knew of the mines (regardless of who had laid them and when) and failed to notify the UK of their existence; and so it did.

The UK had initially claimed that the mines were laid by Albania. However, the Court easily dismissed this contention, since Albania had no navy and only possessed a few launches and motor boats.[55] Similarly, the Court dismissed the Albanian allegation that the mines might have been laid by Greece as mere conjecture.[56] The ICJ also dismissed Albania's submission that the minefield was laid (presumably by the British or the Greeks[57]) after 22 October as too improbable.[58]

More importantly, however, the Court emphasised that the parties agreed 'that the minefield had been recently laid'.[59] In fact, there was sufficient evidence to justify this given the absence of rust and marine growth, the easy unscrewing of the horns, the new paint and clearly visible identification marks, and the grease on the mooring wires.[60] The ICJ considered this agreement as a sufficient basis for examining Albania's responsibility on the ground of knowledge. Thus, the Court did not (need to) establish the exact date of the minelaying and concluded that 'the minelaying, *whatever may have been its exact date*, was done at a time when there was a close Albanian surveillance over the Strait'.[61]

---

55 *ICJ Judgment*, op. cit., p. 15.
56 Ibid., p. 17.
57 In the words of Enver Xoxha: 'The mines could also easily have been laid by British ships or by those of their lackeys in Athens.' E. Hoxha, 'Speech Delivered to the People's Assembly on the Opening of the 3rd Regular Session of the 1st Legislature', 12 July 1947. Online at 'Marxists Internet Archive'. Available at: www.marxists.org/reference/archive/hoxha/works/1947/07/12.htm (accessed 10 June 2010).
58 *ICJ Judgment*, op. cit., p. 14. See also the dissenting opinion of Judge Azevedo, *ICJ Reports 1949*, op. cit., p. 82 ('the Albanian suggestion would involve the successive laying of two minefields at short intervals, and that would be even more extraordinary').
59 *ICJ Judgment*, op. cit., p. 19.
60 Munro, op. cit., p. 365.
61 *ICJ Judgment*, op. cit., p. 22 (emphasis added).

Before discussing the evidence of Albania's knowledge of the minefield, it is useful first to shed some light on the alleged involvement of Yugoslavia, the main 'suspect' in the laying of the mines. Proof of minelaying by Yugoslav warships would imply Albania's connivance and thereby establish her responsibility on that ground. The UK put forward circumstantial evidence and also relied heavily on the testimony of Lieutenant-Commander Kovacic, a Yugoslav army deserter. Strangely, no enquiries were made by the British with a view to obtaining evidence from possible eyewitnesses in Corfu.[62]

Thus, in addition to the very close economic, political and military ties between Albania and Yugoslavia at the time,[63] circumstantial evidence also consisted of Yugoslavia being the only neighbouring State possessing GY mines, like the ones struck by the two British vessels. Both Albania and Yugoslavia contested these propositions.

Kovacic testified before the Court that he saw mines being loaded onto two Yugoslav minesweepers, the *Miljet* and the *Meljine*, at the port of Sibenik (in today's Croatia) and that these two vessels left Sibenik on about 18 October and returned a few days after the explosions.[64] However excellent a witness Kovacic proved to be for the British,[65] his testimony was based on his personal knowledge and on statements attributed by him to third parties, of which the Court received no direct confirmation. In addition, both Albania and Yugoslavia seriously challenged his credibility on a variety of grounds. Despite what was perhaps 'a strong suspicion of connivance',[66] the ICJ could reach no 'firm conclusion' on Yugoslavia's involvement: '[a] charge of such exceptional gravity against a State would require a degree of certainty that has not been reached here'.[67] It ultimately ruled that it had not been legally established that Yugoslavia possessed any German Y mines, that the origin of the mines remained a matter for conjecture and that, in the light of the information available to the Court, the authors of the minelaying remained unknown.[68]

4.3.2 Question answered: Albania's knowledge of the minefield

The Court's judgment with regard to Albania's knowledge of the minefield was quite extensive since it was on this ground that Albania would ultimately

---

62 This was noted with surprise by the Lord Chancellor at a Cabinet meeting of 6 January 1947. Document extract from the British National Archives, Catalogue Reference: CAB/128/9, Secret C.M. (47), 2nd Conclusions, Cabinet 2 (47), p. 16.
63 See above notes 10–12 and accompanying text.
64 *ICJ Judgment*, op. cit., p. 16.
65 Pearson, op. cit., p. 318.
66 *Dissenting Opinion of Judge Badawi-Pasha, ICJ Reports 1949*, p. 58 (concurring on this point).
67 *ICJ Judgment*, op. cit., p. 17.
68 Ibid.

be held responsible for the mine explosions. The series of facts referred to by the ICJ related, first, to Albania's attitude before and after the mine explosions of 22 October 1946 and, second, to the feasibility of observing minelaying from the Albanian coast.

The Albanian government's attitude before the explosions revealed, by *inter alia*, diplomatic notes and official statements,[69] their intention to keep a jealous watch on its territorial waters.[70] Albania had actually acted in accordance with this intention when its coastguard fired upon the British cruisers *Orion* and *Superb* on 15 May 1946.

The ICJ also took pains to establish that it was easy to put such an intention into effect because it was possible to observe minelaying from the Albanian coast. The Court gave great weight to the views of the Experts it had appointed, who visited the area on a fact-finding mission in the presence of the parties' own experts and of Albanian officials and who were meticulously examined by the Court during the hearings of the case. Based on their views, the Court concluded that the minelaying must have lasted between two and two and a half hours; that the minelayers must have passed at no more than 500 metres from the coast; and that the geographical configuration of the area was such that the laying of mines in the North Corfu Channel could easily be watched and heard *under normal weather conditions*, even on a moonless night, by the Albanian coastguards stationed at the look-out posts at Cape Kiephali and St George's Monastery.[71] However, the caveat of 'normal weather conditions' and the fact that the existence of a look-out post at Denta Point (which lies between Cape Kiephali and St George's Monastery and was closer to the minefield than the other two points) was not proved, were the two main points raised by the judges who dissented from that part of the Court's findings, arguing that, just like Albania's connivance, Albania's knowledge was also not judicially proven.[72]

The Albanian government's attitude after the explosions also showed on various occasions that they did not seem unaware of the minefield. Even if they had first become aware of the existence of the minefield when the British swept the Channel on 12 and 13 November 1946 (an argument dismissed by the Court), they failed to protest against the *laying* and/or the existence of the minefield; they only protested against the *sweeping* of the minefield by the British in Albania's territorial waters. They also failed to

---

69 In the words of Enver Xoxha: 'It is quite true that we guard our coastline and our southern borders with the greatest jealousy and determination, for they are sacred for us.' See E. Hoxha, 'Speech Delivered to the People's Assembly', 12 July 1947. Available at: www.marxists.org/reference/archive/hoxha/works/1947/07/12.htm (accessed 10 June 2010).
70 *ICJ Judgment*, op. cit., p. 19.
71 Ibid., pp. 20–22 (emphasis added).
72 See the Declaration of Judge Zoričić, *ICJ Reports 1949*, p. 38, and the dissenting opinions of Judges Winiarski, ibid., p. 50; Badawi-Pasha, ibid., p. 62; Krylov, ibid., pp. 70–71; and Judge *ad hoc* Ečer, ibid., pp. 124–125.

launch any enquiry or judicial investigation into the events surrounding the minelaying. In other words, Albania's reaction demonstrated that they were not taken by surprise by the British discovery of the minefield. The Court logically concluded that '[t]his attitude [did] not seem reconcilable with the alleged ignorance of the Albanian authorities that the minefield had been laid in Albanian territorial waters'; but could rather be explained by Albania's knowledge and its desire to keep the circumstances of the minelaying secret.[73]

On these factual findings the ICJ gave the following replies to the questions put by the parties: 'Albania [was] responsible under international law for the explosions which occurred on October 22nd, 1946, in Albanian waters, and for the damage and loss of human life which resulted from them'[74]; 'the United Kingdom did not violate the sovereignty of Albania by reason of the acts of the British Navy in Albanian waters on October 22nd, 1946';[75] and 'by reason of the acts of the British Navy in Albanian waters in the course of the Operation of November 12th and 13th, 1946, the United Kingdom violated the sovereignty of the People's Republic of Albania'.[76]

4.4 Post-judgment developments

4.4.1 Albanian gold and the long-overdue settlement of the dispute

In the judgment on the Merits of 9 April 1949, the ICJ also decided that it had jurisdiction to assess the amount of compensation due by Albania (the Court having made an award of satisfaction in respect of the UK's *Operation Retail*), but stated that further proceedings on this matter were necessary.[77] Albania disputed the Court's jurisdiction to assess the amount of compensation, did not file any submissions and declined to appear at the public hearing.[78] Instead, it made repeated calls to the British government to negotiate directly on the question of fixing the amount of compensation, but to no avail.[79] The ICJ handed down its judgment on 15 December 1949 and fixed the amount of compensation due by Albania to the UK at £843,947,[80] making the *Corfu Channel* case the only ICJ decision to award a liquidated sum of money to an

---

73 *ICJ Judgment*, op. cit., p. 20.
74 Ibid., p. 23.
75 Ibid., p. 32.
76 Ibid., p. 36.
77 Ibid., p. 26.
78 *Corfu Channel case (United Kingdom v. Albania), Judgment of December 15th 1949, ICJ Reports 1949*, (Assessment of the Amount of Compensation Due from the People's Republic of Albania to the United Kingdom of Great Britain and Northern Ireland), pp. 246–248.
79 Pearson, op. cit., pp. 357, 370, 375.
80 *ICJ Reports 1949*, op. cit., p. 250.

applicant State.[81] Discussions by Albanian and British representatives in Paris on the methods of payment in 1950 were fruitless[82] and an Albanian offer in January 1951 to pay £40,000 was turned down as unsatisfactory.[83] Meanwhile, the British government had compensated the dependants of the dead seamen in accordance with normal pension arrangements.[84]

Although the UK had initially contemplated bringing the question of Albania's non-compliance to the Security Council, they never did so, nor did they take any other enforcement action against Albanian assets or property in the UK – actually, there did not seem to be any – or elsewhere, owing to practical and legal considerations.[85] The British government chose instead to obtain payment of the damages through the Albanian gold held in the Bank of England's vaults since the end of WWII.[86] The gold had been looted by the Germans from the National Bank of Albania in Rome on 16 September 1943, but was recovered by the Allies following the cessation of hostilities and then deposited in the Bank of England. It was claimed by both Albania and Italy. In February 1948, the US-UK-France Tripartite Commission for the Restitution of the Monetary Gold made two preliminary allocations of 1,121.4 kilogrammes to Albania (whose total validated claim was 2,454.9 kilogrammes) but delivery of the gold was suspended on 11 July 1949, that is, between the two ICJ rulings.[87] After a more profound examination of the issue, the Commission eventually annulled its decision in 1951 and decided that it was not competent to determine the ownership of the gold concerned.[88]

The governments represented on the Commission signed the Washington Agreement on 25 April 1951, by which they agreed to have the ownership of the gold determined by an arbitrator appointed by the ICJ President; the parties to this agreement also agreeing to abide by his opinion.[89] They also

---

81 This was also done by the PCIJ in the *Wimbledon* case. See S. Rosenne, 'Decisions of the International Court and the Law of State Responsibility', in S. Rosenne, *Essays on International Law and Practice* (Leiden: Martinus Nijhoff, 2007), p. 548, n. 11. See also P. D'Argent's contribution to this book (Chapter 20).
82 Pearson, op. cit., p. 399.
83 Statement of Mr. Davies, British Under-Secretary of State for Foreign Affairs, *House of Common Debates*, vol. 484, 1 March 1951, c 2511.
84 See the reply of Mr Nutting, *House of Commons Debates*, vol. 517, 14 July 1953, cc 149–150.
85 See the relevant discussion in *House of Common Debates*, vol. 484, 1 March 1951, cc 2504–2514.
86 A. Roselli, *Italy and Albania: Financial Relations in the Fascist Period* (New York: I.B. Tauris, 2006), p. 137.
87 Ibid., pp. 134–137.
88 Pearson, op. cit., p. 425.
89 Agreement between the Governments of the French Republic, the United Kingdom of Great Britain and Northern Ireland and the United States of America for the Submission to an Arbitrator of Certain Claims with respect to Gold Looted by the Germans from Rome in 1943, signed in Washington on 25 April 1951, *United Nations Treaty Series*, vol. 100, p. 21.

declared in a statement of the same date that if the arbitrator were to find in Albania's favour, the gold would be delivered to the UK in partial satisfaction of the ICJ judgment in the *Corfu Channel* case unless either Albania or Italy applied to the ICJ within a certain time-limit, requesting that the Court adjudicate on their claims to the gold. Albania protested strongly against the Washington Agreement and considered the nomination of an arbitrator illegal and arbitrary.[90] In fact, Swiss arbitrator, Georges Sauser-Hall, ruled that the 2,338.7565 kilogrammes of gold looted by the Germans in Rome in September 1943 belonged to Albania.[91] Italy then applied to the ICJ, bringing a claim against France, the UK and the USA within the prescribed time limit, but questioned the Court's jurisdiction to adjudicate upon her first claim against Albania on the ground that the proceedings were in reality directed against Albania and that Albania was not a party to the suit. The Court upheld Italy's objection and found unanimously that, in the absence of Albania's consent, it had no jurisdiction to adjudicate upon Italy's first submission.[92]

British officials had stated on various occasions that the gold was held in the Bank of England on behalf, or in the custody, of the Tripartite Commission and that its disposal was a matter of joint agreement between the three governments represented on the Commission.[93] Since 1956, Albania had indicated that no further discussion on compensation would take place until the resolution of the problem of the gold, which Albania also linked to the restoration of diplomatic relations between the two States. The British government had made it clear that they would be glad to find a way around these obstacles that had prevented the restoration of diplomatic relations.[94]

Diplomatic relations were finally established on 29 May 1991 following the end of the Cold War. The outstanding issues regarding the gold and the ICJ decision were discussed at separate talks. A Memorandum of Understanding was signed in Rome in May 1992.[95] Both sides expressed their regret at the *Corfu Channel* incident of 22 October 1946. They confirmed that all the British Government's financial claims were settled and that 'all matters

---

90 Pearson, op. cit., p. 429.
91 *Affaire relative à l'or de la Banque nationale d'Albanie* arbitration, 20 February 1953, XII RIAA, p. 52.
92 *Case of the Monetary Gold Removed from Rome in 1943 (Italy v. France, United Kingdom of Great Britain and Northern Ireland and United States of America), Preliminary Question, Judgment of 15 June 1954, ICJ Reports 1954*, p. 34.
93 See the reply of Lord Carrington, *House of Lords Debates*, vol. 424, 29 October 1981, c 1185 and the replies of Mr Blaker, *House of Commons Debates*, vol. 2, 10 April 1981, cc 356–357 and vol. 3, 30 April 1981, c 449.
94 Reply of Mr Luard, *House of Commons Debates*, vol. 952, 19 June 1978, cc 80–81.
95 G. Marston, 'United Kingdom Materials on International Law', *British Year Book of International Law*, 63 (1993): 781.

relating to the *Corfu Channel* incident *had been taken note* by both sides'.[96] The UK agreed to approve the delivery of 1,574 kilogrammes of gold to Albania and Albania agreed to pay the UK two million dollars in full and final settlement of the British financial claims. Delivery of the gold was subject to the consent of France and the USA. The USA gave its consent in 1995 and France did so in February 1996. On 29 October 1996, 50 years after the mine explosions, the Tripartite Commission concluded the transfer of the gold to Albania and the Albanian Government settled the British claim for compensation.[97]

4.4.2 *Questions remaining*

As to the authors of the minelaying, there have been no reported investigations by any of the concerned States and only few developments have reached the public eye since the ICJ's 1949 judgment. Undoubtedly, the 40 years of the Cold War had also 'frozen' any serious prospects of successfully doing so. Albania had been almost entirely isolated from both its neighbours and the rest of the world for several decades. Even after the end of the Cold War, Albania has remained one of the few States not to have opened the archives of its communist-era security services.[98] Nor did the British documents that were declassified in the early 2000s provide any evidence as to the perpetrators of the minelaying. One of them revealed the surprise of British officials at the absence of enquiries seeking evidence from persons in Corfu who might have witnessed the minelaying.[99] As to the former Yugoslav archives, the relevant agency (State Archives of the Federal People's Republic of Yugoslavia), located in Belgrade, was only founded in 1950 and began protecting archival holdings in 1952. Although the archival holdings from the period after 1945 are lengthy, the level of preservation of some fonds, especially those before 1953, is unsatisfactory. Minutes and documents from government sessions are missing and the archival holdings from five fonds were destroyed during the NATO bombing of Belgrade in April 1999.[100]

As a result, some questions have remained unanswered. In particular, if the mining was a Yugoslav enterprise, why did Albania refrain from accusing

---

96 See the webpage of the British Embassy in Tirana, 'Full Embassy History (Part Three – since 1991)'. Online. Available at: http://ukinalbania.fco.gov.uk/en/about-us/our-embassy/embassy-history/full-embassy-history-part-three (accessed 15 June 2010) (emphasis added).
97 Maher, op. cit., p. 80.
98 Report of P. Alston, Special *Rapporteur* on Extrajudicial, Summary or Arbitrary Executions, Preliminary Note on the Mission to Albania (15–23 February 2010), UN Doc. A/HRC/14/24/Add.9, para. 37.
99 See also supra note 62.
100 Information taken from the website of the Archives of Yugoslavia. Online. Available at: www.arhivyu.gov.rs/active/en/home.html (accessed 15 June 2010).

the Yugoslavs of the incident after it fell out with Belgrade in 1948?[101] Unofficially this would be done, if only in 1992, by Bedri Spahiu, a senior Albanian leader at the time of the incidents (subsequently purged by Xoxha), who reportedly revealed that 'the mines were laid at the Corfu Channel on Tito's orders and with Enver Xoxha's agreement . . . I welcome [the ICJ] verdict and am ready if need be to testify to its justice.'[102] There does not seem to have been any follow-up to this statement, which was made at a time when the relations between Albania and the former Yugoslavia had begun to deteriorate; they have since been even more hostile because of the Kosovo conflict.

In an interesting development in October 2009, an international team of archaeologists comprising members from the Florida-based RPM Nautical Foundation, the Institute of Nautical Archaeology, the Albanian Institute of Archaeology and the Albanian Ministry of Defence announced the discovery of a wreckage which, in all probability, was the remains of the bow of the *Volage*. The discovery was part of a project that began in 2007 to create an underwater cultural heritage map of the Albanian coastline. The wreckage was found approximately 50 metres under water, in proximity to the Albanian shore near the port of Saranda.[103] In view of the strong likelihood that the wreckage was from the *Volage*, and would therefore be considered a war grave, the artefacts were neither disturbed nor removed, which prevented absolute confirmation. However, the nature of the finds strongly suggested that this was where *Volage* hit the mine that tore off its bow. While largely obscured by mud, the remains showed steel frames, electrical wiring, ammunition, stacks of ceramic plates, and the remains of boots or shoes. Given that the part of the *Volage* blown off by the mine was forward of the deck guns and included the forward mess, where some of the crew ate and slept, the dishes, shoes and ammunition found were evidence that correlated with the speculation that this was indeed that vessel. The discovery was kept secret until both Albania and the UK were officially notified. A report of the investigation, including remotely operated vehicle (ROV) footage, was provided by the RPM Nautical Foundation to both governments.[104]

---

101 D. Floyd, 'Book Review', *International Affairs*, 43 (1967): 373.
102 Statement reportedly published in the Albanian daily *Republika* and included in a letter delivered to the *Independent* on 28 July 1992, as cited in Kola, op. cit., p. 75, n. 252.
103 See http://abcnews.go.com/International/wireStory?id=8975978, 2 November 2009 (accessed 15 June 2010).
104 Press release issued by the Institute of Nautical Archaeology, 'Volage Found!', 21 October 2009. Available at: http://inadiscover.com/news_events/news_events_archives/volage_found (accessed 15 June 2010).

4.5 Conclusion

The factual findings of the *Corfu Channel* case, the methods of deciding disputed facts and the Court's pronouncements on the standards and burden of proof played a cardinal role in the judgment, especially in answering the first question and deciding on Albania's responsibility for the mine explosions. In fact, there was no legal dispute between the parties with regard to the obligations deriving from the knowledge of the minefield. In the words of the ICJ: 'The obligations resulting for Albania from this knowledge are not disputed between the Parties.'[105] What was vehemently disputed was the knowledge of Albanian authorities. This is why the first half of the Court's judgment on Albania's responsibility dealt almost exclusively – with the exception of a few paragraphs – with questions of fact.

The Court had to establish the facts surrounding two incidents, one of which involved the laying of mines, which was, in the words of the ICJ, a criminal act.[106] However, the ICJ, not being a criminal court, it had to reach factual conclusions for the purpose of establishing the responsibility of a State rather than attributing criminal responsibility to individuals. The nature of criminal responsibility is fundamentally different from that of State responsibility for the commission of an internationally wrongful act, even when the wrongful act amounts to a crime. It was therefore possible for the Court to answer the questions put to it in order to decide the case and still leave other questions unanswered, most notably who had laid the mines, which was perhaps the central question.

In the Cold War environment of the late 1940s, answering that question looked like a formidable task, if not an impossible mission. There were too many political issues at stake and little, if any, meaningful cooperation between the States concerned. As a result, part of the evidence was either missing or insufficient, if not misleading. Nevertheless, against the background of such complex and highly disputed facts, the Court rendered a decision of enduring legal interest and relevance. Yet, in assessing the evidence on the question of Albania's knowledge under these circumstances, the Security Council Member States as well as the ICJ judges were influenced by their ideological and political affiliation. Indeed, voting in both the Security Council and the ICJ largely reflected the Cold War divide between the East and the West.

Answering the question of who laid the mines presented other kinds of difficulties in the post-Cold War era: the passage of time, unavailable or missing national archives and a lack of interest, save on the part of a handful of researchers. The dispute is now settled. Compensation has been paid; the Albanian gold is returned; the UK, Greece and Albania enjoy excellent

---

105 *ICJ Judgment*, op. cit., p. 22.
106 Ibid., p. 17.

relations; Yugoslavia no longer exists as a State, whereas Albania's relations with Serbia are hostile because of Kosovo. Nevertheless, the recent discovery of the remains of the bow of the *Volage* has shown that scientific research can possibly provide answers to some of the questions left unanswered by the Court's judgment more than sixty years ago; even if only for the sake of historical knowledge.

5 The International Court of Justice and the Security Council

Disentangling Themis from Ares

Giovanni Distefano and Etienne Henry

Quidquid latine dictum sit, altum sonatur.

5.1 Prologue

This contribution analyses three main issues raised by the *Corfu Channel* case both during the proceedings before the Security Council and later before the International Court of Justice (ICJ). The first relates to the nature and functions of these organs under the United Nations (UN) Charter and the Statute of the ICJ. In this regard, the Security Council shed light on the two organs' respective fields of competence, much like an apprentice sorcerer through the 'learning by doing' approach, as well as on these organs' different functions: the jurisdictional versus the executive. In 1925, the Permanent Court of International Justice (PCIJ) had already affirmed in the *Mossoul* case that the Council of the League of Nations could not be considered a 'tribunal of arbitrators',[1] but was this to apply also in the UN context? The second theme relates to the legal effect of a Security Council recommendation under Article 36(3) of the UN Charter, notably with regard to the establishment of the ICJ's jurisdiction.[2] The *Corfu Channel* case is the first and – until now – the only case for which the Security Council explicitly recommended the referral of a dispute to the ICJ under Article 36(3) of the UN Charter. This raises the question whether a Security Council resolution, adopted in accordance with Article 36(3), can constitute an autonomous head of ICJ jurisdiction. Last, but not the least, the Security Council's role as a fact-finder or 'investigator' will be reviewed, given that the question of whether the Security Council was acting in the context of Article 34 of the Charter had arisen during its meetings. These three topics all share a common ground: the institutional interactions between two of the principal organs of the UN in the pursuit of their

---

1 *Article 3, paragraph 2, of the Treaty of Lausanne (Frontier between Turkey and Iraq), Advisory Opinion of November 21st 1925*, Series B, No. 12, p. 26.
2 The more general question of the ICJ's jurisdiction is dealt with in Henry Burmester's contribution to this volume (Chapter 6).

goals. Moreover, all of them reveal, especially from a perusal of the Security Council's official records, that the UN organ upon which Member States have conferred the 'primary responsibility for the maintenance of international peace and security' (Article 24(1) UN Charter), was then acting in a still uncharted province of the Charter; hence, its practice would most certainly influence the interpretation of its relevant provisions.

5.2 General observations on the respective functions and powers of the Security Council and the ICJ in the light of the *Corfu Channel* case

As the Brazilian representative stressed just before the Security Council's referral of the dispute to the ICJ, the Council's functions 'have been well defined in the Charter, and we can neither broaden them nor reduce them. Should misconception or misapplication bring about an attempt to do so, *the result will be the practical disarticulation of our Organization*.'[3] Nonetheless this distribution of functions had not been so clear when the incident first came before the Council. An attempt at direct negotiations having failed to resolve the dispute, the UK sought to exert greater pressure on Albania by lodging a complaint with the Security Council in January 1947 under Article 35 of the Charter.[4] Initially, the British delegate to the Council, Sir Alexander Cadogan, sought the adoption of a resolution recommending 'under Article 36 of the Charter [the settlement of] the dispute by direct negotiation, after making the finding of fact without which such direct negotiation cannot succeed'.[5] The draft Resolution submitted by the UK contained a paragraph which clearly attributed the laying of the minefield to the Albanian Government. The proposal read:

> *The Security Council* . . . 1. *Finds* that an unnotified [sic] minefield was laid in the Corfu Channel by the Albanian Government or with its connivance, resulting in serious injury to His Majesty's ships and loss of life and injury to their crews.[6]

It then recommended that the parties 'settle the dispute on the basis of the Council's finding'. Acceptance of this proposal would have automatically implied acknowledgement by Albania of its international responsibility. It would have amounted to the Security Council not only 'recommend[ing] appropriate procedures or methods of adjustment' but also 'recommend[ing]

---

3 *Official Records of the Security Council*, Second Year, 125th Meeting, p. 686 (hereinafter *Official Records*). Emphasis added.
4 R. Dennett, 'Politics in the Security Council', *International Organization*, (1949): 424.
5 *Official Records*, op. cit., 107th Meeting, p. 306.
6 Ibid., 120th Meeting, p. 567.

... terms of settlement' within the meaning of Article 37 of the Charter, as it clearly dealt with the substance of the dispute. The British draft went so far as to characterise Albania's deeds as an 'offence against humanity'.[7]

The political tensions and partisan attitude adopted by some Security Council members made it unthinkable that an agreement could be reached as to the merits of the dispute. In this respect, the discussions which later took place, dealing with various more or less complex questions of facts,[8] cast doubt on the Council's ability to reach an impartial finding in this matter.[9] Several Council members seemed to have already made up their mind and expressed their judgment – although not publicly – even before the debates had begun.[10] Moreover, the lack of a formal adversarial procedure, the absence of applicants and defendants, let alone evidentiary standards (see above),[11] raise serious doubts as to the impartiality of the entire process. Thus, paradoxically, the veto power became the only guarantee against an arbitrary Security Council decision. As a matter of fact, the first item to be addressed by the delegates – the apparently innocuous and purely organisational matter of fixing a date for a further meeting on the topic – sparked bitter dispute. Beyond mirroring the growing political tensions of the Cold War, the Soviet reluctance to convene another meeting on the topic before knowing if Albania would or could be represented,[12] illustrates the procedural differences between the Security Council and the ICJ.

Indeed, the interests at stake in a proceeding before the Security Council are not the same as those before the ICJ. Thus there existed at the time of the

---

7 The phrase would ultimately be deleted at the suggestion of the US delegate. Ibid., 125th Meeting, pp. 689–690.
8 For a thorough account of the admitted and disputed facts, see H. Munro, 'The Case of the Corfu Minefield', *The Modern Law Review*, 10 (1947): 363–376.
9 See e.g. L. W. Maher, 'Half Light Between War and Peace: Herbert Vere Evatt, The Rule of International Law, and the *Corfu Channel case*', *Australian Journal of Legal History*, 9 (2005): 81. Online. Available at: http://www.law.mq.edu.au/html/AJLH/vol9/vol9-1_3.pdf (accessed 13 August 2010). On Australia's attitude towards the Council's task of dispute settlement during the first years of the UN, see also Dennett, op. cit., pp. 425–427.
10 Maher, op. cit., p. 56.
11 The Australian representative (Colonel Hodgson), after having strenuously supported the quasi-judicial character of the Security Council's functions in dispute settlement, candidly affirmed that

> in this respect the ICJ can do very fully the very things we are not able to do here. It can collect additional evidence, and particularly in the oral hearings ..., it can call in witnesses, experts, counsels and advocates. It can obtain material witnesses for examination and cross-examination so that justice shall be done.
> (*Official Records*, op. cit., 125th Meeting, p. 722)

It is hard not to subscribe to such a declaration while at the same time it is hard to understand why the Council, so especially encouraged by this same Australian representative, persisted (stubbornly) in adjudicating the dispute, shall we say *more Curia*?
12 Ibid., 95th Meeting, p. 127.

Corfu Channel controversy the perception that the Council had to 'build up [its] authority and prestige ... in the interest of the discharge of its primary responsibility for the maintenance of peace and security in the world',[13] and that this function might collide with third States' rights established by Article 32.[14] In contrast, the non-appearance of a State does not affect the prestige and authority[15] of the World Court in a case where its jurisdiction is established and when it is satisfied that 'the claim is well founded in fact and law',[16] since its jurisdiction rests upon the consent of both parties.

Moreover, the fact that one of the parties to this dispute, the UK, acted in fact as a member of the adjudicating organ, cannot but heighten doubt as to impartiality. Although it refrained from voting on the draft Resolution it had submitted, the UK had considerably more institutional and political weight than Albania. As is well known, the Security Council finally confined itself, in desperation – '*en désespoir de cause*'[17] – to '[*recommending*] that the United Kingdom and Albanian Governments should immediately refer the dispute to the [ICJ] in accordance with the provisions of the Statute of the Court'.[18]

The uncertainty as to the need (the obligation?) to refer the case to the Court led to an interesting exchange of views on the nature and functions of the Council. As the Brazilian representative to that organ aptly stated, the question of the articulation of competences between the Security Council and the ICJ is a 'fundamental [one]. If we do not define it accurately now, and if we do not set the limits for our attributions, *this council will become a lower court for all disputes* [the higher Court being, consequently, the ICJ].'[19] These discussions did not yield definitive answers but raised many questions that would prove – and remain – crucial for the future of the Security Council's mandate: can the Council set aside international law and justice in discharging its duty, in order to reach a settlement? Does the Council have the institutional capacity or even the jurisdiction to settle legal disputes that involve disputed factual aspects or complex legal issues? Or, on the contrary, is it bound to shy away from such cases? What rules and guarantees protect a party to a dispute submitted to the Security Council against the latter's partial findings? It can be maintained that, at the political level, the referral was merely an elegant

---

13 These were the words of Mr Quo Tai-chi. Ibid., 96th Meeting, p. 139.
14 Ibid., p. 141.
15 See *Military and Paramilitary Activities in and against Nicaragua (Nicaragua v. United States of America). Merits, Judgment. ICJ Reports 1986*, p. 22, para. 27.
16 Article 53 ICJ Statute. See *United States Diplomatic and Consular Staff in Tehran, Judgment, ICJ Reports 1980*, p. 24, para. 45.
17 L. Delbez, 'L'évolution des idées en matière de règlement pacifique des conflits', *Revue générale de droit international public*, 55 (1951): 16.
18 Security Council Resolution 22 of 9 April 1947, adopted with the abstention of Poland and the Soviet Union.
19 Ibid., 125th Meeting, p. 687. Emphasis added.

way (from an institutional standpoint) for the Council to avoid these tricky issues.[20] The ICJ certainly offered the possibility of obtaining a definitive and balanced finding while circumventing the veto rule.[21] Furthermore, in expressing the (official) grounds for its decision, the Security Council hardly created a rebuttable interpretation of the rule contained in Article 36(3) of the UN Charter.

Under Article 24 of the UN Charter, Member States confer on the Security Council the 'primary responsibility for the maintenance of international peace and security'. Because its function is phrased in this manner, the Council has generally been considered the 'executive arm' of the UN system. This function is reinforced by the political nature of its composition. Moreover, this was already the case of the Council of the League of Nations, as was asserted by the PCIJ:

> It appears, in fact, that according to the arguments put forward on both sides before the Council, the settlement of the dispute in question depends, at all events for the most part, on considerations not of a legal character; moreover, it is impossible, properly speaking, to regard the Council, acting in its capacity of an organ of the League of Nations, as will be hereinafter described, as a tribunal of arbitrators.[22]

In the framework of the newly adopted Charter, the question was again put on the table, perhaps in even stronger terms than previously, under the League, because of the relatively lesser role attributed to international law under the Charter.[23] Mr Aranha '[even believed] that, within the framework of the [UN], it was this Council that was invested with the power of executive action'.[24]

In the same spirit, Mr Hasluck, the Australian representative, affirmed that the Council had to draw a clear-cut *distinction between the facts and the law*. The fact-finding function was a necessary aspect of the Security Council's political function, but it was to be carried out without any political bias or legal *a priori*. In many of his declarations Hasluck stressed that the proposal to establish a Sub-Committee with a mandate to elucidate the factual circumstances

---

20 In this sense, see E. Jiménez de Aréchaga, 'Le traitement des différends internationaux par le Conseil de Sécurité', *Recueil des cours*, 85 (1954-I): 73.
21 'All questions [before the ICJ] shall be decided by a majority of the judges present' (Article 55 (1) of the ICJ Statute).
22 *Article 3, paragraph 2, of the Treaty of Lausanne (Frontier between Turkey and Iraq), Advisory Opinion of November 21st 1925*, Series B, No. 12, p. 26.
23 Delbez, op. cit., p. 12 ; M. Forteau, 'Le droit international dans la Charte des Nations Unies', in J.-P. Cot, A. Pellet and M. Forteau, *La Charte des Nations Unies: Commentaire article par article*, vol. I (Paris: Economica, 2005), p. 114.
24 *Official Records*, op. cit., 114th Meeting, p. 423. Also see for the position of the US delegate, Mr Johnson, ibid., 125th Meeting, p. 686.

of the incident was not tantamount to proceeding 'to a judgment of the dispute'. There was a need to determine the facts 'in order that [the Council] can determine what is the appropriate method of resolving the dispute'.[25]

These views nonetheless collided with those defended by his successor on the Council, Colonel Hodgson, who advocated for a *quasi-judicial vision of the Security Council's mission*.[26] At the 127th meeting, he quoted an earlier declaration made by one of his predecessors at the 26th meeting according to which:

> in short, the Council is intended to occupy a position . . . comparable to that of the International Court of Justice in relation to justiciable disputes. The Council should govern its actions and decisions accordingly. It should administer impartial justice according to equity and good conscience and the proven merits of the particular case.[27]

Colonel Hodgson was confident, rather belatedly since the Security Council was on the verge of deferring the dispute to the ICJ, of the Council's ability to adopt a fair decision on the merits: '[the members of the Security Council] have to act on the evidence as reasonable men and come to a reasonable conclusion'.[28] In view of the history of the Australian position, that State's incoherence, if not the duplicity – on the one hand, arguing for an ideally a-politicised Security Council basing its decisions on the 'principles of justice and international law', while on the other blindly supporting the UK – seems blatant.[29]

But this vision of a quasi-judicial Security Council function did not attract the support of the other Council members: Mr Johnson declared that '[the] least the Council [could do was] to give the impartial forum, which the [ICJ] constitutes an opportunity to repair, if possible, some of the damage which has been done by the action of the [Council]'[30] and further asserted that 'we all have confidence in the impartiality of the Court',[31] implying that he doubted that the Council could act impartially. The USSR was opposed to a Security Council finding on the merits on two different grounds: (1) the Council should

---

25 Ibid., 111th Meeting, p. 363. See also ibid., p. 365; ibid., 114th Meeting, p. 420.
26 These were also the views of Herbert Vere Evatt (at the time, Australia's Foreign Minister). Maher, op. cit. p. 57.
27 Ibid., 127th Meeting, p. 721.
28 Ibid.
29 C. Bridge, 'Diplomat', in R. Nile, K. Saunders, and T. Stannage (eds), *Paul Hasluck in Australian History: Civic Personality and Public Life* (Brisbane: University of Queensland Press, 1999), pp. 138–140. Maher reports that Evatt had ordered his delegation 'to fall in behind whatever approach the UK took in the Security Council', Maher, op. cit., p. 60.
30 *Official Records*, op. cit., 125th Meeting, p. 686.
31 Ibid., p. 686. The unshackled faith of the United States in this respect is strangely at odds with its later struggle during the *Nicaragua* case proceedings aimed at rebutting the ICJ's jurisdiction. *Military and Paramilitary Activities in and against Nicaragua (Nicaragua v. United States of America), Jurisdiction and Admissibility, Judgment, ICJ Reports 1984*, p. 435, para. 99.

decline its competence because of the lack of previous negotiations;[32] and (2) because there was no threat to the peace.[33] The first argument was dismissed outright by the British delegate.[34] As to the second, while it is hard to find a clear determination as to the legal basis for the Council's seizure, it cannot be easily sustained that an incident such as the Corfu Channel incident, resulting in the death of more than 40 soldiers, could fall outside the notion of a dispute under Article 33(1) of the Charter.[35] It is significant that Mr Gromyko did not rebut the arguments relating to the Council's quasi-judicial function, although he insisted on the fact that the resolution establishing the Sub-Committee could not 'prejudge the case';[36] nor did he refute the views, shared by the majority of the members, advocating a limited role for the Security Council when it had to deal with complex legal issues. In contrast, Mr Michalowski, the Polish delegate, after having asserted that no proof 'at all' existed and that 'the charges contradict one another', observed that 'some questions of law ... [were] in doubt, such as the question of innocent passage through territorial waters' and that it was not the Security Council's task to address them.[37]

Yet, it is not clear whether the Polish delegate was referring to the functional limits of the Council's powers in matters relative to the law-adjudication process or whether he was merely pointing, in support of Mr Gromyko's thesis, to the Council's lack of jurisdiction over the case. Just after having mentioned, for the first time in this context, the possibility of referring the dispute to the ICJ in accordance with Article 36(3) of the Charter,[38] Mr Michalowski, who was clearly aiming at showing the fallacy of the quasi-judicial thesis, further added that '[we] are not a court of justice nor a jury, and we cannot pass a verdict one way or the other on the basis of our convictions alone'.[39]

To sum up, the members, on the one hand, expressed the view (1) that the Security Council's task was not to deal with a 'legal dispute', thus giving substance to the rule enshrined in Article 36(3). Mr Aranha went as far as to assert that the Council had no competence to settle the dispute in its legal aspects.[40] He was also preoccupied by the way the Security Council had entered into discussion on the material aspects of the litigation and concluded that it should instead immediately refer the matter to the ICJ.[41] But at the

32 *Official Records*, op. cit., 111th Meeting, pp. 365–366.
33 See ibid., p. 371.
34 Ibid., pp. 384–385.
35 L. Jully, 'Le premier arrêt de la Cour internationale de Justice', *Die Friedens-Warte*, 48 (1948): 148.
36 *Official Records*, op. cit., 111th Meeting, p. 365.
37 Ibid., pp. 375–376.
38 Ibid.
39 Ibid.
40 Ibid., 125th Meeting, p. 686.
41 Ibid., 125th Meeting, p. 688. See Delbez, op. cit., p. 10.

same time, (2) they underlined the need to adopt legal procedures, and in this context the term quasi-judicial was deemed appropriate, so as to allow the Council to carry out its fact-finding function; even if, it must be recalled, it was not contested that the Council 'is not and cannot be a tribunal'.[42]

5.3 The Security Council's practice of referral to the ICJ

The case concerning the *Corfu Channel* is the first, and until today, the only dispute in which the Security Council has recommended the referral of a dispute to the ICJ under Article 36(3) of the Charter.[43] Such a possibility has sometimes been discussed as, for instance, in 1947 during the Anglo-Egyptian dispute over the allegedly illegal presence of British troops in Egypt and Sudan,[44] on a proposal of Belgium (supported by the UK), but which did not attract the requisite majority.[45] One can also note Security Council Resolution 395 (1976) of 25 August 1976, which was adopted in the context of the crisis between Turkey and Greece and in which the Security Council:

> [invited] the Governments of Greece and Turkey . . . to continue to take into account the contribution that appropriate judicial means, in particular the [ICJ], are qualified to make to the settlement of any remaining legal differences which they may identify in connection with their present dispute.

---

42 Aranha, *Official Records*, op. cit., 125th Meeting, p. 686.
43 G. Guillaume, 'L'Organisation des Nations unies et ses juges', *Pouvoirs*, 2(109) (2004): 92. It ought nevertheless to be remembered that the General Assembly evoked at least once, the possibility for the parties to a dispute to refer it to the ICJ. This happened in conjunction with the South-West African (Namibia) decennial controversy. See General Assembly Resolutions 1142 (XII) and 1361 (XIV). It ought to be stressed that what has been said in regard to the Security Council's power to refer a dispute to the Court is *a fortiori* applicable with respect to the General Assembly. Indeed, the latter cannot but (re-)commend to the Parties a specific means of dispute settlement.
44 See United Nations, *Repertoire of the Practice of the Security Council 1946–1951* (New York: UN, 1954), pp. 314–315. See also H. W. Briggs, 'Rebus Sic Stantibus Before the Security Council: The Anglo-Egyptian Question', *AJIL*, 43 (1949): 762–769. Briggs explained the Egyptians' reluctance to submit the case to the ICJ as follows: 'it is not surprising that Egypt preferred not to rest her case on juridical arguments: she had no legal case' (ibid., p. 768).
45 S. Rosenne, *The Law and Practice of the International Court, 1920–2005*, vol. II: *Jurisdiction* (Leiden: Martinus Nijhoff, 2006), p. 670; M. S. M. Amr, *The Role of the International Court of Justice as the Principal Judicial Organ of the United Nations* (The Hague: Kluwer Law International, 2003), p. 222. Amr points out that 'the US proposal that the Soviet Union's complaint concerning violation of Soviet air space be referred to the ICJ was vetoed by the Soviet Union'; Stein also relates a Colombian proposal in the context of the Indo-Pakistan dispute, T. Stein, 'Article 36', in B. Simma *et al.* (eds), *The Charter of the United Nations: A Commentary*, 2nd edn (Oxford: Oxford University Press, 2002), p. 627; see also, United Nations, *Repertoire of the Practice of the Security Council: Supplement 1989–1992*, Doc. UN ST/PSCA/1/Add. 11, pp. 867–871, for the *Lockerbie Case* as well as the boundary between Iraq and Kuwait.

However, this wording appears to be more of a mere suggestion than a recommendation within the meaning of Article 36(3) of the Charter; provision which, incidentally, the Security Council did not mention.[46] An analysis of the reach of this provision sheds light on the reasons for such scarce practice.[47] The rule it contains, though of limited effect, requires the Council to take into account the fact that 'legal disputes should as a general rule be referred by the parties to the [ICJ]'.[48] Undeniably, the ICJ, in the *Tehran Hostages Case*, confirmed that the rule bears some meaning, thus confirming the *Corfu Channel* precedent:

> It is for the Court, the principal judicial organ of the [UN], to resolve any legal questions that may be in issue between parties to a dispute; and the resolution of such legal questions by the Court may be an important, and sometimes decisive, factor in promoting the peaceful settlement of the dispute. This is indeed recognized by Article 36 of the Charter, paragraph 3.[49]

Would it be an exaggeration to paraphrase the Court's landmark decision in the *Nicaragua* case,[50] and, reversing the roles (of the organs), consequently assert that 'the Security Council should shy away from a case brought before it merely because it has legal implications'? Nothing in the Charter requires the Security Council to refer a dispute to the ICJ for the sole reason that it has legal implications, as indeed most international disputes have. Unlike the Council's relationship with the General Assembly, the ICJ does not benefit from any privilege of primacy in the exercise of its law-adjudicating function. In fact, whereas Article 12 of the Charter prevents the General Assembly from making a recommendation concerning a situation or a dispute as long as the Security Council is seized,[51] Article 95 of the Charter expressly allows State parties to submit their disputes to other tribunals. Admittedly, for the

---

46 S. D. Bailey and S. Daws, *The Procedure of the Security Council*, 3rd edn (Oxford: Oxford University Press, 2003), p. 315.
47 For an account of the question of the binding effect of Security Council recommendations with references to the legislative history of the UN Charter, see H. Kelsen, *The Law of the United Nations: A Critical Analysis of its Fundamental Problems* (London: Stevens & Sons, 1951), pp. 444–450.
48 H. Lauterpacht, *International Law: Being the Collected Papers of Hersch Lauterpacht*, vol. 5: *Disputes, War and Neutrality* (Cambridge: Cambridge University Press, 2004), pp. 224–226 (hereinafter *Collected Papers*). For a rather critical appraisal of this provision, see Delbez, op. cit., pp. 9–10.
49 *United States Diplomatic and Consular Staff in Tehran, Judgment, ICJ Reports 1980*, p. 22, para. 40.
50 'It must also be remembered that, as the *Corfu Channel case* (ICJ Reports 1949, p. 4) shows, the Court has never shied away from a case brought before it merely because it had political implications or because it involved serious elements of the use of force'. *Military and Paramilitary Activities in and against Nicaragua (Nicaragua v. United States of America), Jurisdiction and Admissibility, Judgment, ICJ Reports 1984*, p. 435, para. 96.
51 But see *Legal Consequences of the Construction of a Wall in the Occupied Palestinian Territory, Advisory Opinion, ICJ Reports 2004*, pp. 150–151, para. 30.

Security Council to adopt such a stance would constitute a failure in the exercise of its duties. It could be accused of not discharging its primary responsibility for the maintenance of peace under Article 24. But the rule embodied in Article 36(3) suggests that the Security Council should at least provide compelling explanations when it refuses to refer a 'legal dispute' to the Court.

As regards the States involved in a proceeding, a recommendation under Article 36(3) issues a strong political and moral injunction to give their consent so that the ICJ's jurisdiction can be established. But the lack of binding legal force of such recommendations does not necessarily entail the conclusion that their effects are limited to the political and moral sphere. Lauterpacht suggested that 'the failure to act on them may bring about the enforcement provisions of Chapter VII wherever such failure is held to amount to a breach of the peace'.[52]

Lauterpacht wondered whether the reasons behind the meagre resort to Article 36(3) might not be found in the replacement of the term 'justiciable' by the term 'legal' when the provision was drafted, arguing that the latter is part of an 'unhelpful traditional terminology'.[53] Thus it appears that this topic is closely intertwined with the so-called argument (or theory) of the justiciability of disputes. As Judge Lachs rightly affirmed in his separate opinion in the *Nicaragua* case, the criterion must be sought elsewhere than in 'complex legal issues':

> It is not the purely formal aspects that should in my view be decisive, but the legal framework, the efficacy of the solution that can be offered, the contribution the judgment may make to removing one more dispute from the overcrowded agenda of contention the world has to deal with today.[54]

Furthermore, Judge Schwebel in the same case asserted that, contrary to what the USA had argued before the Court, it was 'not the design of the drafters of the Charter and the Statute to exclude the Court from adjudicating disputes falling within the scope of Chapter VII of the [UN] Charter'; he was thus 'unable to agree that the practice of States in interpreting the Charter and the Statute confirms such a design'.[55] This (sound) affirmation is even more persuasive as Judge Schwebel was far from being tender towards the ICJ in his dissenting opinion.

---

52 Lauterpacht, *Collected Papers*, op. cit., p. 226; see also Kelsen, *The Law of the United Nations*, op. cit., p. 450.
53 Lauterpacht, *Collected Papers*, op. cit., p. 226.
54 *Military and Paramilitary Activities in and against Nicaragua (Nicaragua v. United States of America)*, Separate Opinion, ICJ Reports 1986, p. 168.
55 *Military and Paramilitary Activities in and against Nicaragua (Nicaragua v. United States of America)*, Dissenting opinion, ICJ Reports 1986, p. 289.

As some authors underline, 'all international conflicts are at the same time political and legal; only the balance between the political and legal aspects varies'.[56] Can it consequently be maintained that a criterion for characterising a dispute as a legal dispute within the meaning of Article 36(3) is the fact that the dispute must be predominantly made up of 'complex legal issues', as suggested by some delegates during the discussion of the *Corfu Channel* case? What then would be a complex legal issue? Would it be tenable, for instance, to reword the assumption as following: 'the SC may not shy away from a case brought before it merely because it has legal implications *unless the legal implications are predominant*'?[57] Be that as it may, the question should be answered not in terms of the allegedly legal or political nature of the dispute but rather in terms of the nature and functions of the organ that is more suited to settling the dispute. In other words, the Security Council may decide which disputes are 'legal disputes', by taking into account the effectiveness of the different options for the sake of the maintenance of international peace and security. For example, it can be argued that disputes involving complex legal issues and controversial factual elements may require different means than others in terms of time and procedure. Some disputes may feature a character of urgency that the Security Council would be better placed to address, others requiring a balanced and fair assessment of the different responsibilities; the latter being the province of the ICJ. It has also been submitted that in some cases a Security Council settlement would provide more flexibility, which in some contexts could mean greater effectiveness.[58] Yet, this does not seem to be the practice adopted by the political organs of the UN, which tend to appraise whether States abide by their obligations.[59]

It is plausible that the main reason for the meagre Security Council practice is, trivially, to be found in a fundamental loss of faith in the strength of international justice – the terminological issue, simply furnishing a purely formal legal explanation, and is thus nothing more than an epiphenomenal manifestation – as Remiro Brotóns has bitterly pointed out.[60]

---

56 D. Nguyen Quoc, P. Daillier, M. Forteau and A. Pellet, *Droit international public*, 8th edn (Paris: L.G.D.J., 2009), p. 920 [authors' translation].

57 Similar arguments were used by the Libyan Arab Jamahiriya and some other States in the discussions before the Security Council in the framework of the *Lockerbie* case. See United Nations, *Repertoire of the Practice of the Security Council: 1996–1999 (advance version)*, Chapter X, p. 70; Online. Available at: http://www.un.org/en/sc/repertoire/96-99/96-99_10.pdf (accessed 16 August 2010). See V. Gowland-Debbas, 'The Relationship Between the International Court of Justice and the Security Council in the Light of the Lockerbie Case', *AJIL*, 88 (1994): 648–653.

58 R. Higgins, 'The Place of International Law in the Settlement of Disputes by the United Nations Security Council', *AJIL*, 64 (1970): 16.

59 O. Schachter, 'The Quasi-Judicial Role of the Security Council and the General Assembly', *AJIL*, 64 (1958): 961.

60 A. Remiro Brotóns, *Derecho internacional* (Valencia: Tirant lo Blanch, 2007), p. 1116.

5.4 The legal effects of the Security Council referral in regard to the ICJ's jurisdiction

At the first meeting which dealt with the *Corfu Channel* incident, the Security Council, pursuant to Article 32 of the Charter, decided to invite Albania to take a part in the discussion. On 'summoning' Albania, the Council asked her to abide by all 'those obligations which would apply to a Member of the [UN] in such a case'.[61] This point is worth noting as it would become the touchstone of the legal construction advocated by the UK in order to establish the alleged compulsory jurisdiction of the ICJ. The UK affirmed that having accepted these obligations, Albania was bound to abide by the alleged compulsory jurisdiction flowing from the combined reading of Articles 25 and 36(3) of the UN Charter as well as of Article 36(1) of the ICJ Statute.[62]

In its 1948 *Judgment on Preliminary Objections*, the ICJ considered that it need not 'express an opinion' on the existence of a compulsory jurisdiction arising out of Article 36(1) of the Statute, 'since, ... the letter of July 2nd, 1947, addressed by the Albanian Government to the Court, [constituted] a voluntary acceptance of its jurisdiction'.[63] Nevertheless seven Judges regretfully observed in a joint separate opinion that the Court had not dealt with the issue and contested any view that Article 36 '[had] introduced more or less surreptitiously, a new case of compulsory jurisdiction'.[64] In the same vein, Judge *ad hoc* Daxner noted, after a thorough perusal of the *travaux préparatoires*, that 'the obligatory character of a recommendation under Article 36(3), is inadmissible'.[65]

Most commentators admit without hesitation that the British argument of the alleged binding effect of the Security Council resolution was devoid of legal accuracy – sometimes even terming it 'specious'.[66] Some authors, like

---

61 *Official Records*, op. cit., 95th Meeting, pp. 123–124.
62 See *Corfu Channel case, Judgment on Preliminary Objection: ICJ Reports 1948*, p. 17.
63 Ibid., p. 26.
64 *Corfu Channel case, Judgment on Preliminary Objection, Joint Separate Opinion: ICJ Reports 1948*, p. 32.
65 *Corfu Channel case, Judgment on Preliminary Objection, Dissenting Opinion by Dr. Igor Daxner: ICJ Reports 1948*, p. 33; Also see F. Honig, 'The International Court of Justice 1947– 1950', *Zeitschrift für Ausländisches Öffentliches Recht und Völkerrecht*, 14 (1951/52): 500; Munro, op. cit., p. 375; L. B. Sohn, 'Senate Resolutions Relating to the International Court of Justice', *AJIL*, 69 (1975): 95.
66 H. Waldock, 'Forum Prorogatum or Acceptance of a Unilateral Summons to Appear before the International Court', *International Law Quarterly*, 2 (1948): 390; J.-F. Lalive, 'La jurisprudence de la Cour internationale de Justice', *Annuaire suisse de droit international*, VI (1949): 167; H. Lauterpacht, *The Development of International Law by the International Court* (London: Stevens and Son, 1958), p. 47; Honig, op. cit., p. 500; E. Hambro, 'Some Observations on the Compulsory Jurisdiction of the International Court of Justice', *BYBIL*, 25 (1948): 133; L. Goodrich and E. Hambro, *Charter of the United Nations: Commentary and Documents*, 2nd edn (London: Stevens and Son, 1949), p. 258; Jully, op. cit., p. 151.; M. Dubisson, *La Cour internationale de Justice* (Paris:

Kelsen, were less stringent in their appraisal.[67] Gross, while agreeing with Draxner's dissenting opinion in its dogmatic aspects, nevertheless, found the outcome unsatisfactory.[68]

Hence, what can be said of the reference in Article 36(1) ICJ Statute recognising the Court's jurisdiction for matters 'specially provided for in the Charter of the [UN]'? Can one maintain that a ground of jurisdiction can arise out of this provision despite the lack of binding effect of Security Council recommendations?[69] Following a systemic and literal interpretation, Article 36(3) of the Charter seems to temper the scope of Article 36(1) of the ICJ Statute by providing that recommendations shall be made 'in accordance with the provisions of the Statute of the Court'. Therefore, this provision can hardly be construed as substantiating the *ipso facto* establishment of the ICJ's jurisdiction by virtue of a mere Security Council resolution.

An argument that has been advanced in order to criticise the abovementioned separate opinion is that the interpretation chosen by the minority of the Court left Article 36(1) of the ICJ Statute emptied of any legal meaning given that it establishes the jurisdiction of the Court for 'all matters specially provided for in the Charter of the [UN]'.[70] Yet in this respect, Hambro considered that the Charter contains no 'matters specially provided for' in regard to the jurisdiction of the Court in relation to Article 36(1) ICJ Statute.[71] On a purely logical level,[72] taking into account the 'ordinary meaning to be

---

L.G.D.J., 1964), p. 158; F. Wittman, *Das Problem des Obligatoriums in der internationalen Gerichtsbarkeit unter besonderer Berücksichtigung von Artikel 36 Absatz 2 des Statuts des Internationalen Gerichtshofes*, Dissertation, Munich, 1963, pp. 106–108; K. Herndl, 'Reflections on the Role, Functions and Procedures of the Security Council of the United Nations', *Recueil des Cours*, 206 (1987-VI), p. 326; T. Stein, op. cit., p. 626.

67 Kelsen, *The Law of the United Nations*, op. cit., p. 517; H. Kelsen, 'The Settlement of Disputes by the Security Council', *International Law Quarterly*, 2 (1948), p. 193.

68 L. Gross, 'The International Court of Justice and the United Nations', *Recueil des Cours*, 120 (1967-I), pp. 353–354 (hereinafter 'The International Court').

69 The Australian representative, Hodgson, plainly supported this ground of jurisdiction, albeit without elaborating on it (*Official Records*, op. cit., 125th Meeting, pp. 722–723). We could even infer this as regards the Soviets in view of the terms used by Gromyko just before the adoption of the resolution: 'We have no justification ... for *dragging* Albania before the International Court of Justice, because in order to *bring* any country before the International Court of Justice, some sort of justification is necessary' (ibid., p. 725) [emphasis added].

70 Gross, 'The International Court', op. cit., pp. 353–354. See particularly, J. Mervyn Jones, '*Corfu Channel case*: Jurisdiction', *Transactions of the Grotius Society*, 35 (1949): 95.

71 Hambro, op. cit., p. 133.

72 As stressed by Dionisio Anzilotti, the logical presuppositions and consequences derived from the rules adopted by States actually matter for the purpose of the determination of the sources of international law. D. Anzilotti, *Corso di diritto internazionale, Vol. Primo, Introduzione – Teorie Generalli*, 3rd edn (Padova: Cedam, 1955), p. 67. For an example of such a 'logical interpretation', see ICTY, *The Prosecutor v. Duško Tadić*, Appeals Chamber, Judgment of 15 July 1999, Case No. IT-94-1-A, para. 284.

given to the terms of[73] the Charter, it is indeed quite bold to assert that the Security Council has been vested with the power to issue recommendations that are impossible to implement. In any future cases, it is most likely that a recommendation would be issued only when the parties have no intention of submitting the case to the ICJ. It is possible that the political pressure put on them would influence their will.[74] But this is simply speculation in respect of the effects of the recommendation, as a wide range of other factors might determine their conduct. The plausible alternative is that one of the parties adamantly refuses to submit the dispute. In such a case the Security Council would recommend something that would prove legally impossible. It is submitted that to accept such a nonsense would seriously undermine the Council's prestige and authority, not to say that of the UN as a whole.

Quite strikingly, both the judges who had issued the separate opinion and most of the commentators of the time favoured the historical interpretation,[75] rejecting implicitly the argument arising out of the principle of *effet utile*.[76] The least that can be said is that the separate opinion is unsatisfactory, even from a purely dogmatic point of view, as it does not address the problem of the meaning of the words 'provided for in the Charter of the United Nations' in Article 36(1) ICJ Statute and actually leaves this part of the provision without any legal meaning.

The argument that this provision provides an autonomous ground of compulsory jurisdiction was also raised in the *Ambatielos* case, although in a different, and this time undoubtedly specious, legal construction – for in this case, there had been no recommendation by the Council.[77] The Court did not seize the opportunity this time either to elucidate the issue, instead establishing its jurisdiction on the main ground submitted by Greece, namely Article 37 of the ICJ Statute.

---

73 As suggested by Article 31(1) of the Vienna Convention on the Law of Treaties (1969). *United Nations Treaty Series*, vol. 1155, p. 331.
74 Jully also terms the British argument of the mandatory effect of the recommendation as 'specious' and rebuts the argument of applying the principle *ut res magis valeat quam pereat* to Article 36(3) of the UN Charter in order to confer the power on the Security Council to impose a specific – let alone judicial – means of dispute settlement. He considers that Article 36(3) UN Charter has already an '*effet utile*', namely the political and moral effects of a recommendation issued pursuant to its terms, even if it has no binding force. Refusing this would amount to denying and undermining this persuasive strength. Jully, op. cit., p. 152.
75 In this context, it ought to be remembered that at that time the historical interpretation, notably based on the analysis of the *travaux préparatoires*, constituted one of the main, if not the principal, methods of treaty interpretation.
76 With the notable exception of Jully, op. cit.
77 *ICJ Pleadings, Ambatielos Case (Greece v. United Kingdom)*, p. 25 See also Greece's observations on the preliminary objection. ibid., p. 223. It is interesting to notice that Hartley Shawcross acted this time as counsel for Greece, proving coherent in his argument (in contrast to Sir Eric Beckett). Also see, ibid., p. 285.

It took more than fifty years after the *Corfu Channel* case for the ICJ to end – in an *obiter dictum* – the debate with regard to the interpretation of Article 36(1) of the ICJ Statute in relation to Article 36(3) of the UN Charter:

> The Court observes that the [UN] Charter contains no specific provision of itself conferring compulsory jurisdiction on the Court. In particular, there is no such provision in Articles 1, paragraph 1, 2, paragraphs 3 and 4, 33, 36, paragraph 3 and 92 of the Charter, relied on by Pakistan.[78]

It is curious that after declining to do so twice, for reasons of 'procedural economy', the ICJ eventually decided to take position on Article 36(1) ICJ Statute with such a wide affirmation even though it was not necessary for the sake of the case,[79] as if the judges felt the need to close the door definitively on such a 'surreptitious ground of compulsory jurisdiction'. Nonetheless, and on the basis of what has just been said, was it tenable to sustain back in 1948 the validity of such an autonomous head of jurisdiction? The Court's repeated silences and uncertainties over nearly fifty years prove that it was not absurd to argue in this sense. The fundamental importance of the issue for the rule of law in the international community indicates that it still warrants a more in-depth and up-to-date treatment than that provided for in the reviewed precedents.[80]

Be that as it may, one of the legacies of the Court's judgment in the *Corfu Channel* case lies, as was wisely underlined by Waldock, in the full establishment of the doctrine of *forum prorogatum* in a case where the Security Council had previously recommended deferral to the ICJ.[81] Yet, this is not tantamount to saying that the Court has *ipso facto* jurisdiction over the case; as we have seen, to do so, the Court needs a basis established in accordance with its Statute and these heads of jurisdiction are exhaustively enunciated in its Article 36. In spite of the phrase found in paragraph 1, recognising the Court's jurisdiction for 'all matters specially provided for in the Charter of the [UN]', the ICJ has been silent in this respect, rendering this provision, to date, without effect. Hence, even though the Statute is annexed to the Charter, only the former regulates the establishment of the Court's jurisdiction. This

---

78 *Aerial Incident of 10 August 1999 (Pakistan v. India), Jurisdiction of the Court, Judgment, ICJ Reports 2000*, p. 33, para. 48.
79 There is no trace in Pakistan's memorial of a legal interpretation such as the one used by the UK in 1947 or by Greece in 1952.
80 See e.g. General Assembly Resolutions 60/1, para. 134(f) and 64/116; *Accordance with International Law of the Unilateral Declaration of Independence in Respect of Kosovo (Request for Advisory Opinion), Separate Opinion of Judge Antônio Augusto Cançado Trindade*, para. 28. Thomas Bingham describes the consensual basis of the ICJ's jurisdiction as one of the 'most serious deficiencies of the rule of law in the international legal order'. See T. Bingham, *The Rule of Law* (London: Allen Lane, 2010), p. 128.
81 Waldock, op. cit., p. 390.

conclusion remains correct even in the (highly) hypothetical case of the Council, through a binding resolution, requesting two States to refer their dispute to the ICJ. The latter, in order to verify its jurisdiction, could not be satisfied with the Council's resolution and would need the two States' consent and thus a valid head of jurisdiction under Article 36(1) or (2) of the Statute.[82] Hence, the Security Council cannot obviate the requirement of State consent through the adoption of a resolution. In the absence of such consent, the two States have given their consent to the binding character of certain Security Council resolutions but not to the Court's jurisdiction. The Council cannot avail itself of their consent embodied in Article 25 UN Charter and 'transfer' it to Article 36 of the Statute and thus establish the Court's jurisdiction. Therefore, if the two States – or just one of them – do not go to the Court, they will breach the Security Council resolution, thereby engaging their responsibility, but the Court will not as a consequence have jurisdiction over the dispute.[83]

5.5 Fact-finding in the Security Council and its use by the ICJ

Prior to the adoption of Security Council Resolution 22, the long politically tainted clash over the disputed facts – mainly the alleged Albanian origin of the minefield or at least the knowledge and connivance of Albania in that regard – led the Council's members to a certain sense of disillusionment and to the belief that the Security Council in full session was unable 'to decide on facts'.[84] The Council therefore decided at its 114th meeting to create a Sub-Committee whose task was 'to examine all the available evidence concerning the . . . incidents and to make a report to the Security Council'[85] and decided to appoint Australia, Colombia and Poland as its members.[86] Those who approved the Sub-Committee's creation considered that it possessed 'a certain judiciary competence'; but it still had to be composed of 'a rapporteur and two

---

82 See in this respect Judge Daxner's dissenting opinion, op. cit., p. 38. See Sohn, op. cit., p. 95, arguing *de lege ferenda* that states should be given the 'option to accept a recommendation . . . under Article 36(3) [which] would constitute a sufficient basis for the Court's jurisdiction because of the prior acceptance by the parties of this optional provision'.
83 Quite surprisingly, Albania acknowledged that if the Security Council had adopted a binding resolution referring the dispute to the Court, such a resolution would have 'oblige[d] both parties *ipso facto* and without any other step, to appear before the [ICJ] and . . . would [have] authorized them to approach the [ICJ] without regard to the provisions of the Statute of the Court'. Albanian government's observations reproduced in *Corfu Channel case, Judgment on Preliminary Objection: ICJ Reports 1948*, p. 22.
84 In this context, it is not without interest to recall that Albania had quite inappropriately seized the General Assembly hoping that 'sa requête sera suivie d'une enquête' (Oral argument of Jean Nordmann (Albania), 20/01 (1949, vol. I, p. 608).
85 SC Resolution 19 of 27 February 1947. *Official Records*, op. cit., 114th Meeting, p. 432.
86 Ibid., p. 438.

revisers whose duty is to examine and report upon questions for final judgment of their fellow members'.[87] Even though the Security Council did not take an official position in this respect, Syria's delegate made a statement according to which the Council's decision to set up the Sub-Committee did not constitute the carrying out of an 'investigation' pursuant Article 34.[88] This seems to be consistent with a generally admitted understanding within the Council as it was unchallenged by other members. According to the Soviet delegate, the establishment of the Sub-Committee was not necessary because 'the accusations levelled at Albania by the [UK] Government [were] not proved, and it is impossible to prove them'.[89] Unlike Australia, the USSR did not even try – or did not succeed? – to disguise its political agenda behind its juridical rhetoric.[90] It appears in the judgment on the merits that the evidentiary materials arising out of the proceedings before the Council and subsequently submitted to the Court were, at least partially, taken *ipso facto* into account by the Court.[91]

Be that as it may, the Sub-Committee concentrated its attention on the following two questions: (1) the existence of the minefield; and (2) and, if established, was 'it laid by Albania or with the connivance of the Albanian Government, or was it not?'[92] The Report which was ultimately adopted unanimously, albeit with an additional Report by the Polish representative, answered the first question in the affirmative. As for the second, and more substantial question, the Chairman of the Sub-Committee, Mr. Zuleta Angel (Colombia) maintained that:

> There is no direct evidence and no positive facts from which it may be concluded beyond doubt that the mines were laid by Albania or with her connivance. Nor have we any conclusive and categorical assertions to this effect by the United Kingdom.[93]

He then went on to stress the core of the problem, namely how the mines could be laid 'so close to the coast without Albania's knowledge when that country, especially in view of the incidents which took place in May, had shown such jealous concern for all matters connected with her sovereignty

---

87 Aranha; ibid., 114th Meeting, p. 423.
88 Ibid., p. 430.
89 Ibid., p. 377.
90 It seems that such a reproach can also be formulated in respect of the proceeding before the ICJ. See Z. L. Zile, 'A Soviet Contribution to International Adjudication: Professor Krylov's Jurisprudential Legacy', *AJIL*, 58 (1964): 367, 386–387. A commentator in the *Journal de Genève* of 26 December 1949 ironically expressed his scepticism in respect of Judge Krylov's vote. Online. Available at: http://www.letempsarchives.ch.
91 *Corfu Channel case, Judgment of April 9th, 1949: ICJ Reports 1949*, p. 17.
92 *Official Records*, op. cit., 120th Meeting, p. 544.
93 Ibid., p. 549.

over territorial waters?'.⁹⁴ Consequently, he was ready to vote in favour of a finding on the merits against Albania and added that if no majority could be reached by the Security Council on that point he 'should be inclined to suggest that ... the Council should recommend that the two parties bring their dispute before the [ICJ]'.⁹⁵ This interpretation of the Sub-Committee's findings, while an authoritative one (since by its chairman), was far from unanimously shared by the other Security Council members. Mr Gromyko affirmed that the ascertained facts

> confirm that ... the British charges are entirely unfounded [and] that they should not be taken as the basis for the adoption by the Security Council of an unfair decision. *There is no reason for the Security Council to find Albania guilty.*⁹⁶

In addition to Poland and the USSR, it is worth mentioning Belgium, whose stance is not presumptively tainted in Cold War terms. The Belgium representative noted that there was 'no direct evidence that the mines were laid by the Albanian Government'⁹⁷ and further contended that he could not 'conceive that these mines were laid without that Government's knowledge';⁹⁸ even though this could entail the latter's responsibility, as the Court would subsequently determine in its judgment. It is interesting to observe how, little by little, Albania's responsibility slid from direct responsibility, to connivance and ultimately to its mere knowledge, in parallel with the ever-shrinking robustness of the 'compelling' evidence brought by the UK. The ICJ would ultimately arrive at the same conclusion. Albania rejected by all available means the UK draft Resolution arguing that 'to draw mere assumptions from [arguments devoid of all foundation] is to act contrary to the principles of justice, and is neither a valid nor a serious procedure'.⁹⁹ One of the reasons adduced (by Poland and Albania) to weaken the probative value of the Sub-Committee's findings rested on the variable standards of proof applied respectively before the Security Council and the Sub-Committee. The Australian representative, Hasluck, retorted that:

> The findings which we [i.e. the Sub-Committee] think the Council is justified in making, are simply that the mines must have been laid *with the knowledge* of Albania. We think that that finding is a *reasonable* one because of the *accumulation of evidence* leading to that conclusion, and

---

94 Ibid.
95 Ibid.
96 Ibid., 121st Meeting, pp. 586–587. Emphasis added.
97 Ibid., p. 587.
98 Ibid. This view would be supported by the USA (ibid., pp. 588–589) as well as by France (ibid., p. 595) and China (ibid., pp. 600–601).
99 Ibid., p. 597.

particularly *in the absence of any other reasonable explanation or plausible or practicable theory* as to how the mines got into water at that particular place.[100]

This reply was not deemed satisfactory by the Syrian delegation which correctly assumed that '[t]here must be certainty in the matters [*sic*]'.[101] Finally, the UK representative's last bid to support its draft Resolution made clear that 'although, as I have said several times, I cannot produce eyewitnesses, *the evidence I have given creates such a clear presumption* that I think nobody need do violence to his conscience in adopting the resolution which I have submitted'.[102] The Sub-Committee's work – Poland submitting a dissenting Report[103] – did not further the dispute's settlement but rather revealed the Security Council's incapacity to reach a balanced pronouncement. Yet, on the basis of this Report, the UK submitted a draft Resolution determining that the minefield 'was laid in the Corfu Channel by the Albania Government or with its connivance' (§1) and consequently that the dispute had to be settled 'on the basis of the Council's findings in §1 above', while the Council retained the 'dispute on the agenda'. Such an abrupt request was doomed from the outset; Poland, France and the USA, each of them with their own ends in mind, put forward amendments. At the end of the debates preceding the vote on the UK's draft Resolution, as amended by a US proposal,[104] it was not hard to guess that the USSR would cast its veto. Indeed, the resolution was not adopted and thus the Council's fact-finding was rejected. This is paradoxical since the determination rebutted by the Security Council would ultimately be endorsed by the ICJ in its Judgment on the Merits.[105] Since the 'facts and observations' were roughly the same, can one conclude, in contrast to what was hastily observed above, that the standard of proof in terms of threshold is higher for the Security Council than for the ICJ? That, in the light of this case, the Security Council is 'more Catholic than the Pope'? Or, conversely, that the ICJ (the UN's principal 'judicial organ') proved itself to be bolder – or less demanding – than the Council (a political organ)? Or, more simply and perhaps more pragmatically, that the Security Council, since it is a political organ, can be prevented from discharging its task ... for crude political reasons, that have nothing to do with highly sophisticated theories and constructions on evidence and

---

100 Ibid., p. 603. Emphasis added.
101 Ibid., p. 605.
102 Ibid., p. 607. Emphasis added.
103 Poland challenged more specifically the previously alleged 'strong presumption' incumbent upon Albania's connivance or lack of knowledge, describing the evidence before the Council as being mere 'conjectures, theories and hypotheses' (ibid., pp. 553–555).
104 The relevant part of the US amendment read: 'this minefield could not have been laid without the knowledge of the Albanian authorities' (ibid., p. 609), thus entailing a 'light' responsibility as compared to a 'direct' one suggested by UK.
105 *Corfu Channel case, Judgment of April 9th, 1949: ICJ Reports 1949*, p. 22.

standards of proof. It is nevertheless the case that, in an unexpected – and perhaps unwanted – institutional casting, the Security Council tried to act as the investigator, or better still, the Prosecutor – or, even, as a lower court – while the ICJ acted as itself, namely as a judicial organ.

Be that as it may, veto power and the discordance between different interpretations as to the Sub-Committee's findings rendered impossible the adoption of any adjudicating resolution, be it condemning or acquitting Albania.[106] The end of the story is well known; the Security Council referred the case to the ICJ.

5.6 The Security Council's attempt to act as the ICJ's prosecutor

It must be remembered from the outset that the UK's argument put to the Security Council, according to which Albania could not but have laid the mines itself in the Corfu Channel, was decisive in convincing seven of the Council's members. In this context, one can note – as the Court did not fail to remark – that 'although the [UK] Government never abandoned its contention that Albania herself laid the mines, very little attempt was made by the Government to demonstrate this point'.[107] In the same vein, the Court observed that ultimately the UK 'proposed to show that the said warships, with the knowledge and connivance of the Albanian Government, laid mines in the Corfu Channel just before October 22nd, 1946', adding furthermore that the original UK contention (i.e. Albania having laid the mines) 'was in fact hardly put forward at that time [of the Final submissions] except *pro memoria*, and no evidence in support was furnished'. Hence, the UK actually abandoned, if not formally, its pristine contention which was instrumental, as previously stated, (almost) convincing the Security Council. Why? Was it due to an unavowed, if legitimate, fear that this allegation would not meet the Court's higher standard of proof, especially if compared to that of the Security Council? Be that as it may, Albanian counsel had an easy job dismantling the UK evidence, previously submitted to the Council, and allegedly demonstrating that Albania had laid the mines.

In respect of the required evidentiary threshold,[108] the Australian view was that the Security Council had to decide 'as reasonable men on the basis of all

---

106 For the sake of completeness, the Corfu dispute and in that context the USSR's potential to use the veto, underlined the need for a general discussion on the veto power. The debate took place just before the Security Council deferred the dispute to the ICJ, Gromyko telling Hodgson that Australia 'suffered from the "vetophobia disease"'. Ibid., p. 722 (Hodgson) and p. 725 (Gromyko).
107 *Corfu Channel case, Judgment of April 9th, 1949: ICJ Reports 1949*, p. 15.
108 Albania pleaded that 'les Membres du Conseil de Sécurité reconnaissent qu'on ne saurait condamner le Gouvernement albanais sans preuve et sur des simples présomptions', Reply of Albania (20/IX/1948), vol. II, p. 347.

the available evidence',[109] thus giving rise to a finding of responsibility based on circumstantial evidence.[110] This formulation seems considerably less stringent than the requirement of a 'degree of certainty' in cases concerning grave accusations against States called for by the ICJ in its judgment on the Merits.[111] In fact, in the *Corfu Channel* case the Court did not rely exclusively on the Security Council's fact-finding. The only explicit reference to the Security Council's Official Records is made with respect to an Albanian declaration according to which the latter admitted that its coasts were kept under close vigilance.[112] With regard to this fundamental discrepancy between the ICJ and the Council in matters of fact-finding, one should recall what Judge Schwebel candidly stated in his dissenting opinion in the *Nicaragua* case:

> While the Security Council is invested by the Charter with the authority to determine the existence of an act of aggression, it does not act as a court in making such a determination. It may arrive at a determination of aggression – or, as more often is the case, fail to arrive at a determination of aggression – for political rather than legal reasons. However compelling the facts which could give rise to a determination of aggression, the Security Council acts within its rights when it decides that to make such a determination will set back the cause of peace rather than advance it. In short, the Security Council is a political organ which acts for political reasons. It may take legal considerations into account but, unlike a court, it is not bound to apply them.[113]

The evidentiary threshold, the powers with which the two organs are respectively vested, not to speak of the (political) composition and the veto right, fundamentally distinguish these organs. In this respect, evidence which can be admitted and availed of before the Security Council can be barely alleged before the Court, let alone adjudicated upon. The Court is thus entitled to refuse evidence which does not meet the acknowledged standards of a judicial organ, even if they are upheld by the Security Council. In this regard, the *Corfu Channel* case is emblematic in showing that, contrary to the Security Council's first factual determination, the Court did not consider that Albania had laid the minefield. What if the Council, surrendering to the UK's compelling insistence, had adopted a resolution condemning Albania on the basis of a 'factual error'? This question appears even more crucial since, as is widely admitted, the

---

109 See above note 27.
110 Maher, op. cit., p. 60.
111 *Corfu Channel case, Judgment of April 9th, 1949: ICJ Reports 1949*, p. 17.
112 Ibid., p. 19.
113 *Military and Paramilitary Activities in and against Nicaragua (Nicaragua v. United States of America), Dissenting Opinion, ICJ Reports 1986*, p. 290.

ICJ cannot review Security Council resolutions.[114] Conversely, it is not bound by any factual finding emanating from the Security Council. Incidentally, the latter has not always distinguished itself for the accuracy of its investigations; it suffices to recall, for example, its Resolution 1530 (2004), hastily – and wrongly – attributing instantly the Atocha (Madrid) bomb attacks to the 'terrorist group ETA', while it quickly emerged that it was imputable to one of Al-Qaeda's cells;[115] or its Resolution 731 (1992) straightforwardly endorsing UK, US and France's 'investigations'.[116] From the above, the Court's cautious handling of fact-finding made by the Security Council seems both intelligible and wise, from both a logical and institutional point of view.

Hence, this trend of maintaining a relative distance from the factual findings made by the Security Council, inaugurated by the ICJ in 1949, would ultimately be confirmed in the *Congo v. Uganda* case[117] and later in the *Genocide* case.[118] In both of these cases the Court '[noted] that evidence obtained by examination of persons directly involved, and who were subsequently cross-examined by judges skilled in examination and experienced in assessing large amounts of factual information, some of it of a technical nature, merits special attention'.[119]

More specifically, in the first case, the Court started by stating that '[It] will take into consideration evidence contained in certain [UN] documents to the extent that they are of probative value and are corroborated, if necessary, by other credible sources.'[120] In accordance with the aforementioned line of

---

114 *Questions of Interpretation and Application of the 1971 Montreal Convention arising from the Aerial Incident at Lockerbie (Libyan Arab Jamahiriya v. United States of America), Provisional Measures, Order of 14 April 1992, ICJ Reports 1992*, paras 42–43.

115 In the afternoon of 11 March 2004, the evidence gathered already pointed the investigators to fundamentalist Islamist terrorists. See, e.g., E. Ekaizer, 'Matanza en Madrid: Análisis – En la mira de ETA y de Osama', in *El País*, 12 March 2004. Online. Available at: <http://www.elpais.com/articulo/espana/mira/ETA/Osama/elpepiesp/20040312elpepinac_23/Tes> (accessed 5 October 2010).

116 Resolution 731 (1992), adopted on 21 January 1993, whose fifth recital read:

> Deeply concerned over results of investigations which implicate officials of the Libyan Government and which are contained in Security Council documents that include the requests addressed to the Libyan authorities by France, the United Kingdom of Great Britain and Northern Ireland and the United States of America in connection with the legal procedures related to the attacks carried out against Pan Am flight 103 and UTA flight 772.

117 *Armed Activities on the Territory of the Congo (Democratic Republic of the Congo v. Uganda), Judgment, ICJ Reports 2005*, paras 208–211. See S. Halink, 'All Things Considered: How the International Court of Justice Delegated its Fact-Assessment to the United Nations in the Armed Activities Case', N.Y.U.J. Int'L L. & Pol 40 (2008): 13-52.

118 *Application of the Convention on the Prevention and Punishment of the Crime of Genocide (Bosnia and Herzegovina v. Serbia and Montenegro), Judgment, ICJ Reports 2007*, paras 217–224.

119 Ibid., para. 213. But see *Application of the Convention on the Prevention and Punishment of the Crime of Genocide (Bosnia and Herzegovina v. Serbia and Montenegro), Dissenting Opinion Mahiou*, paras 50–54.

120 *Armed Activities on the Territory of the Congo (Democratic Republic of the Congo v. Uganda), Judgment, ICJ Reports 2005*, para. 205.

conduct, the Court considered that 'there is sufficient evidence of a reliable quality to support the DRC's allegation'.[121] In this regard the Court relied on Security Council as well as MONUC reports. On reading the Court's reasoning, it seems nonetheless quite clear that Security Council reports or reports established under its aegis do not enjoy a predominant probative value as the Court treats all UN-issued documents indiscriminately as it does any factual evidence alleged by the parties, making sure that '[the] above reports are consistent in the presentation of facts, support each other and are corroborated by other credible sources'.[122] In contrast, in the second case, the Court relied heavily on the judgment delivered by the ICTY as well as on the latter's factual determinations.[123]

In condemning the UK for having carried out the so-called *Operation Retail*, the Court in the *Corfu Channel* case not only stressed that it was applying the 'new international law', which flowed from the recently adopted UN Charter, thus adamantly rejecting the 'alleged right of intervention as a manifestation of a policy of force' – this would have been sufficient for the sake of pronouncing a solemn condemnation – but it also insisted that '[intervention] . . . *might easily {have led} to perverting the administration of international justice itself*'.[124] This raises the tricky question of the use by a tribunal of evidentiary material obtained through a breach of the law. Indeed, had the (forcible) intervention aiming to obtain legal evidence been considered lawful – as alleged by the UK – this would have not only emptied Article 2(4) of the UN Charter of meaning, but it would have also entailed a blatant inequality of States before the ICJ. For only those States having the means and the will to use force, could be enabled to collect *corpora delicti*,[125] at the expense of weaker States,[126] thus striking a flagrant imbalance between them in the administration of proof; not to mention, as was argued by the Albanian representative before the Security Council,[127] the crucial question of the 'purity' of the evidence collected in this way by one of the parties to the dispute. Forcibly collected probative material cannot be submitted before an international tribunal in general. In the light of the above, it can be maintained that the Security Council, let alone one of its members being at the same time party to a dispute, is not the judicial police of the ICJ.

---

121 Ibid., para. 208.
122 Ibid., para. 209.
123 *Application of the Convention on the Prevention and Punishment of the Crime of Genocide (Bosnia and Herzegovina v. Serbia and Montenegro), Judgment*, paras 217–224.
124 *Corfu Channel case, Judgment of April 9th, 1949: ICJ Reports 1949*, p. 34. Emphasis added.
125 For an attempt of justification by the UK, see Reply of the UK (30/VII/1948), vol. II, p. 283.
126 For Albania's response to the British arguments, see Reply of Albania (20/IX/1948), vol. II, p. 373. See likewise Mr Pierre Cot's pleadings (Albania), Minutes (18/XI/1948), pp. 405–410.
127 *Official Records*, op. cit., 121st Meeting, p. 574.

5.7 Epilogue

One is tempted to label this concluding section an 'Epitaph', as the *Corfu Channel* case has quite probably sealed for a long time such an impromptu casting of roles between the ICJ and the Security Council. After having determined that such a dispute was not suited to Security Council resolution, the latter referred it to the ICJ, while it could not at the same time establish *motu proprio* the Court's jurisdiction. Regardless of this highly controversial question, it is a pity that such a practice of deferral was not followed in the years to come; this would have enhanced the apparent synergies between the two organs. The Security Council could have dealt primarily with disputes presenting a character of urgency, while others could have been dealt with by the Court. Or, with regard to a single dispute, one might envisage the Security Council being bound to address its most urgent aspects by way of Chapters VI and VII without prejudging the Court's role for the assessment of legal responsibilities and other essentially legal topics. In this context, the Security Council could (have) play(ed) the role of fact-finder or even as a prosecutor, though without these two terms being read in their narrow legal meaning. As for the fact-finding function, the Court relied from time to time on evidence collected, assembled and digested by the Security Council, yet it did so with a lot of precaution. In contrast, for the prosecuting task – nowhere envisaged by the Charter[128] – one could imagine it with a role, notably in certain situations where the use of force is involved and its legal regime is at stake, i.e. rules belonging to *ius cogens*. Well, this could lead the sceptical reader to think that we are talking about 'International Crimes of States', but ... *Honni soit qui mal y pense!*

---

128 As any well-informed international lawyer knows, the Charter has been thoroughly interpreted and modified by subsequent practice, teleological interpretation and the 'implied powers' doctrine (and a mixture of the three); therefore, the absence of specific powers, tasks and functions cannot be considered *per se* a bar to such an argumentation.

Part III
Procedural and evidential issues before the World Court

6 The basis of the Court's jurisdiction and the scope and usefulness of *forum prorogatum*

Henry Burmester

6.1 Introduction

Determining whether the necessary jurisdiction exists has proved to be a contentious issue in a large proportion of the cases brought before the International Court of Justice. The *Corfu Channel* case, the first case before that Court, was no exception. It raised some interesting jurisdictional issues and continues to be a relevant and important source of authority today in this area. This chapter first considers the jurisdictional issues that arose, including the relevance of *forum prorogatum* as a source of jurisdiction. It then considers *forum prorogatum* more generally. Judge Lauterpacht has described the case as 'the principal illustration' of jurisdiction resulting from that process.[1]

An international law student learns very early that consent is essential if two States are to have a dispute adjudicated by an international tribunal. In the case of the International Court, the most familiar forms of consent arise under Article 36(2) of the Statute through reciprocal optional clause declarations, or under Article 36(1) where specially provided in the Charter of the United Nations or through dispute settlement provisions in relevant treaties. Consent can, however, also arise under Article 36(1) on a one-off basis through a Special Agreement whereby the parties jointly refer a case to the Court. This does not, however, exhaust the possible forms of consent.

Despite the silence of the Statute, it is now firmly accepted that consent can also arise by conduct evincing consent. *Forum prorogatum* is the name given to this form of consent. It involves by conduct the acceptance of the court's jurisdiction which cures any lack or imperfection that may otherwise exist in this regard. The *Corfu Channel* case, at the preliminary objection phase,[2] gave this form of consent a wide scope of operation. It is a landmark case in this regard.

---

1 *Application of the Convention on the Prevention and Punishment of the Crime of Genocide (Bosnia and Herzegovina v. Serbia and Montenegro)*, Order of 13 September 1993, Further Requests for the Indication of Provisional Measures, Separate opinion of Judge *ad hoc* Lauterpacht, ICJ Reports 1993, p. 416.
2 *Corfu Channel* case, Judgment on Preliminary Objections: ICJ Reports 1948, p. 15.

The *Corfu Channel* case also provides, however, an illuminating insight into various other jurisdictional twists and turns that can arise in a case before the International Court. While *forum prorogatum* as a basis of jurisdiction, as already mentioned, was relied upon by the Court at the preliminary objection phase, a number of developments occurred with regard to jurisdiction separately from the preliminary objection decision. The jurisdictional base for the merits phase became a Special Agreement, rather than the basis of jurisdiction accepted by the Court in its preliminary objection decision. However, the Special Agreement did not end jurisdictional arguments. There was argument as to whether it was the sole source able to be relied on for the adjudication on the merits, and if so, what was its scope. Whether there was ultimately still some residual reliance on *forum prorogatum* in the case is something which will be explored further below.

6.2 Background to *Corfu Channel* case

The detail of the case has been set out elsewhere. For present purposes it is noted that the *Corfu Channel* case concerned an incident in the Corfu Channel in October 1946, within Albanian territorial waters, when two British destroyers struck mines, causing explosions damaging the vessels and heavy loss of life. The Security Council in a resolution of 9 April 1947 recommended that the United Kingdom and the Albanian Governments should immediately refer the dispute to the International Court in accordance with the provisions of the Statute.[3] Albania was not then a member of the United Nations but it had accepted an invitation to participate in the debate on the dispute on the condition laid down by the Security Council that Albania accept, in this instance, all the obligations which a member of the United Nations would have to assume in a similar case. This includes being a party to the Statute to the Court.

Albania in the debate resisted strenuously the proposal for reference to the Court. Despite this resistance, the resolution was passed. The United Kingdom then in May 1947 unilaterally instituted proceedings in the Court against Albania. Given the Albanian resistance to having the matter referred to the Court, the United Kingdom probably considered the resolution sufficed to establish jurisdiction without the need for any joint action. This was a position with which Albania did not agree. This gave rise to the first preliminary objection phase of the case. That is the primary focus of this chapter.

6.3 The jurisdictional basis

As Professor Waldock remarked, the preliminary objection decision 'may outwardly seem to have been much ado about nothing, since the parties signed

---

3 Resolution set out in *ICJ Reports 1948*, op. cit., p. 17.

a Special Agreement shortly before the Court dismissed Albania's plea to jurisdiction'.[4] In fact, two distinct questions of jurisdiction of considerable importance were involved. The first concerned whether the Security Council resolution conferred jurisdiction. The second was the use of *forum prorogatum*.

The application invoked Article 36(1) of the Statute, on the ground that the matter was one 'specially provided for in the Charter'.[5] It was argued that the Security Council had adopted a 'decision', Albania had accepted the obligations of a Member by its participation in the debate following the conditional invitation, and Article 25 of the Charter provides that members agree to carry out decisions of the Council in accordance with the Charter.

The unilateral application was followed by a communication in July 1947 from Albania to the Court.[6] It first complained that the unilateral institution of proceedings by the United Kingdom did not comply with the Security Council resolution as there first needed, in accordance with the Statute, to be an acceptance by Albania of the Court's jurisdiction under Article 36 of the Statute or some other instrument of international law. Albania denied the existence of any such acceptance or instrument.

Albania also rejected any reliance on Article 25 of the Charter, which had been referred to in the United Kingdom application, as the Security Council had only adopted a recommendation. It was, however, the best provision the United Kingdom could point to at the time of its application. The United Kingdom, at the preliminary objection written phase, reserved its position on this ground and made no substantive argument on it, despite this ground of jurisdiction being that set out in the initiating application. It was fully argued orally by both sides but the majority of the Court decided not to pronounce on it as a basis of jurisdiction. However, in a joint, separate opinion by seven judges (supported on this point by the *ad hoc* judge) any reliance on Article 25 to establish compulsory jurisdiction was rejected.[7] This rejection was clearly correct as Article 25 could not realistically provide any jurisdictional basis in the circumstances.[8]

The second question of jurisdiction, that of *forum prorogatum*, depended on what Albania said in its communication with the Court. Albania stated in its communication to the Court that it would be within its rights in holding that the United Kingdom was not entitled to bring the case before the Court by unilateral application. However, it went on and said that, despite this irregularity, it 'fully accepts the recommendation of the Security Council' and 'it is

---

4 C.H.M. Waldock, 'Forum Prorogatum or Acceptance of a Unilateral Summons to Appear before the International Court', *International Law Quarterly*, 2 (1948): 377.
5 *ICJ Reports 1948*, p. 17.
6 Ibid., pp. 18–19.
7 *ICJ Reports 1948*, p. 31 for the joint opinion, p. 33 for the dissenting opinion.
8 Whether a binding decision taken under Chapter VII of the Charter can effectively confer jurisdiction remains an open question, which is not considered further here.

prepared ... to appear before the Court'. It further said that 'it makes the most explicit reservations respecting the manner in which the United Kingdom has brought the case before the Court' and that 'The Albanian Government wishes to emphasize that its acceptance of the Court's jurisdiction for this case cannot constitute a precedent for the future.' On its face, this appears on a reasonable reading to suggest that Albania did not intend to contest the jurisdiction of the Court in this instance, despite its unhappiness about the unilateral British application.

Following this communication, the President of the Court made an order, reciting the terms of the communication and setting time limits for a Memorial and Counter Memorial.[9] The President appears to have concluded that the terms of the Albanian communication meant jurisdiction was not in dispute. Despite this, following the filing of the United Kingdom memorial, Albania filed a preliminary objection on the ground of inadmissibility.

Albania's principal argument was that in the circumstances a Special Agreement was required to confer jurisdiction and a unilateral application was not permissible. It rejected, as already noted, reliance by the United Kingdom on this being a matter 'specially provided for in the Charter', for purposes of Article 36(1). It did this on the basis that the resolution was not a 'decision' of the Security Council which obliged both parties to appear before the Court without regard to the Statute of the Court. It reiterated its earlier argument that Article 25 of the Charter provided no basis for jurisdiction and that there was no other agreement or basis allowing the unilateral submission of the British application. It followed, it said, that the Court could not consider the application.[10]

Albania sought to distinguish acceptance of jurisdiction in order to dispute jurisdiction and the admissibility of the particular application given the manner in which it was made. This was not, however, a distinction that it had clearly made in its prior communication to the Court in which it appeared generally to accept jurisdiction in relation to this case. In that communication any objection based on the form in which the proceedings had been commenced appeared intertwined with the question of jurisdiction. Thus, when Albania said it would not contest jurisdiction it also appeared to say it would not contest the way in which proceedings had been instituted.

The United Kingdom responded that the Albanian communication to the Court of July 1947, together with the United Kingdom application, constituted a 'reference' to the Court within the terms of the Security Council resolution, and a further Special Agreement was not necessary. In any event, it argued, these same actions amounted to a Special Agreement or, even if there were a formal irregularity in the mode of commencement, 'this irregularity has been cured, because the Albanian Government by its letter of 2 July 1947

---

9 *ICJ Reports 1948*, p. 19.
10 Ibid., pp. 20–23.

has waived any possible objections and has consented to the jurisdiction of the court'.[11] In other words, by Albania's conduct it was argued that the jurisdiction of the Court had been perfected.

6.4 The Court's holding

The Court rejected the Albanian preliminary objection by 15 to 1. Did it do so on the basis that jurisdiction existed as a matter of *forum prorogatum*? It appears that it did.

The Court found that the letter of July 1947 from Albania to the Court 'constitutes a voluntary acceptance of its jurisdiction'.[12] The language in the letter that 'it is prepared, notwithstanding this irregularity in the action taken by the Government of the United Kingdom, to appear before the Court' could not be understood 'otherwise than as a waiver of the right subsequently to raise an objection directed against the admissibility of the application founded on the alleged procedural irregularity of the application'.[13] The Court said that the letter of July 1947 'is no less decisive' as regards the question of the Court's jurisdiction. It constituted 'a voluntary and indisputable acceptance of the Court's jurisdiction'.[14]

6.5 Subsequent developments

This was not, however, the end of the matter as far as jurisdiction was concerned. On the same day that the Court handed down its decision on the preliminary objection, the United Kingdom and Albania concluded a Special Agreement.[15]

This agreement recited that it had been drawn up as a result of the resolution of the Security Council for the purpose of submitting to the Court for decision two questions there set out. One asked about the responsibility of Albania and whether there was any duty to pay compensation. The second asked whether the United Kingdom had violated the sovereignty of Albania and whether there was any duty to give satisfaction.

The Court by order of 26 March 1948 (the day after the preliminary objection decision), after reciting the Special Agreement, placed on record that the Special Agreement 'now formed the basis of the further proceedings, and states the questions submitted to it for decision'.[16] Did this mean there was no

---

11 *ICJ Reports 1948*, pp. 23–25.
12 Ibid., p. 26.
13 Ibid., p. 27.
14 Ibid., p 26.
15 *ICJ Reports 1948*, p. 53.
16 Ibid., p. 26.

need for any further reliance on *forum prorogatum*? It would seem, at first glance, that this was so.

However, during the course of the proceedings on the merits, an issue arose as to the scope of the Special Agreement, and in particular the capacity of the Court to determine the amount of compensation to be paid to the United Kingdom if it found in its favour. This was, however, only raised by Albania in its last oral statement. The United Kingdom did not reply and no argument between the parties on the issue took place. The Court in its judgment on the merits ruled 10 to 6 that it had jurisdiction to determine the question of compensation.[17]

What was the basis for this? The Special Agreement was certainly not entirely clear on the question of compensation, referring only to whether there was a 'duty' to pay compensation. The majority concluded, however, that

> Neither government suggested in any way that the Special Agreement had limited the competence of the Court to a decision merely upon the principle of compensation or that the United Kingdom had abandoned an important part of its original claim.[18]

The original British application and Memorial had contained a claim for compensation and there was no evidence the Special Agreement had been intended to alter this. This was also evident in the subsequent submissions. In particular, Albania had in its rejoinder declared that it was unnecessary, given its position on the United Kingdom claim, to address reparation and it reserved the right, if necessary, to discuss this issue, which should involve expert opinion.

The Court said that, having regard to the previous attitude of the Albanian Government, 'this must be considered an implied acceptance of the Court's jurisdiction' to decide the compensation issue.[19] The Court considered the use of the term 'duty to compensate' rather than any express reference to amount could be explained by reference to the similarity of the wording of the second question in the Special Agreement, and in particular the use of 'duty to give satisfaction'.[20]

This part of the judgment suggests that, as a matter of interpretation, the Special Agreement was construed as encompassing the determination of compensation. However, the Court also referred to the previous attitude of Albania and, in particular, the statement in the Rejoinder reserving the right to discuss the issue of reparation which it said constituted 'an implied acceptance of the court's jurisdiction to decide this question'.[21]

---

17 *ICJ Reports 1949*, pp. 23–26. Those in dissent on this point were President Basdevant and the five judges delivering dissenting opinions.
18 Ibid., p. 24.
19 Ibid., p. 25.
20 Ibid., pp. 25–26.
21 Ibid., p. 25.

This suggests that, in relation to compensation, reliance was not being placed solely on the Special Agreement to establish jurisdiction in this regard but that, once again, if necessary, reliance was also being placed on jurisdiction arising on the basis of *forum prorogatum*. This time the conduct evincing consent was Albania's conduct during the Court proceedings, not any formal communication. Despite the Court's earlier statement in its order of 26 March 1948 that the Special Agreement was now the basis of jurisdiction, and hence implicitly replaced any earlier need to rely on jurisdiction based on *forum prorogatum* arising from Albania's communication, it appears that on this issue of compensation the Court was not precluding the possibility of jurisdiction based on *forum prorogatum* arising from the way in which Albania had conducted itself during the proceedings.

In contrast, the judges in dissent took the view that the Special Agreement had replaced the earlier jurisdictional basis and that as a matter of construction, it provided no basis to assess compensation.[22] They do not appear to address the possible new basis of jurisdiction based on *forum prorogatum* arising from Albania's conduct during the proceedings.

6.6 The scope of *forum prorogatum*

Having outlined the jurisdictional issues that arose in the case, it is appropriate to consider more generally the use of *forum prorogatum* in International Court jurisprudence.[23] In this regard, the *Corfu Channel* case remains significant.

As Rosenne and other commentators have recognised, neither the Charter nor Statute expressly envisage any operation of *forum prorogatum* as a basis of jurisdiction. However, it has developed as an established basis of jurisdiction through the practice of the Permanent Court as developed by the International Court.[24]

Thus, in *Certain Questions of Mutual Assistance in Criminal Matters (Dijbouti v. France)*,[25] citing the *Corfu Channel* case, the court said:

> The jurisdiction of the Court is based on the consent of States, under the conditions expressed therein. However, neither the Statute of the Court nor its rules require that the consent of the parties which thus confers

---

22 Ibid. See particularly Judge Winiarski at p. 57. Judges Badawi Pasha, at p. 67; Krylov at p. 73; Ečer at p. 128.
23 For an overview of developments, see S. Rosenne, *The Law and Practice of the International Court 1920–1996* (1997), v.2, at 695–725; D. W. Greig, *International Law* (2nd edn) (London: Butterworths, 1976), pp. 641–644; S. Yee, 'Forum Prorogatum in the International Court', *German Yearbook of International Law*, 42 (1999): 147.
24 For discussion of debates within the Permanent Court in 1936, see Waldock, op. cit., pp. 358–386.
25 *ICJ Reports 2008*, paras 60–64.

jurisdiction on the Court be expressed in any particular form . . . The Statute of the Court does explicitly mention the different ways in which States may express their consent to the Court's jurisdiction . . . The Court has also interpreted Article 36(1) of the Statute as enabling consent to be deduced from certain acts, thus accepting the possibility of *forum prorogatum*. This modality is applied when a respondent State has, through its conduct before the Court or in relation to the applicant party, acted in such a way as to have consented to the jurisdiction of the Court.

Having accepted the possibility of this form of consent, the issue remains how and when this consent can be manifested.

In the Permanent Court, the doctrine was used to extend the jurisdiction of the Court that already existed between relevant parties, to cover additional matters. This could arise as a result of additional claims made in one party's pleadings that were not contested on jurisdictional grounds by the other party or where jurisdiction was cured by subsequent consent (by ratification of a Treaty) without specific reference to the proceedings before the Court.[26]

However, what the *Corfu Channel* case made clear is that this form of consent is not so confined. As Rosenne says, the 'innovation' lies in the extent to which the principle can be and has been used to found a unilateral application in the nature of a summons to appear before the court.[27] Thus, in the *Corfu Channel* case, while the United Kingdom purported to invoke a jurisdictional basis derived from the Charter, its application was effectively made unilaterally. It was only the Albanian letter in response that provided the necessary consent. That consent did not just extend the dispute but was the essential foundation for the case to proceed at all. Or at least it would have been, absent the Special Agreement concluded at the same time as the Court found it otherwise had jurisdiction as a result of the Albanian letter.

The significant expansion in the potential of *forum prorogatum* to provide a basis of jurisdiction accepted in the *Corfu Channel* case has been matched by a repeated emphasis on the need for the consent to be 'certain' and for 'an unequivocal indication' of the desire of the State concerned to accept the Court's jurisdiction in a 'voluntary and indisputable manner'.[28]

These latter words reflect those used in the *Corfu Channel* case.[29] The Court has, in cases like the *Djibouti* case, emphasised that 'the element of consent must be either explicit or clearly to be deduced, from the relevant conduct of a State'.[30]

---

26 *Mavrommatis*, PCIJ Ser A. No. 2 (1924), Waldock, op. cit., pp. 383–384.
27 Rosenne, op. cit., p. 695.
28 *Djibouti v. France, ICJ Reports 2008*, para. 62.
29 *ICJ Reports 1948*, p. 27.
30 *ICJ Reports 2008*, para. 62.

What is clear from the *Corfu Channel* case is that there is no particular form in which the consent has to be expressed, provided it is unequivocal. Obviously, consent has to be given by someone with appropriate authority, such as a Foreign Minister, if it is to be effective to confer an otherwise wholly non-existent jurisdiction. Consent can, however, also arise from conduct, such as non-objection to an additional claim made in a plaintiff State's memorial. This consent can be explicit or implicit. Thus, pleading on the merits establishes a tacit acceptance of jurisdiction.[31] Once consent is given, it cannot be withdrawn.[32]

Since the 1936 revision of its Rules by the Permanent Court, an initiating party is required in its application to specify 'as far as possible' the legal grounds on which the jurisdiction of the Court is said to be based. This allows for the possibility of jurisdiction being based on *forum prorogatum*. However, since 1978 the Rules also provide in Article 38(5) that, where an applicant State proposes to found the jurisdiction of the Court upon a consent yet to be given, the application is transmitted to the other State but is not entered in the general list nor any action taken in the proceedings unless and until the State concerned consents to the jurisdiction for the purposes of the case. This avoids the need for the Court to take action to remove a case where the jurisdiction not existing at the time of application is not perfected. There were a number of such cases, particularly in the years soon after the *Corfu Channel* case.[33] Consent was not forthcoming in these cases, not surprisingly, given the highly sensitive issues that were sought to be agitated, particularly in the Cold War era.

The *Djibouti v. France* case was the first occasion when the Court was required to decide on the merits of a dispute based on Article 38(5). In that case, France consented to the Court's jurisdiction by letter from the French Minister for Foreign Affairs. Earlier, in 2003, France had consented to jurisdiction in a case brought by the Congo, and an application on provisional measures was heard.[34] However, that case has been removed from the Court's List at the request of the Republic of the Congo in November 2010. Those are, however, the only cases since 1978 where Article 38(5) of the Rules has been applied.

However, as the *Djibouti* case showed, determining the scope of acceptance pursuant to *forum prorogatum* is not without its own problems. France in its letter accepted jurisdiction 'in respect of the dispute forming the subject of the application and strictly within the limits of the claims formulated therein'. Djibouti in its pleadings put in issue certain summonses and arrest warrants not addressed in the application and which were issued after it was filed. The

---

31 *Haya de la Torre* case, *ICJ Reports 1951*, p. 78.
32 *Rights of Minorities in Upper Silesia (Minorities Schools)* PCIJ, Ser A No.15, p. 25.
33 See *Aerial Incident* cases, *Antarctic* cases referred to with full citation in *Djibouti v. France*, *ICJ Reports 2008*, para. 63.
34 *Certain Criminal Proceedings in France (Congo v. France)*, *ICJ Reports 2003*, p. 102.

Court did not approach the question of jurisdiction over these matters by considering the nature of the dispute. Rather, it construed strictly the terms of France's consent and held that the later developments were outside its jurisdiction.[35] It is noticeable that these cases relate principally to matters of international judicial co-operation in relation to criminal matters. The cases are not directed at highly sensitive issues going to fundamental issues affecting relations between the States concerned. This may have made it easier for France to give its consent.

Difficult issues can also arise when a State contesting jurisdiction at the same time also makes a counter-claim or seeks relief of its own. In the *Anglo-Iranian Oil Co (Preliminary Objections)* case, the Court rejected a United Kingdom argument that Iran had consented to jurisdiction by submitting certain issues for decision. The Court said that by filing a Preliminary Objection disputing jurisdiction, and consistently maintaining that objection, it was not possible to infer consent by submission of other Objections designed as measures of defence.[36] A similar issue arose in the *Application of the Convention on the Prevention and Punishment of the Crime of Genocide* case.[37] Judge *ad hoc* Lauterpacht considered that Yugoslavia had, by its own provisional measures request, expanded the jurisdiction of the Court beyond that founded on the Genocide Convention.[38] The Court majority did not agree, considering it could not infer the necessary unequivocal acceptance of the Court's jurisdiction for this purpose.[39]

6.7 The usefulness of *forum prorogatum*

It is not the purpose of this chapter to review all the cases since *Corfu Channel* dealing with *forum prorogatum*. Rather, the aim has been to indicate the way in which *forum prorogatum*, recognised by the International Court in its first case, has become an accepted part of international law jurisprudence. This it clearly has and the principles for its application are widely accepted.

Yet the principle is not without difficulty. Rosenne's conclusion is as follows:

> By a process of autonomous judicial interpretation untrammelled by excessive consideration for the travaux preparatoires of the Statute or for matters of pure form, the Court has created an imposing doctrine which seems to be at some variance with the political attitude of certain States towards what ought to be the basis of the Court's jurisdiction.[40]

---

35 *ICJ Reports 2008*, paras 87–88.
36 *ICJ Reports 1952*, pp. 101, 114.
37 Provisional Measures Order of 13 September 1993, *ICJ Reports 1993*, p. 325.
38 *ICJ Reports 1993*, pp. 416–421 (paras 24–37).
39 *ICJ Reports 1993*, pp. 341–342 (para. 34).
40 Rosenne, op. cit., p. 724.

At the same time, reliance on *forum prorogatum* has been described as 'by far the most flexible' form of consent.[41] Yet this is far from clear. In my view, despite its potential flexibility, it should be regarded as the least satisfactory way in which to establish consent. Unilateral applications rarely succeed in prompting an unequivocal acceptance of consent. This is certainly likely to be the case in relation to matters of national security or importance. Even if it is a useful way in which to try and secure jurisdiction over less critical issues, as *Djibouti v. France* shows, the terms of consent may make it difficult to fully resolve the underlying dispute.

Certainly in the *Corfu Channel* case itself, the parties recognised that the matter was best dealt with on the basis of a Special Agreement that identified the particular issues for resolution. The dispute over the meaning of that Agreement highlights the need for careful drafting of any Special Agreement. It does not mean *forum prorogatum* is a preferable basis for jurisdiction. The same care in drafting is necessary in any unequivocal acceptance of jurisdiction for purposes of reliance on *forum prorogatum*.

What the cases show is that a State should be careful in the way it acts in order to avoid consent being implied. While the Court requires unequivocal indication of consent, often the question of what precisely has been consented to remains contentious. This is not a matter that only arises where consent is by *forum prorogatum*, but it shows there is little advantage, and often just as many problems, with consent that arises this way. The *Corfu Channel* case still contains many lessons relevant today in this regard.

---

41 V. Pouliot, '*Forum Prorogatum* before the International Court of Justice: the *Djibouti v. France* Case, 3 *Hague Justice Journal* (2008): 32, citing M. Bedjaoui *et al.*, 'Le Forum Prorogatum devant la Cour internationale de Justice', *African Yearbook of International Law*, 5 (1997): 91–114.

7 The International Court of Justice and standards of proof

*Katherine Del Mar**

7.1 Introduction

The very existence of the notion of a standard of proof, or a degree of satisfaction with proof, implies that a court can never be 'absolutely certain' (meaning the probability of 1) of establishing on the basis of the facts before it, what occurred. This point was made by Sir Frank Soskice (United Kingdom) during the oral pleadings in the Court's first contentious case, and the catalyst of this edited collection, the *Corfu Channel* case. Sir Frank observed that 'in the nature of things, absolute certainty can never be attained in human affairs. Human beings must order their lives upon the basis of convincing probability.'[1]

A standard of proof or a degree of satisfaction of proof marks a point somewhere along the line between two extremes: a mere conjecture at one end, and absolute certainty at the other.[2] Proof furnished in support of a particular proposition must meet or surpass this point for a judicial finding in favour of the proposition to be made. In practice, this may either constitute a very explicit exercise of applying an objective standard of proof, as occurs in some domestic legal traditions, or it may be simply that the judge is persuaded to make a finding in favour of a particular proposition, based on a number of unarticulated factors concerning the evidence that has been furnished.[3]

---

* This contribution benefited from comments received from participants and the organizers of the workshop held at the Australian National University on 29 October 2009, entitled 'The Continued Relevance of the *Corfu Channel case* 60 Years On'. I would also like to express my gratitude to Professor Marcelo G. Kohen for his invaluable comments on earlier drafts. The usual caveats apply.
1 Sir Frank Soskice (United Kingdom), *Corfu Channel case*, Public sittings of 17 January 1949, *Pleadings, Oral Arguments, Documents*, vol. IV, p. 479.
2 There is of course enormous debate about what is meant by 'absolute certainty'. This is not the place to enter into that discussion.
3 These two different approaches to applying a standard of proof have been labelled by one scholar as the 'external' and the 'internal' approaches: Ho Hock Lai, *A Philosophy of Evidence Law: Justice in the Search for Truth* (New York: Oxford University Press, 2008), pp. 173–229.

Throughout its case law, the Court has consistently applied standards of proof, or it has required that it be satisfied with proof to a given degree. The difficulty, however, is trying to make sense of this judicial practice. A reading of the Court's case law quickly confirms that the Court does not apply one standard of proof across the board, but rather varying standards. Indeed, beginning with the *Corfu Channel* case, the Court has on a number of occasions articulated different standards of proof, sometimes within the same case. In the *Corfu Channel* case the Court employs no less than three expressions to refer to a particular standard of proof: 'a degree of certainty',[4] '*no room* for reasonable doubt',[5] and proof that does not 'fall ... short of conclusive evidence'.[6] In subsequent cases, the Court has used *inter alia* the following formulations: 'on the basis of a balance of evidence',[7] 'on a balance of probabilities',[8] 'in all probability',[9] 'consistent with the probabilities',[10] proof 'to the Court's satisfaction',[11] 'with a high degree of probability',[12] 'beyond any reasonable doubt',[13] 'beyond possibility of reasonable doubt',[14] 'no reasonable

---

4 *Corfu Channel case (United Kingdom of Great Britain and Northern Ireland v. Albania)*, Merits, Judgment, ICJ Reports 1949, p. 17.
5 Ibid., p. 18. Original emphasis.
6 Ibid., p. 17.
7 *Oil Platforms (Islamic Republic of Iran v. United States of America)*, Judgment, ICJ Reports 2001, p. 189, para. 57.
8 *Case Concerning the Land, Island and Maritime Frontier Dispute (El Salvador/Honduras: Nicaragua Intervening)*, ICJ Reports 1992, p. 506, para. 248.
9 *Case Concerning Sovereignty over Pulau Ligitan and Pulau Sipadan (Indonesia/Malaysia)*, Judgment, ICJ Reports 2002, p. 662, para. 72; *Case Concerning the Land, Island and Maritime Frontier Dispute*, op. cit., p. 434, para. 121.
10 *Case Concerning Military and Paramilitary Activities in and against Nicaragua*, ICJ Reports 1986, p. 85, para. 158.
11 *Case Concerning Armed Activities on the Territory of the Congo (Democratic Republic of the Congo v. Uganda)*, Judgment, ICJ Reports 2005, pp. 201, 205, 213 paras 62, 71, 106; *Case Concerning Military and Paramilitary Activities in and Against Nicaragua (Nicaragua v. United States of America)*, Request for the Indication of Provisional Measures, Order of 10 May 1984, ICJ Reports 1984, p. 179, para. 25.
12 *Case Concerning the Land, Island and Maritime Frontier Dispute*, op. cit., p. 456, para. 155.
13 *Oil Platforms*, op. cit., Separate Opinion of Judge Kooijmans, p. 263, para. 56; *Case Concerning the Land and Maritime Boundary between Cameroon and Nigeria (Cameroon v. Nigeria: Equatorial Guinea Intervening)*, Judgment, ICJ Reports 2002, Dissenting Opinion of Judge Ajibola, p. 599, para. 194; *Case Concerning Maritime Delimitation and Territorial Questions between Qatar and Bahrain*, Merits, Judgment, ICJ Reports 2001, Separate Opinion of Judge Kooijmans, pp. 313, 325, 353, 372, 374, 389, paras 157, 195, 268, 324, 327, 369; *Case Concerning the Land, Island and Maritime Frontier Dispute*, op. cit., Separate Opinion of Judge Torres Bernárdez, pp. 683, 725, paras 110, 198; *South West Africa (Ethiopia v. South Africa; Liberia v. South Africa)*, ICJ Reports 1962, Joint Dissenting Opinion of Judges Sir Spender and Sir Fitzmaurice, pp. 473, 474; *Certain Norwegian Loans*, ICJ Reports 1957, Separate Opinion of Judge Sir Lauterpacht, p. 58.
14 *South West Africa*, op. cit., Joint Dissenting Opinion of Judges Sir Spender and Sir Fitzmaurice, p. 511.

doubt',[15] 'little reasonable doubt',[16] 'sufficient certainty',[17] 'with any degree of certainty',[18] 'with certainty',[19] 'with the necessary degree of precision and certainty',[20] 'conclusive' evidence,[21] and 'evidence that is fully conclusive'.[22]

There is a limit as to how much one can make sense of the standards of proof used in the case law of the Court on a purely inductive basis. No further guidance on the applicable standards of proof before the Court is provided in the Statute of the Court, the Rules of Court, or the Court's Practice Directions, to assist the Court in its treatment of evidence, and the parties in their presentation of the evidence. This contribution attempts to provide some rough guidance on the factors that may contribute to either raising or lowering the standard of proof, by endeavouring to identify some of the theoretical underpinnings for the use of standards of proof by the Court.

The theoretical grounds on which matters of procedure and evidence are premised in the work of the Court are very different to the theoretical foundation of evidence law in domestic legal systems; different theoretical considerations are at play in inter-state disputes within the institutional context of the principal judicial organ of the United Nations than are at play in domestic judicial contexts. It is consequently problematic to draw analogies between the standards of proof applied by the Court, and the standard(s) of proof applicable in domestic jurisdictions. For example, it is not the case that because the Court does not adjudicate 'criminal' matters, in the sense of individual criminal responsibility, that the standard of proof the Court applies is analogous to the 'civil' standard applied in some domestic legal systems, any more than it is the case that 'serious claims' alleged before the Court require an application of a 'criminal' standard of proof.[23] That said, it is to be expected that members of the Court may find it useful to draw on their domestic legal experience in their work at the Court, and consequently it is not uncommon for the Court, or individual judges, to use formulations for standards of proof similar to those found in some domestic jurisdictions, or variations thereof.

---

15 *Case Concerning the Temple of Preah Vihear (Cambodia v. Thailand), Judgment, ICJ Reports 1962*, pp. 21, 58; *Case Concerning the Aerial Incident of July 27, 1955 (Israel v. Bulgaria), ICJ Reports 1959*, Joint Dissenting Opinion of Judges Sir Lauterpacht, Wellington Koo and Sir Spender, p. 162.
16 *Case Concerning the Temple of Preah Vihear*, op. cit., p. 55.
17 *Oil Platforms*, op. cit., Separate Opinion of Judge Kooijmans, p. 265, para. 63.
18 *Case Concerning Sovereignty over Pulau Ligitan and Pulau Sipadan*, op. cit. p. 677, para. 120.
19 Ibid., p. 678, para. 124.
20 *Case Concerning Kasikili/Sedudu Island (Botswana/Namibia), Judgment, ICJ Reports 1999*, p. 1106, para. 99.
21 *Oil Platforms*, op. cit., p. 195, para. 71; *Case Concerning Maritime Delimitation and Territorial Questions between Qatar and Bahrain*, op. cit., Separate Opinion of Judge Oda, p. 244, para. 76.
22 *Application of the Convention on the Prevention and Punishment of the Crime of Genocide (Bosnia and Herzegovina v. Serbia and Montenegro), Merits, Judgment of 26 February 2007*, p. 76, para. 209.
23 See the arguments made by the Parties on the standard of proof applicable in *Application of the Convention on the Prevention and Punishment of the Crime of Genocide*, op. cit., summarized in the Judgment of the Court at p. 76, para. 208.

This contribution argues that standards of proof vary depending on the type of matter before the Court, and the phase of the case.[24] Standards of proof are thus intimately linked to the function of the Court. Section 7.2 discusses how the standards of proof applied by the Court vary depending on whether the Court is exercising a 'declarative' or a 'determinative' function in a case. Where the Court is 'declaring' which state has sovereignty over territory, or where it is defining a territorial or maritime boundary, the Court applies a relatively lower standard of proof, compared to the relatively higher standard of proof the Court applies when 'determining' State responsibility. Section 7.3 examines the rule according to which the graver the claim alleged before the Court, the higher the applicable standard of proof. It will be argued that the standard of proof may be relatively higher in a case depending on the manner an international legal obligation is alleged to have been breached, and the importance of the norm allegedly breached. Section 7.4 focuses on a particular stage in proceedings before the Court: the indication of provisional measures. It is submitted that in general, a lower standard of proof applies in incidental proceedings before the Court, compared with the merits phase of a case. It is further argued that the Court applies varying standards of proof in the indication of provisional measures, depending on the nature of the risk of 'irreparable prejudice' claimed.

7.2 Varying standards of proof depending on the function of the Court: declarative and determinative functions

It is submitted that the function of the Court differs depending on the particular matter before it, and that standards of proof must be understood by reference to the particular function being exercised by the Court. Roughly speaking, there are two principal functions exercised by the Court. The first function is *declarative*. This is a function exercised by the Court when it has been requested to define a territorial or maritime boundary, or to declare which State has sovereignty over territory. Delimitation of a boundary, or declaring sovereignty over territory is a 'declaratory' exercise as the Court is effectively recognizing a boundary or sovereignty over territory, rather than performing a constitutive act.[25] As the Court stated in the *North Sea Continental Shelf* case, with respect to the delimitation of the continental shelf:

> Delimitation is a process which involves establishing the boundaries of an area already, in principle, appertaining to the coastal State and not the determination *de novo* of such an area ... the process of delimitation is

---

24 This was a point made by R. Kolb, 'General Principles of Procedural Law', in A. Zimmermann, C. Tomuschat and K. Oellers-Frahm (eds), *The Statute of the International Court of Justice: A Commentary* (Oxford: Oxford University Press, 2006), pp. 829–830.
25 *Contra*: P. Weil, *The Law of Maritime Delimitation – Reflections*, trans. M. MacGlashen (Cambridge: Grotius Publications Limited, 1989), pp. 21–45.

essentially one of drawing a boundary line between areas which already appertain to one or other of the States affected.[26]

In some cases when exercising its declarative function, the Court may choose between two competing claims, selecting the most evidentially plausible by applying a relatively low standard of proof. For example, the location of the provincial boundary, and consequently the *uti possidetis* line, in *El Salvador/ Honduras* was identified by the Chamber of the Court as corresponding to the river Las Cañas 'on the balance of probabilities, there being no great abundance of evidence either way'.[27] Similarly, in his Declaration to the Judgment in the *Sovereignty over Certain Frontier Land* case, Judge Spiropoulos disagreed with the majority and concluded:

> Faced as I am with a choice between two hypotheses which may lead to opposite results with regard to the question to whom sovereignty over the plot belongs, I consider that preference ought to be given to the hypothesis which seems to me to be the less speculative, and that, in my view, is the hypothesis of the Netherlands.[28]

In the *Case concerning Sovereignty over Pulau Ligitan and Pulau Sipadan*, the Court had to effectively choose which State had sovereignty over the islands in accordance with the terms of the Special Agreement concluded between Indonesia and Malaysia. Judge Oda, who voted in favour of the judgment, explained in his Declaration that he applied a relatively low standard of proof in coming to the conclusion that the islands belonged to Malaysia:

> I voted in favour of the Judgment, in which the Court finds that 'sovereignty over Pulau Ligitan and Pulau Sipadan belongs to Malaysia' (para. 150). The present case is a rather 'weak' one in that neither Party has made a strong showing in support of its claim to title to the islands on any basis. While Malaysia has made a more persuasive case on the basis of '*effectivités*', its arguments are still not very strong in absolute terms. The Court, however, has been requested to choose between the two Parties in adjudicating 'whether sovereignty over [the two islands] belongs to . . . Indonesia or to Malaysia' (Special Agreement of 31 May 1997, Art. 2) and, given that choice, the Court has come to a reasonable decision.[29]

---

26 *North Sea Continental Shelf (Federal Republic of Germany/Denmark; Federal Republic of Germany/Netherlands), Judgment, ICJ Reports 1969*, p. 22, paras 18 and 20; *Land and Maritime Boundary between Cameroon and Nigeria*, op. cit., p. 359, para. 84.
27 *Case Concerning the Land, Island and Maritime Frontier Dispute*, op. cit., p. 506, para. 248.
28 *Case Concerning Sovereignty over Certain Frontier Land (Belgium/Netherlands), Judgment of 20 June 1959, ICJ Reports 1959*, p. 232.
29 *Case Concerning Sovereignty over Pulau Ligitan and Pulau Sipadan*, op. cit., Declaration of Judge Oda, p. 687.

In other cases where the Court has exercised its declarative function, the Court has not found in favour of either of the competing claims put forward by one or other party, or not entirely with either of them, but has rather staked out a middle road between them. With respect to the delimitation of a maritime boundary in the *Case Concerning Maritime Delimitation in the Black Sea*,[30] the Court defined the boundary as falling in part between the two lines claimed by Romania and Ukraine, respectively. In relation to competing claims of sovereignty over three maritime features in *Case Concerning Sovereignty over Pedra Branca/Pulau Batu Puteh, Middle Rocks and South Ledge*, the Court declared that the maritime feature of Pedra Branca/Pulau Batu Puteh belonged to Singapore, whereas Middle Rocks belonged to Malaysia.[31]

It is important to stress that when requested to exercise its declarative role, the Court has never failed to fulfil this task, either by finding in favour of a claim made by one or other Party, or by finding a compromise between the two competing claims. The Court has always found sufficient evidence either in support of a claim of title over territory, or in a claim of *effectivités*, when it has been requested to exercise its declarative role.[32] Given that the Court will

---

30 *Case Concerning Maritime Delimitation in the Black Sea (Romania v. Ukraine)*, Judgment of 3 February 2009.
31 In *Case Concerning Sovereignty over Pedra Branca/Pulau Puteh, Middle Rocks and South Ledge (Malaysia/Singapore), Judgment, ICJ Reports 2008*, the Court found that it could not determine which State had sovereignty over South Ledge unless it determined in which State's territorial waters this maritime feature was located, a task the Court was not requested to undertake.
32 *Fisheries case (United Kingdom v. Norway), Judgment, ICJ Reports 1951; The Minquiers and Ecrehos Case (France/United Kingdom), Judgment, ICJ Reports 1953*; in *North Sea Continental Shelf Cases*, op. cit., the Court was requested only to determine the applicable principles and rules of international law pertaining to the delimitation of the continental shelf in the North Sea, and not to define the boundaries; in *Continental Shelf (Tunisia/Libyan Arab Jamahiriya), Judgment, ICJ Reports 1982*, the Court was requested to lay down the applicable principles and rules of international law and the method for their application to the delimitation; *Delimitation of the Maritime Boundary in the Gulf of Maine Area, Judgment, ICJ Reports 1984*; in *Continental Shelf (Libyan Arab Jamahiriya/Malta), Judgment, ICJ Reports 1985*, the Court was requested to specify the principles and rules of international law which should enable the Parties to effect a delimitation of areas of the continental shelf; *Frontier Dispute (Burkina Faso/Republic of Mali), Judgment, ICJ Reports 1986; Case Concerning the Land, Island and Maritime Frontier Dispute*, op. cit.; *Maritime Delimitation in the Area between Greenland and Jan Mayen (Denmark v. Norway), Judgment, ICJ Reports 1993; Territorial Dispute (Libyan Arab Jamahiriya/Chad), Judgment, ICJ Reports 1994; Case Concerning Kasikili/Sedudu Island*, op. cit.; *Maritime Delimitation and Territorial Questions between Qatar and Bahrain*, op. cit.; *Land and Maritime Boundary between Cameroon and Nigeria*, op. cit.; *Sovereignty over Pulau Ligitan and Pulau Sipadan*, op. cit.; *Frontier Dispute (Benin/Niger), Judgment, ICJ Reports 2005*; in *Case Concerning Territorial and Maritime Dispute between Nicaragua and Honduras in the Caribbean Sea, Judgment, ICJ Reports 2007*, the Court left it to the parties to negotiate in good faith a delimitation line connecting the endpoint of the land boundary to the starting point of the maritime boundary. The Court was only requested to define the maritime boundary, and it found that the starting-point for the boundary was three nautical miles out to sea; *Case Concerning Maritime Delimitation in the Black Sea*, op. cit.

always make a positive finding when exercising its declarative function, it appears that the Court applies a relatively lower standard of proof in matters concerning the delimitation of boundaries or sovereignty over territory, than when the Court exercises a different function: its determinative function.

When the Court is exercising the second of its two functions, its *determinative* function, one of its tasks 'is to decide disputes of fact which have to be resolved in determining whether a party to the proceedings has breached its legal obligations'.[33] The Court is not required to make a positive determination in such matters; the Court may make a negative finding, and decide that because of the insufficient or unconvincing nature of the evidence furnished by the parties, it cannot find in favour of a claim of State responsibility. For example, and as highlighted in the Joint Dissenting Opinion of Judges Al-Khasawneh and Simma, the Court concluded in the *Pulp Mills* case that Argentina had not sufficiently demonstrated that Uruguay was in breach of its 'substantive' obligations under the 1975 Statute of the River Uruguay because the (unarticulated) standard of proof had not been met by Argentina:

> In several paragraphs, the Court variously states that it 'sees no need' or 'is not in a position' to arrive at specific conclusions (paragraphs 213, 228), that 'there is no [clear] evidence to support' certain claims (paragraphs 225, 239, 259), that certain facts have 'not . . . been established to the satisfaction of the Court' (paragraph 250), or that the evidence 'does not substantiate the claims' (paragraph 257) that Uruguay is in breach of its obligations under the 1975 Statute.[34]

Given the quantity of evidence submitted by both parties in the *Pulp Mills* case, described by Judge Keith as 'many thousands of items',[35] and the unchallenged quality of the evidence,[36] it appears the Court applied a relatively higher standard of proof in that case, compared with the generally lower standard of proof the Court applies when exercising its declarative function. In other words, the possibility for the Court to make a negative finding in matters involving claims of State responsibility implies that the Court is applying a relatively higher standard of proof when exercising its determinative function, than when it exercises it declarative function.

It is often the case that the Court does not explain its reasoning in a judgment with reference to the applicable standard of proof. This can be frustrating for the parties in cases like *Pulp Mills* where the Court makes a negative finding on the basis of the lack, or the unpersuasive nature, of the evidence,

---

33 *Case Concerning Pulp Mills on the River Uruguay (Argentina v. Uruguay), Judgment of 20 April 2010*, Separate Opinion of Judge Keith, p. 3, para. 8.
34 Ibid., Joint Dissenting Opinion of Judges Al-Khasawneh and Simma, pp. 2–3, para. 5.
35 Ibid., Separate Opinion of Judge Keith, p. 2, para. 7.
36 Ibid.

but the Court does not explain its reasoning, and in particular, the evidence that it would have found sufficient or persuasive. An atypical instance when the Court did make clear the applicable standard of proof that it applied, albeit not before or during the written and oral proceedings, is the *Genocide* case. In this case, the Court went to great lengths to reason its judgment by reference to rules of evidence, and it addressed the applicable standard of proof in a specific section of its judgment.[37]

Conversely, it is more often the case that the Court takes an arguably more subjective or 'internal' approach to the applicable standard of proof.[38] As a former Registrar of the Court has observed, 'The international regime appears to reflect the civil law tradition, in which all that is needed is that the court be persuaded, without reference to a particular standard.'[39] This in turn has led to criticism of the Court's reasoning in cases where the Court exercised its determinative function, even from members of the bench. Indeed, some judges from the common law tradition have found the Court's failure to articulate a clear standard of proof troubling in cases where the Court has not found in favour of a claim of State responsibility because the Court did not consider that the evidence met the applicable (but unarticulated) standard of proof.

Judge Higgins in her Separate Opinion to the *Oil Platforms* case noted that:

> [I]n a case in which so very much turns on evidence, it was to be expected that the Court would clearly have stated the standard of evidence that was necessary for a party to have discharged its burden of proof . . . the principal judicial organ of the United Nations should . . . make clear what standards of proof it requires to establish what sorts of facts. Even if the Court does not wish to enunciate a general standard for non-criminal cases, it should in my view have decided, and been transparent about, the standard of proof required in this particular case.[40]

Similarly, Judge Buergenthal commented in his Separate Opinion to the same case:

> One might ask, moreover, where the test of 'insufficient' evidence comes from . . . and by reference to what standards the Court applies it? What is meant by 'insufficient' evidence? Does the evidence have to be 'convincing', 'preponderant', 'overwhelming' or 'beyond a reasonable doubt' to be

---

37 *Application of the Convention on the Prevention and Punishment of the Crime of Genocide*, op. cit., p. 76, para. 209. See also Ibid., pp. 76–77, paras 209–210.
38 On the 'internal' aspect of standards of proof, see Ho Hock Lai, *A Philosophy of Evidence Law*, op. cit., pp. 185–229.
39 E. Valencia-Ospina, 'Evidence before the International Court of Justice', *International Law Forum*, 1 (1999): 203.
40 *Oil Platforms*, op. cit., Separate Opinion of Judge Higgins, pp. 233–234, paras 30 and 33.

sufficient? The Court never spells out what the relevant standard of proof is.[41]

The relative difference in the standards of proof that the Court applies when exercising its determinative function, in contrast to when it exercises its declarative function, is particularly well illustrated in *Land and Maritime Boundary between Cameroon and Nigeria*, a case that dealt with both a request for a delimitation of a boundary, and claims of State responsibility. Whereas the Court fixed the territorial boundary in the Lake Chad area and the Bakassi Peninsula,[42] and defined the maritime boundary,[43] it did not find either State responsible on the claims and counter-claims presented, considering that 'Cameroon has not established the facts which it bears the burden of proving',[44] and that 'neither of the Parties sufficiently provides the facts which it alleged, or their imputability to the other Party'.[45] Judge Ajibola agreed with the Court's findings that neither Cameroon nor Nigeria incurred State responsibility, and he commented upon the applicable high standard of proof that applied to Cameroon's claim, as follows: 'Cameroon's allegation of the very serious offence of State responsibility must be proved beyond reasonable doubt. This proof is missing.'[46]

7.3 Varying standards of proof depending on the manner by which the norm is allegedly violated, and the content of the norm

It is a well-established rule in the practice of the Court that the more serious the claim alleged by a State against another State, the higher the standard of proof that will apply in establishing that claim. As Judge Higgins noted in her Separate Opinion in the *Oil Platforms* case, there is 'a general agreement that the graver the charge, the more confidence must there be in the evidence relied on'.[47] This was reaffirmed by the Court in the *Genocide* case when it stated that 'The Court has long recognized that claims against a State involving charges of exceptional gravity must be proved by evidence that is fully conclusive.'[48] It is submitted that the 'gravity of the claim' is determined by reference to two elements: (1) the manner by which a norm is allegedly violated; and (2) the importance of the content of the norm allegedly violated.

---

41 Ibid., Separate Opinion of Judge Buergenthal, p. 286, para. 41.
42 *Case Concerning the Land and Maritime Boundary between Cameroon and Nigeria*, pp. 345, 346, 416, paras 57, 60, 61, 225.
43 Ibid., p. 448, para. 307.
44 Ibid., p. 453, para. 322.
45 Ibid., p. 453, para. 324.
46 Ibid., Dissenting Opinion of Judge Ajibola, p. 599, para. 194.
47 *Oil Platforms*, op. cit., Separate Opinion of Judge Higgins, p. 234, para. 33.
48 *Application of the Convention on the Prevention and Punishment of the Crime of Genocide*, op. cit., p. 77, para. 209.

There are a number of reasons why the Court may apply a higher than usual standard of proof for 'serious charges'. The first reason concerns the particular legal consequences that result from a finding of a 'serious breach of a peremptory norm'.[49] The second, and non-legal reason, is the potential political fallout and perception of the State in global public opinion following a finding by the Court of State responsibility for certain very serious violations of international law. With respect to this second reason, it is worth recalling that in the *Genocide* case, the Court quoted in its judgment the following passage from the *Krstić* case before the Appeals Chamber of the International Criminal Tribunal for the Former Yugoslavia, which highlights the particular stigma that attaches to a finding of genocide:

> The Appeals Chamber states unequivocally that the law condemns, in appropriate terms, the deep and lasting injury inflicted, and calls the massacre at Srebrenica by its proper name: genocide. Those responsible will bear this stigma and it will serve as a warning to those who may in future contemplate the commission of such a heinous act.[50]

The 'seriousness of the charge' for evidentiary purposes corresponds roughly to, but does not mirror, the legal test for 'serious breaches of peremptory norms' under Article 41 of the International Law Commission's *Articles on State Responsibility for Internationally Wrongful Acts*, namely (1) a breach of 'an obligation arising under a peremptory norm of general international law'; and (2) where this breach is 'serious' insofar as 'it involves a gross or systematic failure by the responsible state to fulfil the obligation'.[51] Where a case clearly involves a claim of a serious breach of a peremptory norm, the most stringent evidentiary requirements will apply, including a very high standard of proof. For example, in the *Genocide* case, the Court required that 'it be *fully convinced* that allegations made in the proceedings, that the crime of genocide or the other acts enumerated in Article III [of the Genocide Convention] have been committed, have been *clearly established*'.[52]

This section will explore what concretely amounts to a 'serious charge' in the practice of the Court in order for a high standard of proof to apply, and it will consider the factors which may lead to the standard of proof being

---

49 International Law Commission, 'Responsibility of States for Internationally Wrongful Acts', annexed to United Nations General Assembly resolution 56/83 of 12 December 2001, Article 41.
50 *Prosecutor v. Krstić*, IT-98-33-A, Appeals Chamber, Judgment, 19 April 2004, para. 37–38, cited by the International Court of Justice in *Case Concerning the Application of the Convention on the Prevention and Punishment of the Crime of Genocide*, op. cit., p. 106, para. 293.
51 International Law Commission, 'Responsibility of States for Internationally Wrongful Acts', op. cit., Article 41.
52 *Application of the Convention on the Prevention and Punishment of the Crime of Genocide*, op. cit., pp. 76–77, para. 209. Emphasis added.

relatively higher or lower in a given case. Section 7.3.1 will examine the first element of a 'serious charge', namely the manner by which a norm is allegedly violated. It will be argued in this section that claims concerning the commission of acts demand a higher standard of proof than claims concerning omissions. Section 7.3.2 will examine the second element, namely the importance of the norm purportedly violated. It will be argued that even when important norms are violated by omissions, a high standard of proof will apply. It is important to stress that the two elements of a 'serious charge' (the manner by which the violation occurs, and the importance of the norm violated) do not constitute a mathematical formula that must be applied consecutively in every case for a high standard of proof to apply.

7.3.1 Varying standard of proof depending on the manner by which the norm is allegedly violated: acts and omissions

Broadly speaking, the Court treats a claim of a violation of international law stemming from a commission of an act differently than an omission. Whereas the former must generally meet more stringent evidentiary requirements in order for the State to incur responsibility – including a relatively higher standard of proof – the latter can satisfy a lower standard of proof for State responsibility to be incurred. The reason for these varying standards of proof for the commission of acts, and for omissions, is an underlining presumption that, in general, an act of wrongdoing rather than a failure to act leading to wrongdoing, is more reprehensible, and thus should meet more stringent evidentiary requirements in order to be proven.

That omissions may, in general, be considered less reprehensible than the commission of acts has been explored by Tony Honoré in the context of the common law tradition, who argues that while some omissions that violate distinct duties are just as serious as the commission of acts and incur the same level of reprehensibility, omissions in relation to what he terms 'background duties', where there is no distinct duty owed, may indeed be considered not as serious, and the actor not as culpable, than if a positive act had been committed. He writes:

> [P]ositive-harm doing is on the whole viewed as worse than harmful abstention, which threatens our security interests only indirectly. Though in a particular instance a harmful abstention may have equally noxious results, in general, positive acts of intrusion and destruction are the more menacing, and it is reasonable to judge them more severely . . . positive acts have a general destructive significance different from that of harmful abstentions.[53]

---

53 T. Honoré, 'Are Omissions Less Culpable?', in P. Cane and J. Stapleton (eds), *Essays for Patrick Atiyah*, 1991, reproduced in T. Honoré, *Responsibility and Fault* (Oxford: Hart Publishing, 1999), p. 64.

Tony Honoré's theory cannot simply be transposed to the international plane, and to the institutional context of the Court in particular. Nevertheless, the kernel of his idea, i.e. the relative reprehensibility of acts and omissions, is enlightening when reflecting upon the standard of proof that applies in cases of State responsibility before the Court. Indeed, there seems to be something inherently 'worse', for want of a better word, about a State committing a wrongful act, than one failing to act and thereby violating an international obligation. In some, but not all instances, the commission of an act may imply that the conduct was deliberate or intended, and therefore the act appears more reprehensible than an omission – which, in contrast, may not appear to have been maliciously planned in many instances. The International Law Commission's Special Rapporteur on State Responsibility, Professor James Crawford, noted in his commentary to Article 40 of the International Law Commission's *Articles on State Responsibility for Internationally Wrongful Acts*, that 'to be regarded as systematic, a violation would have to be carried out in an organized and *deliberate way*'.[54]

The *Corfu Channel* case is illustrative of the varying standards of proof applied by the Court to the commissions of acts and omissions, as it involved claims of both. This case involved the loss of human life, the loss of one UK warship and damage to another. The Court found that this harm was caused by mines that had recently been moored in the Channel. Of the three claims advanced by the UK in which it argued that Albania was responsible for the harm caused, the UK made two claims that suggested that the mooring of the mines was a deliberate act that Albania had participated in, either by mooring the mines herself, or by colluding with a neighbouring State, Yugoslavia, in their mooring. UK's third submission concerned an omission on the part of Albania: a failure to warn the ships in the area of the presence of mines in the Corfu Channel.

With respect to the claims concerning the commission of acts, the UK first argued that Albania had itself laid the mines, and in the alternative, that Albania had colluded with another State, Yugoslavia, in the laying of the mines in the Channel. The proof furnished by the UK in support of its claim that Albania had participated in the commission of the act of laying the mines was based on circumstantial evidence. In the words of Sir Frank Soskice (UK):

> From the very nature of the case, the United Kingdom cannot furnish the testimony of eye-witnesses who were present when these mines were laid ... The United Kingdom case must rest on inferences from circumstances, and it is only as to these circumstances that the United Kingdom can afford proof by evidence adduced before the Court. My submission is

---

54 International Law Commission, 'Draft Article on Responsibility of States for Internationally Wrongful Acts, with Commentaries', *Yearbook of the International Law Commission*, 2001, vol. II (Part Two), p. 113, para. 8. Emphasis added.

that, if I can prove circumstances from which the inference arises, that these mines could only have been laid by the Albanian Government or with Albanian complicity, the United Kingdom will have discharged the onus which rests upon it.[55]

Both of these arguments failed to convince the Court. The Court dismissed out of hand the UK contention that Albania had itself laid the mines, stating that 'no evidence in support [of the contention that Albania had laid the mines] was furnished' by the UK.[56] There was thus no discussion by the Court of the standard of proof that the UK had to meet in order to demonstrate that Albania itself had laid the mines, because the Court considered there was no proof *tout court*. The standard of proof was, however, discussed in relation to the second UK claim, that Albania had colluded with Yugoslavia in the laying of the mines.[57] In respect to this claim, the Court stated that '[a] charge of such exceptional gravity against a State would require a degree of certainty that has not been reached here', and that the facts alleged 'lead to no firm conclusion'.[58]

The indirect evidence furnished by the UK in support of its contention that Albania had colluded with Yugoslavia in the laying of the mines included the purported motives of Albania and Yugoslavia to carry out such an act, the fact that the minefield consisted of GY mines marked with a swastika and that Yugoslavia had such mines and the means of laying them,[59] and that a witness had seen mines being loaded onto two Yugoslav vessels that had departed some days before and returned some days after the explosions on 22 October 1946 causing harm to the UK vessels in the Channel. The Court held that:

> It has not been legally established that Yugoslavia possessed any GY mines . . . It is clear that the existence of a treaty [of friendship and mutual assistance between Albania and Yugoslavia], however close may be the bonds uniting its signatories, in no way leads to the conclusion that they participated in a criminal act.[60]

Although the lack of any direct evidence in showing collusion between Albania and Yugoslavia was already problematic, not least because the UK

---

55 Sir Frank Soskice (United Kingdom), *Corfu Channel case*, Public sittings of 17 January 1949, *Pleadings, Oral Arguments, Documents*, vol. IV, p. 479.
56 *Corfu Channel case*, op. cit., p. 16.
57 Although Counsel for the UK also claimed that collusion may have occurred between Albania and Greece, he admitted to the Court that this was a mere conjecture: *Corfu Channel case, Judgment*, p. 17.
58 *Corfu Channel case*, op. cit., p. 17.
59 Sir Frank Soskice (United Kingdom), *Corfu Channel case*, Public sittings of 17 January 1949, *Pleadings, Oral Arguments, Documents*, vol. IV, p. 496.
60 *Corfu Channel case*, op. cit., p. 17.

was unable to furnish any proof that established the identity of the entity that had actually laid the mines and much less that it had been Yugoslavia,[61] the task of the UK in advancing this claim was particularly difficult for a further reason, namely that Yugoslavia was not a party to the proceedings before the Court.[62] The Court could thus not find Albania responsible on the basis of collusion if this responsibility was contingent on Yugoslavia's direct involvement in the minelaying. Although this factor may very well explain why the Court did not find that Albania had colluded with Yugoslavia, the very high standard of proof that the Court set in this case, and particularly its implicit requirement for direct proof in order to show that Albania had been involved in the commission of the act of minelaying, has been followed in later cases.

The Court has dealt with claims of States committing the act of minelaying in two other cases. In the *Oil Platforms* case the very high standard of proof of 'conclusive evidence', first posited in the *Corfu Channel* case, also had to be met, this time by the United States to support its claim that Iran had laid mines. In the *Oil Platforms* case, the US had to prove that Iran had 'deliberately' laid the mines with an 'intention' to cause damage to US persons and/or property in order for the US to establish that, together with other acts, Iran had committed an 'armed attack' against the US (thereby justifying the US to use force in self-defence). There was no question that Iran had indeed laid mines, but this had occurred during its armed conflict with Iraq.[63] The Court noted that both Iran and Iraq had been laying mines at the relevant time, and that consequently 'evidence of other minelaying operations by Iran is *not conclusive* as to the responsibility of Iran for this particular mine'.[64] It went on to note that:

> The main evidence that the mine struck by the USS *Samuel B. Roberts* was laid by Iran was the discovery of the moored mines in the same area, bearing serial numbers matching other Iranian mines . . . This evidence is highly suggestive, but not *conclusive*.[65]

---

61 The Court noted that 'the origin of the mines laid in Albanian territorial waters remains a matter for conjecture': *Corfu Channel case*, op. cit., p. 17. Even the UK acknowledged during the oral pleadings that '[t]he United Kingdom, having suffered injury from these mines, is not in a position by precise demonstration to show how and when and by whose hand in fact these mines were laid in the Channel', Sir Frank Soskice (United Kingdom), *Corfu Channel case*, Public sittings of 17 January 1949, *Pleadings, Oral Arguments, Documents*, vol. IV, p. 481.
62 What was later termed the 'Monetary Gold principle' applied: *Case of the Monetary Gold Removed from Rome in 1943 (Preliminary Question), Judgment, ICJ Reports 1954*, p. 32.
63 *Oil Platforms* case, p. 183, para. 44.
64 Ibid., p. 195, para. 71. Emphasis added.
65 Ibid.

This relatively high standard applied by the majority of the Court to evidence furnished in support of Iran's alleged commission of the act of minelaying was also applied by Judge Simma in his Separate Opinion, who wrote:

> The thought that Iran could be held responsible for acts that could not be attributed to it beyond a certain threshold of proof is also troubling. The question we face is thus the following: how can we hold Iran responsible for acts which . . . cannot be attributed to Iran *with certainty*?[66]

The third example of a case before the Court involving the commission of the act of minelaying is *Military and Paramilitary Activities in and against Nicaragua*, where Nicaragua alleged, and ultimately proved, that the US had laid mines. The Court did not articulate a specific standard of proof when finding that it had been

> established that . . . the President of the United States authorized a United States government agency to lay mines in Nicaraguan ports; that in early 1984 mines were laid . . . by persons in the pay and acting on the instructions of that agency, under the supervision and with the logistic support of United States agents.[67]

The Court in the *Nicaragua* case nevertheless applied a high standard of proof as evidenced in two respects. First, in order to connect the actions of the persons that laid the mines for the US, it formulated the rigorous test of 'complete dependency',[68] described by the Court in a later case as 'proof of a particularly great degree of State control over' such persons,[69] and the test of 'effective control' of the US over the persons who laid the mines, or the requirement that the US had provided specific orders for each military operation, in order to attribute the actions of the individuals concerned to the US.[70] Second, the kind of evidence relied upon by the Court, and the Court's careful treatment of the evidence, in order to establish the responsibility of the US for the minelaying evinces the high standard of proof that the Court applied.[71]

---

66 Ibid., Separate Opinion of Judge Simma, p. 353, para. 63. Emphasis added.
67 *Military and Paramilitary Activities in and against Nicaragua, Merits*, op. cit., p. 48, para. 80.
68 Ibid., p. 62, para. 109.
69 *Application of the Convention on the Prevention and Punishment of the Crime of Genocide*, op. cit., p. 141, para. 393.
70 *Military and Paramilitary Activities in and against Nicaragua, Merits*, op. cit., pp. 64–65, para. 115. See also *Application of the Convention on the Prevention and Punishment of the Crime of Genocide*, op. cit., p. 143, paras 399–400.
71 *Military and Paramilitary Activities in and against Nicaragua, Merits*, op. cit., pp. 40–44, paras 62–73.

In addition to the three examples of allegations of minelaying, a very high standard of proof also applied in the *Genocide* case to the claim made by Bosnia and Herzegovina that Serbia had committed genocide. Bosnia-Herzegovina had to furnish the Court with proof of a very special kind of *mens rea*, namely the *dolus specialis* to destroy in whole or in part a protected group. Therefore, Bosnia-Herzegovina not only had to demonstrate that Serbia had committed the acts of genocide, but that it had done so with the necessary *dolus specialis*. This constituted the greatest evidentiary hurdle for Bosnia-Herzegovina to overcome, and it did not succeed. Bosnia-Herzegovina attempted to show a 'pattern of acts' that 'speaks for itself' as evidence of the *dolus specialis*.[72] The Court found that

> The *dolus specialis*, the specific intent to destroy the group in whole or in part, has to be convincingly demonstrated to exist; and for a pattern of conduct to be accepted as evidence of its existence, it would have to be such that it could only point to the existence of such intent.[73]

In light of the above discussion on the relatively high standard of proof that applies to allegations involving the commission of acts, the standard of proof that is applied by the Court to claims concerning omissions seems to be relatively lower. The third, and ultimately successful, argument of the UK in the *Corfu Channel* case concerned a claim of an omission on the part of Albania. This was the contention that Albania 'did not notify the presence of mines in its waters, at the moment when it must have known this'.[74] This obligation of Albania to notify States of the existence of mines in its territorial waters stemmed not from any treaty-based obligation,[75] but rather from

> elementary considerations of humanity, even more exacting in peace than in war; the principle of the freedom of maritime communication; and every State's obligation not to allow knowingly its territory to be used for acts contrary to the rights of other States.[76]

What the UK had to prove in this respect was not the commission of any act by Albania, but that Albania omitted to act by not notifying States of the presence of the mines. It was undisputed that Albania had not notified other States, or at the very least, the UK whose vessels were in the area at the time.

---

72 *Application of the Convention on the Prevention and Punishment of the Crime of Genocide*, op. cit., p. 76, para. 207.
73 Ibid., p. 133, para. 373.
74 *Corfu Channel case*, op. cit., pp. 19–20.
75 The UK claimed it was a violation of the 1907 Hague Convention VIII, but as the Court pointed out, this treaty did not apply during peacetime: *Corfu Channel case*, op. cit., p. 22.
76 Ibid., p. 22.

However, in order for Albania to have been obliged to provide such notification, the Court considered that Albania had to have had knowledge of the presence of the mines. Proof of Albania's omission thus turned on whether it could be demonstrated that Albania had knowledge of the presence of the mines in its territorial waters.

Instead of reiterating the standard of proof it had already established had to be met in order to show that Albania had participated in the minelaying by colluding with Yugoslavia, namely the standard of proof of 'a degree of certainty', the Court articulated a different standard of proof for establishing Albania's knowledge of the minelaying and consequently its omission in failing to notify other States of the mines in its territorial waters. Proof of Albania's knowledge had to be established so as to 'leave *no room* for reasonable doubt.'[77] Although this appears to be a very high standard of proof, it is arguably a relatively less stringent standard when compared with the standard of proof required to establish Albania's participation in the commission of the minelaying. This is indicated by the way in which this 'knowledge' of minelaying on the part of Albania was proven.

Although indirect evidence was not sufficient to establish that Albania had colluded with Yugoslavia in the laying of the mines, as discussed above, indirect evidence amounting to 'a series of facts linked together and leading logically to a single conclusion'[78] was sufficient to establish 'that the laying of the minefield which caused the explosions on 22 October 1946, could not have been accomplished without the knowledge of the Albanian government'.[79] The Court was careful in this double negative assertion not to say that Albania had knowledge of the minelaying. As Judge Winiarski noted in his dissenting opinion, there was no evidence that Albania actually knew of the minelaying.[80] Rather, the UK had to provide a convincing legal narrative through inferences of fact that Albania should have known of the presence of mines in the Channel. The UK thus argued during the oral pleadings that:

> we rely on proof of circumstance in this case. Among those circumstances, we are entitled to draw assistance from the fact that the situation and character of the minefield of itself point strongly towards Albania as at least implicated in the minelaying, or knowing about it. We agree that the presumption so raised can be rebutted by some alternative explanation put forward by our opponents, but we submit that, if we can prove to the point of reasonable conviction that no alternative explanation

---

77 Ibid., p. 18. Original emphasis.
78 Ibid.
79 Ibid., p. 22.
80 Ibid., Dissenting Opinion of Judge Winiarski, p. 50: 'it does not seem to be definitely proved that the local authorities had knowledge of the operation'.

so put forward is credible, then we are entitled to say that our case is proved.[81]

The Court relied particularly on the following inferences of fact that Albania had knowledge of the minelaying, and had consequently omitted to notify other States of the presence of these mines in its territorial waters: (1) the conduct of Albania prior to and following the damage caused by the mines on 22 October 1946; and (2) the feasibility of observing minelaying from the Albanian coast, as determined by the on-site observations made by experts appointed by the Court. Counsel for Albania offered alternative inferences that could be drawn from the same facts. However, these alternative accounts did not satisfy the Court.

Another comparison between the differences in standards of proof applied by the Court to the commission of acts as opposed to omissions is found in the *Genocide* case. In that case, the Court required Bosnia-Herzegovina to meet the highest possible standard of proof in order to establish its claim that Serbia had committed genocide, as discussed above. It required 'fully conclusive evidence'. In contrast, the ultimately successful claim that Serbia had omitted to fulfil its obligation under the Genocide Convention to prevent genocide met the comparatively lesser standard of proof of 'a high level of certainty appropriate to the seriousness of the allegation'.[82] As has been noted, '[b]y the subtle change of wording, the Court tries to convey the message that a differentiation of the standard of proof would be justified'.[83]

7.3.2 *Varying standards of proof depending on the importance of the norm allegedly violated*

The Court applies varying standards of proof depending upon the importance of the norm allegedly violated. If the content of the international obligation purportedly breached has the character of a peremptory norm, the Court will apply a higher standard of proof, compared with an alleged violation of international obligation that does not have the character of a peremptory norm. As discussed above, the reason for the varying standards of proof is arguably the particular legal consequences entailed from a finding of State responsibility for a serious breach of a peremptory norm, and other non-legal consequences.

It must be stressed that although the discussion taking place in this section is separated from the discussion in the section above, on the varying standards

---

81 Sir Frank Soskice (United Kingdom), *Corfu Channel (United Kingdom of Great Britain and Northern Ireland v. Albania), Merits, Judgment, ICJ Reports 1949*, Public sittings of 17 January 1949, *Pleadings, Oral Arguments, Documents*, vol. IV, p. 482.
82 *Application of the Convention on the Prevention and Punishment of the Crime of Genocide*, op. cit., para. 210.
83 A. Gattini, 'Evidentiary Issues in the ICJ's *Genocide* Judgment', *Journal of International Criminal Justice*, 5 (2007): 898.

of proof that are applied by the Court depending on the manner an international obligation is violated, in practice, it may be difficult to neatly separate the two; an imperfect combination of both elements may constitute the 'seriousness' of the claim alleged, thereby demanding a high standard of proof to apply. In this respect, it may be noted that the Special *Rapporteur* on State Responsibility, Professor James Crawford, considered that because of the very nature of some norms, violations of these norms would always be 'serious'. He noted: 'It must be borne in mind that some of the peremptory norms in question, most notably the prohibitions of aggression and genocide, by their very nature require an intentional violation on a large scale.'[84]

The Court confirmed in the *Genocide* case that a State's failure to prevent and punish genocide, albeit 'omissions', constitutes 'serious claims' and a high standard of proof will be applicable.[85] It is less clear whether a high standard of proof would also apply to 'minor' breaches of other peremptory norms. In some instances, such breaches would not fall within the purview of Article 40 of the International Law Commission's *Articles on State Responsibility for Internationally Wrongful Acts*,[86] and in terms of evidentiary requirements, a high standard of proof arguably would not apply in order to establish that the breach occurred. An example may be a claim of one instance of torture, which although highly reprehensible, may not need to meet the stringent evidentiary requirements applicable to a gross and systematic practice of torture. However, other 'minor' breaches of peremptory norms, such as a use of armed force not amounting to an armed attack, may be considered a 'serious claim',[87] that must meet a high standard of proof in order to be established.

However, it will not necessarily be the case that a claim of an omission of an international obligation, that does not have the character of a peremptory norm, and therefore is not a 'serious claim', will be easy to prove. The comparatively lower standard of proof that will apply to such claims does not ensure their success of being proven. For example, in the *Pulp Mills* case, Argentina claimed that Uruguay had breached its substantive obligations under the 1975 Statute of the River Uruguay, which amounted to a series of omissions leading to environmental harm. The Court found that Uruguay was not in breach of these obligations on the basis of the evidence submitted by Argentina in support of its claim.

---

84 International Law Commission, 'Draft Article on Responsibility of States for Internationally Wrongful Acts, with commentaries', op. cit., p. 113, para. 8.
85 *Application of the Convention on the Prevention and Punishment of the Crime of Genocide*, op. cit., p. 77, para. 210.
86 J. Crawford, 'International Crimes of States', in J. Crawford, A. Pellet and S. Olleson (eds), *The Law of International Responsibility* (New York: Oxford University Press, 2010), p. 410.
87 See P. Gaeta, 'The Character of the Breach', in J. Crawford, A. Pellet, and S. Olleson (eds), *The Law of International Responsibility*, op. cit., p. 426.

7.4 Varying standards of proof in requests for the indication of provisional measures

This section will address the standards of proof applied by the Court in the context of the incidental proceedings of a case. It can be stated with some confidence from the outset that the standard of proof that the Court applies in incidental proceedings will generally be lower compared with the standard of proof that the Court applies during the merits phase of a case. The reason for this relatively lower standard of proof in incidental proceedings is simply that these proceedings should not prejudge the merits of a case.[88] As Judge Ranjeva stated in his Separate Opinion to the Decision on Preliminary Objection to the *Oil Platforms* case, 'it is not a matter, at the preliminary objections stage, of stating that the propositions are true or false from the legal standpoint'.[89] Facts during incidental proceedings need not be proven to the standard required in order to make declarations or determinations at the merits stage, and consequently, a relatively lower standard of proof applies across the board in incidental proceedings.

This section will focus on requests for provisional measures, and in particular, the requirement of demonstrating a 'risk of irreparable prejudice' being caused to the rights of the parties. It will be recalled that the requirement of demonstrating a 'risk of irreparable prejudice' to the rights of the parties is a requirement that has developed in the practice of the Court. The Statute of the Court simply provides that 'The Court shall have the power to indicate, if it considers that circumstances so require, any provisional measures which ought to be taken to preserve the respective rights of either party.'[90] The requirement of 'irreparable prejudice' is particularly interesting to examine for the purposes of this contribution as it immediately raises evidentiary concerns, in particular, to what standard of proof must the facts being claimed as constituting the risk of 'irreparable prejudice' to the rights of the parties be established?

A *risk* of 'irreparable prejudice' requires States to demonstrate the likelihood of the irreparable prejudice occurring in the future, rather than a breach of an international obligation that has already occurred. Logically, the Court must deal with probabilities concerning future events, and a lower standard of proof will apply than would otherwise apply to assessing facts or events at the merits stage. As Judge De Cara stated in the *Case Concerning Certain Criminal Proceedings in France*:

---

88 *Certain Phosphate Lands in Nauru (Nauru v. Australia)*, Preliminary Objections, Judgment, ICJ Reports 1992, p. 262, para. 56.
89 *Oil Platforms (Islamic Republic of Iran v. United States of America)*, ICJ Reports 1996, Preliminary Objections, Separate Opinion of Judge Ranjeva, p. 844.
90 Statute of the International Court of Justice, annexed to the Charter of the United Nations, Article 41, para. 1.

As illustrated by the jurisprudence, in assessing the risk of irreparable prejudice, the Court may be led to consider both the probability and the potential consequences of the occurrence of a fact or event. A future event does not have to be a certainty; it only needs to be probable.[91]

It is submitted that the Court applies varying standards of proof with respect to the requirement of demonstrating a 'risk of irreparable prejudice' for a grant of provisional measures. The standard of proof will vary depending on the type of right at risk of 'irreparable prejudice' being claimed. Two types of 'irreparable prejudice' will be used to illustrate this argument. Where the risk of 'irreparable prejudice' concerns rights involving the lives and well-being of persons, the Court appears more willing to grant provisional measures, and consequently, to apply a lower standard of proof. In contrast, the Court less readily grants provisional measures, and it applies a relatively higher standard of proof, where the risk of 'irreparable prejudice' claimed involves damage to the environment.

The Court has granted provisional measures in a number of cases where the lives and well-being of persons were considered to be in imminent danger. Two such cases involved persons on death row in the USA. In *LaGrand*, the Court unanimously indicated *inter alia* the provisional measure that 'The United Nations of America should take all measures at its disposal to ensure that Walter LaGrand is not executed pending the final decision in these proceedings.'[92] Similarly, in the *Case Concerning Avena and Other Mexican Nationals*, the Court unanimously indicated provisional measures requiring 'The United States of America . . . [to] take all measures necessary to ensure that Mr. César Roberto Fierro Reyna, Mr. Roberto Moreno Ramos and Mr. Osvaldo Torres Aguilera are not executed pending final judgment in these proceedings.'[93]

A risk of a use of armed force by States, potentially endangering the lives and well-being of persons within the jurisdictions of the States, may also prompt the Court to indicate provisional measures. In the Request for the Indication of Provisional Measures in *Application of the International Convention on the Elimination of All Forms of Racial Discrimination (Georgia v. Russian Federation)*, the Court noted that:

> *the rights in question in these proceedings*, in particular those stipulated in Article 5, paragraphs *(b)* and *(d)* (i) of [the International Convention on

---

91 *Case Concerning certain Criminal Proceedings in France (Republic of the Congo v. France), Order of 17 June 2003, Request for the Indication of a Provisional Measure*, Dissenting Opinion of Judge De Cara, p. 124.
92 *LaGrand (Germany v. United States of America), Provisional Measures, Order of 3 March 1999*, ICJ Reports 1999, p. 16, para. 29(I)(*a*).
93 *Case Concerning Avena and Other Mexican Nationals (Mexico v. United States of America)*, ICJ Reports 2003, pp. 91–92, para. 59(I).

the Elimination of All Forms of Racial Discrimination], *are of such a nature that prejudice to them could be irreparable*.[94]

However, it is not always the case that a risk of an alleged use of armed force by a State in the territory of another will prompt the indication of provisional measures. In contrast to *Georgia v. Russian Federation*, the Court in the *Case Concerning Armed Activities on the Territory of the Congo* rejected the request by the Democratic Republic of the Congo for provisional measures against Rwanda with respect to

> [the] continuing grave, flagrant, large-scale acts of torture, cruel, inhuman or degrading punishment or treatment, genocide, massacre, war crimes and crimes against humanity, discrimination, violation of the rights of women and children, and the plundering of resources committed on the territory of the Democratic Republic of the Congo.[95]

However, it was not the nature of the risk of 'irreparable prejudice' in this case that precluded an indication of provisional measures. As the Court made clear in its Order, it did not consider that it had 'the prima facie jurisdiction necessary to indicate those provisional measures requested by the Congo'.[96]

The Court has shown a predisposition to grant provisional measures in cases where the risk of 'irreparable prejudice' involves a danger to the lives and well-being of persons. Indeed, the President of the Court effectively requested States to refrain from causing harm to persons even before the Court considered a request for the indication of provisional measures: the day immediately following Georgia's request for an order for provisional measures in its dispute with Russia, and thus before Russia could respond to the request, President Higgins addressed an urgent communication to the parties calling upon them 'to act in such a way as will enable any order the Court may take on the request for provisional measures to have its appropriate effects'.[97] Thus, on the strength of the evidence submitted by Georgia, the Court demonstrated its

---

94 *Application of the International Convention on the Elimination of All Forms of Racial Discrimination (Georgia v. Russian Federation), Request for the Indication of Provisional Measures, Order*, ICJ Reports 2008, p. 396, para. 142. Emphasis added.
95 *Armed Activities in the Territory of the Congo (New Application: 2002) (Democratic Republic of the Congo v. Rwanda), Provisional Measures, Order of 10 July 2002*, ICJ Reports 2002, p. 222, para. 8.
96 *Armed Activities in the Territory of the Congo, Provisional Measures*, op. cit., p. 249, para. 89.
97 Press Release from the International Court of Justice, 'Proceedings instituted by Georgia against Russia. Urgent Communication to the Parties from the President under Article 74, paragraph 4, of the Rules of Court', 15 August 2008, available at: http://www.icj-cij.org. See also Speech by H. E. Judge Rosalyn Higgins, President of the International Court of Justice, to the General Assembly of the United Nations, 30 October 2008, also available on the website of the Court.

willingness to consider favourably a request for provisional measures where the lives and well-being of persons were at stake.

In addition to the nature of the risk of 'irreparable prejudice' at stake, much will turn on proof of an imminent risk to these rights requiring the protection afforded by the indication of provisional measures. In this respect, it was essential in *Georgia v. Russian Federation* that although the armed conflict had ceased, Georgia was able to furnish evidence that 'the situation . . . is unstable and could rapidly change . . . [due to] the ongoing tension and the absence of an overall settlement to the conflict in this region'.[98] Similarly, in *Avena*, the Court decided to grant provisional measures with respect to three of the Mexican nationals on death row because they 'are at risk of execution in the coming months, or possible even weeks . . . [and] their execution would cause irreparable prejudice to any rights that may subsequently be adjudged by the Court to belong to Mexico'.[99]

In contrast to the requests for the indication of provisional measures where the risk of 'irreparable prejudice' has involved imminent danger to the lives and well-being of individuals, the Court has been less forthcoming in indicating provisional measures where the risk of 'irreparable prejudice' alleged involves damage to the environment. The Court has acknowledged that – in principle – irreparable damage may be caused to the environment. In the case of the *Gabčíkovo-Nagymaros Project*, it stated:

> The Court is mindful that, in the field of environmental protection, vigilance and protection are required on account of the often irreversible character of damage to the environment and of the limitations inherent in the very mechanism of reparation of this type of damage.[100]

In the context of other jurisdictions, it is explicitly acknowledged that provisional measures may be indicated in order to counter the risk of damage to the environment, pending a decision at the merits stage. Article 290, para. 1, of the United Nations Convention on the Law of the Sea provides:

> If a dispute has been duly submitted to a court or tribunal which considers that *prima facie* it has jurisdiction . . ., the court or tribunal may prescribe any provisional measures which it considers appropriate under the circumstances to preserve the respective rights of the parties to the dispute or *to prevent serious harm to the marine environment*, pending the final decision.[101]

---

98 *Application of the International Convention on the Elimination of All Forms of Racial Discrimination*, op. cit., p. 39, para. 143.
99 *Avena and Other Mexican Nationals*, op. cit., p. 91, para. 55.
100 *Gabčíkovo-Nagymaros Project (Hungary/Slovakia), Judgment, ICJ Reports 1997*, p. 78, para. 140.
101 Article 209, paragraph 1, United Nations Convention on the Law of the Sea, concluded on 10 December 1982, 1833 UNTS 396. Emphasis added.

However, in the practice of the Court, it is difficult to obtain provisional measures with respect to a risk of environmental damage. In the Request by Argentina for the Indication of Provisional Measures in *Case Concerning Pulp Mills on the River Uruguay (Argentina v. Uruguay)*, Argentina argued that its rights derived *inter alia* from substantive obligations under the 1975 Statute, and it argued that it had demonstrated 'a serious risk that irreparable prejudice or damage might occur', and that 'environmental damage was, at least "a very serious probability" and would be irreparable.'[102] With respect to this request, the Court took care to emphasize the importance of respect for the environment.[103] However, the Court narrowly construed Argentina's request and held that 'there is, however, nothing in the record to demonstrate that the *very decision by Uruguay to authorize the construction of the mills* poses an imminent threat of irreparable damage to the aquatic environment of the River Uruguay',[104] because 'Argentina has not provided evidence at present that suggests that any pollution resulting from the commission of the mills would be of a character to cause irreparable damage to the River Uruguay'.[105]

7.5 Conclusion

In relation to the applicable standard of proof before the Court, the Court's first contentious case, the *Corfu Channel* case, made immediately clear that the Court does not apply one standard of proof across the board in its treatment of evidence, but rather varying standards of proof. This contribution has endeavoured to provide some rough guidance on the factors that may contribute to a standard of proof being relatively higher or lower in a given case. It has been argued that standards of proof vary depending upon the function of the Court in a given case, the gravity of the claim put forward by the parties, and the phase of the case.

It is apparent from the factors contributing to the raising or lowering of standards of proof before the Court, described in this contribution, that the reasoning of the Court in the *Corfu Channel* case has had a lasting impact. First, with respect to the function of the Court in a given case as a factor contributing to raising or lowering a standard of proof, it is clear that the Court continues to apply the relatively high standard of proof enunciated in the *Corfu Channel* case to matters where the Court exercises its 'determinative' function when faced with claims of State responsibility. The very fact that the

---

102 *Case Concerning Pulp Mills on the River Uruguay (Argentina v. Uruguay)*, Request for the Indication of Provisional Measures, Order, ICJ Reports 2006, p. 9, para. 35.
103 Ibid, p. 18, para. 72.
104 Ibid, p. 18, para. 73. Emphasis added.
105 Ibid, p. 18, para. 75.

Court is free to make a negative finding, and not find in favour of a claim of State responsibility because of the inadequacy or insufficient quality of the evidence presented, suggests that the Court applies a relatively high standard of proof in such cases, compared to when it exercises a different function, its declaratory function.

When the court exercises its 'declaratory' function, in cases where it must declare which State has sovereignty over territory, or where it must define a territorial or maritime boundary, the Court applies a relatively lower standard of proof. This is because the Court must make a positive finding if requested to do so: it must declare which State has sovereignty over the disputed territory, and/or define the disputed boundary. Even when faced with rather weak evidence, the Court must nevertheless fulfil the task it has been requested to undertake. In such cases, and depending on the expression of consent to its jurisdiction – particularly if the terms of a Special Agreement govern such a question – the Court may either select the more plausible of two competing claims, or it may find a compromise and attribute different territory to both States, and define the boundary as falling in between the lines claimed by each State respectively.

Another factor that this contribution has discussed as contributing to raising or lowering a standard of proof in a case where the Court is exercising its determinative function, is the gravity of the claim alleged. Two elements of the gravity of a claim fall to be considered. The first is the manner by which a breach of an international obligation is claimed to have occurred. It has been submitted that – in general – the Court applies a relatively higher standard of proof to claims concerning the commission of acts, compared with a relatively lower standard of proof that the Court applies to claims involving a failure to act (omissions). This factor as contributing to the applicable standard of proof was made apparent in the *Corfu Channel* case, which involved both claims of acts and omissions, and it has been followed in subsequent cases.

The last factor discussed in this contribution that contributes to raising or lowering the standard of proof in a particular case before the Court, is the phase of the case. A relatively low standard of proof will apply in incidental proceedings, compared with the relatively higher standard of proof that the Court will apply during the merits phase. This is simply because the incidental proceedings cannot prejudge the facts that will be established at the merits stage, and therefore facts in incidental proceedings do not need to be established to the same standard of proof as facts at the merits stage. In relation to the indication of provisional measures in particular, it was argued that the Court applies a relatively higher standard of proof where the risk of the 'irreparable prejudice' claimed involves imminent danger to the lives and the well-being of persons. In contrast, the Court applies a relatively lower standard of proof, and is more reluctant to indicate provisional measures, where the risk of 'irreparable prejudice' concerns claims of environmental damage.

It is hoped that the insights offered in this contribution, based on a close reading of the case law of the Court, will assist international legal scholars in better understanding the factors that may influence the Court's reliance on a particular standard of proof in a given case. The factors that may contribute to a standard of proof being relatively higher or lower as described in this contribution do not constitute an exhaustive list. There remains much work to be done to provide parties before the Court with greater certainty of the standards of proof that will be applied by the Court to the claims and the supporting evidence they furnish, thereby assisting them in their presentation of the evidence at the written and oral stages of proceedings.

8 'Naval secrets', public interest immunity and open justice

*Kenneth J. Keith**

8.1 Introduction

Courts, national and international, have the function of deciding disputes of fact which have to be resolved as they determine the claims of legal right or breach of legal obligations submitted to them. In principle, the courts should have before them all the evidence which they need to ascertain those facts. That statement of the ideal may be unrealistic, given the nature of the disputed facts, the interests of the litigants and others affected, and issues of cost and delay. This chapter concerns one particular potential obstacle to a court's access to relevant evidence: a claim that evidence should not be made available in order to protect rights to confidentiality or other important public interests. In the *Corfu Channel* case, the United Kingdom refused to produce certain documents, referred to as XCU (explained as Exercise Corfu), pleading naval secrecy. As the pleadings and the judgment of the Court make clear, the documents were seen as relevant to the innocent character of the passage of 22 October 1946.

Such claims present challenges to litigants and their counsel, and to courts which may have to decide the claim in its specific context, and to law makers, including treaty negotiators and courts drafting their rules. Similar claims of confidentiality or public interest may also arise in other inter-state legal contexts, for instance, as limiting cooperation in legal matters or trade obligations.[1]

How, in the evidentiary context, should the law treat the competing claims? Should one interest or the other always prevail? If not, how should the balance be struck? Who should strike it? What procedures should they follow?

---

* My judicial responsibilities as Judge of the International Court of Justice explain the absence of comment on certain issues and cases, notably the *Genocide* case, *ICJ Reports 2007*, at 128–129 (paras 205–206), 254–255 (para. 35) and 412–421 (paras 50–63) on which there is already much commentary. Thanks to Robyn Briese and Chester Brown for comments and Jennifer Cavenagh for research assistance.
1 For example, S. Schill and R. Briese, '"If the State Considers" – Self Judging Clauses in International Dispute Settlement', *Max Planck UNYB*, 13 (2009): 61.

In the sixty years since the *Corfu Channel* case was decided, law and practice in national and international jurisdictions have changed in major ways.

8.2 Changing practice in common law courts

I begin with developments in the common law world, starting at about the time of the *Corfu Channel* case. On 1 June 1939, the Royal Navy submarine *Thetis*, which was undergoing tests, sank in Liverpool Bay with the loss of 99 lives. Survivors of the deceased sued the builders and sought discovery from them of documents which included the contract for the hull and machinery of the submarine, letters written before the disaster relating to the vessel's trim, reports about its condition when raised, a large number of plans and specifications relating to various parts of the vessel, and a notebook of a foreman painter employed by the defendant builders. The First Lord of the Admiralty opposed the production of the documents on the basis of his opinion that it would be injurious to the public interest that any of them should be disclosed to any person. For the Lord Chancellor, Viscount Simon, who had been a Cabinet Minister for much of the 1930s, speaking on behalf of a bench of seven in the House of Lords, the question to be decided was

> of high constitutional importance, for it involves a claim by the Executive to restrict the material which might otherwise be available for the tribunal which is trying the case. This material one party, at least, to the litigation may desire in his own interest to make available, and without it, in some cases, equal justice may be prejudiced.[2]

The House of Lords ruled that the documents were not to be disclosed. Given the apparent content of the documents or at least of most of them and the wartime context in which the decision was given, the particular result is fully understandable. But the House of Lords went further than was necessary in two important respects. First, the public interest ground for withholding could relate, it said, not just to the contents of the particular document, as in this case, but also to 'the class of documents (e.g. departmental minutes) to which they belong':

> the objection is sometimes based upon the view that the public interest requires a particular class of communications with, or within, a public department to be protected from production on the ground that the candour and completeness of such communications might be prejudiced if they were ever liable to be disclosed in subsequent litigation.

Second, the government's objection to disclosure was conclusive; the court could not question it. Viscount Simon did, on the other hand, give some

---

2 *Duncan v. Cammell Laird and Co* [1942] AC, p. 624.

indications to the responsible Ministers, who were, he said, to make the decisions to object personally, and their advisers about how they should go about making the decision:

> It is not sufficient ground that the documents are 'State documents' or 'official' or are marked 'confidential'. It would not be a good ground that, if they were produced, the consequences might involve that department or the Government in Parliamentary discussion or in public criticism, or might necessitate the attendance as witnesses or otherwise of officials who have pressing duties elsewhere ... nor that production might tend to expose a want of efficiency in the administration or tend to lay the department open to claims for Compensation. The Minister ... ought not to take the responsibility of withholding production except in cases where the public interest would otherwise be damnified – for example, where disclosure would be injurious to national defence, or to good diplomatic relations, or where the practice of keeping a class of documents secret is necessary for the proper functioning of the public service.[3]

The range of the information covered by the broader statements, especially about 'the class of documents' and 'the proper functioning', and the conclusive effect of a Government's decision to object soon came under challenge. In 1954, the Supreme Court of Canada held that in a criminal prosecution the court could overrule the Minister's objection to production, and, in 1955, the House of Lords in a Scottish appeal asserted the same power in a civil case, followed by the New Zealand Court of Appeal in 1962, the House of Lords in an English appeal in 1968, the High Court of Australia in 1978 and in a civil case in the Supreme Court of Canada in 1986.[4]

Those and later decisions have relevant features which might inform not just national, but also international, litigation, as, in part, they already have. First, the decisions demonstrated, particularly in England, that the advice given by Viscount Simon in 1942 about the care that Ministers were to take in opposing disclosures – recall his examples of national defence and diplomatic relationships – and the undertakings given to Parliament by Ministers in the 1950s to limit claims to withhold did not lead to the more extensive

---

[3] *Duncan v. Cammell, Laird and Co* [1942] AC, pp. 642–643.
[4] For the cases, see, for instance, P. Hogg and P. Monahan, *Liability of the Crown* (3rd edn, 2000), pp. 89–90. The Scottish case is *Glasgow Corporation v. Central Land Board* 1956 SC (HL) 1. It is notable for its criticism of Lord Simon's reasons. For a splendid critique of the law as it was by the 1920s of the privilege for secrets of state and official communications, see J. H. Wigmore, 5 *A Treatise on the Anglo-American System of Evidence in Trials and Common Law Including the Statutes and the Judicial Decisions of All Jurisdictions of the United States and Canada* (2nd edn, 1923), pp. 186–200, paras 2378–2379, especially pp. 193–196 and 198–200. The United States Supreme Court had in 1952 decided that the executive's claim was not conclusive: *United States v Reynolds* (1952) 345 US 1.

disclosure that many had expected. While careful executive assessment of possible claims might be necessary to facilitate further disclosure, practice had made it clear that it was not sufficient. Judicial control was also required. This development of judicial power occurred along with, and as part of, the development of the courts' powers to review administrative action. That development was encouraged by legislative action and was to be seen in the broader context of moves in many countries and internationally towards more open government.

Second, the courts, in exercising their power of control over executive decisions to withhold evidence, began distinguishing between different categories of information, recognizing, for instance, at first that:

> there are many cases in which documents by their very nature fall in a class which require protection such as, only by way of example, cabinet papers, foreign office despatches, the security of the State, high level interdepartmental minutes and correspondence pertaining to the general administration of the naval military and air force services.[5]

Such broad protections against disclosure soon, however, came under examination. Very importantly, between 1974 and 1986, courts in the United States, Australia, New Zealand and Canada reviewed and, in some cases, rejected claims in respect of cabinet and similar papers.[6]

Third, even in areas in which executive claims not to disclose appeared to be strongest, the courts began to give closer attention to the detail of the claims and to require more careful justification. In a New Zealand case,[7] the Court began by accepting that 'the argument for deference is particularly strong where, as in the present case, immunity is claimed on grounds of national security [which] undoubtedly forms a category of public interest of special importance'. But how is national security to be defined and to be limited? The legislature, the Court noted, had frequently drawn distinctions relating to security (or national security and defence) when addressing intelligence or information relating to security. The Court provided this context to the process for the preparation of the ministerial certificate, its content and the judgment to be made about it by the Court. Those matters:

> are to be seen in the context both of the general movement of the law towards more open government and of the protection of national security.

---

5 Lord Upjohn in *Conway v. Rimmer* [1968] AC 910.
6 *United States v. Nixon* 418 US 683 (1974), *Sankey v Whitlam* (1978) 142 CLR 1, *Environmental Defence Society v. South Pacific Aluminium Company Ltd* [1981] 1 NZLR 146 and *Carey v. Ontario* [1986] 2 SCR 637.
7 *Choudry v. Attorney-General* [1999] 3 NZLR 399.

That general movement appears in the public interest immunity cases decided over the last four decades, . . . in legislation, notably the Official Information Act 1982, and in related official policies and practice. The movement is in turn part of the growth of greater controls over public power developed in recent decades by Parliament and the courts. The development of those wider controls and the movement to more open government have always, of course, been accompanied by balancing factors or limits, in particular in respect of matters of national security, an area which is often associated with defence and international relations.

Both Courts and legislatures have at times seen those areas as non-justiciable, or as barely justiciable, or as requiring judicial deference to ministerial exercises of discretion. Those positions have been seen in Court rulings relating to governmental decisions and processes, for instance:

- Determining foreign and defence policy: . . .;
- Characterising certain goods as urgently required for requisition in connection with the defence of the realm, the prosecution of war, or other matters involving national security . . .;
- Supporting the Court's inherent jurisdiction to protect the names of witnesses who are employed by the Security Intelligence Service . . .;
- Denying or severely limiting natural justice to immigrants or to State employees or the right of unions to be consulted . . .;

But Courts do not of course always abstain or defer. In recent decades they have applied wider powers of review. Thus:

- The Supreme Court of Canada has held that the prerogative power relating to defence may be subject to a challenge under the Charter of Rights . . .;
- Courts in several jurisdictions have rejected challenges, based on claimed threats to Britain's national security, to the release of [the book] Spycatcher . . .; and
- A New Zealand naval officer was held entitled to natural justice in respect of decisions affecting his grading notwithstanding arguments of national security . . .[8]

Fourth, the judges increasingly struck their own balance between the conflicting interests having made their own assessment, for instance, of the impact of disclosure on the candour of officials in the particular context.

Fifth, in terms of procedure courts sometimes asked the Minister to reconsider the reasoning in the certificate and the extent of the claim and to submit a new certificate (as in the New Zealand case) and sometimes inspected the

---

8 *Choudry v. Attorney-General* [1999] 3 NZLR at 403–404 (references omitted).

documents to make their own assessments of the balance of the competing public interests (as proposed in that case but not adopted).

A recent high profile British case shows how far the law in that jurisdiction has moved since the *Thetis* case.[9] It focused on a feature of national security to which the New Zealand Court referred – the protection of sources, in particular intelligence sharing arrangements with the United States. The British Government, with the support of the US Government, was strongly opposed to the publication of some paragraphs of a court judgment. The paragraphs concerned the methods used by American authorities to interview the plaintiff who sought an order, at the time he was detained at Guantanamo Bay, that the UK Government supply certain documents to his lawyers in the United States; the documents were relevant, he said, to his defence against charges which he anticipated would be brought by the US Government and which he said were based on false confessions resulting from torture over a lengthy period. The opinion of the Foreign Secretary in his public interest immunity applications was that:

> the publication of the redacted paragraphs would damage the intelligence sharing arrangements between this country and the USA, between this country and our allies, and the USA and its allies. If the redacted paragraphs are published, the USA will 'review' the workings of the present intelligence sharing arrangements. Quite apart from any formal 'review', publication may also serve to stultify many of the less formal arrangements which currently work to the advantage of the battle against terrorism. Accordingly the control principle must be upheld in its full rigour.[10]

The 'control principle' referred to in the last sentence is a principle of confidentiality which is vested in the country of the services which provide the information; it never vests in the country which receives the information. Because there was nothing in the paragraphs themselves which would involve a breach of security or disclose intelligence material such as names or places or means of communication, the disclosure of which would damage national security, and because the close UK/US intelligence sharing agreement was no secret – it was the essential element in the government's argument – the case, in the words of the Chief Justice, came down to this:

> Unless the control principle prevails, the intelligence sharing arrangement between the USA and the UK will be reviewed, and following the review may, not will, become less 'productive', to presumably, the disadvantage of both countries, although I shall assume to the much greater disadvantage of the UK.[11]

---

9 *Binyam Mohamed v. Foreign Secretary* [2010] EWCA Civ 65.
10 *Binyam Mohamed v. Foreign Secretary* [2010] EWCA Civ 65, para. 12.
11 Ibid., para. 13.

On the other side was the principle of open justice:

> Although expressed in wide and general terms – and perhaps inevitably so expressed – in my judgment the principles of freedom of expression, democratic accountability and the rule of law are integral to the principle of open justice and they are beyond question.[12]

The Chief Justice completed his reasons with this paragraph in which he weighs the competing principles:

> In my view, the arguments in favour of publication of the redacted paragraphs are compelling. Inevitably if they contained genuinely secret material, the disclosure of which would of itself damage the national interest, my conclusion might be different. However, dealing with this appeal as a matter of practical reality rather than abstract legal theory, unless the control principle is to be treated as if it were absolute, it is hard to conceive of a clearer case for its disapplication than a judgment in which its application would partially conceal the full reasons why the court concluded that those for whom the executive in this country is ultimately responsible were involved in or facilitated wrongdoing in the context of the abhorrent practice of torture. Such a case engages concepts of democratic accountability and, ultimately, the rule of law itself.[13]

The other two members of the Court also made it clear that while national security arguments would frequently prevail, the responsibility for decision remained with the judges who would engage in the necessary balancing exercise. The case is also of interest for the detail of the executive certificates provided to the Court and their accompanying documentation.[14] The executive accepts that courts may no longer be persuaded by a statement simply asserting that 'national security', not further defined, will be damaged.

8.3 The role of national and international legislation in regulating disclosure

As already mentioned, courts have been developing these powers at the same time as they were developing their more general powers of judicial review of

---

12 Ibid., para. 41.
13 Ibid., para. 57.
14 For other British instances of government claims which took too broad a form and finally failed, see the D Notice controversy in 1967 discussed by N. Duxbury, 'Lord Radcliffe Out of Time' [2010] CLJ 41, 50–51 and the Matrix Churchill (Arms to Iraq) case, followed by the Scott Inquiry.

administrative action, and legislatures were taking steps towards greater openness, fairness and control in respect of government, for instance, by setting up the office of the Ombudsman, providing for freedom of official information, regulating the procedures of administrative tribunals and providing for appeals from their decisions. Courts, in considering whether to require the disclosure of government documents, have made express reference to the policies included in such legislation. In some cases, the legislature has also regulated challenges on public interest grounds to the disclosure of information in litigation. The Canadian and New Zealand provisions on that matter may be contrasted, with the first making a categorical prohibition on disclosure and the second stating a balancing test with a presumption of disclosure. If a Canadian Minister or the Clerk of the Privy Council objects to the disclosure of information before a court on the grounds that the information constitutes a confidence of the Privy Council disclosure shall be refused without examination or hearing.[15] Under the New Zealand provision:

> A Judge may direct that a communication or information that relates to matters of State must not be disclosed in a proceeding if the Judge considers that the public interest in the communication or information being disclosed in the proceeding is outweighed by the public interest in withholding the communication or information.[16]

Through much the same period, the case for greater openness was also being made and, to a significant extent, was being accepted in many areas of international relations. As early as 1918, President Woodrow Wilson had called, in the first of his Fourteen Points, for 'open covenants of peace, openly arrived at', a call which led among other things to the registration of treaties with the

---

15 Canada Evidence Act s 39; see also ss 38.06 and 38.13. Section 39 was considered in a *Decision {of a NAFTA Tribunal} Relating to Canada's Claim of Cabinet Privilege, United Parcel Service of America Inc and Government of Canada*, 8 October 2004. The Tribunal, noting that the record before it did not demonstrate that the Clerk of the Privy Council in making his claim had weighed the competing interest in disclosure and that the matter had in any event to be determined under the law of the tribunal and not under the law of Canada, directed:

> That Canada consider whether it wishes to assess whether the claims to privilege may be established by reference to particular stated public interests which justify protection and to weigh that justification, if it is made out, against the public interest in disclosure, for the purpose of the arbitration, to UPS and the Tribunal.
>
> A failure to disclose, found by the Tribunal to be unjustifiable, may lead to the Tribunal drawing adverse inferences on the issue in question. Whether it does draw such an inference will depend on the circumstances surrounding that issue.

16 Evidence Act 2006 s 70(1); the 'public interest' is defined by reference to the protected interests set out in the Official Information Act 1982.

League of Nations and the United Nations and their publication in more than 2,000 volumes to date.[17]

I give two contemporary examples of texts supporting greater openness. Under the International Health Regulations 2005, States are obliged:

1. To develop, strengthen and maintain their surveillance capacity and their capacity to respond promptly and efficiently to public health risks (Article 5).
2. To assess events within their territory and to notify the World Health Organization within twenty-four hours of all events which may constitute a public health emergency of international concern; when appropriate the notice is to go to the International Atomic Energy Agency, a reference which highlights the very broad scope of the regulations extending as they do to new threats to public health arising from the releases of radiological as well as biological and chemical materials (Article 6).
3. Following a notification, to continue to communicate timely, accurate and sufficiently detailed information and to report difficulties faced and support needed to respond to the emergency (Article 6).
4. To provide information during unexpected or unusual public health events (Article 7); and
5. To consult about events which do not require notification (Article 8).

The World Health Organization has related powers concerning sources of information, requesting verification and the provision of information (Articles 10 and 11). Its Director General also has the important power to determine the existence of a public health emergency of international concern and to make recommendations to meet the emergency (Article 12). Those powers are subject to careful processes including consultation and the involvement of an emergency committee. It will be noticed that the obligation under these Regulations to disclose information is not subject to any limit, particularly on the grounds of national security.

These regulations, concerned with a specific matter, may be put in the broader context of the draft articles on the prevention of transboundary harm from hazardous activities prepared in 2001 by the International Law Commission. The draft requires the host State authorizing activities which are lawful but which involve a risk of causing significant transboundary harm to provide the State likely to be affected 'with timely notification of the risk and the assessment and to transmit to it the available technical and all other relevant information on which the assessment is based' (Article 8).

---

17. I consider these issues in 'Freedom of Information and International Law', in J. Beatson and Y. Cripps (eds), *Freedom of Expression and Freedom of Information* (Oxford: Oxford University Press, 2000), p. 349.

At the request of any of the States involved, they are: '[to] enter into consultations, with a view to achieving acceptable solutions regarding measures to be adopted in order to prevent significant transboundary harm or at any event to minimize the risk thereof' (Article 9).

They are also

> [To] exchange in a timely manner all available information concerning that activity relevant to preventing significant transboundary harm or at any event minimizing the risk thereof. Such an exchange of information shall continue until such time as the States concerned consider it appropriate even after the activity is terminated.
>
> (Article 12)

And '[To] provide the public likely to be affected by an activity within the scope of the present articles with relevant information relating to that activity, the risk involved and the harm which might result and ascertain their views' (Article 13).

By contrast to the obligations under the International Health Regulations, the obligations of the State of origin under this general text are subject to a limit:

> Data and information vital to the national security of the State of origin or to the protection of industrial secrets or concerning intellectual property may be withheld, but the State of origin shall cooperate in good faith with the State likely to be affected in providing as much information as possible under the circumstances.
>
> (Article 14)

It will be seen that the test is stated at a high level – the information must be vital to the protected interests – and that a limited disclosure may be one way of protecting the national security or other interests.

Such limits on the obligation to provide information also appear in treaties concerned with Court processes. Article 72 of the Statute of the International Criminal Court enables a State, if the disclosure of its information or documents is proposed, to intervene in the proceedings if it is of the opinion that disclosure would prejudice its national security interests. The provision sets out a procedure, not unlike that to be found in some national courts, for reasonable steps to be taken to seek to resolve the matter, for instance, by modifying the request, using another source, providing the information in a summarized or edited form, limiting disclosure, or using *in camera* or *ex parte* hearings. If those efforts fail, the State is to notify the Prosecutor or the Court of the specific reasons for its decision, unless that description of the reasons would itself necessarily result in prejudice to the State's national security interests. If the Court determines that the evidence is relevant and necessary for the establishment of the guilt or innocence of the accused, the Court may request further consultations for the purpose of considering the State's representations, which may include, as appropriate, hearings *in camera* and *ex parte*. If it concludes that the requested State is not acting in accordance with its obligations under the Statute, it may refer the matter to the Assembly of State Parties, or to the Security Council if the matter has been referred to it by the Council, specifying the reasons for its conclusion.

Rule 73 of the ICC Rules of Procedure and Evidence 2002, adopted by the Assembly of State Parties, regulates privileged communications and information, with a general provision for confidential relationships and specific references to lawyers, medical and related personnel, and clergy. It includes this particular provision:

> The Court shall regard as privileged, and consequently not subject to disclosure, including by way of testimony of any present or past official or employee of the International Committee of the Red Cross (ICRC), any information, documents or other evidence which it came into the possession of in the course, or as a consequence, of the performance by ICRC of its functions under the Statutes of the International Red Cross and Red Crescent Movement.

The provision does not apply if the information is contained in public statements or documents of the ICRC, or, if the Court, having decided that the information is of great importance and consulted with the ICRC, the ICRC does not object to the disclosure, or if the ICRC waives the privilege. That rule had been preceded by a ruling in 1999 of an ICTY trial chamber that the evidence of a former employee of the ICRC who was willing to give evidence was not to be given. The chamber divided on the question whether evidence could ever be given by former employees of the ICRC when facts came to their knowledge by virtue of their employment.[18]

Such public interest limits are to be found in many other treaties regulating criminal justice matters. Their interpretation and application may be subject to international adjudication, as in the ICTY case and a recent decision of the International Court of Justice in a dispute between Djibouti and France.[19] In that case, the Court ruled that it had the power to examine the refusal by the competent French authorities to transfer a criminal investigation file to the Djibouti authorities. The French authorities had refused the transfer under a treaty provision, Article 2(c), which makes an exception to the obligation of the requested State to transfer the file if it 'considers that the execution of the request is likely to prejudice its sovereignty, its security, its *ordre public* or other of its essential interests'. That broadly stated power was subject to limits which the Court could police. In the first place, France had

---

18 *Prosecutor v. Blagoje Simi and Others*, Decision of 27 July 1999.
19 *Certain Questions of Mutual Assistance (Djibouti v. France), ICJ Reports 2008*, p. 177.

to give Djibouti a statement of reasons for its refusal. Second, that statement had to go beyond a repetition of the terms of the provision. Third, France had to exercise its power under Article 2(c) in good faith. While France had breached its obligation to give reasons to Djibouti, the reasons that were given by the judge who had authority under French law to decide the matter 'do fall within the scope of Article 2(c)'.[20]

8.4 *Corfu Channel*, behind the scenes

At the risk of anachronism, I return to the *Corfu Channel* case. How in the light of subsequent national and international litigation and legislative practice, a small sample of which I have mentioned, might such a case now be handled? A starting point which has remained constant while much may have and has changed is that the International Court of Justice has no compulsory powers to call witnesses or to require the production of evidence. Article 49 of the Statute provides as follows: 'The Court may, even before the hearing begins, call upon the agents to produce any document or to supply any explanations. Formal note shall be taken of any refusal.' (See also Articles 43 (5), 48, 50 and 51.) Article 62 of the Rules is written in broader terms:

1 The Court may at any time call upon the parties to produce such evidence or to give such explanations as the Court may consider to be necessary for the elucidation of any aspect of the matters in issue, or may itself seek other information for this purpose.
2 The Court may, if necessary, arrange for the attendance of a witness or expert to give evidence in the proceedings.[21]

The lack of coercive powers is paralleled by the law in a number of common law countries in which, at the time of the *Corfu Channel* case, the State (the Crown) was not subject to coercive powers to call evidence; that element of the Crown's immunity from legal suit, along with some immunities from legal liability, remained.[22]

---

20 *ICJ Reports 2008*, pp. 231 and 230 (paras 152 and 148); I saw the assessment by the French judge differently from the way the Court saw it: ibid., pp. 278–282 (paras 4–10).
21 The relevant rule in 1948–49 was Rule 54.
22 The United Kingdom Crown Proceedings Act enacted in 1947 which did subject the Crown to discovery in civil proceedings to which it was party, included this critical proviso:

> Provided that this section shall be without prejudice to any rule of law which authorises or requires the withholding of any document or the refusal to answer any question on the ground that the disclosure of the document or the answering of the question would be injurious to the public interest.
>
> (s. 28(1))

The position internationally was to the same effect, as Sir Eric Beckett, the British Agent, recalled in his final address to the Court in January 1949.[23] The 1899 and 1907 Hague Conventions for the Peaceful Settlement of Disputes give the Tribunals set up under them the power to require the parties to produce documents and to demand necessary explanations, again with the qualification which recognizes that there is no absolute obligation that 'in case of refusal, the Tribunal takes note of it'.[24] The committee which in 1899 was responsible for preparing the text thought that an unqualified right of the Tribunal to require documents was not acceptable and there could be legitimate refusals.[25] The Committee of the PCIJ considering revisions to its rules in 1936 did not think anything could be said, about the duty of a State to produce all the relevant materials in its possession.

> There are great difficulties in the way because in its own courts every government must claim to exercise occasionally the right to refuse to produce a document on the ground of public interest, and of that interest it claims to be the sole judge.[26]

That privilege or immunity of the State continues to be recognized in more recent treaties, but with greater precision and with procedures being prescribed to provide for disclosure if possible. Provisions of the ICC Statute to that effect were mentioned earlier. An ICTY Appellate Chamber has held, by contrast, that States are obliged to comply with orders made by the ICTY for the production of evidence, but that obligation, it said, derives from the provisions of Chapter VII and Article 25 of the Charter. That legal basis for the relevant provision of its statute 'accounts for the novel and indeed unique power granted to the International Tribunal to issues orders to sovereign States'.[27] The ruling does, however, appear to recognize possible national security limits to that obligation and the possibilities of a weighing of the competing interests.

The long-recognized State privilege to refuse to adduce evidence in national and international courts would presumably have been part of the context in which the British lawyers – and politicians – handled the evidentiary issues arising in the *Corfu Channel* case. So too would have been the sensitive character of the information in issue in the context of armed clashes with an ally of the Soviet Union at that very early stage of the Cold War.

---

23 4 Pleadings, pp. 563–564.
24 Article 44 of the 1899 Convention and Article 69 of the 1907 Convention. See similarly Article 24(3) of the Optional Arbitral Rules for two States drawn up by the PCA.
25 Quoted by Beckett, op. cit., p. 563.
26 PCIJ Series D No 2 3d Add, at 768–769 quoted by Beckett, op. cit., pp. 563–564.
27 *Prosecutor v. Blaski* (1997) 110 ILR 688, 699 para. 26. The Trial Chamber provides a detailed survey of the law and practice of other courts and tribunals. See also Chester Brown's valuable discussion, *The Common Law of International Adjudication* (Oxford: Oxford University Press, 2007), pp. 104–110.

The XCU orders, issued on 5 and 13 October 1946, have been declassified and are published as an annex to a valuable article by Anthony Carty in which he reviews the exchanges in London about whether those orders should be disclosed.[28] They were referred to in reports of the events of 22 October prepared the following day by the commander of the *Volage* (Paul), the commander of the *Saumarez* (Selby) and Rear Admiral Kinahan, commanding the first cruiser squadron. Those reports were submitted to the Court on 25 October 1948, following the completion of the written pleadings on 30 September 1948 and before the beginning of the oral argument on 9 November 1948.[29] The first contains this (apparently) intriguing passage, quoted by the Court: 'The most was made of the opportunities to study Albanian defences at close range. Those included, with reference to XCU . . .' and he then gives a description of some coastal defences.[30]

The other two reports say only that the vessels proceeded in accordance with the orders.

As Anthony Carty recounts, in mid-October 1948, as the British team was preparing for the oral argument which was to begin the following month, the Attorney-General, Sir Hartley Shawcross, became concerned about the significance of the XCU documents which had only recently, it seems, come to his attention.[31] In a minute to the Foreign Secretary he said it would be better to disclose the documents. There followed further memoranda and meetings involving the Foreign Office, the Admiralty, the Lord Chancellor and the Prime Minister. For the moment I quote one passage from a letter of 3 November from the Attorney-General to the Prime Minister (also a barrister):

> 6. It is a fundamental principle of the practice of the Courts of our country and of the conduct of our legal profession that parties to litigation are not entitled to use merely those documents which they think will assist their case and to suppress others which are inimical to it. I must make it clear that neither the Solicitor General, nor myself, nor, I am sure, any of the other members of the Bar who are assisting us in this matter, would for a moment contemplate being parties to the course of conduct now forced upon us by the Admiralty's failure to procure and produce these documents earlier had our country's international position not been so gravely

---

28 A. Carty, 'The *Corfu Channel case* – and the Missing Admiralty Orders', *Law and Practice of International Courts and Tribunals*, 3 (2004): 30–34. Another recent interesting article by L. W. Maher, 'Half Light Between War and Peace: Herbert Vere Evatt, the Rule of International Law and the *Corfu Channel case*', *Australian Journal of Legal History*, 9 (2005): 3 raises the hypothetical prospect of that formidable Australian advocate and politician being involved in the London discussions of 1948–49!
29 Special Volume and 5 Pleadings, pp. 48, 53.
30 *ICJ Reports 1949*, p. 32.
31 They appear to have been sent from the Commander in Chief, Mediterranean Station, only on 1 October 1948, Carty, op. cit., pp. 32 and 34.

involved. As it is, we retain great misgiving about the propriety of what is being done, which we can only justify on the principle 'my country . . . right or wrong, my country'. We all feel that we must insist that circumstances such as these are not allowed to recur.[32]

No decision to disclose was made during that period and Sir Eric Beckett, Foreign Office Legal Adviser and Agent in the case, felt himself able to say in the first round of oral hearings, on 12 November 1948, that the operational orders in the XCU documents:

> prescribed action to be carried out in certain eventualities, which did not take place; that is to say if the ships were fired on from the land. As we told the Albanian Government in the note of 2nd August, the ships were, in that event, going to fire back. What matters, after all, is what the ships did and not what they might have done had circumstances been otherwise. We do not produce those XCU documents, no doubt for similar reasons to those which have led Albania not to produce . . . the orders to its own coastal defence units which fired on our ships on 15th May.
> . . .
> We see no necessity for disclosing certain technical matters which navies at all times keep secret. I want to take this opportunity of saying that with these sole exceptions we have responded to the Albanian request for the production of every document they have asked for, in so far as the document exists at all.[33]

The documents are next mentioned on 30 November when the President of the Court asked Commander Paul, the commanding officer of the *Volage* who was giving evidence, 'What do you mean by the words "with reference to XCU" [in his report of 23 October 1946]?' The commander replied that the term referred to a document which, as a serving officer, he had been instructed not to discuss. The President said he was not asking for explanations, simply what was meant by the three letters, to which the reply was that it was simply a short title.[34] On 1 December the navigating officer of the *Mauritius* was asked in cross-examination by Professor Pierre Cot, counsel for Albania, about 'the famous orders referred to as XCU' and received essentially the same reply followed by this comment by counsel:

> I am in complete agreement that you should not answer the question if it is at all embarrassing. I have asked our United Kingdom colleagues to submit these orders to an expert who would work in secrecy and report on

32 Ibid., p. 11.
33 3 Pleadings, p. 291.
34 4 Pleadings, pp. 27–28.

the pertinent matters. I have received no answer to this request, and I might consider asking the Court whether those orders should be shown to the experts – Commander Moullec, for instance – who would work in secrecy, or whether the Court would wish to have these orders submitted to the Court's own experts.[35]

The issue next arose on 6 December when Sir Frank Soskice, the Solicitor-General, was cross-examining an Albanian captain, a coastal defences commander, about correspondence relating to his functions on 15 May 1946 which was not in the record. Professor Cot intervened:

> May I make a proposal? In this particular case – and this incident . . . is only one of the incidents and a secondary one at that – there are many military orders concerned. The offer which I make, and I make it on behalf of Mr. Ylli, the Albanian Agent, is that the Albanian Government is willing to submit to the Court all the military orders which are mentioned or are concerned in this case, even the most secret ones, but we will do so on condition that the Court shall be supplied with all military orders, including the XCU orders and Admiral Kinahan's orders. Our proposal is very clear-cut, and, I feel, a very loyal one. I might add that neither we nor, as you will have noticed, the Albanian Government have given their officers any orders that they are not to mention any particular point on grounds of military secrecy. So I repeat my proposal: we are willing to hand to the Court any documents which the Court may require or which our British colleagues may require, so long as our British colleagues do likewise.[36]

Four days later, referring to the passage in Commander Paul's report of 23 October 1946 which the Court later quoted, Professor Cot on behalf of the Albanian agent withdrew absolutely the right to see the documents.

> We wish only that the Court requests the documents and consults them freely. We do not even request that our expert sees them. We wish only that the Court may know in what conditions and for what purposes the Albanian coastal defences have been studied in the course of the passage of 22 October.[37]

The record shows no United Kingdom response to the Albanian offers. Rather the President of the Court, at the beginning of the hearing on 14 December, addressed a request to the two agents for the production of certain documents.

---

35 Ibid., p. 270.
36 Ibid., p. 270.
37 Ibid., p. 394.

The British agent was asked to communicate to the Court for its use the documents designated as XCU.[38] In early January 1949 there were conferences and exchanges in London between ministers and officials, finally involving the First Lord of the Admiralty, the Attorney-General, the Solicitor-General, the Lord Chancellor and the Prime Minister. To the Attorney-General's proposal of 13 January 1949 that the Solicitor-General have discretion to disclose, if in his view the situation made disclosure practically unavoidable, the Prime Minister, after consulting the Foreign Secretary, responded on 14 January that it was not possible to give such a wide discretion. The views of the Foreign Secretary, the Minister of Defence and the First Lord of Admiralty were all against disclosure after a careful consideration of all the factors. If the contingencies mentioned by the Attorney were to arise, the Solicitor should refer back for instruction. On the same day, the Agent wrote to the Registrar as follows:

> I have to inform the Court that the Government of the United Kingdom regrets that it feels obliged to refuse to produce these documents. The reasons for this refusal have already been briefly indicated in my oral address to the Court on November 12th, 1948. I propose to deal with this matter further in my concluding oral address.[39]

In that address, on 18 January, having recalled the background to Article 49 of the Statute mentioned earlier in this chapter, Sir Eric Beckett expressed the great regret of his Government, that 'since we sincerely wish to show our respect to the Court by complying with every request, it felt obliged to avail itself of this privilege [to refuse disclosure] with regard to XCU'.[40] He then turned to the question whether the Court might draw an inference from that refusal: the Court's readiness to do that must depend, he said, largely on the extent to which the Court considers the reasons for non-disclosure to be legitimate; and any inference drawn had to be consistent with the rest of the evidence. On the first point the Agent must have thought that 'naval secrets' was a sufficient reason. On the second, he traverses, over two pages, aspects of the evidence which he said related to the contents of the documents,[41] beginning with the proposition that the judges had full and clear evidence on all matters relevant to innocent passage; there was no room for conjecture. He accepted it would be legitimate to infer from Commander Paul's report that

---

38 Ibid., p. 428. In terms of the principle of natural justice, Article 43(4) of the Statute requires a certified copy of every document produced by a party to be communicated to the other. How the Court's request was to be reconciled with that requirement in the event was not addressed. Compare the procedure followed in the *Guyana-Suriname* arbitration, outlined in its procedural orders, one instance of the *ex parte* procedures increasingly to be found nationally and internationally.
39 4 Pleadings, p. 255.
40 Ibid., p. 564.
41 Ibid., pp. 564–565.

XCU contained some reference to Albanian gun provisions. He agreed that a deliberate reconnaissance of coast defences is not a thing which a ship exercising its right of innocent passage can lawfully do: it is an act prejudicial to the security of the coastal State. Commander Paul in evidence said that 'we did envisage the possibility that our squadron might be fired on from the shore, and there were given in XCU certain positions from which it seemed possible that fire might be opened'. The much quoted passage from his report stated the action they had taken after the *Saumarez* was mined: he had then looked at the positions he had been told about and reported on his observations. The Agent, commenting on this evidence, 'repeated that there was nothing in XCU ordering any of the ships to engage in any such reconnaissance'. The Agent also addressed, in the context of the XCU documents, the purposes of the passage. There were two:

1   to exercise a right of passage which had been disputed by gunfire in May, as a test of the attitude of the coastal State;
2   as a means of reaching the open water in the Adriatic north-west of Corfu for a rendezvous with *Ocean* and *Raider* for training exercises.

Earlier he had recalled that the telegrams between the Admiralty and the Commander in Chief of August and September 1946 had made it clear, in the first place, that the passage was a 'test' 'in the sense that it was desired to see if Albania would tacitly let the warships pass, it being our intention to establish diplomatic relations if she did so'. Second, it was clear from the 10 August 1946 telegram that if the coastal guns fired at the ships, they should fire back. Third, the same telegram clearly directed that the passage was not to be made in a threatening manner because 'the armament was to be in a fore and aft position'. Fourth, the Navy were to use the Channel 'only when essential' – any passage was not to be a test only. The Court should not, he submitted, infer against the United Kingdom that XCU contained anything inconsistent with those telegrams. The Agent's final reference to the XCU documents was as follows:

> As I said, I wish we were in a position to comply with the Court's request that we should produce XCU, but our actions after all put it completely beyond doubt that our intentions were wholly peaceful and simply to sail through the Straits. I pointed out that no one could ever be subjected to stronger provocation, provocation to resort to any measures that XCU could possibly authorize. The fact that in spite of this temptation our ships did nothing shows that XCU cannot have contained any instructions which authorize anything except a wholly peaceful passage through the Straits, subject to the qualification that our ships, under the orders of the Admiral Commanding, could have fired back if fired upon.[42]

---

42   Ibid., p. 569.

Professor Cot in his reply for Albania was able to place major stress on the absence of the 'famous documents XCU'.[43]

It was against that background that the Court ruled as follows:

> In accordance with Article 49 of the Statute of the Court and Article 54 of its Rules, the Court requested the United Kingdom Agent to produce the documents referred to as XCU for the use of the Court. Those documents were not produced, the Agent pleading naval secrecy; and the United Kingdom witnesses declined to answer questions relating to them. It is not therefore possible to know the real content of these naval orders. The Court cannot, however, draw from this refusal to produce the orders any conclusions differing from those to which the actual events gave rise. The United Kingdom Agent stated that the instructions in these orders related solely to the contingency of shots being fired from the coast – which did not happen. If it is true, as the commander of *Volage* said in evidence, that the orders contained information concerning certain positions from which the British warships might have been fired at, it cannot be deduced therefrom that the vessels had received orders to reconnoitre Albanian coastal defences. Lastly, as the Court has to judge of the innocent nature of the passage, it cannot remain indifferent to the fact that, though two warships struck mines, there was no reaction, either on their part or on that of the cruisers that accompanied them.[44]

8.5 Reading *Corfu Channel* in light of subsequent practice

I set out details of the 1948–49 process for two principal reasons. First, with the material considered earlier in this chapter, those details help suggest practical steps that may be taken when issues arise relating to the disclosure of sensitive information. Second, with the public release of the XCU documents, it is possible to assess the strength of the claim of 'naval secrecy'.

I begin with the second matter, helped by Anthony Carty's careful account of the exchanges in London in late 1948 and early 1949. The Attorney-General's concern as stated in a letter of 15 October 1948 was that it was quite clear from the Admiralty order

> that this was conducted as a naval operation with the deliberate intention of trailing our coats, with the expectation that our ships might be fired upon and with the knowledge (apparently obtained from a previous reconnaissance) of certain existing defences . . . and the object of observing what other defences there might be.

---

43 Ibid., pp. 687, 690–691.
44 *ICJ Reports 1949*, p. 32; to the contrary, see Judges Krylov, p. 75 and Ečer, p. 129.

The telegrams between the Admiralty and the Commander in Chief Mediterranean between 1 August and 22 September 1946, provided to the Court on 27 October 1948,[45] made it clear that one purpose of the intended passage was indeed to test the Albanian position, to trail the British coat. The telegrams also made it clear that Albanian fire would be returned. As Commander Paul's report, also before the Court,[46] showed, XCU indicated at least five Albanian gun positions. The only matters to which the Attorney refers and which were not supported by the record at the time of the hearing were the apparent previous reconnaissance and 'the object of observing other defences'. The Albanian firing of 15 May was one possible basis for the knowledge of the defence points but it is the case that XCU states that after that event 'air photographs of the whole area were obtained'. Aerial reconnaissance in breach of Albanian sovereignty had been denied in the Security Council. Contrary to the Attorney, I cannot see anything in the two documents supporting the object of 'observing' other defences, but no doubt had attacks occurred in October, others might have been identified as a result.

Two comments may be made at this stage. The first is that the principal substantive worry – about the purpose of testing Albania, of trailing the coat – was in the record before the Court by the time of the hearing. Furthermore, the Court saw no problem about that purpose. On the contrary, it said:

> The intention must have been not only to test Albania's attitude, but at the same time to demonstrate such force that she would abstain from firing on passing ships. Having regard, however, to all the circumstances of the case, as described above, the Court is unable to characterize these measures taken by the United Kingdom authorities as a violation of Albania's sovereignty.[47]

The second comment is that none of the matters mentioned by Shawcross are about 'technical matters' of naval secrecy (to use Beckett's term in his first address to the Court), except perhaps the (aerial) reconnaissance. A list of such technical matters was provided in a useful Admiralty memorandum of early January 1949 identifying the matters in the documents which were 'top secret' and 'could not be disclosed'. I include comments on the matters in parentheses.

1. a reference by a number to a secret intelligence report; this appeared in a sentence under *Minefields* saying that a minefield shown on the plan in that report 'can be disregarded'. (The reference or the whole sentence might have been deleted without any alteration to the sense of the document.)

---

45 5 Pleadings, pp. 58–59, 188.
46 Ibid., p. 48 and Special Volume.
47 *ICJ Reports 1949*, p. 31.

2 aerial photography
3 the Greeks should not be informed of the intended passage and 'one does not want to alert the Greeks now [in January 1949] to this policy'. (But the passage and its purposes were by then very well known.)
4 the last sentence of XCU referred to a disguise or deception in respect of the passage. 'Both this practice itself, and the extent to which it is employed, should be kept secret.' (Deception in time of peace as well as war has always existed and what harm could be caused by the disclosure after the event of just one known method?)
5 XCU1 (the second document) disclosed detailed information about signal communications. (Again, those details could have been deleted.)[48]

I finally mention aspects of a conference of the officials principally involved, held on 5 January 1949. In Carty's account, among the 'striking features' of the record of the conference are these:

> It was thought that the strengthening of the squadron and the fact that its intention was to test the autumn cruise worked against disclosure, but were not fatal. The fact that orders showed an expectation of hostilities and called for 'excessive' countermeasures, especially the role of aircraft, also marked against disclosure, but 'could be explained away'. A more decisive consideration was the following: 'Retaliatory action of 1 hour's duration is excessive, yet if we do not reveal XCU, we can show we did nothing'. This point was marked 'much against disclosure'. As to whether all of the above destroyed the innocent character of the passage, Shawcross and Waldock [who was representing the Admiralty] disagreed.[49]

Again it will be observed that those concerns are not about secrets in any technical sense. Rather all are about the (non-)innocent nature of the passage. It is difficult to avoid Professor Carty's conclusion that what was principally motivating the lawyers was the national interest (or one definition of it) and winning the case; 'my country right or wrong'. The ethical issue identified early in the story by Sir Hartley Shawcross remains.[50]

8.6 Lessons for the future

What may be learned from the processes followed in this case and the other developments discussed in this chapter? How can courts and tribunals and the parties appearing before them address the relationship between the right of the court or tribunal and the parties to have access to all relevant material and

---

48 See Carty, op. cit., p. 19.
49 Ibid., p. 20.
50 See also e.g. R. Higgins, 'Ethics and International Law', *LJIL*, 23 (2010), especially pp. 298–299 ('Ethics and the International Lawyer').

the protection of important interests which may call for non-disclosure? As has already appeared, the issues arise as well for law-makers, including courts and tribunals adopting their rules. First, extensive practice shows that those claiming non-disclosure will be required to defend the relevant interests with greater precision than was common at the time of the *Thetis* and *Corfu Channel*. A general claim of military secrets or national security will not serve. The claim in the normal course may be given some precision, if necessary by the Court requiring further consideration and a new certificate. Second, the State considering making the claim should assess in good faith in respect of the particular documents the prejudice likely to be caused by their release and articulate its reasons, with supporting evidence if appropriate. Third, it should consider whether the documents might be edited to facilitate release or their release might be controlled in some way.[51] Fourth, when appropriate, it should consider whether the interest in release outweighs the reason for protection and articulate its justification if it concludes that it does not. Those suggestions are directed at the Parties and their advisers.

That is, however, not the end of the matter. The courts will in general have related responsibilities. They have the power to examine the claim of non-disclosure. It may be that, as with most international courts, they do not have

---

51 One issue raised in London in 1948–49 was whether the release to the Court (but not to the other Party) would mean wider release. According to Carty (op. cit., p. 21) the Solicitor-General's memorandum of 7 January 1949, agreed to by the Attorney-General said that 'the presence of Slav judges means that whatever is disclosed will probably become public property'. This matter also arose in *Nicaragua v. United States* (see the strong statements by Judges Lachs and Jennings, *ICJ Reports 1986*, pp. 158–160 and 528) and more recently in an Appeals Chamber of the ICTY, *Prosecutor v. Blaskić*, Judgment of 29 October 1997, where the Chamber in discussing possible modalities of making allowance for national security concerns proposed that the State in issue may be invited to submit the relevant documents to the scrutiny of one Judge of the Trial Chamber designated by it. 'Plainly the fact that only one judge alone undertakes a perusal of the documents should increase the confidence of the State that its national security secrets will not accidentally become public' (para. 68). Judge Karibi-Whyte disagreed in a vigorous principled separate opinion which concluded as follows:

> The Trial Chamber is the only body vested with jurisdiction to conduct trial proceedings. Accordingly, every issue constitutive of the ultimate decision in the trial of a matter before it must involve the participation of all the members of the Trial Chamber. The suggested modality will result in a conflict between the right of the individual and the protection of national security interests. The modality suggested is an expedient sacrificing the principle of the protection of the rights of the individual on the altar of political expediency of the protection of national security interests. Transparency in the conduct of public affairs is the ideal. It is undoubtedly the most enduring character of the administration of justice. Accordingly, a justified accusation of bias and partiality cannot be discounted or ignored if the procedure of an *ex parte, in camera* application by a single Judge in a trial before the Trial Chamber is adopted in the determination of a claim of national security interests. The aphorism that justice should not only appear to be done but should also be manifestly seen to have been done is still the current universal opinion of purity of the administration of justice.

a final power of decision. They may have only a power of persuasion, but the deliberate following of procedures such as those set out in the previous paragraph and the exercise of that power should result in more extensive disclosure and better enable the court to meet its responsibilities of finding the facts and doing justice according to law.[52]

---

[52] The two words inscribed in stone in the Great Hall of Justice in plain view of the judges are *veritas* and *justitia*.

Part IV
Law of the Sea

9 International straits

Still a matter of contention?

Stuart Kaye

9.1 Introduction

In 1946, when the incident that gave rise to the litigation in the *Corfu Channel* case[1] occurred, almost all international transportation across the world's seas and oceans was by sea. Although air transportation had received a huge boost as a result of its increasing use during World War II, and air power had become a new and vital important element in the armed forces of the victorious allies, ships and shipping were still of tremendous importance. The vast bulk of international trade over water was carried by ships, and international peace and security were directly affected by the ability of warships to transit freely on the world's oceans.

The *Corfu Channel* case, concerned as it was with the access of warships, and, by extension, other vessels, to the territorial sea of other States, was of tremendous significance to the facilitation of freedom of navigation. The confirmation of the International Court of Justice that warships had a right of innocent passage through the territorial sea of a coastal State along a strait used for international navigation was a landmark in the law of the sea. The decision ensured that the International Law Commission's consideration of the law of the sea, in the years leading up to the first large international conference on the subject since World War II, would incorporate provisions dealing with rights of navigation within the territorial sea. Before the war, at the 1930 Hague Conference, no consensus had emerged on the right of innocent passage for warships.[2] This lack of consensus was effectively neutralised by the Court's decision in the *Corfu Channel* case, and ensured the ILC would support the concept.[3] This in turn saw the incorporation of provisions dealing with international straits in the 1958 Convention on the Territorial Sea and

---

1 *Corfu Channel case, Judgment of April 9th 1949, ICJ Reports 1949*, p. 3.
2 See F. Ngantcha, *The Right of Innocent Passage and the Evolution of the International Law of the Sea: The Current Regime of 'Free' Navigation in Coastal Waters of Third States* (New York: Pinter, 1990), pp. 122–123.
3 Ibid., pp. 123–127; M.H. Nordquist (ed.), *United Nations Convention on the Law of the Sea 1982: A Commentary* (Dordrecht: Martinus Nijhoff, 1985), vol. II, pp. 279–280.

Contiguous Zone,[4] and subsequently in the 1982 United Nations Convention on the Law of the Sea.[5]

In the first decade of the twenty-first century, it is still true that the vast bulk of international trade over water travels in ships, whether this is calculated by volume or value. International peace and security are still directly affected by the freedom of the seas being available to warships. The ability of the United States to project military power through the mechanism of the aircraft carrier battlegroup is as important in 2010 as it was in 1946, albeit that the equipment has changed. A right of passage through an international strait is still of great importance, and while the law is more explicit in its nature today than it was in the 1940s, there are still matters in its interpretation and application which vex the international community.

This chapter will first briefly consider the development of the regime for passage through international straits, before turning to the contemporary regime of transit passage under the Law of the Sea Convention. It will then move to examine those elements of transit passage which have proven contentious, namely the obligation not to hamper passage, and the nature of 'normal mode' for ship's passage.

9.2 Developments since the *Corfu Channel* case

The *Corfu Channel* case ensured that a right of passage existed through international straits, provided vessels passing through such straits met certain criteria. These were not precisely defined but included that the passage was 'innocent' and that it should be for the purpose of passing through the waters rather than to undertake other activities such as minesweeping.[6] The International Law Commission (ILC) built upon these foundations and through its deliberations prepared a draft text for consideration by States at the First United Nations Conference on the Law of the Sea in Geneva in 1958. The ILC's text in relation to innocent passage and international straits was adopted

---

4 Convention on the Territorial Sea and Contiguous Zone, done at Geneva on 29 April 1958, entered into force 10 September 1964, 516 UNTS 205.
5 United Nations Convention on the Law of the Sea, done at Montego Bay on 10 December 1982, entered into force on 14 November 1994: 1833 UNTS 396.
6 The Court stated:

> It is, in the opinion of the Court, generally recognized and in accordance with international custom that States in time of peace have a right to send their warships through straits used for international navigation between two parts of the high seas without the previous authorization of a coastal State, provided that the passage is *innocent*. Unless otherwise prescribed in an international convention, there is no right for a coastal State to prohibit such passage through straits in time of peace.
>
> (*Corfu Channel case*, op. cit., p. 28)

almost verbatim by the Conference,[7] and became Article 16(4) of the Convention on the Territorial Sea and Contiguous Zone. It provided:

> There shall be no suspension of the innocent passage of foreign ships through straits which are used for international navigation between one part of the high seas and another part of the high seas or the territorial sea of a foreign State.

The ILC explicitly attributed the language used in this article to that used by the ICJ in the *Corfu Channel* case.[8] The significance of this provision was to indicate that under no circumstances could a right of passage be hampered or suspended in an international strait, whereas some temporary suspension of passage elsewhere in the territorial sea was possible.[9]

The confirmation of the width of the territorial sea to 12 nautical miles during the negotiations at the Third United Nations Conference on the Law of the Sea meant that the number of international straits around the world would increase substantially. Prior to the 1970s, most States maintained territorial seas of 3 or 4 nautical miles, and therefore the widespread adoption of 12 nautical miles meant that a substantially greater number of straits were potentially enclosed by the territorial sea. This encouraged a number of States to pursue a specific regime that provided for greater guarantees of passage rights. The negotiations also saw the acceptance of the concept of the archipelagic State with sovereignty over both the land and waters of an archipelago. The same States who sought guarantees for passage through international straits also sought similar protections for passage through archipelagic waters.[10]

9.3 Regime of transit passage

The 1982 Law of the Sea Convention provides a specific regime that operates for international straits. An international strait is defined in Article 37 as a strait which is 'used for international navigation between one part of the high seas or an exclusive economic zone and another part of the high seas or an exclusive economic zone'. The phrase used in Article 37 is the same as that used in Article 16(4) of the Territorial Sea Convention, which in turn was directly derived from the language used by the ICJ in the *Corfu Channel* case. As such, a strait 'used for international navigation' is not restricted to voyages

---

7 The only difference between the ILC's draft article and that subsequently adopted in Article 16 of the Convention on the Territorial Sea and Contiguous Zone was the removal from the ILC's text of the word 'normally' in relation to the use of the strait for international navigation.
8 *Yearbook of the International Law Commission*, Vol. II (New York: United Nations, 1956), p. 273.
9 Article 16(3), Convention on the Territorial Sea and Contiguous Zone.
10 See Nordquist, op. cit., Vol. I, p. 107.

of ships passing between States, but rather any strait where the traffic using it comes from a variety of flags, as this was the interpretation used by the ICJ. With the possible exception of remote straits that have been closed to international traffic, such as the Vilkitski'i Strait in the Russian far north, it would seem that any strait consisting of territorial sea will qualify as an international strait provided there is sea traffic flagged in more than just the coastal State.[11]

The Law of the Sea Convention deals with international straits in Part III. There are three ways international straits are dealt with:

1. Straits which are subject to international conventions of long-standing.
2. International straits with other routes of similar convenience (the so-called 'Messina Exception').[12]
3. Straits subject to the regime of transit passage.

The categories other than transit passage are all ultimately subject to innocent passage. Under the first category, Article 35(c) of the Law of the Sea Convention was designed to protect well-established arrangements, like those in relation to the Turkish Straits, from being varied by the Convention. However, such arrangements are rare, and the provision appears to preclude the creation of new ones. The second category occurs where the strait effectively does not serve as a significant route for international navigation. The rationale behind it is that if international shipping will not be inconvenienced by the potential withdrawal of an international strait, then there is little reason for the affected coastal State to be burdened with having the care of an international strait.

One advantage of transit passage over innocent passage is the restrictions on vessels exercising a right of transit passage are substantially less than those imposed under the regime of innocent passage. Under innocent passage, a range of activities are listed as being prohibited, including the launching or receiving of aircraft, and a catch-all provision, 'any other activity not having a direct bearing on passage'.[13]

The transit passage regime is far more generous. Most obviously, it is available to aircraft as well as ships. In addition, the list of specific restrictions and the catch-all provision in Article 19 are not found, but rather a more modest set of requirements:

1. Ships and aircraft, while exercising the right of transit passage, shall:

    (a) proceed without delay through or over the strait;

---

11 See W.E. Butler, *The Northeast Arctic Passage* (Alphen aan den Rijn: Sijthoff and Noordhoff, 1978), pp. 122–127.
12 Named because the Straits of Messina are the most often cited example of this concept in application. See generally L.M. Alexander, 'Exceptions to the Transit Passage Regime: Straits with Routes of "Similar Convenience"', *Ocean Development and International Law*, 18 (1987): 479.
13 Article 19(2)(l), Law of the Sea Convention.

(b) refrain from any threat or use of force against the sovereignty, territorial integrity or political independence of States bordering the strait, or in any other manner in violation of the principles of international law embodied in the Charter of the United Nations;
(c) refrain from any activities other than those incident to their normal modes of continuous and expeditious transit unless rendered necessary by force majeure or by distress;
(d) comply with other relevant provisions of this Part.

2   Ships in transit passage shall:

(a) comply with generally accepted international regulations, procedures and practices for safety at sea, including the International Regulations for Preventing Collisions at Sea;
(b) comply with generally accepted international regulations, procedures and practices for the prevention, reduction and control of pollution from ships.

The most significant advantage of transit passage over innocent passage, however, is Article 44 which provides that transit passage shall not be hampered or suspended.[14] This provision was designed to meet the objective of the maritime powers to ensure that key international straits could not be subject to closure. It makes it clear that under no circumstances can a coastal State block an international strait to vessels, although transiting ships must comply with such regulations that can be validly applied to them.[15] This is different to the regime of innocent passage which permits a coastal State to temporarily suspend the right of innocent passage if 'essential for the protection of its security, including weapons exercises'.[16]

While transit passage is advantageous to ships and aircraft, the coastal State is not completely without the ability to regulate activities of transiting vessels. In fact, in terms of the extent of a coastal State's ability to regulate, the range of laws is essentially the same as for innocent passage. Article 42 provides:

1   Subject to the provisions of this section, States bordering straits may adopt laws and regulations relating to transit passage through straits, in respect of all or any of the following:

---

14   Article 44, Law of the Sea Convention provides:

> States bordering straits shall not hamper transit passage and shall give appropriate publicity to any danger to navigation or overflight within or over the strait of which they have knowledge. There shall be no suspension of transit passage.

15   J. Norton Moore, 'The Regime of Straits and the Third United Nations Conference on the Law of the Sea', *American Journal of International Law*, 74 (1980): 102–105.
16   Article 25(3), Law of the Sea Convention.

(a) the safety of navigation and the regulation of maritime traffic, as provided in Article 41;
(b) the prevention, reduction and control of pollution, by giving effect to applicable international regulations regarding the discharge of oil, oily wastes and other noxious substances in the strait;
(c) with respect to fishing vessels, the prevention of fishing, including the stowage of fishing gear;
(d) the loading or unloading of any commodity, currency or person in contravention of the customs, fiscal, immigration or sanitary laws and regulations of States bordering straits.

2 Such laws and regulations shall not discriminate in form or in fact among foreign ships or in their application have the practical effect of denying, hampering or impairing the right of transit passage as defined in this section.
3 States bordering straits shall give due publicity to all such laws and regulations.
4 Foreign ships exercising the right of transit passage shall comply with such laws and regulations.
5 The flag State of a ship or the State of registry of an aircraft entitled to sovereign immunity which acts in a manner contrary to such laws and regulations or other provisions of this Part shall bear international responsibility for any loss or damage which results to States bordering straits.

This regulatory scope only differs from innocent passage in the context of the protection of cables and pipelines.

9.4 Hampering of passage

The obligation not to hamper passage and to ensure that an international strait remains open at all times has proven to be the most contentious aspect of the regime of international straits. As noted above, Article 42(2) of the Law of the Sea Convention provides that the laws of a coastal State may not in fact, form or application have the effect of 'denying, hampering or impairing the right of transit passage', while Article 38 provides that the right of transit passage cannot be impeded. These two exhortations seem very clear, but their clarity has not prevented a number of coastal States from asserting their jurisdiction over vessels passing through their territorial sea, including through an international strait, that have the practical effect of permitting transit passage to be suspended.

A number of coastal States assert jurisdiction in their territorial sea in respect of 'security' matters.[17] The basis for this assertion, at least for some

---

17 See below.

States, appears to be that the territorial sea is part of the coastal State's sovereignty, and that nothing in the Law of the Sea Convention prevents a State taking reasonable security measures to protect its sovereignty from attack. Such States might argue that a security over their territorial sea cannot be displaced by the Law of the Sea Convention, as the Convention is itself obliged to remain consistent with the United Nations Charter, which itself preserves a State's right to self-defence outside of other measures controlling the exercise of the use of force.[18]

A large number of coastal States assert security zones in their territorial sea and beyond, into the EEZ. The range of measures varies considerably, and does not easily lend itself to the type of statistical representation undertaken above. Overall, in excess of 60 coastal States have asserted some form of restriction or notification. It is therefore necessary to summarise the nature of various coastal State measures in Table 9.1, in the context of States with what qualifies as an international strait forming part of their territorial sea:

Table 9.1 State practice – freedom of navigation and security and international straits

State	Type of Rights Asserted	Straits
Albania	Warships require prior special authorisation	Corfu Channel
Cape Verde	Warships require prior authorisation. Prohibition of 'non-innocent use' of the exclusive economic zone, including weapons exercises	ASL
China	Requires prior notice for transports of waste in territorial sea and EEZ. Warships require prior authorisation. Contiguous zone 24 nm Security interests	Taiwan Strait between the Pescadores and Taiwan*
Croatia	Warships must announce their passage; the number of warships is limited	Various in the Adriatic Sea
Denmark	Warships and governmental ships are required to notify the Danish authorities prior to their passage through territorial waters if that involves passage through the Great Belt, the Samsø Belt or the Øre Sound. Prior authorisation is required for more than 3 warships passing through at the same time	Great Belt; Samsø Belt; Øre Sound
Djibouti	Prior notice required of any passage of nuclear-powered ships and ships carrying nuclear or other radioactive material	Bab al Mandeb

(*Continued overleaf*)

---

18 Article 51, United Nations Charter.

156 *Stuart Kaye*

Table 9.1 Continued.

State	Type of Rights Asserted	Straits
Egypt	Warships have to announce their passage in advance. Ships carrying nuclear material or other hazardous substances require prior authorisation. Contiguous zone 24 nm Security interests	Tiran
Estonia	Warships and research vessels must announce their passage 48 hours in advance. Authorisation must be applied for nuclear-powered ships 30 days prior to their passage	Irbe Strait
Finland	Warships and governmental ships have to announce their passage in advance	Various around the Aaland Islands
Greece	Claims only a 6-nm territorial sea but 10 nm of airspace for air traffic control purposes	Corfu Channel*
Grenada	Warships require prior authorisation	Martinique Channel
India	Warships have to announce their passage in advance. Prior consent to military exercises and manoeuvres in the exclusive economic zone and on the continental shelf; Contiguous zone 24 nm Security interests	Palk Strait*
Indonesia	Warships and all vessels other than merchant ships must announce their passage in advance. 100 nm Ships are not allowed to stop, anchor or cruise 'without legitimate cause'.	Malacca; Singapore; Lombok; Sunda
Iran	Warships, submarines, nuclear-powered ships as well as ships carrying nuclear or other hazardous materials require authorisation; Prohibition of 'military activities and practices' in the exclusive economic zone and on the continental shelf. Contiguous zone 24 nm Security interests	Hormuz
Latvia	Reserves the right to regulate the passage of warships	Irbe Strait
Malaysia	Prior consent to military exercises and manoeuvres in the exclusive economic zone and on the continental shelf	Balabac Strait
Maldives	Warships require prior authorisation. With regard to the EEZ, acknowledge only the right of innocent passage; make entry of fishing and research vessels into the exclusive economic zone conditional upon prior consent	ASL
Mauritius	Warships must announce their passage; Apparently makes the passage of warships and submarines through the EEZ conditional upon prior approval	ASL
Oman	Warships, nuclear-powered ships, submarines and ships carrying hazardous loads require prior authorisation	Hormuz

The Philippines	Expressed concern at UNCLOS III in respect of military activities in the EEZ	Balabac Strait
São Tomé and Príncipe	Reserves the right to regulate the passage of warships	ASL
Seychelles	Warships are required to announce their passage in advance	ASL
South Korea	Warships and government ships have to announce their passage three days in advance	Jeju Strait*
Sri Lanka	Warships require prior authorisation; Contiguous zone 24nm Security interests	Palk Strait*
St. Vincent and Grenadines	Warships require prior authorisation	Bequia Channel; Martinique Channel; St Vincent Passage
Venezuela	15 nm National and security interests	Bocas del Dragón*
Yemen	Warships require prior authorisation; nuclear-powered ships or ships carrying nuclear materials must announce their passage in advance; Contiguous zone 24 nm Security interests	Bab el Mandeb

Notes: * denotes may be a strait with a route of similar convenience.
nm = nautical mile.

Source: S.B. Kaye, 'Freedom of Navigation in a Post 9/11 World: Security and Creeping Jurisdiction', in R. Barnes, D. Freestone and D. Ong (eds), *The Law of the Sea: Prospects and Problems*, Oxford: Oxford University Press, 2006, p. 347.

Table 9.1 includes a number of archipelagic States, who have placed similar notification requirements. Since archipelagic sea lanes passage has the same prohibition on hampering passage, archipelagic States that impose analogous security measures have also been included.

While a jurisdiction based on security is apparently compelling for many States, there is little support for it in the Law of the Sea Convention. The language used in Articles 38 and 42 is unequivocal in terms of the right of transit passage. Nor is the Law of the Sea Convention contrary to the United Nations Charter by prohibiting suspension of transit passage. Like innocent passage, transit passage cannot be exercised if such passage constitutes a threat to 'the sovereignty, territorial integrity or political independence of States bordering the strait'.[19] Were transiting vessels posing a threat of this nature to the coastal State, then nothing in the Convention would prohibit a coastal State from defending itself, in a manner consistent with the United Nations Charter.

However, the mere passage of a foreign warship will not qualify as such a threat. This argument was explicitly rejected by the ICJ in the *Corfu Channel*

---

19 Article 39(1)(b) of Law of the Sea Convention.

case, on the basis that the passage of HM Ships *Saumarez* and *Volage* could be innocent – even at action stations.[20] The *travaux préparatoires* of the 1958 Territorial Sea Convention confirms the acceptance of the decision in the *Corfu Channel* case, and nothing in the Law of the Sea Convention suggests a right to prohibit warships.[21] The Convention does provide that a variety of laws can be applied in the territorial sea to vessels exercising a right of innocent passage. However, Article 30 provides that laws on these subjects cannot be applied to a foreign warship or other sovereign immune vessel, although they can provide a basis for a claim by the coastal State against the flag State of the offending warship. A warship or other vessel can only be ordered to depart the territorial sea in the event that it breaches the laws of the coastal State.[22] There is equally nothing in the transit passage regime which suggests it is unavailable to warships, and further the right is explicitly confirmed for State aircraft,[23] which would include warplanes.

In addition to restrictions based on perceived national security, a number of States have also sought to assert the right to deny vessels carrying ultra-hazardous cargoes, such as nuclear waste for reprocessing or disposal. Such restrictions apply not merely to passage through their territorial sea, but also to navigation within their EEZ. These restrictions have often been manifested in the shadowing or redirection of vessels by warships of the coastal States. They have often been motivated by particular incidents, where vessels have been likely to pass through their waters on planned voyages between other States. The voyages of the *Pacific Pintail, Pacific Teal* and *Pacific Swan* and the *Atatsuki Maru* carrying highly radioactive material attracted protests from a number of States. States such as Argentina, Chile, Antigua and Barbuda, Colombia, Dominican Republic, New Zealand, South Africa and Mauritius have all purported to exclude vessels carrying radioactive ultra-hazardous cargo from their EEZs. Voyages were also condemned by Caricom, representing the Caribbean States, and the South Pacific States.[24] States who have

---

20 *Corfu Channel case*, op. cit., p. 28.
21 Ngantcha, op. cit., pp. 122–130.
22 See Article 30, Law of the Sea Convention provides:

> If any warship does not comply with the laws and regulations of the coastal State concerning passage through the territorial sea and disregards any request for compliance therewith which is made to it, the coastal State may require it to leave the territorial sea immediately.

23 Article 39(3)(a), Law of the Sea Convention distinguishes between the obligations owed by civil aircraft and State aircraft when exercising a right of transit passage. The distinction serves to confirm the right exists for State aircraft, including war planes.
24 See generally M. Roscini, 'The Navigational Rights of Nuclear Ships', *Leiden Journal of International Law*, 15 (2002): 251; J.M. Van Dyke, 'Balancing Navigational Freedom with Environmental and Security Concerns', *Colorado Journal of International Environmental Law and Policy*, 15 (2003): 19; J.M. Van Dyke, 'The Legal Regime Governing Sea Transport of Ultra-hazardous Radioactive Materials', *Ocean Development and International Law*, 33 (2002): 77.

Table 9.2 States that have objected to nuclear ships passing through their territorial sea or EEZs[1]

Antigua and Barbuda	Malta
Argentina	Mauritius
Brazil	Nauru
Chile	New Zealand
Colombia	Oman
Dominican Republic	Papua New Guinea
Egypt	Peru
Fiji	Philippines
Guinea	Saudi Arabia
Indonesia	Singapore
Iran	South Africa
Haiti	Venezuela
Kiribati	Yemen
Malaysia	

Source: Kaye (2006, p. 351).

asserted that they do not permit nuclear cargo vessels in the territorial sea or EEZ are noted in Table 9.2.

The Law of the Sea Convention does not appear to provide support for States who wish to assert the right to deny passage to vessels carrying ultra-hazardous cargoes. In the context of innocent passage, Article 23 of the Convention provides for circumstances where voyages by such vessels are envisaged:

> Foreign nuclear-powered ships and ships carrying nuclear or other inherently dangerous or noxious substances shall, when exercising the right of innocent passage through the territorial sea, carry documents and observe special precautionary measures established for such ships by international agreements.

Restrictions of the type contemplated in Article 23 as yet are not well developed, and international agreements restricting the passage of vessels carrying ultra-hazardous cargoes are still to be concluded. This would seem to mean that such vessels continue to have a right of innocent passage, and by extension a right of transit passage regardless of the attitude of the coastal State.

9.5 Torres Strait compulsory pilotage

A recent contentious example of State practice that has been labelled by at least one publicist as hampering the right of innocent passage is in the context of the Torres Strait. The Torres Strait is the body of water between the northernmost point of the Australian continent and the large island of New Guinea.

The Strait is over 80 nautical miles wide, but is dotted with islands which enclose it within the territorial seas of Australia and Papua New Guinea, making it an international strait. The Torres Strait is one of the most treacherous waterways in the world, as it is beset with numerous coral reefs and extremely confined, narrowing to less than 1 kilometre of navigable water. As the tides of the Indian and Pacific Ocean mix in the Strait, they are difficult to predict and there are exceptionally strong tidal flows, sometimes in excess of 8 knots.[25]

Concern about the dangers of navigating these waters and the risk of accident saw Australia and Papua New Guinea lobby the IMO to introduce a voluntary regime for pilotage through the Torres Strait in early 1990s. This led to IMO Resolution A.710(17) and Resolution MEPC 45(30) which provided for a voluntary regime for certain types of vessels to engage the services of a pilot when passing through Torres Strait.[26]

Concerned that the voluntary regime was proving ineffective, in 2003, Australia and Papua New Guinea lodged a proposal at the International Maritime Organization (IMO) to create a Particularly Sensitive Sea Area in the region. After much negotiation Resolution MEPC 133(53) was adopted by the IMO's Marine Environment Protection Committee on 22 July 2005. It provided in part:

> 3. RECOMMENDS that Governments recognize the need for effective protection of the Great Barrier Reef and Torres Strait region and inform ships flying their flag that they should act in accordance with Australia's system of pilotage for merchant ships 70 m in length and over or oil tankers, chemical tankers, and gas carriers, irrespective of size when navigating:
>
> (a) the inner route of the Great Barrier Reef between the northern extreme of Cape York Peninsula (10° 41′ S) and 16° 40′ S and in Hydrographers Passage; and
>
> (b) the Torres Strait and the Great North East Channel between Booby Island (latitude 10° 36′ S, longitude 141° 54′ E) and Bramble Cay (latitude 09° 09′ S, longitude 143° 53′ E).

This resolution explicitly replaced resolution MEPC 45(30) that encouraged a voluntary pilotage regime. The critical element here is the use of the phrase 'Australia's system of pilotage'. It had the effect of empowering Australia to implement a system for pilotage through Torres Strait, which in turn would see a regime of compulsory pilotage introduced.

---

25 S.B. Kaye, *The Torres Strait* (The Hague: Kluwer Law International, 1997), Chapter 1.
26 See R.C. Beckman, 'PSSAs and Transit Passage – Australia's Pilotage System in the Torres Strait Challenges the IMO and UNCLOS', *Ocean Development and International Law*, 38(2007): 329.

In the following year, the Australian Maritime Safety Authority issued Marine Notice 8/2006. This provided in part:

> These decisions are reflected in IMO Resolution MEPC.133(53), which recommends that Governments recognize the need for effective protection of the Torres Strait and inform ships flying their flag that they should act in accordance with Australia's system of pilotage for merchant ships 70m in length and over or oil tankers, chemical tankers, and liquefied gas carriers, irrespective of size, when navigating the Torres Strait and the Great North East Channel.
>
> Amendments to the Commonwealth *Navigation Act 1912* (the Act) make it an offence under new section 186I to navigate in a compulsory pilotage area without a pilot. A new compulsory pilotage area for the Torres Strait will be specified in Marine Orders Part 54 and further details of that area are reproduced below. Significant penalties will apply to a master or owner who fails to comply with the compulsory pilotage requirements in the Navigation Act and Marine Orders Part 54.
>
> Under the new requirements, section 186J of the Act will require the pilot to provide a certificate to the master in the approved form specifying details about the completed piloted voyage before disembarking the ship. Such a certificate will provide an owner and master evidence that they engaged a pilotage service and complied with the compulsory pilotage requirements of the Act.[27]

With the introduction of these measures, concern was expressed by some States that they were inconsistent with notions of transit passage. The United States and Singapore both indicated they felt the Marine Notice was contrary to Part III of the Law of the Sea Convention.[28]

The requirement to have a pilot would seem to be *prima facie* a measure which might hamper transit passage. It would be possible to imagine, during a strike or other form of industrial action, or if use of the strait increased dramatically, that the services of a pilot might be unavailable for a long period. This in turn would effectively hamper transit passage.

The Australian Government's response to this proposition is to point to the manner of enforcement of the Marine Notice and the Navigation Act 1912 (Cth). Although a vessel requiring a pilot under Australian law transiting Torres Strait without such services would be in breach of statutory obligations, there would be no capacity to enforce the law, unless and until that vessel called at an Australian port. As such, there was no direct 'hampering' of the vessel, but rather a penalty imposed at some indefinite time on a different voyage.

---

27 Australian Marine Notice 8/2006. Available at: http://www.amsa.gov.au/Shipping_Safety/Marine_Notices/2006/Marine_Notice_8-2006.asp (accessed 15 April 2010).
28 Beckman, op. cit., p. 326.

One flaw in this approach is that transit passage is available to vessels not merely using a strait for transit, but also vessels coming alongside at a port along the strait. Although Torres Strait is sparsely inhabited, it does have Port Kennedy at Thursday Island where some coastal shipping does stop. If the Australian argument is to be sustained, there would have to be a prohibition upon Australian authorities enforcing the pilotage laws against vessels transiting through the Strait and stopping at Port Kennedy. Given the nature of the anchorage and the volume of shipping calling at Thursday Island, it is submitted this is not a significant problem at this point.

9.6 Normal mode

A second area of confusion is whether there are limitations on the nature of passage as with innocent passage while undertaking transit passage, or whether the regime is more generous than innocent passage. While there is certainly a difference in structure, with the long list of prohibited activities for innocent passage in Article 19 of the Law of the Sea Convention, some coastal States have sought to argue there should be analogous restrictions for vessels exercising rights of transit passage and archipelagic sealanes passage.[29]

Much of the concern focuses on two elements. The first concerns submarines. Article 20 of the Law of the Convention provides: 'In the territorial sea, submarines and other underwater vehicles are required to navigate on the surface and to show their flag.' This provision makes it clear that to exercise a right of innocent passage, a submarine must surface and display its flag. However, the provision is contained within the Part devoted to innocent passage, and there is no reference to submarines at all in those articles devoted to transit passage or archipelagic sealanes passage. The only provision of potential application in the context of transit passage is Article 39:

> 1. Ships and aircraft, while exercising the right of transit passage, shall:
>   (c) refrain from any activities other than those incident to their normal modes of continuous and expeditious transit unless rendered necessary by *force majeure* or by distress.

The reference to 'normal modes of continuous and expeditious transit' is critical here. A number of maritime States have taken the view that this phrase can accommodate the transit of a submarine through an international strait or archipelagic sealane remaining submerged. This is because modern submarines are not designed to navigate on the surface, and typically navigate submerged in normal circumstances.

---

29 See generally J. Astley and M.N. Schmitt, 'The Law of the Sea and Naval Operations', *Air Force Law Review*, 42 (1997): 119.

The *travaux préparatoires* of the Law of the Sea Convention do not provide much assistance in the interpretation of the phrase 'normal mode' and State practice has typically seen the passage of submarines remaining submerged through international straits and archipelagic sealanes as a matter of some dispute.[30] The United States has regularly exercised its rights with respect to submarines and subsequently advised of these voyages under its Freedom of Navigation (FON) program, often with subsequent protests from affected States.[31]

9.7 Conclusion

Although the international community has built on the work done by the ICJ in the *Corfu Channel* case in dealing with rights of passage through international straits, it is fair to say they remain a source of contention. Transit passage may be neatly elucidated in Part III of the Law of the Sea Convention, but it is clearly undermined by States asserting a 'security jurisdiction' to prevent or restrict the use of international straits by warships. The principal contention of Albania in the *Corfu Channel* case was that foreign warships were not permitted to pass as of right through its territorial sea, and the Court, with some provisos, rejected this contention.[32] It is therefore in some respects remarkable that over 60 years on, some States essentially reprise Albania's position, even though the rights enunciated by the Court have changed into part of an extremely widely adopted international agreement. That the States asserting such a security jurisdiction include Albania, which would apply restrictions over warships to the waters of the *Corfu Channel*, does seem to render the Case a nonsense.

Yet to dismiss the relevance of the *Corfu Channel* case on this basis is to underestimate its impact. The Court's consideration of the nature of innocent passage and the availability of passage rights through an international strait were used as the basis for the International Law Commission's work that led to the 1958 Convention on the Territorial Sea and Contiguous Zone and from that much of the Law of the Sea Convention. Contemporary international law on the law of straits owes much to the *Corfu Channel* case, and this is the case regardless of inconsistency of compliance by States.

---

30 Nordquist, op. cit., Vol. II, p. 323 *et seq.*
31 For a brief discussion of the FON program, see G. Galdorisi, 'The United Nations Convention on the Law of the Sea: A National Security Perspective', *American Yearbook of International Law*, 89 (1995): 208–213.
32 *Corfu Channel case*, op. cit., *ICJ Pleadings*, Vol. II, pp. 129ff.

10 Dangerous waters and international law

The *Corfu Channel* case, warships, and sovereignty irritants

Rob McLaughlin[*]

[The UNCLOS I debates] indicate that juridical authority played a subordinate role to other motivations and interests . . . In support of their views, the delegates drew very sparingly from legal authority; rather they argued the issues in terms of the practical consequences. On occasion, they advocated proposals which were, in fact, contrary to earlier declared law on the matter. The issue of warships illustrates the relative disinterest of the delegates in legal precedent.[1]

10.1 Introduction

What is it about ships which so provokes modern international law? In the *Caroline* incident, action by British agents in killing a man on board a US ship, and sending the ship in flames over the Niagara Falls, provoked a diplomatic correspondence which underpins the modern law of national self-defence.[2] Piracy, a crime committed by ships against other ships, became the first modern crime of universal jurisdiction.[3] In the *Muscat Dhows* case, the critical issue of the actual effects of the connection between a State's flag and its sovereignty came to the fore.[4] The *SS Wimbledon* case, concerning a British ship under French charter, carrying a cargo embarked in Greece, destined for Poland for use in her conflict with the Soviet Union, through a German canal, provided

---

[*] The views expressed in this chapter are those of the author and should not be taken to be the views or official position of the Department of Defence or the Royal Australian Navy.
[1] S. Slonim, 'The Right of Innocent Passage and the 1958 Geneva Conference on the Law of the Sea', *Columbia Journal of Transnational Law*, 5 (1966): 126–127.
[2] See R. Jennings, 'The *Caroline* and *McLeod* Cases', *American Journal of International Law*, 32 (1938): 82.
[3] See *The Case of the SS Lotus, Judgment No. 10 of 7 September 1927, PCIJ*, Series A, *Dissenting Opinion of Judge Moore*, p. 62; M.N. Shaw, *International Law* (Cambridge: Cambridge University Press, 2003), p. 234; A.P. Rubin, 'The Law of Piracy', *US Naval War College International Law Studies*, 63 (1988): 1.
[4] *Muscat Dhows Case (France v. Great Britain), Arbitral Award*, The Hague, 8 August 1905, available at: http://www.haguejusticeportal.net/eCache/DEF/6/926.html.

the backdrop for the PCIJ's first judgment.[5] And in the *Corfu Channel* case, the ICJ's first judgment, the Court was called upon, in effect, to make an early postwar declaration (either positively, or by inference – depending upon one's interpretation) that consciously and intentionally generating friction by irritating another State's sovereignty is a legitimate and lawful act, regardless of its purpose, so long as it does not transgress any applicable international law. Indeed, it is arguable that the underpinning rationale of the majority judgment is that an act in accordance with law, regardless of the sovereign intent behind it, by definition cannot rise to the level of a legally condemnable threat to international peace and security.

10.2 Outline

The intent in this short study is to examine two closely related issues, raised in the *Corfu Channel* case, which are of particular interest to the conduct of naval operations. The first is the political and legal utility of using ships to provoke sovereignty frictions. The second is debate about blanket 'characterisation' of warship conduct – most particularly through the medium of warship passage and regimes of special authorisation. I will undertake this review by outlining the context of each debate, determining what it is that the *Corfu Channel* case had to say about each issue, and then briefly recounting some developments since 1949.

10.3 The political and legal utility of ships as sovereignty irritants

There are two closely related reasons why ships provide such rich opportunities to provoke and sponsor the formation or crystallisation of international law. Both are very clearly exhibited in the *Corfu Channel* case.

10.3.1 *Ease of interaction*

First, it is very easy for ships to interact with another State's ships or with the territory or territorial seas of other States. Ships unavoidably interact with other sovereignties, thus creating the potential for immediate international frictions because they represent (if not actually are) themselves moving units of sovereignty. As Robin Churchill and Vaughan Lowe note:

> The ascription of nationality to ships is one of the most important means by which public order is maintained at sea. As well as indicating what rights a ship enjoys and to what obligations it is subject, the nationality of a vessel indicates which State is to exercise flag State jurisdiction over the vessel. Nationality also indicates which State is responsible in

---

5 *The SS Wimbledon, Judgment No.1 of 17 August 1923, PCIJ*, Series A.

international law for the vessel in cases where an act or omission of the vessel is attributable to the State, and which State is entitled to exercise diplomatic protection on behalf of the vessel.[6]

Furthermore, whereas many highly visible sovereign acts that touch so tangibly upon the sovereignty of another State are committed or authorised at high levels, a ship can readily blunder into such incidents with little or no planning, and indeed while controlled by a person who may not even be a national of that flag State. It can even be the case that warships are placed in situations where interaction with another State's ships can unexpectedly escalate or intensify through mere proximity. Indeed this is the very reason that the then USSR and the USA negotiated the 1972 INCSEA Agreement.[7] As the US Navy's *Annotated Commanders Handbook on the Law of Naval Operations* explains:

> In order to better assure the safety of navigation and flight of their respective warships and military aircraft during encounters at sea, the United States and the former Soviet Union in 1972 entered into the [INCSEA Agreement]. This navy-to-navy agreement . . . has been highly successful in minimizing the potential for harassing actions and navigational one-upmanship between US and former Soviet units operating in close proximity at sea.[8]

In 1973, certain provisions of the 1972 INCSEA were extended via a Protocol to cover non-military shipping. Additionally – providing yet another indication of the high visibility and unpredictability of ships as sovereignty irritants – similar agreements were concluded between the then USSR and the

---

6 R.R. Churchill and A.V. Lowe, *The Law of the Sea* (Manchester: Manchester University Press, 1999), p. 257. See also, Shaw, op. cit., p. 545:

> The foundation of the maintenance of order on the high seas has rested upon the concept of the nationality of the ship, and the consequent jurisdiction of the flag state over the ship. It is, basically, the flag state that will enforce the rules and regulations not only of its own municipal law but of international law as well.

As Judge Moore held in his dissent in the case of the SS *Lotus*, op. cit., p. 60:

> It is universally admitted that a ship on the high seas is, for jurisdictional purposes, to be considered as a part of the territory of the country to which it belongs; and there is nothing in the law or in the reason of the thing to show that, in the case of injury to life and property on board a ship on the high seas, the operation of this principle differs from its operation on land.

7 *Agreement Between the Government of the United States of America and the Government of the Union of Soviet Socialist Republics on the Prevention of Incidents On and Over the High Seas*, Moscow, 25 May 1972, 23 UST 1168. 852 UNTS. 151 ('Incidents at Sea Agreement' or 'INCSEA').
8 US Navy, *Annotated Supplement to the Commander's Handbook on the Law of Naval Operations*, publicly available as *International Law Studies*, 73 (1999): 187. The *Annotated Commander's Handbook* has undergone a number of revisions since 1999, but remains consistent as to the references made in this regard.

UK (1986); the then Federal Republic of Germany (1988); and Canada, France, and Italy (1989). The INCSEA Agreement continues in force between the USA and Russia and the USA and Ukraine.[9]

10.3.2 Conscious political agency

Second, and conversely, it is equally clear that this very attribute of a ship as a moving expression of a State's sovereignty makes ships very useful as proxies for conscious political acts. But the affront provoked by the fact of a ship's presence or its navigational conduct is clearly, and very conveniently, a lesser form of 'provocation' than crossing a land border. As Judge Alvarez observed in his separate opinion in the *Corfu Channel* case:

> Sovereignty confers rights upon States and imposes obligations on them. These rights are not the same and are not exercised in the same way in every sphere of international law. I have in mind the four traditional spheres – terrestrial, maritime, fluvial and lacustrine – to which must be added three new ones – aerial, polar and floating (floating islands). The violation of these rights is not of equal gravity in all these different spheres.[10]

This is particularly so with warships, which can both create a significant level of affront, while simultaneously preserving for the ship itself a greater degree of sovereign protection. This is well expressed in Marshall CJ's judgment in *The Schooner Exchange v. McFaddon* (US Supreme Court, 1812):[11]

> She [a public armed ship] constitutes a part of the military force of her nation; acts under the immediate and direct command of the sovereign; is employed by him in national objects. He has many and powerful motives for preventing those objects from being defeated by the interference of a foreign State. Such interference cannot take place without affecting his power and his dignity.

In terms of offence caused by presence, the warship – as the Chief Justice observed – is thus an entirely different proposition to that of an army. By comparison, a warship's presence carries with it maximum protections and minimum immediate legal consequences:

> But the rule which is applicable to armies [that they can never gain immunities of any other description than those which war gives by entering a

---

9 Ibid., pp. 147–149.
10 *Corfu Channel case, Judgment of April 9th 1949, ICJ Reports 1949*, Separate Opinion of Judge Alvarez, p. 43.
11 *The Schooner Exchange v. McFaddon*, US 7 Cranch 116 (1812), p. 144. Online edition. Available at: HTTP: supreme.justia.com/ us/ 11/116/case.html (accessed 16 December 2010).

foreign territory against the will of its sovereign] does not appear to be equally applicable to ships of war entering the ports of a friendly power. The injury inseparable from the march of an army through an inhabited country, and the dangers often – indeed generally – attending it do not ensue from admitting a ship of war without special license into a friendly port.[12]

As such, sending a ship – and most especially a warship – to harass another State's ships, to sail through that State's waters, or to do some act that is sure to provoke a response from that State is (certainly legally, and also generally politically) a less risky means of sending a message than deploying forces on the ground in another State's land territory, or an aircraft into its national airspace. A warship steaming a few nautical miles off the coastline – that is, within the Territorial Sea of the coastal State – is a very powerful exhibition of latent force.

10.3.3 *The* Corfu Channel *case . . .*

This conscious use of warships, and their ready capacity to interact with other sovereignties as a very public agent of their own sovereign, is simply gunboat diplomacy – a concept that was well recognised, and endorsed, in the *Corfu Channel* case, and which remains useful to and well utilised by States today. Indeed, the UK was quite open about the political aim of the Corfu Channel transit – the instructions from the Admiralty to the Commander-in-Chief Mediterranean that the government wished 'to know whether the Albanian Government have learnt to behave themselves'[13] could not be more clearly, if

---

12 Ibid., p. 141.
13 *Corfu Channel case*, op. cit., pp. 27–82. That such transits are overtly political, calibrated for specific political effects and messages, and accepted as such in international practice, is also evident in the clear UK statement that a planned return transit by HM Ships *Orion* and *Superb* was cancelled 'so as to avoid the possibility of a fresh incident while tempers were hot' – Reply Submitted, Under the Order of the Court of 26th March, 1948, by the Government of the United Kingdom of Great Britain and Northern Ireland, *ICJ Reports 1950*, p. 259 (*UK Reply*). Similarly, the UK overtly recognised the political utility of using warship interactions with elements of coastal state sovereignty as a means of conducting international relations, in its response to the allegation (contained in the Albanian Counter-Memorial) that the UK laid mines in the Corfu Channel on 12 November 1946. Albania argued that the UK laid these mines in order that they could then sweep for them on 13 November, while monitored by the invited French Naval observer, in order to generate a pretext for UK action against Albania. The Albanian allegation, the UK asserted, was that:

> [T]he United Kingdom, in other words, fabricated evidence, in order to have the incident examined meticulously by an international organ or by the International Court and then obligingly disclosed to the Court, which is investigating the matter, the evidence from which these machinations are clearly to be seen. Leaving aside the aspersions thus made . . . the suggestion implies on the part of the Government of the United Kingdom an almost incredible naiveté and the reckless taking of risks extraordinarily disproportionate to the end desired.
>
> (Ibid., pp. 263–264)

undiplomatically, expressed. The ICJ explicitly recognised this as both an international fact of practice and a legitimate political motive:

> It is shown by the Admiralty telegram of September 21st . . . admitted by the United Kingdom Agent, that the object of sending the warships through the Strait was not only to carry out a passage for the purposes of navigation, but also to test Albania's attitude . . . The legality of this measure taken by the Government of the United Kingdom cannot be disputed, provided that it was carried out in a manner consistent with the requirements of international law. The 'mission' was designed to affirm a right which had been unjustly denied.[14]

10.3.4 . . . and since

This conscious, calculated, and overt use of the broad capacity for one State's warships to interact so easily with another State's sovereignty – so clearly expressed by the UK, and so categorically accepted by the ICJ in the *Corfu Channel* case – has continued apace since. Nowhere is this more evident than in the most public, co-ordinated, and wide-ranging example of this recognition today – the US Freedom of Navigation (FON) program. The purpose of the FON program, formally commenced in 1979, was expressed by then President Reagan in his 1983 *Oceans Policy Statement*:

> [T]he United States will exercise and assert its navigation and overflight rights and freedoms on a worldwide basis in a manner that is consistent with the balance of interests reflected in the [1982 UN Convention on the Law of the Sea]. The United States will not, however, acquiesce in unilateral acts of other States designed to restrict the rights and freedoms of the international community in navigation and overflight and other related high seas uses.[15]

As many incidents attest, the presence of warships asserting an international right still has the capacity to both send a message and provoke assessable responses – the 'Black Sea Bumping incident' on 13 March 1986, when US Ships *Yorktown* and *Caron* transited within six nautical miles of the Soviet Crimean coast, leading to a response involving Soviet naval, air and coastguard forces, being but the best-known example.[16] Similarly, assertions of other rights – such as intelligence collection operations outside the Territorial Sea – also continue to provide a mechanism by which States provoke or irritate

---

14 *Corfu Channel case*, op. cit., p. 30.
15 Extracted in Annex A2–7 of the US Navy's *Annotated Commander's Handbook*, op. cit., p. 187.
16 W. E. Butler, 'Innocent Passage and the 1982 Convention: The Influence of Soviet Law and Policy', *American Journal of International Law*, 81(2) (1987): 343–346.

sovereignty friction points in a very physical and tangible manner, in order to assert or deny a claim, or to assess reactions and responses with an eye to wider political purposes or circumstances. The most famous example is the USS *Pueblo* incident on 23 January 1968, when North Korean forces seized a US Navy intelligence gathering vessel, claiming it was within DPRK territorial waters.[17] The USNS *Impeccable* incident (navigational harassment between a US ocean surveillance vessel and Chinese vessels off Hainan Island on 8 March 2009), the sinking of a North Korean 'spy ship' by the Japan coastguard in December 2001, and the sinking of the Republic of Korea Ship *Cheonan* on 26 March 2010, are but three of a number of even more recent examples.[18]

For these reasons (and others), ships are, consequently, very useful agents for testing and forming international law. As the *Corfu Channel* case so clearly illustrates and asserts, the use of ships to irritate sovereignty friction points – as opposed to violating sovereignty and claiming an excuse (as the UK did in relation to *Operation Retail*, the 12–13 November 1946 minesweeping operation condemned by the Court) – is not only a legitimate and lawful act, but also a routine political act. Indeed, one suspects that it was precisely because such transits were (and remain) so useful and widespread as a political tool that the ICJ, if honest to the provenance of the law, would have been hard pressed to have found otherwise.

10.4 The 'characterisation' of warship conduct

Infinitely more significantly than a commercial ship bearing a State's flag, the conduct of a warship bearing a State's flag is considered indivisible from the conduct of the State as a sovereign entity. The *prima facie* assumption – particularly with the speed and quality of modern communications – will always be that what a warship does, it does because it has been instructed to do so, and thus that its acts are directly attributable to a conscious political decision of its sovereign. The adjunct to this assumption is that the warship carries with it a greater level of 'sovereignty' than other ships under the same flag. While this is undoubtedly true in a political sense, it is not necessarily

---

17 See A. P. Rubin, 'The Impact of the *Pueblo* Incident in International Law', *Oregon Law Review*, 49(1) (1969): 1. See also, D.P. O'Connell, *The Influence of Law upon Seapower* (Manchester: Manchester University Press, 1975), p. 65. The vessel was never returned to the USA, but the ship's company were released from DPRK detention on 22 December 1968.
18 On the USNS *Impeccable* incident, see '"Reckless" Chinese ships harassed US navy vessel', *Australian Broadcasting Authority*, 10 March 2009, available at: http://www.abc.net.au/news/stories/ 2009/03/10/2511825.htm. On the sinking of a 'North Korean spy ship' by the Japan coastguard in December 2001, see Marcus Warren, 'Japan sinks "North Korea spying ship"', *The Telegraph*, 24 December 2001, available at: http://www.telegraph.co.uk/news/worldnews/asia/northkorea/1366227/Japan-sinks-North-Korea-spying-ship.html. On the ROKS *Cheonan*, see "Joint Civilian-Military Investigation Group: Statement", 20 May 2010, available at: http://www.globalsewrity.org/military/library/report/2010/100520_jcmigroks-cheonan.htm

true in a pure legal sense. A prime example is the HMS *Danae* incident alongside Rio de Janeiro in April 1977. A number of junior ratings from *Danae* had proceeded ashore on leave and had met up with an apparently wealthy British expatriate who invited them to his home for dinner. In return they invited him on board *Danae*. He was asked to leave the ship soon thereafter when the officers identified him as Ronald Biggs, the 'great train robber' who had fled British jurisdiction. In response to a question as to what article of the Queen's Regulations and Admiralty Instructions had allowed that Mr Biggs be 'invited to leave' rather than arrested, the Secretary of State for Defence (Mr Duffy) responded that:

> Whilst one of Her Majesty's ships in a foreign jurisdiction has extra-territoriality – that is, it is immune from local jurisdiction and enforcement of local laws – it is not correct to regard it as floating United Kingdom territory, and all laws of the United Kingdom do not necessarily apply to all persons on board that ship. The relevant provisions of the Criminal Law Act [1977 – powers of citizens arrest, applicable in England and Wales] are such an example.[19]

The modern view of 'sovereign immunity' of warships does not markedly differ from this, however the degree to which flag State law applies on board warships does still vary significantly between States.[20]

10.4.1 Special authorisation for warships

It is important to recognise that the ICJ's *Corfu Channel* case merits judgment only addresses the specific situation applicable to the Corfu Channel – what would now be called transit passage through a strait used for international navigation.[21]

> It is, in the opinion of the Court, generally recognized and in accordance with international custom that States in time of peace have a right to send their warships through straits used for international navigation between two parts of the high seas without the previous authorization of a coastal State, provided that the passage is *innocent*. Unless otherwise prescribed in

---

19 Mr Duffy, in response to a question from Rear-Admiral Morgan-Giles, HC Deb 29 April 1977, vol. 930 cc449-50W. For the background to the incident, see Mr Duffy in response to a question from Mr Woodall, HC Deb 22 April 1977, vol. 930 cc167-8W. Both can be found at: http://hansard.millbanksystems.com/written_answers/1977/apr.
20 On sovereign immunity, see *Law of the Sea Convention* 1982, Articles 32, 58(2), 95, and 236.
21 *Law of the Sea Convention* 1982, Article 37, more precisely, 'straits which are used for international navigation between one part of the high seas or an exclusive economic zone and another part of the high seas or an exclusive economic zone'.

an international convention, there is no right for a coastal State to prohibit such passage through straits in time of peace.[22]

The UK recognised this factual limitation to straits in its memorial.[23] However, to bolster their respective claims as to the State of the applicable law, both the UK and Albania addressed the broader issue of warship innocent passage through territorial waters generally,[24] and it is upon this broader canvas that the issue of special authorisation regimes for warships is best assessed.

10.4.2 'Character' and 'innocence'

The *Corfu Channel* case – most particularly through the memorials of the two parties in relation to the 22 October 1946 transit by two cruisers and two destroyers – discloses two fundamental debates touching upon the issue of prior authorisation regimes. The first fundamental debate relates to the Albanian claim that it was the 'offensive character' of the warships that is central to defining 'innocence'. There were two core elements of the Albanian claim.[25]

---

22 *Corfu Channel case*, op. cit., p. 28. See also, p. 29, where the Court further reiterated this limitation of scope in its judgment to 'international highways through which passage cannot be prohibited by a coastal State in time of peace'. And, again, p. 30:

> In these circumstances, it is unnecessary to consider the more general question, much debated by the Parties, whether States under international law have a right to send warships in time of peace through territorial waters not included in a strait.

23 For example: Memorial Submitted by the Government of the United Kingdom of Great Britain and Northern Ireland, *ICJ Reports 1950*, p. 42 (*UK Memorial*); *UK Reply*, op. cit., p. 256 and pp. 295–299. See, for example, p. 289:

> The Government of the United Kingdom will discuss the legal position with regard to the passage of warships both through territorial waters, which are not straits forming international highways, and also through such straits, because the Albanian Counter-Memorial has done so. It is, however, strictly only the latter question which is relevant to the present case and the former is pertinent only in so far as it throws light upon the latter.
>
> (*Corfu Channel case*, op. cit., p. 27)

24 *UK Memorial*, op. cit., pp. 42–46; *UK Reply*, op. cit., pp. 289–295.
25 There were other, more specific and incidental, elements to the Albanian claim. One of these was that the UK violated Albania's sovereignty by intentionally entering Albanian internal waters. However, this claim raised no real legal issues as the UK agreed that warships have no right of innocent passage in internal waters, and argued that even if either *Volage* or *Saumarez* had briefly entered Albanian internal waters as they exited the channel, it was only due to *force majeure* as *Volage*, herself just struck by a mine, manoeuvred to tow (stern first) the crippled *Saumarez* (also stern first) back to port. Manoeuvrability going astern – even without the added complexities of significant damage, and towing another vessel – is very different to that when steaming ahead. See *UK Memorial*, op. cit., p. 44; *UK Reply*, op. cit., p. 260. This is, of course, a different argument to that employed by the UK in attempted justification of the later minesweeping operation.

Element one was the general assertion that the UK Government failed to give notice of the intended transit. Element two rested on a number of specifically 'offensive' components of the actual transit: The transit was a 'political mission'; there were 'troops' in the ships; the crews were at action stations; and the ships were in 'combat formation' and carrying out 'manoeuvres'.[26] However, both these claims are different to, and much more limited than, claims based in the broader assertion that warships are by definition never in a position to claim 'innocent' passage precisely because their inherently offensive character precludes it. This is a much more general, ambit objection, which traces its modern heritage to statements such as Judge Elihu Root's assertion in the *North Atlantic Coast Fisheries Arbitration* that, in relation to the territorial sea, 'warships may not pass without consent into this zone because they threaten. Merchant ships may pass and repass because they do not threaten.'[27]

The ICJ did not engage with this debate in detail – as O'Connell noted on this point, the ICJ's opinion was 'dogmatically stated and the Court eschewed any rationalisation of the principle'.[28] It is clear that they rejected the first Albanian claim to the effect that the offensive character of the transit was to be found in the fact that the UK did not notify Albania in advance. As noted previously, the Court explicitly affirmed for States the 'right to send their warships through straits used for international navigation between two parts of the high seas without the previous authorization of a coastal State, provided that the passage is *innocent*'.[29] In relation to the second Albanian assertion as to defining the transit as 'offensive', the Court (tantalisingly) referred to the concept of 'manner' as a definitive element of assessing innocence: 'It remains, therefore, to consider whether the *manner* in which the passage was carried out was consistent with the principle of innocent passage . . .'.[30] The Court concluded that:

> In view of the firing from the Albanian battery on May 15th, this measure of precaution [steaming through the Channel at action stations] cannot, in itself, be regarded as unreasonable. But four warships – two cruisers and two destroyers – passed in this manner, with crews at action stations, ready to retaliate quickly if fired upon. They passed one after another through this narrow channel, close to the Albanian coast, at a time of political tension in this region. The intention must have been, not only to test Albania's attitude, but at the same time to demonstrate such force

---

26 *UK Reply*, op. cit., pp. 278–279; *Corfu Channel case*, op. cit., p. 30.
27 'Proceedings' (1912) 11 *US North Atlantic Fisheries Arbitration: Proceedings Before the Permanent Court of Arbitration in The Hague* at 2007.
28 D.P. O'Connell, *The International Law of the Sea* (ed. Ivan Shearer) (Oxford: Clarendon Press, 1982), pp. 312–313.
29 *Corfu Channel case*, op. cit., p. 28.
30 Ibid., p. 30.

that she would abstain from firing again on passing ships. Having regard, however, to all the circumstances of the case ... the Court is unable to characterize these measures taken by the United Kingdom authorities as a violation of Albania's sovereignty.[31]

Additionally, the Court explicitly recognised that the UK's open admission that '[T]he most was made of the opportunities to study Albanian defences at close range'[32] – was not sufficient to characterise the transit as 'offensive':

> With regard to the observations of coastal defences made after the explosions, these were justified by the fact that two ships had just been blown up and that, in this critical situation, their commanders might fear that they would be fired on from the coast, as on May 15th.[33]

As an aside, it could be claimed that this finding by the Court is at direct odds with where the law has since progressed in terms of the *Law of the Sea Convention* 1982 Article 19(2)(c) assertion that 'any act aimed at collecting information to the prejudice of the defence or security of the coastal State' is an act prejudicial to the peace, good order and security of that coastal State.[34] However, this would be the wrong conclusion to draw – it is clear that the Court's approval of the warships' actions in this case was intimately linked to unit self-defence, not a general statement of authorisation as a component of innocent passage.

10.4.3 Distilling the law

The second debate touching upon the issue of prior authorisation regimes is of a more theoretical nature, and goes to both the sources of law and the weight to be attributed to those sources. It is a debate the ICJ did not engage with in detail, except to the extent that it is implicit in its narrow findings as to the existence of an international right of warship transit through straits, without prior notification or permission, provided it is innocent.[35] But it is nevertheless significant in that it provided an early indication of the two main, and continuing, schools of thought on the juridical nature of the right of innocent passage – particularly for warships. Indeed the battlelines in terms of legal argument have shifted little since the *Corfu Channel* case, even while a number of States have nevertheless changed sides in the debate as a whole (including the then USSR, twice – after 1958, from 'no' to 'yes' as to a prior

---

31 Ibid., p. 31. The cruisers were HM Ships *Mauritius* and *Leander*; the destroyers were HM Ships *Saumarez* and *Volage*.
32 *Corfu Channel case*, op. cit., p. 32.
33 Ibid.
34 *Law of the Sea Convention* 1982 Article 19(2)(c).
35 *Corfu Channel case*, op. cit., p. 28.

authorisation/notification requirement, and then back to 'no' in 1989).[36] There are, however, still a number of States – including, it should be noted, Albania – which still assert that warships may be subject to a regime of prior authorisation or notification for innocent passage.[37] Syria's legislation is indicative of a prior *authorisation* regime:

Article 9
(a) Foreign warships, ships of a dangerous nature, submarines and other diving vessels shall enjoy the right of innocent passage only upon obtaining the approval of the Ministry of Defence and provided that they satisfy all the conditions, standards and reservations in force internationally.[38]

South Korea provides an example of a prior *notification* regime:

Article 5
(1) Foreign ships enjoy the right of innocent passage through the

---

36 On 1954–58, see Soviet Academy of Sciences Department of Law, *International Law*, 1947, quoted in O.G. de Vries Reilingh, 'Warships in Territorial Waters: Their Right of Innocent Passage', *Netherlands Yearbook of International Law*, 2 (1972): 48–49; and W. E. Butler, 'Soviet Concepts of Innocent Passage', *Harvard International Law Journal*, 7 (1965–66): 118, discussing the 1960 *Soviet Statute on the Protection of the State Borders of the USSR*, Article 16. On 1989, see *Joint Statement by the United States of America and the Union of Soviet Socialist Republics: Uniform Interpretation of Rules of International Law Governing Innocent Passage*, Jackson Hole, Wyoming, 23 September 1989, operative paragraph 2 – 'All ships, including warships, regardless of cargo, armament or means of propulsion, enjoy the right of innocent passage through the territorial sea in accordance with international law, for which neither prior notification nor authorization is required.'

37 One recent assessment (J. Ashley Roach, in July 2007) was that 39 States still impose some form of impermissible restriction on warship innocent passage: Albania, Algeria, Antigua and Barbuda, Bangladesh, Barbados, Brazil, Bulgaria, Cambodia, Cape Verde, China, Congo, Croatia, Denmark, Egypt, Finland, Grenada, Guyana, India, Indonesia, Iran, South Korea, Libya, Maldives, Malta, Mauritius, Myanmar, Oman, Pakistan, the Philippines, Poland, Romania, St Vincent, Seychelles, Somalia, Sri Lanka, Sudan, Syria, UAE, Vietnam. See http://www.authorstream.com/Presentation/Peppar-9552-Roach-Internal-Waters-TS-Innocent-Passage-INTERNAL-WATERS-TERRITORIAL-SEA-INNOCENT-PASSAGE-roach-internal-waters-ts-and-innocent-passage-ppt-powerpoint/. For a post-1982 expression of the continuing nature of the debate, see S. Jin, 'The Question of Innocent Passage of Warships After UNCLOS III' *Marine Policy*, 13(1): (1982): 67:

> State practice has been dualistic rather than monistic. One group of states, mostly European and North American, have made no distinction between warships and merchant ships or left the matter unregulated. Another group of states, mainly Asian, African and Latin American, have made some requirements for the passage of warships. And both groups of states hold the conviction that their own practice is in accordance with international law.

38 *Law No. 28, dated 19 November 2003 – Definition Act of Internal Waters and Territorial Sea Limits of the Syrian Arab Republic*, Article 9, available at: http://www.un.org/Depts/los/LEGISLATIONANDTREATIES/PDFFILES/syr_2003e.pdf.

territorial sea of the Republic of Korea so long as the passage is not prejudicial to the peace, public order or security of the Republic of Korea. When a foreign warship or a government ship operated for non-commercial purposes intends to pass through the territorial sea, it shall give a prior notice to the authorities concerned under the conditions as provided for by the Presidential Decree.[39]

Denmark provides an example of a more targeted and specific regime incorporating both authorisation and notification elements, although the authorisation ('permission') elements merely reflect the State of the law as regards internal waters, and (almost) as regards stopping or anchoring in the Territorial Sea:

> 3 (2) Simultaneous passage of the Great Belt, Samsoe Belt or the Sound of more than three warships [of] the same nationality shall be allowed, however, but subject to prior notification through diplomatic channels...
> 4 (2) Passage of Hollaenderdybet/Drogden and passage of the Little Belt and, in connection therewith, the necessary navigation by the shortest route through internal waters between Funen, Endelave and Samsoe shall be allowed, however, subject to advance notification through diplomatic channels.[40]

This particular debate is evident in the *Corfu Channel* case on two levels: The prudential concern as to the weight which the practice of States is to hold in relation to inference from theory on the legal nature of 'territory'; and whether the right for warships is an expression of law, or mere international comity. The essence of this debate is captured in the UK and Albanian memorials in their discussions of the 1930 Hague Codification Conference, and the writings of Gilbert Gidel. The UK position was that both the records of the 1930 Hague Conference, and State practice, clearly indicated that the right of warship innocent passage was considered to be a general rule of law, not a mere 'matter of comity'. The Albanian position, placing reliance on Gidel, was

---

39 *Territorial Sea and Contiguous Zone Act: Law No. 3037*, Promulgated on 31 December 1977, Amended by Law No. 4986, which was promulgated on 6 December 1995, Article 5, available at: http://www.un.org/Depts/los/LEGISLATIONANDTREATIES/PDF-FILES/KOR_1996_Decree.pdf.

40 *Ordinance Governing the Admission of Foreign Warships and Military Aircraft to Danish Territory in Time of Peace*, 1999, Part 2, Articles 3, 4, available at: http://www.un.org/Depts/los/ LEGISLATIONANDTREATIES/ PDFFILES/DNK_1999_Ordinance.pdf. On prior authorisation for passage in internal waters, and stopping or anchoring in the territorial sea, see Article 3(1). The Ordinance excuses stopping or anchoring by warships engaged in innocent passage so long as it is '*essential* for ordinary navigation'. The *Law of the Sea Convention* 1982 Article 18(2) definition of continuous and expeditious passage permits stopping and anchoring 'in so far as the same are *incidental* to ordinary navigation'.

that both the records of the Conference, and logical reasoning from the broader concept of 'territory', indicated the opposite. The UK response was based on three elements, aimed at the critical propositions inherent in the Albanian claim. The first was to explain the 'proper' construction of Draft Article 12 from the 1930 Hague Codification Conference, placing significant weight on the negotiating history of the Article and emphasising that the settled text was clearly a result of compromise between the (at that time) primary advocate and the primary denier of the right of warship innocent passage without prior authorisation or notification – the UK and the USA respectively.

The second element of the UK response was that Gidel himself had recognised that his view was a 'small minority' view among writers.[41] It is clear that Judge Alvarez (along with the perhaps more partisan Dr Ecer) sympathised with the Albanian position. Judge Alvarez – arguably the more eloquent advocate for this view – was not convinced that the law required warships and merchant ships to be treated similarly in relation to innocent passage. In his Separate Opinion, Judge Alvarez found that although merchant ships were possessed of an international right, not a mere coastal State concession, to innocent passage through both straits and territorial seas, '[T]he position is not the same in the case of warships':

> As war has been outlawed henceforward, the mission of these ships can only be to ensure the legitimate defence of the countries to which they belong. Therefore, although they may effect an innocent passage through straits forming an international highway between two free seas, in other cases the coastal States are entitled to regulate the passage, especially with a view to the protection of their own security or interests, but they are not entitled to forbid it.[42]

That Judge Alvarez was an advocate of the 'comity' view of warship innocent passage (to the extent of permitting regimes of prior notification or authorisation, so long as they did not ultimately 'forbid' passage) is reinforced by his obiter on the issue of UN operations and their impact on innocent

---

41 *UK Reply*, op. cit., pp. 289–292. The specific debate concerned the records of the 1930 Hague Codification Conference in relation to Draft Article 12:

> As a general rule a coastal State will not forbid the passage of foreign warships in its territorial sea and will not require a previous authorisation or notification. The coastal State has the right to regulate the conditions of such passage. Submarines shall navigate on the surface.

The UK claim was that Gidel (*Le droit international public de la Mer*) had incorrectly assessed Draft Articles 4 and 12, leading him to conclude that 'the liberty of passage of warships is not a right, but a tolerance on the part of the territorial State'.

42 *Corfu Channel case*, op. cit., Individual Opinion of Judge Alvarez, p. 47.

passage. In dealing with this exception to the comity rule, he observed that warships 'only enjoy an unrestricted right of passage when they are engaged in an international mission assigned to them by the United Nations'.[43]

Gidel, and to a lesser extent Alvarez, remained the touchstones for the prior authorisation or notification argument for decades following the *Corfu Channel* case. Jaroslav Zourek (Czechoslovakia), for example, referred approvingly to Gidel during the International Law Commission's 1954 session, where he asserted that 'the passage of foreign warships through the territorial sea [is] a concession on the part of the coastal State'.[44] He was not alone in this view, being echoed in its essence by Roberto Cordova (Mexico). But this view was itself challenged at the ILC by Sir Gerald Fitzmaurice and Sir Hersch Lauterpacht (UK), Georges Scelle (France), JPA François (The Netherlands), and Carlos Salamanca (Bolivia) on the grounds (*inter alia*) that the right was one of law, not mere coastal State comity.[45] However, the question has continued to bedevil discussions with little change to the post-war lines first drawn in the *Corfu Channel* case: Draft Article 24 on warship innocent passage at UNCLOS I (subsequently not included in the 1958 Convention) was altered at the ILC's 1956 session to include a text affirming that such passage 'may' be subject to a previous notification or authorisation regime, but that such approval would 'normally' be granted;[46] and as late as 1982 at UNCLOS III, Algeria, Bahrain, Benin and 25 other States proposed an amendment to the draft text which would have allowed coastal States to add 'security' to the list of matters upon which they could adopt laws and regulations regarding innocent passage – a stealthy means of introducing grounds for a regime of prior notification for warship innocent passage.[47] This debate, and the potential for sovereignty irritants by warships which it provides, continues still.

---

43 Ibid., p. 47. He explains his views thus (p. 41):

> Suppose that the Security Council of the U.N.O. decided to take measures of coercion against a State and, with that object, despatched warships, belonging to different countries – for the U.N.O. has no naval forces of its own. If this international squadron desired to pass through the territorial waters of certain States, the latter cannot do anything to impede its passage, under any pretext, not even if their national laws require a previous authorization, or other formalities.

44 *Yearbook of the International Law Commission* (1954), Vol. I (Summary of Records, 6th Session, 3 June–28 July, 1954), 20 July 1954, para. 47, p. 158.
45 See, for example, *Yearbook of the International Law Commission* (1954), Vol. I (Summary of Proceedings), 8 July 1954, paras 25–43, pp. 109–116; *Yearbook of the International Law Commission* (1956), Vol. I (Summary of Proceedings, Eighth Session, 23 April–4 July 1956), 15 June 1956, para. 23, p. 214.
46 *Yearbook of the International Law Commission* (1956), Vol. II, p. 276.
47 'Proposed Amendment to Draft Article 2', Algeria [*et al.*], *Third United Nations Conference on the Law of the Sea: Official Records*, Vol XVI (Summary of Records of Meetings, Eleventh (New York) Session, 8 March–30 April 1982), A/CONF.62/L.117, 13 April 1982.

It is, however, the third element of the UK response to this challenge which is most significant:

> In any event, as has already been stated, it is the practice of States which is of decisive importance in this matter, and the writers who oppose a right of passage for warships do not draw their conclusions from an analysis of that practice but *a priori* from their concepts of territorial sovereignty.[48]

The UK then recounted that 34 of 37 States assessed in the US Office of Naval Intelligence survey in 1916 did not indicate any general prohibitions on warship passage, and that two of the three which did – Denmark and The Netherlands – had altered their view by the 1930 Hague Codification Conference (Romania was the third). Similarly, in responses to the questionnaire used to inform the 1930 Hague Conference debates, 15 States recognised the right of warship innocent passage, with the US, Bulgaria, and Latvia joining Romania in the 'no' camp. This response underlined that practice should prevail over theory – a sentiment reinforced during the preliminary negotiations preceding the four 1958 Conventions related to the Law of the Sea – in particular the *Convention on the Territorial Sea* 1958. As the Yemeni Delegate declared at UNCLOS I, the 'codification of the international law of the sea had political implications' and could not be considered merely from a 'technical point of view'.[49] Similarly, for Fitzmaurice at the ILC, reference back to the political and practical, rather than the theoretical, was clearly overt in his assertion that it 'would be both dangerous and potentially controversial to leave it to the coastal State to decide such issues' as whether a warship could transit its territorial sea.[50] This is a refreshing reminder – clearly expressed in the *Corfu Channel* case, but often forgotten or overlooked even, or perhaps even more regularly, today – that it is State practice, not aspiration, which lies at the hard and sometimes harsh core of international law.

10.5 Conclusion

Intuitively, the *Corfu Channel* case, decided so soon after the conflagration of 1939–45, and the birth of the United Nations, could readily have resulted in a majority decision along the lines of Judge Alvarez's erudite and highly symbolic reading of the 'the new international law'. Indeed, as Judge Alvarez explained, the 'profound changes that had taken place in international

---

48 *UK Reply*, op. cit., p. 292.
49 United Nations, *United Nations Conference on the Law of Sea: Official Records*, Vol. III, p. 16.
50 See, for example, *Yearbook of the International Law Commission* (1955), Vol. I (Summary of Records, 7th Session, 2 May–8 July, 1955), 8 June 1955, paras 16–21, pp. 145–146; 9 June 1955, para. 30, p. 151.

relations', leading to a consequent focus upon 'social interdependence' as the cornerstone of this new international law could not but make this new law attractive, and bring it into 'collision' with the 'old law, which was strictly juridical'.[51] But the majority did not take this path — perhaps equally influenced by other, less aspirational, post-World War II realities such as the drawing of the Iron Curtain, and the shadow of bi-polar antagonism and one-upmanship which would come to define the next half century. Instead (and whether it was evidence of holding to 'the old law', or of adopting a 'strictly juridical' approach, is itself highly contestable), the majority decision represents what international law then, and still, must fundamentally achieve if it is to retain its status, utility, and power — the practical regulation of relationships and issues. This is nowhere more economically, yet assertively, expressed than in the ICJ's clear, pragmatic, and sensible acceptance of the prudential and categorical fact that sovereignty irritants exist, and that their exploitation can be both useful for States, and lawful as between them. Arguably, the decision's self-evident acknowledgement of the political and legal utility of warships as sovereignty irritants, and its fundamentally practical approach to characterising warship conduct, is one of its signal achievements, in that it provided an early indication of a pragmatic sensibility and willingness to engage with issues in their practical contexts. This is not to say that the ICJ has always been as well anchored to context as the *Corfu Channel* case suggests, but it was an early and very crucial statement of fundamental character and intent which undoubtedly shaped international law, and discourse between States, then and since.

---

51 *Corfu Channel case*, op. cit., Individual Opinion of Judge Alvarez, p. 40.

11 Peacetime maritime operations

Donald R. Rothwell

11.1 Introduction

One feature of the modern law of the sea as it has evolved following the *Corfu Channel* case, the 1958 Geneva Conventions, the 1982 United Nations Convention on the Law of the Sea (LOSC), and State practice in the twentieth and early part of the twenty-first century has been the ability to balance the rights and interests of coastal States with those of maritime States, which includes military powers with large naval fleets. Initially, when the territorial sea developed as part of the law of the sea, the interests of coastal States were conceived in terms of national security and the limited assertion of State sovereignty over a narrow band of adjacent waters. However, those interests have expanded over time to include concerns over the marine environment, health of marine living resources, threats posed by non-State actors such as terrorist groups, and the management of ocean space extending from the territorial sea to the edge of the continental shelf. This has especially become a prominent issue as the maritime domain of coastal States has steadily expanded from a relatively narrow territorial sea of approximately 3 nautical miles at the turn of the twentieth century, to one that now in the early twenty-first century can extend to an outer continental shelf that may be 350 nautical miles from the coast. A counter-balance to this so-called 'jurisdictional creep', has been the effort within the law of the sea generally and especially within the LOSC to ensure a careful balance between the interests of coastal States and maritime States. This was an issue that was uppermost in the negotiating positions of the major maritime powers during 1970s, and was even reflected in the mutual cooperative positions taken by the two global superpowers at the time.[1] In this respect, peacetime navigational rights and freedoms through the territorial sea were at the sharp edge of this debate, reflecting the concerns of coastal States over the security of the territorial

---

1 D.G. Stephens, 'The Impact of the 1982 Law of the Sea Convention on the Conduct of Peacetime Naval/Military Operations', *California Western International Law Journal*, 29 (1998–99): 286.

sea and those of maritime powers over increased interference with innocent passage through the territorial sea and transit passage through international straits.[2]

In this context, the influence of the *Corfu Channel* decision on the development of the law of the sea with respect to navigation in general, and peacetime maritime operations in particular should not be underestimated. The ICJ was confronted with a volatile peacetime situation arising only one year after the conclusion of World War II when security concerns for both coastal States and maritime powers such as the United Kingdom remained high. It is significant then that the court did not rely upon the 1907 Hague Convention[3] in its findings against Albania regarding its responsibilities to notify users of the strait as to the existence of the minefield. Rather, the court relied upon what it referred to as 'general and well-recognized principles' being

> elementary considerations of humanity, even more exacting in peace than in war; the principle of the freedom of navigation; and the State's obligation not to allow knowingly its territory to be used for acts contrary to the rights of other States.[4]

The ICJ's finding that the freedom of navigation is enjoyed by warships in peacetime was subsequently reflected in deliberations at UNCLOS I and III and in both the Geneva Conventions and the LOSC.[5] That it was considered a general principle further elevates its significance and needs to be taken into account when interpreting the international law of the sea concerning navigation by warships.

Three aspects of the decision in *Corfu Channel* therefore justify further consideration in the context of the contemporary international law of the sea. The first is the ongoing importance of the decision regarding the categorisation and characterisation of international straits. The Court in *Corfu Channel* made reference to the strait being an 'international highway',[6] and this immediately raises issues as to how such bodies of water are to be identified, especially given the sensitivity for littoral States of having foreign vessels

---

2 See discussion in S. Bateman, D.R. Rothwell and D. Vander Zwaag, 'Navigational Rights and Freedoms in the New Millennium: Dealing with 20th Century Controversies and 21st Century Challenges', in D.R. Rothwell and S. Bateman (eds), *Navigational Rights and Freedoms and the New Law of the Sea* (The Hague: Martinus Nijhoff, 2000), pp. 317–318.
3 1907 Hague Convention (VIII) Relative to the Laying of Automatic Submarine Contact Mines.
4 *Corfu Channel case, Judgment of April 9th 1949, ICJ Reports 1949*, p. 22.
5 See also the discussion of these principles in the *Case Concerning Military and Paramilitary Activities in and Against Nicaragua (Nicaragua v. United States of America) Merits, Judgment, ICJ Reports 1986*, pp. 111–112, with respect to the freedom of communications and maritime commerce; Stephens, op. cit., pp. 293–304 compares the ICJ decisions in *Corfu Channel* and *Nicaragua* on their observations regarding the freedom of navigation.
6 *Corfu Channel case*, op. cit., p. 29.

passing through these waters enjoying certain special status. The second is the manner in which the transit passage regime, the contemporary LOSC-based framework of some of the components of the *Corfu Channel* decision, has developed. The third remains the general question of peacetime maritime operations by warships within the territorial sea and international straits. Each will be considered below in the context of *Corfu Channel*.

11.2 International straits

Unlike the 1958 Convention on the Territorial Sea and Contiguous Zone, the LOSC devotes considerable attention in Part III to the regime of straits used for international navigation. Reference is made to a 'regime of passage through straits used for international navigation',[7] suggesting that the intention was to create a comprehensive legal framework for such straits. This is what is ultimately achieved by the transit passage regime, however, there are many potential categories of straits which depending on their history, geographic configuration, and usage may be subject to different characterisations for the purposes of the law of the sea. The International Court of Justice in the *Corfu Channel* case hinted that a variety of factors may need to be taken into account in determining which navigational rights applied within a particular strait. Accordingly, one of the initial issues that needed to be addressed in the LOSC was distinguishing between various navigational regimes that apply in the different bodies of water that may comprise a strait. One of those factors is clearly the width of the strait and surveys have estimated that there are 52 international straits less than 6 nm in width, 153 international straits between 6 and 24 nm in width, and 60 other international straits in excess of 24 nm.[8]

11.2.1 Categories of straits

The starting point for an analysis of Part III is its title – 'Straits Used for International Navigation' – a descriptor repeated in various articles found within this Part of the Convention. This immediately raises for consideration what the convention classifies as a strait used for international navigation. Using terminology similar to that found in the *Corfu Channel* case, by the ILC, and in the Geneva Convention on the Territorial Sea and Contiguous Zone, this phrase suggests both a geographical and functional element. The geographical element relates to a strait being a body of water which lies between two areas of land, either continental land masses,[9] a continent and an

---

7 LOSC, Article 34 (1).
8 A.R. Thomas and J.C. Duncan (eds), 'Annotated Supplement to The Commanders Handbook on the Law of Naval Operations', *International Legal Studies*, 73 (1999): 207–208, Table A2–5.
9 An example is the Bering Strait separating continental Asia and North America.

island,[10] or two islands.[11] However, there is no guidance as to how proximate the bodies of land must be to one another, or at which point the width of the body of water which separates the two areas of land is no longer considered a strait but rather a sea or an ocean.[12] For practical purposes this distinction may not be of great relevance as most bodies of water that separate sufficiently proximate areas of land are referred to as straits, or have equivalent titles.[13] One limited exception applies in the case of so-called 'dead end' straits where two bodies of adjoining land separated by a large body of water provide navigational access to land areas at the end of the strait. Examples include the Strait of Tiran, Gulf of Bahrain, and the Gulf of Honduras.[14] Nevertheless, the recognition of a body of water as a strait is an important starting point in the application of the Part III legal regime.[15]

In addition to the geographical criterion, in the *Corfu Channel* case the ICJ placed emphasis on the strait being one that was 'used for international navigation'.[16] While there was no analysis as to what volume of navigation through the strait would be required to meet the usage requirement, reference was made to the volume of navigation through the Strait between 1936 and 1937 which in the view of the Court assisted it in determining that the Corfu Channel had been 'a useful route for international maritime traffic'.[17] Therefore, while this functional element remains a feature of the LOSC, it is unclear as to what level of international navigation is required for a strait to be appropriately classified as an 'international strait'. However, it is doubtful whether infrequent or irregular use of a strait would suffice to meet the functional criterion. Likewise, the strait must have been used by foreign flagged

---

10 The Dover Strait lies between the continent of Europe and an island comprising Great Britain.
11 The Cook Strait separates the North and South Island of New Zealand.
12 R.R. Baxter, *The Law of International Waterways* (Cambridge, MA: Harvard University Press, 1964), pp. 3–4; G. K. Walker, 'Definitions for the 1982 Law of the Sea Convention – Part II: Analysis of the IHO Consolidated Glossary', *California Western International Law Journal*, 33(2003): 298, observes that 'The geographic definition of a strait is a narrow passage of water between two land masses or islands, or groups of islands connecting two sea areas.'
13 Of which the term 'channel' is in State practice used as an alternate to 'strait', as in the Corfu Channel; alternate terms which are used include 'Belt', 'Mouth', and 'Sound'.
14 In these instances, LOSC, Article 45 provides for a right of non-suspendable innocent passage through those waters.
15 For example, the Tasman Sea separates the continent of Australia with the islands that make up New Zealand, similar to the manner in which the English Channel separates the continent of Europe from the United Kingdom. However, the Tasman Sea at its narrowest point is 1250 miles, while the English Channel at its narrowest point between Dover and Calais is 21 miles. The Tasman Sea has never been considered a strait while the English Channel has always been considered a strait once that concept was known to the law.
16 *Corfu Channel case*, op. cit., p. 28.
17 Ibid.

vessels and not only by through or cross-strait local vessel traffic. These are issues which are increasingly becoming relevant in the context of the impacts upon navigation caused by climate change. The most significant of these is occurring in the Arctic, where long-standing debates over the status of the Northwest Passage along the Canadian coast and the Northeast Passage (or Northern Sea Route) along the Russian coast[18] now need to be considered in light of the increasing access available to those navigational routes as a result of the melting of sea ice.[19] Likewise, the consequences of sea level rise need to be accounted for with some navigational routes becoming hazardous as a result of land features becoming submerged and placing constraints on the ability of certain ships to use some straits. The potential therefore exists for the status of a strait – whether it be considered international or non-international in the traditional *Corfu Channel* sense – to vary as a result of climatic conditions and navigational factors.[20]

The principal focus of Part III is upon straits used for international navigation between one part of the high seas and the exclusive economic zone (EEZ), and another part of the high seas or EEZ, and the regime of transit passage applies within these straits.[21] However, Part III also makes reference to other categories of straits. These include the following:

- Straits which are regulated in whole or in part by long-standing international conventions.[22]
- Straits where there exists a route through the high seas or EEZ of similar convenience.[23]
- Straits which exist between the mainland and an island where there exists seaward of the island a route through the high seas or EEZ of similar convenience.[24]

---

18 See discussion in D. Pharand, *Canada's Arctic Waters in International Law* (Cambridge: Cambridge University Press, 1988); E. Franckx, *Maritime Claims in the Arctic: Canadian and Russian Perspectives* (The Hague: Martinus Nijhoff, 1993).
19 See discussion in A. Chircop, 'The Growth of International Shipping in the Arctic: Is a Regulatory Review Timely?' *International Journal of Marine and Coastal Law*, 24 (2009): 355–380; and more generally R. Rayfuse, 'Melting Moments: The Future of Polar Oceans Governance in a Warming World', *Review of European Community and International Environmental Law*, 16 (2007): 196–216.
20 The status of a strait may also vary as a consequence of modified maritime claims. Bass Strait, which separates the island of Tasmania from the Australian mainland was not considered to be an international strait until such time as Australia proclaimed a 12 nautical mile territorial sea, as prior to that a high seas corridor existed through the strait with the result that international shipping did not have to enter the Australian territorial sea to pass through the strait: D.R. Rothwell, 'International Straits and UNCLOS: An Australian Case Study', *Journal of Maritime Law and Commerce*, 23(1992): 461–483.
21 LOSC, Article 37.
22 LOSC, Article 35 (c).
23 LOSC, Article 36.
24 LOSC, Article 38 (1).

- Straits used for international navigation between one part of the high seas or EEZ and the territorial sea of a foreign State.[25]

All of these categories of straits are ones in which the principal regime of transit passage as created under the LOSC does not apply, but in its place alternate navigation regimes are recognised.

11.3 Transit passage through international straits

The regime of transit passage which exists between straits used for international navigation between one part of the high seas and EEZ and another part of the high seas and EEZ is one which all ships enjoy.[26] The right of transit passage is also one that is not to be 'impeded',[27] implying that the strait State must not bar or suspend transit passage or otherwise engage in activities that may have the practical effect of doing so. This raises a number of important practical issues for peacetime maritime operations which build upon some of the matters addressed in the *Corfu Channel* case.

11.3.1 The act of transit

Article 38 (2) of the LOSC identifies the physical act of transit passage as including the freedom of navigation 'solely for the purpose of continuous and expeditious transit of the strait'. This reflects the objective of ensuring that the regime facilitates the movement of vessels physically through the strait from an entrance to an exit point and builds upon the ICJ's notion in *Corfu Channel* of a strait being an 'international highway'.[28] Allowance is also made in the case of where passage through the strait is undertaken for the purpose of 'entering, leaving or returning from a State bordering the strait',[29] thereby facilitating ships which are seeking to dock at a facility within a State adjoining a strait, of which Singapore is one of the most prominent examples.[30] Transit passage is therefore enjoyed by ships which seek to pass through the strait, or which are entering or exiting the strait after having stopped at or on their way to a State which borders the strait.

---

25 LOSC, Article 45.
26 LOSC, Article 38 (1).
27 LOSC, Article 38 (1).
28 *Corfu Channel case*, op. cit., p. 29.
29 LOSC, Article 38 (2).
30 The only way in which Singapore can be approached by ship is via either the Straits of Malacca and Singapore, or the Straits of Jahore; similarly for an aircraft making an approach by sea and not overflying the territory of adjoining states, these Straits provide the only means of air access.

11.3.2 Duties of ships and aircraft in transit

Once engaged in transit passage, under Article 39 of the LOSC, ships have certain duties that are reflective of some of the elements of innocent passage, though these are by no means as extensive. They include the requirement to proceed without delay, to refrain from any use or threat of force against the sovereignty, territorial integrity or political independence of the strait State, or in any other manner in violation of principles of international law found in the United Nations Charter, and to refrain from activities other than those which are incidental 'to their normal mode' of transit, unless rendered necessary by *force majeure* or distress.

These duties of ships reflect an important balancing of rights and interests within the straits regime. On the one hand, transit passage was developed to permit the free and unimpeded passage of ships through international straits, thereby ensuring the continuation of important guarantees of the freedom of navigation recognised in *Corfu Channel*. On the other hand, strait States have legitimate security concerns relating to the presence of foreign ships within their territorial sea in what may be relatively confined waters as was highlighted by Albania's response to the passage of the British warships through its waters in 1946. Balancing those competing rights and objectives has at times proven to be a major challenge, and during the Cold War the United States and Soviet Union occasionally engaged in maritime clashes in incidents which arose from US attempts to robustly exercise a right of navigation within Soviet-controlled waters.[31] This has certainly been the case with respect to warships, in particular in interpreting what constitutes the 'normal modes of continuous and expeditious transit' for such vessels.[32]

11.3.3 Obligations of strait States

Article 44 of the LOSC makes clear that strait States are not to 'hamper' transit passage and are to give appropriate notification of any dangers to navigation within or over the strait of which they may be aware, which would extend to cases of shipwreck blocking parts of the strait, or as was also highlighted in *Corfu Channel*, mines that may be in the water. It is also made clear that strait States are not to suspend transit passage. Here one of the important distinctions that exists between the regime of transit passage in an international strait and innocent passage within the territorial sea is made clear – while transit passage cannot be suspended by the strait State, a coastal State

---

31 The 12 February 1988 Black Sea 'bumping incident' involving the USS *Yorktown* and USS *Caron* and a Soviet frigate is a prominent example of such an incident: J.A. Roach and R.W. Smith, *United States Responses to Excessive Maritime Claims* 2nd ed (The Hague: Martinus Nijhoff, 1996), pp. 245–251.
32 See further discussion in Chapter 9 in this volume by S. Kaye.

may temporarily suspend innocent passage.³³ Therefore, even if a strait State has concerns regarding its national security because of the potential for transiting traffic to be caught up in internal disturbances, it may not suspend the right of transit passage. However, it may seek to issue a warning to ships of the potential hazards that exist within its waters at any particular point in time.³⁴ This implies that even if certain waters are known to be favoured by pirates, or used by non-State actors such as terrorists, a coastal State remains under an obligation to continue to permit transit, though it would be under obligations to warn maritime traffic of the dangers.

The obligation upon the strait State not to 'hamper' transit passage suggests that no obligations or requirements may be imposed upon ships that create a burden for them. One traditional interpretation of this requirement is that the strait State may not impose tolls or any other fees in return for a right of passage.³⁵ However, some strait States such as Indonesia have expressed concerns about the financial burdens they face in maintaining navigational aids and other safety and marine environmental protection measures within the waters of an international strait without receiving any recompense and have argued there should be an entitlement to charge tolls or at least a fee-for-service that relates directly to the benefits they provide to international shipping that passes through the strait.³⁶

11.3.4 Enforcement of strait State laws and regulations regulating transit passage

Within the limits of the above obligations imposed upon strait States, they enjoy the capacity to enact laws and regulations relating to transit passage.³⁷ Yet the LOSC is unclear as to the level of enforcement action a strait State may undertake against a delinquent vessel engaged in transit passage. One scenario arises when a vessel is not complying with the requirements of transit passage and its actions are in breach of Article 39 such that it is posing a threat to the strait State or it is not engaging in 'normal mode' passage. A strait State retains its capacity of self-defence under international law and could rely upon that right in the face of a hostile act by a transiting ship. It also has the capacity, consistent with the LOSC, to prohibit passage by a ship which is not

---

33 LOSC, Article 25 (3).
34 Note that LOSC, Article 44 refers to 'any danger to navigation or overflight within or over the strait of which they have knowledge', which is a direct reference to the issues that arose in *Corfu Channel* regarding whether Albania did or did not have knowledge as to the existence of mines in the strait: see *Corfu Channel case*, op. cit., pp. 22–23.
35 LOSC, Article 26; *Virginia Commentaries*, vol. II, p. 236.
36 M. J. Valencia and Abu Bakar Jaafar, 'Environmental Management of the Malacca–Singapore Straits: Legal and Institutional Issues', *Natural Resources Journal*, 25 (1985): 195–232.
37 LOSC, Article 42.

engaging in transit passage in conformity with Part III. Accordingly, even if the ship poses no threat to the national security of the strait State, a delinquent ship could be prevented from continuing its passage.

Another enforcement scenario arises when a ship undertaking transit consistent with Article 39 breaches the laws and regulations of the strait State. Part III is silent on the actual enforcement capacity of the strait State in such circumstances, which raises issues as to how a strait State may go about seeking to enforce its law in a manner that does not have the practical effect of hampering or impairing transit passage. Nevertheless, Article 34 makes clear that the Part III straits regime does not in other respects affect the legal status of the waters of a strait with regards to the coastal State's sovereignty and jurisdiction. This would extend to the coastal State's criminal and civil jurisdiction within the territorial sea of the strait. This view is supported by the text of Articles 27 and 28 which respectively deal with coastal State criminal and civil jurisdiction in the case of 'a foreign ship passing through the territorial sea'. These provisions make clear that in the case of criminal jurisdiction, there is a limited right to board a ship and effect an arrest while that ship is within the territorial sea, which would also extend to a ship engaged in transit passage.

If the infraction by the transiting ship relates to a marine environmental measure, other provisions in the LOSC will also apply. Article 233 makes clear that ships that commit violations of certain environmental laws and regulations while undertaking transit passage and which are 'causing or threatening major damage to the marine environment of the straits' may be subject to 'appropriate enforcement measures' by the strait State.[38] The context of the provision suggests that law enforcement against delinquent foreign ships engaged in transit passage is permitted, which by implication would extend to stopping and barring further passage of a vessel to contain any threat to the marine environment. Spain indicated upon both its signature and ratification of the LOSC that it also interpreted Article 221 as providing a basis of intervention against international navigation following a maritime casualty,[39] a position apparently endorsed by the United States.[40] Given increased coastal State concern over the environmental impacts resulting from a major maritime incident such as the 2002 *Prestige* shipwreck off the Spanish coast, it would have to be anticipated that the coastal States will take a more robust attitude to these interventions in the future.

---

38 E. Jaap Molenaar, *Coastal State Jurisdiction over Vessel-Source Pollution* (The Hague: Kluwer Law International, 1998), pp. 295–298.
39 Spain 'Upon Ratification' (15 January 1997), United Nations Division for Ocean Affairs and the Law of the Sea 'Declarations and Statements'. Available at: www.un.org/Depts/los/convention_agreements/convention_declarations.htm (accessed 7 November 2009).
40 Roach and Smith, op. cit., pp. 303–304.

11.4 Peacetime maritime operations by warships

11.4.1 Innocent passage

Notwithstanding the variable approaches taken towards innocent passage for warships by the ILC and at UNCLOS I and III, the LOSC retains a right of innocent passage for warships in their capacity as 'ships of all States' under Article 17. Nevertheless, Articles 29–32 specifically apply to some aspects of innocent passage through the territorial sea by warships. A warship is defined under Article 29 as being a ship belonging to the armed forces of a State, with distinguishing external marks, under the command of a commissioned officer and manned by a crew under regular armed forces discipline.[41] Article 30 then addresses how a coastal State may respond to a warship which is not complying with relevant laws and regulations applicable to innocent passage; potentially one of the most sensitive issues which can arise in the innocent passage regime. A graduated response from the coastal State is envisaged: first, requesting compliance with the relevant laws, and, second, requiring the warship to immediately leave the territorial sea if the request is disregarded. Articles 31 and 32 address questions relating to international responsibility arising from any loss or damage to the coastal State as a result of non-compliance by a warship or other government non-commercial vessel, and the immunities those vessels enjoy under general international law. Therefore, while a foreign warship could not be prosecuted for an oil spill within the territorial sea, State responsibility would rest with the flag State for any damage which resulted for the coastal State.

Some States maintain the position that foreign warships are only able to enter the territorial sea and undertake innocent passage with permission,[42] which is difficult to reconcile with the Convention. The LOSC is clear that warships are capable of undertaking innocent passage, again consistent with how the ICJ viewed this issue in *Corfu Channel*, and by and large that right may be exercised in the same manner as merchant ships. Nevertheless, there are three particular types of constraints in the innocent passage regime that have relevance for warships.

The first is that warships need to take particular care that while in passage they do not engage in acts which are considered non-innocent under Article 19. A number of limitations on passage found in Article 19 (2) have particular application to warships including that they do not engage in actions considered to constitute any threat or use of force against the coastal State, any form of weapons exercise, acts aimed at collecting information to the prejudice of

---

41 This definition is broadly consistent with that which applies under international humanitarian law, see L. Doswald-Beck (ed.), *San Remo Manual on International Law Applicable to Armed Conflicts at Sea* (Cambridge: Cambridge University Press, 1995), p. 9, Rule 13 (g).
42 See discussion in Chapter 9 in this volume by S. Kaye.

the defence or security of the coastal State, acts of propaganda, research or survey activities, acts aimed at interfering with the communications systems of the coastal State, and the launching, landing or taking on board of any aircraft or military device. This is clearly an extensive list of requirements, which, if complied with, will ensure that the possible security threats to coastal States posed by foreign warships are neutralised as far as possible while they are within the territorial sea. In contrast to the transit passage and archipelagic sea lanes passage regimes, there is no reference in the right of innocent passage to 'normal mode' of navigation, therefore precluding warships undertaking activities which would otherwise be permissible in other settings. A clear limitation in this respect is the inability of aircraft carriers to launch or receive aircraft while undertaking innocent passage, as such activity conflicts with Article 19 (2)(f). However, some aspects of warship operations remain ambiguous, such as the activation of radar while in passage. Radar is clearly an aid to navigation for all vessels and as such also promotes safety at sea, but also may be used for defensive purposes.[43] By way of contrast, there is nothing in the innocent passage regime, the LOSC, or general international law which suggests that warships do not enjoy the right of self-defence while within the territorial sea of a foreign State.[44] This issue has been highlighted since the October 2000 terrorist attack on the USS *Cole* while in port at Aden, Yemen, and the subsequent US response to ensuring security of its warships while within potentially hostile waters.[45]

The second constraint relates to compliance by warships with the laws and regulations of a coastal State relating to innocent passage that may have been adopted under Article 21 of the LOSC. In the case of warships, relevant provisions would be those relating to the safety of navigation and regulation of maritime traffic, the preservation of the environment and the prevention of pollution. The LOSC makes clear that '[f]oreign ships exercising the right of innocent passage . . . shall comply' with such laws and regulations.[46] While coastal States would encounter difficulty in applying their civil and criminal laws to warships because of the principles of sovereign immunity,[47] the LOSC in recognition of this legal reality makes clear in Article 30 that if a non-compliant warship disregards a request for compliance, the coastal State may require the warship to leave the territorial sea with the effect that the right of innocent passage has been lost. While the LOSC is silent as to how full compliance with a request to leave the territorial sea could be achieved, there are a

---

43 J. Astley and M.N. Schmitt, 'The Law of the Sea and Naval Operations', *Air Force Law Review*, 42 (1997): 131.
44 See discussion in A.V. Lowe, 'Self-Defence at Sea', in W.E. Butler (ed.), *The Non-Use of Force in International Law* (Dordrecht: Martinus Nijhoff, 1989), pp. 185–202.
45 See Department of Defense *USS Cole* Commission (United States) *USS Cole Commission Report* (Washington, DC: Department of Defense, 2001).
46 LOSC, Article 21 (4).
47 LOSC, Article 32.

range of options open to the coastal State consistent with the convention and international law. Further guidance on State practice in this area is provided by the 1989 United States and Soviet Union Uniform Interpretation of Rules which makes clear that:

> If a warship engages in conduct which violates such law or regulations or renders its passage not innocent and does not take corrective action upon request, the coastal State may require it to leave the territorial sea . . . In such case the warship shall do so immediately.[48]

This joint statement which came only a year after the 1988 Black Sea 'bumping incident' involving the USS *Yorktown* and USS *Caron* and a Soviet frigate, was clearly designed to facilitate a better understanding on this sensitive issue between the two naval superpowers and remains a powerful example of relevant State practice.

The third restraint found in the LOSC relates to the particular situation of submarines, which under Article 20 are 'required to navigate on the surface and show their flag'.[49] This recognises the very particular sensitivities associated with the presence of foreign submarines within the territorial sea, but also takes into account the navigational safety issues that may arise from a submarine navigating submerged within busy territorial sea shipping channels.

A number of issues arise from these provisions. One is the capacity of the coastal State to interpret the LOSC unilaterally and determine that either the mere presence of a warship within the territorial sea constitutes a threat to its security, or that the actions of the warship while engaged in passage are not innocent. There is a widely held view that a presumption of innocence exists, which can only be rebutted by proof from the coastal State, relying upon the objective and specific criteria in Article 19, of a non-innocent act.[50] This is a position which the United States and Soviet Union endorsed in their 1989 Uniform Interpretation of Rules.[51] However, while maintaining a balance between a coastal State's sovereign rights and its duty to respect innocent

---

48 USA-USSR Joint Statement on the Uniform Interpretation of Rules of International Law Governing Innocent Passage, *Law of the Sea Bulletin*, 14 (1989): 13, para. 7.
49 S.N. Nandan and S. Rosenne (eds), *United Nations Convention on the Law of the Sea 1982: A Commentary*, vol. II (Dordrecht: Martinus Nijhoff, 1985), p. 183, observing the use of the term 'are required' is unusual, leaving open the possibility that the coastal State may waive the requirement.
50 F.D. Froman, 'Uncharted Waters: Non-innocent Passage of Warships in the Territorial Sea', *San Diego Law Review*, 21 (1984): 658; J.W. Rolph, 'Freedom of Navigation and the Black Sea Bumping Incident: How "Innocent" Must Innocent Passage Be?', *Military Law Review*, 135 (1992): 159.
51 USA-USSR Joint Statement on the Uniform Interpretation of Rules of International Law Governing Innocent Passage, para. 3.

passage would suggest that only an objective standard is acceptable when interpreting Article 19,[52] categories such as 'propaganda' are difficult to define and assess objectively when national interests are at stake. This was highlighted by the response of the Indonesian Navy in 1991 to the voyage of the Portuguese ferry, *Lusitanio Expresso*, from Darwin to Dili (East Timor), in which the ferry was asked not to enter the Indonesian territorial sea because it was engaged in a 'peace voyage' to highlight the plight of the East Timorese peoples.[53] Commentators such as Ngantcha emphasise that the coastal State's subjective appraisal of passage as non-innocent should be limited by the objective requirement that any violation which is alleged to have occurred has taken place while the vessel is in passage.[54] Capacity to engage in undesirable conduct should therefore be insufficient, and actual conduct within the territorial sea by a foreign warship should be the test, and such an approach would be consistent with Article 19 which anticipates a positive 'act' having taken place while the vessel is within the territorial sea.

11.4.2 Transit passage by warships

Given the issues and sensitivities associated with innocent passage by warships, it is not surprising that similar and even more acute issues arise in the context of transit passage through international straits. This is illustrated by the pre-LOSC codification efforts in relations to straits, and the ongoing sensitivities associated with naval navigation through pivotal 'choke points' which have persisted. The 1936 Montreux Treaty[55] is a prominent illustration of a pre-LOSC initiative to address questions of navigation through an international strait by warships containing a range of measures which made distinctions between different types of naval vessels depending on their capacity and size, flag of origin, and overall maximum aggregate tonnage of a naval force exercising passage. A right of transit through the straits could be enjoyed with or without significant limitations and constraints, though any transit was to be preceded by notification to Turkey.[56] The *Corfu Channel* case is another prominent example in this respect given the ICJ directly endorsed the innocent passage by warships through an international strait without prior

---

52 G. Fitzmaurice, 'Some Results from the Geneva Conference on the Law of the Sea', *International and Comparative Law Quarterly*, 8 (1959): 96–97.
53 See D.R. Rothwell, 'Coastal State Sovereignty and Innocent Passage: The Voyage of the *Lusitania Expresso*', *Marine Policy*, 16 (1992): 427–437.
54 F. Ngantcha, *The Right of Innocent Passage and the Evolution of the International Law of the Sea* (London: Pinter, 1990), p. 51.
55 173 UNTS 213.
56 Convention Regarding the Regime of the Straits, Article 13; see further discussion in N. Ünlü, *The Legal Regime of the Turkish Straits* (The Hague: Martinus Nijhoff, 2002), pp. 87–100.

authorisation.⁵⁷ With an obvious reference to the Montreux Treaty, the Court observed that: 'Unless otherwise prescribed by an international convention, there is no right for a coastal State to prohibit such passage through straits in time of peace.'⁵⁸

These pre-LOSC precedents need to be measured against the impact of the convention recognising the legitimacy of a 12 nm territorial sea and the impact of that upon the high seas corridor which would have once existed through a number of international straits around the world. The effect of the 12 nm territorial sea was that 116 international straits potentially became enclosed within a territorial sea which even though subject to the regime of innocent passage had the potential to place considerable constraints upon the freedom of military operations and especially the capacity of navies to speedily move from one maritime domain to another.⁵⁹ Particularly sensitive strategic 'choke points' where maritime traffic converges to move from one ocean or sea to another include the Straits of Gibraltar, Dover, Hormuz, Malacca, Sunda, Lombok, and Formosa (Taiwan).⁶⁰

The LOSC makes clear that transit passage is a right enjoyed by 'all ships' with respect to straits used for international navigation where warships pass through the territorial sea between one part of the high seas or EEZ and another part of the high seas or EEZ.⁶¹ Warships while engaged in transit passage are bound by the same constraints as merchant ships. Two particular constraints apply to warships. The first is that they are to refrain from any activity constituting a threat or use of force against the coastal State, and likewise refrain from any activities not incidental to their normal mode. The second of these is that they are to comply with generally accepted international rules and regulations regarding safety of life at sea and pollution prevention.

Of particular significance here is what constitutes 'normal mode' of operations for a warship and when would such operations be considered to cross the boundaries so as to constitute a threat to the coastal State? In the *Virginia Commentaries* to the LOSC, the observation has been made that

> it is clear from the context and from the negotiating history that the term was intended to refer to that mode which is normal or usual for navigation for the particular type of ship ... making the passage in given circumstances. In the case of surface ships, this means navigation on the surface in ordinary sailing conditions.⁶²

---

57 *Corfu Channel case*, p. 28.
58 Ibid., p. 28.
59 K. Booth, *Law, Force and Diplomacy at Sea* (Boston: George Allen & Unwin, 1985), pp. 97–119.
60 Ibid., pp. 98–99.
61 LOSC, Article 38 (1).
62 Nandan and Rosenne, op. cit., p. 342.

Some guidance on this point can again be found in *Corfu Channel*, where the ICJ was satisfied that even when the British warships passed through the channel with crews at action stations, and ready to retaliate if fired upon, this was consistent given the tensions that then existed between Albania and the United Kingdom at the time with the right of passage.[63] It is doubtful, however, whether this would be an acceptable mode of navigation on all occasions as the Court gave weight to the context of when the passage was being exercised and its manner. At the other end of the spectrum, in the case of the actions of the British warships several weeks later when minesweeping operations were conducted in the strait, the ICJ did not accept those actions as being legitimate under either the law of the sea or other general principles of international law.[64] For modern warships, the normal mode for surface vessels would extend to the launching and recovering of aircraft and the deployment of radar, sonar and depth-finding devices. For submarines, navigation through the strait could be submerged.[65] The conduct of weapons exercises, however, would not be consistent with normal mode as such an activity would constitute a threat of the use of force against the coastal State.

The second constraint is the expectation that all ships, including by implication warships, also comply with legitimate coastal States' laws and regulations relating to transit passage. Laws of particular relevance would be those relating to safety to navigation, including passage through sea lanes and traffic separation schemes, and pollution control.[66] In recognition of the immunities enjoyed by warships and the difficulties therefore associated with the enforcement of any coastal State laws against warships, the LOSC makes clear that the flag State will bear international responsibility for any loss or damage that may arise as a result of the warship acting contrary to those laws and regulations.[67]

11.4.3 Exercise of the right of assistance entry

One exceptional right which exists under customary international law and the LOSC, and which has particular application to warships during peacetime, is the unilateral right to enter the territorial sea of a foreign State on a temporary basis to provide assistance to vessels or persons in distress at sea. This right of 'assistance entry' is founded upon fundamental principles of the law of the sea and maritime law to provide humanitarian assistance to persons in distress at sea and is generally reflected in the Article 98 obligation in LOSC to render assistance on the high seas, and more generally in the 1979 International

---

63 *Corfu Channel case*, op. cit., p. 31.
64 Ibid., pp. 33–35; see comment in Stephens, op. cit., pp. 306–307.
65 Nandan and Rosenne (eds), op. cit., pp. 342–343; Astley and Schmitt, op. cit., p. 133.
66 LOSC, Article 42.
67 LOSC, Article 42 (5); see also Article 236.

Convention on Maritime Search and Rescue.[68] Part of the difficulties for warships in this situation is that while they are often uniquely equipped to engage in search and rescue operations, any unilateral undertaking of such an activity has the potential to raise sovereignty tensions which, depending on the State of bilateral relations between the coastal and flag State, may have diplomatic consequences. Nevertheless, Article 18 (2) does recognise the potential for innocent passage to be interrupted while rendering assistance to persons, ships or aircraft in distress, and the practice of assistance entry is reflected in the doctrine of some navies.[69] This right has been expressly extended in the case of pirate attacks off the coast of Somalia by UN Security Council Resolution 1816 (2008) which expressly provides for States to 'render assistance to vessels threatened by or under attack by pirates or armed robbers'.[70]

11.5 Conclusion

Peacetime maritime operations have evolved considerably since the *Corfu Channel* case was decided in 1949. The full emergence of the United Nations and the development of its Chapter VI and VII powers opened the door for multiple naval operations following the end of the Cold War, which give effect to UN sanctions regimes and new peace enforcement mechanisms.[71] NATO and other regional organisations, including loose coalitions, have also become actively engaged in naval operations ranging from counter-piracy to counter-terrorism. This has especially been highlighted by the responsiveness of NATO and the European Union to UN Security Council Resolutions 1816 (2008), 1846 (2008), 1851 (2008) and 1897 (2009) which provided the international community with a counter-piracy mandate off the coast of Somalia, authorising in some instances interdiction of suspected pirates within the territorial sea. At the other end of the spectrum, concerned over the safety and security of shipping and the environment in strategic straits, cooperative initiatives have also been taken in Southeast Asia between littoral States, maritime States and the International Maritime Organization to enhance maritime security in the Malacca and Singapore Straits.[72]

These contemporary initiatives, built upon the foundation of the modern law of the sea of which the LOSC is the basis, would have been impossible to foresee by either the International Court of Justice or the major coastal and

---

68 1405 UNTS 97.
69 Thomas and Duncan, op. cit., p. 120, outlining United States practice.
70 United Nations Security Council Resolution 1816 (2008), para. 3.
71 See generally R. McLaughlin, *United Nations Naval Peace Operations in the Territorial Sea* (The Hague: Martinus Nijhoff, 2009).
72 J.H. Ho, 'Enhancing Safety, Security, and Environmental Protection of the Straits of Malacca and Singapore: The Cooperative Mechanism', *Ocean Development and International Law*, 40 (2009): 233–247.

maritime States at the time of the *Corfu Channel* decision. Nevertheless, they reflect the continued development and expansion of the law of the sea as it applies to peacetime maritime operations in which respect for the freedom of navigation is balanced against the recognition of legitimate coastal States' rights and interests, and also the wider interests of the international community in the maintenance of peace and security. These interests will no doubt continue to evolve over coming decades but the significance of the *Corfu Channel* case will remain because of the manner in which the International Court was able to address the delicate balancing of the rights and interests of coastal and maritime States at such a crucial time for the post-war development of international law.

Part V
Fundamental rules of international law

12 The Court's decision *in silentium* on the sources of international law

Its enduring significance

Akiho Shibata

12.1 The issue of sources in the *Corfu Channel Judgment*

Anyone reading the *Corfu Channel Judgment*[1] would notice the extreme brevity of its discussion of the sources of international law. In fact, the Court did not even once mention Article 38, paragraph 1 of the Statute of the International Court of Justice (ICJ). This is particularly noticeable if one compares it to the Court's second substantive judgment, handed down a year later in 1950 in the *Asylum* case.[2] In that case, the Court, composed of the same judges as in the *Corfu Channel* case[3], expressly referred to Article 38 of the Statute and made an extensive deliberation on the two necessary elements of custom and determined that the right of diplomatic asylum could not be recognised as established under regional customary law.[4] This highlights the Court's almost complete lack of substantive discussion on the issue of sources in the *Corfu Channel Judgment*.

The Court's brief reference in the *Corfu Channel Judgment* to the sources of international law appears only twice: one referring to 'international custom' and another to 'the general and well-recognized principles'. As regards the former, the Court in one sentence confirmed that:

---

1 *Corfu Channel case, Judgment of April 9th 1949*, ICJ Reports 1949, p. 4.
2 *Colombian-Peruvian Asylum case, Judgment of November 20th 1950*, ICJ Reports 1950, p. 266.
3 The Court was composed as follows: Guerrero (El Salvador: Acting President), Basdevant (France: President), Alvarez (Chile), Fabela (Mexico), Hackworth (USA), Winiarski (Poland), Zoricic (Yugoslavia), de Visscher (Belgium), McNair (UK), Klaestad (Norway), Badawi Pasha (Egypt), Krylov (Russia), Read (Canada), Hsu Mo (China), Azevedo (Brazil), and Ečer (Czechoslovakia, judge *ad hoc*).
4 The Court said:

> The Party which relies on a custom of this kind must prove that this custom is established in such a manner that it has become binding on the other Party. The Colombian Government must prove that the rule invoked by it is in accordance with a constant and uniform usage practised by the States in question, and that this usage is the expression of a right appertaining to the State granting asylum and a duty incumbent on the territorial State. This follows from Article 38 of the Statute of the Court, which refers to international custom 'as evidence of a general practice accepted as law'.
>
> (*Asylum* case, op. cit., note 2, pp. 276–277)

> It is generally recognized and in accordance with international custom that States in time of peace have a right to send their warships through straits used for international navigation between two parts of the high seas without the previous authorization of a coastal State, provided that the passage is *innocent*.[5]

Here we can already observe one feature of the Court's treatment of the sources issue that has since become recurring in its jurisprudence: the Court's application of 'source requirements' when establishing a custom has been more relaxed than when denying its existence. For example, in the *Asylum* case and the *North Sea Continental Shelf* cases,[6] the Court strictly applied the two requirements for the establishment of custom, namely State practice and *opinio juris*, and denied its existence. The question is how the Court's apparent silence in its proof of establishment of custom could be justified in the context of the *Corfu Channel* case, and how that justification could be examined in light of the Court's current jurisprudence.

As regards 'general and well-recognized principles', the Court said:

> The obligations incumbent upon the Albanian authorities consisted in notifying, for the benefit of shipping in general, the existence of a minefield in Albanian territorial waters and in warning the approaching British warships of the imminent danger to which the minefield exposed them. Such obligations are based, not on the Hague Convention of 1907, No. VIII, which is applicable in time of war, but on certain general and well-recognized principles, namely: elementary considerations of humanity, even more exacting in peace than in war; the principle of the freedom of maritime communication; and every State's obligation not to allow knowingly its territory to be used for acts contrary to the rights of other States.[7]

Here again, we can observe a couple of features of the Court's treatment of the sources issue that has become recurring in the Court's jurisprudence. First, the Court has been extremely reluctant to declare a *non-liquet*. It has endeavoured to find the norms that could legitimately be applied in each specific case, utilising where necessary, innovative legal reasoning and creative interpretation of Article 38(1) of the Statute. The only exception, in which the Court came very close to declaring a *non-liquet*, was in the *Nuclear Weapons* case in 1996.[8] However, this case was an advisory opinion. Second, the Court has been reluctant to apply explicitly the source listed in Article 38(1)(c),

---

5 *Corfu Channel Judgment*, op. cit., note 1, p. 28.
6 *North Sea Continental Shelf, Judgment, ICJ Reports 1969*, p. 3.
7 *Corfu Channel Judgment*, op. cit., note 1, p. 22.
8 *Legality of the Threat or Use of Nuclear Weapons, Advisory Opinion, ICJ Reports 1996*, p. 226.

namely 'the general principles of law as recognized by civilized nations'.[9] Article 38(1)(c) was specifically inserted into the Statute of the Permanent Court of International Justice (PCIJ) in 1921 as a kind of 'last resort' for the Court to avoid a *non-liquet*, allowing it to look for principles generally recognised under domestic laws of civilised nations. The *Corfu Channel* decision did not expressly refer to Article 38(1)(c); nor did the Court make any effort to demonstrate that the principle of 'elementary considerations of humanity' is generally recognised under domestic laws of nations.

The question, therefore, is whether and how the Court's above line of argument, referring to and applying 'general and well-recognized principles', can still be explained in terms of the sources of international law.

12.2 Establishment of custom

In the *Corfu Channel* case, the Court had reasonable grounds for its brevity in dealing with the requirements for establishing the customary nature of the right of innocent passage of warships through straits. As both parties had made extensive analysis of the customary nature of the relevant rules, the Court was able to rely on the arguments and evidence presented to the Court. As regards the right of innocent passage of warships through territorial waters, at issue was the legal status of draft Article 12 prepared by a Sub-Committee of the 1930 League of Nations Codification Conference. Draft Article 12 provided that:

> As a general rule a coastal State will not forbid the passage of foreign warships in its territorial sea and will not require a previous authorization or notification. The coastal State has the right to regulate the conditions of such passage.

Albania, in its Counter-Memorial, argued that, based on the stipulations of the Draft, especially its second sentence, innocent passage of warships was a tolerance by the coastal State and was recognised only as international comity.[10] The United Kingdom, on the other hand, argued that, based on the government's replies to a questionnaire prepared for the Conference and the actual practice of States, the right of innocent passage of warships through territorial waters was established as a right under customary international law.[11]

---

9 A. Pellet, 'Article 38', in A. Zimmermann, C. Tomuschat and K. Oellers-Frahm (eds), *The Statute of the International Court of Justice: A Commentary* (Oxford: Oxford University Press, 2006), pp. 764–773.
10 'Contre-Mémoire soumis par le gouvernement de la République populaire d'Albanie (15 juin 1948)', in *The Corfu Channel case, ICJ Pleadings, Oral Arguments, and Documents 1950*, Vol. II, p. 129.
11 'The Reply', submitted by the United Kingdom, in ibid., pp. 289–290. Statement by Sir Eric Beckett (UK) on 11 November 1948, *The Corfu Channel case, ICJ Pleadings, Oral Arguments, and Documents 1950*, Vol. III, pp. 269–276.

As regards the right of innocent passage of warships through straits, at issue was the so-called 'Observation' attached to draft Article 12. This 'Observation' stated that: 'Under no pretext, however, may there be any interference with the passage of warships through straits constituting a route for international maritime traffic, between two parts of the high seas.' Unlike draft Article 12 itself, the United Kingdom argued, based on the *travaux préparatoires*, that this part of the 'Observation' was regarded by the delegates to the Conference as an accepted rule of international law. In support of such a claim, the United Kingdom also referred to the *travaux préparatoires* of the 1907 Hague Convention VIII and to the relevant resolutions adopted in 1895 and 1922 by the International Law Association.[12] Albania, on the other hand, did try to undermine the significance of the 'Observation' attached to draft Article 12, but her main argument as regards the passage of warships through straits was that such right, if there was any, would apply only to international straits and that in its view, the Northern Corfu Channel was not such international strait.[13]

The Court must have noticed Albania's attitude which, rather than categorically denying the rule as stipulated in the 'Observation', instead concentrated on arguing that the Corfu Channel was not a strait used for international navigation. Thus, from the arguments put forward by the parties and the evidence presented to the Court, the Court was satisfied of the customary nature of the right of innocent passage of warships through *straits*. The relatively uncontroversial nature of this determination could also be verified by the fact that there was only one judge, the judge *ad hoc* appointed by Albania, who seemed to cast doubt on its customary nature, indicating that the practice of States was so varied.[14] On the contrary, the establishment of the customary right of innocent passage of warships in *territorial waters* might have been more controversial, but the Court wisely did not touch on this thorny issue.[15]

---

12 The Reply submitted by the United Kingdom, op. cit., note 11, pp. 295–298.
13 'Contre-Mémoire soumis par le gouvernement de la République populaire d'Albanie', op. cit., note 10, pp. 130–131. 'Exposé de M. Pierre Cot (Albanie)', 18 November 1948, *The Corfu Channel case, ICJ Pleadings, Oral Arguments, and Documents 1950*, vol. III, pp. 382–384.
14 Opinion dissidente du juge *ad hoc* Ečer, *ICJ Reports 1949*, pp. 115, 128. Judge Alvarez, in his individual opinion, stated that, although warships may effect an innocent passage through straits forming an international highway between two free seas, 'in other cases the coastal States are entitled to regulate the passage, especially with a view to the protection of their own security or interests, but they are not entitled to forbid it', Opinion individuelle de M. Alehandro Alvarez, *ICJ Reports 1949*, p. 39, pp. 46–47. While clearly denying the customary nature of the right of innocent passage of warships through territorial waters, the dissenting opinion of Judge Azevedo, rather than denying the same for straits, emphasised that the Corfu Channel was not a strait serving for international navigation. Opinion dissidente de M. Azevedo, *ICJ Reports 1949*, pp. 78, 99, 103–108.
15 The Court said: 'In these circumstances, it is unnecessary to consider the more general question, much debated by the Parties, whether States under international law have a right to send warships in time of peace through territorial waters not included in a strait', *Corfu Channel Judgment*, op. cit., note 1, p. 30.

Under such circumstances, the Court was justified, in its judgment, briefly to confirm the customary nature of the right of innocent passage of warships through straits used for international navigation between two parts of the high seas. As the Court would later itself state in the *Nicaragua* case:

> in the field of customary international law, the shared view of the Parties as to the content of what they regard as the rule is not enough. The Court must satisfy itself that the existence of the rule in the *opinio juris* of States is confirmed by practice.[16]

In the *Corfu Channel* case, rather than expounding in its judgment, the Court *in silentium* deferred to the arguments made by the parties for the establishment of *opinio juris* and States' practice. It is worth emphasising that the Court seemed to accept the argument that the proceedings of law-making conferences and views expressed by governments during those meetings could be taken into account as evidence of customary law. This reliance on *opinio juris* expressed in, and during the negotiation of, normative instruments to establish customary law would culminate in the Court's judgment in the *Nicaragua* case.[17]

12.3 General principles: their significance for the sources' discussion

There is already a wealth of work on the concept of 'general principles' in general and that of 'elementary considerations of humanity' in particular. The purpose of examining these concepts in this chapter is solely to analyse the reasons why the Court had to refer to these concepts without indicating under which of the listed sources under Article 38(1) they fall, and to examine the significance of the Court's reasoning for the general discussion on the sources of international law.

Regarding the obligation of the coastal State to notify the existence of minefields in its territorial waters, the United Kingdom argued first that this obligation was based on the 1907 Hague Convention, and, second, knowing that Albania was not a party to this Convention, that the rules provided in the Hague Convention were already declaratory of pre-existing international law, the practice of States confirming such status.[18] The United Kingdom also argued that, even in times of peace, the obligation to notify derived from the

---

16 *Military and Paramilitary Activities in and against Nicaragua (Nicaragua v. United States of America)*, Merits, Judgment, *ICJ Reports 1986*, p. 14, p. 98 para. 184.
17 O. Schachter, 'New Custom: Power, *Opinio Juris* and Contrary Practice', in J. Makarczyk (ed.), *Theory of International Law at the Threshold of the 21st Century* (The Hague: Kluwer Law International, 1996), pp. 531–540.
18 Memorial submitted by the Government of United Kingdom, *The Corfu Channel case*, *ICJ Pleadings, Oral Arguments, and Documents 1949*, vol. I, pp. 38–39 paras. 67–70.

general principles declared in the 1907 Hague Convention relevant to the laying of automatic contact mines.[19] In fact, Albania concurred with the United Kingdom that the rules in the 1907 Hague Convention were declaratory of existing international law, and stated that laying of mines even in times of peace was a violation of international law. However, Albania denied the applicability of the obligation to notify in this case because Albania neither laid, nor participated in laying, nor knew of the laying of mines.[20] It stated: 'If Albania would have known of the fact of laying of the mines in its territorial waters, it would have notified and would have, in the first place, protested against such breach of its sovereignty.'[21] Thus, the contentious issue between the United Kingdom and Albania, and indeed among the judges, as can be seen from their dissenting opinions, was less the existence or even the content of the law applicable in this case, but rather the alleged facts of whether Albania knew of, or had connived in, the laying of mines within its territorial waters.

In this context, the United Kingdom put forward the following argument specifically to cover the possibility of some other State having laid the mines in Albania's territorial waters without Albania's positive assent or indeed the reception of any information by Albania on the matter. The United Kingdom agent, at the very end of his oral statement, argued that Albania would still be responsible for her failure to notify other States of the existence of a new minefield because, according to the UK, 'the *basic principles on which the Hague Convention VIII is founded* as well as *general principles of law* oblige a State to make a notification in such circumstances'.[22] The UK then went on to state that the whole purpose of Hague Convention VIII is to prevent all shipping from being endangered by mines; and a State cannot at the same time claim rights of sovereignty in its territorial waters and disclaim any obligation to give warning of a new minefield in those waters which it knows to constitute a danger to shipping.[23] The UK continued that '[t]he principles declared in the Hague Convention VIII are absolute principles based on *considerations of common humanity*'.[24]

The United Kingdom knew that the 1907 Hague Convention itself was not binding on Albania, but with Albania's declaration that she would respect

---

19 Reply by Sir Frank Soskice (UK), 18 January 1949, *The Corfu Channel case, ICJ Pleadings, Oral Arguments, and Documents*, vol. IV, p. 535.
20 'Contre-Mémoire soumis par le gouvernement de la République populaire d'Albanie (15 juin 1948)', op. cit., note 10, pp. 84–85 para. 84, p. 104 para. 107.
21 'Duplique présentée par le gouvernement de la République populaire d'Albanie', in *The Corfu Channel case, ICJ Pleadings, Oral Arguments, and Documents 1950*, vol. II, p. 325 para. 27.
22 Reply by Sir Frank Soskice (UK), 18 January 1949, op. cit., note 19, p. 538. Emphasis added.
23 Ibid.
24 Ibid. Emphasis added.

the Convention even in times of peace and accept the Convention as declaratory of existing international law, the United Kingdom nonetheless tried to base its argument as much as possible on the Hague Convention. Why, then, did the United Kingdom refer to the basic principles on which the Hague Convention was founded? This was because the Hague Convention did not specifically provide for the obligation to notify the minefield when the coastal State came to know of its existence but it itself did not lay the mines. In order to fill this gap in the Convention, the United Kingdom needed to refer to: (1) the whole purpose of the Hague Convention, namely freedom of maritime communication, which, according to the United Kingdom, had been recognised as general international law; and, (2) The State's obligation not to allow knowingly its territory to be used for acts contrary to the rights of other States. This was, according to the United Kingdom, a general principle of law, in the sense of Article 38(1)(c). Finally, (3) according to the UK, all these principles were based on considerations of common humanity. Of course, the Court slightly paraphrased it and called it 'elementary considerations of humanity'.

The UK's elaboration on 'general principles', including 'elementary considerations of humanity', was firmly grounded on the Hague Convention; it could even be said that it was a result of an interpretation of the Convention. The British deductive logic of extracting the specific obligation of notification from these 'general principles' was a result of meticulous referencing to the provisions of the Hague Convention;[25] interpreting the Convention as not excluding from its scope the case in which the coastal State simply knew of the minefield and in times of peace.

Unfortunately, the Court's relevant passage as cited at the beginning of this chapter, did not reflect this link between the Hague Convention, on one hand, and the elaboration of 'general principles' founded on deductive logic and used to fill the gap in the Convention, on the other. Unfortunate as this may be, if the above reading of the judgment is correct, the Court, following the reasoning of the United Kingdom *in silentium*, elaborated the 'general principles' from a treaty; thus, these principles are not natural law principles or principles of ethics or morality. The Court then extracted a specific rule of international law from such general principles, by reference to the treaty provisions, in order to fill the gap in that treaty and broaden its scope.

Arguably, this legal reasoning could be based generally on Article 38(1) of the Statute, especially on the Court's exercise of its power to decide in accordance with international law, even though each element of such reasoning does not squarely come under any of the listed sources from (a) to (c) of Article 38(1).

The gap-filling function of the 'foundational' or 'basic' principles elaborated from relevant treaties or from generally recognised rules of international

---

25 Ibid., pp. 538–539.

law, coupled with a reasoned deductive inference to find an applicable norm has become a recurring method used by the Court.[26] In the *North Sea Continental Shelf* cases, the Court found that the 'agreement/equitable principle rule' for delimitation of adjacent continental shelves could be derived from the basic notion of the continental shelf as a natural prolongation of the territory of coastal States.[27] In 2002, in the *Arrest Warrant* case, the Court found a basic principle of effective functioning of foreign ministers in international relations, as enunciated in the Vienna Convention on Diplomatic Relations, and from that principle, through deductive inference, found a norm of immunity of incumbent foreign ministers from the criminal jurisdiction of other States even with regard to war crimes.[28]

12.4 Conclusion: towards a functional concept of sources of international law?

Sixty years ago, although *in silentium*, the Court had already admitted the need to interpret Article 38, paragraph 1 of the Statute creatively and flexibly. When the parties to the case were virtually in agreement on the existence and the content of rules of international law and when support for such rules (*opinio juris*) was fairly evident from the discussion in law-making conferences, the Court tended to be satisfied by simply declaring such rules as established, without itself proving their existence. The reference to the concept of 'elementary considerations of humanity' in its judgment had a similar function. As Pierre-Marie Dupuy rightly stated, this concept of 'elementary considerations of humanity' allowed the Court to dispense with the need to make any reference to the actual behaviour of States to support the eminent legal authority of such a 'cardinal' principle. And, according to the same author, this approach to the sources of international law by the Court influenced it for more than a decade and a half from 1969 (*North Sea Continental Shelf* cases) until 1986 (*Nicaragua* case) in its jurisprudence.[29]

---

26 S. Murase, 'Nippon no Kokusaihogaku niokeru Hogenron no Iso (Studies on the Sources of International Law in Japan)', *Kokusaiho Gaiko Zasshi (Journal of International Law and Diplomacy)*, 96(4–5) (1997): 196–197.
27 *North Sea Continental Shelf*, op. cit., note 6, pp. 46–47.
28 *Arrest Warrant of 11 April 2000 (Democratic Republic of the Congo v. Belgium), Judgment, ICJ Reports 2002*, pp. 3, 21–24. For an interesting analysis, see: T. Mizushima, 'Gaimudaijin no Keijikankatsukenmenjo nikansuru "Kanshukokusaiho": Taihojo Jiken Hanketsu niokeru Kokusai Rippo no Sokumen (Customary International Law in Relation to the Immunity from Criminal Jurisdiction of Foreign Ministers: An Aspect of Law-Making in the Arrest Warrant Case)', in S. Sakamoto (ed.), *Kokusai Rippo no Saizensen (Current Issues of International Lawmaking)* (Tokyo: Yushindo, 2009), pp. 29–44.
29 P-M. Dupuy, 'Between the Individual and the State: International Law at a Crossroads?', in L. Boisson de Chazournes and P. Sands (eds), *International Law, the International Court of Justice and Nuclear Weapons* (Cambridge: Cambridge University Press, 1999), p. 456. He then continued: 'But which has almost completely disappeared since, giving way to the

According to Vaughan Lowe, writing in 2000, the prominence of 'interstitial norms' would increase over next decade or two in the field of norm-creation.[30] Interstitial norms are those norms that do not by themselves provide for specific rights or obligations, but exist at the foundation of those rules or between those rules to fulfill a variety of functions. For example, they may fill a gap; they may provide coordination between seemingly conflicting rules; they may provide an interpretative direction for rules; and they may provide 'additional force'[31] to those rules. Indeed, in the *Nicaragua* case, the concept of 'elementary considerations of humanity' assumed a different function from that in the *Corfu Channel* case. In a manner similar to the *Corfu Channel* case, the Court in the *Nicaragua* case elaborated on the same well-recognised principle of 'elementary considerations of humanity', but in this case as the foundation of common Article 3 of the Geneva Conventions. According to the Court, because these conventional rules are based on such a general principle, the rules enunciated in those Conventions could also be recognised as forming a part of customary international law.[32] Thus, in the *Nicaragua* case, elementary considerations of humanity, being the foundation of a provision of a treaty and recognised as a general principle, assumed the function of transforming a treaty obligation into one of a customary nature.

The concept of 'interstitial norms' is one example of the functional view of the sources of international law. Those interstitial norms may take the form of custom, or general principles of law common to domestic laws of major legal systems of the world, or something different. But since interstitial norms provide only, for instance, for gap-filling and do not oblige States directly, it may not be significant for the States and for the Court to stipulate which particular form of source they take. States would be more interested in the persuasiveness of the Court's legal reasoning in their elaboration and application.

Article 38, paragraph 1 of the Statute is founded on a formal conception of the sources of international law. This formalistic conception of sources focuses on the satisfaction of conditions and requirements for the fulfilment of certain forms. This has in turn stimulated the 'source requirements' discussion. The Court has taken this discussion seriously since as early as 1950 in the *Asylum* case, and Article 38(1) continues to be the pivotal provision in this discussion. At the same time, as this chapter has tried to demonstrate, the Court has also

---

narrow and more formalistic approach to the applicable sources of law, strictly linked with what the judges consider, case by case, as being supported by the manifest will of the concerned states.' Ibid.

30 V. Lowe, 'The Politics of Law-Making: Are the Method and Character of Norm Creation Changing?', in M. Byers (ed.), *The Role of Law in International Politics* (Oxford: Oxford University Press, 2000), p. 207, pp. 212–221.
31 M. Shaw, *International Law*, 6th edn (Cambridge: Cambridge University Press, 2008), p. 109.
32 *Nicaragua* case, op. cit., note 16, p. 114 (para. 218).

recognised a functional conception of sources of international law since as early as 1949 in the *Corfu Channel* case. If Vaughan Lowe's prediction is correct, admitting the near completeness of the international legal order with complex and multilayered networks of treaty regimes and customary international law, a more exciting study for the next decade or so will be the functional conception of the sources of international law. The *Corfu Channel Judgment* will be an important beacon for such a study.

13 Intervention and self-help

Theodore Christakis

13.1 Birth of a new era? The Corfu Channel incident as a passage from the 'old' to the 'new international law'

The aim of this chapter is to focus on one of the most famous passages of the *Corfu Channel Judgment*, one of the most often quoted and the most admired pieces of international jurisprudence – the passage concerning the condemnation of the alleged right of intervention and self-help in international law.

From various points of view, this case appears a turning point in the history of international law. As H. Munro wrote in 1947:

> Sixty years ago, a Balkan incident like the mining of the destroyers in the Corfu Channel would probably have led to an immediate British ultimatum to Albania, with limitless vistas of punitive war and Great Power intervention on opposite sides.[1]

Is it really necessary to be reminded of the frequent cases of Great Power intervention that had occurred up until the beginning of the twentieth century for reasons often less important than this? We do know, as a matter of fact, that during the eighteenth and nineteenth centuries and prior to the first real limitations of the use of force in international relations, which only appeared with the Covenant of the League of Nations in 1919 (which had many gaps) and the Treaty of Paris for the Renunciation of War of 1928 (the famous Briand–Kellogg Pact), the right to resort to war was a 'question of morality and policy outside the sphere of Law'.[2] Indeed, military intervention was a privileged means of settling a dispute and Great Powers could, with perfect impunity, conduct terrestrial or naval operations (such as blockades, bombing of coastal towns and ports, reprisals, etc.) against weaker States in order to obtain satisfaction for an alleged injury to their rights or to their citizens' rights or because 'their honor' or 'dignity' had been violated or, even, because

---

1 H. Munro, 'The Case of the Corfu Minefield', *Modern Law Review*, 10 (1947): 363.
2 I. Brownlie, *International Law and the Use of Force by States* (Oxford: Clarendon Press, 1963), p. 20.

'the glory of the State' was at stake.³ Who has forgotten the (in)famous 'gunboat diplomacy' (*politique de la canonnière*') exercised by European States during the nineteenth century in order to intimidate weak States such as Greece (during the blockade by British forces of the port of Piraeus in 1850 in retaliation for the damage suffered by a British subject, David Pacifico) or Venezuela (during the blockade and the shelling of Venezuelan ports in 1902–1903 by Germany, Great Britain and Italy as a coercive measure in order to compel Venezuela to repair the injuries suffered by the subjects of these States)?

But all this was, to quote H. Munro once again, 'in the dark days before observance of international law had developed into the standard of conduct for civilized States'.⁴ From this point of view the attitude of the British Government in the *Corfu Channel* case was to a certain extent a mark of progress. Instead of having recourse to anarchic reprisals, naval blockades and bombardments of the Albanian ports, the UK undertook a careful mine-sweeping operation, after having informed the Albanian Government several times and after having obtained the presence of foreign observers – while submitting at the same time the case to the UN Security Council and then to the ICJ. This feeling of 'progress', of the 'difference between the old and the new International Law', to quote Judge Alvarez,⁵ was apparent in the pleadings in front of the International Court of Justice and this despite the 'strong language' used against *Operation Retail* in the final stage by Albania.⁶ Thus,

---

3 In an article published in 1939, when World War II had already started, Joachim von Elbe wrote:

> The majority of writers during the nineteenth and at the beginning of the twentieth century who, following the positivistic school, rejected the distinction between just and unjust wars, considered war as an act entirely within the uncontrolled sovereignty of the individual state. By applying armed force as the ultima ratio in international politics, a State creates a factual situation where the rules governing the peaceful intercourse among nations are replaced by the law of war. As to the origin and the merits of the act, international law remains silent . . . Another group of writers conceive war as an institution of international law. Thus it is said that 'in the absence of an international organ for enforcing the law, war is a means of self-help, an arm of the law,' a remedy against a legal wrong; it is in international law 'the mode of giving effect to its decisions.' War is the exercise of 'the international right of action,' the highest trial of right in the sense of Bacon's famous saying.
>
> (J. Von Elbe, 'The Evolution of the Concept of the Just War in International Law', AJIL, 33 (1939): 684–685)

4 Munro, op. cit., p. 363.
5 *Corfu Channel case (United Kingdom of Great Britain and Northern Ireland v. Albania), Merits, Judgment, ICJ Reports 1949*, Individual opinion of Judge Alvarez, part IV, p. 42.
6 Albania qualified *Operation Retail* as '*une opération de grand style*', '*une invasion typique*' (*Contre-Mémoire du Gouvernement Albanais du 15 juin 1948*, para. 120, p. 119), 'une action menée sans finesse, sans doigté, avec une brutalité inutile et déconcertante' (*Duplique* of P. Cot of 22 January 1949, ICJ, *Corfu Channel, Pleadings, Oral Arguments, Documents*, Oral Proceedings (Second Part), p. 698).

Sir Eric Beckett, Counsel for the United Kingdom, said during the oral arguments of the UK:

> If you remember the two violent attacks made upon us by Albania and the grave injuries which we had suffered, you may perhaps think that the restraint exercised by the United Kingdom in this case in confining itself to the protective measures which I have described, and then applying to the United Nations, has few, if any parallels in history . . . Do the Albanian Government think that before the days of the League of Nations or the United Nations a State in the position of the United Kingdom would have contented itself with operations the sole purpose of which was to ascertain the truth and to preserve the evidence, if any, in order to bring Albania before the bar of international justice?[7]

Operation Retail was nonetheless still a unilateral action, and a very controversial one from an International Law point of view, and that is why the UK had to invoke the old theories of intervention and self-help in order to justify its operation.

13.2 A State has no right, in modern international law, to intervene in the territory of another State in order to redress an *'injuria'* or to secure possession of evidence

The UK accepted that it had removed the mines without Albanian consent and inside the territorial waters of Albania. Moreover, the UK accepted that, in principle, International Law did not allow a State to assemble a large number of warships in the territorial waters of another State and to carry out minesweeping in these waters. However, the UK position was that it was responding to a situation of extreme urgency and that it was entitled to carry out the minesweeping without anybody's consent.[8]

In his oral pleadings, Sir Eric Beckett characterized his nation's intervention theory as a 'well-recognized principle of international law':

> There is recognized in international law the right of a State, when a state of affairs involving a serious and flagrant breach of the law has been brought about by another State or has been permitted to come about, to intervene by direct action. The purpose of such intervention may be to prevent the continuance of the situation which is in breach of the law, or, where the intervening State has suffered an injury of a nature capable of

---

7 Oral Statement of 12 November 1948, ICJ, *Corfu Channel, Pleadings, Oral Arguments, Documents*, Oral Proceedings (First Part), pp. 296–297.
8 See *Corfu Channel Judgment*, op. cit., pp. 33–34.

being redressed, to further the administration of international justice by preventing the removal of the evidence.[9]

Although the first purpose advanced by the UK was obvious from the beginning (the UK asserted in its notes to Albania a right to act unilaterally in order to clean an international waterway), the second purpose seemed much more as an 'afterthought':[10] having omitted to advance this argument in its diplomatic correspondence with Albania or even in the Security Council debates, it was only in the *Memorial* submitted to the Court one year later that the UK contended that *Operation Retail* was undertaken for the purpose of collecting and preserving evidence (the mines) before it disappeared.

Thereby for the UK, the nature of self-help, was limited: the objective was the abatement of an international nuisance and the preservation of the *'corpora delicti'*. 'We recognize that the right of self-help has been restricted and controlled by the provisions of the Charter,' said Sir Eric Beckett, 'but I am arguing for a limited right of self-help.'[11]

The Court, nonetheless, was not convinced. It followed instead the brilliant argumentation of the Albanian Counsel, French Professor Pierre Cot, who tried to explain how anachronistic the British arguments were on intervention and self-help which had no ground in law. It could be extremely dangerous for the Court to follow the British argument, said Pierre Cot, because intervention can only be the privilege of Great Powers against weak States.[12] Could you imagine Albania undertaking such an operation in the UK's territorial waters? asked Albania in its Rejoinder.[13] This State warned that support of the UK position would create a serious threat to world order and constitute *'la négation même de la justice internationale'*.[14]

The Court thus unanimously rejected the doctrines of 'intervention', 'protection' and 'self-help' as being incompatible with the proper conduct of international relations in the post-World War II era. It said that:

> The Court cannot accept such a line of defence. The Court can only regard the alleged right of intervention as the manifestation of a policy of force, such as has, in the past, given rise to most serious abuses and such as cannot, whatever be the present defects in international organization, find a place in international law. Intervention is perhaps still less admissible

---

9 *Reply of the United Kingdom* of 30 July 1948, p. 282, para. 82.
10 N.H. Shah, 'Discovery by Intervention: The Right of a State to Seize Evidence Located Within the Territory of the Respondent State', *AJIL*, 53 (1959): 599.
11 ICJ, *Corfu Channel, Pleadings, Oral Arguments, Documents*, Oral Proceedings (Second Part), p. 584.
12 ICJ, *Corfu Channel, Pleadings, Oral Arguments, Documents*, Oral Proceedings (First Part), p. 408.
13 'Duplique du Gouvernement Albanais du 20 septembre 1948', p. 373, § 153.
14 Ibid., p. 371, § 147.

in the particular form it would take here; for, from the nature of things, it would be reserved for the most powerful States, and might easily lead to perverting the administration of international justice itself.

The United Kingdom Agent, . . . has further classified 'Operation Retail' among methods of self-protection or self-help. The Court cannot accept this defence either. Between independent States, respect for territorial sovereignty is an essential foundation of international relations. The Court recognizes that the Albanian Government's complete failure to carry out its duties after the explosions, and the dilatory nature of its diplomatic notes, are extenuating circumstances for the action of the United Kingdom Government. But to ensure respect for international law, of which it is the organ, the Court must declare that the action of the British Navy constituted a violation of Albanian sovereignty.[15]

It is thus clear that the fact that Albania's actions were violations of international law engaging its international responsibility did not by itself justify forcible intervention by the United Kingdom. In other terms, the UN era leaves no place for a *'just war'*, or any other military action in order to redress an *'injuria'* – unless of course if there is a specific legal exception such as self-defense or UN Security Council authorization.

13.3 The use of forcible measures by a State to remedy the 'defects' of the UN Charter's collective security machinery is not permitted in international law

Corfu Channel is also an authority for the proposition that the prohibition of forcible intervention does not depend on whether, or how effectively, the UN Charter's collective security machinery functions and that States cannot be relieved of their international obligations because of an eventual failure of the Security Council or the UN.

In order to convince the Court that *Operation Retail* was compatible with international law, the UK said that this unilateral action was the only remedy, because there was no way to obtain interim measures of protection from the ICJ while a reference to the Security Council would have involved delay and would have probably produced nothing but a veto. As Sir Eric Beckett said to the Court:

> It is surely a truism that in proportion as the machinery of justice and police is deficient, self-help must be given a larger scope. We hope for better things, but what is the position today? Your Court has a jurisdiction which depends on consent . . . We could not have come to this Court on the 23rd October with an urgent request for an interim order against Albania to preserve evidence. You would have no jurisdiction . . . [T]he

---

15 *Corfu Channel Judgment*, op. cit., p. 35.

Security Council can only make compulsory orders in the event of a threat to the peace under Chapter VII of the Charter ... And how slowly and uncertainly it works! Does anyone think that the United Kingdom could have got even a recommendation out of the Security Council in ten days or a week if the United Kingdom had applied on 23rd October, and yet, for all we knew, those mines might have been swept or had a flooding device and been descending to the deep sea bed at any time. Will your Court be assisting law, order and justice if it denies in *principle* the existence of the limited right of self-help for which we contend? Such a decision can only favour the law-breaker, great or small. It would be out of keeping with the present state of the world organization. It would be impractical law.[16]

The Court nonetheless clearly rejected this line of defense emphasizing, as we have seen, that 'it can only regard the alleged right of intervention as the manifestation of a policy of force, such as has, in the past, given rise to most serious abuses and such as cannot, whatever be the present defects in international organization, find a place in international law'.[17] This position of the Court has been hailed as a very important step forward in the evolution of International Law by many scholars, both at the time of the judgment[18] and continuously since then.[19] It is nonetheless interesting to observe that this important position taken by the Court did not prevent some commentators from advancing the argument that 'in the absence of collective United Nations machinery, the opportunity for States to resort to self-help in an abusive and unprincipled way continues'.[20] Indeed, as Christine Gray shows in Chapter 14 in this volume, the argument has been openly used by the UK Prime Minister Tony Blair in order to justify the war against Iraq in 2003. But, as both Christine Gray and Olivier Corten have demonstrated in their books on the use of force in international law, the prohibition of intervention is not conditional on the proper functioning of the collective security machinery of the

---

16 ICJ, *Corfu Channel, Pleadings, Oral Arguments, Documents*, Oral Proceedings (Second Part), p. 584.
17 *Corfu Channel Judgment*, op. cit., p. 35.
18 See J. Mervyn Jones, 'The *Corfu Channel case*: Merits', *BYBIL*, 26 (1949): 453.
19 See, for example, C. Greenwood, 'The International Court of Justice and the Use of Force', in V. Lowe and M. Fitzmaurice (eds) *Fifty Years of the International Court of Justice* (Cambridge: Cambridge University Press, 1996), p. 379. But see R. Sloane, 'The Cost of Conflation: Preserving the Dualism of Jus ad Bellum and Jus in Bello in the Contemporary Law of War', *Yale Journal of International Law*, 34 (2009): 81 (arguing that this position of the Court was 'inevitable, for as a creature of the U.N. Charter, it would be remarkable for the Court to declare the Charter a dead letter'. 'Yet', according to this scholar, 'Corfu Channel created a disconnect between the formal law of the Charter, as elaborated by the ICJ, and actual State practice').
20 L. Malone, ' "Green Helmets": A Conceptual Framework for Security Council Authority in Environmental Emergencies', *Michigan Journal of International Law*, 17 (1996): 535.

UN Charter and there is no 'presumed authorization' to intervene in case of unwillingness or impossibility of the UN Security Council to act, unless, of course, once again, if a specific exception (such as a situation of self-defense), authorizes a State to do so.[21]

13.4 The problem of admissibility of evidence obtained by illegal intervention or other unlawful means

Although the Court unanimously rejected the right of intervention and self-help as a legal remedy in order to collect and secure evidence, it is very interesting to notice that the Court admitted at the same time this illegally procured evidence. Indeed, while the Court found that the United Kingdom had clearly violated international law during *Operation Retail*, evidence resulting from that operation was not only taken into account by the Court but was in fact of capital importance.[22] This pushed some scholars to advance the idea that the illegally gained evidence would not be deemed inadmissible by the ICJ or, more generally, by International Courts, on the basis of the *Corfu* precedent. Thus, in an article published in 1982, M. Reisman and E. Freedman observed that the 'phenomenon of a Judgment that affirms a norm, while allowing the illegal fruits of its violation to be enjoyed by the violator, is not unusual'[23] and concluded that:

> For precedential purposes one may say that unlawfully gathered evidence may at least on the facts of the *Corfu Channel* case be deemed admissible. More broadly construed, the only practical interpretation of this aspect of the *Corfu Channel Judgment* would seem to be that certain unlawful collections of evidence will be declared violations of international law, yet no sanction will be imposed on the gatherer, nor will the illegally gained evidence be deemed inadmissible.[24]

---

21 O. Corten, *The Law Against War* (Oxford: Hart, 2010), pp. 348–400 and Christine Gray, *International Law and the Use of Force*, 3rd edn (Oxford: Oxford University Press, 2008), pp. 348–369. See also Christine Gray's contribution to this book (Chapter 14).

22 See N.H. Shah, 'Discovery by Intervention: The Right of a State to Seize Evidence Located Within the Territory of the Respondent State', *AJIL*, 53 (1959): 606:

> As a result of this it was established: (1) that the mines striking the British warships on October 22 were moored contact mines of the GY type; (2) that these mines had been recently laid; (3) that they were laid in Albanian territorial waters and in the exact spot where the British ships were blown up on October 22 and were of the same type as those which struck the British ships on that day; (4) that it was thus clear that the explosions on October 22 were due to the mines belonging to the mine-field discovered by 'Operation Retail'.

23 M. Reisman and E. Freedman, 'The Plaintiff's Dilemma: Illegally Obtained Evidence and Inadmissibility in International Adjudication', *AJIL*, 76 (1982): 747.

24 Ibid., p. 748 (footnotes omitted).

Other scholars challenged this assertion emphasizing that

> At no time did Albania as respondent challenge the admissibility of the evidence derived from the mines swept by the British Navy during *Operation Retail*, or seek to have that evidence excluded on the grounds that it had been obtained unlawfully.[25]

According to these scholars,

> If Albania had offered the plea that the Court should not have permitted the introduction of evidence seized by the United Kingdom Government by an act contrary to international law, it might have prevented the Court from relying on this evidence.[26]

Therefore, and taking into consideration that there is probably no duty on international tribunals to consider *ex officio* the possibility of excluding evidence if there is suspicion that it was unlawfully obtained, the ICJ made no pronouncement on this subject. From this point of view, the judgment in the *Corfu Channel* case is only a precedent for the fact that there is no right of intervention in order to obtain evidence or to secure the '*corpora delicti*' and that such an action should be considered as an internationally wrongful act engaging the responsibility of the State. But, to quote Thirlway: 'On the possibility of excluding evidence because in the course of its collection an act was done that was in itself contrary to international law, the Judgment in the *Corfu Channel* case has nothing whatever to say.'[27]

It is needless to emphasize the continuous importance of this conclusion for some contemporary theories concerning the 'war on terror' and the admissibility of torture-obtained evidence. Indeed, we do know that in these past years some commentators have supported either the use of torture or, at least, the admissibility of illegally obtained evidence in a 'ticking bomb scenario', in order to get crucial information and avert an imminent terrorist attack.[28] This position has nonetheless been rejected not only by an overwhelming

---

25 H. Thirlway, 'Dilemma or Chimera? Admissibility of Illegally Obtained Evidence in International Adjudication', *AJIL*, 78 (1984): 632.
26 A.V.W. Thomas and A.J. Thomas, *Non Intervention: The Law and its Import in the Americas* (Dallas, TX: Southern Methodist University Press, 1956), p. 136. See also Shah, op. cit., p. 607.
27 Thirlway, op. cit., p. 633.
28 See, for example, E. Posner and A. Vermeule, 'Should Coercive Interrogation Be Legal?', *Michigan Law Review*, 106 (2006): 674:

> Coercive interrogation is justified in certain circumstances, even narrow circumstances, there is no sense in treating it as 'illegal' but subject to ex post political or legal defenses. It should be made legal, albeit subject to numerous legal protections – again, in this way like police shootings, wartime killings, preventive detentions, capital

majority of legal academics,[29] but also by the UN General Assembly[30] or national Courts expressing their attachment to the rule of exclusion of torture-obtained evidence.[31] It is clear that the *Corfu Channel Judgment* can in no way be used in order to assist the theories in favor of the admissibility of torture-obtained evidence.[32]

13.5 The problem of the 'threshold' of Article 2§4 of the UN Charter

Contrary to what has often be said, *Corfu* does not seem to be a judgment about Article 2§4 of the UN Charter and the prohibited use of force in International Relations.

It must be emphasized that the Court never mentioned, in this judgment, Article 2§4 and the prohibition of the use of force in international relations. This was criticized at that time by some judges in their separate or dissenting

> punishment, and other serious harms. The law should treat coercive interrogation the way it typically treats coercive governmental practices.
>
> See also M. Bagaric, and J. Clarke, *Torture: When the Unthinkable Is Morally Permissible* (Albany, NY: State University of New York Press, 2007) where the authors take the position that 'the ostensibly brutal act of torture may be permissible if it has the potential to achieve compassionate outcomes in the form of saving innocent lives'.

29 See, for example, D. Hamer, 'The Admissibility of Torture-Obtained Evidence', *International Law Reporter*, May 8, 2010, *Sydney Law School Research Paper* No. 10/19 (available at SSRN: http://ssrn.com/abstract=1548183); T. Thienel, 'The Admissibility of Evidence Obtained by Torture under International Law', *EJIL*, 17(2) (2006): 349–367; R. Pattenden, 'Admissibility in Criminal Proceedings of Third Party and Real Evidence Obtained by Methods Prohibited by UNCAT', *International Journal of Evidence and Proof*, 1 (2006): 40f.; for a more flexible approach, see M. Scharf, 'Tainted Provenance: When, If Ever, Should Torture Evidence Be Admissible?', *Washington & Lee Law Review*, 65 (2008): 169f.

30 See A/RES/59/182 (2005) on *Torture and Other Cruel, Inhuman or Degrading Treatment or Punishment* where the UN General Assembly:

> 1. Condemns all forms of torture and other cruel, inhuman or degrading treatment or punishment, including through intimidation, which are and shall remain prohibited at any time and in any place whatsoever and can thus never be justified . . .; 6. Urges States to ensure that any statement that is established to have been made as a result of torture shall not be invoked as evidence in any proceedings.

31 Such as the House of Lords in the *A v. Secretary of State (No. 2)* case [2006] 2 AC 221.
32 It also goes without saying that the facts in the *Corfu Channel case* were completely different from a situation where torture is used in order to obtain evidence. In the first case only the interests and rights of Sovereign States were at stake, while the latter case involves violations of a fundamental human right having a *jus cogens* character. The practice of international tribunals, such as the International Criminal Tribunal or the International Criminal Tribunal for the Former Yugoslavia, seems to indicate that there is no systematic inadmissibility of 'tainted evidence' when the rules violated are not of a fundamental importance. For an analysis of this point, see A. Lagerwall, *Le principe ex injuria jus non oritur en droit international contemporain*, Thèse soutenue à l'ULB, 2008, pp. 80ff.

opinions[33] and is still criticized today by some scholars who consider that the *Corfu Channel Judgment* initiated a very 'cautious approach to the question of use of force' by the ICJ which is also to be found in subsequent jurisprudence and till today, such as in the judgments in the *Land and Maritime Boundary between Cameroon and Nigeria* (2002) case, the *Oil Platforms* case (2003) and the *Armed Activities on the Territory of the Congo (DRC v. Uganda)* (2005) case.[34] With due respect, we do not agree with these criticisms.

It should be noted that the general rule of prohibition of the use of force of Article 2§4 never appeared in the diplomatic correspondence between the UK and Albania. In the multiple UN Security debates, no State, including Albania, ever presented *Operation Retail* as a violation of Article 2§4, but simply mentioned an 'incident'.[35] And even the second question submitted to the Court by the Special Agreement between the two States only spoke about a probable violation of Albania's sovereignty – not about Article 2§4. It was only in its Rejoinder and in the Oral proceedings that Albania presented, for the first time, this case as a violation of the rule prohibiting the use of force,[36] but the UK firmly rejected this allegation[37] and the ICJ did not even mention this rule it in its judgment.

---

33 See *Corfu Channel Judgment*, op. cit., Judge Ečer, Dissenting Opinion (pp. 130–131):

> The Judgment should mention . . . the provisions of the United Nations Charter, in particular, Article 2, para. 4, and Article 42. The International Court's task as the juridical instrument of the UN is more far-reaching than that of a domestic court . . . The International Court's task is therefore to help to strengthen the cohesion of the international community. The instrument of cohesion of the international community is the United Nations Charter . . . In referring to the Charter, the Judgment would emphasize that the supreme task of the International Court of Justice is: that its jurisdiction should contribute to the technical development of international law and also promote peaceful relations between the States of the world, and thus help to maintain peace.

See also Judge Krylov, Dissenting Opinion (pp. 76–77), Judge Azevedo, Dissenting Opinion (p. 108), and Judge Alvarez, Separate Opinion (pp. 42 and 47).

34 See in particular the analysis of Christine Gray in Chapter 14 of this volume.

35 See Security Council, 2nd year, 109th meeting (19 February 1947); 111th meeting (24 February 1947) and 121st meeting (21 March 1947).

36 'Duplique du Gouvernement Albanais du 20 septembre 1948', para. 154, p. 373. It is interesting to note that Albania made no reference to Article 2§4 of the UN Charter and the prohibition of the use of force in its Counter-Memorial, talking there only about a 'flagrant violation' of 'Albania's sovereignty'. See 'Contre-Mémoire du Gouvernement Albanais du 15 juin 1948', pp. 116–122 and 138–146.

37 See, for example, statements by Sir Eric Beckett in ICJ, *Corfu Channel, Pleadings, Oral Arguments, Documents*, Oral Proceedings (First Part), p. 296 or ICJ, *Corfu Channel, Pleadings, Oral Arguments, Documents*, Oral Proceedings (Second Part), p. 595 insisting that 'we retract nothing from our whole-hearted acceptance of paragraph 4 of Article 2 of the Charter', but the 'measure of self-help' used during *Operation Retail* had nothing to do with this because this operation 'was a sweeping of a strait for mines against the will of Albania, the Power whose territorial waters this part of the strait was' and with 'no interference with the lives of the people of this very non-maritime Power'.

This is of great significance as there is a major dilemma in International Law concerning the threshold of applicability of Article 2§4. On the basis of the *Corfu* judgment we could argue that some limited interventions in a territory of a third State, with no real gravity, with no use of force against this State and not even any *will* to use such force, probably do not meet the threshold of applicability of Article 2§4. We could then apply, under some important restrictions and conditions, this reasoning in operations such as: forcible police measures undertaken by a State in zones under its jurisdiction (whether on land, at sea or in the airspace); some incursions into foreign territory to forestall harmful operations by an armed group (including terrorists) which was preparing to attack the territory of the State or in pursuit of an armed band of criminals who had crossed the frontier and perhaps had their base in foreign territory; limited commando operations in foreign territory in order to protect the lives of nationals; limited operations outside the State's territory in order to eliminate or neutralize a source of troubles (including pollution) which threatens to occur or to spread across the frontier; and even a forcible abduction of a terrorist in a foreign country.

Following some articles published on the admissibility of these very limited operations in International Law,[38] Olivier Corten analyses in depth this question

---

38 In two articles published after the 9/11 attacks we defended the idea, relying on the ILC's work and the intellectual constructions of one of its *Rapporteurs* on state of necessity, Roberto Ago, that limited military actions and counter-terrorist operations abroad, such as the ones examined above, which clearly do not constitute aggression, could be justified by a state of necessity, assuming of course that the requirements of this circumstance are met in a specific case (see T. Christakis, 'Unilatéralisme et multilatéralisme dans la lutte contre la terreur: l'exemple du terrorisme biologique et chimique', in K. Bannelier *et al.* (eds), *Le droit international face au terrorisme* (Paris: Pedone, 2002), pp. 173–176 and, especially, T. Christakis, 'Vers une reconnaissance de la notion de guerre préventive?' in K. Bannelier *et al.* (eds), *L'intervention en Iraq et le droit international* (Paris: Pedone, 2004), pp. 28–44. See also T. Christakis, 'Existe-t-il un droit de légitime défense en cas de simple "menace"? Une réponse au "Groupe de personnalités de haut niveau" de l'ONU', in *Les métamorphoses de la sécurité collective. Droit, pratique et enjeux stratégiques* (Paris: Pedone, 2005), p. 221. Articles available at: http://cesice.upmf-grenoble.fr/35333675/0/fiche___pagelibre/&RH=1265280570220). Olivier Corten reacted to those articles demonstrating that an interpretation of the UN Charter, as it was devised and then construed by several General Assembly resolutions, confirms that the prohibition of the use of force represents a legal regime from which there is 'no way out' and that, as a *jus cogens* rule, the prohibition of the use of force cannot be circumvented by reference to exceptional circumstances and secondary rules such as state of necessity (O. Corten, 'L'état de nécessité, peut-il justifier un recours à la force non constitutif d'agression?', *The Global Community Yearbook of International Law & Jurisprudence*, I (2004): 11–50). At the same time, nonetheless, O. Corten seems to agree with our conclusion that 'under certain circumstances, a State cannot be held internationally responsible for an "antiterrorist" military operation or a military action to rescue nationals' (O. Corten, *The Law Against War* (Oxford: Hart, 2010), p. 247). The only difference is that O. Corten considers that in those cases state of necessity could *only* be operative if there is no applicability of Article 2§4 (because the threshold of applicability of this article is not met). But as soon as we enter the domain of

in his recent book, *The Law Against War*[39] and concludes that, on the basis of the *Corfu Channel* precedent[40] and the subsequent practice of States, 'such a violation of sovereignty should not systematically be considered a violation of the prohibition of the use of force between States, but will depend on the circumstances of each case'.[41] The great merit of Corten's work is that he also tries to identify *when* a limited coercive action could be considered as not meeting the threshold of applicability of Article 2§4, announcing six criteria that need to be taken into consideration in this respect.[42]

What precedes must not lead to any kind of confusion: the fact that a very limited coercive action undertaken in a foreign State's territory and giving rise to no confrontation between the agents of the two States, might sometimes be considered as not meeting the threshold of applicability of Article

> the use of force as regulated by the UN Charter and Article 2§4, it is no longer possible to invoke state of necessity or other circumstances precluding wrongfulness or responsibility. See also Section 13.6 in this Chapter.

39 O. Corten, *The Law Against War*, pp. 52–92.
40 Ibid., p. 70
41 Ibid., p. 85.
42 According to Corten:

> Practice suggests that six questions can be asked in this respect: 1. Where was the coercive action carried out? If a State acts within its own territorial boundaries, it will be presumed to be implementing police measures as part of the normal exercise of its sovereignty . . . If, however, the coercive action is conducted in another State's territory or in zones that are not subject to any jurisdiction, there will be a greater tendency to characterise the act as serious and to apply Charter article 2(4); 2. In what context does the military action occur? If the two States involved are engaged in armed conflict or if tension is high, the military action will probably be seen in the context of Charter article 2(4), even if the action does not seem serious in absolute terms. The case of the failed US military operation in Iran in 1980, of the Israeli commando in Tunis in 1988 or of certain aerial incidents (USS Vincennes or the 1999 incident between India and Pakistan in 1999) illustrate the importance of this question; 3. Who decided on the military operation and who carried it out? . . .; 4. What is the target of the military operation? If it is the infrastructure, the agents or a fortiori the leaders of another State, things will more easily come within the ambit of article 2(4) than for purely private targets (as in the Rainbow Warrior case) . . .; 5. Has the military operation given rise to confrontation between the agents of two States? If so, it seems difficult to set aside article 2(4), even if the fighting remained limited. The Entebbe raid or the Mayaguez case, which can be contrasted with the Rainbow Warrior or the Liberia (1990) cases, are instructive on this point; 6. What is the scope of the means implemented by the intervening State? If confronted with a straightforward abduction or the despatch of a few men who do not open fire (Eichmann affair), there will be less of a tendency to apply article 2(4) than if faced with troop landings, bombardments, or bombings (Mayaguez or Entebbe precedents). The greater the means used, the more the State in whose territory the action takes place will be affected, even if the State is not the main target of the operation and there is no fighting between its armed forces and those of the intervening State. This criterion can therefore have decisive effects.
>
> (Ibid., pp. 91–92)

2§4 of the Charter, does not mean that this is not a violation of International Law, nor does it mean that the State 'victim' of such a violation should stay like 'a sitting duck' while this violation occurs.

On the first point, it is clear that such an action, even if not considered as a violation of Article 2§4 of the Charter, is still an illegal intervention and a violation of the sovereignty of the State where this coercive action occurs. There was no need to invoke Article 2§4 of the Charter in order to condemn *Operation Retail* in the *Corfu Channel* case, as there was no need to invoke this article in order to condemn the forcible actions of French agents in New Zealand in the *Rainbow Warrior* case.

On the second point it is also clear that there is no 'gap' in International Law concerning the possibility of reaction of the State on the territory of which the limited coercive action occurs. Of course, somebody could argue that given the fact that Article 2§4 of the Charter is not applicable, the State victim of a violation of its sovereignty cannot invoke self-defense and Article 51 of the UN Charter. While this is true, nothing prohibits this State from resisting and reacting to the coercive action of foreign agents on its territory under the usual police powers conferred on it by territorial jurisdiction in land, sea or its air space. In other words, it is not necessary to try desperately to seek a 'licence to react' in Articles 2§4 and 51 of the UN Charter, as this authorization already exists under the classic sovereign rights of every State. Indeed, the exercise of such police measures in order to stop the illegal operations of foreign agents on its territory could 'trigger' the applicability of Article 2§4 of the Charter if the foreign agents resist and if there is an important armed confrontation between the agents of the two States. This can easily be illustrated, for example, by the famous *Entebbe raid* case where, whatever the arguments used to justify this operation, there was no doubt about the applicability of Article 2§4 of the UN Charter.[43]

13.6 Self-help and the concept of 'state of necessity' today

This brings us to a final question which is: what is the difference after all? If in both cases there is a violation of international law, then what is the point in

---

43 An Israeli commando engaged in action at Entebbe airport on 4 July 1976 in order to free the hostages held by a group of the Popular Front for the Liberation of Palestine. This action took place without the consent of the government of Uganda and the Israeli commando killed 20 Ugandan soldiers on duty at the airport who tried to oppose the operation. The matter was raised before the UN Security Council, which was unable to adopt any resolution. But the military operation was considered by all States to be a use of force, with Israel invoking Charter Article 51, and most States condemning the action as an armed attack. For exact quotations of the debates in the UN Security Council, see O. Corten, ibid., p. 87 and pp. 225–227.

making this distinction between violation of Article 2§4 and violation of the principle of sovereignty, non-intervention and non-interference?

As we have already hinted above,[44] there might be an important consequence of this distinction. According to Article 26 of the ILC Articles on State responsibility, it is impossible to invoke any kind of circumstance in order to preclude the wrongfulness of any act of a State which is not in conformity with an obligation arising under a peremptory norm of general international law.[45] Article 2§4 of the UN Charter is widely considered such a peremptory norm.[46] Respecting the sovereignty of States is of course a major rule of international law but not a *jus cogens* rule. This means that in some cases,[47] and especially in the case of a state of necessity, a State violating the sovereignty of another State under such a limited intervention (which does not meet the threshold of Article 2§4 of the UN Charter), could avoid international responsibility or, at least, use the circumstances of Article 25 of the ILC Draft Articles as *attenuating* circumstances.

We have argued extensively elsewhere about the fact that state of necessity should not be considered as a 'circumstance excluding wrongfulness', but instead as a *'circumstance excluding or attenuating responsibility'*.[48] The *Corfu Channel* case could seem to offer a hint in this respect, but in reality it is not extremely useful. The Court found indeed that Albania's 'failure to carry out its duties after the explosions, and the dilatory nature of its diplomatic notes' were *'extenuating circumstances'* for the UK.[49] This gives the impression that the Court did accept the theory of mitigation of damages under the doctrine of

---

44 *Supra*, note 38.
45 'Nothing in this chapter precludes the wrongfulness of any act of a State which is not in conformity with an obligation arising under a peremptory norm of general international law', *International Law Commission's Draft Articles on State Responsibility for Internationally Wrongful Acts*, Annexed to GA Res. 56/83 of 12 December 2001.
46 The best analysis is provided by O. Corten, *The Law Against War*, op. cit., pp. 200–213.
47 We will not discuss here the hypothesis of countermeasures (article 22 of the ILC Articles) or distress (article 24) which are other forms of 'self-help' admitted as 'secondary rules' of contemporary international law.
48 T. Christakis, 'Les "circonstances excluant l'illicéité": une illusion optique?', in *Droit du pouvoir, pouvoir du droit, Mélanges offerts à Jean Salmon* (Bruxelles: Bruylant, 2007), pp. 223–270. See also: T. Christakis, '"Nécessité n'a pas de Loi"? Rapport général sur la nécessité en droit international', in *La nécessité en droit international*, colloque de la Société française pour le droit international (Paris: Pedone, 2007), pp. 9–62, and T. Christakis, 'Quel remède à l'éclatement de la jurisprudence CIRDI sur les investissements en Argentine? La décision du Comité ad hoc dans l'affaire *CMS c. Argentine*', *Revue Générale de Droit International Public*, 4 (2007): 879–896. Those articles are available at: http://cesice. upmf-grenoble.fr/35333675/0/fiche___pagelibre/&RH=1265280570220. But see S. Heathcote, *State of Necessity and International Law*, thesis No. 772, Université de Genève, Genève, 2005 (denying altogether the existence of a general secondary rule on state of necessity in contemporary customary international law).
49 *Corfu Channel Judgment*, op. cit., p. 35. Emphasis added.

extenuating circumstances.⁵⁰ The problem is nonetheless that Albania was not 'innocent' in this case, so it becomes an intricate one to resolve: Is the *Corfu Channel* case a casuistic recognition of the fact that necessity in order to safeguard an essential interest against a grave and imminent peril can act as an *'extenuating circumstance'*? Or was this just a case about 'clean hands' and contribution, by Albania, to the injury similar to that described by Article 39 of the ILC Draft?⁵¹

Whatever the answer, the conclusion must be that while the Court clearly and definitely rejected in the *Corfu Channel Judgment* the alleged right of intervention or the right of self-help as *primary rules* of international law, the Court said nothing about the state of necessity, a contemporary form of self-help which could still be admitted today as a *secondary rule* of International Law, capable, under some strict conditions, to exclude or extenuate the responsibility of a State who has violated a non-peremptory rule of international law.

---

50 See J. Mervyn Jones, 'The *Corfu Channel case*: Merits', *BYBIL*, 26 (1949): 452.
51 According to Article 39: 'In the determination of reparation, account shall be taken of the contribution to the injury by wilful or negligent action or omission of the injured State or any person or entity in relation to whom reparation is sought'. *Loc. cit.*

14 A policy of force

Christine Gray

14.1 Introduction

The International Court of Justice's warning against a 'policy of force' in the *Corfu Channel* case seems to have been forgotten by some States and commentators in recent years. But it is as important today as it was in 1949 when the Court rejected the United Kingdom's arguments that it was justified in using force on behalf of the international community. In recent years the prohibition on the use of force in Article 2(4) has been challenged by States and writers seeking to justify a wide right to use force. In so doing, many of them echo the arguments of the United Kingdom in the *Corfu Channel* case. Too often since the end of the Cold War, writers and States have turned to the threat or use of force as an appropriate method of resolving differences. We have seen this in the NATO action over Kosovo; in the doctrine of revived authorization to use force used to justify the use of force against Iraq; in the 'Bush doctrine' of pre-emptive self-defence against a non-imminent attack; and in the claims since the terrorist attacks of 9/11 for a wide right to use force against terrorists in third States not involved in the terrorist attack. Such wide justifications for the resort to force can indeed be seen as a 'policy of force'; international law and policy do not support such claims, but commentators in search of something new often seem too ready to countenance such arguments on the basis of the practice of just a few States.

The *Corfu Channel* case – the first judgment on the merits given by the new International Court of Justice – was to prove an unusual case in so far as it concerned the use of force.[1] It thus for the first time raised the question as to the role of the Court in such cases. There were no further decisions on the merits by the Court on the use of force until nearly 40 years later in the *Nicaragua* case.[2] The question of force arose before the Court in the *Corfu*

---

1 *Corfu Channel case, Judgment of April 9th 1949, ICJ Reports 1949*, p. 4 (hereafter 'Judgment').
2 *Military and Paramilitary Activities in and against Nicaragua (Nicaragua v. United States of America), ICJ Reports 1986*, p. 14. C. Greenwood, 'The International Court of Justice and the Use of Force', in V. Lowe and M. Fitzmaurice (eds), *Fifty Years of the International Court*

Channel case through Albania's counter-claim. The issue was set out in Question 2 of the Special Agreement: has the United Kingdom under international law violated the sovereignty of the Albanian People's Republic by reason of the acts of the Royal Navy in Albanian waters on the 22nd October and on the 12th and 13th November 1946 and is there any duty to give satisfaction?

This chapter will focus on *Operation Retail* of 12–13 November 1946. After Albania had challenged the right of passage of warships through the Corfu Channel, the United Kingdom sent ships through the Channel claiming the right of innocent passage on 22 October 1946; its warships were blown up by mines in the Corfu Channel. HMS *Saumarez* was a total loss; HMS *Volage* was seriously damaged; 44 sailors were killed and 42 injured. In response, the United Kingdom undertook *Operation Retail*: on 12–13 November 1946 it sent minesweepers into the Corfu Channel, claiming that it was entitled to recover mines from Albania's territorial waters in order to secure evidence as to who was responsible for laying the mines which had blown up the British ships. It also sent an aircraft carrier, cruisers and other war vessels to accompany the minesweepers.

Albania said that any minesweeping undertaken inside its territorial waters without its consent could only be considered as a deliberate violation of Albanian territory and sovereignty; Albania called this an invasion. The United Kingdom argued that it had a right of intervention.

14.2 The Court's rejection of a policy of force

At the end of its judgment in the *Corfu Channel* case the International Court of Justice clearly rejected the United Kingdom's claim that it was justified in using force, saying in the final part of its reasoning that the alleged right of intervention was the 'manifestation of a policy of force, such as has, in the past, given rise to most serious abuses and such as cannot, whatever be the present defects in international organization, find a place in international law'.[3]

The Court's language and reasoning in this regard were clearly influenced by Albania's pleadings, especially by the persuasive and amusing Oral Pleadings of Pierre Cot. It was he who referred to the United Kingdom's 'politique de force',[4] and this phrase was adopted by the Court in its judgment.

---

of Justice (Cambridge: Cambridge University Press, 1996), p. 373; C. Gray, 'The Use and Abuse of the International Court of Justice: Cases Concerning the Use of Force after Nicaragua', *European Journal of International Law*, 41 (2003): 867.

3 Judgment, op. cit., p. 35.
4 Albania, 'Exposé', 19 November 1948, p. 422.

14.3 The United Kingdom's pleadings

The arguments of the United Kingdom presented to the Court prefigure those adopted by States and commentators seeking to justify a wide right to use force or pursuing a 'policy of force'. The Court said in its judgment on the merits that the United Kingdom's main line of defence for *Operation Retail* was that the remaining mines – the *corpora delicti* – must be secured as soon as possible for fear that they should be taken away, without leaving traces, by the authors of the minelaying or by the Albanian authorities. The Court described this as a new and special application of the theory of intervention by means of which the State intervening would secure possession of evidence in the territory of another State, in order to submit it to an international tribunal.[5] Albania strongly denied that the United Kingdom was acting on behalf of the International Court of Justice or the Security Council in its military intervention in Albania.[6] This argument (as set out at greater length in the United Kingdom's pleadings) that the United Kingdom was really acting on behalf of the International Court of Justice or of the Security Council clearly resembles the doctrine of implied or revived authority used by those involved in *Operation Iraqi Freedom* in 2003.

The Court also said that the second justification offered by the United Kingdom for *Operation Retail* was that its actions were justified as self-protection or self-help. The Court rejected this, saying that between independent States respect for territorial sovereignty is an essential foundation of international relations. Although the Court recognized that the Albanian government's complete failure to carry out its duties after the explosions, and the dilatory nature of its diplomatic notes, were extenuating circumstances for the action of the United Kingdom government, '[t]o ensure respect for international law, of which it is the organ, the Court must declare that the action of the British Navy constituted a violation of Albanian sovereignty'.[7] These two justifications – one that the United Kingdom had been acting on behalf of the international community and the other that it had been acting on its own behalf – had been intertwined in the United Kingdom's pleadings.

14.4 The language of the Court

It is immediately striking that in the *Corfu Channel* case the Court did not expressly refer to Article 2(4) of the UN Charter in its reasoning and made no mention of Article 2(4) in its judgment. The UN Charter had entered into force on 24 October 1945; the events in question took place less than a year later. But, rather than refer to Article 2(4), the Court in its reasoning used the

---

5 Judgment, op. cit., p. 34.
6 Cot, 'Oral Duplique', 22 January 1949, pp. 675–679.
7 Judgment, op. cit., p. 35.

language of Question 2 of the Special Agreement, that the United Kingdom had violated Albania's sovereignty under international law. And it was this language that the Court echoed in the operative part of its judgment.[8] The Court did not explicitly address the issue of what amounts to use of force, or of its relation to forcible intervention.[9] In this way the International Court of Justice took a cautious approach to the question of the use of force.[10]

The Court was similarly cautious in its choice of language relating to the issue of the use of force in later cases such as *Land and Maritime Boundary between Cameroon and Nigeria* (2002).[11] In this case the Court not only did not mention Article 2(4) of the UN Charter, it totally avoided pronouncing on the question whether either party had illegally resorted to force. The Application of Cameroon had expressly asked the Court to declare that Nigeria was in violation of Article 2(4) of the UN Charter.[12] However, Nigeria argued that it was not appropriate for the Court to decide on issues concerning State responsibility in a boundary case.[13] In its later Counter-claim Nigeria did accuse Cameroon of responsibility for incidents involving the use of force, but it did not expressly call for a decision under Article 2(4).[14] Nor did the Separate Opinions mention Article 2(4), apart from that of *ad hoc* Judge Ajibola (Nigeria) who said that the Court as a principal organ of the UN had a cardinal duty to encourage, by its judgments, all member States to observe Article 2(4).[15]

The Court was also cautious in its choice of language in the *Oil Platforms* case (2003)[16] and *Armed Activities on the Territory of the Congo (DRC v. Uganda)* (2005).[17] In *Oil Platforms*, Iran's Application had made no reference to the UN Charter; the Court's jurisdiction was based on the 1955 Treaty of Amity. But

---

8 Ibid., p. 36.
9 See T. Christakis' contribution to this book (Chapter 13).
10 But it was probably not as cautious as H. Lauterpacht suggested ten years later in *The Development of International Law by the International Court* (London: Stevens and Sons Ltd, 1958), p. 317, when he said that:

> It is probable that these observations (on the policy of force), so comprehensive in scope, were limited to the particular circumstances of the case before the Court. There is in general international law no absolute prohibition of intervention; traditional international law permits intervention in a number of cases.

But Lauterpacht did not provide any convincing justification for this interpretation, and he continued, 'It is possible – and perhaps probable – that inasmuch as intervention takes the form of physical force it is, by virtue of Article 2(4) of the Charter of the United Nations, no longer open to its Members.'
11 *ICJ Reports 2002*, p. 303.
12 Ibid., at para. 310; Cameroon, Application, paras 18–19.
13 Nigeria, Preliminary Objections, Ch. 6, at 6.15; Counter-Memorial, para. 25.3.
14 Nigeria, Counter-Memorial, Vol. III, Counterclaims, Ch.25, para. 26.3.
15 Dissenting Opinion, para. 4.
16 *ICJ Reports 2003*, p. 161.
17 *ICJ Reports 2005*, p. 168.

the Court held that it was able to consider whether there had been unlawful use of force in violation of the UN Charter and international law.[18] The USA had justified its actions under the Treaty of Amity as lawful self-defence. The Court rejected this claim, but did not expressly find the USA guilty of a violation of Article 2(4);[19] it limited its judgment to the terms of the Treaty of Amity.

In *DRC v. Uganda*, the Court found by 16 to 1 in its judgment on the merits that Uganda had violated the principle of non-use of force in international relations and the principle of non-intervention.[20] But it did not expressly refer to Article 2(4) in the operative part of its judgment, even though the DRC in its Application had specifically asked the Court to declare that Uganda was guilty of an act of aggression contrary to Article 2(4) of the UN Charter. In its reasoning the Court did refer expressly to Article 2(4).[21]

This cautious approach by the International Court of Justice contrasts with the lack of restraint shown by arbitral tribunals in the recent *Eritrea/Ethiopia*[22] and *Guyana/Suriname*[23] cases. In those cases the arbitration tribunals did expressly find violations of Article 2(4), and they did so even though it was controversial whether their jurisdiction extended this far. Arguably it would have been possible and even preferable for them to have avoided venturing into such difficult and sensitive territory and coming to their rather unusual and surprising conclusions on the use of force.

14.5 The role of the Court in the cases concerning the use of force

As was mentioned above, in the *Corfu Channel* case the Court itself did not mention Article 2(4) of the UN Charter. But some Separate and Dissenting Opinions took a different view of the role of the Court, and said that the Court should have expressly mentioned Article 2(4), just as separate and dissenting judges argued later in *Oil Platforms* and *DRC v Uganda* that the Court's role required it to take a more assertive role in this regard.

Thus in the *Corfu Channel* case some separate and dissenting judges argued that the Court should have made express mention of the new regime in the UN Charter. Judge Azevedo (Brazil) in his Dissenting Opinion still used some old language indicating that it was not only the United Kingdom which had not yet fully adjusted to the Charter regime: 'Apart from legitimate defence, a

---

18 *ICJ Reports 2003*, para. 42.
19 Ibid., para. 78.
20 *ICJ Reports 2005*, para. 345.
21 Ibid., para. 148, 153, 165.
22 Ehiopia's *ius ad bellum* claims, *International Legal Materials*, 45 (2006): 430.
23 Award of arbitral tribunal constituted pursuant to Article 287 of the UN Convention on the Law of the Sea, 17 September 2007, paras 425–447, *International Legal Materials*, 47 (2008): 164.

counter-stroke confestim, "hot pursuit", or an emergency, nothing justifies the use of force, not even the pretext of reprisals.' But he went on to add that 'it would be absolutely contrary to the spirit of the San Francisco Charter and to several of its articles for a country to become judge in its own case.' So, even if Albania's refusal of passage was unlawful, the United Kingdom was not justified in its resort to force.[24] As regards *Operation Retail*, the minesweeping should have been done under the auspices of the UN. The collection of evidence was repugnant to the letter and the spirit of the San Francisco Charter:

> The world of today will no longer tolerate a practice which has never been sincerely regarded as lawful, and one which allows the noblest aims of humanity to be used, all too easily, as a cloak for the worst abuses.[25]

Judge *ad hoc* Ečer (Czechoslovakia, for Albania) was more specific in his Dissenting Opinion:

> The Judgment should mention the provisions of the UN Charter, in particular, Article 2(4) and Article 42. The International Court's task as the juridical instrument of the UN is more far-reaching than that of a domestic court . . . The International Court's task is therefore to help to strengthen the cohesion of the international community. The instrument of cohesion of the international community is the UN Charter . . . In referring to the Charter, the Judgment would emphasize that the supreme task of the International Court of Justice is: that its jurisdiction should contribute to the technical development of international law and also promote peaceful relations between the States of the world, and thus help to maintain peace.[26]

Judge Krylov (USSR), in his Dissenting Opinion, focused more directly on the Charter, and specifically ruled out unilateral military action by State. He said that the acts undertaken by the British Navy were nothing else but the intervention of a foreign Power in the affairs of another State – a weak State which possessed no means *vim vi repellere*. There was no right of intervention or self-help in international law:

> The British argument on this point relies on assertions which had already been outstripped by the further development of international law, especially since the ratification of the Charter of the UN. Since 1945, i.e., after the coming into force of the Charter, the so-called right of

---

24 Dissenting Opinion, para. 38.
25 Ibid., para. 42.
26 Dissenting Opinion, Part II.

self-help, also known as the law of necessity (Notrecht), which used to be upheld by a number of German authors, can no longer be invoked. It must be regarded as obsolete. The employment of force in this way is forbidden by the Charter (para 4 of Art. 2) ... According to the UN Charter (Art. 42) demonstrations and other operations carried out by the air, sea or land forces of Members of the UN may only be undertaken in pursuance of a decision by the Security Council. The Charter, therefore, prohibits unilateral military action by its Members.[27]

Finally Judge Alvarez (Chile) in his Individual Opinion said that 'The Charter of the UNO (para. 4 of Article 2) forbids the employment of force except in the case of legitimate self-defence (Art. 51).' In other cases a State must have recourse not to force, but to the Security Council or to the International Court of Justice. 'Here we see clearly the difference between the old and the new international law.'[28] The intervention of a State had long been condemned. It is expressly forbidden by the Charter of the UN. The same applies to other acts of force, and even to a threat of force. The United Kingdom's acts were not justifiable self-help, but a violation of Albanian sovereignty.[29]

This contrast between the silence with regard to Article 2(4) in the majority judgment of the Court in the *Corfu Channel* case and the express support for Article 2(4) in certain separate and dissenting judges reflects a difference of view on the proper role of the Court. Such differences have been apparent also in subsequent cases. Judges disagree on the general question as to how far the Court's role as principal judicial organ of the UN requires it to be assertive in its pronouncements on the law on the use of force; and more specifically they have disagreed as to how far the Court should be radical in its development of the law on controversial subjects such as self-defence against terrorists.

In the *Oil Platforms* case, even though there was controversy over the Court's jurisdiction to pronounce on the use of force, the Court was prepared to consider this issue. It said in justification of its examination of self-defence that 'the self-defense issues presented in this case raise matters of the highest importance to all members of the international community'.[30] But in the operative part of its judgment, the Court only:

> [f]inds that the actions of the United States of America against Iranian oil platforms on 19 October 1987 and 18 April 1988 cannot be justified as

---

27 Dissenting Opinion, para. 6.
28 Individual Opinion, Part IV.
29 Ibid., Part VIII.
30 *ICJ Reports 2003*, para. 38.

measures necessary to protect the essential security interests of the United States of America under Article XX, paragraph 1 (d), of the 1955 Treaty of Amity, Economic Relations and Consular Rights between the United States of America and Iran, as interpreted in the light of international law on the use of force.

It did not make any more general and more serious finding on the violation of the UN Charter by the USA. Judges Elaraby (Egypt), Simma (Germany) and Judge *ad hoc* (for Iran) Rigaux (Belgium) all said that as the case was being considered in the context of the lead-up to 2003 Iraq War, the Court should have gone further: having rejected the USA's claim to be acting in self-defence, it should expressly have pronounced on the UN Charter. Judge Simma was critical of the 'half-heartedness' of the Court in not restating and thus reconfirming the fundamental principles of the law of the UN on the prohibition of the use of force at a time when such a reconfirmation was called for with the greatest urgency. The opaque language used by the Court – 'international law on the question' – might be seen as a downgrading of the relevance and the importance of the rules of the Charter on the use of force.[31] Judge Rigaux was even more outspoken. The Court needed to make the position on the use of force clear because some had challenged the prohibition on the use of force in Article 2(4).[32] He singled out the writing of John Bolton (US Under-Secretary of State for Arms Control and subsequently US representative at the UN) in this regard. Accordingly it was appropriate for the principal judicial organ of the UN to take the opportunity to recall the binding force of Article 2(4). In contrast the US, UK and Japanese judges (whose States supported the legality of the use of force against Iraq) said that the Court should not have pronounced on the use of force at all.

Again in *Armed Activities on the Territory of the Congo (DRC v. Uganda)* Judges Elaraby and Simma said that the Court should have been bolder in its judgment and snould have pronounced on the DRC's claim that Uganda was guilty of aggression in violation of Article 2(4). The latter asked:

> Why not call a spade a spade? If ever there was a military activity before the Court that deserves to be qualified as an act of aggression, it is the Ugandan invasions of the DRC. Compared to its scale and impact, the military adventures the Court has had to deal with in earlier cases, as in *Corfu Channel* and *Military and Paramilitary Activities in and against Nicaragua* or *Oil Platforms*, border on the insignificant.[33]

---

31 Separate Opinion, paras 5–8.
32 Separate Opinion, paras 31–33.
33 Separate Opinion, para. 2.

14.6 The contrasting pleadings of the United Kingdom and Albania

The Pleadings in the *Corfu Channel* case on *Operation Retail* show a strong contrast between the approaches of the United Kingdom and Albania to the use of force. The United Kingdom's arguments are reminiscent of a passing world: they stress the right to intervene by direct action. In both its written and oral pleadings the language is that of self-redress, self-help and necessity. The United Kingdom even stresses its own restraint with regard to *Operation Retail*. For example, Sir Eric Beckett, Counsel for the United Kingdom, said that in the light of the violent attacks by Albania and the grave injuries to the United Kingdom, 'you may perhaps think that the restraint exercised by the United Kingdom in this case in confining itself to the protective measures which I have described and then applying to the UN, has few, if any parallels in history.' He asked:

> Do the Albanian Government think that before the days of the League of Nations or the United Nations a State in the position of the United Kingdom would have contented itself with operations the sole purpose of which was to ascertain the truth and to preserve the evidence, if any, in order to bring Albania before the bar of international justice?[34]

But the United Kingdom's tone altered during the Court proceedings. In the later oral proceedings there is a clear shift away from the earlier assertive language insisting on a right of intervention, and away from the stress on past practice and reliance on pre-Charter writers, to reliance on a more limited right restricted to very specific facts. The United Kingdom indeed stated that this was 'absolutely the first case' of this type of intervention to secure evidence on behalf of the Court.[35]

In contrast, Albania stressed that a new world had come into existence since the creation of the UN:

> [T]he right of intervention is outmoded, and has, in fact, completely disappeared since the adoption of the Charter of the United Nations ... Self-redress is only a part of primitive law and has been displaced, at any rate in most cases, by collective action through the UNO.[36]

Albania repeatedly stressed that it was a weak State, without a navy; this was a premeditated United Kingdom operation, 'une opération de grand style', 'une invasion typique', a war fleet presented as a mere covering force. The aim

---

34 Oral Statement, 12 November 1948, pp. 296–297.
35 Beckett, Oral Reply, 19 January 1949, pp. 579–582; as noted by Cot, Statement, 19 November 1948, p. 410.
36 Albania, 'Duplique', 20 September 1948, paras 145, 151, 153–154; Beckett, Statement, 12 November 1948, p. 295.

of *Operation Retail* was intimidation, to impose by force a decision of the United Kingdom.[37]

Albania also claimed that the United Kingdom did not see Albania as its equal in law,[38] and argued that the right of intervention asserted by the United Kingdom was open only to powerful States.[39] The United Kingdom tried to address this point.[40] It said that it was not true that the limited principle of a narrow right of self-help could be invoked only by powerful States against weak ones. The United Kingdom accepted that Albania could not have staged *Operation Retail*, but it did not accept that the principle was inherently one-sided. It claimed that small powers would not hesitate to use the right of intervention against the United Kingdom.[41]

In its rejection of a policy of force, the Court supported the position that laws should be equally applicable to powerful and weak States alike. The Court took account of Albania's argument on this point in its judgment when it stated that the right of forcible self-help claimed by the United Kingdom would in practice be available only to 'the most powerful States'.[42] Part of the United Kingdom's counter-argument was that it was not challenging the universal nature of the rules of international law on the use of force, because weak States could persuade other powerful States to act on their behalf.[43] This may have been persuasive during the Cold War, but it is less so today. Now a State which is hostile to the aims or actions of the USA may turn to Russia or China for political support, but is unlikely to secure military support as had occurred in the proxy conflicts of the Cold War.

14.7 Subsequent use of the arguments in the *Corfu Channel* case

Since the end of the Cold War, and particularly since 9/11, the USA and her allies such as the United Kingdom, Israel and Ethiopia have seemed to follow 'a policy of force', sometimes as part of a 'global war on terror', and arguably one that has demonstrated that even for powerful States the use of force rather than the use of peaceful settlement and resort to the Security Council to secure their ends has generally proved ineffective and even counter-productive. They have sought to resolve disputes by the use of force in Kosovo, Afghanistan,

---

37 Albania, Counter-Memorial, 15 June 1948, paras 120, 122, 143; 'Duplique', 20 September 1948, paras 132–141.
38 Albania, 'Duplique', 20 September 1948, paras 156–157.
39 Albania, 'Oral Exposé', 18 November 1948, p. 408; 'Duplique', 22 January 1949, pp. 675–677.
40 UK, 'Oral Reply', pp. 582–583.
41 This was rejected by Albania in its Duplique, 22 January 1949, pp. 675–677.
42 Judgment, p. 35.
43 Beckett, Reply, 19 January 1949, p. 582.

Iraq, Lebanon, Somalia and Gaza, on the bases of humanitarian intervention, Security Council authorization, or a wide right of self-defence. These military actions pose a challenge to the *ius cogens* prohibition on the use of force in Article 2(4), but there is no express consensus among States that could support any transformation of *ius cogens*.

In order to justify their use of force in the episodes mentioned above, States have used arguments that were pre-figured in the *Corfu Channel* pleadings. We have seen that in the pleadings of both Albania and the United Kingdom there was also almost no reference to Article 2(4) in particular, or to the UN Charter provisions on the use of force in general. However, a fundamental disagreement on the interpretation of Article 2(4) – one which was to become significant later and is still important today – did emerge in these pleadings.

The only United Kingdom reference to Article 2(4) came in Sir Eric Beckett's oral statement.[44] Here we find a narrow interpretation of Article 2(4):

> It is well known that even the most highly developed systems of law recognize certain rights of self-defence and self-redress . . . International law, unhappily, cannot yet be regarded as a fully developed system of law either as to the certainty of its principles or more particularly as to its machinery for enforcing the law . . . The Security Council can be rendered powerless by a single vote. Consequently it is only natural that the rights of self-defence and self-help which are recognized in municipal law should have a somewhat greater importance in international law.

The United Kingdom accepted that the large rights of forcible intervention and action to obtain redress by self-help which formerly existed had now become more restricted and controlled with the growth of international organization. It also claimed that: 'Our actions on the 12th–13th November threatened neither the territorial integrity nor the political independence of Albania. Albania suffered thereby neither territorial loss nor any part of its political independence.'

The United Kingdom proclaimed its 'whole-hearted acceptance' of Article 2(4). But two United Kingdom arguments limiting the scope of Article 2(4) are clear. First, the UK claimed that defects in international organization justify a right of forcible intervention, in this instance in order to help preserve evidence. Where the Security Council is slow to act, then a State may act unilaterally in order to help the International Court of Justice to carry out its functions. The United Kingdom claimed that it was acting 'within the spirit of the Charter', that its forcible intervention was justified in order to help the International Court of Justice and the Security Council. In its Reply, the United Kingdom said: It is argued that the right of self-help or intervention can only be exercised when there is an immediate necessity and that in this

---

44 Oral statement, 12 November 1948, para. 296.

case the proper course for the United Kingdom was to have applied to the Security Council immediately after the incident on 22nd October and to have asked the Security Council to arrange for the sweeping on the Channel under international auspices. The answer is that it was urgent to take this action quickly. The Security Council took many weeks to deal with the Corfu issue; consequently there would have been every opportunity for the removal of the evidence.[45]

Albania's response was that Article 2(4) over-rode any earlier right of intervention.[46] It rejected any claim that a State could act unilaterally to implement international justice or to act on behalf of 'the appropriate international organization' as particularly dangerous.[47] As regards the humanitarian mandate and international benefit claimed by the United Kingdom, international law did not recognize that even a Great Power had the power to give itself unilaterally the mandate to invade another State. There was no legal basis for such an invasion.[48] On the particular facts, *Operation Retail* was not an operation taken on the Court's behalf or on behalf of the Security Council; it was the British government's own enterprise. The United Kingdom had put forward an ingenious and seductive argument, but not one that was acceptable in international law. It was contrary to the UN Charter and to the general trend in international politics and international law which was to substitute collective action for unilateral action and to outlaw self-help.[49]

The International Court of Justice adopted the Albanian position and rejected the United Kingdom's argument that defects in international organization could justify the unilateral use of force: the right of intervention was the 'manifestation of a policy of force, such as has, in the past, given rise to most serious abuses and such as cannot, *whatever be the present defects in international organization*, find a place in international law'.[50] The United Kingdom's argument on Article 2(4) was apparently also rejected by the International Court of Justice in the *Nicaragua* case where the Court said that:

> The principle of non-use of force may thus be regarded as a principle of customary international law, not as such conditioned by provisions relating to collective security, or to the facilities or armed contingents to be provided under Article 43 of the Charter.[51]

---

45 UK, 'Written Reply', 30 July 1948, p. 284, para. 82(g).
46 Albania, 'Written Duplique', 20 September 1948, para. 154; Cot, 'Oral Exposé', 18 November 1948, p. 408.
47 'Oral Duplique', 22 January 1949, p. 677.
48 Counter-Memorial, 15 June 1948, paras 142, 145 at p. 144(e).
49 Cot, 'Oral Statement', 19 November 1948, p. 417; Cot, 'Duplique', 22 January 1949, pp. 675–679.
50 Judgment, p. 35.
51 *ICJ Reports 1986*, p. 214, para. 188.

Therefore, those who claim an exceptional right to use force 'on behalf of the international community', either for the USA or for 'democratic States', run counter to the approach of the International Court of Justice in the *Corfu Channel* case.

Nevertheless we see the United Kingdom's argument – that Article 2(4) should be interpreted to allow the unilateral use of force when the UN collective security system is ineffective – being put forward by commentators such as Michael Reisman during the Cold War.[52] And even after the end of the Cold War, there was a brief re-emergence of the United Kingdom argument that, if the Security Council could not function because of a single veto, a State could take action to implement the wishes of the international community. This was the suggestion of United Kingdom Prime Minister Tony Blair with regard to Iraq: he notoriously suggested that an unreasonable veto preventing the adoption of a Security Council resolution authorizing force against Iraq might justify the use of force by the USA and the United Kingdom on behalf of the Council in order to implement the Council's earlier resolutions.[53] This argument of the unreasonable veto was rejected by the United Kingdom Attorney-General in his legal advice of March 2003 on the use of force against Iraq,[54] and it was not maintained by United Kingdom government ministers giving evidence to the 2009–10 Iraq Inquiry.[55]

The claim to be acting on behalf of the international community was used more broadly with regard to Kosovo in 1999 and Iraq in 2003. Some States involved in the use of force in Kosovo relied not on humanitarian intervention, but on implied Security Council authorization under a series of resolutions determining that Serbia was in material breach of its obligations.[56] This argument was taken further with regard to Iraq in 2003, when the States involved in *Operation Iraqi Freedom* claimed that their use of force was based on revived Security Council authorization in order to secure Iraqi compliance with its disarmament obligations as laid down by the Council. This policy split NATO; several major member States wanted to continue UN weapons inspections of Iraq rather than resort to force. The claim by the States using force that they were acting on behalf of the international community with

---

52 M. Reisman, 'Coercion and self-determination', *American Journal of International Law*, 78 (1984): 642; for a reply, see Schachter, 'The Legality of Pro-democratic Invasion', ibid., p. 646.
53 See C. Gray, *International Law and the Use of Force* (Oxford: Oxford University Press, 2008), 3rd edn, p. 358, note 151.
54 'Memorandum of Advice on the Use of Force against Iraq', *International and Comparative Law Quarterly*, 54 (2005): 415.
55 See, for example, *Written Transcript of Evidence of Jack Straw*, former Secretary of State for the Foreign and Commonwealth Office, 8 February 2010, pp. 47–49.
56 Gray, *International Law and the Use of Force*. op. cit., p. 351; J. Lobel and M. Ratner, 'Bypassing the Security Council', *American Journal of International Law*, 93 (1999): 124.

regard to Kosovo and Iraq was rejected by many States.[57] The lasting impact of the US arguments on Security Council authorization of force may be seen in the Security Council's subsequent resolutions on Iran and North Korea with regard to non-proliferation; members of the Security Council have taken care to avoid any wording that could be taken as authority for the use of force.[58]

In its letter to the Security Council in justification of *Operation Iraqi Freedom*, the USA also invoked self-defence.[59] It seemed to US State Department legal advisers that this operation could be seen as an example of pre-emptive action to stop Iraq from acquiring weapons of mass destruction, in line with the 'Bush doctrine' of pre-emptive self-defence as outlined in the 2002 and 2006 US National Security Strategy.[60] But many commentators concluded that the use of force against Iraq in 2003 showed the dangers of the doctrine of pre-emptive self-defence. Since the end of the George W. Bush Presidency there has been little sign of any continuing support for pre-emptive self-defence where there is no imminent armed attack, one of the most dangerous examples of a policy of force.

The second argument limiting the scope of Article 2(4) in the *Corfu Channel* case appeared when Sir Eric Beckett said: 'Our action on 12/13 November threatened neither the territorial integrity nor the political independence of Albania. Albania suffered thereby neither territorial loss nor any part of its independence.'[61] The Court in finding that the United Kingdom's minesweeping action was unlawful rejected this narrow interpretation of Article 2(4).[62]

This argument – that it is legally possible to use force in the territory of another State without violating Article 2(4) if the aim is not to overthrow the government or to seize its territory – was rarely made expressly by States during the Cold War.[63] But it may be seen as underlying two recent and controversial doctrines. First, it may be seen as underlying the arguments of those who claim that a State may use force in self-defence against non-State actors in a third State in response to past terrorist attacks, even in the absence of complicity in the actions of the non-State actors by the third State. Commentators have suggested that *Operation Enduring Freedom* against Al Qaida in Afghanistan after the terrorist attacks of 9/11 marked a shift in the law of self-defence; they claim that the use of force by Turkey against the PKK in Iraq, by Israel against Hizbollah in Lebanon (2006), Hamas in Gaza

---

57 O. Corten, *Le droit contre la guerre* (Paris: Pedone, 2008), p. 561.
58 C. Gray, 'The Use of Force to Prevent the Proliferation of Nuclear Weapons', *Japanese Yearbook of International Law*, 52 (2009), p. xx.
59 UN document S/2003/351.
60 W. H. Taft and T. F. Buchwald, 'Pre-emption, Iraq and International Law', *American Journal of International Law*, 97 (2003): 553.
61 Oral statement, 12 November 1948, p. 296.
62 Greenwood, op. cit., p. 379.
63 C. Gray, *International Law and the Use of Force*, op. cit., pp. 31–33.

(2008–09), and by Ethiopia against Somalia (2006) constitute the emergence of a wider right of self-defence and hence a limit on the prohibition of the use of force in Article 2(4).[64]

But such claims are difficult to justify. Most importantly, the States taking this type of action have not offered a clear legal justification that their actions are self-defence against non-State actors even in the absence of State complicity in the armed attack.[65] Their military operations have not always been discussed in open Security Council meetings. When debates have been held, there has been little by way of legal discussion. These operations, like their controversial predecessors during the Cold War, look more like self-help than self-defence.[66] Attempts to revive or transform the doctrine of necessity to justify the use of force against non-State actors seem problematic.[67] The question arises whether it is possible to narrow the prohibition in Article 2(4), generally accepted as *ius cogens*, without express discussion and universal acceptance. Moreover, the International Court of Justice has been distinctly cautious in its pronouncements on self-defence in the *Wall* Advisory Opinion[68] and in *DRC v. Uganda*.

The United Kingdom's argument for a narrow interpretation of Article 2(4) in the *Corfu Channel* case can also be seen with regard to Kosovo, in the argument by some States and commentators that the use of force in 'humanitarian intervention' does not violate Article 2(4), but is rather a new right which has emerged because of the development of human rights since World War II. The 1999 NATO bombing campaign to protect the ethnic Albanians of Kosovo has been invoked by some as a paradigm for humanitarian intervention; for others, it should be seen rather as a failure of negotiation which led to a deterioration rather than an improvement of the situation. The United Kingdom Attorney-General in his advice on the use of force against Iraq later acknowledged that 'humanitarian intervention' was a controversial doctrine; he rejected the use of the doctrine to justify resort to force in that particular case.[69] The Non-Aligned Movement has maintained its steadfast opposition to the doctrine of humanitarian intervention.[70]

---

64 See, for example, C. Tams, 'The Use of Force against Terrorists', *European Journal of International Law*, 20 (2009): 359.
65 See T. Ruys, *Armed Attack and Article 51 of the UN Charter* (Cambridge: Cambridge University Press, 2010), Chapter 1.
66 Gray, op. cit., p. 195.
67 See, for example, K. Trapp, 'Back to Basics: Necessity, Proportionality and the Right of Self-Defence against Non-State Terrorist Actors', *International and Comparative Law Quarterly*, 56 (2007): 141; J. A. Green, *The International Court and Self-Defence in International Law* (Oxford: Hart Publishing, 2009).
68 *Legal Consequences of the Construction of a Wall in Occupied Palestinian Territory, ICJ Reports 2004*, p. 136, para. 139.
69 'Memorandum of Advice on the Use of Force against Iraq', *International and Comparative Law Quarterly*, 54 (2005): 415.
70 Though the inclusion of a reference to 'humanitarian intervention' in the *Constitutive Act of the African Union*, Article 4(h), has added to the controversy.

Thus, since the end of the Cold War justifications based on humanitarian intervention, self-defence against non-State actors and preemptive self-defence may all be seen as echoing the UK's arguments for a limited prohibition on the use of force in the *Corfu Channel* case. The dangers in these wide claims to use force are apparent in Russia's rejection of US criticism of its forcible intervention in Georgia in 2008. In the Security Council meetings on this conflict Russia made deeply sarcastic reference to what it saw as the hypocrisy of the USA: the USA now called on States to refrain from the use of force, but had itself used force unlawfully in Iraq; the USA now invoked territorial integrity, but had itself intervened unlawfully in Kosovo.[71] And when the USA accused Russia of seeking regime change, it replied that regime change was an American expression.[72] This reminds us that a State's actions and arguments may be invoked by other States in support of their own use of force.[73] Albania's arguments in the *Corfu Channel* case – that powerful States should not be allowed to claim that they are acting on behalf of the international community and that such arguments are not compatible with the collective security system created by the UN Charter – remain convincing to all those concerned to limit the use of force as a means of resolving disputes.

---

71 UN document S/PV.5969, pp. 16–17.
72 UN document S/PV.5953, p. 18.
73 See T.M. Franck and E. Weisband, *Word Politics* (New York: Oxford University Press, 1972).

15 Foundational judgment or constructive myth?

The Court's decision as a precursor to international environmental law

Karine Bannelier

15.1 Introduction

The history of the International Court of Justice begins in Corfu with an amazing judgment which, undoubtedly, marked its time and the future generations. This impression is particularly evident with regard to the fundamental principles of international environmental law, especially regarding the consecration of the famous principle of due diligence as a principle of customary international environmental law. The story is both strange and topical of what a permanent Court can achieve over time and of this special irreplaceable situation conferred by the 'permanence' of its status.

At first sight, it is strange to realize how the *Corfu Channel*'s judgment is often considered by many scholars as one of the three foundational judgments[1] (with the *Trail Smelter* and the *Lake Lanoux* arbitrations), for the subsequent development of international environmental law.

This trilogy is said to have built the backbone of international environmental law by giving it its well-known cardinal principle *sic utere tuo ut alienum non laedas* ('one should use one's own property so not to injure another').[2] In reality, these three decisions did not 'invent' this principle. Borrowed from Roman law, this principle was transposed to international law by Max Huber in the Island of Palmas's arbitration as a corollary of sovereignty. According to this well-known Award:

---

1 According to Alexandre Kiss and Jean-Pierre Beurier, these three judgments 'fourniront les fondements juridiques aux développements qui domineront pour une large part la période suivante, "l'ère de l'environnement" ', in A. Kiss and J-P. Beurier, *Droit international de l'environnement* (Paris: Pedone, 2000), p. 29, para. 23.
2 Quoting the *Corfu Channel Judgment* as an 'authority', the *Rapporteur* of the International Law Commission, Stephen C. McCaffrey, wrote in his *Second Report on the Law of the Non-Navigational Use of International Watercourses*: 'The maxim sic utere tuo alienum non laedas ... is a generally accepted principle of law governing the relations between States', A/CN.4/399 and Add. 1 and 2, 19 March, 12 and 21 May 1986, p. 131.

Territorial sovereignty, as has already been said, involves the exclusive right to display the activities of a State. This right has as corollary a duty: the obligation to protect within the territory the rights of other States, in particular their right to integrity and inviolability in peace and in war, together with the rights which each State may claims for its nationals in foreign territory.[3]

But if these three decisions did not invent this principle, these decisions used it in such a way that it became the spring from which flowed many rules and principles of international environmental law, such as, especially, the 'due diligence principle' popularized many years later by the Stockholm Conference,[4] the principle of 'good neighbourliness' or 'the obligation to notify other States of the risk of significant harm to which they are exposed'.

What is strange and should be underlined here, is that the *Corfu Channel* case is different from both the others, because the dispute in this case did not deal with an environmental problem – contrary to the *Trail Smelter* case and the *Lake Lanoux* case: there was here no transboundary pollution, nor a dispute concerning the management of shared natural resources. This singularity, however, never prevented the most qualified scholars from referring to the *Corfu Channel Judgment* abundantly. As underlined by the Special *Rapporteur* of the International Law Commission (ILC), Stephen C. McCaffrey in its *Second Report on the Law of the Non-Navigational Use of International Watercourses*:

> The case thus does not deal at all with international watercourses, nor strictly speaking, with environmental injuries such as those suffered through air pollution. Nonetheless, certain aspects of the Court's opinion have been cited repeatedly in connection with legal analyses of international environmental problems.[5]

The ILC thus quoted the Court's judgment several times in support of its comments concerning the *Draft Articles on the Law of the Non-Navigational Uses of International Watercourses* as well as the *Draft Articles on Prevention of Transboundary Harm from Hazardous Activities* in order to attest to the existence of general principles in the field of international environmental law.

In this context one can ask: how this judgment, which was *not* the first one claiming the existence of a due diligence principle and which was *not* about environmental concerns, was propelled to a kind of mythical foundation of international environmental law? Was it just an illusion? Or does this judgment contain in essence some innovating and fertile proposals?

---

3 *Island of Palmas* case, Award of 4th April 1928, *RIAA* II, p. 839.
4 See our development *infra*.
5 *Second Report on the Law of the Non-Navigational Uses of International Watercourses*, op. cit., p. 115.

Our answer is definitively positive: *Corfu Channel* was a rich and modern judgment which incorporated important potentialities for the development of international environmental law. Despite the iconic *status* of the dictum of the *Trail Smelter* Award,[6] the content of the obligation of due diligence given here by the Court is much more convincing and useful for international environmental law than the one given by the *Trail Smelter* Award[7] or the *Palmas Island* case. This judgment seems to go much further than these two arbitrations, giving to international environmental law the true contemporary dimension of the due diligence principle. From this point of view, the *Corfu Channel* case could be held as a foundational judgment for international environmental law (see Section 15.2).

But what makes the richness of this ruling is that the Court has subsequently taken up and developed the principle of due diligence into a customary principle of international environmental law. The Court thus succeeded in turning this foundational judgment into a constructive myth for the protection of the environment (see Section 15.3).

15.2 A foundational judgment

In order to understand the contribution of the Court in this field, it is important to recall briefly the reasoning of this judgment.

In its judgment, the Court held that Albania had violated its obligation to notify and warn by not informing the United Kingdom of the danger of the minefield. According to the Court, this obligation to notify and warn was:

> based . . . on certain general and well-recognized principles, namely: elementary considerations of humanity, even more exacting in peace than

---

6 Quoting A. P. Rubin who wrote that 'Every discussion of the general international law relating to pollution starts and must end, with a mention of the Trail Smelter Arbitration', (A. P. Rubin, 'Pollution by Analogy: the Trail Smelter Arbitration', *Oregon Law Review*, 50 (1971): 259), Karin Mickelson underlines that 'the *Trail Smelter* case is more an object of reverence than a subject of analysis', K. Mickelson, 'Rereading *Trail Smelter*', in R. M. Bratspies and R. A. Miller, *Transboundary Harm in International Law: Lessons from the Trail Smelter Arbitration* (Cambridge: Cambridge University Press, 2006), p. 79 and note 1.

7 Many authors have highlighted the shortcomings of this Award. According to Jay Ellis:

> There is little agreement on how its holding should be interpreted and applied, and its persuasive value is often called into question . . . [I]t is difficult to discover the basis on which Canada would be responsible at international law for the damage caused by the smelter. The Tribunal did not identify the nature of the international legal obligation that Canada breached in this case, and in any event this question was not put to it . . . However, we still need a basis on which to impute liability to the *State*. This could be provided by a generally applicable due diligence obligation, such as was articulated in *Corfu Channel*.
>
> (J. Ellis, 'Has International Law Outgrown *Trail Smelter?*' in Bratspies and Miller, op. cit., pp. 56, 60–61)

in war ; the principle of the freedom of maritime communication; *and every State's obligation not to allow knowingly its territory to be used for acts contrary to the rights of other States.*[8]

In this reasoning, three points should be underlined. First, the Court gave to the principle of due diligence a broad dimension, a dimension without borders (see Section 15.2.1). Second, this geographical extension of the principle is also clearly accompanied by a condition, which is knowledge (see Section 15.2.2), and third, the due diligence principle is accompanied by an obligation to inform and notify (see Section 15.2.3).

15.2.1 *The Court gave to the principle of due diligence a new dimension, a dimension without borders*

One remembers that in the *Trail Smelter* case, the dispute was about transboundary harm. It was about fumes from a smelter located in Canada that was polluting the US territory. This specific case led to a rather limited dictum in the Award, relevant only to transboundary pollution that causes damage in the territory of another State. According to the *Trail Smelter* Award:

> under principle of international law, as well as of the law of the United States, no State has the right to use or permit the use of its territory in such a manner as *to cause injury by fumes in or to the territory of another or the properties or persons therein*, when the case is of serious consequence and the injury is established by clear and convincing evidence.[9]

However, in the *Corfu Channel* case, the damage is not transboundary since it is carried out on ships and British citizens inside the territorial waters of Albania and in an international strait. Thus, the *Corfu Channel Judgment* does not include any territorial limit and extends potentially to all areas located under State sovereignty, as well as beyond national jurisdiction.

And it is in this dimension given by the Court that the principle was recognized as a cornerstone principle of international environmental protection. According to the famous Principle 21 adopted at the Stockholm Conference in 1972:

> States have, in accordance with the Charter of the United Nations and the principles of international law, the sovereign right to exploit their own resources pursuant to their own environmental policies, and the responsibility

---

8 *Corfu Channel case*, Judgment of April 9th 1949, *ICJ Reports 1949*, p. 22. Emphasis added.
9 *Trail Smelter* case, Award of 11 March 1941, *RIAA* III, p. 1965.

to ensure that activities within their jurisdiction or control do not cause damage to the environment of other States or of areas beyond the limits of national jurisdiction.[10]

This principle without borders was then reaffirmed 20 years later in Principle 2 of the Rio Declaration.[11]

15.2.2 The geographical extension of the principle is accompanied by a condition which is knowledge

In the reasoning of the Court, due diligence is clearly expressed as an obligation of conduct and its violation is subordinated to the knowledge which a State had, or ought to have, of the activities taking place on its territory.[12] According to the Court, the fact that a State has the control of its territory does not imply automatically the knowledge of all that is happening on its territory. The ICJ underlines that:

> it cannot be concluded from the mere fact of the control exercised by a State over its territory and waters that that State necessarily knew, or ought to have known, the authors. This fact by itself and apart from other circumstance neither involves *prima facie* responsibility nor shifts the burden of proof.[13]

And, following this reasoning, the Court concluded that it is because the laying of the minefield could not have been accomplished without the knowledge of the Albanian government that Albania violated its obligation of due diligence.

This point is really interesting because the Court seems here to contradict the holding of the *Trail Smelter* arbitration: that a State is responsible for every transboundary harm when it exceeds a certain threshold of gravity. On the contrary, the reasoning of the Court in the *Corfu Channel* case is not exclusively based on the gravity of the harm but also clearly on the knowledge of the unlawful activities or situation. And, once again, we should underline that it is in this dimension given by the Court that the principle of due diligence was recognized. For example, by the International Law Commission in its

---

10 Principle 21 of the *Declaration of the United Nations Conference on the Human Environment*, Stockholm, UN Doc. A/CONF/48/14/REV.1.
11 See *infra* note 20.
12 For example, according to Birnie, Boyle and Redgwell, the true significance of this judgment 'may be confined to a narrower point about warning other States of known dangers', in P. Birnie, A. Boyle and C. Redgwell, *International Law and the Environment* (Oxford: Oxford University Press, 2009), p. 144.
13 *Corfu Channel case*, op. cit., p. 18.

commentary on Article 8 of the *Draft Articles on the Law of the Non-Navigational Uses of International Watercourses*:

> 8. A watercourse State can be deemed to have violated its due diligence obligation only if *it knew or ought to have known* that the particular use of an international watercourse would cause significant harm to other watercourse States.
>
> 9. As observed by the ICJ in the *Corfu Channel* case ... it cannot be concluded from the mere fact of control exercised by a State over its territory and waters that that State necessarily knew, or ought to have known, of any unlawful act perpetuated therein ...[14]

15.2.3 The due diligence principle is accompanied by an obligation to inform and notify

The Court has also held that the 'obligation not to allow knowingly its territory to be used for acts contrary to the rights of other States' implied an obligation to inform and notify. And it is precisely the violation of this obligation (because Albania did nothing to warn the UK) which engaged the responsibility of Albania. Here again one can note that this obligation to inform and notify, which is of particular importance for international environmental law, was not disclosed by the *Trail Smelter* Award, but by the *Corfu Channel Judgment*. The paternity of *Corfu* for the development of this obligation has been widely recognized, and today 'it is legitimate to view the *Corfu Channel* case as authority for a customary obligation to give warning of known environmental hazards'.[15] According to the ILC:

> The obligation to notify other States of the risk of significant harm to which they are exposed is reflected in the *Corfu Channel* case *where the ICJ characterized the duty to warn as based on* 'elementary considerations of humanity'.[16]

And finally, what is very interesting in the case of *Corfu* is that the Court adopted a much broader approach than the one expressed in the *Trail Smelter* Award or in the *Lake Lanoux* Award. While these *two* awards forcefully

---

14 *Draft Articles on the Law of the Non-Navigational Uses of International Watercourses and Commentaries Thereto and Resolution on Transboundary Confined Groundwater*, Report of the International Law Commission on the work of its forty-sixth session, 1994, p. 104. Emphasis added.
15 Birnie *et al.*, op. cit., p. 182.
16 *Draft Articles on Prevention of Transboundary Harm from Hazardous Activities with Commentaries*, Report of the International Law Commission on the work of its fifty-third session, 2001, p. 159.

expressed the 'no harm rule',[17] the Court judgment seems to express a principle of respecting the right of third States which is 'a broader, [but] less precise obligation'.[18]

15.3 A constructive myth

Today, nobody disputes the customary character of the due diligence principle in international environmental law nor its status as the cornerstone of international environmental law. The success of this collective construction would not have been possible without the Court's contribution. But the Court took a long time to address directly the issue of environmental protection in international law. It is only from the second half of the 1990s, with the *Legality of the Threat or Use of Nuclear Weapons* case and the *Gabcikovo-Nagymaros Project* case that the Court anchored authoritatively the due diligence principle into customary international environmental law (see Section 15.3.1).

But that anchor was just the first step in the life of this principle. To make it effective, it was necessary to define its contours and content. That is what the Court began to do 60 years after *Corfu* in the *Pulp Mills* case (see Section 15.3.2).

15.3.1 The consecration of the principle of due diligence as a principle of customary international environmental law

As we have already mentioned, it is well known that the role of the principle of due diligence in protecting the environment was clearly recognized by the international community in 1972 in Principle 21 of the Stockholm

---

17 The *Trail Smelter* Award expressed an obligation not 'to cause injury by fumes' (see *supra* note 9). The *Lake Lanoux* Award similarly stated:

> 13. Le Gouvernement espagnol s'est efforcé d'établir également le contenu du droit international positif actuel (Mémoire espagnol, p. 65; Contre-Mémoire espagnol, p. 105). Certains principes dont il fait la démonstration sont, à supposer celle-ci acquise, sans intérêt pour le problème actuellement examiné. Ainsi, en admettant qu'il existe un principe interdisant à l'Etat d'amont d'altérer les eaux d'un fleuve dans des conditions de nature à nuire gravement à l'Etat d'aval, un tel principe ne trouve pas son application à la présente espèce, puisqu'il a été admis par le Tribunal, à propos de la première question examinée plus haut, que le projet français n'altère pas les eaux du Carol.
>
> (*Lake Lanoux* case, Award of 16 November 1957, *RIAA* XII, p. 308)

18 E. Brown Weiss, 'Opening the Door to the Environment and to Future Generations', in L. Boisson de Chazournes and P. Sands (eds), *International Law, the International Court of Justice and Nuclear Weapons* (Cambridge: Cambridge University Press, 1999), p. 345.

Declaration[19] and reaffirmed 20 years later in 1992 in Principle 2 of the Rio Declaration[20] and also in many other treaties.[21]

The repetition of the principle in instruments of different legal nature has often raised questions about the legal nature of the principle itself. Namely, the question was whether or not the due diligence principle was a customary principle of international environmental law.[22]

This issue was decided by the Court itself. In this regard, the Court expressed a very consistent approach, a true judicial policy. The Court recognized and then recalled, whenever a case permitted, the customary international law status of the due diligence principle for the protection of the environment.[23]

First, in 1996 in its Advisory Opinion relating to the *Legality of the Threat or Use of Nuclear Weapons*, the ICJ recognized the customary character of the due diligence principle, stating that:

> the existence of the general obligation of States to ensure that activities within their jurisdiction and control respect the environment of other States or of areas beyond national control is now part of the corpus of international law relating to the environment.[24]

Then, the following year, in the *Gabcikovo-Nagymaros* case, the Court 'pushed the nail'. Quoting itself, the Court stated that:

---

19 See *supra* note 10.
20 Principle 2 of the Rio Declaration repeats almost word for word Principle 21 of the Stockholm Declaration. It stated that

> States have, in accordance with the Charter of the United Nations and the principles of international law, the sovereign right to exploit their own resources pursuant to their own environmental and developmental policies, and the responsibility to ensure that activities within their jurisdiction or control do not cause damage to the environment of other States or of areas beyond the limits of national jurisdiction.
> (*Rio Declaration on Environment and Development*, Rio de Janeiro, 3–14 June 1992, UN Doc. A/CONF.151/26 (Vol. I))

21 See examples given by J. Brunnée, 'Sic utere tuo ut alienum non laedas', in *Max Planck Encyclopedia of Public International Law* (Oxford: Oxford University Press, 2008), para. 11; T. Koivurova, 'Due Diligence', in ibid., paras 29–30.
22 See J. E. Vinuales, 'The Contribution of the International Court of Justice to the Development of International Environmental Law: A Contemporary Assessment', *Fordham International Law Journal*, 32 (2008–09): 240.
23 For the importance of the contribution of the Court in recognizing the existence of customary rules, see P. Weil, 'Le droit international en quête de son identité', in *Collected Courses of The Hague Academy of International Law*, 237 (1992): 160–201.
24 *Legality of the Threat or Use of Nuclear Weapons*, Advisory Opinion, *ICJ Reports 1996*, pp. 241–242, para. 29.

The Court recalls that it has recently had occasion to stress, in the following terms, the great significance that it attaches to respect for the environment, not only for States but also for the whole of mankind:

> 'the environment is not an abstraction but represents the living space, the quality of life and the very health of human beings, including generations unborn. The existence of the general obligation of States to ensure that activities within their jurisdiction and control respect the environment of other States or of areas beyond national control is now part of the corpus of international law relating to the environment' (*Legality of the Threat or Use of Nuclear Weapons, Opinion, ICJ Reports 1996*, pp. 241–242, para. 29).[25]

More recently, in its judgment of 20th April 2010 in the *Pulp Mills* case, the Court highlighted twice the relationship between *Corfu* and the principle of prevention and diligence applied in the protection of the environment:

> The Court points out that the principle of prevention, as a customary rule, has its origins in the due diligence that is required of a State in its territory. It is 'every State's obligation not to allow knowingly its territory to be used for acts contrary to the rights of other States' (Corfu Channel (United Kingdom v. Albania), Merits, Judgment, *ICJ Reports 1949*, p. 22). A State is thus obliged to use all the means at its disposal in order to avoid activities which take place in its territory, or in any area under its jurisdiction, causing significant damage to the environment of another State. This Court has established that this obligation 'is now part of the corpus of international law relating to the environment' (*Legality of the Threat or Use of Nuclear Weapons, Advisory Opinion, ICJ Reports 1996 (I)*, p. 242, para. 29).[26]

Then a few paragraphs further, the Court reminded once again that:

> The existence of the general obligation of States to ensure that activities within their jurisdiction and control respect the environment of other States or of areas beyond national control is now part of the corpus of international law relating to the environment (*Legality of the Threat or Use of Nuclear Weapons, Advisory Opinion, ICJ Reports 1996 (I)*, pp. 241–242, para. 29).[27]

---

25 *Case Concerning the Gabcikovo-Nagymaros Project*, Judgment of 25th September 1997, *ICJ Reports 1997*, para. 53.
26 *Case Concerning Pulp Mills on the River Uruguay (Argentina v. Uruguay)*, Judgment of 20th April 2010, *ICJ Reports 2010*, para. 101.
27 Ibid., para. 193.

15.3.2 Clarifying the contours and the content of the principle

Neither the *Gabcikovo-Nagymaros* case nor the *Threat or Use of Nuclear Weapons* case gave the opportunity for the Court to clarify the contours and content of the due diligence applied to the protection of the environment.

On the contrary, this incantatory repetition clouded the understanding of due diligence. The variations in terminology in the expression of the principle raised some doubts about its exact scope. In the *Pulp Mills* case, the Court seemed to give two different understandings of the same principle.

At first, the Court seemed to refer to the 'no harm rule' as it was revealed by the *Trail Smelter* case. Stating that the due diligence principle 'obliged a State to use all the means at its disposal in order to avoid activities ... causing significant damage to the environment of another State', the Court limits the scope of the due diligence principle to environmental damage to other States.[28] But, a bit later, the Court seems to go beyond the concept of 'damage' and considers that due diligence obliged 'States to ensure that activities within their jurisdiction and control respect the environment of other States or of areas beyond national control'.[29]

This same case was also the occasion for the Court to clarify the contours and content of the principle. In this case, the protagonists (Argentina and Uruguay) agreed to consider that the Statute of the River Uruguay signed by Argentina and Uruguay on February 1975 (the '1975 Statute'), which was the subject of the dispute, should be interpreted in a dynamic way, in accordance with customary principles of international environmental law.[30]

The principle of dynamic interpretation of environmental provisions of international treaties (and evolutionary interpretation of treaties in general so that it will be possible to take into consideration new developments in

---

28 Ibid., para. 101.
29 Ibid., para. 193.
30 According to the Court,

> Argentina contends notably that the 1975 Statute must be interpreted in the light of principles governing the law of international watercourses and principles of international law ensuring protection of the environment. It asserts that the 1975 Statute must be interpreted so as to take account of all 'relevant rules' of international law applicable in the relations between the Parties, so that the Statute's interpretation remains current and evolves in accordance with changes in environmental standards.
>
> (*Pulp Mills* case, op. cit., para. 55)

The Court added that:

> Uruguay likewise considers that the 1975 Statute must be interpreted in the light of general international law and it observes that the Parties concur on this point. It maintains, however, that its interpretation of the 1975 Statute accords with the various general principles of the law of international watercourses and of international environmental law, even if its understanding of these principles does not entirely correspond to that of Argentina.
>
> (Ibid., para. 57)

environmental law) had already been developed by the Court itself in 1997 in the *Gabcikovo-Nagymaros* case[31] and repeated in 2009 in the *Dispute Regarding Navigational and Related Rights* case.[32] Thus the Court had no difficulty in accepting the proposal of both States and adopting a dynamic interpretation of the 1975 Statute in particular by using the principle of due diligence.

Regarding the contours of the principle, the Court held that the obligation of States to act with due diligence in respect of all activities which take place under the jurisdiction and control of each party was an obligation of conduct and not an obligation of result.[33] This is a clear confirmation of the position of the ILC in this field and of the *Corfu Channel Judgment*. In its commentary on Article 7 of the *Draft Articles on the Law of the Non-Navigational Uses of International Watercourses*, the ILC stated that:

> The obligation of due diligence contained in article 7 sets the threshold for lawful State activity. It is not intended to guarantee that in utilizing an international watercourse significant harm would not occur. It is an obligation of conduct, not an obligation of result.[34]

This obligation of conduct entails an obligation of due diligence in its enforcement:

---

31 The Court

> wishes to point out that newly developed norms of environmental law are relevant for the implementation of the Treaty and that the parties could, by agreement, incorporate them through the application of Articles 15, 19 and 20 of the Treaty. These articles do not contain specific obligations of performance but require the parties, in carrying out their obligations, to ensure that the quality of water in the Danube is not impaired and that nature is protected, to take new environmental norms into consideration when agreeing upon the means to be specified in the Joint Contractual Plan. By inserting these evolving provisions in the Treaty, the parties recognized the potential necessity to adapt the Project. Consequently, the Treaty is not static, and is open to adapt to emerging norms of international law. By means of Articles 15 and 19, new environmental norms can be incorporated in the Joint Contractual Plan.
>
> (*Gabcikovo-Nagymaros Project* case, op. cit., para. 112)

32 In this case, the Court observed that:

> There are situations in which the parties' intent upon conclusion of the treaty was, or may be presumed to have been, to give the terms used – or some of them – a meaning or content capable of evolving, not one fixed once and for all, so as to make allowance for, among other things, developments in international law.
>
> (*Dispute Regarding Navigational and Related Rights (Costa Rica v. Nicaragua)*, Judgment of 13 July 2009, *ICJ Reports 2009*, para. 64)

33 *Pulp Mills* case, op. cit., para. 187.
34 *Draft Articles on the Law of the Non-Navigational Uses of International Watercourses and Commentaries Thereto and Resolution on Transboundary Confined Groundwater*, op. cit., p. 103.

It is an obligation which entails not only the adoption of appropriate rules and measures, but also a certain level of vigilance in their enforcement and the exercise of administrative control applicable to public and private operators, such as the monitoring of activities undertaken by such operators, to safeguard the rights of the other party.[35]

But the most important contribution of the Court to the development of the due diligence principle is the requirement of an environmental impact assessment. The Court held that an impact assessment was required even though it was not expressly provided for in the Statute of 1975 because it was binding on States as a customary rule of international environmental law derived from the principle of due diligence. The Court said that:

[T]he Statute, has to be interpreted in accordance with a practice, which in recent years has gained so much acceptance among States that it may now be considered a requirement under general international law to undertake an environmental impact assessment where there is a risk that the proposed industrial activity may have a significant adverse impact in a transboundary context, in particular, on a shared resource. *Moreover, due diligence*, and the duty of vigilance and prevention which it implies, *would not be considered to have been exercised*, if a party planning works liable to affect the régime of the river or the quality of its waters did not undertake an environmental impact assessment on the potential effects of such works.[36]

Indeed, contemporary practice in impact assessment is now abundant. Besides the famous Espoo Convention,[37] environmental impact assessment requirements have been introduced into a great number of national environmental regulations as well as in international binding and non-binding legal instruments and in the practice of many international agencies.[38] Far from being prophetic, the Court has followed the position adopted by the ILC, which codified the requirement of impact assessment in Article 7 of its *Draft Articles on Prevention of Transboundary Harm from Hazardous Activities* adopted in 2001.[39]

---

35 *Pulp Mills* case, op. cit., para. 197.
36 Ibid., para. 204. Emphasis added.
37 Convention on Environmental Impact Assessment in a Transboundary Context, Espoo, 1991.
38 For a detailed presentation of international practice, see A. Epiney, 'Environmental Impact Assessment', in *Max Planck Encyclopedia of Public International Law* (www.mpepil.com). See also Birnie *et al.*, *International Law and the Environment*, pp. 164–175.
39 According to Article 7: 'Any decision in respect of the authorization of an activity within the scope of the present article shall, in particular, be based on an assessment of the possible transboundary harm caused by that activity, including any environmental impact assessment', in *Draft Articles on Prevention of Transboundary Harm from Hazardous Activities, with Commentaries*, Report of the International Law Commission on the work of its fifty-third session (A/56/10), p. 157.

But the Court did not go very far in determining the scope and the content of the obligation. The Court said that 'an environmental impact assessment must be conducted *prior* to the implementation of a project'[40] and that 'once operations have started and, where necessary, throughout the life of the project, continuous monitoring of its effects on the environment shall be undertaken'.[41] But the Court refused to identify more accurately the content of the obligation on the basis of the argument that neither the 1975 Statute nor general international law specified the scope and content of an environmental impact assessment and that Argentina and Uruguay were not parties to the Espoo Convention. Following once again the solution given by the ILC,[42] the Court decided 'that it is for each State to determine in its domestic legislation or in the authorization process for the project, the specific content of the environmental impact assessment required in each case'.[43]

One could regret here the timidity of the Court. As long as the impact assessment is determined by national legislation of each State, this requirement is likely to remain a formal one that does not guarantee that future projects will not cause significant damage to the environment of another State.

But the purpose of the Court is not to create the rule but only to identify its existence. On the eve of the *Pulp Mills* judgment, there was still a lot of controversy on whether the impact assessment was part of international environmental customary law. As noted by P. Birnie, A. Boyle and C. Redgwell a few months before the judgment, 'some of the literature appears to think that [environmental impact assessment] can be customary law only if a Court spells this out in black and white'.[44]

15.4 Conclusion

The Court has played a major role in the recognition and implementation of the principle of due diligence for the protection of the environment. However, too many grey areas still remain: what is the exact meaning of a 'significant harm', what is the content of the 'respect of the environment'?

In their joint dissenting opinion in the *Pulp Mills* Judgment, Judges Al-Khasawneh and Simma underlined the problem, stating that:

---

40 *Pulp Mills* case, op. cit., para. 205.
41 Ibid.
42 In its commentary of article 7, the ILC stated that 'the question of who should conduct the assessment is left to States' and that 'the specifics of what ought to be the content of assessment is left to domestic laws of the State conducting such an assessment', in *Draft Articles on Prevention of Transboundary Harm from Hazardous Activities, with Commentaries*, op. cit., pp. 158– 159, para. 5, para. 7.
43 *Pulp Mills* case, op. cit., para. 205.
44 Birnie *et al.*, *International Law and the Environment*, op. cit., p. 170.

> [I]n matters related to the use of shared natural resources and the possibility of transboundary harm, the most notable feature that one observes is *the extreme elasticity and generality* of the substantive principles involved. Permanent sovereignty over natural resources, equitable and rational utilization of these resources, the duty not to cause significant or appreciable harm, the principle of sustainable development, etc., all reflect this generality.[45]

As it is often the case with the 'infinitely obscurantist possibilities of legal language and the wondrous opacities of legal syntax',[46] these substantive principles add sometimes to the confusion. Without clarification of these terms, it is questionable whether the Court will be able to rule on the question of whether the harm is or is not significant. Given the uncertainty and the subjectivity which surround terms such as 'significant or appreciable' harm, one may wonder, like Judges Simma and Al-Khasawneh, if the Court should not accept the use of experts as it did in the *Corfu Channel* case.[47]

---

45 *Joint Dissenting Opinion, judges Al-Khasawneh and Simma, ICJ Reports 2010*, para. 26. Emphasis added.
46 In the words of W. M. Reisman, 'International politics and international law-making: reflections on the so-called "politicization" of the International Court', in W. Heere (ed.), *International Law and its Sources: Liber Amicorum Maarten Bos* (The Hague: Asser Institut, Kluwer, 1988), p. 88.
47 According to them,

> The conclusions of scientific experts might be indispensable in distilling the essence of what legal concepts such as 'significance' of damage, 'sufficiency', 'reasonable threshold' or 'necessity' come to mean in a given case. For this reason, in a case concerning complex scientific evidence and where, even in the submissions of the Parties, a high degree of scientific uncertainty subsists, it would have been imperative that an expert consultation, in full public view and with the participation of the Parties, take place.
> (*Joint Dissenting Opinion Judges Al-Khasawneh and Simma*, op. cit., para. 17)

16 The interaction between international humanitarian law and human rights law and the contribution of the ICJ

Djamchid Momtaz and Amin Ghanbari Amirhandeh

16.1 Introduction

The year between December 1948 and December 1949 was clearly an important one for international law. Within that twelve-month period, both the Universal Declaration of Human Rights (UDHR) as well as the four Geneva Conventions were adopted. Moreover, the underlying link between these instruments was not lost on the President of the Geneva conference, when he stated:

> [I]t is, we think, interesting to compare the Declaration with the Geneva Conventions. Our texts are based on certain of the fundamental rights proclaimed in it – respect for the human person ... the Universal Declaration of the Rights of Man and the Geneva Conventions are both derived from one and the same ideal.[1]

Within the very same year, the International Court of Justice (ICJ) handed down its merits decision in the first case referred to it, the *Corfu Channel* case.[2] In paying tribute to the ICJ's first contentious decision, it is fitting that consideration be given here to that case's impact on the interaction between the two bodies of law to which the President of the Geneva conference had alluded; namely, international human rights law (HRL) and international humanitarian law (IHL). Indeed, one of the Court's contributions in the *Corfu Channel* case was to engage with the ideals underlying both the UDHR and the Geneva Conventions. In the Court's judgment this would find expression in the concept of 'elementary considerations of humanity'. Indeed, the Court's recognition of this principle can be regarded as a breakthrough in HRL.

---

1 *Final Record of the Diplomatic Conference of Geneva of 1949*, vol. II, Section A, p. 536.
2 *Corfu Channel case, Judgment of April 9th 1949*, ICJ Reports 1949, p. 4.

16.2 The Court's use of principles

16.2.1 *Elementary considerations of humanity*

It can be recalled that in the *Corfu Channel* case, the United Kingdom (UK) claimed that Albania was responsible for the damage caused by mines in the latter's territorial waters to two British Royal Navy destroyers and the subsequent loss of life among the crew. The UK based its claims on 'articles 3 and 4 of Hague Convention No. VIII of 1907, by the general principles of international law *and* by the ordinary dictates of humanity'.[3] For its part, the ICJ, admitting Albania's responsibility, concluded that:

> Such obligations are based, not on the Hague Convention of 1907, No. VIII, which is applicable in time of war, but on certain *general and well-recognized principles*, namely: *elementary considerations of humanity*, even more exacting in peace than in war.[4]

The divide between IHL and HRL had thus been breached and this was done by recourse to principles.

As is well known, in hard cases, a judge will often fall back on principles[5] – especially to avoid a *non-liquet*, which the law abhors.[6] For at least one of the ICJ judges, it appears there was in fact a risk of a *non-liquet* in the *Corfu Channel* case or, if this is overstating the matter, there was for that same judge a perceived need to comment on such a possibility. Judge Alvarez would write in his separate opinion that 'the law which the Court has to apply' was one adapted to a 'new era' – a 'new international law' – and this in turn led him to divide international law into two eras, that before 1939 and that after, the latter defined as a 'realization of social justice . . . entirely different from the old law, which was strictly judicial'.[7] Then, in his enumeration of the Court's functions, Judge Alvarez mentions a new function, 'that of creating and formulating new precepts, both for old problems where *no rules exist* and also for new problems'.[8]

Indeed, as summed up by Alain Pellet, 'the first purpose of paragraph 3 [of the Permanent Court of International Justice Statute and now Article 38(1)(c) ICJ Statute] was to avoid a *non liquet*[9] without giving the Court the possibility

---

3 *ICJ Reports 1949*, vol. 1 p. 9. Emphasis added.
4 *ICJ Reports 1949*, p. 22. Emphasis added.
5 R. Dworkin, *Taking Rights Seriously* (Cambridge, MA: Harvard University Press, 1978), p. 81.
6 H. Lauterpacht, *The Function of Law in the International Community* (New Jersey: The Lawbook Exchange Ltd, 2000), pp. 60–70; see also D. Bodansky, 'Non liquet and the Incompleteness of International Law', in L. Boisson de Chazournes and P. Sands (eds), *International Law, the International Court of Justice and Nuclear Weapons* (Cambridge: Cambridge University Press, 1999), pp. 153–170.
7 *Corfu Channel case, Individual Opinion of Judge Alvarez, ICJ Reports 1949*, pp. 39–40.
8 Ibid. Emphasis added.
9 *Procés-Verbaux of the Proceedings of the Advisory Committee of Jurists* (1920), p. 318 (Descamps), p. 311 (Loder), pp. 312–313 (La Pradelle), pp. 307 and 317 (Hagerup).

to legislate'.[10] In other words, when exercising its competence, the Court does not invent principles in the exercise of a discretion, but rather applies the content of such principles. The very right and obligation contained therein, is to be inferred from an already-existing rule of international law. It is useful then, to consider what those pre-existing rules of international law were before the ICJ handed down its 1949 decision.

16.2.2 Roots of the principle

In considering the origins of the Court's enunciation of the principle of elementary considerations of humanity, one can refer first, to one of the oldest principles of international law, the Martens Clause. It provides that:

> Until a more complete code of the laws of war has been issued, the High Contracting Parties deem it expedient to declare that, in cases not included in the Regulations adopted by them, the inhabitants and the belligerents remain under the protection and the rule of the principles of the law of nations, as they result from the usages established among civilized peoples, from the laws of *humanity*, and the dictates of the public conscience.[11]

If between the two World Wars, HRL was mainly confined to minority rights,[12] the United Nations Charter (UN Charter) can be regarded as the point of departure in a chain of events making HRL universal. Aside from its Preamble's direct reference to *fundamental human rights*, its Article 1, designating the

---

10 A. Pellet, 'Article 38', in A. Zimmermann, C. Tomuschat, K. Oellers-Frahm *et al.* (eds), *The Statute of the International Court of Justice* (Oxford: Oxford University Press, 2006), p. 765, referencing *Procés-Verbaux of the Proceedings of the Advisory Committee of Jurists* (1920) p. 296 (La Pradelle), p. 309 (Root), p. 314 (Rici-Busatti), p. 316 (Phillimore), p. 319 (Hagerup).

11 Emphasis added. Rephrased and repeated in Article 1, para. 2, of the Additional Protocol I of 1977. For a brief reading on the Martens Clause, see T. Meron, 'The Martens Clause, Principles of Humanity, and Dictates of Public Conscience', *AJIL*, 94 (2000), pp. 78–89; A. Cassese, 'The Martens Clause: Half of a Loaf or Simply Pie in the Sky?', *EJIL*, 11 (2000): 187–216. Emphasis added.

12 N. Quenivet, 'The History of Relationship between International Humanitarian Law and Human Rights Law', in R. Arnold and N. Quenivet (eds) (Leiden: Martinus Nijhoff Publishers, 2008), p. 5; see: S. Bedi, *The Development of Human Rights Law by the Judges of the International Court of Justice* (Portland, OR: Hart Publishing, 2007), p. 31; S. Schwebel, 'Human Rights in the World Court', *Vanderbilt Journal of International Law*, 24 (1991); also see: Advisory Opinion No. 6, *German Settlers in Poland*, 1923 PCIJ (ser. B) No. 6, at 20, available online at: http://www.icj-cij.org/pcij/serie_B/B_06/Colons_allemands_en_Pologne_Avis_consultatif.pdf (10 September 2010); Advisory Opinion No. 44, *Treatment of Polish Nationals in Danzig*, 1932 PCIJ (ser. A/B) No. 44, at 28 (Feb. 4); Advisory Opinion No. 46, *Minority Schools in Albania*, 1935 PCIJ (ser. A/B) No. 64, at 17, available online at: http://www.icj-cij.org/pcij/serie_AB/AB_64/01_Ecoles_minoritaires_Avis_consultatif.pdf (6 April 2010).

purposes of the Organization, encourages 'respect for human rights and for fundamental freedoms for all' and Article 13 vests in the General Assembly the power and the responsibility for 'assisting in the realization of human rights and fundamental freedoms for all without distinction as to race, sex, language, or religion'.

As the only legal framework for HRL, the Charter constituted an assurance for States of the exclusiveness of HRL to times of peace, of 'which the United Nations was the guarantor';[13] this perception started to shatter after the adoption of the UDHR, which gave HRL an embodiment apart from and independent of the UN Charter. As a matter of fact, consideration of the UDHR's *travaux préparatoires* reveals that delegations were concerned with the applicability of HRL in times of armed conflict. So too, in the process of the elaboration of the four Geneva Conventions, reference was made to human rights, even if such references were 'few and far between',[14] highlighting the problem more boldly than ever before. The Charter of the International Military Tribunal, annexed to the Four-Power Agreement of 8 August 1945, by including *crimes against humanity*, was of course another step forward in creating an international law for *humanity*. Its Article 6 provides that the Tribunal:

> shall have the power to try and punish persons who acting in the interests of the European Axis countries, whether as individuals or as members of organizations, committed any of the following crimes: . . . (c) Crimes against humanity: namely, murder, extermination, enslavement, deportation, or other inhumane acts committed against any civilian population, before or during the war.

The provision was originally designed to vest in the Tribunal the authority to try crimes committed by the Nazis against German citizens.[15]

From these above-mentioned foundations, one can draw the conclusion that when deciding the *Corfu Channel* case, the Court had at its disposal a series of

---

13 R. Kolb, 'The Relationship between International Humanitarian Law and Human Rights Law: A Brief History of the 1948 Universal Declaration of Human Rights and the 1949 Geneva Conventions', *International Review of the Red Cross*, 324 (1998): 409–419; D. Momtaz, 'Conflit armé non international: interaction des differents régimes juridiques', in G. Ravasi and J.L. Bezuto (eds), *Current Problems of International Humanitarian Law: International Humanitarian Law and Other Legal Regimes: Interplay in Situations of Violence* (Rome: Nagard, 2005), p. 109. As Quentin-Baxter put it, it is 'easy to see why they [the two branches of IHL and HRL] departed. The United Nations was dedicated to the principle of peace', in R. Quentin Baxter, 'Human Rights and Humanitarian Law – Confluence or Conflict?' *Australian Yearbook of International Law*, 9 (1980): 97.
14 Kolb, op. cit, 412; Lebanon's delegate held that HRL should be guaranteed in times of war.
15 See for a short reading on the history of the notion, E. Schwelb, 'Crimes against Humanity', *British Year Book of International Law*, 23 (1946): 178–226.

material sources, already applied in cases concerned with protection of the human person both in times of war and in times of peace.

16.3 Application of human rights in armed conflicts

After the *Corfu* judgment a series of other practices accepted the Court's 1949 reasoning and this would grow into a trend. In this regard, mention must *inter alia* be made of the Tehran Conference of 1968 which 'marked the UN's first foray in the domain of humanitarian law, a field considered up to then incompatible with the very purpose of the organization and the prohibition of use of force in article 2(4) of the UN Charter',[16] as well as Article 72 of the first Additional Protocol (AP) to the four Geneva Conventions of 1949, and last but not least, to the reference to common Article 3 – deemed a 'parent provision'[17] – in the preamble of APII of 1977 relating to the Protection of Victims of Non-International Armed Conflicts.

If, as seen above, principles can serve a normative function in that they convey rights or obligations, they also – and simultaneously – serve a second function; namely, as an aid in the interpretation of a rule, which results, seemingly, from the omnipresence of principles in the normative structure.[18] This second function of principles in legal reasoning becomes operational the moment that the existence of the principle is affirmed by the Court concerned.

16.3.1 Interpretation of a rule in light of a principle

To understand the role of principles for the interpretation of rules, it is necessary to understand the position of the principle in the structure of international law. Were there an absence of principles in the legal order, the whole structure of international law would collapse into disparate solitary commands. Put otherwise, there is no rule without a principle in its company. Principles fill the spaces between rules and teach us where to turn to find other relevant rules to a given question. This is comforted by Article 31 of the 1969 Vienna Convention on the Law of Treaties, which is a reflection of customary international law[19] and regulates the general rule of interpretation which provides

---

16 R. Provost, *International Human Rights and Humanitarian Law* (Cambridge: Cambridge University Press, 2002), p. 3; see also United Nations Secretary General, 'Respect for Human Rights in Armed Conflicts' UN Doc. A/8052 (1970) and 'Report of the Secretary General on Respect for Human Rights in Armed Conflicts', UN Doc. A/7720 (1969). http://daccess-dds-ny.un.org/doc/UNDOC/GEN/N69/254/40/PDF/N6925440.pdf?OpenElement (accessed 7th Jan. 2011).
17 Y. Sandoz, C. Swinarski and B. Zimmermann, op. cit, p. 1339.
18 On interpretive function of principles, or to be exact general principles of law, see Geza Herczegh, *General Principles of Law and International Legal Order* (Budapest: Akadémiai Kiado, 1969), pp. 68–73.
19 See, for instance, *Territorial Dispute (Libyan Arab Jamahiriya/Chad), Judgment, ICJ Reports 1994*, pp. 21–22, para. 41.

that 'there shall be taken into account, together with the context: any relevant rules of international law applicable in the relations between the parties'.

A vivid example is the Court's treatment in the *Nicaragua Case* of common Article 3 to the four Geneva Conventions, which is referred to as 'convention in miniature'. In that case, the Court concluded that:

> [A]rticle 3 . . . defines certain rules to be applied in the armed conflicts of a non-international character. There is no doubt that, in the event of international armed conflicts, these rules also constitute a minimum yardstick, in addition to the more elaborate rules which are also to apply to international conflicts; and they are rules which, in the Court's opinion, reflect what the Court in 1949 called *'elementary considerations of humanity'*.[20]

This application to common Article 3 of the principle enunciated in the *Corfu Channel* case reveals how interpretation of a principle is of use when the Court examines the scope of a rule, or a set of rules to be applied in a given dispute.

16.3.2 *The ICJ and the application of HRL in armed conflicts*

The ICJ has played a leading role in determining the extent to which human rights instruments are applicable in times of armed conflict. It was first in the context of the 1996 Advisory Opinion on the *Legality of the Threat or Use of Nuclear Weapons*, where the issue of the applicability of the International Covenant on Civil and Political Rights (ICCPR) in times of armed conflict was brought before the Court. With the potential conflict between use of weapons of mass destruction and the very right to life as a fundamental and non-derogable right being the object in focus, the Court provided the international community with its understanding of the 'relevant rules and principles of international law'[21] and determined that:

> [T]he protection of the International Covenant of Civil and Political Rights does not cease in times of war, except by operation of Article 4 of the Covenant whereby certain provisions may be derogated from in a time of national emergency. Respect for the right to life is not, however, such a provision.[22]

While in this Opinion, the Court seemingly limited its reasoning to the ICCPR's field of application and the wording of the judgment was confined to

---

20 *Military and Paramilitary Activities in and against Nicaragua (Nicaragua v. United States of America), Merits, Judgment, ICJ Reports 1986*, p. 114, para. 218. Emphasis added.
21 *Legality of the Threat or Use of Nuclear Weapons, Advisory Opinion, ICJ Reports 1996*, pp. 233–234, para. 13.
22 ibid, p. 240, para. 25.

the ICCPR's provisions concerning non-derogable rights, it was in the *Wall Advisory Opinion* that the Court found itself free to consider a wider horizon, by interpreting Article 2(1) of the Covenant on Economic, Social and Cultural Rights (CESCR), in a manner similar to the United Nations Human Rights Committee's General Comment no. 31.[23]

Article 2(1) of the CESCR reads: 'Each State Party to the present Covenant undertakes to respect and to ensure to all individuals within its territory and subject to its jurisdiction the rights recognized in the present Covenant.'

The Court, with reference to the Committee's 'constant practice', decided that:

> [T]his provision can be interpreted as covering only individuals who are both present within a State's territory and subject to that State's jurisdiction. It can also be construed as covering both individuals present within a State's territory and those outside that territory but subject to that State's jurisdiction.[24]

The Court held that the continuing occupation of a territory by a State, indicating the existence of an international armed conflict, meant that the relevant provisions of the CESCR were to be applied by the occupying power to the occupied territory and people subject to its jurisdiction.[25]

One year later in its Judgment of 19 December 2005 in the *Case Concerning the Armed Activities on the Territory of the Congo*, the Court recalling its position in the *Wall Advisory Opinion*[26] was again inclined to apply HRL in times of armed conflicts,[27] holding Uganda responsible for the atrocities committed by its forces on the claimant's territory.[28]

In the recent case of *Georgia v. Russia*, the issue of the application of HRL abroad was brought to the Court's attention. The parties' disagreement on the territorial scope of the HRL instruments led the Court to hold that provisions of the Convention on the Elimination of all Forms of Racial Discrimination also applies to those cases in which a State chooses to act beyond its national borders. This trend has been taken up by regional human rights courts, as, for instance, by the European Court of Human Rights which has in several

---

23 Human Rights Committee, General Comment No. 31 [80]: The Nature of the General Legal Obligation Imposed on States Parties to the Covenant, *26/05/2004, CCPR/C/21/Rev.1/Add.13. (General Comments)*, para. 10.
24 *Legal Consequences of the Construction of a Wall in the Occupied Palestinian Territory, Advisory Opinion, ICJ Reports 2004*, p. 179, para. 109, [hereafter *Wall Advisory Opinion*]
25 Ibid., p. 165, para 70; see also paras 178–181, 107–113.
26 *Armed Activities on the Territory of the Congo (Democratic Republic of the Congo v. Uganda), ICJ Reports 2005*, para. 216, [hereafter *Armed Activities* case]
27 *Armed Activities* case, para. 217; the Court includes in the same paragraph 'Convention on the Rights of the Child of 20 November 1989' and 'Optional Protocol to the Convention on the Rights of the Child on the Involvement of Children in Armed Conflict of 25 May 2000'.
28 *Armed Activities* case, para. 180.

proceedings regarded the application of human rights instruments and rules they contain.[29]

16.4 Conclusion

It is perhaps appropriate by way of conclusion to focus on the reasoning to be applied in articulating HRL and IHL. This was established in general terms by the Court in its 2004 *Wall Advisory Opinion*:

> as regards the relationship between international humanitarian law and human rights law, there are thus three possible situations: some rights may be exclusively matters of international humanitarian law; others may be exclusively matters of human rights law; yet others may be matters of both these branches of international law. In order to answer the question put to it, the Court will have to take into consideration both these branches of international law, namely human rights law and, as lex specialis, international humanitarian law.[30]

Writers hold that the Court's contribution to the relationship between the two *branches* of IHL and HRL can be expressed in a single term, namely the *principle* as an integral part of a *strong lex specialis regime* or *self-contained regime*.[31] The question of the interrelation between IHL and HRL owes its credibility to the recognition given in the *Corfu Channel Judgment* to the principle of 'elementary considerations of humanity' around which rules of HRL and IHL as branches of the law, revolve.

---

29 *Bankovi and Others v. Belgium and Others*, Application No. 52207/99, 12 December 2001; *Loizidou v. Turkey*, Application No. 15318/89, Preliminary objections, 23 March 1995; *Issa and Others v. Turkey*, Application No. 31821/96, 16 November 2004; *Ilascu and Others v. Moldova and Russia*, Application No. 48787/99, 8 July 2004.
30 *Wall Advisory Opinion*, p. 178, para. 106.
31 *Report of the Study Group of the International Law Commission*, 'Fragmentation of International Law: Difficulties Arising from the Diversification and Expansion of International Law,' A/CN.4/L.682, 13 April 2006.

17 Elementary considerations of humanity

Matthew Zagor

17.1 Introduction

In reaching its conclusion that an obligation lay upon the Albanian authorities to notify of the existence of a minefield in Albanian territorial waters, the International Court of Justice found:[1]

> Such obligations are based, not on the Hague Convention of 1907, No. VIII, which is applicable in time of war, but on certain general and well-recognized principles, namely: elementary considerations of humanity, even more exacting in peace than in war; the principle of the freedom of maritime communication; and every State's obligation not to allow knowingly its territory to be used for acts contrary to the rights of other States.

The statement has become one of the Court's best-known passages, enjoying a currency in subsequent domestic, regional and international decisions in humanitarian, environmental, human rights, refugee, and maritime law, and forming the basis of what some consider to be a constitutionalist, value-oriented formulation of international law. By conjuring up 'elementary considerations of humanity, even more exacting in peace than in war', the Court deliberately echoed the Martens Clause from the 1899 and 1907 Hague Conventions, extracting and adapting to peacetime one of the core components of the clause – the 'laws of humanity'[2] – and transforming it into what appears to be a free-standing general principle of international law.

Less commonly cited is the analogous passage in the separate opinion of Judge Álvarez, in which he referred in kind to acts contrary to the '*sentiments*

---

1 *Corfu Channel case (United Kingdom v. Albania), Judgment of April 9th 1949, ICJ Reports 1949,* p. 22.
2 *Laws and Customs of War on Land (Hague II),* opened for signature 29 July 1899, Preamble (entered into force 4 September 1900); *Laws and Customs of War on Land (Hague IV),* opened for signature 18 October 1907, Preamble (entered into force 26 January 1910). The formulations of the clauses differ slightly in the two Conventions, and in its adoption in the denunciation clauses of the four Geneva Conventions; see Articles 63, 62, 142 and 158 respectively.

of humanity'[3] – a term *prima facie* less objective than 'elementary considerations', but nonetheless consistent with the affective and empathetic nature of any interpretative exercise with humanity at its rhetorical and analytic core. Although different in their articulation, both 'elementary considerations' and 'sentiments' of humanity evince a discernible intention to set a tone for the judicial approach to international law and the judicial role more broadly. For Judge Álvarez, who before joining the court had promoted a dynamic and progressive international law emerging out of a 'universal juridical conscience',[4] this agenda was explicit: here was an opportunity to present the contours of a new evolutionary international law, founded upon 'social interdependence' and characterized by a purpose, or telos, of realizing 'social justice', where acts contrary to sentiments of humanity could be condemned as 'international delinquencies'.[5]

The majority decision is not so overt. Nonetheless it remains significant that the Court relied upon or at least invoked humanity in its very first decision. The phrase 'elementary considerations of humanity', after all, stands as a Jeffersonian-type statement of normative humanism, a declaration of *inter*dependence, presuming a common humanity that may be judicially protected by the application of universally applicable norms derivable from humanity's shared existence.

Those seeking further enlightenment as to the nature and status of the principle or the process by which the judges reached their conclusion will find

---

3 *Corfu Channel case*, op. cit., p. 45 (Judge Álvarez). Emphasis added.
4 A. Álvarez, *Exposé de motifs et Déclaration des grands principes du Droit international moderne* (Paris: Éditions Internationales, 1938), pp. 8–9, 16–23, 27, 51, cited in *Pulp Mills on the River Uruguay (Argentina v. Uruguay)* (ICJ, General List No. 135, 20 April 2010) [36] (Judge Trindade) ('*Pulp Mills*'). Judge Álvarez's use of 'juridical consciousness of peoples' in the *Corfu Channel case* is an anomaly; 'consciousness' and 'conscience' are not identical notions. The term disappeared from his subsequent judgments, to be replaced by 'juridical conscience'. Judge Álvarez's position on international law had already been expressed in his individual opinion in the *Conditions of Admission of a State to Membership in the United Nations (Article 4 of the Charter) (Advisory Opinion), ICJ Reports 1948* (Judge Álvarez). He maintained his 'international law as social justice' agenda throughout his time on the court, notably in his separate opinion in *Anglo-Norwegian Fisheries (United Kingdom v. Norway), ICJ Reports 1951*, pp. 148–150, in which he elaborated what D.M. Johnston called the 'law of social independence':

> the great principles, have their origin in the legal conscience of peoples (the psychological factor). This conscience results from social and international life; the requirements of this social and international life naturally give rise to certain norms considered necessary to govern the conduct of States *inter se*.

The idea of a juridical conscience discernible by judges in their elaboration of norms has occasionally been adopted by other judges. See, for instance, the Declaration of President Bedjaoui in *Legality of the Threat or Use of Nuclear Weapons (Advisory Opinion), ICJ Reports 1996*, p. 271 ('*Nuclear Weapons*'); and more recently, Judge Trindade's opinion in the *Pulp Mills* case. See also I. Hussain, *Dissenting and Separate Opinions at the World Court* (Dordrecht: Martinus Nijhoff, 1984), pp. 82–125.
5 *Corfu Channel case*, op. cit., p. 45 (Judge Álvarez).

little assistance in the main judgment or the arguments put to the Court. Other than the reference to the inapplicable but clearly inspirational Hague Convention,[6] the majority fail to refer to precedent, evidence or any familiar authority to support the effortless assertion that the principle is 'well recognized', essentially adopting with minor amendment the equally unelaborated and categorically confused British memorials and oral argument of Frank Soskice QC.[7] The Martens Clause itself is notably missing from the decision, although the 'laws of humanity' which the clause insists apply to situations not covered specifically by The Hague Conventions is distinctly echoed in the formulation adopted by the Court.[8] Nonetheless, the content, scope and status of the principle are left unexamined, as is the methodology for its future elaboration and application.

The result is some considerable confusion in the commentary on the case. Even the concept's place in the topology of sources remains uncertain,[9] commentators describing it variously as a general principle binding in itself,[10] an equitable principle,[11] a non-binding general principle from which other norms can be derived, a rule of custom,[12] a soft-law norm sitting outside tradi-

---

6 The reference is to those provisions raised by the Government of the United Kingdom, notably Articles 3–4 of the *Convention Relative to the Laying of Automatic Submarine Contact Mines (Hague VIII)*, opened for signature 18 October 1907 (entered into force 26 January 1910), which concern the laying of mines and the duty of notification.
7 'Memorial submitted by the United Kingdom', *Corfu Channel case (United Kingdom v. Albania), ICJ Pleadings 19*, p. 21 ('(4) that the Albanian Government did not notify the existence of these mines as required by Articles 3 and 4 of The Hague Convention No. VIII of 1907, by the general principles of international law, and by the ordinary dictates of humanity'). The categorical confusion arises as a result of the references on one hand to principles of international law in distinction to 'dictates of humanity', and on the other to an 'offence' and 'crime against humanity'. Similar arguments had been made on behalf of the United Kingdom to the UN Security Council by Sir Alexander Cadogan. See I. Yung Chung, *Legal Problems Involved in the Corfu Channel Incident* (Geneva: E. Droz, 1959), p. 33.
8 The idea that the principle articulated in the *Corfu Channel case* 'underlies' specific provisions of relevant treaties was eventually made explicit in the *Nicaragua* case. See below, note 79.
9 The issue of sources is addressed more fully in the contribution in this volume by Professor Akiho Shibata (Chapter 12).
10 Fitzmaurice, in one of the earliest commentaries, described an 'obligation to act in accordance with elementary considerations of humanity' in the context of discussing 'general principles of good conduct'. See G. Fitzmaurice, 'The Law and Procedure of the International Court of Justice: General Principles and Substantive Law', *British Yearbook of International Law*, 27 (1950): 4. See also Lauterpacht, who notes somewhat equivocally that '[i]t is probable that these "general principles of law" include elementary considerations of humanity'.
11 M. Akehurst, 'Equity and General Principles of Law', *International and Comparative Law Quarterly*, 25 (1976): 806.
12 T. Meron, *Human Rights and Humanitarian Norms as Customary International Law* (Oxford: Clarendon Press, 1989); M. Koskenniemi, 'The Pull of the Mainstream', *Michigan Law Review*, 88 (1990): 1946–1962.

tional statute sources,[13] or a merely rhetorical device of little if any legal import.[14] This ambiguity was evident early on. Writing in *Recueil des Cours* in 1962, Sir Humphrey Waldock, who had appeared for the United Kingdom in the case, accused the Court of blurring custom and general principle, using phraseology reminiscent of paragraph (c) of Article 38 of the ICJ Statute (on general principles of international law) while simultaneously presenting elementary considerations as part of custom, 'though again not making itself clear on the question of the source'.[15] Attempting to resolve this uncertainty, Waldock relied on a contextual reading of the decision, finding it significant that 'elementary considerations of humanity' appears alongside two other 'well-recognized' principles belonging to customary law – freedom of maritime communication and every State's obligation not to allow knowingly its territory to be used for acts contrary to the rights of other States. For Waldock, this reflected an understanding of both sources as 'a single corpus of law', where the addition of a general principle provides a 'flexible element' that 'enables the court to give greater completeness to customary law and in some limited degree to extend it'.[16]

The Court has, of course, built upon the notion of elementary considerations of humanity in subsequent cases, although not always in an illuminating fashion. Most commentators trace its trajectory from the *Corfu Channel* case to the *Nicaragua* judgment and *Nuclear Weapons* Advisory Opinion (a task this chapter similarly undertakes below). Inevitably, the *erga omnes* jurisprudence often appears as a related discourse. The logical step from 'elementary considerations of humanity' in 1949 to the rhetorically-related 'elementary principles of morality' identified in the *Genocide Convention Reservation Advisory Opinion* two years later[17] lies partly in their shared 'elementary' or 'fundamental' and

---

13 F. Francioni, 'International "Soft Law": A Contemporary Assessment', in V. Lowe and M. Fitzmaurice (eds) *Fifty Years of the International Court of Justice: Essays in Honour of Sir Robert Jennings* (Cambridge: Cambridge University Press, 1996), p. 169 ('it would be difficult to imagine a softer body of law than "elementary considerations of humanity" '). For Francioni, the decision 'reveals an explicit recognition that principles of soft law may be drawn from an unwritten source' (p. 169).

14 This, at least, has been said about the Martens Clause, which Cassese describes as a *lex specialis* of the broader rule in the *Corfu Channel case*. Raimondo notes the early scepticism about whether the principle expressed by the Court possessed either normative character or assisted in the formation of customary rules. See F.O. Raimondo, 'The International Court of Justice as a Guardian of the Unity of Humanitarian Law', *Leiden Journal of International Law*, 20 (2007): 597.

15 H. Waldock, 'General Course on Public International Law', *Recueil des Cours*, 106 (1962): 63. Waldock's use of the term 'again' refers to a discerned tendency to neglect to identify the source, or to invoke different sources simultaneously as in the *Chorzów Factory* case.

16 Ibid, p. 64.

17 *Reservations to the Convention on the Prevention and Punishment of the Crime of Genocide (Advisory Opinion), ICJ Reports 1951*, p. 23.

thus superior nature,[18] and partly in the shared meta-juridical normativity found in the idea of 'inhumane conduct' inherent to both concepts.[19] Both were also eventually to engage a specific if ill-defined idea of the international community as a touchstone.[20] It is therefore unsurprising that scholars and judges mention elementary considerations of humanity and *erga omnes* obligations in almost the same breath.[21] For Ragazzi, this synergy is apparent in the *Corfu Channel* case itself. Notably, the inclusion of elementary considerations alongside two additional sources is again considered to be instructive: unlike these more established grounds, no 'exceptional circumstances' could be pleaded against an obligation of notification based on considerations of humanity: after all, they are 'even more exacting in peace than in war'. As a result, the concept of elementary considerations of humanity, Ragazzi argues, 'is functionally equivalent to the concept of obligations *erga omnes*',[22] opposable to all States at all times.

The intersection of these two concepts begs further questions about the nature of the law being espoused, and the concomitant judicial role and method necessary for its elucidation. And behind these questions lie further assumptions – philosophical, cultural and attitudinal – about the legal import of the idea of 'humanity' which lies at the heart of both the Martens Clause and the Court's famous statement. This chapter therefore provides a brief history of humanity as a modern juristic concept, from its birth in the anti-slavery

---

18 See, for instance, *Fragmentation of International Law*, Report of the International Law Commission, 58th session (2006), para. 31:

> Some rules of international law are more important than other rules and for this reason enjoy a superior position or special status in the international legal system. This is sometimes expressed by the designation of some norms as 'fundamental' or as expressive of 'elementary considerations of humanity' or 'intransgressible principles of international law'.

It can also be argued that 'general principles' invariably appeal to both reason and morality, and can therefore 'be presented as normatively superior to rules or goals'. See O. Schachter, *International Law in Theory and International Practice* (Dordrecht: Martinus Nijhoff, 1991), p. 49.

19 M. Ragazzi, *The Concept of International Obligations Erga Omnes* (Oxford: Oxford University Press, 2002), p. 102. For Ragazzi, elementary considerations of humanity is understood as 'aimed, as such, at protecting basic values such as human life' (p. 475) where value 'denot[es] something that is intrinsically worthy' (note 80).

20 *Barcelona Traction, Light and Power Co. Ltd. (Belgium v. Spain)*, ICJ Reports 1970, p. 32 ('*Barcelona Traction*'). The discussion of the international community is taken up below.

21 See, for instance, V. Gowlland-Debbas, 'Judicial Insights into the Fundamental Values and Interests of the International Community', in A. Sam Muller, D. Raič and J. M. Thuránszky (eds), *The International Court of Justice: Its Future Role after Fifty Years* (The Hague: Kluwer Law International, 1997), p. 346. See also, *Pulp Mills*, op. cit. (Judge Trindade).

22 Ragazzi, *Concept of International Obligations Erga Omnes*, pp. 85–86, further supported by his analysis of the *Nicaragua* case. The *ILC Report*, op. cit., similarly implies an equation between the 'intransgressible' and the 'elementary'.

treaties to its formulation in the Martens Clause, its liberation from the contextual shackles of The Hague Conventions in the *Corfu Channel* case and subsequent elaboration in the jurisprudence of both the ICJ and the international criminal tribunals, to its extension beyond the humanitarian law field. The aim is to provide a better understanding of why an appeal to considerations of humanity carries with it such legal and normative gravitas, and how it has taken centre stage in contemporary conceptualizations of the function of international law and the role of its principal practitioners.

17.2 Humanity as a normative concept in the age of reason

The central place of a concept of humanity in international legal thought has a lengthy pedigree. As Simma has pointed out, the view that 'mankind as a whole forms a moral-legal unity' – which for current purposes is assumed to underpin a normative notion of humanity – can be traced from the Stoic-Christian philosophies of law of Cicero, St Augustine and Thomas Aquinas, through the natural law theories of De Vitoria, Suarez and Wolff, to its modern articulation in the writings of scholars such as Verdross and even Kelsen.[23] Humanity from this perspective is a universalistic and ethical idea, assuming a shared social nature and 'community' that stands above the artificial divides of nation.[24]

The eighteenth century saw humanity as a normative-legal idea endorsed by the social and political thinkers of the age, not least in the emerging rights discourse. It found particular favour among the *philosophes*, featuring prominently in Diderot's famous entry on *Droit Naturel* in the *Encyclopédie* where it was presented as the basis of a theory of natural law and 'inalienable natural rights'.[25] However, its first major substantive transition from theory and political rhetoric to positive legal reality arose in the context of the antislavery movement in England. 'Humanity' had long appeared as a central

---

23 See B. Simma, 'The Contribution of Alfred Verdross to the Theory of International law', *European Journal of International Law*, 6 (1995): 38–43. For the shift in the natural law thinking of De Vitoria and Suarez towards 'the idea of a law of nature innate to humanity as a whole, and on which an international legal community extending to all nations was founded,' see W. G. Grewe and M. Byers, *The Epochs of International Law* (Berlin: Walter de Gruyter, 2000), pp. 141f.

24 See, for instance, Simma, 'The Contribution of Alfred Verdross', op. cit., pp. 42–43. Simma does not use the term 'humanity' in this context, preferring expressions such as 'the *normative* idea of the moral unity of mankind' (p. 40).

25 D. Diderot, 'Volume 5, *Encyclopédie*', in J. Mason and R. Wokler (eds) *Diderot, Political Writings* (Cambridge: Cambridge University Press, 1992), p. 20 ('I have no other truly inalienable natural rights except those of humanity'). According to Mason and Wokler, Diderot's law of nature was based on 'a rational principle of common humanity which restrained the selfishness of individuals and made the establishment of civil society both necessary and possible' (p. 20). This view was common to natural law philosophers, especially Samuel von Pufendorf, whose *De Jure Naturae et Gentium* was liberally pillaged by Diderot.

affective trope in the speeches of the main proponents of reform. Thomas Paine, for instance, in his influential pamphlet on 'African Slavery in America' in 1772, had argued that slavery was 'contrary to the natural dictates of reason, and feelings of Humanity',[26] famously signing off the pamphlet: 'These are the sentiments of Justice and Humanity.'[27] Almost identical language is found in the parliamentary debates of 1788 that resulted in the *Slave Trade Regulation Act*, and the many statutes that followed, including the *Abolition Bill* of 1807 which declared the trade to be 'contrary to the principles of justice, humanity and sound policy'.[28]

Given England's pivotal role in pursuing the anti-slave trade agenda on the international stage, it is unsurprising to find in the *Declaration against the Slave Trade*, signed at the Congress of Vienna in 1815, echoes of the domestic political rhetoric now writ large as a universalistic sentiment: '[The] Trade is repugnant to the principles of humanity and of universal morality . . . at length, the public voice in all civilized countries calls aloud for its prompt suppression.'[29] A similar form of words is replicated in the many bilateral treaties which were to follow.

Slavery was therefore the location of what Clark has termed a 'normative shift' in international society around the idea of shared humanity.[30] Its formulation as a principle linked to universal morality and demanded by the fictive public voice of all nations, not just Christendom, is significant, as is the geopolitical imbalance and historical 'moment' which brought it into being.[31] The characterization of an international legal rule as reflecting what would later in the Martens Clause be termed the 'dictates of public conscience' is as unique as it is disingenuous. The world society whose normative voice can be heard in the 1815 Declaration was essentially that of Britain, the emerging hegemon after the Napoleonic wars, where an organized and politicized public had demanded international action. Indeed, the ground-breaking treaties which codified the trade's prohibition were effectively sponsored and paid for by the victorious British in exercise of their considerable financial and diplomatic

---

26 T. Paine, 'African Slavery in America', in M. Ishay (ed.) *The Human Rights Reader* (New York: Routledge, 1997), p. 133.
27 Ibid.
28 The phrase was eventually dropped from the preamble. Interestingly, the same language was used to *support* the trade, with emphasis falling on the 'sound policy' element. See S. Farrell, ' "Contrary to the Principles of Justice, Humanity and Sound Policy": The Slave Trade, Parliamentary Politics and the Abolition Act 1807', *Parliamentary History*, 26 (2007): 141.
29 'Declaration against the Slave Trade', in *Parliamentary Debates from 1803 to the Present Time*, vol. 32 (London: T.C. Hansard, 1816), p. 200.
30 I. Clark, *International Legitimacy and World Society* (Oxford: Oxford University Press, 2007), p. 173.
31 The Declaration marks the first appearance of the term *'nations civilisées'* in an international treaty. As Grewe points out, 1815 marks the end of references in treaties to 'Christendom'. See Grewe and Byers, op. cit., p. 445.

post-war muscle.³² With little enthusiasm for abolition outside of Britain, the treaties can hardly be characterized as a reflection of any 'spontaneous sharing of moral conviction' such as purportedly characterized the domestic movement.³³ Nonetheless, by the end of the century, the practice would be universally accepted as both immoral and unlawful in what was a remarkable international institutionalization of a new normative logic.

The adoption by the British of a normative rhetoric of humanity in international affairs had other less salubrious manifestations. As Crawford demonstrates, the 'aggressive humanitarianism' which characterized British diplomatic efforts was soon to be applied to the colonial enterprise. Indeed, the same anti-slavery arguments relied upon to ban the trade were used to justify international cooperation in the colonization of Africa, as witnessed in the deliberations at the Berlin West Africa Conference of 1884.³⁴ A not dissimilar ethical and universalistic rhetoric of civilized humanity was employed by the United States to justify intervention in the Americas, where the principle of humanity created a perceived moral imperative. Thus, for President McKinley, there was 'a duty imposed by our obligations to ourselves, to civilization and humanity, to intervene with force' in the region. As Emerson has argued, 'By justifying their action in Cuba as consistent with the promotion of civilisation and the betterment of humanity, the U.S. would essentially convert Latin America into their own moral protectorate.'³⁵

Nor was normative humanity philosophically uncontentious. The nineteenth century in particular saw a tension within the very idea of humanity between reason and sentiment that it retains to this day. At one level, it was understood that conceiving humanity as unified by a shared rationality, as Di Vitoria had argued, could have important ramifications for the extension of rights.³⁶ However, such arguments often sat uncomfortably alongside reason, even in the slavery debate. Thus, Lord John Russell, despite finding slavery repugnant to his 'feelings', viewed abolition as 'delusive', a feeble attempt to serve the cause of humanity which would only see the trade taken up by other States.³⁷ It is an

---

32 See N. Crawford, *Argument and Change in World Politics: Ethics, Decolonization, and Humanitarian Intervention* (Cambridge: Cambridge University Press, 2002), p. 185 for an overview of the strategies used by the British to reach agreements with Spain and Portugal, and the costs involved. Crawford makes the argument that it is crucial to understand the ethical arguments against slavery used domestically and internationally, not just the material and economic explanations for its demise.
33 Ibid, p. 184, noting the 800 petitions (and one million signatures) made to Parliament in 1814 alone.
34 Ibid, pp. 201–248.
35 G. Emerson, 'Seeds of Liberty', *ANU Centre for European Studies*, 25 May 2010, p. 14. For a critique of the tendency for contemporary neo-conservatives to equate America's national interests with those of humanity, see C. Reus-Smit, *American Power and World Order* (Cambridge: Polity Press, 2004), pp. 48–55.
36 The connection between humanity and human rights law is explored below.
37 W. Jay, *Miscellaneous Writings on Slavery* (Boston: John P. Pewett, 1853), p. 142.

argument not dissimilar to the contemporary contention that taking unilateral greenhouse gas abatement action is bad policy, despite its honourable motivation.[38] Rationality also clashed with principles of humanity in the torture debate, with Bentham infamously decrying the torture prohibition as 'blind and vulgar humanity'.[39] Again, this argument has unfortunately retained some currency, with Alan Dershowitz citing Bentham in his crude utilitarian defence of judicial torture warrants.[40] More profoundly, Proudhon saw the normative elevation of humanity as a deification of man, and argued that those who employ the term want to cheat, a phrase picked up by the twentieth-century legal theorist Carl Schmitt, and cited repeatedly since in the literature.[41] Schmitt aptly captured the long-standing critique of humanity, noting 'the possibility of deep inequality when one's enemy can be portrayed as against and therefore an "outlaw of humanity"'.[42]

For its nineteenth-century critics, the idea of humanity thus spoke less of rationality than unsupportable and dangerous sentimentality. In many respects, however, this was a response to the rhetoric of the age. Appeals to humanity-grounded norms were invariably accompanied by references to sentiment. Indeed, the rational and the empathetic went hand-in-hand in establishing humanity's position as a normative concept; both aspects were essential to its norm-creating potential. By itself, rational humanity lacked normative persuasiveness. This need to engage with a motivation for agency was apparent to David Hume who noted 'if the principles of humanity are

---

38 These arguments have effectively stalled the implementation of effective climate change legislation in the United States and Australia.
39 W.L. Twining and P.E. Twining, 'Bentham on Torture', *Northern Ireland Legal Quarterly*, 24 (1973): 347.
40 See A. Dershowitz, 'The Torture Warrant: A Response to Professor Strauss', *New York Law School Law Review*, 48 (2003): 275–276.
41 Schmitt warned about States that seek to 'usurp a universal concept against a military opponent' by identifying themselves with and misusing the ethical-humanitarian concept of humanity. See C. Schmitt, *The Concept of the Political: Expanded Edition* (Chicago: University of Chicago Press, 2007) (trans. G. Schwab). The impact of Schmitt's ideas on contemporary international legal theory is evident, for instance, in M. Koskenniemi, *The Gentle Civilizer of Nations: The Rise and Fall of International Law 1870–1960* (Cambridge: Cambridge University Press, 2001); and G.J. Simpson, *Great Powers and Outlaw States: Unequal Sovereigns in the International Legal Order* (Cambridge: Cambridge University Press, 2004). For a critique of the use of Schmitt both as an inspiration and counter-point, see D. Chandler, 'The Revival of Carl Schmitt in International Relations: The Last Refuge of Critical Theorists', *Millennium: Journal of International Studies*, 37 (2008): 27–48.
42 See C. Schmitt, 'The Legal World Revolution', *Telos*, 72 (1987): 88, cited by T. B. Strong, 'Foreword: Dimensions of the New Debate around Carl Schmitt', ibid, p. xxii.

capable, in many instances, of influencing our actions, they must, at all times, have some authority over our sentiments'.[43]

At the core of the notion of sentimental humanity lies empathy. As philosopher Charles Taylor and historian Lynn Hunt have separately argued, empathy was a core ingredient of European Enlightenment thought, motivating an expanded egalitarian idea of humanity which had developed by the end of the eighteenth century into a cultural trait.[44] Such universal empathy was evident in the birth of universal human rights law, not least in the idea that such rights are 'self-evident' – a statement of logic that only makes sense when a shared ethical sentiment of empathy is assumed to characterize the human condition.

As humanity consolidated its place in both international law and foreign policy, these same themes were to find repeated articulation: the dynamic movement between the rhetorical and the norm-generating, the formulation of a principle against which conduct might be deemed 'repugnant' (a term which in English constitutional practice meant unlawful), responding to the putative 'voice' of international society, the 'civilizing' role of the principle, the tension between its rational and affective components, and suspicion surrounding its ethically ambivalent and politically expedient use in the realm of international affairs.

By the end of the nineteenth century, the historical and cultural forces identified above were to have an impact on a new movement of international lawyers for whom, as Martti Koskenniemi has argued in his *Gentle Civilizer of Nations*, 'humanity' had become a guiding principle. Koskenniemi traces the

---

[43] D. Hume, 'An Inquiry Concerning the Principles of Morals', cited in L. May, *War Crimes and Just War* (Cambridge: Cambridge University Press, 2007), p. 75. A similar argument has been made more recently by Richard Rorty, see below at note 138. See also, May, op. cit., p. 89. May has noted the various ways in which 'humanity' is understood, arguing that, in the context of international humanitarian law, it refers primarily to *characteristic attitudes* such as 'compassion and mercy' rather than a *shared quality*, such as rationality.

> It is not just the rational side of human nature that gives rise to these prohibited behaviors, but also the sentiment or feeling side ... Humane treatment in both humanitarian and human rights law promotes the minimum amount of compassionate and merciful treatment that humans characteristically do, and should, display towards fellow human beings.
>
> (p. 89)

[44] See L. Hunt, *Inventing Human Rights* (New York: W. W. Norton, 2007), pp. 35ff; C. Taylor, *Sources of the Self: The Making of Modern Identity* (Cambridge, MA: Harvard University Press, 1989). Although Taylor employs the semantically different term 'sympathy', his arguments about the development of sentiment as a touchstone of morality, manifested in a new egalitarian consciousness and reflected in literature and the arts, has striking similarities to Hunt's account, which sees the trait reflected in the development of the epistolary novel and portraiture. Taylor's sophisticated treatment of the relationship between rationality, sympathy, naturalism and sensualism, throws light on some of the trends noted in this chapter.

first manifestation of this professional self-awareness to the manifesto of the *Revue de Droit International* in 1868, especially its espousal of the 'superior unity of the great human society', and its depiction of a new 'science or rather the conscience of humanity' as '[the] source, the tribunal and the sanction of positive law'.[45] This 'science', practised by a new breed of international lawyer,[46] was to be based upon the sober reflections of the 'civilized conscience', which in turn would influence public opinion, ultimately forming the basis of international legal norms.[47]

In other words, international lawyers – including judges – saw themselves as the shapers and arbiters of humanity's conscience, taking the place of the absent international legislator, and steadily steering international society towards its realization of core liberal ideals. It is Victorian (or perhaps more accurately Whiggish) evolutionary liberalism at its most idealistic and, as Koskenniemi points out, potentially imperialistic.[48]

This is the context within which the Martens Clause should be considered. It stands as the first manifestation of humanity as a positive normative principle in its own right,[49] a precursor to the ICJ's eventual reification of the related general principle of international law in the *Corfu Channel* case. Despite being drafted to break a diplomatic deadlock and receiving little attention in its early years,[50] the Clause nonetheless gave expression to the very purpose of the profession within which the framers of the Convention were engaged, and to their conceptualization not just of the laws of war, but of international law itself.[51] Its subsequent history, although riddled with uncertainty in interpre-

---

45 G. Rolin-Jacquemyns, 'De l'étude de la législation comparée et de droit international', *Revue de Droit International*, 1 (1869): 225, cited in Koskenniemi, *The Gentle Civilizer of Nations*, op. cit., p. 16.
46 As Martineau has commented (drawing upon and extending the work of Kennedy), 'the last half of the nineteenth century saw a self-confident period of invention and renewal among international lawyers'. See A. Martineau, 'The Rhetoric of Fragmentation: Fear and Faith in International Law', *Leiden Journal of International Law*, 22 (2009): 3 (note 7).
47 Koskenniemi, *The Gentle Civilizer of Nations*, op. cit., pp. 15–16. A similar argument was made by Grewe: 'the equation of the international legal community with the community of civilized nations . . . was essentially a product of British policy and theory concerning international law.' See Grewe and Byers, op. cit., p. 446.
48 The evolutionary and idealistic view of Whig history was famously identified by Herbert Butterfield in *The Whig Interpretation of History* in 1931, and subsequently developed in the historical and political literature. Victorianism could also, however, be very pessimistic.
49 Or, as Cassese puts it, 'an ingenious blend of natural law and positivism'. See A. Cassese, 'The Martens Clause: Half a Loaf or simply Pie in the Sky?', *European Journal of International Law*, 11 (2000): 188–189.
50 For an overview of the drafting history, see Cassese, ibid.
51 As Grewe noted, the clause manifested the clearest expression of the British theory of international law which identified the international community with the 'community of civilised nations'. Grewe and Byers, op. cit., p. 446. However, it should also be noted that a nascent 'principle of humanity' already featured prominently in the early influential work on the laws of war, especially the codes developed by Johann Caspar Bluntschli and

tation, bears this out.[52] As Cassese observes, 'In spite of its ambiguous and its undefinable purport, [the Martens Clause] has responded to a deeply felt and widespread demand in the international community.' It has, claims Cassese, '*struck a chord with the sentiments prevailing in the world community*'.[53] This 'chord,' presumably, is one discernible by international lawyers, those 'keepers of the international juridical conscience' (to quote Weeramantry) whose faculties are finely tuned to discern the world community's sentiments.

These same sentiments also underpin the Court's distillation of elementary considerations of humanity 50 years after Martens famously penned his 'inspiring fudge words'.[54] The Court was not, of course, alone in expressing such attitudes at the time. Acting on behalf of an evolving idea of humanity characterized the post-war moment, not least among those international lawyers negotiating the Genocide and Geneva Conventions.[55] It is discernible, for instance, in the speech of Max Petitpierre, Head of the Swiss Federal Political Department, who in opening the first Plenary Meeting of the Conference of the drafters of the Geneva Conventions on 21 April 1949 called upon delegates to 'join us on that higher impartial plane of pure humanity where differences of a political nature should have no place'.[56]

Pure humanity – spiritual, transcendent, apolitical and universal – is the hidden theme evident in much of the commentary on both the Martens Clause and elementary considerations of humanity, the 'animating and motivating principle of the law of war, *and indeed all law*', as Quincy Wright put it in one

---

Francis Lieber. See D. Schindler, 'J.C. Bluntschli's Contribution to the Law of War', in M. G. Kohen and L. Caflisch (eds), *Promoting Justice, Human Rights and Conflict Resolution through International Law* (Leiden: Koninklijke Brill, 2007), p. 444. Lieber's Code is replete with references to humanity, including (in Article 29) the infamous recommendation to pursue what nowadays might be called shock and awe: 'The more vigorously wars are pursued, the better it is for humanity. Sharp wars are brief' (p. 444).

52 Cassese, op. cit., pp. 189–192; T. Meron, 'The Martens Clause, Principles of Humanity, and Dictates of Public Conscience', *American Journal of International Law*, 94 (2000): 78–89; R. Ticehurst, 'The Martens Clause and the Laws of Armed Conflict', *International Review of the Red Cross*, 37 (1997): 126ff.
53 Cassese, op. cit., p. 212. Emphasis added.
54 A. Roberts, 'Land Warfare: From Hague to Nuremberg', in M. Howard, G. Andreopoulos and M.R. Shuman (eds,) *The Laws of War: Constraints on Warfare in the Western Worlds* (New Haven CT: Yale University Press, 1996), p. 122.
55 Humanity occupies a central rhetorical position in the discussions surrounding other major developments including the Nuremberg Charter, the Universal Declaration of Human Rights, and even the Refugee Convention. The language is apparent in the *travaux* of these important documents, as well as in General Assembly discussions.
56 *Final Record of the Diplomatic Conference of Geneva (Vol. II Section A)* (Berne: Federal Political Department, 1949), p. 10. Interestingly, Petitpierre described the Convention of 1864 as representing 'the spiritual heritage of mankind . . . one of the steps mankind has climbed in its endeavours to raise the standard of civilization' (p. 9).

of the earliest commentaries on the case.[57] It betrays an attitude which may in part explain the Court's relative silence in identifying and establishing the rule. Not unlike the declarations of rights in the eighteenth century, elementary considerations of humanity are presented as self-evident, in no need of elaboration, explanation, or support from traditional sources, other than by oblique reference.[58]

The Court's failure to provide detailed reasons, of course, is not that unusual,[59] especially in the elucidation of general principles.[60] As Gaja notes, 'The assertion by the ICJ of a general principle of law . . . is only rarely accompanied by an adequate demonstration of its existence in international law.'[61] Such reticence may therefore be a function of the source, providing the necessary judicial flexibility to gap-fill where necessary.[62] Yet for those judges relying upon the general principle of humanity to reveal, confirm or develop specific rules of international law, this presents peculiar challenges to judicial method. In relying upon elementary considerations of humanity in the *Corfu Channel* case itself, as Louis Henkin observed, the Court 'invoked moral standards based on values other than State consent'.[63] Subsequent cases relying upon humanity as a self-evident moral principle have similarly

---

57 Q. Wright, 'Foreword', in UN War Crimes Commission, *Law Reports of Trials of War Criminals* (London: His Majesty's Stationery Office, 1949), p. xiii. Emphasis added. The statement was cited with approval by Judge Weeramantry in his strong dissent in the *Nuclear Weapons Advisory Opinion*. See *Nuclear Weapons*, op. cit., p. 264 (Judge Weeramantry). Cassese also uses the term 'animating' in his article. See Cassese, op. cit., p. 192. The natural law resonances are irresistible.

58 See, for instance, Q. Wright, 'The *Corfu Channel case*', *American Journal of International Law*, 43 (1949): 494 ('The opinion is notable for the extent to which the court relied upon broad principles of law, apparently deemed to be self-evident and stated without citation of precedent or authority. It is also notable that these principles referred to rights of humanity . . .').

59 This tendency was recognized early on. See Waldock, op. cit. In 1976, Kearney demonstrated that the Court had repeatedly reached its conclusion by stating rather than establishing those very rules whose existence and content were in controversy. See R. Kearney 'Sources of Law and the International Court of Justice', in L. Gross (ed.) *The Future of the International Court of Justice* (Dobbs Ferry: Oceana, 1976), p. 610. Kearney notes at p. 653 that the rules are largely treated as 'self-evident' (cited by M. Koskenniemi, *From Apology to Utopia: The Structure of International Legal Argument* (Cambridge: Cambridge University Press, 2005), p. 397).

60 As J. Kammerhofer and A. de Hoogh point out in 'All Things to All People? The International Court of Justice and its Commentators', *European Journal of International Law*, 18 (2007): 979, '[t]he problem with "general principles" lies not with their substantive content, but in how their existence is justified, and how the "source" is traced'.

61 G. Gaja, 'General Principles of Law', in *Max Planck Encyclopedia of Public International Law*, 2007, para. 20. See also Lauterpacht, op. cit., p. 71: 'prior judicial or arbitral authority is not a condition of valid recourse to general principles of law'.

62 That general principles of international law provide an answer to *non liquet* is well covered in the literature.

63 L. Henkin, *International Law: Politics and Values* (Dordrecht: Martinus Nijhoff, 1995), p. 103.

resulted in a reframing of the approach to the elucidation of relevant customary norms.[64]

Before examining this case law in more detail, it is worth returning to one last component of the translation of humanity into the discourse of international law: the relationship between humanity (either as a general principle or in its Martens Clause formulation) and various conceptualizations of the 'international community'. As already noted, the replacement of Christendom with humanity in the early slavery prohibition treaties was significant, not just for its universalization of international legal norms outside the traditional European club, but also for purportedly responding to the demands of the so-called 'public voice' which was portrayed as an expression of universal conscience and empathy for humanity. The notion of an international community, of course, took on more juristic relevance in the twentieth century. Given its roots, it is unsurprising to see it acting to connect the jurisprudence of elementary considerations of humanity, a principle 'derived from the specific nature of the international community', with *erga omnes* obligations, which are owed to 'the international community as a whole'.[65]

In both areas, the courts have pronounced upon the validity of norms independently from State practice, 'seeming to recognize a spontaneous social process generating general principles of international law'.[66] Indeed, the link between a creative judicial role, the application of general principles, and the force of a normative notion of the international community, is irresistible. Thus, for Lauterpacht, 'international practice recognizes, and the very existence of the international community necessitates, a residuary source of law on which States are entitled to act and by reference to which international courts are bound to render decisions'.[67] According to this formulation, judicial

---

64 See also D. Lefkowitz, 'Sources of International Law', in S. Besson and J. Tasioulas, (eds) *The Philosophy of International Law* (Oxford: Oxford University Press, 2010), pp. 187, 189–190:

> Arguably, the claim that correctness as a moral principle currently provides a sufficient condition for the legal validity of certain human rights norms, better accounts for claims made in a number of opinions issued by the ICJ – such as its appeal to elementary considerations of humanity ... than do alternative explanations drawing on custom or general principles of law.

65 See Mosler's discussion of general principles, notably his second category of 'principles and rules derived from the specific nature of the international community', in H. Mosler, 'The International Society as a Legal Community', *Recueil des Cours*, 140 (1974): 148f. And *Barcelona Traction*, op. cit., p. 32, for the nature of *erga omnes* obligations. Note also Judge Tanaka's earlier reference, in his dissent in the *South West Africa* cases, to a law which 'cannot be abolished or modified, because it is deeply rooted in the conscience of mankind'. See *South West Africa (Ethiopia v. South Africa; Liberia v. South Africa) (Second Phase), ICJ Reports 1966*, p. 298 (Judge Tanaka).

66 Gowlland-Debbas, op. cit., p. 344 ('Drawing on the underlying moral, ethical or constitutional foundations of the international community, the ICJ has ... considered the validity of certain fundamental norms independently from state practice, seeming to recognize a spontaneous social process generating general principles of international law.').

67 Lauterpacht, op. cit., pp. 68–69.

recognition of the international community (by which Lauterpacht meant a 'deeper community' transcending values and interests, and characterized by a 'higher unity')[68] requires the existence of a source of law that can fill legal gaps. In such a value-oriented model of international law, the principle of 'elementary considerations of humanity' is utilizable by judges by reference to notions such as 'the dictates of public conscience' or 'universal juridical conscience' to implement the values of, and simultaneously strengthen and forge, the so-called international community.[69]

Elementary considerations of humanity thus carry considerable historical and methodological baggage. It stands at the threshold of discussion about the role of international judiciary, and the nature and function of international law. The following section will examine some of these underlying tensions by examining the judicial approach to the principle.

17.3 Norm creating, norm exposing, or norm enhancing?

As noted, jurists and judges have struggled to place elementary considerations of humanity in the firmament of international legal categories or to agree on its role in the interpretation, elucidation and creation of new international norms.[70] At one extreme, it has been promoted as a distinct source of international law in its own right, whether as manifested alongside 'dictates of public conscience' in the Martens Clause or expressed as a general principle of international law liberated from its treaty context.[71] For others, such appeals are merely rhetorical flourishes which only have substance, if at all, when accompanied by positive law. In between are those who see the principle primarily as an interpretative device, supporting liberal constructions of treaty provisions, establishing a presumption to be raised in cases of doubt about the existence of a norm, operating to exclude *a contrario* arguments when hitherto unforeseen circumstances arise,[72] or merely endowing existing norms with

---

68 Lauterpacht's understanding of 'community' is predicated on his concept of international law as 'developing and protecting through international action the interests of human personality as the ultimate purpose of the international society ... Such international law requires a deeper community of moral and political outlook.' Ibid, p. 264. This idea of 'deeper community' is echoed by Simma and Paulus, who refer to a 'higher unity' in international relations. See B. Simma and A. Paulus, 'The "International Community": Facing the Challenge of Globalization', *European Journal of International Law*, 9 (1998): 268.
69 As Judge *ad hoc* Ečer put it, in his dissenting opinion, the role of the Court is 'to help strengthen the cohesion of the international community'. See *Corfu Channel case*, op. cit., p. 130 (Judge Ečer).
70 See Cassese's comprehensive overview of the various interpretations of the Martens Clause in the literature, Cassese, op. cit., pp. 189f. Cassese considers *inter alia* the work of Binz, Roling, Strebel, Munch, Sperduti, and in particular Judge Shahabuddeen.
71 Although for some commentators the two limbs of the Martens Clause represent 'two new sources of law'. See Cassese, op. cit., p. 191.
72 That is, the view that the absence of a positive prohibition provides an implicit licence.

what Shaw, citing the *Corfu Channel* case and the *Nuclear Weapons Advisory Opinion*, calls 'an additional force within the system'.[73]

From a judicial perspective, the opinions on the principle's norm-generative character are inconsistent. Thus, in the *South West Africa* cases, the Court asserted:

> Humanitarian considerations may constitute the *inspirational basis* for rules of law, just as, for instance, the preambular parts of the United Nations Charter constitute the moral and political basis for the specific legal provisions thereafter set out. Such considerations do not, however, in themselves amount to rules of law . . . [I]t is necessary not to confuse the moral ideal with the legal rules intended to give it effect . . . It is not permissible to import new [legal incidents] by a process of appeal to the originating idea – a process that would, *ex hypothesi*, have no natural limit.[74]

The suggestion that considerations of humanity are a moral and political ideal, not a legal or even norm-generative principle, would seem to be incompatible with its juridical elevation in the *Corfu Channel* case.[75] The judgment also relies upon the sticky dichotomy between law and politics, with the inescapable implication that some humanitarian concerns will be non-justiciable – a proposition strongly contested by those, led intellectually by Lauterpacht, who see no such gaps in international law, and for whom the principle of humanity is the ultimate 'gap-filler'.[76]

Standing in sharp contrast to the somewhat anomalous *South West Africa* cases is the *Nicaragua* case where, in another failure to notify of the existence and location of mines, the Court repeatedly stated that conventional rules and obligations are 'merely' or 'no more than' a reflection of '*fundamental* general principles of humanitarian law'.[77] This phrase, immediately followed by reference to the Martens Clause (as it appears in the denunciation provisions of the

---

73 M. Shaw, *International Law* (Cambridge: Cambridge University Press, 2003), p. 103, citing the *Corfu Channel case* and in particular the *Nuclear Weapons* advisory opinion, op. cit., pp. 257, 262, where the court insisted that at the heart of the rules and principles of international humanitarian law lay 'overriding considerations of humanity'.
74 *South West Africa*, op. cit., pp. 34–35. Emphasis added.
75 See, for instance, Henkin, op. cit., p. 186; Gowlland-Debbas, op. cit., p. 346. The 'ideal' at issue in the *South West Africa* cases was the 'sacred trust of civilization' which appeared in Article 22 of the League Covenant.
76 It is uncontentious that the Martens Clause fulfils this function. See, for instance, Meron, who notes that it provides 'an additional argument against a finding of non liquet'. See Meron, 'The Martens Clause', op. cit., p. 88.
77 *Military and Paramilitary Activities in and Against Nicaragua (Nicaragua v. United States of America)*, ICJ Reports 1986, pp. 112–114 ('*Nicaragua*').

Geneva Conventions),[78] echoes the essentialism hinted at in the *Corfu Channel* case which the Court here recognized as having expressed '*principles underlying* the specific provisions of Convention No. VIII of 1907'. These principles, moreover, were considered to be binding in themselves.[79] As Jørgensen notes, in concluding that common Article 3 of the Geneva Conventions reflects elementary considerations of humanity, '[T]he Court's choice of words ... seems to confirm Fitzmaurice's early view of considerations of humanity as a source of law.'[80] According to Jørgensen, 'The Court seems to have had in mind principles which are so fundamental that they do not require translation into customary law in order to be applicable.'[81] Criticism of the Court understandably targeted what was considered by Meron to be 'perfunctory and conclusory references to the practice of States'.[82]

An elaboration of humanity's norm-creating potential was subsequently provided by Judges Shahabuddeen and Weeramantry in their dissenting opinions in the Advisory Opinion on the *Legality of the Threat or Use of Nuclear Weapons*. Judge Shahabuddeen found evidence for Fitzmaurice's suggestion that 'considerations of humanity give rise in *themselves* to obligations of a legal character' in the jurisprudence of various courts and tribunals, including in the *Corfu Channel* case.[83] His attempt to address many of the problems which such

---

78 Convention for the Amelioration of the Condition of the Wounded and Sick in Armed Forces in the Field, adopted 12 August 1949, 75 UNTS 31, art 63 (entered into force 21 October 1950); Convention for the Amelioration of the Condition of Wounded, Sick and Shipwrecked Members of Armed Forces at Sea, adopted 12 August 1949, 75 UNTS 85, art 62 (entered into force 21 October 1950); Convention Relative to the Treatment of Prisoners of War, adopted 12 August 1949, 75 UNTS 135, art 142 (entered into force 21 October 1950); Convention Relative to the Protection of Civilian Persons in Time of War, adopted 12 August 1949, 75 UNTS 287, art 158 (entered into force 21 October 1950).
79 The Court referred to a 'breach of the principles of humanitarian law *underlying* the specific provisions of Convention No. VIII of 1907', noting that 'the conduct of the United States *may be judged* according to the fundamental general principles of humanitarian law ...' Nicaragua, op. cit., pp. 112–114. Emphasis added.
80 N.H.B. Jørgensen, *The Responsibility of States for International Crimes* (Oxford: Oxford University Press, 2003), p. 128. This may be the reason why Judge Jennings in his dissenting opinion noted that 'the Court's view that the common Article 3, laying down a "minimum yardstick" ... for armed conflicts of a non-international character are applicable as "elementary considerations of humanity", is not a matter free from difficulty'. See *Nicaragua*, op. cit., p. 537 (Judge Jennings).
81 Jørgensen, op. cit., p. 128. Jorgensen notes further: 'Consequently, these principles of humanitarian law must either be a source of obligations or one of the general principles in the sense of Article 38, paragraph 1(c) of the ICJ's Statute.'
82 Meron, *Human Rights and Humanitarian Norms*, op. cit., p. 42. See also p. 36 ('The Nicaragua court completely failed to inquire into whether opinio juris and state practice actually does support the crystallisation of articles 1 and 3 into custom ...').
83 *Nuclear Weapons*, op. cit., p. 407 (Judge Shahabuddeen), citing G. Fitzmaurice, *The Law and Procedure of the International Court of Justice*, vol. 1 (Cambridge: Cambridge University Press, 1986), p. 17 (note 4). The emphasis, it is worth noting, is in the original. Shahabuddeen also applied the advice from the Court in the *Barcelona Traction* case that one should test the soundness of a principle by the consequences which would flow from its application.

a characterization of the general principle generates, however, is only partially persuasive. For instance, the problems associated with judge-made law, or 'government by judges', were countered by insisting that judges are merely 'evaluating a standard embodied in an existing principle'.[84] And the judge was guided in evaluating these embodied standards by the views of States themselves.[85] Interestingly, Shahabuddeen equated these views with 'public conscience', studiously distinguishing the task of divining such an ephemeral substance from ascertaining *opinio juris*, a presumably more arduous task.[86]

With respect to the *content* of principles of humanity and the dictates of public conscience, Judge Shahabuddeen relied upon an evolutionary picture of international law, built on certain essential constants:[87]

> [This is] to be ascertained in the light of changing conditions, inclusive of changes in the means and methods of warfare and the outlook and tolerance levels of the international community. The principles would remain constant, but their practical effect would vary from time to time.

The reference to the 'tolerance levels of the international community' is intriguing. It may be partly understood by reference to the aforementioned 'dictates of public conscience' of the Martens Clause, which Judge Shahabuddeen re-introduced to the principle after its omission in the *Corfu Channel* case formulation.[88] It is a crucial consideration. After all, Judge Shahabuddeen found – on the evidence – that nuclear weapons are unlawful because of their 'repugnance to the conscience of the international community'.[89] But on what basis – moral, political, practical – the international community fails to tolerate something, and how a judge can glean from such intolerance a legal obligation or prohibition, is left largely unexamined. A judge must somehow measure this level of tolerance on behalf of the ill-defined community (presumably not to be equated with the community of States as this would require

---

84 *Nuclear Weapons*, op. cit., p. 409 (Judge Shahabuddeen).
85 For Judge Weeramantry, accusations of judicial activism were similarly allayed by claiming that what is at work is the application of the general principle to specific situations, out of which 'a rule of greater specificity emerges'. See *Nuclear Weapons*, op. cit., p. 493 (Judge Weeramantry).
86 This may also explain why the 'international community' he is concerned with is not the community of States, which would require a closer analysis of state practice. A more radical approach was called for by Australia's Minister of Foreign Affairs who argued before the Court that the dictates of public conscience could outlaw a means of warfare irrespective of State consent through custom or treaty, thereby keeping the Court in step with community values not necessarily reflected in the *opinio juris* of States. See 'Public Sitting', *Nuclear Weapons (Advisory Opinion)* [1996] ICJ, 30 October 1995, paras 9–11 (Gareth Evans QC).
87 *Nuclear Weapons*, op. cit., p. 406 (Judge Shahabuddeen)
88 Ibid, p. 403 (Judge Shahabuddeen).
89 Ibid, p. 386 (Judge Shahabuddeen).

closer attention to State practice) and translate it into the legal content of the *constant* principle of humanity when 'written rules [have] proved to be inadequate'.[90] For Shahabuddeen, this is exactly what happened in the *Corfu Channel* case.[91]

The majority in *Nuclear Weapons Advisory Opinion*, while not expressly rejecting elementary considerations of humanity as a freestanding norm-creating general principle, provided more confusing guidance as to its status. They affirmed the view, for instance, that the rules of international humanitarian law are 'fundamental to the respect of the human person and "elementary considerations of humanity" ',[92] thus adding to the appearance of hierarchical essentialism which the considerations conjure. The Martens Clause, moreover, was depicted as 'an effective means of addressing the rapid evolution of military technology',[93] relevant to the development of humanitarian law, although only conventional rules are cited as examples. And while the Court agreed that these principles apply to nuclear weapons,[94] the use of which was 'scarcely reconcilable' with respect for the 'requirements' (an odd word to use in such circumstances) of the 'overriding consideration of humanity',[95] it nonetheless found there were not 'sufficient elements to enable it to conclude with certainty that the use of nuclear weapons would necessarily be at variance with the principles and rules of law applicable in armed conflict in any circumstance'.[96]

Lofty as the somewhat muddled humanity-centred rhetoric of the majority may be, 'the yardsticks used by the court', as Meron has noted, 'were the principle of distinction and the prohibition of unnecessary suffering, rather than principles of humanity and the dictates of public conscience'.[97] Humanity discourse thus acted as a principled smokescreen for what was in effect a pragmatic and conservative conclusion.

Nonetheless, it is significant that the Court continued to consolidate the principle of humanity as a foundational element in the elevation of particular norms. In this sense, the various decisions and opinions reflect a movement towards

---

90 See Meron, 'The Martens Clause', op. cit., p. 83.
91 *Nuclear Weapons*, op. cit., p. 407 (Judge Shahabuddeen). It is a view far from shared by all commentators. Writing in his academic capacity, Antonio Cassese, who otherwise admires the judge's reasoning, insists that the laws of humanity and dictates of the public conscience have never been treated as distinct sources in the case law. See Cassese, op. cit., pp. 202–212.
92 *Nuclear Weapons*, op. cit., p. 257.
93 Ibid, p. 257.
94 Ibid, p. 260.
95 Ibid, p. 262.
96 Ibid, p. 263.
97 See also Cassese's critique of the reasoning on the Martens Clause as 'obscure', 'far from illuminating' and 'difficult to grasp', begging more questions than it answers. Cassese, op. cit., pp. 205–207.

what Meron has famously described as the 'humanisation' of international humanitarian law, inaugurated at the judicial level by the *Corfu Channel* case itself. They also consolidate a simultaneously evolutionary and essentialist characterization of international law. Indeed, the depictions of various layering of norms in the judgments can become quite dizzying; a 'standard', for instance, can be discerned by judges as 'embodied' in 'constant' principles which themselves 'underlie' treaty provisions, some of which are so 'fundamental' as to be intransgressible.

As might be expected, the decisions of the International Criminal Tribunal on the Former Yugoslavia (ICTY) have been a particularly fertile ground for an elaboration of the humanization phenomenon, with elementary considerations of humanity featuring prominently alongside the Martens Clause in the elaboration of new norms and new methodologies for their identification. Most spectacularly, the seminal *Tadic* judgment drew upon these sources in concluding that individual criminal responsibility during non-international armed conflict can arise under custom – a conclusion based on reasoning that in turn reflected the long-standing agenda of the presiding judge, Antonio Cassese.[98] Again, the language is essentialist in tone. Although the Court asserted that not all the rules applicable to international armed conflict are applicable to civil wars, it concluded that 'the *general essence* of those rules, and not the detailed regulation they may contain, has become applicable to internal conflicts'.[99] More specifically, the Court found that:[100]

> elementary considerations of humanity *and common sense* make it preposterous that the use by States of weapons prohibited in armed conflicts between themselves be allowed when States try to put down rebellion by their own nationals on their own territory. What is inhumane, and consequently proscribed, in international wars, cannot but be inhumane and inadmissible in civil strife.

Thomas Paine, one can imagine, would have been pleased by this reasoning, not least the conjoined reference to humanity and common sense – an assumption of a natural convergence of rationality and humanity which, as noted

---

98 T. Meron, 'Cassese's Tadic and the Law of Non-International Armed Conflicts', in L.C. Vohrah *et al.* (eds), *Man's Inhumanity to Man: Essays in Honour of Antonio Cassese* (The Hague: Kluwer Law International, 2003), p. 533. For a history of Cassese's attempts to influence the direction of the law of non-international armed conflict leading up to the decision, see T. Hoffmann, 'The Gentle Humanizer of Humanitarian Law: Antonio Cassese and the Creation of the Customary Law of Non-International Armed Conflicts', in C. Stahn and L. van den Herik (eds), *Future Perspectives on International Criminal Justice* (The Hague: T.M.C. Asser Press, 2010), p. 58. Hoffmann persuasively argues that Cassese went from progressive scholar to revolutionary judge.
99 *Prosecutor v Tadic* (ICTY, Case No. IT-94-1-AR72, 2 October 1995), para.126. Emphasis added.
100 Ibid, para. 119. Emphasis added.

above, is neither logically necessary nor universally endorsed. As Cassese's later reflections indicate, this commonsensical attitude (or perhaps sentiment?) characterized the judicial mindsets of the *Tadic* judges who were singularly motivated to overturn the 'stupid distinction' between types of conflict wars.[101] The result was a decision that rewrote the rules for establishing customary international law, relaxing the approach to evidence of State practice and placing unprecedented reliance on sometimes rather thin *opinio juris*. That humanity was defined by reference to inhumane conduct is similarly significant. Unnecessary brutality and individual human suffering are presented as carrying a presumption of illegality, or 'delinquency', to use Judge Álvarez's earlier evocative term. Such conduct is inherently, even archetypically prohibited, as Jeremy Waldron might say: it offends against a principle – or perhaps an 'essence' – that purportedly underpins this entire body of law.[102] It is, of course, a small step from here to the *erga omnes* jurisprudence which similarly relies upon obligations absolutely prohibited 'by nature'.[103]

The case law that was to follow in the wake of *Tadic* pursued a similar humanity-focused agenda, albeit with significant exceptions.[104] Importantly, the Appeals Chamber in *Celebici* found that the rules and values entailed in common Article 3 of the Geneva Conventions also found expression in international human rights law. Linked by their mutual considerations of human

---

101 I am indebted to Tamás Hoffmann for bringing to my attention the 2003 lecture in which Cassese made these retrospective observations on the decision. See Hoffmann, op. cit., p. 10. I concur with Hoffmann's observation that Cassese's judicial reasoning is more radical than his academic musings in which humanity is presented as an interpretative rather than norm-generative device. See Cassese, op. cit., pp. 189ff.

102 J. Waldron, 'Torture and Positive Law', *Columbia Law Review*, 105 (2005): 1723. For Waldron, an archetype, such as the torture prohibition, makes more 'vivid' such a principle. The principle of non-brutality espoused by Waldron is analogous to humanity law's fundamental principle that inhumane conduct is inherently prohibited. As Hoffmann puts it, Cassese's reasoning results in a position whereby custom prescribes the prohibition of conduct based on its 'inherent repulsiveness'. See Hoffman, op. cit., p.18.

103 See *Barcelona Traction*, op. cit., p. 32. Ragazzi has noted the analogous language used by Judge Jennings in the *Nicaragua* case that unnotified minelaying is 'of itself' unlawful, noting that 'the absolute value attached to the prohibition ... is grounded in the very essence of the prohibition and the values it protects'. See M. Ragazzi, 'International Obligations *Erga Omnes*: Their Moral Foundation and Criteria of Identification in Light of Two Japanese Contributions', in G.S. Goodwin-Gill and S. Talmon (eds), *The Reality of International Law: Essays in Honour of Ian Brownlie* (Oxford: Clarendon Press, 1999), pp. 472–473.

104 The 'imperatives of humanity' have not always resulted in an elevation of *opinio juris* over State practice, as the Appeal court noted in the *Ojdanic* decision where the particular gravity or heinousness of an international crime was not considered sufficient to establish its customary nature. See *Prosecutor v Ojdanic* (ICTY, Caso No. IT–99–37–AR72, 21 May 2003), para. 42.

dignity, these two bodies of law formed the 'basis of fundamental minimum standards of humanity',[105] containing a common 'core' of non-derogable standards applicable at all times, in all circumstances and to all parties, and from which no derogation was permitted.[106] The Court thus expressly joined by way of humanity the general principle with its *erga omnes* counterpart.

In cases like *Tadic, Celebici, Kupreskic* and their successors, humanity law arguably reached its judicial apotheosis, courtesy of its judge practitioners.[107] International law is undoubtedly changed as a result. However, the humanity-based reasoning has not met with universal acclaim. In addition to criticism received from academic commentators,[108] the influence of cases such as *Tadic* on subsequent positive norm development is chequered. As Hoffmann points out, one response was the deliberate restriction by negotiators of the Rome Statute of judicial discretion, and the codified expression of a hierarchy of applicable sources in Article 21.[109] The reaction of the international legal fraternity displays an internal struggle between welcoming the commonsensical result and dismay at the mechanism for achieving it. This response to the ramifications of the 'interpretative turn' towards what Teitel calls 'humanity law'[110] goes to the heart of one of the most pressing dilemmas within the discipline.

17.4 Immanent humanity unbound

The portrayal of international law as the preeminent vehicle by which to promote fundamental normative and transformative values 'demanded' by humanity continues to enjoy considerable currency among its practitioners. Theodor Meron, discussing the nature of those dictates of public conscience by which a Court can recognize the existence of unwritten norms, has encouraged interna-

---

105 *Celebici* (ICTY, Case No. IT–96–3–A, 20 February 2001), para. 149. As Schleutter notes, the ICRC had used similar language in its commentary on the Additional Protocols. See B. Schleutter (2006) *Constitutionalisation at its Best or at its Worst? Lessons from the Development of Customary International Criminal Law*, Online. Available at: <http://www.esil-sedi.eu/english/Paris_Agora_Papers/Schleutter.PDF>.
106 *Celebici*, op. cit., para. 149.
107 For cases invoking elementary considerations of humanity to establish the customary character of key norms, see the cases listed by Schleutter, op. cit., p. 5 (note 27), including *Kupreskic, Celebici,* and *Halilovic*. In *Kupreskic*, for instance, the Court found a prohibition on reprisals based *inter alia* on the imperatives of humanity. However, as Schleutter points out, these considerations 'were hardly ever employed on their own to evidence the customary character of a certain norm' (p. 5).
108 See Hoffmann, op. cit., note 160 for the many articles rejecting the reasoning with respect to custom.
109 Ibid, p. 19.
110 R. Teitel, 'Humanity's Law: Rule of Law for the New Global Politics', *Cornell International Law Journal*, 35 (2002): 355–387.

tional lawyers to 'mold public opinion through the infusion of moderating and humanitarian views to make it worthy of public conscience'.[111] For Meron, '[t]his is a challenge that we [international lawyers] cannot ignore'.[112] As seen, some judges of the ICJ and ICTY have advanced Meron's humanization of humanitarian law by jurisprudential use of elementary considerations of humanity and the dictates of public conscience. ICRC jurists have similarly engaged in an exercise of identifying 'fundamental standards of humanity' to fill protection gaps – a practice assisted and applauded more recently by the (then) UN Commission on Human Rights, extending the humanity-based identification program to 'the protection of persons in all circumstances'.[113] Some scholars have looked to the cross-fertilization potential of the humanitarian law jurisprudence to identify the crystallization of specific rights. Guy Goodwin-Gill, for instance, has employed elementary considerations of humanity and the related *jus cogens* jurisprudence to support the existence of a new State obligation to *grant* asylum to a person facing breaches of their fundamental rights in their country of origin, not least because protection of these rights must be 'even more exacting in peace than war'.[114] Other scholars have appealed to humanity to found moral and legal rights of distributive justice, for instance, in the form of specific obligations to alleviate poverty.[115]

That human rights discourse makes use of a free-standing principle of

---

111 Meron, 'The Martens Clause', op. cit., p. 85. See also C.G. Weeramantry, *Universalising International Law* (Leiden: Martinus Nijhoff, 2004), pp. 149–150, who describes the great responsibility that falls to the 'invisible college of international lawyers' as the 'keepers of the international juridical conscience' to further the 'international rule of law'.
112 Ibid.
113 Commission on Human Rights, *Promotion and Protection of Human Rights: Fundamental Standards of Humanity*, UN ESCOR, 62nd session, Agenda Item 17, UN Doc E/CN.4/2006/87 (3 March 2006) [29]. See also ICRC, *Commentary on the Additional Protocols of 8 June 1977 to the Geneva Conventions of 12 August 1949* (Norwell: Martinus Nijhoff, 1987), p. 1340.
114 G.S. Goodwin-Gill, 'Europe and the Right to be Granted Asylum' (speech delivered at Australian National University, 29 September 2010), cited with permission of author. The right to be granted asylum appeared in René Cassin's original draft of article 14 of the Universal Declaration of Human Rights, but met with considerable resistance amongst negotiators. The 'right to seek and to enjoy' asylum which resulted has been criticized as not imposing a correlative duty on States to give effect to that right. See Lauterpacht, *International Law and Human Rights* (New York: F. A. Praeger, 1950), p. 422. See also G. Goodwin-Gill and J. McAdam, *The Refugee in International Law* (Oxford: Oxford University Press, 2010), pp. 358–362.
115 See H. Shue, *Basic Rights: Subsistence, Affluence and US Foreign Policy* (Princeton, NJ: Princeton University Press, 1996), p. 19. 'Basic rights . . . are everyone's minimum reasonable demands upon the rest of humanity' (p.19). See discussion of principles of humanity and justice in S. van Hooft and W. Vandekerckhove (eds), *Questioning Cosmopolitanism (Studies in Global Justice)* (Dordrecht: Springer, 2010).
116 See also I. Brownlie, *Principles of Public International Law* (Oxford: Clarendon Press, 1998), who noted with respect to the Universal Declaration of Human Rights that 'some of its provisions either constitute general principles of law or represent elementary considerations of humanity' (p. 575).

humanity should come as no surprise.¹¹⁶ At a theoretical level, an affective notion of common shared humanity is often posited as the touchstone principle for the universality and fundamentality of human rights.¹¹⁷ The position faces very real philosophical and practical obstacles. As Raz has persuasively argued, deriving actual norms from attributes of a shared humanity, such as agency or autonomy, 'misconceives the relation between value and rights'.¹¹⁸ However, such philosophical objections do not necessarily undermine the methodology of rights identification which can now be founded upon the flexible approach taken by the courts themselves, as seen in the jurisprudence of the ICTY explored above.

Humanity has also become a yardstick for international lawyers outside these traditional fields, although usually where there are human rights or humanitarian law elements at stake. Nordquist, for instance, has described elementary considerations of humanity as underpinning the principle of humanitarian assistance at sea.¹¹⁹ Bernard Oxam has gone further, arguing that 'the Convention [UNCLOS] as a whole seeks to advance the interests of humanity'.¹²⁰ Again, this can be seen in judicial practice, where the principle of humanity has been used to fill gaps where UNCLOS is otherwise silent, an approach endorsed by ITLOS in the context of the use of force in the arrest of ships. In concluding that such force must not go beyond what is reasonable and necessary in the circumstances, the Tribunal noted, '[c]onsiderations of humanity must apply in the law of the sea, as they do in other areas of international law'.¹²¹ International environmental lawyers have taken a similar approach to their discipline, finding humanity implicated in principles making up the explicitly anthropocentric doctrine of sustainable development.

---

117 See, for instance, J. Donnelly, *Universal Human Rights in Theory and Practice* (Ithaca, NY: Cornell University Press, 2003). 'Human rights would appear to have humanity or human nature as their source' (p. 13) and 'the essential insight of human rights is that the worlds we make for ourselves . . . must conform to relatively universal requirements that rest on our common humanity' (p. 123); John Vincent, *Human Rights and International Relations* (Cambridge: Cambridge University Press, 1986), p. 13 ('Human rights are the rights that everyone has, and everyone equally, by virtue of their very humanity.')
118 J. Raz, 'Human Rights', in S. Besson and J. Tasioulas (eds), *The Philosophy of International Law* (Oxford: Oxford University Press, 2010), p. 324. Raz's main target is Gewirth's theory that humans have rights to 'the proximate necessary conditions of human action', and Griffin's theory that rights are protections of our personhood and capacity for agency which constitute that personhood.
119 M.H. Nordquist, *The United Nations Convention on the Law of the Sea 1982: A Commentary* (The Hague: Martinus Nijhoff, 1985), p. 193.
120 B. Oxam, 'Human Rights and the United Nations Convention on the Law of the Sea', *Columbia Journal of Transnational Law*, 36 (1998): 404.
121 *M/V Saiga (No. 2) (St Vincent and the Grenadines v. Guinea)* (Judgment) (ITLOS, Case No. 2, 1 July 1999), para. 155.

Intra- and inter-generational equity, the protection of cultural heritage, and even the precautionary principle can each be read as founded upon an 'awareness of the unity of humankind" as Judge Trindade has recently claimed.[122]

That 'elementary considerations of humanity' codified in the *Corfu Channel* case might have import outside the laws of war has long been claimed by commentators, from Wright's early view that it is the 'animating and motivating principle' of 'all law',[123] to Cassese's assertion that it 'embraces the whole body of international law'.[124] Yet it is in the hands of international legal theorists that an essentialist principle of humanity has become truly unbound. A volume of the *European Journal of International Law*, for instance, was recently dedicated to a discussion of Anne Peters' argument that humanity has superseded sovereignty as the first principle of international law, replacing it as the Grundnorm or *Letztbegründung* upon which all other aspects of international law are ultimately based.[125] As Peters put it:

> [T]he normative status of sovereignty is derived from humanity, understood as the legal principle that human rights, interests, needs, and security must be respected and promoted, and that this humanistic principle is also the telos of the international legal system. Humanity is the A and Ω of sovereignty.[126]

This would complete what Peters insists has been a process of 'humanisation of sovereignty'[127] in recent times, not least evident in the discourse of humanitarian intervention and the theories surrounding the 'responsibility to protect'. The result, at the very least, is a 'presumption' in favour of humanity,[128] a conclusion that marries neatly the interpretative function ascribed by Cassese (in his writings, at least) to the Martens Clause.

The metaphor which forms the title of Peters' article is itself revealing, although nowhere commented upon. Drawn from a New Testament reference

---

122 *Moiwana Village v. Suriname* (Inter-American Court of Human Rights, Case No. 145, 15 June 2005), para. 23 (Judge Trindade). Judge Trindade borrowed the phrase from the Preamble and Article 1 of the 2001 Universal Declaration on Cultural Diversity.
123 Wright, 'Foreword', op. cit., p. xiii.
124 By contrast, Cassese describes the Martens Clause as a sort of *lex specialis* vis-à-vis the general principle. See Cassese, op. cit., p. 213.
125 A. Peters, 'Humanity as the A and Ω of Sovereignty', *European Journal of International Law*, 20 (2009): 513–544.
126 Ibid, p. 514.
127 Ibid.
128 A not dissimilar attitude was adopted by Justice Higgins in her dissent in the *Nuclear Weapons* advisory opinion in which she argued that where there are competing norms, the 'judicial lodestar . . . must be those values that international law seeks to promote and protect. In the present case, it is the physical survival of peoples that we must constantly have in view'. See *Nuclear Weapons*, op. cit., p. 592 (Judge Higgins).
129 See Book of Revelation, 22:13 (King James Version): 'I am Alpha and Omega, the beginning and the end, the first and the last.'

to the place of Christ in the universe,[129] it evokes a quasi-theological and Christian natural law of an immanent humanity.[130] For those suspicious of humanity-law's implicit Judaeo-Christian and Eurocentric bias, such a reference is perhaps unfortunate. Nonetheless, as seen, it draws upon a healthy tradition, from the 'universal morality' of the slave trade treaties to Petitpierre's 'higher impartial plane of pure humanity'.

Such formulations also sit alongside the now abundant literature positing the existence of a new constitutional, cosmopolitan international law espoused by scholars such as Tomuschat, Simma and Slaughter.[131] At the risk of being reductionist, the constitutionalism project is loosely based on what Habermas has called the juridification (to use another contentious term) of international relations[132] through which sovereign power is restrained by law and its core values. For some, this constitutionalization was the deeper agenda of the ICTY judges in their invocation of elementary considerations of humanity and the dictates of public conscience, reflecting the juristic use of certain humanizing principles which 'exist on a hierarchically higher level than other norms of international law' and from which other norms can legitimately be derived.[133] In this sense, it is arguable that in the *Corfu Channel*, *Nicaragua* and *Tadic* cases, bolstered by the strong dissents in the *Nuclear Weapons* advisory opinion, judges helped establish 'the structural principle of unnecessary suffering' as a constitutional norm in the emerging international order.[134]

The *Corfu Channel* case formulation itself, despite its ambiguities and

---

130 The OED explains that 'immanent', in the sense of 'indwelling, inherent', is 'in recent philosophy applied to the Deity regarded as permanently pervading and sustaining the universe'. A similar Stoic-Christian view of mankind as forming a moral-legal unity is a foundational concept in natural law. See, for instance, Simma, 'The Contribution of Alfred Verdross', op. cit.

131 See B. Simma, 'From Bilateralism to Community Interest in International Law', *Recueil des Cours*, 250 (1994): 221; C. Tomuschat, 'International Law: Ensuring the Survival of Mankind on the Eve of a New Century, General Course on Public International Law', *Recueil des Cours*, 281 (1999): 9–438. This development is variously described in the literature. The diversity of views is found in R. Macdonald and D. Johnston (eds), *Towards World Constitutionalism: Issues in the Legal Ordering of the World Community* (Leiden: Martinus Nijhoff, 2005) and J.L. Dunoff and J.P. Trachtman (eds), *Ruling the World? Constitutionalism, International Law, and Global Governance* (Cambridge: Cambridge University Press, 2009). See discussion of critiques of these trends in J. Cohen, 'Empire Versus International Law', in C. Barry and T. Pogge (eds), *Global Institutions and Responsibilities: Achieving Global Justice* (Oxford: Blackwell Publishing, 2005).

132 See L. Blichner and A. Molander, 'Mapping Juridification', *European Law Journal*, 14 (2008): 36–54.

133 See Schleutter, op. cit., p. 5. See also Hoffmann's analysis of Cassese's view of post-World War II international law as 'idealistic', reflecting 'the need to transform relations as they now stand and proclaim a duty to do more than merely consecrate things as they are' (p. 5, citing A. Cassese, *Violence and Law in the Modern Age* (Princeton, NJ: Princeton University Press, 1988, p. 4)).

134 N. Tsagourias, *Transnational Constitutionalism: International and European Models* (Cambridge: Cambridge University Press, 2007), p. 78.

inconclusiveness, thus finds resonance at several universalist levels. Indeed, for Nicholas Tsagourias, the elementary considerations of humanity expressed by the ICJ is a 'normative-ideational' constitutional principle, encapsulating the values and goals, and reflecting the 'creator spirit' and *raison d'être* behind the international legal order.[135]

This elevation of humanity can be seen as merely a continuation (or perhaps revival) of the same Kantian Victorianism that gave birth to humanity as a normative legal principle in the first place. After all, many contemporary international lawyers see themselves as both responding to progress in human civilization, and attempting to shape its direction through the values inherent in the law. This explains in part why the Martens Clause and the general principle are described by writers and judges using expressions such as dynamic, evolving, motivating, animating, essentialist, fundamental, protecting basic values, intrinsically worthy, and even constitutional. As Koskenniemi has observed, while realism has injected a certain level of discomfort when we speak in 'the (paternalistic) language of the "harmony of interests" ', nonetheless 'international law remains one of the few bastions of Victorian objectivism, liberalism and optimism'.[136] And hand-in-glove with this Victorian theme is the affective, rhetorical aspect of humanity – the 'sentiment' which Judge Álvarez espoused, generated out of 'universal juridical conscience' and the 'demands' of the international community. The persuasive impact of humanity is not to be underestimated or too readily delegitimized. As Meron noted with respect to the Martens Clause formula, its 'rhetorical and ethical code words' exert a 'strong pull toward normativity'.[137] After all, as Hume (and more recently Richard Rorty) recognized, appeals to common humanity retain that motivating ethical element which appeals to common rationality lack.[138] In this sense, an effective principle of humanity both incorporates and necessitates a sentiment of empathy.

Just as the international constitutionalism movement has been the target of those suspicious of European normative hegemony, so has contemporary humanity-law met with considerable opposition. Some target the distillation and reification of a free-standing, norm-generative principle and its unsettling effect on traditional legal categories. For others, humanity law in the guise of constitutionalism represents an attempt to universalize a specifically European

---

135 Ibid, p. 76.
136 Koskenniemi, *The Gentle Civilizer of Nations*, op. cit., p. 360. For an examination of the systemic continuity between contemporary international constitutionalism and nineteenth-century international legal thought, and the centrality to each of a narrative of progress, see R. Collins, 'Constitutionalism as Liberal-Juridical Consciousness: Echoes from International Law's Past', *Leiden Journal of International Law*, 2 (2009): 251–287.
137 Meron, 'The Martens Clause', op. cit., p. 89.
138 Referring to the 'manipulation of sentiment', Rorty notes: 'Most people are simply unable to understand why membership in a biological species is supposed to suffice for membership in a moral community'. See R. Rorty, 'Human Rights, Rationality and Sentimentality', in O. Savic and B. Krug (eds) *The Politics of Human Rights* (London: Verso, 1999), p. 75.

legal paradigm. Commentators have also attempted to explain the trend structurally by reference to questions of unity and disunity in the discipline. Thus, for Martineau, the move towards a teleological international law 'directed towards the greater fulfilment of mankind' evident in international cosmopolitanism and constitutionalism is a response to the 'post-modern anxiety' of fragmentation.[139] The most strident criticisms draw upon the tradition of Proudhon and Bentham. Just as these nineteenth-century thinkers distrusted the humanity-based rhetoric of their age, so do critics of constitutional cosmopolitanism — especially as manifested in humanitarian intervention — see it as one of a related set of 'deformalised mechanisms by which empire aims to rule (and to legitimate its rule) rather than ways to limit and orient power by law'.[140] Koskenniemi's more recent return to formalism betrays a similar distrust.[141] Complemented by Schmitt's portrayal of humanity as an 'asymmetrical counter concept' allowing States to usurp universal concepts against the inhumane 'enemy', these concerns retain their resonance.

Regardless of the ultimate impact of these critiques and caveats, what is undeniable is that the principle espoused 60 years ago in such laconic terms foreshadowed debates that go to the heart of the nature and function of the discipline of international law, and the motivation of its practitioners. For its adherents, considerations of humanity are truly 'elementary',[142] and the Court's decision itself a seminal constitutional moment.[143] By linking general principles of international law to a foundational, essentialist and affective notion of humanity, the Court injected an ideological and empathetic element into this rather amorphous source of law. It took general principles, to borrow the words of Judge Tanaka in his dissent in the *South West Africa* cases, 'beyond the limit of legal positivism', thus providing them with 'a supra-national and supra-positive character'.[144] Contemporary debates are merely commentaries on the Court's original formulation of this 'well-recognized' principle.

---

139 See Martineau, op. cit., pp. 5–6, who argues that the 'constitutionalist vocabulary' helps 'soothe the anxiety over fragmentation', and that the 'cosmopolitan narrative ... respond[s] to perceptions of chaos by further reliance on the universal teleology'. See also M. Koskenniemi and P. Leino, 'Fragmentation of International Law? Postmodern Anxieties', *Leiden Journal of International Law*, 15 (2002): 553–579.
140 J. Cohen, 'Empire Versus International Law', in C. Barry and T. Pogge (eds) *Global Institutions and Responsibilities: Achieving Global Justice* (Oxford: Blackwell Publishing, 2005), p. 160. For Cohen's view on Schmitt, see p. 162.
141 Koskenniemi, *From Apology to Utopia*, op. cit.
142 The *Oxford English Dictionary* defines 'elementary' as '[o]f the nature of an (absolutely or relatively) ultimate constituent'.
143 The term, common in constitutional history, is used in the cosmopolitan context in A. Slaughter and W. Burke-White, 'An International Constitutional Moment', *Harvard International Law Journal*, 43 (2002): 1–22. See discussion and critique in J. Cohen, 'Sovereignty in the Context of Globalization: A Constitutional Pluralist Perspective', in S. Besson and J. Tasioulas (eds), *The Philosophy of International Law* (Oxford: Oxford University Press, 2010), pp. 268–272.
144 *South West Africa*, op. cit., p. 298 (Judge Tanaka).

Part VI
Issues of state responsibility

18 State omissions and due diligence

Aspects of fault, damage and contribution to injury in the law of state responsibility

Sarah Heathcote

18.1 Introduction

A lot has been written about due diligence in international law and since 1949 the *Corfu Channel* case is invariably cited as authority for the principle. Yet the concept was far from new to the law of State responsibility when the International Court of Justice (ICJ) handed down its first contentious decision.[1] Through its appreciation of the due diligence principle, the decision has nonetheless served to anchor, if with some dissent and nuance, an objective appreciation of the law of State responsibility. The case equally illustrates the role of the external event (in this case by a third State) in relation to both the subjective and objective elements of the internationally wrongful act. Finally, while an analysis of the due diligence principle as it emerges from the *Corfu Channel* case is invariably drawn from the first part of the Court's 1949 decision, the second part of that judgment in fact also bears on the concept. This contribution will conclude by considering this latter aspect of the case.

18.2 How due diligence was raised and deployed by the Court in the *Corfu Channel* case

18.2.1 *The general context: a decision in two connected parts*

Neatly divided into two parts, each reflecting the questions put to the ICJ in the *compromis*, the Court's conclusions in the *Corfu Channel* decision equally articulate two mutually reinforcing sets of principles. In response to the first question, the ICJ held Albania responsible for the damage to two British warships (and ensuing loss of life) after they struck mines in Albania's territorial waters on 22 October 1946. This was not premised on Albania having

---

1 The term was used in, and would ground responsibility under, Article 6 of the Washington Treaty (1871) between the United States of America and the United Kingdom, concluded to settle the *Alabama Claims*.

laid the mines or 'connived' in their laying by a third party, but rather on 'certain general and well-recognized principles': elementary considerations of humanity (even more exacting in times of peace than war), freedom of maritime communication and 'every State's obligation not to allow knowingly its territory to be used for acts contrary to the rights of other States',[2] this latter principle expressing a due diligence obligation: Albania knew (or should have been aware) of the mines in its territorial waters, had time to notify the United Kingdom (UK) warships of their presence and failed to do so.[3] It can be seen that having set out a basic premise of humanity (perhaps inspired by the United Nations' contemporaneous work on both human rights and individual criminal responsibility[4]), the Court affirms State freedoms in common spaces as well as their obligation to respect other States' rights, even on their own territory. Cumulatively these principles express State freedoms (and their limits) within a framework of coexisting sovereignties.

Subordinating the exercise of exclusive territorial jurisdiction to the respect of others States' rights, necessarily means that those other States cannot interfere in that exclusive sphere without an enabling rule; hence the mutually reinforcing aspect of the second part of the Court's decision. Thus in reply to the second question, whether the UK had violated Albanian sovereignty by reason of its naval operation known as *Operation Retail* to demine Albanian waters that lay (allegedly, at the time) in an international strait, the Court affirms the postwar legal limits on self-help in the light of the newly adopted UN Charter. Non-intervention is thus emphasised, reinforcing the fundamental principle codified in Article 2 of the Charter, whether or not on the facts of the case the UK operation was forcible[5] and 'whatever be the present defects in international organization'[6] (namely the absence of the envisaged collective security system). The law thus modelled in the light of the *de jure* presence of a collective security system, the implication is that (even despite its *de facto* absence) these institutional provisions were binding on the UK *vis-à-vis* Albania – for although the latter was not a party to the Charter (despite its attempts), it had accepted the obligations under it for the purposes of resolving the dispute.[7]

---

2 *Corfu Channel case, Judgment of April 9th, 1949: ICJ Reports 1949*, p. 22.
3 Ibid.
4 Universal Declaration of Human Rights, adopted by the General Assembly in Resolution 217 A (III) of 10 December 1948 and the Draft Code of Offenses Against the Peace and Security of Mankind (ultimately adopted in 1954, in what would become Part I; Part II being adopted in 1996).
5 While commentators have generally understood the Court to have been referring to the prohibition on the use of force, it has been pointed out that this was not necessarily the case: O. Corten, *Le droit contre la guerre* (Paris: Pedone, 2008), pp. 372–373.
6 *Corfu Channel case, Judgment of April 9th, 1949: ICJ Reports 1949*, p. 35.
7 Letter of Albanian President Mr Hoxha of 24 January 1947, Security Council Official Records, No. 6, p. 123 and No. 7, p. 131, cited in I. Y. Chung, *Legal Problems Involved in the Corfu Channel Incident* (Geneva/Paris: Droz/Minard, 1959), p. 32.

In any event, by setting out such broad principles, it appears the ICJ was doing, whether by design or coincidence, that which the UN's other legal organ, the International Law Commission (ILC), would soon be in the midst of (arguably) failing adequately to achieve; namely the codification of fundamental rights and duties of States;[8] to articulate them in a context outside the Charter, binding on both UN members and those States not yet members of that organisation – such as Albania. This was particularly important given that the ICJ was diffusing an early Cold War dispute that threatened to degenerate into open hostilities.

18.2.2 Due diligence as a general principle

Yet cast as a general principle, the statement of law relative to due diligence had in fact already been affirmed by international tribunals, most famously in three prior decisions. Thus in 1925, Max Huber in the *Spanish Zone* case stated that '[t]he responsibility for events which may affect international law and which occur in a given territory goes hand in hand with the right to exercise, to the exclusion of other States, the prerogatives of sovereignty'.[9] The same Swiss jurist would affirm in similar terms in the 1928 *Island of Palmas* award that by virtue of their territorial sovereignty States have 'the obligation to protect within the territory the rights of other States'.[10] Finally, in that part of its decision rendered in 1941, the tribunal stated in the *Trail Smelter* Award that:

---

8 General Assembly Resolution 375(IV) of 6 December 1949, to which the ILC's Draft Declaration on the Rights and Duties of States is annexed, states *inter alia*:

> *Considering* that at the present time it has encountered some difficulties in formulating basic rights and duties of States in the light of new developments of international law and in harmony with the Charter of the United Nations, and recognizing the need of continuing study with regard to this subject.

The ILC project was discontinued. One can note that the ICJ's *Corfu Channel* Merits decision is dated 9 April 1949 and the ILC met to discuss its topic from 12 April to 9 June 1949. On the preparatory work to the Draft Declaration, including the various similar codification projects of the time, see *Preparatory Study Concerning a Draft Declaration on the Rights and Duties of States* A/CN.4/2. Available at: http://untreaty.un.org/ilc/documentation/english/a_cn4_2.pdf (10 November 2010). In particular note the comments of Mr Alfaro in the Commission: 'The principle that a State should not injure another State was the very foundation of the draft Declaration of the Rights and Duties of States', 5th Meeting, Tuesday 19 April 1949, *ILC Yearbook*, 1949, p. 37, para. 45.

9 *British Claims in the Spanish Zone of Morocco Case* (1 May 1925), United Nations, *Reports of International Arbitral Awards*, vol. II, p. 649; English translation of quoted extract in 'Report of the International Law Commission on its 31st Session', *ILC Yearbook*, 1979, vol. II, Part Two, p. 98, note 505.

10 *Islands of Palmas case (Netherlands v. USA)*, 4 April 1928, United Nations, *Reports of International Arbitral Awards*, vol. II, p. 839.

under the principles of international law, as well as of the law of the United States, no State has the right to use or permit the use of its territory in such a manner as to cause injury by fumes in or to the territory of another or the properties or persons therein, when the case is of serious consequence and the injury is established by clear and convincing evidence.[11]

This last statement – together with the *Corfu Channel* case statement under consideration here – has formed a cornerstone of international environmental law and would be reiterated by the ICJ in later cases.[12] In the light of the above cases, it is no surprise that both parties in the *Corfu Channel* proceedings accepted the principle. As the ICJ stated in its judgment:

The obligations resulting for Albania from this knowledge are not disputed between the Parties. Counsel for the Albanian Government expressly recognized that [translation] 'if Albania had been informed of the operation before the incidents of October 22nd, and in time to warn the British vessels and shipping in general of the existence of mines in the Corfu Channel, her responsibility would be involved.'[13]

In addition to the above statements of general principle, which are really no more than statements of what sovereignty means, a whole series of arbitral awards had, prior to the *Corfu Channel* decision, applied specific primary rules of due diligence relative both to the protection of aliens and foreign State representatives.[14] Moreover, numerous conventional due diligence obligations exist, although in the *Corfu Channel* case itself, the *Hague Convention VIII of 1907 Relative to the Laying of Automatic Submarine Contact Mines* was, contrary to UK pleadings, not held to be applicable, since it was confined to times of war.[15]

---

11 *Trail Smelter* case *(United States v. Canada)*, 16 April 1938 and 11 March 1941, United Nations *Reports of International Arbitral Awards*, vol. III, p. 1965.
12 Thus in the *Legality of the Threat or Use of Nuclear Weapons*, the ICJ would state that the 'general obligation of States to ensure that activities within their jurisdiction and control respect the environment of other States or of areas beyond national control is now part of the corpus of international law relating to the environment', *ICJ Reports 1996*, p. 242, para. 29; a passage reiterated a year later in the *Case Concerning the Gabcikovo-Nagymaros Project (Hungary/Slovakia), Judgment, ICJ Reports 1997*, p. 41, para. 53, and more recently in the *Case Concerning Pulp Mills on the River Uruguay, (Argentina v. Uruguay), Judgment, ICJ Reports 2010*, para. 193.
13 *Corfu Channel* case, *Judgment of April 9th, 1949: ICJ Reports 1949*, p. 22.
14 See for illustrations, R. Ago, 'Fourth Report on State Responsibility', *ILC Yearbook*, 1972, vol. II, pp. 100–106, paras 74–90; more specifically in relation to foreign state representatives: R. Ago, 'Seventh Report on State Responsibility', *ILC Yearbook*, 1978, vol. I, Part One, p. 35, para. 13, note 18.
15 *Corfu Channel* case, *Judgment of April 9th, 1949: ICJ Reports 1949*, p. 22.

Finally, one can note from the cases cited above, that when it comes to responsibility for wrongful acts, it is only in relation to established rights that an obligation of due diligence is owed by one State to another (in the *Corfu Channel* case, the right of innocent passage).[16] In relation to mere interests – such as, for instance, a failure to take adequate measures to prevent the collapse of a banking system leading to a global financial crisis, a field in which only soft obligations exist[17] – it is arguable that if responsibility for a wrongful act were to be invoked, then if at all possible, it would need to rest on an abuse of rights.[18] More broadly, the juncture and inter-play between the various principles enunciated by the Court – humanity, due diligence, freedom of maritime communication and non-intervention – are often the tools for embarking on an analysis of inter-State disputes.

18.3 An objective approach to responsibility: due diligence and fault

The application of the due diligence principle in the *Corfu Channel* case has prompted considerable comment on the role of fault in the law of State responsibility. This has been done from various perspectives, ranging from whether fault is required by the secondary rules of responsibility for internationally wrongful acts, to whether the case leans towards – even if it does not alone support – a more absolute (or no-fault) form of liability.

18.3.1 Inclinations towards no-fault liability rejected

In respect of a more absolute form of liability, the literature invariably notes that the Court rejected both a *prima facie* responsibility of Albania entailing a reversal of the burden of proof;[19] as well as the less extreme position (more clearly back within the realm of responsibility for wrongful acts), that the mere control by Albania of its territory gave rise to a presumption of

---

16 The *Trail Smelter* Award is sometimes considered as having laid down specific obligations in relation to trans-frontier pollution: R. Pisillo-Mazzeschi, 'The Due Diligence Rule and the Nature of the International Responsibility of States', *German Yearbook of International Law*, 35 (1992): 39. If in contrast, it dealt with an impact on a neighbouring state's mere interests, this then raises the question of whether liability might exist for acts not prohibited by international law.
17 The principal instruments, which are non-binding, being at the time the Basel II Accord (and since 2010, the Basel III Accord); both devised by the Basel Committee on Banking Supervision, consisting of regulators of (only) 27 States.
18 Expressing scepticism: P-M. Dupuy, *La responsabilité internationale des états pour les dommages d'origine technologique et industrielle* (Paris: Pedone, 1976), pp. 26–30; in contrast, favourable: R. Kolb, *La bonne foi en droit international public* (Geneva/Paris: Graduate Institute of International Studies/PUF, 2000), p. 442 *et seq.*.
19 *Corfu Channel case, Judgment of April 9th, 1949: ICJ Reports 1949*, p. 18.

knowledge of the mines' presence (embedded in the rejected UK argument of *res ipsa loquitur*).[20] As the Court acknowledged:

> It cannot be concluded from the mere fact of the control exercised by a State over its territory and waters that the State necessarily knew or ought to have known, of any unlawful act perpetrated therein, nor yet that it necessarily knew or should have known, the authors.[21]

It was only because of a sufficient lapse of time between the laying of the mines and the explosions, enabling Albania to gain knowledge of their presence, either constructive or actual, that its responsibility was incurred. That awareness or knowledge, even if only constructive, is required for a breach of a due diligence obligation was reaffirmed by the ICJ in the 2007 *Genocide* decision.[22]

Nonetheless, even if Albania was not responsible merely because the explosions took place in its waters, the location of that event on the wrongful State's territory appears to give a 'preliminary indication' of where responsibility might lie. Hence the Court stated in the *Corfu* decision: 'a State on whose territory or in whose waters an act contrary to international law has occurred, may be called upon to give an explanation'.[23] This helps to explain the lower threshold of proof in the judgment and the Court's use of circumstantial evidence.

The same reasoning applies when it comes to areas over which the State is not sovereign but over which, as a matter of fact (or effectively), it exercises exclusive control, as for instance, in relation to obligations under a Mandate,[24] or under rules of international humanitarian law.[25] When the State's control

---

20 Ibid.
21 Ibid.
22 *Application of the Convention on the Prevention and Punishment of the Crime of Genocide (Bosnia and Herzegovina v. Serbia and Montenegro), Judgment, ICJ Reports 2007*, para. 432. See also *United States Diplomatic and Consular Staff in Tehran, Judgment, ICJ Reports 1980*, p. 32, para. 68.
23 *Corfu Channel case, Judgment of April 9th, 1949: ICJ Reports 1949*, p. 18, as also pointed out by the literature: C. de Visscher, *Theory and Reality in Public International Law* (translation from the French, P.E. Corbett) (Princeton, NJ: Princeton University Press, 1957), p. 277, D. Lévy, 'La responsabilité pour omission et la responsabilité pour risque en droit international public', *Revue générale de droit international public*, XXXII (1961): 744; L. Condorelli, 'L'imputation à l'état d'un fait internationalement illicite: solutions classiques et nouvelles tendances', *Recueil des Cours*, 189 (1984-IV): 108; M. Fitzmaurice, 'The *Corfu Channel case* and the Development of International Law', in N. Ando, E. McWhinney, and R. Wolfrum (eds.) *Liber amicorum Judge Shigeru Oda* (The Hague: Kluwer, 2002), p. 133. However, this may depend on the primary rule in question: I. Brownlie, *System of the Law of Nations: State Responsibility*, Part I (Oxford: Clarendon Press, 1983), p. 165.
24 *Legal Consequences for States of the Continued Presence of South Africa in Namibia (South West Africa) Notwithstanding Security Council Resolution 276(1970), Advisory Opinion, ICJ Reports 1971*, p. 54, para. 118.
25 See generally, Condorelli op. cit., pp. 109–111.

is not over a location but an activity, for instance, over activities in outer space, in Condorelli's view, negligence is harder to prove; both because there is no territory to serve as an initial indicator of potential responsibility, but also because it is harder to show that the State had the means at its disposal to prevent the injury.[26] The notable feature of the 2007 *Genocide* case was that the Court affirmed that the obligation of due diligence, at least as it applies in relation to the prevention of genocide, is applicable as soon as there is a 'capacity to influence effectively'[27] the actions of persons likely to commit genocide. This loose connection would appear, however, to be confined to the particular primary rule in question – indeed, the Court stressed that due diligence had to be assessed *in concreto*.[28] A more traditional approach would be adopted in 2010 by the same Court when, in the *Pulp Mills* case, it found that a particular conventional due diligence obligation relative to a shared watercourse entailed an obligation in respect of 'all activities which simply take place under the jurisdiction and control of each party'.[29]

It can be seen that implicit in the above is the fact that breaches of due diligence obligations can involve (though this is just one hypothesis) a State's own organs' failure to prevent damage caused by third parties, the important point here being that the latter's acts are non-attributable. They simply have the function of revealing or 'catalysing' the State's own directly attributable omission to fulfil an obligation.[30] This position had been encapsulated by draft Article 11 – and notably in its paragraph 2 – of the ILC's Draft Articles on State Responsibility as provisionally adopted on first reading which provided that:

1 The conduct of a person or a group of persons not acting on behalf of the State shall not be considered as an act of the State under international law.
2 Paragraph 1 is without prejudice to the attribution to a State of any other conduct which is related to that referred to in that paragraph and which is to be considered as an act of that State by virtue of [then] articles 5 to 10.[31]

---

26 Ibid, pp. 112–114.
27 *Case Concerning the Application of the Convention on the Prevention and Punishment of the Crime of Genocide (Bosnia and Herzegovina v. Serbia and Montenegro), Judgment,* 2007, para. 430.
28 Ibid, para. 430.
29 *Case Concerning Pulp Mills on the River Uruguay (Argentina v. Uruguay), Judgment, ICJ Reports 2010,* para. 197.
30 The first phase of the *Tehran Hostages* case is generally cited in this regard: the students' storming of the US Embassy revealed that Iran had failed to protect it as required by the Vienna Convention on Diplomatic Relations. *United States Diplomatic and Consular Staff in Tehran, Judgment, ICJ Reports 1980,* pp. 29–33, paras 57–68.
31 'Report of the Commission to the General Assembly on the Work of its Forty-Eighth Session', *ILC Yearbook,* 1996, vol. II, Part Two, p. 59, para. 65.

Ultimately the provision was deemed superfluous by the ILC as it simply envisages attribution *via* the rules currently codified in Articles 4–11 of the 2001 *Articles on State Responsibility (Articles)*.[32] Nonetheless it was inserted to cater precisely for that situation in which 'for example, the simple fact that they [the third parties causing harm] are in its territory'[33] – in other words, to acknowledge the *indicia* (though not a presumption) that location might and can provide in respect of responsibility.[34]

18.3.2 Fault (dolus *or* culpa) *as an additional condition for the internationally wrongful act also rejected*

Given that awareness or knowledge is required, the question becomes whether Albania's real or constructive knowledge indicates that the system of State responsibility for internationally wrongful acts is fault based, requiring the injured State to demonstrate at the level of the secondary rules of State responsibility a *dolus* (malicious intent) or a *culpa* (negligence).

In response to the *Corfu Channel* decision, the literature has in fact raised the question in terms of whether the 1949 judgment *revived* fault in the law of State responsibility.[35] For a minority of writers, the most frequently cited being H. Lauterpacht and Hostie, the 1949 decision does indeed stand for this proposition.[36]

In the traditional doctrine, as reflected, for instance, in the writings of Grotius, fault was perceived as a requirement for responsibility and this was to be found in the psychological attitude of the State organ, thus making it an aspect of attribution (or imputation as the traditional terminology would express it). However, since Triepel and Anzilotti – the latter said to have 'assassinated' fault in international law[37] – the view gradually lost credence. But this took some time to be established by the generality of commentators. Thus, Article 1 of the 1927 Institute of International Law resolution on a State's responsibility for damage caused on its territory to foreign persons and their property, after some controversy, made fault the default position in that it was deemed a requirement unless the primary rule indicated

---

32 Assuming that all these rules of attribution reflect customary international law, which may not be the case. See *Case Concerning the Application of the Convention on the Prevention and Punishment of the Crime of Genocide (Bosnia and Herzegovina v. Serbia and Montenegro), Judgment*, 2007, para. 414.
33 Ago, 'Fourth Report on State Responsibility', op. cit., p. 95, para. 62.
34 Condorelli, op. cit., p. 104.
35 Lévy, op. cit., p. 747.
36 H. Lauterpacht, *Oppenheim's International Law*, 8th edn, vol. I (London: Longmans, Green & Co., 1955), p. 343, para. 154; J. Hostie, 'The *Corfu Channel case* and International Liability of States', *Liber amicorum Algot Bagge* (Stockholm: Norstedt, 1956), p. 93.
37 P-M. Dupuy, 'Faute de l'état et "fait internationalement illicite"', *Droits*, 5 (1987): 51.

otherwise.[38] It has also been said that in 1940 the majority of writers considered that international responsibility depended on the fault of the author[39] and this would be maintained by a number of writers after World War II.[40]

Yet in 1949 the World Court chose continuity with its predecessor, the Permanent Court of International Justice (PCIJ), its case law sustaining the position that fault need not be demonstrated for responsibility to be incurred. Basdevant and Guggenheim point out that in its first judgment the PCIJ adopted an objective approach to State responsibility: in the *Wimbledon* case,[41] in which the question was whether Germany was in breach of its obligations relative to passage in the Kiel Canal by refusing passage, the Court did not consider the culpability of the German organs in question but merely ascertained that there was a discrepancy between what was required by Article 380 of the Treaty of Versailles and Germany's conduct.[42] Max Huber in the *Spanish Zone* case (a Permanent Court of Arbitration case) also considered that the degree of diligence required by a State depends on objective conditions, such as peace, war or revolution and not on the psychological state of the individual.[43]

Likewise, in 1949, the Court did not enquire into Albania's subjective intentions. Indeed, the dissenting opinions in the *Corfu Channel* case notably by Judges Krylov and Ečer,[44] all placed emphasis on the need for subjective fault, confirming for authors,[45] the fact that the judgment itself was premised on objective responsibility. Moreover, in the second part of the judgment relative to *Operation Retail*, the Court rejected the UK argument that it had no intention of infringing Albania's territorial integrity or political independence,[46] thus providing some additional authority that the ICJ excluded fault as a requirement for an internationally wrongful act.

Thus, objective responsibility was maintained, today the element of fault in the view of the 2001 *Articles* being considered relevant at the level of the

---

38 *La résponsabilité internationale des Etats à raison des dommages causés sur leur territoire à la personne et aux biens des étrangers* (Session de Lausanne, 1927), Article 1, para. 4.
39 ILC Secretariat, ' "*Force majeure*" and "Fortuitous Event" as Circumstances precluding wrongfulness: Survey of State Practice, International Judicial Decisions and Doctrine', *ILC Yearbook*, 1978, vol II, Part One, p. 192.
40 Ibid., pp. 193–194.
41 *Case of the SS Wimbledon, 1923, PCIJ, Series A, No. 1*, p. 15.
42 P. Guggenheim, *Traité de droit international public*, vol. II (Geneva: Librairie Georg, 1954), pp. 52–53; Basdevant gives other illustrations drawn from arbitral awards in his 1936 Hague General Course: J. Basdevant, 'Règles générales du droit de la paix', *Recueil des Cours*, 58 (1936-IV): 668–670.
43 Guggenheim, op. cit., p. 53, citing Huber in the *Spanish Zone* case, op. cit. p. 642.
44 *Corfu Channel case, Judgment of April 9th, 1949: ICJ Reports 1949*, pp. 71–72 (Dissenting Opinion of Judge Krylov) and pp. 128–129 (Dissenting Opinion of Judge Ečer).
45 For instance, Lévy, op. cit., pp. 747–748; Chung, op. cit., pp. 166–167.
46 Point made by Chung, ibid., p. 273.

primary norm[47] and indeed, Anzilotti's position is now accepted that due diligence is a primary norm that *consists of* fault (negligence).[48] While this 'objectivised fault'[49] is the dominant approach, it can be noted that for the principal architect of the ILC's work on State responsibility, Roberto Ago, fault in the sense of a psychological attitude is a necessary condition for imputing a breach to a State[50] and, one can note, it consists in the organ's attitude towards the rule being broken (rather than towards the material injury caused).[51]

Even on the dominant view, fault is not absent from the rules relative to the generation of State responsibility, nor indeed those relative to its content.[52] Instead it has a surreptitious presence: the absence of fault can remove the objective element of wrongfulness (on Ago's personal view as just described, it would instead negate imputation) once *a priori* the breach is established by the injured State, or fault can impact upon the level of reparations (the latter being dealt with further below). Thus *force majeure*, including fortuitous event (in the sense of lack of foreseeability or mistake of fact),[53] precludes wrongfulness because of the very absence of awareness or voluntariness that is inherent in an absolute impossibility; *force majeure* being variously expressed as: an 'absence of subjective fault', 'absence of a breach of an obligation' (fault being part of the primary rule) or 'lack of wilfulness or knowledge' (especially since the *Corfu dictum*).[54] Indeed, much of the ILC's (and its Secretariat's) discussion

---

47 Commentary to Article 2, *Articles on State Responsibility for Internationally Wrongful Acts*, J. Crawford, *The International Law Commission's Articles on State Responsibility* (Cambridge: Cambridge University Press, 2002), pp. 81–82, para. 3.
48 D. Anzilotti, 'La responsabilité internationale des états à raison des dommages soufferts par des étrangers', *Revue générale de droit international public*, XIII (1906): 291; D. Anzilotti, *Cours de droit international* (translation from the Italian by G. Gidel) (Paris: LGDJ, 1999), p. 501.
49 On the various nuances in relation to 'fault', 'objectivised fault' and 'objective' responsibility, of which space precludes an analysis here, see Pisillo-Mazzeschi, op. cit., *passim*.
50 R. Ago, 'Le délit international', *Recueil des Cours*, 68 (1939-II): 486.
51 Ibid.
52 For an overview, see J. Salmon, 'La place de la faute de la victime dans le droit de la responsabilité internationale', *International Law at the Time of its Codification: Essays in Honour of Roberto Ago* (Milan: Giuffrè, 1987), p. 371. In respect of the content of state responsibility (the obligation to make reparation), see G. Arangio Ruiz, 'Second Report on State Responsibility', *ILC Yearbook*, 1989, vol. II, Part 1, pp. 47–54, paras 164–190.
53 Note that the 1978 ILC Secretariat Survey defines fortuitous event as lack of foreseeability whereas *force majeure* is lack of voluntariness: '"Force majeure" and "Fortuitous Event" as Circumstances precluding wrongfulness: Survey of State Practice, International Judicial Decisions and Doctrine', op. cit., p. 219. Thus fortuitous event relates to constructive knowledge – the State should be aware; while *force majeure* relates to actual knowledge.
54 Ibid., p. 207, para. 530, where there is a general list. Note in this regard, that in the *Corfu Channel case*, dissenting judge Krylov in essence considered Albania to be in a situation of *force majeure*: 'even if Albania had known of the existence of the minefield before October 22nd, 1946 . . . the Albanian coastal guard service could not have warned the

of due diligence cases before jurisdictional bodies relates to *force majeure*. This absence of fault is for the wrongful State to establish. Thus whether one sees fault as relevant to the subjective element of the internationally wrongful act, as did Ago, or to the objective element (breach) and hence residing in certain primary rules, the secondary rules of responsibility nonetheless cater to it, even if indirectly.

18.4 The objective element of the internationally wrongful act: breach and damage

If fault is objectivised in that its presence is to be found in the relevant primary obligation, then it is appropriate to consider due diligence from the perspective of the objective element of the internationally wrongful act. This is interesting in light of the prevalence of due diligence obligations, as well as from a more theoretical point of view in that it can shed light on their nature; otherwise stated, their place within a 'theory of obligations'.

18.4.1 Prevalence of due diligence obligations

A due diligence obligation as referred to thus far is an obligation to prevent an event perpetrated by a third State (as in the *Corfu* case), though it could be by a person (as in the first phase of the *Tehran Hostages* case[55]) or indeed a natural event. When the external event is a third State, there may in addition to a due diligence breach be scope for responsibility for aid and assistance, although the requirements are stricter,[56] and a jurisdictional body might be precluded from hearing the matter on the basis of the *Monetary Gold* principle.

The number of due diligence obligations of the type described here, as commentators have for quite some time indicated, is ever on the increase.[57] This is certainly true as non-State actors take on an increasingly prominent role, as has been the case since the end of the Cold War and in particular the attacks of 11 September 2001. One finds this type of obligation in respect of

---

British ships of the fact on that day . . . [they] had neither sufficient time nor the necessary technical means for giving such a warning'. *Dissenting Opinion by Judge Krylov, Corfu Channel case, Judgment of April 9th, 1949: ICJ Reports 1949*, p. 72.

55 *United States Diplomatic and Consular Staff in Tehran, Judgment, ICJ Reports 1980*, pp. 29–33, paras 57–68.
56 The ICJ explained in the 2007 *Genocide* case that complicity always requires some positive action to provide aid or assistance, whereas a due diligence breach results from a 'failure to adopt and implement suitable measures to prevent genocide' (op. cit., para. 432). Moreover, complicity requires 'full knowledge of the facts' and not simply awareness, constructive or actual (ibid.). See further the contribution by O. Corten and P. Klein in this volume (Chapter 19).
57 Thus in 1984, Condorelli, op. cit., p. 175.

human rights generally and more specifically in relation to corporate social responsibility[58] or again corruption[59] – any area in which international law's direct control of non-State actors remains tenuous. One also finds such obligations in other fields, thus the responsibility of States themselves for the activities of international organisations.[60]

Perhaps most contentious of all, is the question of prevention of terrorist activities perpetrated by non-State actors from a State's territory. Thus, in 2001 the United States asserted that Afghanistan's (due diligence) failure to prevent Al-Qaeda from using its territory to carry out, what can be classified in terms of scale and gravity, as an armed attack (attribution to Afghanistan being, however, exceptionally hard if not impossible to establish), enabled action in self-defence against Afghanistan:

> The attacks of 11 September 2001 and the ongoing threat to the United States and its nationals posed by the Al-Qaida organization have been made possible by the decision of the Taliban regime to allow the parts of Afghanistan that it controls to be used by this organization as a base of operation. Despite every effort by the United States and the international community, the Taliban regime has refused to change its policy. From the territory of Afghanistan, the Al-Qaida organization continues to train and support agents of terror who attack innocent people throughout the world and target United States nationals and interests in the United States and abroad. In response to these attacks, and in accordance with the inherent right of individual and collective self-defense, United States armed forces have initiated actions designed to prevent and deter further attacks on the United States. These actions include measures against Al-Qaida terrorist training camps and military installations of the Taliban Regime in Afghanistan.[61]

This attempt to extend self-defence on grounds of a due diligence failure, in a manner quite similar to the UK's *Operation Retail* in the *Corfu Channel* case, is difficult to reconcile with the law; though turning on the question of

---

58 See the Report of UN Special Representative of the Secretary General on the issue of Human Rights and Transnational Corporations and Other Business Enterprises, J. Ruggie, 'Protect, Respect and Remedy: A Framework for Business and Human Rights', A/HRC/8/5 (7 April 2008).
59 See, for instance, numerous provisions in the *United Nations Convention Against Corruption* (2003), 2349 UNTS 41 (entered into force 14 December 2005).
60 P. Klein, 'The Attribution of Acts to International Organizations', Crawford *et al.* (eds), op. cit., pp. 310–311.
61 *Letter dated 7 October 2001 from the Permanent Representative of the United States of America to the United Nations addressed to the President of the Security Council*, S/2001/946, 7 October 2001.

the interpretation to be given to the primary norms in question (or alternatively – as indicated – to the general rules of attribution), it is not dealt with here.[62]

Nonetheless, as a general proposition, the ICJ affirmed in the 2007 *Genocide* case, that in exercising due diligence – in that case, to prevent genocide – 'it is clear that every State may only act within the limits permitted by international law'.[63] Thus, a breach of the law cannot be justified on grounds of due diligence. This has potential application in respect of the so-called responsibility to protect insofar as it might be invoked to ground a unilateral humanitarian intervention on the basis of a due diligence failure (not that States have accepted it as allowing intervention without UN Security Council authorisation[64]). On the Court's 2007 *dictum*, such a 'justification' would fail; indeed, the 1949 *Corfu Channel* case more implicitly founds this conclusion.

18.4.2 Due diligence obligations in a theory of obligations

As a type of obligation, due diligence can be categorised in various ways. It is well known that Ago's categorisation of obligations in general led to considerable criticism and many of his proposed provisions were omitted or at best abbreviated by the ILC in its 2001 *Articles*. They were deemed, among other things, to lack clarity and more pragmatically, did not necessarily assist in determining when there was a breach of an obligation.[65] Nonetheless, to the extent they can shed light on due diligence obligations, they will be briefly considered here.

18.4.2.1 Obligations of conduct and result

It is well established today, as recently reaffirmed by the ICJ in the 2007 *Genocide*[66] and 2010 *Pulp Mills*[67] cases, that a due diligence obligation is an

---

62 The argument can be asserted on the basis of an extension to the rule in Article 51, UN Charter (see O. Corten, *Le droit de la guerre*, op. cit., p. 245 *et seq*.) or as affecting the rules on attribution (see Corten, ibid., p. 669 *et seq*.). Steven Ratner presents this US 'harbouring theory' as affecting attribution: S. Ratner, '*Jus ad bellum* and *jus in bello* after September 11', *American Journal of International Law*, 96 (2002): 908.
63 *Application of the Convention on the Prevention and Punishment of the Crime of Genocide (Bosnia and Herzegovina v. Serbia and Montenegro), Judgment, ICJ Reports 2007*, para. 430.
64 International Commission on Intervention and Sovereignty of States, *The Responsibility to Protect*, December 2001, at, for instance, para. 6.14 and para. 6.36; 2005 World Summit Outcome, A/Res/60/1, 24 October 2005, para. 139.
65 See generally P-M. Dupuy, 'Reviewing the Difficulties of Codification: On Ago's Classification of Obligations of Means and Obligations of Result in Relation to State Responsibility', *European Journal of International Law*, 10(2) (1999): 371.
66 *Application of the Convention on the Prevention and Punishment of the Crime of Genocide (Bosnia and Herzegovina v. Serbia and Montenegro), Judgment, ICJ Reports 2007*, para. 430.
67 *Case Concerning Pulp Mills on the River Uruguay (Argentina v. Uruguay), Judgment, ICJ Reports 2010*, para. 187.

obligation of conduct, rather than result; meaning that it is an obligation on States to deploy their best efforts to achieve a desired outcome (which might be to prevent a given event), even if that outcome need not be ensured. This is of course different to what was envisaged by Roberto Ago, even though his vision was premised on international law literature;[68] the distinction as now accepted by the ICJ being based instead on the domestic civil law system's understanding.

Ago's obligations of conduct (then draft Article 20) are those requiring the State actually to achieve a specific result and to do so by particular means, while his obligations of result (then draft Article 21), simply require the State to achieve a particular result by whatever means it chooses. The interesting feature of this distinction is that under his classification, obligations of conduct are far more intrusive than obligations of result, as the former 'invades the sphere of the State by requiring one or other specified component of the State machinery to adopt a particular course of conduct'.[69] The obligation of result on the other hand, is not only far more common, but also 'entirely different' as:

> international law stops short at the outer boundaries of the State machinery and . . . [being] concerned with respect for the internal freedom of the State, merely requires the State to ensure a particular situation or result and leaves it free to do so by whatever means it chooses.[70]

Thus Ago's obligations of result, of which due diligence is a type, enables the State to choose the means by which to achieve a particular outcome, thereby respecting the State's freedom to organise itself as it pleases.

While draft Articles 20 and 21 no longer appear as such in the 2001 *Articles*, the commentary to current Article 12 relative to the existence of a breach alludes to the distinction, even if the examples provided illustrate the inconsistency to which the distinction can give rise in practice.[71] Aware of the domestic civil law distinction,[72] Ago had defended his classification as necessary to appreciate rules in which the State had an opportunity to rectify an inchoate breach[73] (codified in then draft Article 21(2) – the case of complex

---

68 H. Triepel, *Völkerrecht und Landesrecht* (Leipzig: Hirschfeld, 1899), p. 299, cited by R. Ago, 'Fourth Report on State Responsibility', *ILC Yearbook*, 1977, vol. II, Part One, p. 4, para. 3, note 3.
69 R. Ago, 'Sixth Report on State Responsibility', *ILC Yearbook*, 1977, vol. II, Part One, p. 8, para. 14.
70 Ibid, p. 8, para. 15.
71 Commentary to Article 12, *Articles on State Responsibility for Internationally Wrongful Acts*, J. Crawford, *The International Law Commission's Articles on State Responsibility*, op. cit., p. 129, para. 11.
72 Ago, 'Sixth Report on State Responsibility', op. cit., p. 8, para. 12.
73 Ibid, p. 4, para. 4. For a detailed analysis, see G. Distefano, 'Fait continu, fait composé et fait complexe dans le droit de la responsabilité', *Annuaire français de droit international*, LII (2006): 1.

acts, which no longer figure in the 2001 *Articles*) as well as those rules whose breach requires exhaustion of local remedies; Ago considering, quite logically,[74] but contrary to the case law[75] and the majority of writers,[76] that exhaustion of local remedies is a rule of substance and not of procedure. But Ago's reasoning had the merit of clearly revealing that both complex acts and those requiring exhaustion of local remedies can be due diligence obligations – even if they are not exhaustive of the latter category – the *Corfu Channel* scenario being an illustration of a situation in which Albania could not 'catch up' and remedy a mere inchoate breach, nor one in which exhaustion of local remedies was required. Such a classification is, like the following one, particularly important for ascertaining the moment of the breach.

18.4.2.2 Omissions

In Ago's categorisation, not only are obligations of due diligence, obligations of result (or in the ICJ's current classification, best efforts obligations – obligations of conduct), but some of these are of a particular type: namely, obligations to prevent an event, originally dealt with in draft Article 23 and today, finding a place in Article 14(3) of the ILC's 2001 *Articles*. It can be recalled, as indicated above, that due diligence obligations can also be an obligation to deploy best efforts to achieve something positive, such as putting in place an infrastructure, for instance, an education system. Thus, due diligence obligations to prevent are merely a sub-category of best efforts obligations.[77]

As confirmed by the ICJ in the 2007 *Genocide* case, the 'violation of the obligation to prevent results from omission'.[78] In fact, whether or not they are obligations to prevent an event, due diligence obligations are always breached by omission: in Ago's understanding, either by a total failure to act when a positive action is required or, and it remains an omission, they are breached by a positive action other than the action required by the rule, as, for instance, when goods are destroyed rather than returned to the State that owns them.[79] Thus, an omission is not simply inaction.[80]

---

74 For Ago, were exhaustion of local remedies merely procedural, a state organ could remedy an internationally wrongful act, which, from the standpoint of international law is clearly not possible: 'Le délit international', op. cit., p. 517, note 1.
75 See review of decisions by J. Duggard, 'Second Report on Diplomatic Protection', A/CN.4/514 (28 February 2001), pp. 21–25, paras 44–50.
76 See, for instance, C. Economides, 'Content of the Obligation: Obligations of Means and Obligations of Result', in Crawford *et al.* (eds), *The Law of International Responsibility*, op. cit., p. 376.
77 P-M. Dupuy, 'Reviewing the Difficulties of Codification: On Ago's Classification of Obligations of Means and Obligations of Result in Relation to State Responsibility', op. cit., p. 380.
78 *Application of the Convention on the Prevention and Punishment of the Crime of Genocide (Bosnia and Herzegovina v. Serbia and Montenegro), Judgment, ICJ Reports 2007*, para. 432.
79 Ago, 'Le délit international', op. cit., p. 501.
80 Ibid.

They are to be contrasted to rules requiring an abstention and in which a State necessarily breaches the obligation by commission, such as for instance when a State drops a bomb on another State's territory when a rule requires the former not to use force. In these scenarios, due diligence is never relevant[81] and there is, moreover, a 'natural causality' between the conduct and the event giving rise to responsibility.[82] This need not be the case with an omission.

If a State drops a bomb on a hospital because it failed to take the necessary precautions, legally, this is a breach by omission (failure to take precaution and prevent damage), even though the breach was undertaken by the State organ by a positive act. Quite clearly, the acts in this scenario are directly attributable to a State organ: 'the direct and natural cause [is] in an action of the State'.[83] An illustration of this type of obligation, which remains a type of due diligence obligation, is to be found in the 2005 *Armed Activities* case, in which Uganda failed to exercise vigilance and prevent looting by its military forces as required by specific obligations of international humanitarian law.[84]

On the other hand, and slightly different, is an obligation to prevent an external event (that is, by a third State, person or natural cause); the event revealing the State's breach by its organs as defined under Articles 4–11 of the *Articles* and as discussed above. What distinguishes the obligation to prevent an event is that there is no direct causality between the State's failure to fulfil its obligation and the event giving rise to responsibility – this is the fact of a third party or catalyst. Because natural causality is absent, 'normative causality' needs to be established and this is done by comparing the actual conduct of the State with what is abstractly required by a diligent State.[85] This is far harder to do than in cases of natural causality.[86] Ago would oscillate as to whether all obligations of omission lacked natural causality – in 1939, he seemed to consider this was the case,[87] but appears to have changed his mind in his report on draft Article 23 dealing with failure to prevent an event by distinguishing situations in which no external event intervenes[88] (like the one which later arose in the *Armed Activities* case).

The significance of the category envisaged by draft Article 23 was, in Ago's view, that the breach only materialises and responsibility only arises at the moment when the external event occurs (the explosions in the *Corfu Channel*

---

81 Pisillo-Mazzeschi, op. cit., pp. 23–25.
82 Ago, 'Le délit international', op. cit., pp. 500–501.
83 R. Ago, 'Seventh Report on State Responsibility', *ILC Yearbook*, 1978, vol. I, Part One, p. 32, para 2
84 *Case Concerning Armed Activities on the Territory of the Congo (Democratic Republic of the Congo v. Uganda) Judgment, ICJ Reports 2005*, paras 245–248.
85 Ago, 'Le délit international', op. cit., p. 503; Pisillo-Mazzeschi, op. cit., p. 50.
86 Ibid.
87 Ago, 'Le délit international', ibid., pp. 447 and 500.
88 Ago, 'Seventh Report on State Responsibility', op. cit., p. 32, para. 2.

State omissions and due diligence 311

case) and there has been a lack of foresight or vigilance by the State. In other words, responsibility only arises once there is damage, in the sense of injury, and not merely when there is a lack of foresight.[89] As Ago stated:

> To our knowledge, decisions of international tribunals have never affirmed, even indirectly or incidentally, that failure to adopt measures to prevent the occurrence of a possible event sufficed in itself – i.e., without the actual occurrence of such an event – to constitute a breach of the obligation incumbent on the State.[90]

Special *Rapporteur* Crawford would criticise Ago on this point, maintaining that whether or not damage is required depends on the primary rule, citing *inter alia* a passage from the *Tehran Hostages* case in support:

> In the opinion of the Court ... the failure of the Iranian Government to take such steps was due to more than mere negligence or lack of appropriate means ... This inaction of the Iranian Government *by itself* constituted clear and serious violation of Iran's obligations ...[91]

Yet the ICJ in the 2007 *Genocide* case appears to agree with Ago insofar as damage is concerned:

> [A] State can be held responsible for breaching the obligation to prevent genocide only if genocide was actually committed. It is at the time when commission of the prohibited act ... begins that the breach of the obligation of prevention occurs. In this respect, the Court refers to a general rule of the law of State responsibility, stated by the ILC in Article 14, paragraph 3, of its Article on State Responsibility ... This obviously does not mean that the obligation to prevent genocide only comes into being when perpetration of genocide commences; that would be absurd, since the whole point of the obligation is to prevent, or attempt to prevent, the occurrence of the act. In fact, a State's obligation to prevent, and the corresponding duty to act, arise at the instant that the State learns of, or should normally have learned of, the existence of a serious risk that genocide will be committed.[92]

---

89 Ibid., p. 32, para. 3.
90 Ibid., p. 34, para. 11.
91 *United States Diplomatic and Consular Staff in Tehran, Judgment, ICJ Reports 1980*, pp. 31–32, paras 63 and 67, reproduced in J. Crawford, 'Second Report on State Responsibility', A/CN.4/498 (17 March 1998), p. 43, para. 87. Emphasis added.
92 *Application of the Convention on the Prevention and Punishment of the Crime of Genocide (Bosnia and Herzegovina v. Serbia and Montenegro), Judgment, ICJ Reports 2007*, para. 431.

It is not clear whether this is in fact a function of the primary rule in question. However, it does mean that a State can be acting not in conformity with its obligations prior to there being a breach for the purposes of responsibility, which is truly disconcerting!

Applying the above distinctions one can see that in the scenario in which a State has an obligation to prevent (by legislating) the establishment on its territory of non-State actors engaged in subversive activities, the breach is complete simply by the State tolerating those actors on its territory: this is an obligation to prevent and in Ago's terminology is an obligation of conduct (thus not covered by draft Article 23). This is different to those situations in which an external event is required for the breach to be complete; where, for instance, the State is to prevent those actors from perpetrating an attack on a third State – it is only in the event of such an attack that the due diligence obligation is breached and only if the State did not demonstrate the required diligence to prevent it.[93] It is moreover, the time of the event that constitutes the moment at which the breach is realised.[94] In short, when Albania was found responsible for knowingly allowing its territory to be used in a manner contrary to the rights of other States, this breach only occurred when the explosions actually took place – and not before; not even from the moment when it had knowledge but did not warn of the mines.

Yet perhaps the most overlooked aspect of due diligence as it arose in the *Corfu Channel* case is the question of when that particular breach came to an end.

18.5 By way of conclusion: Albania's continuing breach and contribution to injury

The second part of the *Corfu Channel* case relates to the UK's *Operation Retail* to demine Albanian waters ostensibly for the purposes of both abating a danger to navigation and preserving evidence of Albania's responsibility. For the Court, it was a prohibited intervention:

> The Court can only regard the alleged right of intervention as the manifestation of a policy of force, such as has, in the past, given rise to most serious abuses and such as cannot, whatever be the present defects in international organization, find a place in international law. Intervention is perhaps still less admissible in the particular form it would take here; for, from the nature of things, it would be reserved for the most powerful States, and might easily lead to perverting the administration of international justice itself.[95]

---

93 Ago, 'Seventh Report on State Responsibility', op. cit., pp. 35–36, para. 15.
94 As noted, now embodied in Article 14(3) *Articles*.
95 *Corfu Channel case, Judgment of April 9th, 1949: ICJ Reports 1949*, p. 35.

This is a particularly strong ICJ condemnation of self-help outside the Charter framework and indirectly of the natural law doctrine, prevalent in nineteenth-century writings and in the practice of stronger States, of the so-called fundamental right of self-preservation. Nonetheless, the Court would go on to say:

> Between independent States, respect for territorial sovereignty is an essential foundation of international relations. The Court recognizes that the Albanian Government's complete failure to carry out its duties after the explosions, and the dilatory nature of its diplomatic notes, are extenuating circumstances for the action of the United Kingdom Government.[96]

The argument made by some authors is that this passage is an acknowledgment that the UK was acting in a state of necessity and that this 'extenuated' the UK's responsibility.[97] This is hard to sustain for several reasons. First, the Court's judgment is a particularly strong condemnation of unilateral self-help and it is difficult to reconcile the strength of the Court's position with an implied acknowledgement that nonetheless state of necessity – precisely, as pleaded by Albania, a unilateral act of self-help which has in power political terms served the strongest against the weakest – was to be conceded and upheld. Second, the conditions for a state of necessity by the United Kingdom were not present, notably the presence of a grave and imminent peril threatening an essential UK interest and in respect of which the UK had but a sole means at its disposal to avert the danger.

Third, and most importantly, in referring to an 'extenuating circumstance' for the UK, the Court was in fact taking into account Albania's behaviour rather than that of the UK; namely, Albania's 'complete failure to carry out its duties after the explosions, and the dilatory nature of its diplomatic notes'. Albania had indeed refused to give its consent to the Central Mine Clearance Board for the sweeping of its waters. Having the means at its disposal to remove any remaining mines (even if it could not do this itself), Albania's due diligence breach appears to have been of a continuing character, although there was not direct scope for the ICJ to state as much given the manner in which the *compromis* was framed. Moreover, Albania's failure to exercise due diligence to prevent injury after the explosions was arguably a wilful or negligent

---

96 Ibid.
97 Tentatively, J. Combacau and S. Sur, *Droit international public*, 8th edn (Paris: Montchrestien, 2008), pp. 544–555; and assertively: T. Christakis, 'Les "circonstances excluant l'illicéité": une illusion optique?', in N. Angelet, O. Corten, E. David and P. Klein (eds), *Droit du pouvoir, pouvoir du droit. Mélanges offerts à Jean Salmon* (Bruxelles: Bruylant, 2007), pp. 264–265, note 114; T. Christakis, ' "Nécessité n'a pas de loi"? La nécessité en droit international', in T. Christakis and K. Bannelier (eds), *La nécessité en droit international. Société française pour le droit international colloque de Grenoble* (Paris: Pedone, 2007), p. 60. On necessity generally, see S. Heathcote, 'State of Necessity and International Law', thesis no. 772, University of Geneva, 2005.

omission and as such a contribution to injury, otherwise known as contributory fault.[98] Formerly provided for in draft Article 42(2) – that is, part of the general provision on reparation – on the proposition of Special *Rapporteur* James Crawford,[99] it was expanded into a separate article, today, Article 39 of the 2001 *Articles*. Article 39 reads: 'In the determination of reparation, account shall be taken of the contribution to the injury by wilful or negligent action or omission of the injured State or any person or entity in relation to whom reparation is sought.'

Article 39 is based on equitable considerations and in Special *Rapporteur* Crawford's view is separate to concurrent causes, the wrongful State's behaviour (here the UK's) remaining the efficient cause of the injury.[100] This reading of the *Corfu Channel* case, though overlooked, is consistent with the general tenor of the Court's judgment, something which the state of necessity argument certainly is not. Moreover, it shows that in more than one respect, both the first and second parts of the *Corfu Channel* decision are intrinsically linked and indeed, constitute a whole.

---

98 J. Crawford, 'Third Report on State Responsibility', A/CN.4/507 (15 March 2000), p. 17, para. 33.
99 Ibid, p.11, para. 19.
100 Ibid, p. 17, para. 33, footnote 67. The *Special Rapporteur*'s more detailed consideration of contribution to injury is found in 'Third Report on State Responsibility, Addendum', A/CN.4/507/Add.1 (15 June 2000), pp. 52–54, paras 216–221.

19 The limits of complicity as a ground for responsibility

Lessons learned from the *Corfu Channel* case

Olivier Corten and Pierre Klein

19.1 Introduction

The *Corfu Channel* case is sometimes referred to as the first precedent in which the International Court of Justice established the existence in general international law of a principle of due diligence.[1] This aspect of the judgment is discussed in another chapter of this book.[2] On the other hand, reference is not usually made to the *Corfu Channel* case in relation to the notion of 'complicity', in spite of the numerous allusions that were made to it in the course of the proceedings.[3] While complicity has since been retained – albeit under a different name, that of 'aid or assistance' (Article 16)[4] – by the International Law Commission in its Articles on the Responsibility of States for internationally wrongful acts, as one of the situations in which a State may incur responsibility 'in connection with the act of another State', the Commentary

---

1 See e.g. J. Combacau and S. Sur, *Droit international public*, 8th edn (Paris: Montchrestien, 2008), p. 430 and J. Salmon (ed.), *Dictionnaire de droit international public* (Brussels: Bruylant, AUF, 2001), under 'obligation de prévention', p. 768.
2 See Sarah Heathcote's contribution in this volume (Chapter 18).
3 In a book exclusively dedicated to the case, Il Yung Chung deals with the issue of complicity in a single page (*Legal Problems Involved in the Corfu Channel Incident* (Paris: Droz, Minard, 1959), p. 105).
4 According to this Article ('Aid or assistance in the commission of an internationally wrongful act'),

> A State which aids or assists another State in the commission of an internationally wrongful act by the latter is internationally responsible for doing so if: (*a*) that State does so with knowledge of the circumstances of the internationally wrongful act; and (*b*) the act would be internationally wrongful if committed by that State.

It is by reference to this provision that the notion of complicity will be defined in the framework of the present study; see e.g. Salmon (ed.), *Dictionnaire de droit international public*, op. cit., p. 218.

to this provision makes no mention of the Court's 1949 judgment,[5] nor do authors who have addressed the notion of complicity.[6]

This is all the more surprising as complicity is a notion closely related to the *Corfu Channel* case. It hardly needs to be recalled that Albania was not held responsible by the Court for having itself laid the mines that damaged the two British ships, HMS *Saumarez* and HMS *Volage*, causing a significant number of casualties. It is rather for conduct adopted in connection with the laying of mines – the failure to notify their presence to other States – that the Defendant State ultimately incurred responsibility in that case.[7] As the mines could have only been laid by another State – a fact undisputed by the parties, and admitted by the Court – it would clearly have been arguable that Albania was engaged in complicity in the sense that it had helped or assisted the State which had committed the principal wrongful act.[8] And, as shall be seen, the United Kingdom indeed built a significant part of its legal argumentation before the Court on the notion of complicity.

Against this background the question arises as to why the Court did not base its reasoning on the notion of complicity. It will be argued in the following pages that the reason lies in the fact that the notion of complicity raises so many difficulties that it generally appears preferable to resort to the concept of due diligence. The latter is more manageable and leads, to a large extent, to similar results. This argument is based not only on the analysis of the *Corfu Channel* case (see Section 19.2), but also on the Court's more recent case-law, and in particular on the 2007 Judgment in the *Application of the Convention on the Prevention and Punishment of the Crime of Genocide* case, where a problem similar to that encountered by the Court in 1949 led to a solution akin to that upheld at that time (see Section 19.3). More fundamentally, the very usefulness of the notion of complicity may be called into question, considering the existence of the concept of due diligence which appears more manageable both in terms of procedure and of the criteria that have to be met to engage the responsibility of a State on that basis (see Section 19.4).

---

5 ILC, *Report on the Work of its fifty-third session (23 April–1 June and 2 July–10 August 2001)*, GA Official Records, 56th session, Suppl. No.10 (1/56/10), pp. 65–67.
6 J. Quigley, 'Complicity in International Law: A New Direction in the Law of State Responsibility', *BYBIL*, 57 (1986): 77–131; B. Graefrath, 'Complicity in the Law of International Responsibility', *RBDI*, 29 (1996): 370–380.
7 *ICJ Reports 1949*, pp. 17–23; see also dissenting opinion of Judge Winiarski, ibid., pp. 52–56; Dissenting Opinion of Judge Krylov, ibid., pp. 71–72.
8 The notion of complicity is associated with an obligation of vigilance by Judge Alvarez; individual opinion, *ICJ Reports 1949*, pp. 44–45.

19.2 The difficulties raised by the notion of complicity in the *Corfu Channel* case and the ensuing preference given to due diligence

Generally speaking, the parties' written and oral pleadings in the *Corfu Channel* case show that the notion of complicity held a privileged – and perhaps even a central – position in the legal argumentation presented to the Court – at least as far as the first question put to the Court in the Special Agreement was concerned.[9] As noted above, complicity is, in marked contrast, completely set aside in the Court's judgment and is hardly mentioned in individual or dissenting opinions.[10] It is our hypothesis that this could be the result of a deliberate choice by the judges. The appropriateness of such a reading of the Court's reasoning will now be assessed by showing how the relative importance given to the notion of complicity evolved in the course of the proceedings.[11]

In its Application, the United Kingdom claimed that

> the Albanian Government either caused to be laid, or had knowledge of the laying of, mines in its territorial waters in the Strait of Corfu without notifying the existence of these mines as required by Articles 3 and 4 of Hague Convention No. VIII of 1907, by the general principles of international law and by the ordinary dictates of humanity.[12]

The applicant State further argued that '[i]t is certain that no minefield could have been laid in the Channel within a few hundred yards of the Albanian batteries without the connivance or at least the knowledge of the Albanian authorities'.[13] In its Memorial, the United Kingdom reiterates the three distinct legal foundations of its claim: Albania 'either caused to be laid, connived at [*sic*] or had knowledge of the laying of mines in certain areas of its territorial waters in the Strait of Corfu'.[14] 'Complicity' – the term is used on several occasions[15] – therefore appears to constitute a legal basis of the British claim, occupying an intermediary position between a 'strong' hypothesis – Albania being the State that laid the mines itself – and a 'weak' hypothesis – the mere knowledge

---

9 See Written and Oral Proceedings. Online. Available at: http://www.icj-cij.org/docket/index.php?p1=3&p2=3&code=cc&case=1&k=cd&lang=en (accessed 8 October 2010).
10 See Individual Opinion of Judge Alvarez, *ICJ Reports 1949*, pp. 44–45; Dissenting Opinion of Judge Badawi Pasha, pp. 61–64; Dissenting Opinion of Judge Ečer, pp. 116–117.
11 For discussions within the Security Council, see Chung, *Legal Problems Involved in the Corfu Channel Incident*, op. cit., pp. 17 *et seq*.
12 *ICJ Reports 1949*, vol. I, p. 9.
13 Note to the Albanian Government, 9 December 1946, at para. 18, annexed to the application.
14 Memorial of the UK, 30 September 1947, p. 21.
15 Ibid., pp. 41, 42, 48.

of the facts by Albanian authorities, without it being possible to establish any form of complicity. The distinction between complicity and the two other legal foundations of the claim is, however, far from always being clear, as the following quote from the British Memorial reveals:

> The responsibility of Albania rests, firstly, upon a direct complicity in the existence of the minefield which is created by her knowledge of it, *whether or not she laid it or connived in its actual laying*. Secondly, it rests upon a failure – which was, in the submission of the Government of the United Kingdom, a wilful failure – to discharge an imperative international duty to notify the existence of this dangerous minefield.[16]

On the other hand, at the end of the written phase of the proceedings, it became obvious that the hypothesis according to which Albania had itself laid the mines had lost all credibility. Considering the very limited material means that this State had at its disposal in the aftermath of World War II (in particular as far as its navy was concerned), it quickly became apparent that Albania could not technically have laid the mines itself. This explains why another State was then suspected of having laid the mines in the Corfu Channel in October 1946. The following excerpt from the British Reply aptly reflects this change of view:

> The Government of the United Kingdom takes note of the Albanian Government's formal statement that it did not lay the minefield and was not in a position to do so. It observes the statement in paragraph 8 of the Counter-Memorial (bottom of p. 35) that Albania possesses no navy, and that on the whole Albanian littoral the Albanian authorities only disposed of a few launches and motor boats. In the light of these statements, the Government of the United Kingdom calls upon the Albanian Government to disclose the circumstances in which two Yugoslav war vessels, *Meljt* and *Meljine*, carrying contact mines of the German Y type, sailed southwards from the port of Sibenik on or about 18th October, 1946 and proceeded to the Corfu Channel. The Government of the United Kingdom will allege, and will seek leave to call evidence to show, that the said vessels, *Meljt* and *Meljine* with the knowledge and connivance of the Albanian Government, laid mines in the Corfu Channel just before 22nd October, 1946.[17]

Complicity thus becomes a central tenet of the British argument, in which Yugoslavia emerges as the State that laid the mines, with Albania 'conniving' in this act. In their oral pleadings, counsel for the United Kingdom empha-

---

16 Ibid., pp. 48, para. 94. Emphasis added.
17 Reply of the United Kingdom, 30 July 1948, pp. 257–258.

sised the close ties between the two States to substantiate their claim,[18] while carefully asserting that their case in this Court is against Albania and not against Yugoslavia'.[19] The British line of argumentation may therefore be depicted in the following terms: two Yugoslav ships, the *Meljt* and the *Meljine*, sailed from the Yugoslav port of Sibenik carrying German mines. These two ships subsequently laid the mines in the Corfu Channel, at the Albanian authorities' request. This argument mainly rests on the testimony of a former Yugoslav officer, Commandant Kovacic, who had supposedly seen the two ships sailing from Sibenik carrying mines and learned from a source that he did not wish to disclose that mines had indeed been laid in the Channel shortly before the British ships entered the area. A significant part of the oral proceedings was indeed devoted to the examination and cross-examination of that witness, whose testimony was considered crucial by the Applicant State.[20] At that stage of the proceedings, while no more attempts are clearly made at arguing that Albania itself laid the mines, the arguments based on complicity and on mere knowledge respectively do not appear to be clearly distinguished by counsel for the United Kingdom.[21] Indeed, in their argument Albania's knowledge of the presence of mines in the Channel is inferred from the ties between the Albanian and Yugoslav governments.[22] According to the United Kingdom, it was not necessary to establish that Albanian authorities actually saw the Yugoslav ships lay mines in the Channel; such evidence would indeed have been particularly difficult to produce in the circumstances. Inasmuch as the decision to lay mines had been taken at a governmental level, knowledge could be said to exist even before the mines were actually laid.[23] In that context, complicity is not understood as requiring any intentional element. All that matters is the existence of a common undertaking by Yugoslavia and Albania, which caused damage to the United Kingdom. The purpose of this joint undertaking and the joint perpetrators' intentions are not seen as constitutive elements of the wrongful act.[24] To that extent, responsibility for acts of complicity could be established objectively, as in the case of responsibility based on a failure to exercise due diligence. Ultimately, points 2 and 3 of the final oral conclusions presented on behalf of the United Kingdom envisaged two (alternative) grounds for establishing Albania's responsibility:

(2) That the aforesaid minefield was laid between 15th May, 1946, and 22nd October, 1946, by or with the connivance or knowledge of the Albanian Government.

---

18 Statement by Sir Hartley Shawcross, 9 November 1948, CR 1949/1, pp. 239–240, 262.
19 Statement by Sir Hartley Shawcross, 9 November 1948, CR 1949/1, p. 240.
20 25–27 November 1948, pp. 521–679.
21 See Reply by Sir Frank Soskice, 17 December 1948, p. 470; see also p. 479.
22 See Dissenting Opinion of Judge Badawi Pasha, *ICJ Reports 1949*, pp. 61–64.
23 See British Reply, 17 December 1948, pp. 499, 510, 537.
24 Ibid., p. 539.

(3) That (alternatively to (2)) the Albanian Government knew that the said minefield was lying in a part of its territorial waters.[25]

Complicity therefore constitutes one of the main legal foundations of the United Kingdom's line of argumentation, even though the term itself is not used (but rather those of 'connivance or knowledge'). But mere knowledge is nevertheless argued as an alternative ground for establishing responsibility. The Applicant State therefore takes care not to base its claim solely on the notion of complicity. On the one hand, and even though it had seemed to do so in the course of the proceedings, it does not give up the argument according to which Albania had laid the mines itself (as the expression 'by the Albanian Government' shows). On the other hand, the United Kingdom relies on another autonomous ground of responsibility – mere knowledge – the establishment of which would not depend on demonstrating complicity or 'connivance' between Albania and Yugoslavia. While it emerges as the central component of the British scenario, complicity thus appears to constitute too uncertain a ground of responsibility to be relied on exclusively.

A close examination of the arguments put forward by Albania confirms the risks inherent in invoking complicity. From the outset, the Defendant State had endeavoured to show – not without success, as shown above – that it could not possibly have laid the mines itself.[26] The next step of the argument consisted in refuting the complicity theory, which had become central to the United Kingdom's line of argumentation. At that stage, Albania pointed out two issues that appeared particularly problematic in the context of the proceedings before the Court. First, in terms of procedure, the Defendant State formally asked the United Kingdom why it had not presented a claim directly against Yugoslavia since that State had allegedly laid the mines in the Corfu Channel.[27] It is true that Yugoslavia had not accepted the Court's compulsory jurisdiction, but neither had Albania. Thus nothing would have prevented the United Kingdom from attempting to settle its dispute with Yugoslavia, following the same *modus operandi* it had used with Albania. Be that as it may, the net result was Yugoslavia's absence from the proceedings. In spite of this, Yugoslavia extended active cooperation as far as fact-finding was concerned. The Yugoslav Government produced several documents in an attempt to challenge former Commandant Kovacic's testimony – or that of other witnesses; a representative from the Yugoslav Government attended the hearings; the Court sent a team of experts not only to Albania, but also to Yugoslavia. However, the effects of such cooperation proved to be limited since Yugoslavia had made the choice not to intervene in the proceedings

---

25 Ibid., p. 540.
26 Albania's Counter-Memorial, 15 June 1948, p. 36.
27 Albania's Reply, 20 September 1948, p. 352; see also Pierre Cot, 16 November 1948, p. 344.

under Article 62 of the Court's Statute and was not therefore a party to the proceedings. It could therefore not be judged, directly or indirectly.[28] This was all the more problematic as in order to establish complicity, the probative force of the evidence presented by Yugoslavia necessarily had to be assessed. This line of reasoning, which emerges in Albania's reply,[29] gained its full strength during the oral proceedings, as the British line of argument evolved. It is readily apparent from the following excerpt from Professor Pierre Cot's oral pleadings on behalf of Albania:

> Le Gouvernement britannique ne met pas en cause le Gouvernement yougoslave dans la procédure; c'est un fait, mais il l'a mis en cause – et avec quelle vigueur – dans les débats oraux ... Le plus fort de l'argumentation présentée par sir Hartley est une attaque contre le Gouvernement yougoslave. La thèse du Gouvernement britannique, d'après ses avocats eux-mêmes et d'après la logique, suppose donc que le Gouvernement yougoslave aurait adressé à la Cour un communiqué mensonger et une déclaration inexacte. La Cour ne peut pas éviter de se prononcer sur ce point ... On ne peut pas éviter la rigueur de ce raisonnement. Le Gouvernement albanais, vous le savez, ne possède ni mines ni mouilleurs de mines. Le Gouvernement britannique l'a reconnu, et il déclare que la seule puissance qui a pu agir pour le compte de l'Albanie est la Yougoslavie. Mais admettre que l'Albanie soit responsable, c'est au moins admettre que les mines ont été posées sur son ordre ou avec sa complicité ... Par conséquent, le Gouvernement britannique a mis la Cour dans la position suivante: la Cour ne peut pas condamner l'Albanie sans proclamer du même coup, peut-être pas nécessairement dans son arrêt, mais par le rapprochement de son arrêt et des déclarations de sir Hartley, que le communiqué yougoslave n'est qu'un tissu de mensonges. Excusez-moi, Messieurs, de parler franchement, mais vous ne pouvez pas faire cela.[30]

---

28 See Pierre Cot, 16 November 1948, p. 371.
29 Albania's Reply, 20 September 1948, p. 375.
30 Pierre Cot, 16 November 1948, pp. 373–374.

> The British Government does not implicate the Yugoslav Governement in the proceedings; this is a fact, but it implicated it – and vigorously so – in the oral proceedings ... The core of Sir Hartley's argumentation is an attack against the Yugoslav Government. The British Government's thesis, according to its counsel and according to logic, thus supposes that the Yugoslav Government has presented the Court with a misleading communiqué and an inaccurate statement. The Court cannot but pronounce on this issue ... One cannot avoid the harshness of this reasoning. The Albanian Government, as you know, does not possess mines nor minelayers. The British Government has acknowledged that, and claims that the sole power that could have acted on Albania's behalf is Yugoslavia. But accepting that Albania is responsible is at least accepting that the mines have been laid on its orders or with its complicity ... As a consequence, the

Thus, the first difficulty raised by the notion of complicity is of a procedural nature: it touches upon the issue of third States, and this would give rise to further developments in the Court's subsequent case-law. The establishment of complicity by a court does indeed necessarily presuppose a judgment on the responsibility of the principal author of the internationally wrongful act at stake, which is highly problematic when the latter does not take part in the proceedings.

While to a certain extent related to that procedural difficulty, a second difficulty raised by the notion of complicity has more to do with the merits of the dispute, and more specifically with the issue of evidence. Establishing complicity indeed amounts to establishing two unlawful acts: the 'principal' wrongful act, on the one hand and the 'incidental' wrongful act on the other. To make out the complicity argument in the case at hand, it was necessary to demonstrate not only that Albania was, in one way or another, involved in the laying of the mines, but also that the mines had been laid by Yugoslavia. The latter aspect of the dispute proved to be particularly delicate, as noted above in reference to the – highly controversial – testimony of a former officer of the Yugoslav navy. Albania did not fail to put forward other explanations for the presence of mines in the Strait, which excluded any form of Yugoslav involvement. Counsel for Albania thus successively argued that old German mines could have remained in the Corfu Channel despite minesweeping operations,[31] or that the mines could – at least potentially – have been laid by another State, such as Greece.[32] No evidence was produced to substantiate these claims, but the Defendant State was thereby nevertheless showing the extent to which the invocation of complicity amounted to opening a Pandora's box. It is, as a result, easy to understand why the United Kingdom wisely chose to rely on a much simpler ground of responsibility – mere knowledge of the laying of the mines – as an alternative argument to that based on complicity. And it is equally easy to understand why, in such a context, the Court opted for this alternative argument, even though it had not been put forward with as much emphasis as complicity – far from it – in the written and oral pleadings.

After reviewing the three legal foundations upon which the United Kingdom based its claim – Albania having laid the mines, Albania being an

---

> British Government has put the Court in the following position: the Court cannot hold Albania responsible without proclaiming by the same token – maybe not necessarily in its judgment, but by putting together its judgment and Sir Hartley's statement – that the Yugoslav communiqué is nothing but a tissue of lies. Excuse me, Gentlemen, for being blunt, but you cannot do that.
>
> (Authors' translation)

31 Albania's Counter-Memorial, 15 June 1948, pp. 37–38.
32 Albania's Counter-Memorial, 15 June 1948, pp. 76–77, 89; Albania's Reply, 20 September 1948, p. 346.

accomplice to the laying of mines, and Albania being aware of the laying of mines – the Court quickly set aside the first two. It first observed that

> In fact, although the United Kingdom Government never abandoned its contention that Albania herself laid the mines, very little attempt was made by the Government to demonstrate this point ... In these circumstances, the Court need pay no further attention to this matter.[33]

The Court then turned to the 'connivance' or 'collusion' argument:

> Without deciding as to the personal sincerity of the witness Kovacic, or the truth of what he said, the Court finds that the facts stated by the witness from his personal knowledge are not sufficient to prove what the United Kingdom Government considered them to prove ...
>
> Apart from Kovacic's evidence, the United Kingdom Government endeavoured to prove collusion between Albania and Yugoslavia by certain presumptions of fact, or circumstantial evidence, such as the possession, at that time, by Yugoslavia, and by no other neighbouring State, of GY mines, and by the bond of close political and military alliance between Albania and Yugoslavia, resulting from the Treaty of friendship and mutual assistance signed by those two States on July 9th, 1946.
>
> The Court considers that, even in so far as these facts are established, they lead to no firm conclusion. It has not been legally established that Yugoslavia possessed any GY mines, and the origin of the mines laid in Albanian territorial waters remains a matter for conjecture. It is clear that the existence of a treaty, such as that of July 9th, 1946, however close may be the bonds uniting its signatories, in no way leads to the conclusion that they participated in a criminal act.
>
> On its side, the Yugoslav Government, although not a party to the proceedings, authorized the Albanian Government to produce certain Yugoslav documents, for the purpose of refuting the United Kingdom contention that the mines had been laid by two ships of the Yugoslav Navy. As the Court was anxious for full light to be thrown on the facts alleged, it did not refuse to receive these documents. But Yugoslavia's absence from the proceedings meant that these documents could only be admitted as evidence subject to reserves, and the Court finds it unnecessary to express an opinion upon their probative value ...
>
> In the light of the information now available to the Court, the authors of the minelaying remain unknown. In any case, the task of the Court, as defined by the Special Agreement, is to decide whether Albania is responsible, under international law, for the explosions which occurred on

---

33 *ICJ Reports 1949*, pp. 15–16.

October 22nd, 1946, and to give judgment as to the compensation, if any.[34]

This part of the judgment reveals a certain uneasiness by the Court. On the one hand, it held that the complicity thesis had to be set aside for lack of evidence – which seems to imply *a contrario* that such evidence could have been produced, in spite of Yugoslavia's absence from the proceedings.[35] On the other hand, the Court refused to assess the probative value of the Yugoslav documents which it had nevertheless accepted to add to the file, and emphasised that according to the first question put to it in the Special Agreement it may only pronounce on the responsibility of Albania, which seems to exclude pronouncing on the responsibility of any other State.[36] The difficulties raised by the complicity argument are therefore quite obvious. It is easy to understand why, under such circumstances, the Court devoted much more attention to the 'mere knowledge' argument and concluded on that basis that Albania could be held responsible for a breach of the general obligation of due diligence.[37] Thus, since it was judicially established – mainly on the basis of the report submitted by the team of experts appointed by the Court – that Albania had had knowledge of the laying of mines, that State had breached its duty to notify those mines' presence to ships sailing through the Strait. The existence and breach of this obligation could be established independently of the answer to the question of who had laid the mines, and under what circumstances. The difficulties raised by the notion of complicity (such as the absence of a third State from the proceedings, and the difficulties in proving its involvement) can clearly be avoided by the use of the more traditional concept of due diligence.

All in all, the main teachings of the *Corfu Channel* case regarding the notion of complicity are twofold: this argument raises serious practical difficulties, and these can easily be overcome by resorting to another – well-established – concept, that of due diligence. This is confirmed by the Court's subsequent case-law.

---

34 Ibid., pp. 16–17.
35 Compare the Dissenting Opinion of Judge Ečer, *ICJ Reports 1949*, pp. 116–117; *East Timor (Portugal v. Australia)*, *ICJ Reports 1995*, Separate Opinion of Judge Shahabuddeen, pp. 121–122; Dissenting Opinion of Judge Weeramantry, pp. 164–167. See Barbara Delcourt, 'Un seul Etat vous manque ... (L'application de la jurisprudence de l'*Or monétaire* à l'affaire du *Timor oriental*)', *RBDI*, XXIX (1996): 208–209.
36 See Dissenting Opinion of Judge Azevedo, p. 90.
37 See Chung, *Legal Problems Involved in the Corfu Channel Incident*, op. cit., pp. 169–172; E. Jimenez de Arechaga, 'International Responsibility', in M. Sorensen (ed.), *Manual of Public International Law* (London: Macmillan, 1968), p. 537; E. Jimenez de Arechaga and A. Tanzi, 'International State Responsibility', in M. Bedjaoui (ed.), *International Law: Achievements and Prospects* (Dordrecht/Paris: Martinus Nijhoff/UNESCO, 1991), pp. 350–351.

19.3 Confirmation of the Court's approach in its subsequent case-law: the *Application of the Convention on the Prevention and Punishment of the Crime of Genocide* case

Several rulings of the International Court of Justice can be interpreted as confirming the preference given to the concept of due diligence over the notion of complicity, as a consequence of the difficulties raised by the latter. In the *Military and Paramilitary Activities in and against Nicaragua* case, the Court thus referred to Nicaragua's main line of argumentation according to which acts of the *contras* should be attributed to the United States and pointed out that '[i]f such a finding of the imputability of the acts of the *contras* to the United States were to be made, no question would arise of mere complicity in those acts, or of incitement of the *contras* to commit them.'[38] It appears from the judgment taken as a whole that the 'complicity' referred to here actually has more to do with the notion of due diligence – and this may find confirmation in the fact that the term 'complicity' is not used by the Court thereafter. The acts of the *contras* not being attributable to the United States, what is upheld against that State is not strictly speaking complicity, nor aid or assistance in the commission of an internationally wrongful act; but rather the State's own internationally wrongful act: the failure to prevent and punish violations of international humanitarian law committed by individuals upon which that State was in a position to exert its influence.[39]

As far as the Court's advisory jurisdiction is concerned, reference can be made to the opinions on the *Legal Consequences for States of the Continued Presence of South Africa in Namibia (South West Africa) notwithstanding Security Council Resolution 276* and on the *Legal Consequences of the Construction of a Wall in the Occupied Palestinian Territory*. In both opinions, the Court sets out the obligation not to aid or assist in the commission of internationally wrongful acts, which may be taken as an application of the notion of complicity – more specifically inasmuch as it entails a general duty not to recognise the effects of a wrongful act.[40] It should, however, be observed that the Court does not ground this duty on Article 16 of the ILC's Articles on State responsibility, but rather on the obligation to comply with resolutions of the Security Council in the first case[41] and on the obligation to respect and ensure respect of international humanitarian law in the second case.[42] Be that as it may, to the extent that they deserve to be mentioned, these precedents have not given rise to developments that shed much light on the relations between the notion of complicity and that of due diligence. This is not the case, however, of the Court's 2007 decision in the

---

38 *ICJ Reports 1986*, p. 64, para.114.
39 Ibid., pp. 114–115, para. 221, pp. 129–130, paras 255–256.
40 See Article 41(2) of the ILC Articles on State Responsibility.
41 *ICJ Reports 1971*, paras 117 *et seq.*
42 *ICJ Reports 2004*, paras 158–159.

Application of the Convention on the Prevention and Punishment of the Crime of Genocide case which is of the greatest interest in this regard.

In contrast to the *Corfu Channel* case, which was essentially grounded in general international law, the *Genocide Convention* case is centred on the interpretation of a specific treaty. Yet as will be seen, this did not prevent the parties from drawing numerous analogies between the Convention as a *lex specialis* and customary international law as a *lex generalis*. An analysis of the arguments put forward by the parties in this latter case – and the way these arguments were handled by the Court – reveal that they followed a logic similar to that followed by the judges almost 60 years earlier: complicity being more difficult to establish in legal terms, preference was given to the notion of due diligence – as it translates here in the obligation to prevent genocide.

From the outset, Bosnia and Herzegovina based its claim on three different legal grounds: first, Yugoslavia being responsible for the crime of genocide; second, Yugoslavia being responsible for complicity in the crime of genocide; third, Yugoslavia being responsible for failing to prevent and punish the crime of genocide. The similarities between this line of argumentation and that put forward by the United Kingdom in the *Corfu Channel* case are obvious; they should not, however, be over-emphasised, in the sense that complicity is explicitly relied on as a subsidiary basis of responsibility in the *Genocide Convention* case only. Indeed, Bosnia and Herzegovina firmly maintained its principal thesis up to the conclusion of the proceedings: the acts of General Mladic were directly attributable to Yugoslavia – an argument that logically deprived the notion of complicity of any practical effect. Complicity was nevertheless relied on by the Applicant State as a possible basis for responsibility, both – and this deserves to be emphasised – in the specific meaning given to that notion in the 1948 Convention and under customary international law, as the following excerpt from Bosnia's Memorial clearly shows:

> The 1978 Report of the International Law Commission, commenting on its work on State responsibility, has noted that, in its own draft of Article 27, 'complicity' may take the form of 'assistance' such as the 'provision of weapons or other supplies to assist another State to commit genocide' . . . Where a government has a legal duty to protect persons against violation of their rights under international law by other persons within that government's jurisdiction, this Court has clearly established that 'inaction' by the Government itself constitutes a serious violation of that State's legal obligation, whether or not the persons acting unlawfully were doing so in explicit complicity or as agents of the Government.
> [*U. S. Diplomatic and Consular Staff in Teheran, Judgment, ICJ Reports 1980*, p. 3, at 32–33, paras 66–68][43]

---

43 Memorial of the Government of Bosnia and Herzegovina, 15 April 1994, p. 234.

Bosnia and Herzegovina also referred later on to the general and customary notion of complicity as it had been retained in the ILC's Articles by stating that

> in the *Nicaragua* case, this Court has clearly recognised that a State entails its responsibility by 'training, arming, equipping, financing and supplying' paramilitary forces 'or otherwise encouraging, supporting and aiding . . . paramilitary activities in and against' a foreign State.
>
> *[ICJ Reports 1986*, p. 146][44]

While reference is undeniably made to complicity in the Applicant State's written pleadings, the distinction between this notion and that of due diligence is not readily apparent, and the fragments quoted above tend to show that reference seems actually to be made to the latter concept rather than to the former.[45] This apparent confusion probably finds an explanation in considerations of judicial strategy, complicity being particularly difficult to establish in the specific context of the Genocide Convention. Indeed, according to Article III(e) of the Convention, the establishment of complicity in genocide 'requires the demonstration of the accomplice's specific intention to destroy the targeted group as such'.[46] In other words, the main perpetrator's intention must be shared by the accomplice. Bosnia and Herzegovina, however, contended that even if the Yugoslav State's intention as an accomplice 'in genocide' in the meaning of Article III(e) could not be established, it was possible to do so as far as complicity 'for genocide',[47] in the sense of general international law is concerned, namely, devoid of any intentional element.[48] Relying on complicity under general international law would therefore allow for a lowering of the evidentiary requirements, should the notion be interpreted in such a way that it would not require any element of intention.[49]

As one might have expected, Yugoslavia followed quite a different line of argumentation and from the outset put the emphasis on the specificities of the Convention on Prevention and Punishment of the Crime of Genocide. According to the Defendant State, it was only on the basis of this instrument

---

44 Reply of the Government of Bosnia and Herzegovina, 23 April 1998, p. 829, at paras 183–184.
45 The *Corfu Channel case* is mentioned in the section of the written pleadings dedicated to the failure to prevent genocide (ibid., pp. 838–839); the *Nicaragua* and *Hostages* cases, on the other hand, are not, and it is difficult to ascertain why.
46 The two parties agreed on this specific point; for Bosnia-Herzegovina, see Pellet, 3 March 2006, CR 2006/8, p. 27; for FRY, see de Roux, RFY, 15 March 2006, CR 2006/19, pp. 29–31; Fauveau-Ivanovic, 4 May 2006, CR 2006/42, p. 38.
47 The French original reads: 'complicité de génocide'.
48 Pellet, 3 March 2006, CR 2006/8, pp. 27–28; Pellet, 6 March 2006, 2006/10, pp. 58–62; Pellet, 18 April 2006, CR 2006/31, pp. 39–43.
49 See also Condorelli, 21 April 2006, CR 2006/35, p. 45.

that the Court could entertain Bosnia's claim on the Merits, Article IX of the Convention providing the only basis of jurisdiction. As far as the notion of complicity was concerned, it would have been abusive to circumvent the requirement of intention set out in Article III(e) by resorting to complicity under general international law – a notion that was deemed inapplicable in the context of the proceedings before the Court.[50] Yugoslavia called into question the customary character of Article 16 of the ILC's Articles on State Responsibility,[51] and argued that it was in any event inapplicable whenever a relevant primary rule governed the issue of complicity as a *lex specialis*.[52] In any event, Yugoslavia argued that aid or assistance within the meaning of the ILC's Articles could not be envisaged if the intention of the accomplice was not established.[53] Whether complicity 'in' or 'for genocide' was at stake, the Yugoslav State's genocidal intention had to be established – but such intention had never existed and could therefore not possibly be established.

The Court's judgment of 26 February 2007 can be read as confirming the fact that the use of the notion of complicity raises far more difficulties than that of due diligence. One can note first, that the Court expressly drew a parallel between complicity in the context of the Genocide Convention and the notion of aid and assistance retained in Article 16 of the ILC Articles on State Responsibility.[54] The Court quoted in full the latter provision, characterising it as a reflection of customary law. It then held that:

> In other words, to ascertain whether the Respondent is responsible for 'complicity in genocide' within the meaning of Article III, paragraph *(e)*, which is what the Court now has to do, it must examine whether organs of the respondent State, or persons acting on its instructions or under its direction or effective control, furnished 'aid or assistance' in the

---

50 See Brownlie, 3 May 2006, CR 2006/40, p. 49; see also p. 60.
51 Counter-Memorial of the FRY, 22 July 1997, p. 336.
52 '[T]he secondary rules of State responsibility cannot be employed as a replacement for the express primary rules of treaty provisions'; Brownlie, 3 May 2006, CR 2006/40, p. 59; see also Fauveau-Ivanovic, 8 May 2006, CR 2006/43, pp. 62–65.
53 Counter-Memorial of the FRY, 22 July 1997, pp. 337; Fauveau-Ivanovic, 8 May 2006, CR 2006/43, pp. 63–64.
54 According to *ICJ Reports 2007*:

> There is no doubt that 'complicity', in the sense of Article III, paragraph *(e)*, of the Convention, includes the provision of means to enable or facilitate the commission of the crime; it is thus on this aspect that the Court must focus. In this respect, it is noteworthy that, although 'complicity', as such, is not a notion which exists in the current terminology of the law of international responsibility, it is similar to a category found among the customary rules constituting the law of State responsibility, that of the 'aid or assistance' furnished by one State for the commission of a wrongful act by another State.
>
> (*ICJ Reports 2007*, para. 419)

commission of the genocide in Srebrenica, in a sense not significantly different from that of those concepts in the general law of international responsibility.[55]

It was thus also in reference to general international law that the Court subsequently contended that:

> The question arises whether complicity presupposes that the accomplice shares the specific intent (*dolus specialis*) of the principal perpetrator. But whatever the reply to this question, there is no doubt that the conduct of an organ or a person furnishing aid or assistance to a perpetrator of the crime of genocide cannot be treated as complicity in genocide unless at the least that organ or person acted knowingly, that is to say, in particular, was aware of the specific intent (*dolus specialis*) of the principal perpetrator.[56]

According to the Court, such knowledge could not be established in the case at hand and complicity could not therefore be retained as a basis of Yugoslavia's responsibility. On the other hand, it proved possible to establish the Defendant State's failure to prevent genocide, precisely because such demonstration is less demanding in legal terms. The excerpt of the judgment in which the Court clarifies the distinction between both concepts deserves to be quoted in full:

> In the first place, as noted above, complicity always requires that some positive action has been taken to furnish aid or assistance to the perpetrators of the genocide, while a violation of the obligation to prevent results from mere failure to adopt and implement suitable measures to prevent genocide from being committed. In other words, while complicity results from commission, violation of the obligation to prevent results from omission; this is merely the reflection of the notion that the ban on genocide and the other acts listed in Article III, including complicity, places States under a negative obligation, the obligation not to commit the prohibited acts, while the duty to prevent places States under positive obligations, to do their best to ensure that such acts do not occur.
>
> In the second place, as also noted above, there cannot be a finding of complicity against a State unless at the least its organs were aware that

---

55 Ibid., para. 420. Thus, the Court 'sees no reason to make any distinction of substance between "complicity in genocide", within the meaning of Article III, paragraph *(e)*, of the Convention, and the "aid or assistance" of a State in the commission of a wrongful act by another State within the meaning of the aforementioned Article 16'. See also the Dissenting Opinion of Judge Mahiou, para. 124.
56 Ibid., para. 421. See also the Declaration of Judge Keith, paras 1–7.

genocide was about to be committed or was under way, and if the aid and assistance supplied, from the moment they became so aware onwards, to the perpetrators of the criminal acts or to those who were on the point of committing them, enabled or facilitated the commission of the acts. In other words, an accomplice must have given support in perpetrating the genocide with full knowledge of the facts. By contrast, a State may be found to have violated its obligation to prevent even though it had no certainty, at the time when it should have acted, but failed to do so, that genocide was about to be committed or was under way; for it to incur responsibility on this basis it is enough that the State was aware, or should normally have been aware, of the serious danger that acts of genocide would be committed.

... the Court recalls that although it has not found that the information available to the Belgrade authorities indicated, as a matter of certainty, that genocide was imminent (which is why complicity in genocide was not upheld above: paragraph 424), they could hardly have been unaware of the serious risk of it once the VRS forces had decided to occupy the Srebrenica enclave.[57]

The comparison drawn by the Court between the two notions is telling. It clearly shows how much more difficult it is in practice to engage a State's responsibility on the basis of complicity, as opposed to due diligence. It is worth observing that this is the case even though the Court favoured a – relatively – objective conception of complicity, one not requiring that the accomplice share the intention of the principal perpetrator of the wrongful act, but more simply that it provide aid or assistance with 'full knowledge' of the facts.[58] In that respect, the distinction made by the Court between 'full knowledge' of the facts – that would be required to establish complicity – and 'awareness' of a 'serious danger' that a wrongful act would be committed – that would be required to establish failure to exercise due diligence – is certainly open to debate.[59] It has indeed been observed that awareness of a 'serious danger' that a genocide will be committed logically presupposes a knowledge of the genocidal intent of the principal perpetrator.[60] Be that as it may, what clearly emerges from this reasoning is that the Court favoured

---

57 *ICJ Reports* 2007, paras 432 *et seq.*; see also the Declaration of Judge Bennouna.
58 Such a conception is in line with the wording of Article 16(a), which requires that the aiding or assisting State 'does so with knowledge of the circumstances of the internationally wrongful act'. This confirms that the reference to the intention of the State that provides aid or assistance found in paragraph 5 of the Commentary to that provision does not adequately reflect the state of the law.
59 O. Corten, 'L'arrêt rendu par la CIJ dans l'affaire du *Crime de génocide (Bosnie-Herzégovine c. Serbie)*: vers un assouplissement des conditions permettant d'engager la responsabilité d'un Etat pour génocide?' *AFDI*, 53 (2007): 278.
60 See Dissenting Opinion of Judge Mahiou, para. 128.

the 'due diligence' approach over that based on complicity as a result of the obvious practical and legal difficulties raised by the latter.[61]

All in all, one appears to be faced with the following alternative whenever the matter is considered from the perspective of general international law. Either the notion of complicity is interpreted as requiring the establishment of a specific intention on the part of the accomplice,[62] and it will therefore be far more convenient to turn to the concept of due diligence, which does not require such an element of intention. Or the notion of complicity is interpreted as not requiring the establishment of such a specific intention,[63] but this notion then appears equivalent to – or could even be said to merge with – the concept of due diligence. Whichever alternative is taken, there are serious reasons to question the very usefulness of the notion of complicity, which it appears, can always be substituted with the far more manageable concept of due diligence. This conclusion can be drawn on the basis of the two ICJ judgments rendered at a 60-year interval in two very different cases, but which nevertheless seem to have adopted the same logic. One can therefore ask whether this logic cannot be articulated in broader and more general terms.

19.4 Is complicity a meaningful notion in the law of international responsibility?

At this stage, it appears crucial to schematise the complicity and due diligence concepts in order to better assess the former's relevance in relation to the latter (see Table 19.1).

According to these definitions, the concept of due diligence appears to have a much broader scope, since it generally requires States to protect the rights of other States and the rights they may claim for their nationals. Complicity, on the other hand, appears to require much stricter conditions of application.[64] This perception tends to be confirmed when the elements highlighted in the ICJ's judgments of 1949 and 2007 – which appear to adequately reflect the state of general international law – [65] are set out, as in Table 19.2.

---

61 See also P. Gaeta, 'Génocide d'Etat et responsabilité individuelle', *RGDIP* (2007): 274, and A. Cassese, 'On the Use of Criminal Notions in Determining State Responsibility for Genocide', *JICJ* (2007): 885–887; E. Savarese, 'Complicité de l'Etat dans la perpétration d'actes de génocide: les notions contiguës et la nature de la norme', *AFDI*, 53 (2007): 286–287.
62 See on this point the difficulties raised by James Crawford, *Second Report on State Responsibility*, A/CN.4/498/Add.1, 1 April 1999, paras 178–179.
63 See e.g. Declaration of Judge Keith, para. 7 and Dissenting Opinion of Judge Mahiou, para. 125.
64 See also James Crawford, *Second Report on State Responsibility*, op. cit., paras 166–186.
65 See *ILC Yearbook*, 1978, vol II, Part Two, p. 104. Concerning due diligence, see e.g. the *Institut de droit international*'s Resolution of 1927 on the 'Responsabilité internationale des Etats à raison des dommages causés sur leur territoire à la personne et aux biens des étrangers', Session de Lausanne. Online. Available at: #ofhttp://www.idi-iil.org#cf (accessed 8 October 2010).

Table 19.1 Comparison of complicity and due diligence

Complicity (aid or assistance)	Due diligence
Aid or assistance in the commission of an internationally wrongful act 'A State which aids or assists another State in the commission of an internationally wrongful act by the latter is internationally responsible for doing so if: (a) That State does so with knowledge of the circumstances of the internationally wrongful act; and (b) The act would be internationally wrongful if committed by that State.'[1]	'Territorial sovereignty . . . involves the exclusive right to display the activities of a State. This right has a corollary, a duty: the obligation to protect within the territory the rights of other States, in particular their right to integrity and inviolability in peace and in war, together with the rights which each State may claim for its nationals in foreign territory.'[2]

Notes: [1] Article 16 of the ILC Articles on State Responsibility.
[2] *Island of Palmas* case *(the Netherlands v. the U.S.A.), RIAA*, vol. II, p. 839.

Table 19.2 Scope of complicity compared to scope of due diligence

Complicity (aid or assistance)	Due diligence
The existence of a principal internationally wrongful act must be established	The risk of a breach of an international obligation occurring must be established
The principal internationally wrongful act must be committed by a State (or an international organization)[1]	The risk of breach may result from actions undertaken by private persons[2]
An action by the accomplice must be established	A failure to act when the circumstances so required must be established
According to certain views, the specific intention of the accomplice must be established	Intention is not taken into account
The absence of a third State (the principal perpetrator) may constitute an obstacle in judicial proceedings[3]	No procedural problem arises

Notes: [1] See Article 57 of the Draft Articles on Responsibility of International Organizations (ILC Report to the General Assembly, 2009).
[2] On this point, see e.g. R. P. Barnidge, 'The Due Diligence Principle Under International Law', *International Community Law Review*, 8 (2006): 81–121.
[3] This problem was raised by the ILC in its comments to Article 16 (para. 11).

Against this background, it should come as no surprise that in both the *Corfu Channel* and the *Genocide Convention* cases, the ICJ judges favoured the concept of due diligence over that of complicity. More generally, the following hypothesis may be put forward: whenever complicity can be established, the principle of due diligence has been breached; in contrast, the principle of due diligence can be breached in numerous situations where complicity – within the meaning given to this notion in the law of international responsibility – cannot be established. The ICJ case-law (the *Corfu Channel* and *Genocide Convention* cases, but also the *Nicaragua* case) illustrate the latter part of this hypothesis. As for its first part, reference can be made to the various instances of complicity mentioned by the ILC, which could just as well be listed as cases where the principle of due diligence has been breached.[66] In the Commission's work, mention is mostly made of situations where a State extends aid or assistance to another State in a use of force prohibited by the United Nations Charter.[67] And yet many instruments relating to the *jus contra bellum* set out an obligation that may be characterised as a specific expression of the principle of due diligence. Hence, according to the Declaration on Friendly Relations annexed to General Assembly Resolution 2625 (XXV),[68] for instance:

> Every State has the duty to refrain from organizing, instigating, assisting or participating in acts of civil strife or terrorist acts in another State or acquiescing in organized activities within its territory directed towards the commission of such acts, when the acts referred to in the present paragraph involve a threat of force.[69]

It thus appears that the practice relied on to assert the customary character of the rule set out in Article 16 of the ILC Articles on State Responsibility evidences at least as much the existence of a general principle of due diligence as the presence in contemporary international law of a notion of complicity. In any event, as underlined by several commentators, the practice mentioned by the Commission does not reflect any requirement of a specific intention on the part of the State providing aid or assistance.[70] Instead it correlates with the

---

66 See *ILC Yearbook*, 1978, vol. II, pp. 53–60; *ILC Yearbook*, 1978, vol. II, Part Two, pp. 99–105.
67 Ibid., p. 103, para. 15; Crawford, *Second Report on State Responsibility*, op. cit., *passim*.
68 Declaration on Friendly Relations and Co-operation Among States in Accordance with the Charter of the United Nations, annexed to General Assembly Resolution 2625 (XXV).
69 Similarly, Article 3(f) of the Definition of Aggression annexed to General Assembly Resolution 3314 (XXIX) refers to '[t]he action of a State in allowing its territory, which is placed at the disposal of another State, to be used by that other State for perpetrating an act of aggression against a third State'. GA Res 42/22 ('Declaration on the Enhancement of the Effectiveness of the Principle of Refraining from the Threat or Use of Force in International Relations') provides that: 'States have the duty not to urge, encourage or assist other States to resort to the threat or use of force in violation of the Charter' (para. I, 4). For more details, see O. Corten, *Le droit contre la guerre* (Paris: Pedone, 2008), pp. 265–289.
70 Quigley, 'Complicity in International Law: A New Direction in the Law of State Responsibility', op. cit., pp. 109–117; Graefrath, 'Complicity in the Law of International Responbility', op. cit., p. 376; Corten, *Le droit contre la guerre*, op. cit., pp. 274–276.

'objective' logic followed by the law of international responsibility (i.e. devoid of 'subjective' elements, such as the notion of fault), which may also be found in the concept of due diligence. Be that as it may, it appears that the concept of due diligence covers in an adequate manner all the examples mentioned by the ILC on complicity. Thus the conclusion reached on the basis of an examination of the *Corfu Channel* case seems to find confirmation: complicity constitutes a notion whose usefulness is open to serious doubt. The principle of due diligence makes it possible to establish the responsibility of a State that is not the principal perpetrator of an internationally wrongful act in most situations where that State has adopted a particular course of conduct in relation to the wrongful act and has made it possible for this act to take place. This is at least the hypothesis that can legitimately be put forward after confronting the *Corfu Channel* precedent with the Court's subsequent case-law and contemporary practice.

20 Reparation and compliance

Pierre d'Argent[1]

20.1 Introduction

Insofar as the rules of international law on reparation are concerned, the *Corfu Channel* case is most notably remembered for its declaration of wrongfulness as a form of satisfaction.[2] Having ruled that the British Navy's *Operation Retail* of 12–13 November 1946 could not be justified on the grounds of self-preservation or self-help, nor by 'the alleged right of intervention'[3] – despite the fact that the 'Albanian Government's complete failure to carry out its duties after the explosions, and the dilatory nature of its diplomatic notes [were] extenuating circumstances for the action of the United Kingdom' – the Court considered that, in order 'to ensure respect for international law' of which it viewed itself as 'the organ', it 'must declare that the action of the British Navy constituted a violation of Albanian sovereignty'. The Court stated that '[t]his declaration ... [was] in itself appropriate satisfaction'.[4] That unanimous finding was reached not without stressing that such a declaration was 'in accordance with the request made by Albania through her Counsel'. It is to be recalled that the Special Agreement by which the case was, finally, jointly submitted by the Parties to the Court also referred to the possible 'duty to give satisfaction' if the Court were to find one of the UK naval operations in breach of Albania's sovereignty.[5]

Since 1949, the finding of the *Corfu Channel Judgment* on satisfaction has provided strong authority for other courts and tribunals;[6] it has been cited in

---

1 The views expressed herein are those of the author and do not necessarily reflect the views of the United Nations or the International Court of Justice.
2 *Corfu Channel case, Judgment of April 9th 1949, Merits, ICJ Reports 1949*, p. 36 (hereinafter '*Judgment of 9 April 1949*').
3 Ibid., p. 35.
4 Ibid.
5 Ibid., p. 6.
6 For a recent reference to the *Corfu* finding on satisfaction, see e.g. Eritrea Ethiopia Claims Commission, *Final Award Eritrea's Damages Claims*, 17 August 2009, p. 87, para. 386. Very similar words are reproduced in the parallel *Final Award Ethiopia's Damages Claims*, also dated 17 August 2009, p. 60, para. 269, but with an erroneous reference to the compensation Judgment of 15 December 1949, instead of the merits Judgment of 9 April 1949. Online. Available at: www.pca-cpa.org (accessed 16 August 2010).

textbooks as the *locus classicus* for satisfaction as a form of reparation,[7] and for a declaration of illegality as a form of satisfaction; it has of course found its way and its place in the International Law Commission's work on State responsibility.[8]

All this might convey the impression that the famous judgment of 9 April 1949 was a bitter judicial defeat for the United Kingdom. This impression would, however, be incorrect. By in effect articulating a British claim and an Albanian counter-claim, the Special Agreement of 25 March 1948 was a clear invitation to the Court to deliver a balanced decision, one in which both Parties could find reasons for being content. One might question whether such an open invitation was really necessary in order to achieve such a result, as few judicial institutions understand better than the ICJ what the ingredients of a balanced ruling are. The fact that the *Corfu Channel* case was the very first one submitted to the 'new' World Court could explain the care taken by both Parties to send such a message about its role as the principal – but nevertheless non-compulsory – judicial organ of the (then young) United Nations entrusted with the duty of settling international disputes. This might suggest that, in such fragile conditions, effective settlement can only be reached by some (more or less sophisticated) form of Solomon's judgment. The resort to a balanced Special Agreement leading to a balanced judgment is all the more telling in that it was agreed on the very day that the Court decided, in rather strong terms, that it had jurisdiction to entertain the British application of 22 May 1947.[9] Surely the Court fully understood the implicit message conveyed by the Special Agreement: the satisfaction offered to Albania echoed

---

[7] See e.g. P. Daillier, M. Forteau and A. Pellet, *Droit international public*, 8th edn (Paris: LGDJ, 2009), p. 894, no. 490 ; however, I. Brownlie, *Principles of Public International Law*, 7th edn (Oxford: Oxford University Press, 2008), pp. 462–463 considers that:

> in spite of the terminology [used by the ICJ in the *Corfu Channel* merits Judgment of 9 April 1949], this is not an instance of satisfaction in the usual meaning of the word: the declaration is that of a court and not a party, and is *alternative* to compensation. No pecuniary compensation had been asked for by Albania, and a declaration of this kind was therefore the only means of giving an effective decision on the matter.

It is nevertheless difficult to see how this form of reparation could be alternative to compensation when no compensation was claimed, as no material damage had been suffered by Albania as a consequence of *Operation Retail*. In other cases, satisfaction has been awarded by the ICJ in the form of a declaration, as requested by the claimant, in order to make good a non-pecuniary damage (for the latest case at the time of writing, see *Case Concerning Pulp Mills on the River Uruguay (Argentina v. Uruguay)*, Judgment of 20 April 2010, paras 269 and 282, 1).

[8] J. Crawford, 'Third Report on State Responsibility', 15 March 2000, A/CN.4/507, *ILC Yearbook*, 2000, Vol. II, Part I, p 55, and references to the work of the previous *Special Rapporteurs*.

[9] *Corfu Channel case, Judgment of March 25th 1948, Preliminary Objection, ICJ Reports 1947–1948*, p. 15. On the relatively strong wording used by the Court, see p. 27:

> The Albanian contention that the Application cannot be entertained because it has been filed contrary to the provisions of Article 40, paragraph I, and of Article 36, paragraph I, of the Court's Statute, is essentially founded on the assumption that the institution of proceedings by application is only possible where compulsory jurisdiction exists and

Reparation and compliance 337

the affirmation that it bore responsibility for the damages caused to British destroyers *Saumarez* and *Volage* and for the loss of human life and injuries resulting from the mine explosions which occurred in its waters.

There is no need to recall here the reasons for which the Court found Albania internationally responsible, knowing that the laying of the mines had not been proven to be attributable to it. As this contribution focuses on the issue of reparation, it will concentrate first on the judicial developments following that finding in order to then assess the legacy of the *Corfu Channel* case in making good damages. Finally, a short account of the frustrated history of the effective implementation of the compensation ruling of 15 December 1949 will then serve to address issues of compliance.

20.2 The compensation phase

20.2.1 *The obligation to pay compensation and jurisdiction to assess the damage*

Having found Albania responsible for the explosions which occurred on 22 October 1946 in its waters 'and for the damage and loss of human life that resulted from them', the Court considered that, as a consequence, 'there is a duty upon Albania to pay compensation to the United Kingdom'.[10] However, Albania argued that, under the Special Agreement, the Court's jurisdiction fell short of encompassing the assessment of the amount of compensation. This was because the Special Agreement only asked the Court to answer the question: 'is there any duty to pay compensation?', in the event that Albania was to be found internationally responsible. The Court rejected that interpretation of the Special Agreement and found that it had jurisdiction to assess the amount of compensation. That conclusion was reached by taking into account the procedural history of the dispute, starting with the Security Council resolution of 9 April 1947 which was said to aim at a 'final adjustment of the whole dispute'; the subsequent attitude of the Parties; the undisputed jurisdiction of the Court to rule on the form of satisfaction in favour of Albania and the parallelism between the provisions of the Special Agreement on satisfaction and on compensation; the interpretation rule according to which a provision (i.e. the question of the Special Agreement on the duty to pay compensation) should not be devoid of its purport and effect.[11]

As a matter of law, this last point deserves some attention. It is not that this rule of interpretation might be questionable, or require elaborate comments.

> that, where it does not, proceedings can only be instituted by special agreement. This is a mere assertion which is not justified by either of the texts cited . . .
>
> The French authoritative text reads: 'C'est là une pure affirmation qui ne trouve de fondement ni dans l'un ni dans l'autre des textes invoqués.'

10 *Judgment of 9 April 1949*, op. cit., p. 23.
11 Ibid., pp. 23–26.

Rather, its application by the Court conveyed an understanding of the law of State responsibility which is worth mentioning, even if it is now undisputed: the Court found that the Special Agreement's question on the duty to make compensation would be superfluous if it were not interpreted as conferring jurisdiction to assess the damage, since 'it follows from the establishment of responsibility that compensation is due'.[12] By this finding, the Court thus held that the duty to make good the damage automatically flows from the wrongful act and does not require any distinct agreement. So, in accordance with the famous *Chorzów* dictum,[13] the Court clearly rejected the (early) Kelsenian theory according to which the wrongful act would only give rise to a right of the injured State to take sanctions against the wrongful State, whereas the duty to compensate for the damage would distinctively flow from an agreement between those States, by which the right to sanction would be traded against the contractually created duty to compensate.[14]

20.2.2 Appointment of experts

Although the Court ruled that it had jurisdiction to assess the amount of compensation owed by Albania for the damage sustained by the UK, it reserved that question 'for further consideration'[15] and regulated the procedure on this subject by an order issued on the same day as the judgment on the merits. By that order, the Court decided that Albania's observations on the various sums claimed in the British memorial of 1947 were to be filed by 25 June 1949; that the United Kingdom had one month to respond to these observations, while Albania had another month to reply again. This remarkably tight schedule was subject to further procedural arrangements, 'including the appointment of experts in case of agreement being reached by the Parties both as to the subject of the expert opinion and as to the names of the experts'.[16] This invitation addressed to the Parties to reach an agreement on an expert mission was not taken up.

A few days after the Court extended by one week the various time-limits at Albania's request,[17] its agent opined (again) that the Special Agreement conferred jurisdiction to the Court:

---

12 Ibid., pp. 23–24.
13 *Chorzów Factory, Judgment no. 13, 1928, Merits, PCIJ Series A*, no. 17, p. 47.
14 H. Kelsen, 'Unrecht und Unrechtsfolge im Völkerrecht', ZÖR (1932): 481–608; see also P. Guggenheim, *Traité de droit international public*, vol. II (Geneva, 1954), p. 64. This theory is clearly abandoned and never represented the law. For an early rebuttal of the Kelsenian view, see e.g. A. Roth, *Schadensersatz für Verletzungen Privater bei völkerrechtlichen Delikten* (Berlin: Heymann, 1934), p. 178; L. Reitzer, *La réparation comme conséquence de l'acte illicite en droit international* (Paris: Sirey, 1938), p. 239.
15 *Judgment of 9 April 1949*, p. 36.
16 *Corfu Channel case, Order of April 9th, 1949, ICJ Reports 1949*, p. 172, (hereinafter *Order of April 9th, 1949*).
17 *Corfu Channel case, Order of June 24th, 1949, ICJ Reports 1949*, pp. 222–223, (hereinafter *Order of June 24th, 1949*).

solely to consider the question whether Albania was, or was not, obliged to pay compensation . . . [but that it] did not provide that the Court should have the right to fix the amount of compensation and, consequently, to ask Albania for information on that subject.[18]

On 15 November 1949, Albania reasserted the same opinion and stated that it would not be represented at the hearings scheduled to start two days later.

The Albanian absence led the United Kingdom to ask the Court to decide in favour of its claims,[19] as envisaged by Article 53, paragraph 1, of the Statute. This triggered the Court's duty to make sure that the British claim was 'well founded in fact and law' (Article 53, para. 2). Hence, because the British 'estimates and figures . . . raise[d] questions of a technical nature', the Court acted under Article 50 of the Statute and designated two members of the Dutch Navy (Rear-Admiral J. B. Berck and Mr. G. de Rooy, Director of Naval Construction) as experts in order to examine the estimates and figures.[20]

With the assistance of the Registry, the experts had to file their report within two weeks of the order establishing their mission. On 1 December 1949 (a day before the rather tight time-limit fixed by the Court!), the experts handed over their report, which was communicated to the Parties. The Court maintained that hasty pace: it held a private meeting with the experts on 3 December 1949 in order to answer some of the judges' questions; it received on 6 December a telegram from the British Government stating that it did not wish to make any observations on the particular calculations of the experts, as they found the British claim to be a fair and accurate estimate of the damage sustained; and, on 15 December, it ruled on the amount of compensation to be awarded to the United Kingdom.[21] That judgment was reached despite the fact that Albania asked the Court to change or extend the procedure for the submission of its observations. The Court dismissed this late Albanian request and proceeded on the issue of compensation.[22] It also recalled that, as a matter of *res judicata*, its jurisdiction extended to assessing the damage.

Because the Court had previously resorted to experts in order to clarify factual issues related to the merits of the *Corfu Channel* case,[23] this second appointment of experts might seem quite normal. It should, however, be kept in mind that it is only because Albania defaulted that the Court felt compelled

---

18 *Corfu Channel case, Judgment of December 15th, 1949*, ICJ Reports 1949, (assessment of the amount of compensation) p. 246 (hereinafter 'Judgment of 15 December 1949'); see the Albanian letter of 29 June 1949 referred to therein.
19 As presented in the UK's final submissions contained in its written observations dated 28 July 1949.
20 *Corfu Channel case, Order of November 19th, 1949*, ICJ Reports 1949, p. 238.
21 *Judgment of 15 December 1949*, p. 244.
22 Ibid., p. 248.
23 *Corfu Channel case, Order of December 17th, 1948*, ICJ Reports 1947–1948, p. 124, see the expert reports of 8 January 1949 and 8 February 1949, Annex 2 to the *Judgment of 9 April 1949*, p. 142.

to do so, due to the nature of the British compensation claim. This does not mean that, had Albania appeared, the Court would have acted differently or that it would have lacked the power to appoint an expert panel, either at the request of one of the Parties, or of both of them, or even *proprio motu*. As Article 50 of the Statute makes clear, the Court has the broadest possible power to resort to experts, whatever the views of the parties on that issue might be.[24] So, during the merits phase, the Court decided to resort to experts at its own initiative, without any specific request from the Parties. It is also worth noting that, contrary to what common opinion might suggest, resorting to experts did not delay the resolution of this case, but allowed for its speedy conclusion, due to the tightly fixed time-limits.

However, this (double) positive experience of resorting *proprio motu* to experts appointed by the Court under Article 50 of the Statute has, so far, remained exceptional. This is not to say that disputing parties have never resorted to experts, quite the contrary. In some cases, the Court has been presented with hundreds, if not thousands, of pages of reports written by experts retained by a claimant or a respondent State. Sometimes, the Court has heard such experts during the oral phase of the pleadings, either as experts under Articles 63–65 of the Rules, or as counsel because they were included in that capacity in the delegations – a practice the Court has recently criticised.[25] Be that as it may, after *Corfu* and thus far, the Court has never considered it necessary to resort, on its own initiative,[26] to the assistance of expert reports submitted to observations by the parties. Due to the variety of cases heard by the Court over the past sixty years, this might seem quite extraordinary. In the *Pulp Mills* case – which raised highly complex scientific issues – Judges Al-Khasawneh and Simma criticised the fact that the Court did not resort to an independent expert report under Article 50 of the Statute, considering that this case presented itself as a 'textbook example'[27] for that purpose. This statutory possibility was distinguished from the practice according to which, in some cases, the Court has resorted to the services of 'invisible' experts[28] in order to help it understand very technical issues, such as stating geographic coordinates of a boundary line in accordance with a decision it has reached. In the same case, Judge Keith – who supported the findings of the Court on the non-violation by Uruguay of its substantive obligations under the 1975 Statute of the Uruguay River, and the conclusions of the Court on the issues of evidence – recalled that neither Argentina nor

---

24 See C. J. Tams, 'Article 50', in A. Zimmerman, C. Tomuschat and K. Oellers-Frahm, *The Statute of the International Court of Justice: A Commentary* (Oxford: Oxford University Press, 2006), pp. 1109–1118.
25 *Case Concerning Pulp Mills on the River Uruguay (Argentina v. Uruguay)*, Judgment of 20 April 2010, para. 167.
26 On the practice of the Court when an expert report had been requested by the parties: Tams, op. cit.; *Separate Opinion of Judge Keith, Pulp Mills* case, op. cit., para. 9.
27 *Joint Dissenting Opinion of Judges Al-Khasawneh and Simma, Pulp Mills* case, op. cit., para. 3.
28 Called 'internal *experts fantômes*', ibid., para. 14.

Uruguay had ever asked the Court to appoint experts.[29] It is true that such a passive attitude could weaken the case of a claimant – not requiring the appointment of an expert might be interpreted as some form of reluctance to have a transparent debate over the facts –; it could hence discourage the Court from acting *proprio motu* if the evidence presented by the defendant is relatively strong.

20.2.3 Experts' report and compensation ordered by the Court

The experts' Report of 1 December 1949 is a rather short document of three pages, dealing with two issues: the replacement value of the *Saumarez* and the assessment of the damage sustained by the *Volage*.[30] Shortly after having handed over their Report, the experts answered some questions posed by Members of the Court. The records of that meeting[31] should be considered as an integral part of the Report, as it highlights the methodology used by the experts.

As far as the *Saumarez* was concerned, the experts calculated the replacement value of the destroyed ship by making an estimate of the cost of construction of a similar destroyer. The estimate was first based on Dutch shipyards' prices, and then checked and recalculated according to British prices and labour costs.[32] The lower of the two figures was taken into consideration; that amount was then reduced in accordance with the depreciation over the years.[33] So assessed, the replacement value of the *Saumarez* in 1946 included a sum in respect of insurance calculated on a post-War basis, but no 'interest on the growing capital outlay'.[34] To this amount, the experts added an estimated value of the stores contained in the bows of the ship, and deducted from it an estimated value of the still serviceable equipment, together with the scrap value.[35] They arrived at the figure of £716,780 for the loss of the *Saumarez*.

---

29 *Separate Opinion of Judge Keith*, op. cit., para. 11.
30 *Experts' Report of December 1st, 1949*, Annex 2 to the *Judgment of 15 December 1949*, pp. 258–260.
31 *Questions Put by Members of the Court and Replies of the Experts (Meeting of December 3rd, 1949)*, Annex 3 to the *Judgment of 15 December*, p. 261.
32 See the explanation given by Rear-Admiral Berck to Judge De Visscher's question relating to the two evaluations of the construction costs of the destroyer: *Questions Put by Members of the Court and Replies of the Experts*, ibid, p. 261.
33 It was estimated that the decrease in value of such a warship would be 0 per cent in the first year, 1 per cent in the second year, 2 per cent in the third year, 3 per cent in the fourth year, 4 per cent in the fifth year, 7 per cent in the sixth to tenth years, 10 per cent in the eleventh to fifteenth years, thus leaving a residual value of 5 per cent after the estimated 15 years of service: see ibid., the reply to Judge Azevedo's question.
34 Because builders of warships are paid by successive instalments (rather than at delivery), it might seem correct to add an amount of interest to the building costs. However, the experts stated that, in their experience, such interest was never added: ibid., see answer to Judge *ad hoc* Ečer's question, p. 264.
35 'Taking into consideration the necessary costs of salvaging and cutting up, as well as the cost of transporting the material from Malta to scrap plants': *Experts' Report of December 1st, 1949*, ibid, p. 259.

Concerning the damage sustained by the *Volage* as a direct consequence of the mine explosion,[36] the experts based themselves on their experience and on the fact that the repairs required 205 days in dock. Taking into account the cost of transport of material and the cost of the trials after the completion of the repairs as an integral part of extensive repairs, they arrived at an estimated total of the repair costs. To this sum, the estimated value of the stores, including the loss of anti-submarine equipment, was added. The experts arrived at a total figure of £90,800 for the damage sustained by the *Volage*.

The total British claim for the damaged ships (£793,899) being lower than the addition of those two figures (£807,580), the experts considered the UK's assessment to be 'a fair and accurate estimate of the damage sustained'.[37]

This statement allowed the Court to consider that the UK's estimate of the damage sustained by the *Volage* was 'well founded',[38] despite being slightly superior to the evaluation by the experts. Thus, the Court awarded the British claim of £93,812. For the *Saumarez*, it was the experts' assessment which was superior to the British claim. Considering that 'it cannot award more than the amount claimed in the submissions of the United Kingdom Government', and that such an amount had been 'justified',[39] the Court awarded the British claim of £700,087 for the loss of that destroyer. The Court further awarded £50,048, being the amount claimed by the United Kingdom for 'the cost of pensions and other grants made by it to victims or their dependants, and for costs of administration, medical treatment, etc'.[40] The Court soberly considered that this expenditure, which had not been checked by the experts, had been proved to its satisfaction by the British documents produced. The total amount to be paid by Albania to the United Kingdom was fixed by the Court at £843,947. In 2008, this corresponds to an average value of US$27,800,000 when using the GDP deflator, the method best indicated for government expenditure.[41]

The application of the *non ultra petita* rule to the quantum of damages should not come as a surprise,[42] the Court being required to address only the final submissions of the Parties, as they define the dispute submitted to it. This elementary *principe dispositif*, which generally governs the judicial function when it is not entrusted with the keeping of some form of *ordre public*, also has a substantive dimension, as every claim potentially entails a partial, even if silent, renunciation in relation to the underlying facts. Thus, the duty of the

---

36 On this direct causal link, see the answer of Rear-Admiral Berck to Judge *ad hoc* Ečer's question, *Questions Put by Members of the Court and Replies of the Experts*, op. cit., p. 265.
37 *Experts' Report of December 1st, 1949*, op. cit., p. 260.
38 *Judgment of 15 December 1949*, p. 249.
39 Ibid.
40 Ibid.
41 See http://www.measuringworth.com/exchange/index.php.
42 See, however, the criticism of Judge *ad hoc* Ečer in his *Dissenting Opinion, ICJ Reports 1949*, p. 253.

Court to fully make good the damage by applying the rules of international responsibility is limited by the claim(s) presented to it, not so much because of the fundamental rules presiding over its judicial function, but rather because, by submitting its claim, the claimant – implicitly but necessarily – has waived any additional rights as far as the facts forming the subject-matter of the dispute to be settled are concerned.

As is clear by now, the entrusted experts were actually asked to assess the reasonableness of the British claim in light of the Albanian decision not to appear before the Court, rather than to strictly assess the quantum of the damages to be awarded. As the Order of 19 November 1949 reads, their mission was to '*examine* the figures and estimates' claimed by the UK. This explains why it was that, when part of the British claim was higher than the experts' assessment, the Court did not reduce it in accordance with the experts' estimate, but awarded it as such for the reason that the overall claim was found to be 'fair' and 'accurate' by the experts. The experts did not help the Court to get the facts right, in the sense that they did not have to assess the damage *ex nihilo*; they allowed the Court to award the claim presented by the British Government with a certain degree of confidence thanks to such an outside and 'learned' examination. There was no effort made by the Court to precisely describe the damage and evaluate the amount that would adequately compensate it – the Court simply used the experts in order to assess whether the sum claimed was roughly adequate.

20.3 Legal issues relating to reparation: causality, heads of damage and compensation

Neither the Judgment of 9 April 1949 on the merits, nor the Judgment of 15 December 1949 on compensation, dwell on the notion of reparation. There are no theoretical developments, not even a reference to the *Chorzów* dictum. In the judgment on the merits, satisfaction is given in the form of a declaration, but nowhere is it underlined that satisfaction is a form of reparation for an injury that 'cannot be made good by restitution or compensation', as Article 37 of the ILC Articles on State Responsibility now reads.[43] As far as compensation is concerned, the same Judgment assumes, rather than explains, that 'compensation is due' by a State found responsible of a wrongful act, *in casu* Albania's 'grave omissions'[44] consisting of not having warned of the presence of mines. In the later Judgment of December 1949, compensation is awarded without any explanation as to its articulation with restitution and satisfaction, nor as to the principles governing causality, the extent or heads of damage that can be compensated for, the moment to be taken in evaluating a loss, or the currency in which compensation is to be paid. The decision of

---

43 A/RES/56/83.
44 *Judgment of 9 April 1949*, p. 23.

Albania not to appear before the Court in the compensation phase may explain the paucity of the Judgment in that regard, as the Court did not have to answer more theoretical arguments that might otherwise have been presented.

There are nevertheless a few lessons to be learned from the *Corfu Channel* case on issues linked to reparation. They relate to causality, heads of damage and also to various questions arising from compensation, including the monetary assessment of damage.

20.3.1 Causality

From the text of the judgments, causality does not seem to have been a big issue in the *Corfu Channel* case. This might seem all the more astonishing since the very laying of mines was not found to be attributable to Albania, but rather was most probably the act of a third State which remained unidentified. Thus, it appears that two causes produced the damage: the laying of mines (which was not attributed to any specific State) and the failure to warn of their presence (for which Albania was said to be responsible). Despite this apparent combination of causes, labelled as 'concurrent' by James Crawford,[45] the Court did not apportion percentages of the damage according to the importance of each cause; rather, it held Albania responsible for the entire damage suffered by the United Kingdom. In both the reasoning and the operative clauses of the Judgment on the merits, the Court found Albania 'responsible under international law for the explosions [of 22 October 1946] and for the damage and loss of human life that resulted from them'. This might be explained by the fact that no State, other than Albania, was respondent in the case brought before the ICJ. Such a finding of responsibility is, however, not so much based on a logic of attribution[46] – which, for specialists of international law and following the reports of Roberto Ago to the ILC, has become common to the point of unconsciousness – but rather on a hidden understanding of causality. But what was it?

Because of its silence, it is difficult to identify precisely the theory of causality the Court applied. What may, however, be inferred from the judgments is that all the damage suffered by the UK was considered to be a normal and foreseeable consequence of Albania's omission, as if that wrongful act was the only cause of the entire damage. This may lead one to think that the Court relied on some form of adequate or efficient causality: among the various possible causes, the most decisive one is selected, and the author of the illegal act constituting that cause must make reparation for all the damage. However,

---

45 J. Crawford, 'Third Report on State Responsibility', 15 March 2000, A/CN.4/507, *ILC Yearbook*, 2000, Vol. II, Part I, p. 19, paras 31, 34.
46 By definition, a failure to act never raises any question of attribution, not even 'negatively': pointing out a failure to act requires one to identify who had to act, so that the 'subjective' element at stake in the search for attribution is always satisfied by finding the wrongful omission.

one might also think that the Court considered that the damage suffered by the UK would not have occurred, as it occurred, if it were not for the unlawful failure to warn of the presence of the mines, despite the fact that their laying was not (proven to be) attributable to Albania. Does this mean that, instead of relying on the theory of adequate or efficient cause, the Court approached the issue of causality from the perspective of what French (and Belgian) law calls the theory of '*l'équivalence des conditions*'? This theory considers that every event without which the damage would not have occurred, as it occurred, is a cause. Every event which presents itself as a *sine qua non* condition of the damage is considered as a cause; all causes so understood being said to be equivalent to one another. This understanding of causality allows for an eventual sharing of the damage among the causes so identified, according to the importance of their respective causal effect. But it is not because that theory allows for such sharing that it must be considered that the Court, having not ventured into such an exercise, ruled it out. No rule of international law excludes the taking into account of several causes when it appears that they have concurrently produced, each of them in a normal and foreseeable way, the damage. Indeed, it is only 'unless some part of the harm can [not] be shown to be severable in causal terms from that attributed to the responsible State' that, as a matter of principle, a State 'should be held responsible for all the consequences (not indirect or remote) of its wrongful conduct'.[47]

In his dissenting opinion, Judge *ad hoc* Ečer did not explicitly address the issue of multiple causes, but considered that, if the responsibility of Albania was the result of 'grave omissions', the Court should have added 'a few words' in order to explain 'the relationship between the degree of culpability and the amount of compensation'.[48] Judge Ečer did not express doubt as to the existence of a causal relationship between the wrongful omissions of Albania and the damage sustained by the United Kingdom as a consequence of the explosions; he only raised a question as to the degree of causality. This can be understood as another way of phrasing the issue of apportionment of causal percentages, which multiple concurrent causes could call for if the theory of equivalent conditions were followed. Be that as it may, the dissenting opinion seems to confirm that the Court never doubted that there existed a causal nexus between Albania's wrongful omissions and the damage sustained by the United Kingdom. Nowhere is it discussed whether an omission, being a

---

47 J. Crawford, op. cit., note 45, para. 35. On the issue of multiple causes, and the differences between the *Special Rapporteurs* Crawford and Arangio-Ruiz, see P. d'Argent, *Les réparations de guerre en droit international public. La responsabilité internationale des Etats à l'épreuve de la guerre* (Bruxelles: Bruylant-LGDJ, 2002), pp. 636–641, and also the remarks of A. Gattini, 'Breach of the Obligation to Prevent and Reparation Thereof in the ICJ's Genocide Judgment', *EJIL* (2007): 710. When the same internationally wrongful act is committed by several States (this hypothesis being different from the one of multiple causes), see Article 47 of the ILC Articles on State Responsibility (A/RES/56/83).
48 *Dissenting Opinion of Judge* ad hoc *Ečer*, op. cit., p. 254.

wrongful act, can be considered as a cause of damage. Nor did the Court elaborate on what would be the test to be applied in order to decide on the causal relationship between a wrongful omission and the damage sustained. What seemed to have been decisive was that Albania was the sole respondent and that its wrongful omissions were sufficient to explain the occurrence of the damage.

The Court's silence on this point contrasts with what it decided some 58 years later in the *Genocide* (Bosnia v. Serbia) case. In 2007, the Court also had to deal with a wrongful omission, namely Serbia's violation of the obligation to prevent genocide.[49] The Court addressed the issue as to whether Serbia had to make reparation for the Srebrenica genocide as a consequence of its wrongful omission. It ruled that Serbia's wrongful omission could be considered to have a causal nexus with the Srebrenica genocide committed by the Bosnian Serb military, only if it were able to conclude 'from the case as a whole and with a sufficient degree of certainty that the genocide at Srebrenica would in fact have been averted if [Serbia] had acted in compliance with its legal obligations'.[50] The Court found that, 'clearly', it could not so conclude. In the absence of a 'sufficiently direct and certain causal nexus' between the Serbian breach of the obligation to prevent genocide and the injury suffered by Bosnia, Serbia was found not to be under an obligation to make reparation for the Srebrenica genocide. Only satisfaction, in the form of a declaration by the Court, was awarded for the breach by Serbia of the obligation of prevention.[51]

As sensible as it may sound at first glance, the causality test elaborated by the Court is actually quite a puzzling legal construction. Its appropriateness

49 *Application of the Convention on the Prevention and Punishment of the Crime of Genocide (Bosnia and Herzegovina v. Serbia and Montenegro), Judgment*, ICJ Reports 2007, p. 223 (hereinafter '*Judgment of 26 February 2007*'): at para. 432, the Court underlines the difference between the obligation to prevent genocide and complicity in genocide, considering that the latter 'results from commission', while a 'violation of the obligation to prevent results from omission'. For a critical appraisal of the findings of the Court on the question of complicity, see A. Cassese, 'On the Use of Criminal Law Notions in Determining State Responsibility for Genocide', *JICJ* (2007): 875–887. See also the contribution of Pierre Klein and Oliver Corten to this volume (Chapter 19).
50 *Judgment of 26 February 2007*, p. 234, para. 62.
51 In para. 463 of the *Judgment of 26 February 2007* (p. 234), the Court specifically refers to the *Corfu Judgment of 15 April 1949* in order to justify the measure of satisfaction. This reference has been criticised for lack of appropriateness, due to the profoundly different nature of both cases and the injuries involved: see in particular C. Tomuschat, 'Reparation in Cases of Genocide', *JICJ* (2007): 905–912. As noted by A. Gattini, Bosnia's final submissions did not clearly require a form of reparation other than satisfaction for the breach of the obligation to prevent genocide: Gattini, op. cit., pp. 706–707.

to the nature of the obligation to prevent genocide, as identified by the Court to be an obligation of conduct and not one of result,[52] is doubtful.[53]

In 1949, the Court never required that it be proven to its satisfaction that the explosions would not have occurred had Albania warned the British fleet of the presence of the mines. Rather, the Court tacitly assumed that it would have been so – or that the UK would have to bear its own damage if, after having been informed of the presence of mines, it nonetheless had decided to recklessly venture into the Channel. As a matter of common sense, such an assumption is difficult to contest. As a matter of law, it tends to blur the distinction between the omission, as an act, and its causal effect; more fundamentally, it also helps to mould the wrongful nature of such an omission, and hence to shape the content and scope of the obligation of conduct that was not complied with. As a nexus, causality permanently oscillates between the wrongful act and the damage: it is an 'extrinsic' element of the damage (the other, 'intrinsic', element of the damage being the infringement of a legally protected interest[54]), but, in some ways, it also appears to be an 'intrinsic' element of the wrongful act, in the sense that the understanding of the content and scope of the obligation at stake greatly depends on the causality test applied. In the *Genocide* case, the Court carefully described what the obligation to prevent genocide consisted of before addressing the question of the causal link between genocide and the violation of the obligation to prevent it, knowing that such a violation can only exist if genocide occurs.[55] This analytical sequence seems perfectly logical. It is, however, difficult to overlook the fact that the causality test used by the Court was tailored according to what it considered as having to be done in order to comply with the obligation to prevent genocide. Because, undoubtedly, if that obligation had meant a duty to intervene in Bosnia in order to stop the ongoing bloodshed, failing to do so would have had to be considered as satisfying the causality test used by the Court, whatever its flaws might be.

---

52 *Judgment of 26 February 2007*, para. 430, p. 221. Among the many studies on the distinction between obligations of result and obligations of conduct, and their meaning, see P.-M. Dupuy, 'Reviewing the Difficulties of Codification: On Ago's Classification of Obligations of Means and Obligations of Result in Relation to State Responsibility', *EJIL* (1999): 371–385.

53 It is particularly demanding to require that it be established that compliance with the obligation to prevent would have resulted in something that is not required to be achieved under the said obligation, i.e. averting genocide. If the obligation to prevent can be fulfilled despite the occurrence of genocide (if that were not the case, the obligation to prevent would be an obligation of result, not of conduct), it is logically rather strange to require that the absence of genocide be the result of the compliance with the obligation to prevent in order for the breach of such obligation to be considered a cause of genocide. See also Gattini, op. cit., p. 709.

54 J. Combacau and S. Sur, *Droit international public*, 2nd edn (Paris: Montchrestien, 2002), p. 539.

55 *Judgment of 26 February 2007*, para. 431, pp. 221–222, referring to Article 14, para. 3 of the ILC Articles on State Responsibility, A/RES/56/83.

20.3.2 Heads of damage (and causality again . . .)

The fact that the mine explosions occurred at sea and impacted two warships limited not so much the extent of the damage (which remained quite dramatic, as 44 sailors died and 42 were injured), but the type of damage resulting, in an obvious fashion, from those events.

First, all damage was directly caused to the United Kingdom itself. State property was destroyed or damaged, in the form of two warships, but the material damage suffered by the United Kingdom also took the form of the loss of serving seamen (by death or injury), that is, of State organs. There was no cause of action on the basis of diplomatic protection. Also, as the explosions affected non-commercial activities of a State, there was no basis for any claim relating to *lucrum cessans*.[56] The numerous and tricky problems relating to the evaluation of loss of profits did not arise. It is of course quite natural that, in light of the facts of the case, the damages to the two warships were regarded as *damnum emergens*. This deserves no lengthy explanation.

It is nevertheless worth noting that the Court held Albania responsible for the full amount of the damage sustained by both destroyers, despite the fact that the *Volage* was ordered to give assistance to the *Saumarez* after it struck a mine and to take her in tow. Because the *Volage* struck a mine while towing the *Saumarez*, it could have been argued (or considered by the Court) that the UK had to bear part, if not all, of the damage sustained by the *Volage*: after a first mine struck the *Saumarez*, the existence of a mine field would necessarily be suspected and ordering such a rescue mission, involving various ship movements, could have been considered as unnecessarily endangering the remaining fleet. It is a fact that the damage would not have occurred, as it occurred, had the *Volage* not been ordered to tow the *Saumarez*. However, it would have been grossly inappropriate in human and military terms, but also legally unsound, to consider the British Admiralty's order issued to the *Volage* as a decision of the victim having as its effect either the breaking of the causal chain (resulting in Albania not bearing any responsibility for the losses to that ship and its crew), or of being a contributory factor to the damage (resulting in the UK having to sustain part of the damage suffered by the *Volage*). There was of course nothing illegal in the Admiralty's order to the *Volage* and it would be quite far-fetched to consider that it could have had one of those legal effects. The order directed to the *Volage* was rightly not considered as contributory fault within the meaning of what is now Article 39 of the ILC Articles on State Responsibility, nor as the cause of the second explosion. The failure to warn of the presence of the mines was the legal cause of the first and second explosions, as it was fully foreseeable to Albania that its wrongful omissions could result in a mine explosion, which in turn called for an immediate rescue of the damaged ship, despite the risks for the rescuing vessel. The damage to

---

56 See note 61: the UK declined to claim losses resulting from the non-use of the ships. Strictly speaking, those losses are not expected profits lost.

the *Volage* was thus a 'normal', albeit not 'natural', consequence of Albania's wrongful omission, and not the result of a British act which interfered in legal causal terms with the initial Albanian omissions.

Another element worth noting is the fact that the Court awarded the British claim relating to the 'cost of pensions and other grants made by [the UK Government] to victims or their dependants, and for costs of administration, medical treatment, etc.'.[57] According to Christine Gray, 'such an award is unprecedented in international practice'.[58] Strangely enough, the various heads of damage to which the sum of £50,048 corresponded were listed by the Court in an illustrative, and not exhaustive or precise, way. More fundamentally, those different costs had to be borne by Albania despite the fact that their very existence and amount depended on the UK legislation. The administration and medical expenditures were of course straightforwardly linked to the mine incidents – but their precise amount was the result of how much the UK paid its civil servants and medical services. This is even more obvious for pensions and other grants paid to victims or their dependants: the death and injuries physically caused by the mine explosions triggered the application of various domestic legislations fixing entitlements for killed or injured servicemen. Those entitlements were solely a matter of UK law, and its application was clearly not the natural result of the explosions. The fact that the Court considered this expenditure 'proved to [its] satisfaction' and that, consequently, it awarded the amount claimed, is fairly significant as to what causality means in (international) law – a mental construction, rather than an historical or natural process.[59] As in the case of the *Volage*, the interference of an action by the victim State (here, various UK regulations) was (implicitly) not considered by the Court as a decisive concurrent cause having the effect of interrupting the causal chain, nor as a contributory fault requiring some proportional reduction of the compensation awarded. It is of course beyond doubt that, had the explosions not occurred, the UK would not have had to bear the administration and medical costs it claimed. Nevertheless, as far as the pensions costs are concerned, the analysis could have been somewhat more subtle: pensions to soldiers and sailors are normal expenditures for the State when they retire; it is only when those payments have to be anticipated, following an unexpected event, that a specific financial loss occurs. Hence, the Court could have decided to limit the British loss relating to pensions to the cost resulting from their anticipation.[60]

---

57 *Judgment 15 December 1949*, p. 249.
58 C. Gray, *Judicial Remedies in International Law* (Oxford: Clarendon Press, 1987), p. 85. Another (this time unsuccessful) occurrence of pension claims was the one presented by Eritrea to the Eritrea Ethiopia Claims Commission, *Final Award, Pensions, Eritrea's Claims 15, 19, 23*, 19 December 2005 (see note 6).
59 Crawford, op. cit., para. 27, p. 18; see also our developments in P. d'Argent, op. cit., pp. 564–57, 622–626.
60 P. d'Argent, op. cit., p. 644.

350 *Pierre d'Argent*

In its written observations of 28 July 1949, the UK stated that it was entitled to claim compensation in respect of certain additional damages, but renounced doing so. The heads of damage not claimed related to 'sailors who were killed but had no dependants', 'the cost of training other sailors to replace those killed, or for loss of clothing and personal effects', 'the loss of use of the HMS *Volage* during repairs, or the loss of the use of a destroyer during the period which would necessarily elapse before a new destroyer could be put into commission to take the place of the HMS *Saumarez*'.[61] As no compensation was claimed in that regard, 'the Court [concluded that it] need therefore express no view on this subject'.[62] The question whether such heads of damage are compensable was thus left undecided.

20.3.3 *Compensation and monetary assessment of damage*

One of the few authoritative findings contained in the Judgment of 15 December 1949 relates to the moment to be taken in evaluating the damage: '[t]he Court considers the true measure of compensation in the present case to be the replacement cost of the *Saumarez* at the time of its loss'.[63] This moment in time (1946) was also used by the experts in their Report.[64] Even if not entirely clear, nor consistent, practice tends to favour the evaluation of the damage at the time it occurred.[65]

It seems beyond doubt that when a warship has sustained so much damage that it cannot be fixed, its replacement cost fully compensates for such loss. Since compensation serves as a substitute to restitution,[66] the cost of replacing lost property can be considered as the true measure of the damage, at least when such property does not serve any commercial activity. When the property is assigned to a commercial activity, lost profit (*lucrum cessans*) is part of the damage[67] and its value should be added to the replacement value of the lost property (being the cost alternative to restitution) in order to fully compensate for the damage.

The question then arises as to the moment when the replacement cost must be assessed. In the *Corfu Channel* case, three temporal bases of calculation were possible:[68] the construction year of the ship (1943); the time of the loss (1946);

---

61 *Observations Submitted under the Order of the Court of 9th April 1949, by the Government of the United Kingdom of Great Britain and Northern Ireland*, The Corfu Channel case, Pleadings, Oral Arguments, Documents, 1950, Vol. II, para. 6, p. 302.
62 *Judgment of 15 December 1949*, p. 250.
63 Ibid., p. 249.
64 Experts' Report of December 1st, 1949, op. cit., p. 258.
65 C. Gray, op. cit., pp. 80–81. On this question, see generally P. d'Argent, op. cit., pp. 705–707.
66 ILC Articles 34–36, Articles on State Responsibility, A/RES/56/83.
67 Ibid., Article 36, para. 2, Articles on State Responsibility, A/RES/56/83.
68 See *Dissenting Opinion of Judge* ad hoc *Ečer*, op. cit., p. 255.

or the moment of the ruling of the Court (1949). As recalled above, the Court favoured the moment when the loss occurred. Though principled, the Court's assertion on that point is relative, as it appears from the quote itself: it was 'in the present case' that the measure of compensation for the wrecked destroyer was said to be its replacement cost at the time of the loss. It would therefore be wrong to conclude from this judgment that a loss must always be evaluated at the time of its occurrence. Actually, any moment may serve as the temporal reference point in order to evaluate a loss, as long as the necessary adjustments are made in order to truly achieve reparation.

One need simply return to basic premises in order to explain this. From the famous *Chorzów* dictum, it appears that reparation does not mean to re-establish the situation which existed just before the commission of the wrongful act, but rather 'the situation which would, in all probability, have existed if that act had not been committed'.[69] By requiring that reparation result in 'the situation which would . . . have existed' without the wrongful act, international law does not equate the duty to make good the damage with the establishment of the *status quo ante*: restitution is only a form of reparation, and is not tantamount to it.[70] So conceived, reparation seems to be an impossible task, as it requires one to imagine the evolution of a past which actually never existed, having been disrupted by the wrongful act.[71] In order to overcome such an impossible task, the duty to make good the damage may take various forms (restitution, compensation, satisfaction), through (the addition of) which, reparation is legally presumed to be achieved.

The question, however, remains: when is 'the situation which would . . . have existed', and which presumably is achieved through full reparation? The duty to make good the damage is an ongoing obligation: it arises from the day of the wrongful act and it stops after full reparation has been made.[72] Therefore, obviously, it is when it discharges its obligation to make good the damage that the author of the wrongful act must make full reparation – in other words, it is when it is performed that the duty to make good the damage can be said to achieve 'the situation which would . . . have existed' in the absence of the wrongful act. It is only at that moment in time that the completeness of reparation – i.e. compliance with the secondary rule to make up for the all damage – can be assessed. This means that the moment chosen in order to evaluate a loss in monetary terms may vary according to the available evidence, and that once such assessment is made at a certain point in time, interest will have to be added from that point (*dies a quo*) up to 'the date the obligation to pay is fulfilled'[73] (*dies ad*

---

69 *Chorzów Factory (merits), Judgment no. 13, 1928*, PCIJ series A no.17, p. 47.
70 ILC Article 34, Articles on State Responsibility, A/RES/56/83.
71 On the difference between restitution and reparation, and the temporal dimension of reparation, see d'Argent, op. cit., pp. 662–669.
72 The victim of the wrongful act may of course waive, in part or in full, its right to reparation. But this is another matter, which would deserve lengthier developments.
73 ILC Article 38, para. 2, Articles on State Responsibility, A/RES/56/83.

quem). Computing interest is necessary in order to update the past evaluation of the loss, up to the actual performance of the obligation to make good the damage, as monetary erosion exists and as the deprivation of capital over time must be compensated for. Of course, if the loss is evaluated on the day of the judgment, rather than at any previous moment in time, there is no need to add (compensatory) interest in order to update the damage. In such a case, only interest on arrears might be due, from the day of the judgment (*dies a quo*) up to the day of the payment (*dies ad quem*), because delaying payment has a cost for the creditor.

In the *Corfu Channel* case, no interest was added by the Court. The absence of (compensatory) interest computed from the moment chosen to evaluate the loss, i.e. the moment when the damage occurred (22 October 1946), up to the judgment on compensation (15 December 1949) might seem to contradict what has just been explained above. However, if no interest was added, it is simply because, as recalled above, the amount claimed by the United Kingdom was lower than the replacement cost of a destroyer similar to the *Saumarez*, as estimated by the experts. Adding interest would have resulted in some form of *ultra petita* that the Court refused to envisage. Moreover, had interest been computed from October 1946 up to December 1949, such added value would have had to be compensated by the depreciation of the ship over those three years. All in all, one may consider that those calculations – adding interest and deducting depreciation value – would have had a null effect in financial terms. Again, this shows that the Court did not really assess the damage: it just awarded the amount claimed by the British Government, after having checked its reasonableness through an expert opinion.

As far as the absence of interest on arrears from the day of the judgment up to the day of the payment is concerned, the fact that the United Kingdom did not formally request any such interest was certainly decisive. The silence of the operative part of the judgment on interest on arrears does not imply, however, that the UK was barred from claiming, under the general rules of State responsibility, interest on arrears in case of undue delay in payment by Albania. Interest on arrears is not part of the damage on the day of the judgment; hence, it can always be claimed by the creditor after the judgment, from that date to the date of full payment. It is therefore not certain that the ICJ would ever award such interest, even if so requested. One might consider that the Court would be well advised to order interest on arrears if so requested, so as to avoid that the settled dispute be prolonged for that reason. But litigation over the execution of a judgment is always a possibility, being a new dispute different from the one previously settled. The possible reluctance of the Court in that regard might also be explained by some sort of institutional presumption according to which it is understood that States will comply with ICJ decisions in good faith; that is, promptly. Maybe that presumption is too generous, or perhaps even naïve, as the troubled history of compliance in that very case would show. It seems, however, to be central in the reasoning of the

Court when it recently decided not to order appropriate assurances and guarantees of non-repetition.[74]

The amount claimed by the UK and awarded by the Court was in British pounds. The choice of that currency was of course only natural for the claimant. That choice does not seem to have been contested by Albania; it is not discussed by the Court and the experts presented figures in the same currency. Hence, the issue of the choice of currency in the *Corfu Channel* case does not deserve lengthy development.[75]

20.4 Compliance and payment

The fact that Albania declined to appear before the Court at the compensation phase of the proceedings did not augur well for compliance with the final judgment. Non-compliance by Albania with the 1949 compensation judgment[76] was prolonged for over nearly half a century. The long and frustrated story of compliance is briefly summarised here.

In late March 1950, the press reported that, though the date for the discussions had not been fixed, Albania had agreed to initiate talks with the United Kingdom about the implementation of the payment ordered by the Court.[77] Due to the lack of diplomatic relations between the two countries, exchanges were to proceed in Paris between the two embassies. The precise content and scope of those talks remain unknown. It seems that an offer was made by Albania but rejected by the British Government, because it was well below

---

74 *Case Concerning Pulp Mills on the River Uruguay (Argentina v. Uruguay)*, Judgment of 20 April 2010, para. 278, making reference to *Dispute Regarding Navigational and Related Rights (Costa Rica v. Nicaragua)*, Judgment of 13 July 2009, para. 150.
75 The only rules which may exist as far as the currency in which compensation payment is to be made are twofold, and flow from the very notion of reparation as recalled above (see P. d'Argent, op. cit., pp. 714–716): on the one hand, the currency chosen must be easily available to the debtor State, so that it does not incur an additional financial loss by paying the compensation owed (it has been suggested that Albania lacked easy access to sterling currency and that this could have been one of the reasons why it did not comply with the judgment: C. Schulte, *Compliance with Decisions of the International Court of Justice* (Oxford: Oxford University Press, 2004), p. 95, quoting research by J.C.R. Gray, *Much Fine Gold: The History of a Fifty-Year Negotiation* (Cambridge, MA: Harvard Centre for International Affairs Fellow Paper, 1997)); on the other hand, the currency chosen must be stable and worthy enough, otherwise the compensation awarded, despite its nominal value, could quickly become insufficient to make good the damage.
76 By 1958, Albania seemed to have complied with its duty to grant innocent passage in the Corfu Channel, as affirmed in the judgment of 15 April 1949, though this appears only in the reasoning of the Court and not in the operative part: Schulte, op. cit., p. 96.
77 *The Times*, 30 March 1950, *Daily Telegraph*, 31 March 1950.

the amount awarded by the Court.[78] By January 1951, the talks had broken down.[79]

In reaction to the Albanian refusal to pay the full amount awarded, the UK did not resort to Article 94, paragraph 2, of the UN Charter, in light of a highly probable Soviet veto in the Security Council. Instead, it opposed Albania's admission to the United Nations (UN). Then, in 1955, it changed its policy and Albania was admitted to the UN, together with 15 other countries.[80] In 1981, the UK Government proposed to its Albanian counterpart the restoration of diplomatic relations without reaching a settlement on the *Corfu Channel* compensation as a precondition.[81] The Albanian communist authorities declined to do so. Direct diplomatic relations between the two countries were not established before 29 May 1991, after the end of the Cold War.[82]

That major geopolitical change finally allowed for the resolution of the outstanding British claim. On 8 May 1992, after having 'expressed their regret at the Corfu Channel Incident of 22 October 1946',[83] representatives of both governments signed in Rome a memorandum of understanding in order to settle all matters relating to the incident. According to that agreement, the UK was to receive from Albania the sum of US$2 million. The British government agreed to regard the payment of that sum 'as fully and finally settl[ing] [its] financial claims', despite the fact that it was much lower than the sum awarded by the Court (see above). Thus, the Rome Agreement contains a British renunciation of all compensation sums exceeding the US$2 million to be paid by Albania. For its part, the UK Government approved 'the delivery to Albania of some 1574 kgms of gold previously identified for allocation to Albania from the gold pool maintained by the Tripartite Commission for the Restitution of Monetary Gold'.[84] As noted by the agreement, such delivery also required the consent of the French and US governments, the two other

---

78 A. Azar, *L'exécution des décisions de la Cour internationale de Justice* (Bruxelles: Bruylant, 2003), p. 197 affirms that Albania finally offered to pay £40,000 for the final settlement of the dispute. No source is quoted in that regard, but the same amount is mentioned by Schulte, op. cit., p. 96, who refers to the study by J.C.R. Gray, op. cit., pp. 27–28.

79 See the communication of Mr. Ernest Davies, then Foreign Under-Secretary, made to the House of Commons on 29 January 1951, *Keesing's Record of World Events*, vol. VIII, February 1951, United Kingdom, p. 11294, and also Schulte, op. cit., p. 96.

80 See Security Council Resolution 109 (1955) of 14 December 1955. The UK did not abstain nor vote against that resolution.

81 In the 1980s, new efforts were made to try to reach an agreement on compensation: see Schulte, op. cit., p. 97.

82 See http://ukinalbania.fco.gov.uk/en/about-us/our-embassy/embassy-history/ (last accessed May 2010).

83 Albania-United Kingdom Joint Press Statement, Rome, 8 May 1992, reprinted in 'UK Materials on International Law', *BYBIL* (1992): 781.

84 *Albania-United Kingdom, Memorandum of Understanding, Rome, 8 May 1992, ICJ Yearbook, 1995–1996*, p. 257 and also reprinted in 'UK Materials on International Law', *BYBIL* (1992): 781–782.

members of the Tripartite Commission. Three more years were needed in order for agreements to be reached by the US and France with Albania,[85] paving the way for the return of the Albanian gold in October 1996,[86] for an estimated market value of £6.5 million.[87]

The return of the Albanian gold is not to be considered legally as having been made in exchange for the Albanian payment of US$2 million. Indeed, the legal cause of that final, though partial, payment is the ICJ Judgment of 15 April 1949. Nevertheless, that gold had been retained by the United Kingdom by way of a counter-measure, in reaction to Albania's refusal to implement the ICJ ruling in the *Corfu Channel* case.[88] It has to be recalled that, after the fall of the Italian fascist regime, the German occupying forces looted a large quantity of monetary gold from Rome. After having been discovered in Germany in 1945, that gold was taken into the custody of the Western Allied powers. They established the Tripartite Commission for the Restitution of Monetary Gold and entrusted it with the responsibility of deciding on various claims relating to that gold.[89] In 1950–51, the Commission and its three Allied governments were unable to decide on the respective claims by Italy and Albania in respect of a substantial share of that gold. By the Washington Agreement of 25 April 1951, the matter was referred to arbitration. The sole arbitrator, Mr. Sauser-Hall, decided in favour of Albania.[90] According to the terms of the Washington Agreement, the UK was in that case to receive part of the Albanian gold in payment of the 1949 ICJ award, unless Italy or Albania referred the matter to the ICJ. On 19 May 1953, Italy filed an application with the ICJ and asked the Court to order the three Allied governments to deliver to it 'any share of the monetary gold that might be due to Albania . . ., in partial satisfaction of the damage caused to Italy by the Albanian law of January 13th, 1945' and that 'Italy's right to

---

85 *Agreement between the US and Albania on the Settlement of Certain Outstanding Claims*, 34 *ILM* (1995) 597; *Accord relatif au règlement de l'Or monétaire (France-Albanie)*, *RGDIP* (1996): 898 and R. Goy, 'Le sort de l'or monétaire pillé par l'Allemagne pendant la seconde guerre mondiale', *AFDI* (1995): 384.
86 M. Waibel, '*Corfu Channel case*', in *Max Planck Encyclopedia of Public International Law*, Online. Available at: www.mpepil.com (consulted 10 August 2010); Schulte, op. cit., p. 98.
87 *The Independent*, 23 February 1996. In 1996, the worth of the gold held in the Bank of England since 1945 on behalf of the Tripartite Commission was approximately £13 million (US$19 million): 'UK Materials on International Law', *BYBIL* (1996): 818.
88 The idea of obtaining 'payment from frozen Italian funds held in the Bank of England, part of which are due to Albania as war reparations' was concomitant with the Court's ruling on compensation and made public by Maurice Reed, counsel for the British Government: *New York Herald Tribune*, 16 December 1949.
89 *Paris Agreement on Reparation*, open for signature on 14 January 1946, reprinted in M. Hudson, *International Legislation*, vol. IX, 1942–45 (New York: Oceana, 1950), no. 658a, p. 585.
90 *Affaire relative à l'or de la Banque nationale d'Albanie (Etats-Unis d'Amérique, France, Italie, Royaume-Uni)*, 20 February 1953, *RIAA*, vol. XII, pp. 13–52.

receive the said share... must have priority over the claim of the United Kingdom to receive the gold in partial satisfaction of the Judgment in the *Corfu Channel* case'.[91]

As is well known, absent the consent of Albania to its jurisdiction, the Court found – at the subsequent and somewhat paradoxical request of Italy – that it was not authorised to adjudicate upon the Italian submissions.[92] As a result, the Albanian gold remained in the custody of the Bank of England in the name of the Tripartite Commission until the implementation of the 1992 Rome Agreement. The fact that the gold was pooled under the responsibility of the Tripartite Commission prevented the UK from unilaterally appropriating the Albanian gold, but it also allowed it to oppose its early return.

It is rather speculative to wonder whether the symbolic sum of US$2 million was agreed because the income generated by the keeping of the Albanian gold over nearly five decades, and not relinquished by the UK, was considered part of the overall financial settlement. Interest on arrears theoretically accumulated since 1949 are not mentioned either. The minimal content of the Rome Agreement is most certainly a sign that, after so many years, pragmatism prevailed. Such pragmatism stands out against the 'question of principle' approach taken by the British diplomacy during so many years. That approach was of course due to the prevailing geopolitical division of the world, but the authority of the Court – a long-term goal that the UK might have been willing to pursue – indirectly benefited from it. Be that as it may, 'questions of principle' are always diplomatically relative and, often, the law only serves to dress them in clothes of permanency. But political priorities, like fashions, change, and law makes way for other kinds of lastingness.

---

91 *Case of the Monetary Gold Removed from Rome in 1943 (Preliminary Question), Judgment of June 15th, 1954, ICJ Reports 1954*, p. 22.
92 Ibid., p. 34.

21 Conclusion

Hilary Charlesworth

The *Corfu Channel* case occupies a significant place in the history of international law simply by virtue of being the first case decided by the International Court of Justice (ICJ). The Court handed down the judgment in 1949, along with 11 other decisions (judgments, orders and opinions), making that year exceptionally productive at the Peace Palace, as former ICJ President Mohammed Bedjaoui reminds us in his contribution to this volume (Chapter 1). Given the complexity of the issues at stake, the *Corfu Channel Judgment*'s economy of language and analysis is also striking. Quincy Wright pointed out at the time that the Court deployed a broad statement of legal principles 'apparently deemed to be self-evident and stated without citation or precedent or authority'.[1] This suggests a bold and confident Court embarking on a new epoch of international jurisprudence. The buoyant mood is most explicitly expressed by Judge Alvarez in his concurring opinion in the case, rejecting the United Kingdom's assertion of a right to intervene through mine-sweeping in Albania's territorial waters. He refers to the international community entering 'a new era in the history of civilization' and of the 'profound changes [that] have taken place in every sphere of human activity, and above all in international affairs and in international law.' In such a milieu, the Court's role was to develop nothing less than 'the new international law'.[2]

The contributions to this volume indicate, however, that the *Corfu Channel Judgment* has many other claims to significance. It offers a panorama of both procedural and substantive questions that would come before the ICJ over the next 60 years. Here we have discussion of the bases of the ICJ's jurisdiction, the international laws of evidence, reparations and the assessment of damages, the extent of state sovereignty, state responsibility, the law of the sea, the legality of intervention, the limits of self-help and the conditions for the recourse to force in international relations. Some contributors read the judgment as prescient in areas that had not been developed or even imagined in 1949. For

---

1 Q. Wright, 'The *Corfu Channel case*', *American Journal of International Law*, 43 (1949): 494.
2 *Corfu Channel case (United Kingdom v Albania), ICJ Reports 1949*, p. 40.

example, Judge Mohamed Bennouna finds Judge Alvarez's concept of 'social interdependence' a harbinger of the concept of the responsibility to protect, articulated in the first decade of the twenty-first century.[3] Djamchid Momtaz and Amin Ghanbari Amirhandeh similarly explore the concept of 'elementary considerations of humanity' as a watershed in the interaction between human rights law and international humanitarian law as it articulated a principle common to both regimes to be used as a bridge between them. Karine Bannelier focuses on the *Corfu Channel Judgment*'s contributions to international environmental law through enunciating the 'due diligence' principle that no State has the right to use or permit the use of its territory in such a manner as to cause damage to others.[4] Theodore Christakis highlights the continuing relevance of the Court's condemnation of the use of unilateral forcible intervention by a State to redress an *injuria* to secure possession of evidence or to remedy the defects of the UN Charter's collective security machinery. Sarah Heathcote argues that the case both reaffirmed the fundamental international law principle of due diligence and helped to shape its place in the International Law Commission's future architecture on the law of state responsibility. Olivier Corten and Pierre Klein examine another aspect of the Court's use of due diligence, as a type of substitute for the difficult concept of complicity. Don Rothwell uses the case to discuss the development of the law regulating passage through international straits. Although many of the issues that have arisen in this area could not have been predicted by the *Corfu Channel* Court, he suggests that the ICJ's concern to balance the rights of coastal and maritime states is an enduring one. And Stuart Kaye emphasises the way that the *Corfu Channel Judgment* continues to shape disputes over freedom of navigation. Whatever the Court's success in foreshadowing the future of international law, the *Corfu Channel Judgment* at least planted some seeds that have since grown and flowered.

While there is much to be lauded in the *Corfu Channel Judgment*, this rich collection also subjects the opinions of the court to searching critique and analysis. For example, Katherine Del Mar highlights the ICJ's awkward jurisprudence relating to standards of proof: while the Court claims that charges of exceptional gravity 'must be proved by evidence that is fully conclusive', it in fact relies on implied knowledge from the circumstances of the case. Henry Burmester criticises the Court's use of the principle of *forum prorogatum* to overcome tricky questions of consent. Christine Gray suggests that the judgment offers little clarity on the international norms relating to the use of force and she notes the strange absence of references to Article 2(4) of the United Nations (UN) Charter with its prohibition on the use of force in international relations. Matthew Zagor contends that the Court's invocation of the notion of 'essential considerations of humanity' is left both vague and essentialised. Akiho Shibata observes the ICJ's lack of attention to the sources of interna-

---

3 Ibid.
4 Ibid., p. 22.

tional law, while Pierre d'Argent exposes the Court's lack of clarity with respect to causality.

The *Corfu Channel Judgment* illustrates nicely a tension in modern international law perceptively elucidated by Martti Koskenniemi in *From Apology to Utopia: the Structures of International Legal Argument*.[5] The apologetic, or positivist, tendencies emerge, for example, in the Court's reliance on state practice as a source of law. The interwoven utopian strands of argument are found in the articulation of the post-UN Charter international legal order, including concepts such as 'elementary considerations of humanity' and 'social interdependence'. The result is a complex fusion of arguments justifying state behaviour and arguments resting on grand normative visions of the international order. This is both an appealing and frustrating aspect of international legal argument. Rob McLaughlin's chapter examines apologetic and utopian arguments in the *Corfu Channel* case in the context of innocent passage of warships, preferring the pragmatic apologists in the majority who endorsed a right of passage without authorisation or notification.

More broadly, this collection shows that the *Corfu Channel Judgment* can be understood as a microcosm of issues implicated in all international adjudication. For example, recourse to the Court is always a product of a particular political context and, although the ICJ generally avoids articulating it, this context shapes the arguments presented to and the decision made by the Court. In the *Corfu Channel* case the simmering politics of the Cold War, described in this book in valuable detail by Aris Constantinides, steer the ICJ towards a judgment that allows both parties to claim a legal victory. The Court avoids ruling on who laid the mines in the Corfu Channel, but finds on the one hand that Albania was responsible for the mine explosions and the damage that they caused to the British ships; on the other hand, the Court rejects the United Kingdom's claim of a right to intervention and self-help through minesweeping Albania's territorial waters in *Operation Retail*.

At the same time, the *Corfu Channel* case is also testament to the power of international law. Theodore Christakis reminds us that, even a few years earlier, the dispute between the United Kingdom and Albania might well have been resolved through the use of force. The adoption of the UN Charter in 1945 made recourse to force more complicated. The United Kingdom was unable to obtain a remedy for Albania's mining of the Corfu Channel in the UN Security Council and the UN's new judicial institution appeared a useful method of achieving some resolution of the United Kingdom's grievances. For its part, Albania's agreement to submit the dispute to the ICJ's jurisdiction provided a form of international respectability.

As Judge Kenneth Keith shows us in this book, the *Corfu Channel* case is relevant to objections to the disclosure of evidence, an issue of considerable

---

5 M. Koskenniemi, *From Apology to Utopia: The Structures of International Legal Argument* (Cambridge: Cambridge University Press, 2006).

modern relevance in our security-conscious age. The ICJ did not challenge the United Kingdom's refusal to disclose certain documents on the grounds of protecting naval secrecy and Judge Keith traces a trend towards greater governmental openness since the case. He also proposes some valuable guidelines to promote democratic accountability. Another recurring issue in international adjudication illustrated in the *Corfu Channel* case is that of enforcement of judgments. In this case the ICJ's award of damages against Albania was not realised until after the end of the Cold War. An agreement in 1992 between the United Kingdom and Albania stipulated that Albania would pay US$2 million for the damage caused and that the United Kingdom would deliver 1,576 kilogrammes of gold looted by the Germans during the Second World War to Albania. Despite the forty-year delay, the Court's judgment provided a form of political pressure on Albania over that period.

The conference on which this book is based was held at the Australian National University in Canberra in October 2009 and this makes it appropriate to recall Australia's earlier connections with the *Corfu Channel* case. Australia was a member of UN Security Council at the time of the Corfu Channel incidents in 1946 and successfully pressed for the Council to establish a sub-committee of enquiry into them, under Article 35 of the UN Charter. The sub-committee's report disappointed both Australia and the United Kingdom by failing to make any clear finding on responsibility for laying the mines that had damaged the British ships in the Corfu Channel.[6] A Security Council resolution condemning Albania for laying the mines, or allowing them to be laid, was vetoed by the Soviet Union, but the Council later recommended that the dispute be submitted to the ICJ. The background to these events is helpfully recounted in this book in Chapter 5 by Giovanni Distefano and Etienne Henry. They point out that the Security Council's encouragement for the United Kingdom to take its case to the ICJ was an unusual step and one that has not been repeated since. Henry Burmester's chapter in turn considers whether the Security Council resolution successfully conferred jurisdiction on the Court.

Australia then sought to become involved in the United Kingdom's preparations for the ICJ case. Laurence Maher has provided a detailed account of the role of Australia's mercurial and controversial Deputy Prime Minister, Attorney-General and Minister for External Affairs, Herbert Vere Evatt, leading up the oral arguments in the case. Dr Evatt offered to appear as counsel for the United Kingdom when the case was argued in the ICJ, causing both alarm and embarrassment in the British Foreign Office. Evatt's offer appears to have been based on his sense that the case would involve significant legal issues: for him, 'international good behaviour' was at stake as well as the question of

---

6 L.W. Maher, 'Half Light between War and Peace: Herbert Vere Evatt, the Rule of International Law, and the *Corfu Channel case*', *Australian Journal of Legal History*, 3 (2005): 29–42.
7 Ibid., p. 95.

circumstantial evidence.[7] One British objection to Dr Evatt's appearance before the ICJ was the public confusion it might cause: '[p]eople in England, indeed the whole world, would be startled and puzzled at the inclusion in the team of an Australian lawyer who is also Australia's Foreign Minister' wrote the British Legal Adviser to the Foreign Office, W.E. Beckett, to Sir Hartley Shawcross, the British Attorney-General.[8] Another objection was based on Evatt's maverick personality, making him difficult for the British legal team to control.[9] In the end, Dr Evatt received a carefully phrased response from the British government, tactfully refusing his offer in the *Corfu Channel* litigation, but suggesting that he might like to appear before the ICJ in the Advisory Opinion on *Conditions of Admission of a State to Membership in the United Nations*[10] representing both Australia and the United Kingdom's views.[11] He accepted this rebuff with good grace. This book provides a fuller context to this Australian story in Judge Jean-Pierre Cot's lively account of the litigation's atmospherics.

This book celebrates 60 years of a case decided by the ICJ. Why do we seize on anniversaries as the catalyst for assessment of people, events or ideas? The literary critic Frank Kermode has pointed out that anniversaries are milestones that everyone understands and that they provide a 'complex comfort', allowing us to 'project our existential anxieties onto history'.[12] And so it is with the *Corfu Channel Judgment*. Looking back at the reasoning and repercussions of the case allows international lawyers to understand that their modern anxieties have a history, a pedigree, and that their discipline can only ever provide partial and imperfect solutions to complicated political problems.

8 Quoted in ibid., p. 79.
9 Ibid.
10 *ICJ Reports 1948*, p. 61.
11 Quoted in Maher, op. cit., p. 89.
12 F. Kermode, *The Sense of an Ending* (Oxford: Oxford University Press, 1967), p. 11.

Index

In this index notes are indicated by n.

1975 Statute 251, 252, 254, 340
9/11 attacks, and due diligence 306

Abolition Bill 1807 270
abstention, harmful 108
acts/omissions, and standard of proof 108–15
Aden, Yemen 191
aerial reconnaissance, *Corfu Channel* case 143
Afghanistan, and due diligence 306
Africa, colonisation of 271
African Slavery in America 270
agency (political), and warships 167–8
aggressive humanitarianism 271
Ago, Roberto 304, 308, 309, 310, 311, 344
aircraft, and transit passage 152–3, 187
aircraft carriers, and innocent passage 191
Ajax, HMS 38
Ajibola, Judge 106, 229
Albania; communist 42; and Greece 43; opening fire on British cruisers 21, 31; and Yugoslavia 22, 24, 42–3, 46, 51, 57
Albanian Ministry of Defence 57
Albanian territorial waters 44
Al-Khasawneh, Judge 104, 254–5, 340
Al-Qaida, and due diligence 306
Alvarez, Judge 16, 167, 177, 178, 179–80, 212, 264, 284; Individual Opinion of 232
Ambatielos case 73
Angel, Zuleta 76
Anglo-Iranian Oil Co (Preliminary Objections) case 96
Anzilotti, D. 302, 304

Application of the Convention on the Prevention and Punishment of the Crime of Genocide case *see Genocide* case
Application of the International Convention on the Elimination of All Forms of Racial Discrimination; (Georgia v. Russian Federation) see Georgia v. Russian Federation
Aranha, Mr 64, 66
archipelagic sealanes passage, restrictions for vessels 162
archipelagic States; and right of passage 151; security measures of 157
Argentina v. Uruguay see Pulp Mills case
Armed Activities on the Territory of the Congo (DRC v. Uganda) see Congo v. Uganda case
armed conflicts, international human rights law 261–3
Arrest Warrant case 208
Assembly of State Parties 134
Asylum case 201, 202, 209
asylum, right to be granted 201, 286
attenuating circumstances, and responsibility 224, 313
Australia, and *Corfu Channel* case 360–1
Australian Maritime Safety Authority, Marine Notice 8/2006 161
Australian representative, Security Council 48–9, 62n.11, 64–5, 77–8
authorisation/notification requirements, warships 175–6
Avena case 118, 120
awareness of the unity of humankind 288
Azevedo, Judge: Dissenting Opinion of 230–1

Barcelona Traction case 18, 268, 277, 280, 284
bar, the 21–38

Basdevant, J. 303
Beckett, Eric 23, 24–5, 31, 32, 33, 36, 136, 138, 140, 213, 214, 215, 234, 236, 239
Belgrade, bombing of 19
Berck, J.B. 339
Berlin West Africa Conference 1884 271
best efforts obligations 309
Biggs, Ronald 171
Black Sea Bumping Incident 169, 192
Black Sea, *Case Concerning Maritime Delimitation in the Black Sea* 103
Blair, Tony 216, 238
Bolton, John 233
Bosnia and Herzegovina v. Serbia and Montenegro 7, 81–2, 87, 100, 113, 115, 300–2, 307, 309, 311, 326–7, 346–7
Brazilian representative, Security Council 63
breaches of peremptory norms 115–16; *jus cogens* 17
breach of obligations 122, 309, 311, 324
Briand-Kellogg Pact 211
British Memorial 32–3
Buergenthal, Judge 105
burdon of proof 10, 11
Bush, George W. 239

Cadogan, Alexander 3–4, 61
Cameroon and Nigeria, *Land and Maritime Boundary between Cameroon and Nigeria* 106, 220, 229
Canada; and disclosure 131; International Commission on Intervention and State Sovereignty 19
Canal, Kiel 303
Cape Kiephali 52
Caricom 158
Caroline incident 164
Caron, USS 169, 192
Carty, Anthony 32, 137, 142, 144
Case Concerning Armed Activities on the Territory of the Congo see Congo v. Uganda case
Case Concerning Avena and Other Mexican Nationals see Avena case
Case Concerning Certain Criminal Proceedings in France 117–18
Case Concerning Maritime Delimitation in the Black Sea 103

Case Concerning Pulp Mills on the River Uruguay (Argentina v. Uruguay) see Pulp Mills case
Case Concerning Sovereignty over Pedra Branca/Pulau Batu Puteh, Middle Rocks and South Ledge 103
Case concerning Sovereignty over Pulau Ligitan and Pulau Sipadan 102
Cassese, Antonio 275, 283–4, 288
causality 349; *Corfu Channel* case 344–7; natural/normative 310
causes, multiple 345
Celebici case 285
Central International Mine Clearance Board 46, 313
Certain Questions of Mutual Assistance in Criminal Matters (Djibouti v. France) see Djibouti v. France
character of transit, and innocent passage 173–4
charges: serious, and standard of proof 107
Charter of International Military Tribunal 259
Cheviot, HMS 38
Childers, HMS 38
choke points, international straits 194
Chorzów dictum 338, 343, 351
Chorzów Factory 15
Churchill, Robin 165
claims, gravity of claim 106, 122
Clark, I. 270
climate change, and navigation 185
coastal States; and innocent passage 188; rights/interests of 181, 196; security threats to 191; and transit passage 154–5; and warship compliance 191–2
coercive action, and sovereignty 222, 223
Cold War 3, 14, 21–2, 24, 43, 46, 56, 58, 62, 95, 136, 187, 235, 238–41, 297, 354, 359–60
Cole, USS 191
collusion, and *Corfu Channel* case 323
Colombian representative, Security Council 76
colonisation of Africa 271
comity view, warship innocent passage 177
common law courts, changing practice in 125–30
common law rules 28
common sense, and humanity 283

compensation; *Corfu Channel* case 53–6, 337–43, 350–6; and *forum prorogatum* 92; and ICJ jurisdiction 5, 14–15, 53, 92
complete dependency 112
complicity; concept of 330–1; and *Corfu Channel* case 315–24; difficulties with 322, 328–31; and due diligence 332; and *Genocide case* 305n., 326–31; and the ICJ 325; and *Nicaragua v. USA* 325, 327; usefulness of 334
comprehensive/complete case, *Corfu Channel* case as 5
Conditions of Admission of a State to Membership in the United Nations 361
Condorelli, L. 301
Congo v. Uganda case 81, 99n., 119, 220, 229, 230, 233, 240, 262, 310
connivance 25, 51, 323
conscious political agency, and warships 167–8
consent; and *Corfu Channel* case 8–9, 94–5; and *forum prorogatum* 97; State 75, 87
considerations of common humanity 206
constitutional cosmopolitanism 291
contentious case, *Corfu Channel* case as 4–5
contribution to injury 313–14, 348
control principle 129, 130
Convention on the Elimination of all Forms of Racial Discrimination 262
Convention on the Prevention and Punishment of the Crime of Genocide *see* Genocide Convention
Convention on the Territorial Sea and Contiguous Zone 1958 149–50, 151, 158, 163, 179, 183
Cordova, Robert 178
Corfu Channel; as international strait 31, 204; prior to mine explosions 43–5
Corfu Channel case; and attitude of British Government 212; background 21, 31, 41–9, 88; contrasting pleadings in 234–5; distinguishing features of 3–15; ICJ's factual findings 50–3; in light of subsequent practice 142–4; institution of proceedings 7–9; jurisdictional basis 88–91; language of the Court 228–30; Merits phase 25; oral pleadings 25; processing period 6;

risk of *non liquet* 257; and satisfaction 335–6; Separate and Dissenting Opinions 230–2; significance of 357–61; sources in 201–10; written pleadings 25; *see also Operation Retail*; Special Agreement 1948
Corfu Channel question, Security Council 47–9
corporate social responsibility 306
corruption, and due diligence 306
Corten, Oliver 216, 220–1, 222
Cot, Pierre 3, 23, 24–5, 27, 28, 29, 30, 32, 37, 138, 139, 142, 214, 227, 321
Council of the League of Nations 60, 64
court responsibilities, disclosure 145
Courts, and standards of proof 101–6
Covenant of the League of Nations 1919 211
Covenant on Economic, Social and Cultural Rights (CESCR) 262
Crawford, James 109, 116, 311, 314, 344
Crawford, N. 271
crimes against humanity 4, 259
criminal responsibility 58
Crown immunity 135
Cuba, and United States 35
culpa, and State responsibility 302
customary international law 203, 205, 209, 237
customary law, and *opinio juris* 205
custom, establishment of 201–2, 203–5

damages; Albanian responsibility for 337; computing interest 352; *Genocide case* 311; heads of 348–50; ICJ jurisdiction to assess 337–8; mitigation of/extenuating circumstances 224–5; monetary assessment of 350–3
damnum emergens 348
Danae, HMS 170–1
De Cara, Judge 117–18
Declaration against the Slave Trade 270
Declaration on Friendly Relations 333
declarative function of Court, and standards of proof 101–4, 122
delimitation; of maritime boundary 103; territorial 101–2
Denmark, and warships 176
Denta Point 52
determinative function of Court, and standards of proof 104–6, 121
Diderot, D. 269

Dijbouti v. France 93–4, 95–6, 97, 134–5
diplomacy, gunboat 168
diplomatic asylum, right of 201
diplomatic protection; and human rights 18–19; of ships 166
diplomatic relations, UK/Albania 55–6, 353–4
disclosure; and Canada/New Zealand 131; changing practices in 128; and *Corfu Channel* case 136–42; court responsibilities 145; of documents 126–7; and judicial power 127; limited 133; role of legislation in regulating 130–5
Dispute Regarding Navigational and Related Rights case 252
doctrine of humanitarian intervention *see also* humanitarian intervention 18
documents *see also* evidence; XCU documents; disclosure of 126–7; withholding of 125–6
dolus, and State responsibility 302
dolus specialis 113
Draft Articles on Prevention of Transboundary Harm from Hazardous Activities 132, 243, 253
Draft Articles on the Law of the Non-Navigational Uses of International Watercourses 243, 247, 252
draft resolution 1947 49, 61, 77, 78
Droit Naturel 269
due diligence; and breaches of obligations 301; categorisation of 307–12; and complicity 328–31, 332; concept of 330–1; contours/content of 251–4; and *Corfu Channel* case 244–8, 295–9, 312, 324; and corruption 306; customary character of 248–50; a dimension without borders 245–6; and environmental law 243, 254; and fault 299–305; and *Genocide* case 326–31; justifying a breach of law 307; and knowledge of unlawful activity/situation 246–7; and *Nicaragua v. USA* 325; and minelaying 319; and non-State actors 305–6, 312; and obligation of conduct 308; obligation to inform/notify 247–8; and omissions 16, 309–12; *Operation Retail* 313–14; prevalence of obligations 305–7; principle 242–3, 297–9; and sovereignty 298; and *Trail Smelter* case 244, 247–8, 251, 297–8, 299n.

Dupuy, Pierre-Marie 208
duty of humanitarian intervention 16, 17, 19, 240

Economic Agreement 1946, Albania/Yugoslavia 42–3
Ečer, Judge 303, 345; Dissenting Opinion of 231
Egypt, and British troops in Egypt/Sudan 67
Elaraby, Judge 233
Elbe, Joachim von 212
elementary considerations of humanity 208, 286; *Corfu Channel* case 13, 207, 296; ICJ use of 257–60; *Nicaragua V. USA* 209, 261, 279; *see also* chapter 17
elementary principles of morality 267
El-Salvador/Honduras 102
empathy, universal 273
Encyclopédie 269
enforcement of laws/regulations, strait States 189
Entebbe raid case 223
environmental impact assessments 253–4
environmental issues 196; ships/marine environment 189; and strait States 188
environmental law 15; and *Corfu Channel* case 244, 298; development of 242; and humanity 287–8
environmental protection 120–1; and due diligence principle 254; and ICJ 248
environment, marine 120–1
équivalence des conditions? l' 345
erga omnes obligations 267, 268, 277, 284
Eritrea/Ethiopia case 230
Espoo Convention 253, 254
European Court of Human Rights 262–3
European Journal of International Law 288
Evatt, Herbert Vere 23–4n., 360–1
evidence *see also* documents; XCU documents; circumstantial 300; *Corfu Channel* case 9–12, 26–9, 124, 217–19; disclosure of 359–60; obtained by unlawful means 217–19; *Operation Retail* 24–5, 37, 214, 217–19, 228; withholding of 127
exclusive economic zones (EEZs) 185–6; and ultra-hazardous cargoes 158

executive decisions, to withhold evidence 127
Exercise Corfu 45–6
experts, *Corfu Channel* case 29–30, 338–43
extenuating circumstances; and mitigation of damages 224–5; *Operation Retail* 313

fact-finding, Security Council 75–9, 80, 81
fault; and due diligence 299–305; and level of reparations 304; objectivised 304; and State responsibility 302–5
Fitzmaurice, Gerald 178, 179
Fitzmaurice, M.A. 16
flag State law, and warships 171
force majeure 304–5
forum prorogatum 8, 74, 87–97, 358
Four-Power Agreement 1945 259
Fourteen Points, for 'open covenants of peace, openly arrived at' 131–2
France, *Case Concerning Certain Criminal Proceedings in France* 117–18
François, JPA 178
Freedman, E. 217
freedom of navigation 13, 182, 196
Freedom of Navigation (FON) program 162, 169
French Communist Party 24
From Apology to Utopia: The Structures of International Legal Argument 359
fundamental human rights 258
fundamental standards of humanity 286

Gabcikovo-Nagymaros Project case 120, 248, 249–50, 252
Gaja, G. 276
gap-filling function; of general principles 207–8, 209; of law 278; principle of humanity 279
General Assembly, and human rights violations 19
General Assembly Resolution 2625 (XXV) 333
Geneva Conference 12
Geneva Conventions 1958 181; Article 3 209, 261, 280, 284; Article 72 Additional Protocol 260; and freedom of navigation 182; and human rights 259
Genocide case; and acts/omissions 115, 116; and complicity 305n., 316, 326–31; and *Corfu Channel* case 7; and damage 311; and due diligence 300, 301, 305n., 307–8, 309, 326–31; fact finding 81; and omission 346–7; and standards of proof 105, 106, 107, 113, 115
Genocide Convention 96; Article III(e) 327, 328; Article IX 328; and Serbia 115
Genocide Convention Reservation Advisory Opinion 267
genocide, failure to prevent 329
Gentle Civilizer of Nations 273–4
Georgia v. Russian Federation 118–20, 262
German Y mines 51, 318
Germany v. United States of America 118n.
Gidel, Gilbert 176–7, 178
global war on terror 235
gold, Albanian as compensation 5n.5, 54–6, 355–6
good neighbourliness, obligations/ principle of 13, 243
Goodwin-Gill, Guy 286
grants, to victims/dependants 349
gravity of claim, and standards of proof 106, 122
Gray, Christine 216
great train robber 171
Greece; and Albania 43; and Turkey 67
Greek civil war 22
Greek Government, and *Operation Retail* 34
Gromyko, Andrei 4, 66, 77
Guantanamo bay 129
Guerrero, Acting President 29–30
Guggenheim, P. 303
gunboat diplomacy 168, 212
Guyana/Suriname case 230

Hague Codification Conference 1930 149, 176, 179; Draft Article 12 177
Hague Conference debates 1930 179
Hague Conventions 1899/1907, laws of humanity 264, 266
Hague Conventions for the Peaceful Settlement of Disputes 136
Hague Convention VIII 1907; and obligation to warn others 13, 30, 182, 205–7; *Relative to the Laying of Automatic Submarine Contact Mines* 298; and right of intervention 35; *travaux préparatoires* 204
Hague Court, interpretation in 22
Hague, The 14

Index

hampering of passage 154–9; and Marine Notice 8/2006 161
harmful abstention 108
Hasluck, Mr 64–5, 77
hazardous activities, *Draft Articles on Prevention of Transboundary Harm from Hazardous Activities* 132, 243, 253
Henkin, Louis 276
Higgins, Judge 105, 106
High-level Panel on Threats, Challenges and Change 2003 19
Hodgson, Colonal 62n.11, 65
Hodja (Hoxha), Enver 22, 42
Honoré, Tony 108–9
Hostie, J. 302
Huber, Max 242–3, 297, 303
humanitarian assistance at sea, and humanity 287–8
humanitarian intervention 16, 17, 19, 240–1, 236, 238, 288, 291, 307
humanitarian law, humanization of 286
humanity; and common sense 283; considerations of common 206; elevation of 290; fundamental standards of 286; and humanitarian assistance at sea 287–8; idea of 268; and inhumane conduct 284; and international community 277; law 285; as normative concept 269–78; principle of 279, 281, 282, 286–7; sentiments of 264–5; and sovereignty 288
humanity-based identification program 286
human rights 18; in armed conflicts 260–3; law/universal empathy 273; violations/and General Assembly 19; violations/duty of intervention 17
human security 18
Hume, David 272–3
Hunt, Lynn 273

ICJ; coercive power of 135; and compensation 53, 92; *Djibouti v. France* 134–5; and due diligence/complicity 325, 332–3; functions/power of 61–7; and HRL in armed conflicts 261–3; ideological/political affiliation of judges 58; institution of proceedings 7–9; and international human rights law/international humanitarian law 256–63; jurisdiction of 7–9, 15, 71–5, 88, 90, 94–5, 337–8; and policy of force 227; referral of Corfu Channel incident to 49; and Security Council 3–4, 8, 21, 63–4, 67–70, 67–75, 75–82, 83; and use of force 226, 229, 230–3
ICTY; and evidence 134, 136; and humanity 283, 286, 289
ILC *see* International Law Commission
immunity, State/Crown 135, 136
impact assessments, environmental 253–4
impartiality, and Security Council 63, 65, 78
Impeccable, USNS 170
incidental proceedings, and standard of proof 117
incidental wrongful acts 322
INCSEA Agreement 1972 166–7
Indonesian Navy, and *Lusitanio Expresso* 193
information, categories of 127 *see also* documents; evidence; XCU documents
inhumane conduct 268, 284
injuria: redress of, and right of intervention 213–15
innocence, defining 172–3
innocent passage 30–3; and character of transit 173–4; and coastal States 188; *Corfu Channel* case 140–1, 144, 163, 173, 176–7; and international straits 151; and normal mode of navigation 191; presumption of innocence 192; right to 12–13; and security 178; and submarines 162–3, 192; and transit passage 152–4; and ultra-hazardous cargoes 159; and warships 31, 149, 157–8, 174–5, 177, 190–3, 204
Institute of International Law 302
Institute of Nautical Archaeology 57
intelligence collecting operations, at sea 169–70
intelligence sharing arrangements, UK/US 129–30
interest; on arrears 356; computing 352
International Atomic Energy Agency 132
International Central Mine Clearance Board 43
International Committee of the Red Cross (ICRC) 134
international community, and humanity 277
International Convention on Maritime Search and Rescue 196

International Convention on the Elimination of All Forms of Racial Discrimination 118–19
International Court of Justice *see* ICJ
International Covenant on Civil and Political Rights (ICCPR) 261
International Criminal Court; Article 72 133–4; Rule 73 134
International Criminal Tribunal on the Former Yugoslavia (ICTY); and evidence 134, 136; and humanity 283, 286, 289
international environmental law *see* environmental law
International Health Regulations 2005 132
international humanitarian law (IHL), and international human rights law 256–63
international human rights law (HRL); and international humanitarian law (IHL) 256–63; and UN Charter 259; and Universal Declaration of Human Rights (UDHR) 259
international law; and acts/omissions 108–15; customary 203, 209; development of and ICJ 15, 17; and humanity 259, 288; new 82, 179–80, 212, 357; primary/secondary rules of 225; sources of 201–10; teleological 291; and *Trail Smelter* case 242; use of force 216; and war 212; *see also* individual laws
International Law Association 204
International Law Commission (ILC); *Articles on State Responsibility for Internationally Wrongful Acts* 17, 109, 116, 224, 311, 315, 328, 343, 348; Articles 4–11 302; Article 12 308; Article 14(3) 309, 311; Article 16 325, 328, 333; Article 25 224; Article 26 224; Article 37 343; Article 39 225, 348; Article 40 109, 116; Article 41 107; *Draft Articles on State Responsibility for Internationally Wrongful Acts* – as provisionally adopted 1996; draft Article 11 301; draft Article 20 308; draft Article 21 308; draft Article 21(2) 308–9; draft Article 23 309; draft Article 27 326; *Draft Articles on the Law of the Non-Navigational Uses of International Watercourses* 243, 247, 252; *Draft Articles on the Prevention of Transboundary Harm from Hazardous Activities* 132, 243, 253; and law of the sea 149; and right of passage 150–1; Special *Rapporteur* on State Responsibility 109, 116, 243, 311, 314
internationally wrongful acts 325
International Maritime Organization (IMO) 196; Marine Environment Protection Committee 160; Resolution A.710(17) 160; Resolution MEPC 133(53) 160, 161
international obligation 10
international relations; juridification of 289; use of force 211
international responsibility 9, 10–11, 13, 61
International Routeing and Reporting Authority 44
international straits; categories of 182, 183–6; Corfu Channel as 31, 204; defined 151–2; and increasing size of territorial sea 194; and Law of the Sea Convention 1982 151; provisions dealing with 149; right of passage 150; State restrictions on 155–7; transit passage through 186–9; and warships 163
international trade, and ships 150
international transportation 149
international watercourses, *Draft Articles on the Law of the Non-Navigational Uses of International Watercourses* 243, 247, 252
interpretation, in Hague Court 22
interstitial norms 209
intervention, right of *see* right of intervention
Iran, minelaying 111–12
Iraq war 216, 226, 238
irreparable prejudice, risk of 117–18
Island of Palmas case 242, 243n., 244, 297, 332t.19.1
Italy, and Albanian gold 355–6
ITLOS, and use of force to arrest ships 287

Jacquier, Marc 24
Johnson, Mr 65
Jones, Mervyn 23
Jørgensen, N.H.B. 280
Judgement on Preliminary Objections 1948 71
judgement on the Merits 1949 53

Judges; ideological/political affiliation of 58; role of 9–10; *see also* names of individual Judges
judicial power, and disclosure 127
jurisdiction; and *Corfu Channel* case 88–91; criminal/civil of coastal States 189; exclusivity of 14; and *forum prorogatum* 92, 93; of ICJ 7–9, 71–5, 94, 95, 337–8
jurisprudence, and *Corfu Channel* case 6–7
jus cogens, breaches of peremptory norms 17
justiciability of disputes 69

Karibi-Whyte, Judge 145
Keith, Judge 104, 340
Al-Khasawneh, Judge 104, 254–5, 340
Kinahan, Rear Admiral 137
Koskenniemi, Martti 273–4, 290, 291, 359
Kosovo 19, 57, 226, 238–9, 240
Kovacic, Commander 28, 29, 51, 319, 320, 323
Kravchenko, Victor 22
Kristi case 107
Krylov, Judge 303; Dissenting Opinion of 231
Kupreskic case 285

Lachs, Judge 69
LaGrand case 118
Lake Lanoux case 242, 243, 247–8
Land and Maritime Boundary between Cameroon and Nigeria 106, 220, 229
Lapenna, Professor 24
Latin America, and U.S. 271
Lauterpacht, Hersch 23, 69, 96, 178, 277–8, 302
Law Against War, The 221–2
law of necessity *see* state of necessity
law of non-navigational uses of international watercourses, *Draft Articles on the Law of the Non-Navigational Uses of International Watercourses* 243, 247, 252
law of self-defence 239–40
law of State responsibility 338
law of the sea 149; and *Corfu Channel* case 182; and humanity 287; modern 196
Law of the Sea Convention 1982; Article 17 190; Article 18(2) 196; Article 19 162, 190, 192, 193; Article 19(2)(c) 174; Article 19(2)(f) 191; Article 20 192; Article 21 191; Article 23 159; Article 27 189; Article 28 189; Article 29–32 190; Article 30 158, 191; Article 34 189; Article 35(c) 152; Article 37 151–2; Article 38 154, 157; Article 38(2) 186; Article 39 162, 187, 188, 189; Article 41 154; Article 42 153, 157; Article 42(2) 154; Article 44 153, 187; Article 98 195; Article 221 189; Article 233 189; Article 290 120; and coastal/maritime States 181; and freedom of navigation 182; and international straits 151; and jurisdiction based on security 157; navigational regimes 183; part III 183–6; and submarines 162–3; and transit passage 163, 194; and UN Charter 155; and warships 158
League of Nations; Council of 60, 64; Covenant of 211
League of Nations Codification Conference 1930, draft Article 12 203, 204
Leander, HMS 21, 45
Legal Consequences for States of the Continued Presence of South Africa in Namibia (South West Africa) notwithstanding Security Council Resolution see South West Africa case
Legal Consequences of the Construction of a Wall in the Occupied Palestinian Territory see Wall Advisory Opinion
legality, and UN reform process 19
Legality of the Threat or Use of Nuclear Weapons case *see Nuclear Weapons* case
LeGrand case 118n.
liability, no-fault 299–305
litigating parties, role of 9–10
LOSC *see* Law of the Sea Convention 1982
Lotus, SS 166n.6
Lowe, Vaughan 165, 209
lucrum cessans 348
Lusitanio Expresso, and Indonesian Navy 193

Madrid bombings 81
Malacca Straits 196
Marine Environment Protection Committee; (IMO) 160
marine environment, ships causing damage to 189

Marine Notice 8/2006, Australian Maritime Safety Authority 161
Marine Orders Part 54, *Navigation Act 1912* 161
maritime boundaries, delimitation of 103
maritime delimitation, *Case Concerning Maritime Delimitation in the Black Sea* 103
maritime security 196
maritime States, rights/interests of 181
Martens Clause; dictates of public conscience 270, 278; and evolution of military technology 282; and humanity 258, 264, 268, 288; as positive normative principle 274–5
Martineau, A. 291
Mauritius, HMS 21, 38, 45, 138
McCaffrey, Stephen C. 243
McKinley, President 271
Mediterranean, mines in 43–4
Mediterranean Route Instructions (MEDRI) Charts/booklets 44
Mediterranean Zone Board (Medzon) 34, 44, 46
Meljine 51, 318, 319
Meljt 318, 319
Memorandum of Understanding 1992 55
Meron, Theodor 282–3, 285–6, 290
Messina Exception 152
Mestre, Commander 47
Michalowski, Mr 66
Middle Rocks, *Case Concerning Sovereignty over Pedra Branca/Pulau Batu Puteh, Middle Rocks and South Ledge* 103
Military and Paramilitary Activities in and against Nicaragua see Nicaragua v. USA
Miljet 51
mine clearing operation, United Kingdom 14 *see also* Operation Retail
mine explosions, in Corfu Channel 45
minefields, obligation to notify 205–6, 207
minelaying; *Nicaragua v. USA* 112; *Oil Platforms* case 111–12; responsibility for 50–1, 56–7, 58, 318; by Yugoslavia 29, 51
mines; Albanian knowledge of 30, 51–3; Albanian territorial waters 9, 26; German Y mines 51, 318; in Mediterranean post WWII 43–4

minesweeping operations; Mediterranean 43–4; UK/Corfu Channel *see* Operation Retail
minority report, Polish 49, 76, 78
mitigation of damages, and extenuating circumstances 224–5, 313–14
mixed commission 48n.41
Mladic, General 326
Monetary Gold principle 305
Montreux Treaty 1936 193, 194
Moore, Judge 35, 166n.6
More Secure World: Our Shared Responsibility, A 19
Mossoul case 60
Moullec, Admiral 24, 28
Munro, H. 211, 212
Muscat Dhows case 164

nationality, and ships 165–6
national security *see* security
NATO 19, 196
natural causality 310
natural law doctrine 313
naval secrets 140 *see also* XCU documents
Navigation Act 1912, Marine Orders Part 54 161
navigational regimes 183
navigation, and climate change 185
new international law 82, 179–80, 212, 357
New Zealand, and disclosure 131
Nicaragua v. USA; and complicity 325, 327; and *Corfu Channel* case 7, 14; and customary international law 205, 237; and due diligence 325; and elementary considerations of humanity 209, 261, 279; and ICJ 226; and international law 208; minelaying 112; and principle of unnecessary suffering 289; and Security Council/ICJ 63, 68, 69, 80; and standard of proof 112
no-fault liability, and *Corfu Channel* case 299–305
no harm rule 248, 251
Non-Aligned Movement 240
non-innocent acts 192
non-intervention, and *Operation Retail* 296
non-liquet, and ICJ 202–3, 257
non-State actors, and due diligence 305–6, 312

Nordmann, Joë 22, 24, 25, 30
Nordquist, M.H. 287
normal mode of continuous and expeditious transit 162–3
normal mode of navigation, and innocent passage 191
normal mode of operation, and warships 194
normative causality 310
norms; new international 278–85; and standard of proof 106–16; unwritten 285
North Atlantic Coast Fisheries Arbitration 173
North Corfu Channel; as international strait 31, 204; prior to mine explosions 43–5
Northeast Passage 185
Northern Epirus 43
North Korean spy ship, sinking of 170
North Sea Continental Shelf case 101–2, 208
Northwest Passage 185
notification regime, warships 175–6
nuclear ships, States objecting to 159
nuclear waste, shipping of/restrictions 158–9
Nuclear Weapons case 202, 248, 249, 250, 261, 280, 282, 289, 298n.

objectivised fault 304
obligation, international 10
obligations; best efforts 309; by commission 310; of conduct 308, 312; of good neighbourliness 13; to prevent an event/external event 309, 310, 312; of prevention 346; of result 308, 309; to warn others 13, 243, 244, 245, 247–8
Ocean, HMS 38, 141
Oceans Policy Statement 169
Oda, Judge 102
Official Information Act 1982 128
Oil Platforms case 105, 106, 111–12, 220, 229–30, 232–3
omissions; Albania's wrongful 345–6; and due diligence 16, 309–12; and *Genocide* case 115, 116, 346–7; and standard of proof 108–15
'open covenants of peace, openly arrived at', Fourteen Points for 131–2
open government 127, 128, 131; and International Health Regulations 2005 132

open justice, principle of 130
Operation Enduring Freedom 239
Operation Iraqi Freedom 228, 238–9
Operation Retail; and Albanian sovereignty 10, 17; and Article 2§4 223; background 21, 47, 227; collecting evidence 24–5, 37, 214, 217–19, 228; condemnation of 82; and due diligence 313–14; and fault/State responsibility 303; and international law 212; as prohibited intervention 312–14; and right of innocent passage/use of force 31; and right of intervention 33–8, 213–15; and self-help/non-intervention 220, 228, 296, 313; self-protection 215, 228; United Kingdom's pleadings 228
opinio juris, and customary law 205
Orion, HMS 21, 31, 44, 168n.13
Oxam, Bernard 287

Paine, Thomas 270, 283
Palmas Island case 242, 243n., 244, 297, 332t.19.1
passage, hampering of 154–9
passage rights, international straits 150, 163
Paul, Commander 137, 138, 140–1, 143
Pavlov, Zizan 28
Pedra Branca/Pulau Batu Puteh, *Case Concerning Sovereignty over Pedra Branca/Pulau Batu Puteh, Middle Rocks and South Ledge* 103
Pellet, Alain 257
pensions, to victims 349
peremptory norms; and Article 2§4 224; serious breaches of 107, 115–16
Permanent Court of International Justice (PCIJ) 60, 64, 303
Peters, Anne 288
Petitpierre, Max 275
pirate attacks, Somalia 196
Poincaré, Raymond 23
policy of force 226–41; *Operation Retail* 312; and right of intervention 216; and USA 235
Polish delegate, Security Council 66
political agency, and warships 167–8
Port Kennedy 162
positive-harm 108
poverty, and rights of distributive justice 286

pre-emptive self-defence 239
Preparatory Study Concerning a Draft Declaration on the Rights and Duties of States 297n.
prevention, obligation of *see also* obligations 346
prevention of harm, *Draft Articles on Prevention of Transboundary Harm from Hazardous Activities* 132, 243, 253
principal and incidental wrongful acts 322
principle of humanity 279, 281, 282, 286; and UNCLOS I and III 287
principle of open justice 130
principle of the freedom of maritime navigation and communication 13 *see also* freedom of navigation
principle of unnecessary suffering 289
principles; general/well-recognized 202; and rules 260–1
proof, standard of *see* standard of proof
Protection of Victims of Non-International Armed Conflicts 260
provisional measures, and standards of proof 117–21
public interest(s); competing 129; and disclosure 131; immunity application 129; limits 134
public order, at sea 165
public power 128
Pueblo, USS 170
Pulau Ligitan, *Case concerning Sovereignty over Pulau Ligitan and Pulau Sipadan* 102
Pulau Sipadan, *Case concerning Sovereignty over Pulau Ligitan and Pulau Sipadan* 102
Pulp Mills case 104–5; and acts/omissions 116; and due diligence 248, 250, 251, 301, 307–8; and environmental protection 121; and expert reports 340; joint dissenting opinions 254–5

radioactive material, shipping of/restrictions 158
Ragazzi, M. 268
Raider, HMS 38, 141
Rainbow Warrior case 223
Ranjeva, Judge 117
Raz, J. 287
Reagan, President 169
recommendations, Security Council 72, 73

Reed, E. 23
regime of evidence, *Corfu Channel* case *see* evidence
Reisman, M. 217
reparations; *Corfu Channel* case 314; and fault 304; and *Genocide* case 346; legal issues 343–53; meaning of 351; and satisfaction 336n.
Republic of the Congo v. France see Case Concerning certain Criminal Proceedings in France
responsibility; circumstances excluding/attenuating 224, 313; international 9, 10–11, 13, 61; and mere knowledge of minelaying 320, 322
responsibility to protect 16, 307
Responsibility to protect populations from genocide, war crimes, ethnic cleansing and crimes against humanity 19
Responsibility to Protect, The 19
restitution 351
Revue de droit International 274
Rigaux, Judge 233
right of assistance entry, and warships 195–6
right of intervention; *Corfu Channel* case 14, 211, 225, 234–5, 236–7; *Operation Retail* 33–8, 213–15, 312, 335; and policy of force 216
right of passage; and *Corfu Channel* case 12, 150–1; international straits 150, 163; warships 179
right of self-help 211, 214, 216, 225, 232, 236–7
rights/duties of States, codification of 297
rights identification 287
rights of distributive justice, and poverty 286
right to board a ship 189
right to resort to war 211–12
Rio Declaration, Principle 2 245, 249
risk assessment, transboundary harm 132–3
risk of irreparable prejudice 117–18
Rome Agreement 354, 356
Root, Elihu 31, 173
Rooy, G. de 339
RPM Nautical Foundation 57
rules, and principles 260–1
Russia, and Security Council 65–6

Salamanca, Carlos 178
Samuel B. Roberts, USS 111
San Francisco Charter 231
Saranda 31, 44, 45, 57
satisfaction, duty to give 335–6
Saumarez, HMS 9, 21, 45, 137, 141, 227, 341, 348, 350
Sauser-Hall, Georges 55, 355
Scelle, Georges 178
Schmitt, Carl 272
Schooner Exchange v. McFaddon 167
Schwebel, Judge 69, 80
Second Report on the Law of the Non-Navigational Use of International Watercourses 243
security; and coastal States 181, 191; concerns of strait States 187; and disclosure 127, 133; and innocent passage 178; national/and ultra-hazardous cargoes 158–9; post war 182
Security Council; Corfu Channel question 47–9; and disclosure 134; draft resolution 1947 49, 61, 77, 78; fact-finding 75–9, 80, 81; functions/power of 61–7; and ICJ 3–4, 8, 21, 63–4, 67–75, 79–82, 83; impartiality of 65, 78; and military intervention 19; obligations to respect resolutions 325; recommendations 72, 73; Resolution 19 48; Resolution 22 49; Resolution 731 81; Resolution 1816 (2008) 196; Resolution 1846 (2008) 196; Resolution 1851 (2008) 196; Resolution 1897 (2009) 196; Sub-Committee 48–9, 64–5, 66, 75–9; and U N Charter, Chapter VII 20; veto 4, 20, 62, 64, 79n., 238
security matters, and coastal States jurisdiction 154–5
security zones, and coastal States 155
Selby, Commander 137
self-defence; law of 239–40; and *Oil Platforms* case 232–3; and violation of sovereignty 223
self-defence capacity; of strait States 188; warships 191
self-help; and *Operation Retail* 220, 228, 296, 313; redress by 236; right of 211, 214, 216, 225, 232, 236–7; and state of necessity 223–5, 313–14
self-preservation, right of 313
self-protection, *Operation Retail* 215, 228

Separate and Dissenting Opinions, *Corfu Channel* case 230–2
Serbia, *Genocide case* 115
serious breaches of peremptory norms 107
Shahabuddeen, Judge 280–2
Shawcross, Hartley 22–3, 25, 26, 27, 33, 137, 143, 144
ships/shipping; duties of in transit 187; importance of 149; and nationality 165–6; as sovereign irritants 165–70, 180; and transit passage 152–3; violating laws/regulations 189
Sibenik 51, 318, 319
sic utere tuo ut alienum non laedas 242–3
Simma, Judge 104, 112, 233, 254–5, 269, 340
Simon, Viscount 125–6
Singapore 186
Singapore Straits 196
slavery 270–1
Slave Trade Regulation Act 270
social interdependence 16–17
social justice 265
social responsibility 13; corporate 306
solutions, ICJ issuing of 6
Somalia 196
Soskice, Frank 23, 25, 28, 29, 98, 109, 139, 266
South Korea, and warships 175–6
South Ledge, *Case Concerning Sovereignty over Pedra Branca/Pulau Batu Puteh, Middle Rock and South Ledge* 103
South West Africa case 276, 279, 291, 325
sovereign equality of States 18
sovereign immunity, of warships 171
sovereign irritants, warships as 165–70, 180
sovereign protection, of ships 167
sovereign rights, of States 223
sovereignty; *Case Concerning Sovereignty over Pedra Branca/Pulau Batu Puteh, Middle Rock and South Ledge* 103; *Case concerning Sovereignty over Pulau Ligitan and Pulau Sipadan* 102; and coastal States 155; and *Corfu Channel* case 12, 16–20, 41n.2, 165; and due diligence 298; and humanity 288; and limited coercive action 222, 223; respect for territorial 14; ships creating friction 165–70; and State freedoms 296; territorial 179, 181; and transit passage 157; UK violation of

Albanian 14, 53, 143, 174, 335; and violation/self-defence 223; and warships 169, 170
Sovereignty over Certain Frontier Land case 102
Spahiu, Bedri 57
Spanish Zone case 297, 303
Special Agreement 1948; and balanced judgement 336–7; and compensation 92, 337–8, 338–9; *Corfu Channel* case 10, 25, 41; and duty to give satisfaction 335; and *forum prorogatum* 91–2; and jurisdiction of ICJ 15, 88, 90; and Yugoslavia 323
Special Agreement, a 87
Special *Rapporteur* on State Responsibility 109, 116, 243, 311, 314
Spiropoulos, Judge 102
Srebrenica genocide 346–7
SS Wimbledon case 164–5
standard(s) of proof 98–101; *Corfu Channel* case 99, 109–11, 113–15, 300; and declaratory/determinative functions 122; and function of the Court 101–6; *Genocide case* 105, 106, 107, 113, 115; and incidental proceedings 117; and norms/acts/omissions 108–15; and phase of case 122; and provisional measures 117–21; varying 121, 122; and violation/content of norm 106–16
State consent, and Security Council 75
State freedoms, and sovereignty 296
State immunity 136
state of necessity; and self-help 223–5, 313–14; and sovereignty 224
State power, and transit passage 153, 154–5
State practice, restrictions over international straits 155–7
State responsibility; and criminal responsibility 58; and fault 302–5; ILC Articles on State Responsibility 328; and international organizations 306; law of 338; and *Trail Smelter* case 246
States; diplomatic protection of ships 166; power of small/large 24, 36, 38, 82, 211–12, 214, 231, 235, 237, 241; rights/duties of 297; *see also* maritime States; strait States
Statute of the River Uruguay 1975 *see* 1975 Statute

St. Austell Bay, HMS 38
St. Brides Bay, HMS 33, 38
St George's Monastery 52
Stockholm Conference 243
Stockholm Declaration, Principle 21 245, 248–9
strait States; enforcement of laws/regulations 188–9; financial burden of 188; obligations of 187–8; security concerns of 187
Sub-Committee, Security Council 48–9, 64–5, 66, 75–9
submarines; and innocent passage 162–3, 192; and Law of the Sea Convention 162–3
Superb, HMS 21, 31, 44, 168n.
Syria, and warships 175

Tadic judgment 283, 284, 285
Taliban regime, and due diligence 306
Tanaka, Judge 291
Taylor, Charles 273
Tehran Conference 1968 260
Tehran Hostages Case 68, 301n., 305, 311
territorial sea; coastal States jurisdiction 154–5; size of 181, 194; width of 151
Territorial Sea Convention 1958 *see* Convention on the Territorial Sea and Contiguous Zone
territorial waters, Albanian 44
territory, legal nature of 176–7
terrorism, 129, 196, and due diligence 306
Thetis, HMS 125
Third Conference on the Law of the Sea 12
third State rights 63
Thirlway, H. 218
threshold of proof 300
Thursday Island 162
Tito, General 57
Torres Strait, compulsory pilotage 159–62
torture 272
torture-obtained evidence 218–19
Trail Smelter case; and due diligence 244, 247–8, 251, 297–8, 299n.; and international law 242; and State responsibility 246
transboundary damage, and due diligence 245–6

transboundary harm 132–3; *Draft Articles on Prevention of Transboundary Harm from Hazardous Activities* 132, 243, 253
transit, act of 186
transit passage; coastal States laws/regulations relating to 195; and *Corfu Channel* case 171; delinquent ships 189; enforcement of strait States laws/regulations 188–9; and innocent passage 152–4; and Law of the Sea Convention 163, 194; and Marine Notice 8/2006 161–2; regime of 151–4; and restrictions for vessels 162; and sovereignty 157; and State power 153, 154–5; and strait States 187–9; and submarines 162–3; through international straits 186–9; and warships 158, 193–5
travaux préparatoires 204; Territorial Sea Convention 1958 158
Treaty of Amity 1955 229–30, 233
Treaty of Friendship and Mutual Assistance 1946 42–3
Treaty of Paris for the Renunciation of War 1928 211
Treaty of Versailles, Article 380 303
Trial Chamber 145
Triepel, H. 302
Trindade, Judge 288
Tripartite Commission for the Restitution of the Monetary Gold 54, 55, 56, 354–5
Truman Doctrine 21
Truman, President 21
Tsagourias, Nicholas 290
Turkey; and Greece 67; transit passage/warships 193
Turkish Straits 152

ultra-hazardous cargoes, and national security 158–9
UN Charter 19; Article 1 258–9; Article 2 18, 296; Article 2(4) 82, 219–23, 226, 228–9, 231, 232, 233, 236, 237, 238, 239, 240, 260; Article 12 68; Article 13 259; Article 24 64, 69; Article 25 75, 89, 90; Article 32 63; Article 32/33 48; Article 33(1) 66; Article 35 47–8, 61, 360; Article 36 61, 71, 74, 75, 89; Article 36(1) 71, 72, 73, 74, 75, 87, 89, 90; Article 36(1)/(2) 75; Article 36(2) 87; Article 36(3) 60, 64, 66, 67, 68, 69, 70, 72, 74; Article 37 62; Article 38(5) 95; Article 42 231; Article 51 223; Article 94 354; Article 95 68; Chapter VII/and Security Council 20; Chapter VI/VII powers 20, 196; and international human rights law 259; right of intervention 36–7, 38 *see also* right of intervention; security machinery 215–17; and veto 4, 20, 62, 64
UNCLOS 150, 155, 157, 181; Article 290 120
UNCLOS I; Draft Article 24 178
UNCLOS I and III; and freedom of navigation 182; and principle of humanity 287
UNCLOS III 151, 178
UN Commission on Human Rights 286
unilateral application 8
United Nations Conference on the Law of the Sea 1958 *see* UNCLOS
United States; and Cuba 35; and Latin America 271; National Security Strategy 239; and policy of force 235; and submarines 163
United States and Soviet Union Uniform Interpretation of Rules 1989 192
Universal Declaration of Human Rights (UDHR) 256, 259
universal empathy 273
universal juridical conscience 265
unnecessary suffering, principle of 289
UN Security Council *see* Security Council
use of force; and *Corfu Channel* case 219–23, 234; and ICJ 226, 229, 230–3; international relations 211; justifying 236; and UN Charter 233 *See also* UN Charter Article 2(4) and *Right of Intervention*
Use of the North Channel, Corfu. The *see* XCU documents
USSR, and Security Council 65–6

veto, Security Council 4, 20, 62, 64, 79n.106
Vienna Convention on the Diplomatic Relations 208
Vienna Convention on the Law of Treaties 1969, Article 31 260–1
Villard, Paul 24
Virginia Commentaries, LOSC 194

Volage, HMS 21, 45, 59, 137, 138, 227, 341, 342, 348, 350
Von Elbe, Joachim 212

Waldock, Humphrey 23, 144, 267
Waldron, Jeremy 284
Wall Advisory Opinion 240, 262, 263, 325
war; Cold War 3, 14, 21–2, 24, 43, 46, 56, 58, 62, 95, 136, 187, 235, 238–41, 297, 354, 359–60; and international law 212; Iraq 216, 226, 238; and redress of an *injuria* 215; right to resort to 211–12; on terror 218–19, 235; WWII looting of gold 54
warships; characterisation of conduct of 170–9; conscious use of 168–9; constraints applied to 194; and flag State law 171, 195; and innocent passage 31, 149, 157–8, 174–5, 175n.37, 177, 190–3, 204; and international straits 163; and normal mode of operation 194–5; peacetime maritime operations 190–6; political agency of 167–8; political/legal utility of 180; right of passage 179; sovereign immunity of 171; as sovereign irritants 180; and sovereignty 169, 170; special authorisation for 171–2; and transit passage 158, 193–5
Washington Agreement 1951 54, 55, 355
Weeramantry, Judge 280
Wilberforce, R.O. 23

Wilson, Woodrow 131
Wimbledon, S.S. case 164–5
Winiarski, Judge 114
witnesses, *Corfu Channel* case 27–8
Wochac, Professor 24
World Court, and fault/State responsibility 303
World Health Organisation 132
World Summit Outcome 2005 19–20
Wright, Quincy 275–6, 357
written reply 34
wrongful acts, *see also* State Responsibility *and* obligations *and ILC* Articles on Responsibility for Internationally Wrongful Acts; full knowledge of 330; internationally wrongful acts 325; principal/incidental 322
WWII, looting of gold 54

XCU documents 11, 32–3, 124, 137–42
Xoxha, Enver 50n.57, 52n.69, 57

Yemen 191
Ylli, Mr 139
Y mines 51, 318
Yorktown, USS 169, 192
Yugoslav Government, and *Corfu Channel* case 320
Yugoslavia; and Albania 22, 24, 42–3, 46, 51, 57; and genocide 326–30; and the ICJ 323; and minelaying 9, 51, 318–19

Zourek, Jaroslav 178